DATE DUE

JUN 17 1993			
SEP 2 5 1993			
OCT 1 3 1995			
FEB 4 - 1996			
JAN 2 1997			
NOV 3 0 2002			
JUN 1 9 2004			
GAYLORD			PRINTED IN U.S.A.

Modern Latin American Fiction

Titles in the CRITICAL COSMOS series include

THE CRITICAL COSMOS SERIES

Modern Latin American Fiction

Edited and with an introduction
by *HAROLD BLOOM*
Sterling Professor of the Humanities
Yale University

CHELSEA HOUSE PUBLISHERS
New York ◇ Philadelphia

Printed and bound in the United States of America

10 9 8 7 6 5 4 3 2 1

Library of Congress Cataloging-in-Publication Data

Modern Latin American fiction / edited and with an
introduction by Harold Bloom.
        p.   cm.—(The Critical cosmos series)
    Bibliography: p.
    Includes index.
    ISBN 1-555-46096-8
    1. Latin American literature—20th century—History and
criticism. I. Bloom, Harold. II. Series: Critical cosmos.
PQ7081.M53   1987
863—dc19   87-18336
                                                        CIP

DEC 1 7 1991

Contents

Editor's Note

This book gathers together a representative selection of the best criticism available in English upon the principal authors of modern Latin American fiction. We have taken the term "Latin American" to include authors from Puerto Rico, Central America, and Brazil. Three essays each are given to Borges, Carpentier, Cortázar, and García Márquez, as they are clearly the four most eminent figures. Lezama Lima, Rulfo, Donoso, Lispector, Fuentes, and Vargas Llosa each receive two discussions, and the remaining novelists a single examination each. I am grateful to Bernice Hausman, Viviana Daiz Balsera, Johann Pillai, and Frank Menchaca for their help in editing this volume.

My introduction centers upon García Márquez's *One Hundred Years of Solitude*, not in the mistaken notion of regarding it as a representative novel, but because it is now the most widely read single work of modern Latin American fiction. Its scriptural aspect is stressed in my appreciation.

Carter Wheelock discusses the short stories of Borges's late phase, with an emphasis on the symbolism of blindness and death, and on Borges's characteristic philosophical skepticism. The story "The Immortal" is read by Sophia S. Morgan as a parable of literature transformed into ritual, while Bella Brodzki interprets "Emma Zunz" as Borges's least characteristic tale, since its protagonist is a woman, and sees it as "a tragedy of restricted choices."

The Chilean critic Ariel Dorfman studies *Men of Maize* by Miguel Angel Asturias, finding in it a unity that other readers have overlooked. Alejo Carpentier is examined in an overview by Roberto González Echevarría, who shows how *The Kingdom of this World*, *The Lost Steps*, and *Explosion in a Cathedral* demonstrate the tragic flaws of history without departing from their own coherent aesthetic designs. José Piedra reads Carpentier's Afro-Cuban tale, *Histoire de Lunes*, as the turning of an imperialist code against itself, while Julie Jones examines *El recurso del método* as a parable of the trickster tricked.

The demolition of realism by João Guimarães Rosa is Allan Englekirk's subject, after which George Levine compares *A Brief Life* by Juan Carlos Onetti to *Madame Bovary*. The novels of María Luisa Bombal are seen as transitional or crossroads works by Phyllis Rodríguez-Peralta, since their women suffer human estrangement, yet go on longing for the Romantic role once assigned to them by Hispanic society.

Lezama Lima is praised by two fellow novelists, Julio Cortázar and Severo Sarduy. Cortázar celebrates *Paradiso* for its unabashed appropriation of tradition, while Sarduy compares the book to Proust.

A sequence upon Cortázar himself follows, with Saúl Sosnowski regarding the novelist's personae as pursuers, marked by signs of searching. Barbara L. Hussey centers upon chapter 55 in *Rayuela* as a kind of negative epiphany, while Lois Parkinson Zamora relates Cortázar's recent techniques to allied temporal structures in film and photography.

Juan Rulfo's *Pedro Páramo* is studied by Paul B. Dixon in terms of metaphors of visual ambiguity, after which Steven Boldy ponders the relations between authority and identity in Rulfo's *El llano en llamas*. Harry Enrique Rosser, analyzing Elena Garro's *Los recuerdos del porvenir*, praises the novel for its universal projection of the role that the consciousness of death plays in the human condition.

Severo Sarduy compares Manuela in Donoso's *Hell Has No Limits* to Goya's portraits, while Alfred J. MacAdam considers *The Obscene Bird of Night* as a triumph of monstrosity. Clarice Lispector's story "Sunday Before Going to Sleep" is read by Hélène Cixous as a series of systems of symbolic value, after which Lispector's *Family Ties* is seen by Marta Peixoto as a bleak vision of female possibilities, lightened only by the wry symbol of "the smallest woman in the world, alone in her tree house," who has successfully developed.

Susanne Kappeler finds in the epic mode of García Márquez's *One Hundred Years of Solitude* a sequence of "voices of patriarchy," while Patricia Tobin praises *The Autumn of the Patriarch* for being always ahead of all our contemporary critical moments, and Claudette Kemper Columbus returns us to Macondo as a contemporary realm of the Gothic.

Carlos Fuentes becomes the focus in Jaime Alazraki's appreciation of *Terra Nostra* for its bold grasp of history, and in Wendy B. Faris's tracing of the erotic lineaments of Fuentes's fiction. The role of language in *Tres tristes tigres* by Cabrera Infante is studied by Stephanie Merrim, after which Frances Wyers (Weber) accompanies Manuel Puig to the movies.

Bell Gale Chevigny sees Elena Poniatowska's work as a kind of alchemy that transforms empty privileges into responsibilities. Mario Vargas Llosa is read by Ronald Christ as a revolutionary who converts "mere" rhetoric into the action of his plots, and then is praised by Roger Kaplan as a lucid democrat of the Latin American novel.

Stacey Schlau studies the use of mass media images by Luis Rafael Sánchez, after which Roberto González Echevarría returns with an analysis of Severo Sarduy's *Cobra*. Giovanni Pontiero provides notes on Nelida Piñón, while Luisa Valenzuela is saluted by Patricia Tobin for her varied art.

The highly advanced art of Reinaldo Arenas is praised by Julio Ortega for its spontaneity and freedom. In this volume's final essay, Doris Meyer finds a new departure in the feminist second novel of Inés Malinow, *Free Entry*, which conveys the life force of a woman, and the images of the female unconscious, with a true clarity.

Introduction

Macondo, according to Carlos Fuentes, "begins to proliferate with the richness of a Columbian Yoknapatawpha." Faulkner, crossed by Kafka, is at the literary origins of Gabriel García Márquez. So pervasive is the Faulknerian influence that at times one hears Joyce and Conrad, Faulkner's masters, echoed in García Márquez, yet almost always as mediated by Faulkner. *The Autumn of the Patriarch* may be too pervaded by Faulkner, but *One Hundred Years of Solitude* absorbs Faulkner, as it does all other influences, into a phantasmagoria so powerful and self-consistent that the reader never questions the authority of García Márquez. Perhaps, as Reinaldo Arenas suggested, Faulkner is replaced by Carpentier, and Kafka by Borges in *One Hundred Years of Solitude*, so that the imagination of García Márquez domesticates itself within its own language. Macondo, visionary realm, is an Indian and Hispanic act of consciousness, very remote from Oxford, Mississippi, and from the Jewish cemetery in Prague. In his subsequent work, García Márquez went back to Faulkner and Kafka, but then *One Hundred Years of Solitude* is a miracle, and could happen only once, if only because it is less a novel than it is a scripture, the Bible of Macondo. Melquíades the Magus, who writes in Sanskrit, may be more a mask for Borges than for the author himself, and yet the gypsy storyteller also connects García Márquez to the archaic Hebrew storyteller the Yahwist, at once the greatest of realists and the greatest of fantasists, but above all the only true rival of Homer and Tolstoy as a storyteller.

My primary impression, in the act of rereading *One Hundred Years of Solitude*, is a kind of aesthetic battle fatigue, since every page is rammed full of life, beyond the capacity of any single reader to absorb. Whether the impacted quality of this novel's texture is finally a virtue, I am not sure, since sometimes I feel like a man invited to dinner who has been served nothing but an enormous platter of Turkish Delight. Yet it is all story,

1

where everything conceivable and inconceivable is happening at once, from creation to apocalypse, birth to death. Roberto González Echevarría has gone so far as to surmise that in some sense it is the reader who must die at the end of this story, and perhaps it is the sheer richness of the text that serves to destroy us. Joyce half-seriously envisioned an ideal reader cursed with insomnia who would spend his life unpacking *Finnegans Wake*. The reader need not translate *One Hundred Years of Solitude,* a novel that deserves its popularity, as it has no surface difficulties whatsoever. And yet, a new dimension is added to reading by the book. Its ideal reader has to be like its most memorable personage, the sublimely outrageous Colonel Aureliano Buendía, who "had wept in his mother's womb and had been born with his eyes open." There are no waste sentences, no mere transitions in this novel, and so you must notice everything at the moment that you read it. It will all cohere, at least as myth and metaphor, if not always as literary meaning.

In the presence of an extraordinary actuality, consciousness takes the place of imagination. That Emersonian maxim is Wallace Stevens's, and is worthy of the visionary of "Notes toward a Supreme Fiction" and "An Ordinary Evening in New Haven." Macondo is a supreme fiction, and there are no ordinary evenings within its boundaries. Satire, even parody, most fantasy—these are now scarcely possible in the United States. How can you satirize Ronald Reagan or Jerry Falwell? Pynchon's *The Crying of Lot 49* ceases to seem fantasy whenever I visit Southern California, and a ride on the New York City subway tends to reduce all literary realism to an idealizing projection. Some aspects of Latin American existence transcend even the inventions of García Márquez. I am informed, on good authority, that the older of the Duvalier dictators of Haiti, the illustrious Papa Doc, commanded that all black dogs in his nation be destroyed when he came to believe that a principal enemy had transformed himself into a black dog. Much that is fantastic in *One Hundred Years of Solitude* would be fantastic anywhere, but much that seems unlikely to a North American critic may well be a representation of reality.

Emir Monegal emphasized that García Márquez's masterwork was unique among Latin American novels, being radically different from the diverse achievements of Julio Cortázar, Carlos Fuentes, Lezama Lima, Mario Vargas Llosa, Miguel Angel Asturias, Manuel Puig, Guillermo Cabrera Infante and so many more. The affinities to Borges and to Carpentier were noted by Monegal as by Arenas, but Monegal's dialectical point seemed to be that García Márquez was representative only by joining all his colleagues in not being representative. Yet it is now true that, for most North American readers, *One Hundred Years of Solitude* comes first to mind when they think of the Hispanic novel in America. Alejo Carpentier's *Explosion in a Cathedral* may be an even stronger book, but only Borges has dominated the North American literary imagination as García Márquez has with this grand fantasy. The paperback translation I have just reread is in its thirtieth printing, and the novel's popularity seems certain to be permanent. It is inevitable that we are fated to identify *One Hundred Years of Solitude* with an entire culture, almost as though it were a new *Don Quixote*, which it most definitely is not. Comparisons to Balzac and even to Faulkner are also not very fair to García Márquez. The titanic inventiveness of Balzac dwarfs the later visionary, and nothing even in Macondo is as much a negative Sublime as the fearsome quest of the Bundrens in *As I Lay Dying*. *One Hundred Years of Solitude* is more of the stature of Nabokov's *Pale Fire* and Pynchon's *Gravity's Rainbow*, latecomers' fantasies, strong inheritors of waning traditions.

Whatever its limitations may or may not be, García Márquez's major narrative now enjoys canonical status, as well as a representative function. Its cultural status is likely to be enhanced by the end of this century, and it would be foolish to quarrel with so large a phenomenon. I wish to address myself only to the question of how seriously, as readers, we need to receive the book's scriptural aspect. The novel's third sentence is: "The world was so recent that many things lacked names, and in order to indicate them it was necessary to point," and the third sentence from the end is the long and beautiful

> Macondo was already a fearful whirlwind of dust and rubble being spun about by the wrath of the biblical hurricane when Aureliano skipped eleven pages so as not to lose time with facts he knew only too well, and he began to decipher the instant that he was living, deciphering it as he lived it, prophesying himself in the act of deciphering the last page of the parchment, as if he were looking into a speaking mirror.

The time span between this Genesis and this Apocalypse is six generations, so that José Arcadio Buendía, the line's founder, is the grandfather of the last Aureliano's grandfather. The grandfather of Dante's grandfather, the crusader Cassaguida, tells his descendant Dante that the poet perceives the truth, because he gazes into that mirror in which the great and small of this life, before they think, behold their thought. Aureliano, at the end, reads the Sanskrit parchment of the gypsy, Borges-like, Magus, and looks into a speaking mirror, beholding his thought before he thinks it. But does he, like Dante, behold the truth? Was Florence, like Macondo, a city of mirrors (or mirages), in contrast to the realities of the *Inferno*, the *Purgatorio*, the *Paradiso*? Is *One Hundred Years of Solitude* only a speaking mirror? Or does it contain, somehow within it, an *Inferno*, a *Purgatorio*, a *Paradiso*?

Only the experience, and disciplined reflections, of a great many more strong readers will serve to answer those questions with any conclusiveness. The final eminence of *One Hundred Years of Solitude* for now remains undecided. What is clear to the book's contemporaries is that García Már-quez has given contemporary culture, in North America and Europe, as much as in Latin America, one of its double handful of necessary narratives, without which we will understand neither one another nor our own selves.

Borges's New Prose

Carter Wheelock

In 1966, some ten years after "God's magnificent irony" had given him "books and the night," apparently ending his career as a writer of prose fiction, Jorge Luis Borges published a short story, "The Intruder." His devotees sat up with interest, but many leaned back again because the new story—devoid of brain-rattling sophistry and erudite allusions—was not like the old Borges, whose three dozen gripping "fictions" published up to 1953 had made him the most important living writer in the Spanish language. Since "The Intruder," Borges has written more than a dozen new narratives, most of them collected under the title of one in the series, *Doctor Brodie's Report*. Two of them, along with several other short prose pieces, are interspersed with the poetry of *Elogio de la sombra* (1969). A long story, "The Congress," was published separately in 1971.

This new prose has yet to be fully appraised. My effort here can be only a superficial beginning, and we must start by remembering the old Borges.

THE FORMER BORGES

Toward the end of the 1930s Borges turned from poetizing Buenos Aires and fictionalizing the hoodlums of the city's outlying slums (as in "Street-corner Man," 1933) and took to playing literary games with time, infinity, destiny, and the nature of reality. He was well equipped for it, being multilingual and having spent most of his forty years as an eclectic reader, absorbing everything from Burns's *The Saga of Billy the Kid* to Berkeley and the Panchatantra. His life, he has said, has been devoted less to living than to reading. In the following ten or so years he produced three small col-

From *TriQuarterly* no. 25 (Fall 1972). © 1972 by Northwestern University Press.

lections of compact fiction (the first two are now combined as *Ficciones* [1944; enlarged 1956]; the third is *The Aleph* [1949; enlarged 1952]). These stories, suggestive of highbrow detective fiction and of symbolist poetic theory applied to prose, are utterly lacking in social consciousness or moral implication; unemotional, sexless, and uncontemporary, they wave no banners and press no points. They allude to everything and recommend nothing.

For the most part, these highly intellectual creations of the 1940s are clinical, cosmic tales peopled with almost faceless characters who are not really people but archetypal miniatures that move about in a purely cerebral universe. They often act like mythical beings in primitive cosmologies, or like dream figures: two men can be one, they can be dead but alive, and they can be only half real; they can pass in and out of mortal life ("The Immortal"), stare at magic coins until they go mad ("The Zahir"), behold the universe under the cellar stairs ("The Aleph"), live a year in a moment ("The Secret Miracle"), or dream other people into being ("The Circular Ruins"). Borges's people live in ignorance of the secret laws, or the secret will, which guide their destinies, and their actions are not finally their own. Borges surrounds them with the dicta of metaphysical philosophers who make all things logical, and their behavior is told in deftly ambiguous language. The reader finds himself acclaiming with emotion what he doesn't quite grasp and perhaps doesn't believe. He is floated into a kind of esthetic hysteria, feeling spoofed but also sublimated. Although Borges insists that he does not push a philosophical viewpoint (or any other), his underlying skepticism, or idealism, comes through.

Far from being verbose in proportion to their intricacy, these earlier stories are written in a wondrously frugal and exact style—richly suggestive, poetic, and full of ironic humor, baroque artifice, and rhetorical sleight of hand. Prominent symbols—mirrors, labyrinths, tigers, towers, knives—are repeated with unabashed regularity (Borges calls himself monotonous), and the repetition of other images or secondary symbols suggests an esoteric pattern with a meaning: circles, coins, pyramids, horses, swamps, cards.

But again, no messianism intrudes into Borges's work. The ideas of men are arbitrary formulations with infinite alternatives. Certitude is intellectual death; therefore, for Borges, even his basic philosophy is a conjecture. Speculation is the law of intellectual life. Out of this view come the irony and humor of Borges's prose. He mocks knowledge by displaying it lavishly, finally turning it against itself. But his jibes are gentle, because he relishes all ideas for their esthetic value.

Every strange figment of thought implies a whole new structure of reality, a realm in which the errant idea would not be strange at all. By piling up these pieces of heretical "fact," Borges overpowers us with the illusion that we almost understand that realm and that if we did we would know everything. The creation of this illusion of near-understanding seems, on the surface, to be the whole esthetic motive of Borges's older fiction.

By attacking our conception of reality and implying another—a secret order in our chaos—he stalks the "esthetic occurrence" in an Olympian arena. In a short essay, "The Wall and the Books" (*Other Inquisitions* [1952]), he tentatively defined the esthetic event or fact (*el hecho estético*) as "the imminence of a revelation, which never comes." But to say that Borges fabricates esthetic situations is a fundamental error; for he has not believed, apparently since the early 1920s when he split with Ultraism, that the esthetic is man-made.

Much light is thrown on Borges's fiction by his essays, his short prose thoughts, and his poems, where he often centers his attention on literature and philosophy, but where he just as often focuses upon a natural, historical, or literary event that strikes the sensitive intellect as marvelous because of what it implies (that is, what it does not reveal) of time, destiny, or reality. For example, a gaucho murdered by his son does not know that perhaps he died only to repeat Caesar's death along with the words "And thou, my son"; or when a man dies, an infinite number of things in his memory die with him and leave the world poorer, as when the last man died who had seen Woden's rites or the living Christ. These are not intellectual fabrications of an esthetic illusion but simple wonder at the mystery and suggestiveness of real facts. When Borges adds metaphysical half-explanations, the little miracle he is pointing to is only heightened. When he marvels at the strange spiritual likeness between Omar and FitzGerald, there are inevitable overtones of circular time, reincarnation, and Platonic form, or of the primordial metonymy that makes two men one if they share merely a characteristic. When Borges writes that Shakespeare is nobody because he so long pretended on the stage to be other men, he conjures the old theological platitude that God, being everything, is not any one thing, therefore is no thing—nothing. Such logic is a trick of language—both intellectually palliative and spiritually cathartic. Such deliberate speciousness is rare in fiction, and its proliferation in Borges's prose has moved critics to treat it as an esthetic principle. Most readers of the old Borges, if pressed for a quick characterization of his typical stories, would call them dramatizations of intellectual propositions. This makes Borges a coiner of abstruse parables or fables, an allegorist; he is frequently defined as a writer who allegorizes heretical ideas, and more often than not there is the implication that he is some kind of truth-seeker who uses literature as a megaphone for his anxieties or his agnostic faith. Borges knows this. In his new fiction he seems to be telling us that his strange literature of the past is not an intellectual destruction of reality but an esthetic affirmation of it.

THE NEW BORGES

The excellence of "The Intruder" appears to have been somewhat overlooked because many were disappointed that Borges's first story in many years was not of the old vintage. Borges punctured any hope that he would return to the "type" by telling an interviewer in 1967 that he was fed up with "labyrinths and mirrors and tigers and all that." In the future he would write "straightforward" stories, somewhat after the manner of Kipling's early tales, with "little vocabulary" and "without tricks." What caused this change? Anyone who reads such recent stories as "Doctor Brodie's Report," "Guayaquil," or "The Gospel According to Mark" soon realizes that near-blindness has hardly impaired Borges's ability to produce organized intricacy in precise and frugal language. No, the real cause was visible as early as 1962, when James Irby noted that Borges regarded his older fictions as baroque and vain. Even before taking up fiction, Borges had abandoned (with Ultraism) the idea that literature can show us the essences of things or that art is any kind of key to metaphysical knowledge. He had abandoned faith in the reality of the "revelations" that can come out of new metaphors, contrived paradoxes, or juxtaposed antinomies. Now he has abandoned Ultraism's essentially baroque style; but he continues to espouse the idea that literature should "show us our own face," by which he means that it should show us *its* face, for to him the world and literature are the same thing: "If art is perfect, the world is superfluous." The "imminence of a revelation" is perhaps the ultimate knowable reality, and men do not create it. They comprise it, behold it, and try to transmute it into language. This idea precludes any esthetic theory—that is, any rule or formula for producing an imminent revelation.

Borges writes in the preface to *In Praise of Darkness* that he is not the possessor of an esthetic; and in the preface to *Doctor Brodie's Report* he seems to disclaim the attribution to him, by others, of an "esthetic of the intelligence":

> The art of writing is mysterious; the opinions we hold are ephemeral, and I prefer the Platonic idea of the Muse to that of Poe, who reasoned, or feigned to reason, that the writing of a poem is an act of the intelligence.

In the same preface, in answer to those critics who have deplored his lack of artistic concern for national and social issues, he says:

> I want to make it quite clear that I am not, nor have I ever been, what used to be called a preacher of parables or a fabulist and is now known as a committed writer. I do not aspire to be Aesop. My stories, like those of the Thousand and One Nights, try to be entertaining or moving but not persuasive.

This may also be understood as Borges's justification for deserting those metaphysical fictions which have been taken as essentially allegorical, for Borges is well aware of the bad connotations of "allegory." He has called allegory "an error," although he admits to allegorizing. (In the foreword to the second part of *Ficciones* he calls "The Sect of the Phoenix" an allegory.) Apparently he does not mind being called an allegorist if only the implication of didacticism is removed. Stripped of its moralism, allegory becomes a valid and powerful esthetic device, a long metaphor rich in suggestion. In a recent interview Borges characterized himself as a former parabolist turned storyteller; speaking of the new stories he would write (those of *Doctor Brodie's Report*), he said: "They will not be like my former work, parables or pretexts for writing essays. I want to be a storyteller, a narrator of real stories, without tricks."

In "The Approach to al-Mu'tasim" (*Ficciones*), Borges says of the fictitious novel he is "reviewing" that the version of 1932 was somewhat symbolic, but that the 1934 version "declines into allegory." In the foreword to Robert Lima's translation of Ana María Barrenechea's work on Borges (*Borges the Labyrinth Maker* [New York, 1965]), Borges acknowledges his occasional recourse to allegory: "My best writings are of things that were striving to come to life through me, and not simply allegories where the thought comes before the sign." In other words, Borges strives for a true symbolism but thinks that he, too, may occasionally "decline into allegory."

NEW NARRATIVES

Borges's new manner is indeed more straightforward. Much of the stylistic complexity has disappeared, leaving his themes and plots more conspicuous. In these narratives the plots—the *fabulae*, tales as tales—are in my opinion superior to those of *Ficciones* and *El aleph*, not because they are less fantastic but because truth itself is fantastic and these new tales, for the most part, are closer to it than are the stories about the equivocal verities of our mental life. In the eleven stories of *Doctor Brodie's Report* we do not get lost in limitless libraries or go wandering around inside the mind of the Minotaur. We go back, mainly, to the straggling outskirts, or *arrabales*, of Buenos Aires and to the pampa. These are the suburbs and plains as they were, or could have been, at the close of the nineteenth century or the early years of the twentieth, when *compadritos* (Argentine hoodlums, or gang toughs, with a lot of the classical gaucho in them) would hang around the saloons deciding who was the toughest, often by fighting with knives. Thus Borges continues to show his lifelong fascination with the cult of physical courage, which is present in "The Intruder" and commands at least five other *Brodie* stories.

These narratives about blustering *compadres* are among the eight in *Brodie* that are based on some type of interpersonal rivalry. Of the ruffians of the *arrabal* the most conspicuous is Rosendo Juárez ("Rosendo's Tale")—not because he is the toughest but because he is the same Rosendo Juárez who turned coward (apparently) in "Streetcorner Man," a story Borges wrote as far back as 1933. In the new story, Rosendo explains to Borges that his refusal to fight when challenged was due to disillusionment and disgust with his style of life. The most pathetic of the duelers are the gauchos Manuel Cardoso and Carmen Silveira of "The End of the Duel."

These are two longtime rivals who have often faced each other knife in hand but have avoided killing each other because their rivalry gives meaning to their "poor and monotonous lives" (*Doctor Brodie's Report*; hereafter referred to *DBR*). Drafted into the army, they fight side by side, without speaking, until they are finally captured by the enemy. A sadistic captain, knowing their rivalry, orders that they die in competition. Their throats cut, they run a race to see who can go farthest before collapsing.

Borges plays many variations on the rivalry theme. "The Intruder" gives us a rivalry caused by a woman and transcended by a murderous brotherly love. The Nilsen brothers, a pair of illiterate Saturday-night brawlers, pick up and share a country wench, sell her to a brothel to quiet their growing jealousy, and later retrieve her when each of them begins going to the brothel on the sly. Unable to save their comradeship and affection with the girl between them, the older brother kills her. When the younger is told, the two embrace, almost in tears.

In "Juan Muraña" the personal conflict is more fanciful; it is hardly a rivalry, but it involves a tough whose knife was feared. Muraña, long dead, is a bloody legend, and his widow, sister, and nephew are about to be dispossessed by their landlord Luchessi. Muraña's widow, Aunt Florentina, is a bit daft; she keeps assuring the others that her beloved husband will not let the gringo throw them out. Luchessi is butchered one night in his doorway by an unknown knifer. Later, Aunt Florentina shows her nephew her beloved husband—the notorious knife of Juan Muraña.

In "Juan Muraña" the fanciful equation of a man with his knife is explicable as Florentina's mental aberration or as a symbol of Muraña's continuing influence. But in "The Meeting," Borges goes straight to the fantastic—to a mystical, metonymical equation of men with their instruments. Two men—not *compadres* but civilized upper-class Argentines—get tipsy at a stag party and quarrel over a card game. As if driven by something beyond themselves, they do the unthinkable. They go to a display cabinet, take out two knives made famous by a pair of rivals long dead, and fight. Neither knows anything about knife fighting, but they fight like experts. One is killed; the other is incredulous and ashamed. In a kind of postscript, Borges suggests that it was not the men who fought, but the knives; the men were instruments of an ancient enmity inherent in the weapons.

But of all these tales of the mythic outskirts of the city, "The Unworthy Friend" is perhaps the most ambiguous and intriguing. Don Santiago Fischbein (whose real name is Jacobo) tells his story to Borges. He was a Jewish boy and a confessed coward in a neighborhood where the physical courage of the *compadre* was admired. He was terribly eager to be accepted thereabouts, but also to be accepted as an Argentine and a good citizen. He fell in with a gang of hooligans headed by one Francisco Ferrari, not because he had what it took to run with that crowd but because he adulated the leader, who lured him in. Ferrari planned to break into a textile factory one night and assigned Fischbein to keep watch outside. But before the time came, Fischbein went to the police and told all, causing Ferrari's death.

After reading "The Unworthy Friend," one does not know who betrayed whom, who is really judged unworthy, and unworthy of what. In one way this story reverses the plot of "The South" (*Ficciones*), whose nameless old gaucho appears to correspond to the old man of "The Unworthy Friend," Eliseo Amaro, the only gang member who is named. Fischbein's betrayal of Ferrari is prefigured in his verbal denial, at one point, that he knows Ferrari (he feels unworthy of knowing him); this vaguely suggests Peter's denial of Jesus. (Borges's interest in Christ's betrayal is shown in "Three Versions of Judas" [*Ficciones*] and other places, and in his new fiction it is most prominent in "The Gospel According to Mark.")

The possible reasons why Fischbein betrayed Ferrari are numerous. He wanted to prove himself a good Argentine; his hero had tried to corrupt and use him; he lost respect for his idol when he saw him pushed around by the police; he saw him as a punk, the way Rosendo Juárez saw himself; he had to justify his own cowardice by causing his hero's courage to destroy him. The ostensible reason is psychological; men often betray those of whom they feel unworthy. The most probable explanation of the treachery is purely Borgesian: the inscrutable cosmos somehow required it; it repeated the Great Betrayal. Ferrari is a subverted Christ figure. Adored by his followers and persecuted by the authorities, he is first denied, then sold out, then killed.

Why is Peter suggested, however remotely, along with Christ's real betrayer, Judas? I think it is because the betrayal has somehow saved the traitor. The key to this lies in the reasoning of the strange Gutre, or Guthrie, family of "The Gospel According to Mark." Father, son, and daughter, all illiterate, work on a ranch being visited by the protagonist, a medical student named Baltasar Espinosa. Isolated with this rather stupid trio when the ranch is surrounded by floodwaters, Espinosa passes the time in the evenings by reading them the Gospel of St. Mark. Ordinarily unresponsive to the student, they listen with deep interest; when he treats their pet lamb for an injury, he wins their devotion. The rains destroy part of the roof of the toolshed attached to the house, and, according to the Gutres, this accounts for the hammering that goes on while Espinosa sleeps and dreams of the building of the Ark. One night the girl, a virgin, comes to his room naked and has intercourse with him without embracing or kissing him. The next day the father asks him whether even those who crucified Jesus were saved from hell, and Espinosa, whose theology is vague, says yes. After lunch Espinosa leaves his room to find the Gutres kneeling and asking his blessing; then they curse him and spit on him and push him to the door of the wrecked toolshed, from the timbers of which they have built a cross.

The transference of identity from Christ to Espinosa (whose name suggests Baruch Spinoza and also the word "thorny," like a crown of thorns) is plausible, given the superstitious mentalities of the Gutres. But the matter lies deeper. The idea of being saved by killing one's redeemer is a reversal of the idea of being killed *by* him, Job-like, as in "The House of Asterión" (*El aleph*), where the Minotaur is "redeemed" by Theseus. While Borges equates salvation with death in that case, he makes it equivalent to life in this one, where the Gutres appropriate the virtues of their sacrificial victim through the symbolic ritual of cannibalism. Fischbein's cowardice, likewise, is somehow mitigated by the deatl. of his superior, his "redeemer." In the story of the Gutres there are suggestions of correspondences between the death of Christ and the human sacrifices of primitive peoples. Just as the Gutre girl gave herself to Espinosa without the enthusiasm of love, as if in obeisance, the Aztecs (for example) chose sacrificial victims whom they coddled for a time, giving them luxury and women, before killing them. In a higher sense of the word, Jesus was "coddled" for a while, as during the triumphal entry into Jerusalem. The Gutres petted Espinosa, who, like Jesus, was thirty-three years old, a healer, bearded, and noted for oratory and goodness.

The cannibalism in these two stories is finally of an abstruse and philosophical kind, echoing the interplay of order and chaos that characterizes much of Borges's older work. Let me illustrate. The Gutres, who remind me of the oxlike Troglodytes of "The Immortal" (*El aleph*), are of part-Scotch ancestry and are a mixture, Borges tells us, of Calvinist fanaticism and the superstition of the pampa Indian. Let us say they have a fixed and limited world-view. In words that paraphrase a reference in his confessional essay "The Maker" (*Dreamtigers*) and that allude to the Odyssey of Homer, Borges compares the Gutres to a lost ship searching the seas for a beloved island. The Odyssey and the Crucifixion are called the two histories which men, down through the ages, have repeated. On the symbolic level they are contrasted: the voyage of men lost in chaos, seeking a center, versus the exaltation through death (dissolution) of a supreme centrality on Golgotha. The medical student's mentality is contrasted with that of the Gutres; he is a freethinker who has no overriding or centered viewpoint, and no need for one. He likes to gamble, but not to win or to argue; he has "an open intelligence" and an "almost unlimited goodness." Unlike the world-view of the Gutres, then, his fluid and easy outlook seems magnanimous and noble. The Gutres, the lost ship, are searching for a secure idea, but Espinosa is not looking for anything. The Gutres see the Gospel as a conveyor of terribly important truth, but Espinosa reads it for its esthetic value. The Gutres seek order and meaning, but Espinosa is happy with a kind of agnostic equivocality, and, paradoxically, he is more ordered, more saved, than they. The narrow and fanatical Gutres believe that the sacrifice of their new pet, this other lamb, will redeem them.

How will it redeem them? We have to look back at Borges's older "system." Borges has made both salvation and hell equivalent to intellectual obsession (the inability to forget), as in "The Zahir" (*El aleph*) where the narrator cannot forget a coin and goes happily, painlessly mad; or as in "Deutsches Requiem" (*El aleph*) where the poet David Jerusalem is driven insane by an unnamed obsession inculcated by his tormentor, Otto zur

Linde, who observes that any common thing, if not forgettable, is the germ of a possible hell; or as in "The House of Asterion" (*El aleph*), where the Minotaur, bewildered by a house-universe that has too many galleries and doors, is "saved" by the world-simplifying sword that takes his life. In the story of the Gutres, as in Christian dogma, the death of the "Christ" is the vicarious death (redemption) of lost men; "Christ" becomes for the Gutres the holy obsession, the beloved island. Paradoxically, he represents not a limited, obsessive world-view, but its erasure.

"The Gospel According to Mark" is not one of the stories of rivalry. I want to go back to that type in order to mention "The Duel" and "Guayaquil." The first is a kind of parallel story to "The End of the Duel," mentioned earlier; the rivalry depicted is one that enriches the lives of the competitors. Two society women, Clara Glencairn and Marta Pizarro, compete in a friendly way in the field of painting. Painting is here analogous to literature, and I think we can infer that Borges is contrasting his own work—imaginative, ambiguous—both with the almost unintelligible literature of the vanguardist and with the clear-cut, rational literature of the *engagé* writer who tries to mirror the world and push a message. The story is humorous and satirical; in the artist Clara Glencairn we can perhaps see a caricature of Borges himself as he is seen, or thinks he is seen, by some Argentine men of letters who, on the one hand, have criticized his work for its universalism and aloof unconcern with national issues and, on the other hand, do not include him among the really "far out." Clara tried to be an abstract artist—a vanguardist—but that school rejected her work. She smiled and went on. Eventually she won a prize because some judges could not decide between two other artists, one of them too conventional and the other too "modern." Her friend and rival was the "straight" artist Marta Pizarro, a painter of portraits and patios with a nineteenth-century look. The two women painted against and for each other, and when Clara died, Marta's life lost its meaning. She painted Clara's portrait and laid her brushes aside for good. In that delicate duel, says Borges, there were neither defeats nor victories.

"Guayaquil" consists largely in the dialogue of two historians who are thrust into momentary rivalry. The narrator is a scholar whose specialty is the Independence movement and the life of the Argentine hero General San Martín. His adversary is a German Jew from Prague who has fled Hitler's tyranny, one Eduardo Zimmerman. Zimmerman is not a specialist in South American history but has proven himself adept at cleansing the biased histories of others (he has written on the Carthaginian Jews, who formerly were known only through the accounts of their enemies, the Romans). The two men are contending for the privilege of being officially chosen to go to another country to copy, appraise, and publish a newly discovered letter presumably written by Bolívar, which could clear up a famous historical mystery: what was said between San Martín and Bolívar, when they met in Guayaquil, which caused the former to retire from revolutionary activity and leave the destiny of the continent in Bolívar's hands. By conventional standards the narrator is better qualified to appraise the letter (a specialist, he is also the proud scion of revolutionary heroes), but he surrenders the privilege to Zimmerman after the two scholars converse. On leaving, Zimmerman divines that the narrator has conceded the honor because he intimately willed to do so. Still showing his penchant for alluding to philosophers, Borges weaves into the story a mention of Schopenhauer's "law" that no human action is involuntary; this serves a central purpose in the structure of the tale, which is about will and implies that volition—commitment—causes bad literature. I will comment on this story later in connection with Borges's esthetic ideas.

"The Elder Lady" shows Borges's ability to write in a charming and delicate way, with nostalgia for the glories of Argentine history and with both sympathy and satire of the *criollo* sensibility. The story is about the hundredth birthday of the last person who can claim to be the daughter of a revolutionary hero. The bustle and excitement of her anniversary celebration, which her countrymen turn into a celebration of national history and which she probably does not comprehend because she lives in the distracted world of the senile, hastens her end. She has long partaken of the glory of her famous father, hero of the battle of Cerro Alto; now she is somehow the last victim of that battle, for its celebration brings on her death.

Among the more ingenious of Borges's earlier stories are those in which he enumerates the irrational characteristics of some fantastic thing, apparently allegorizing an unnamed common reality. In "The Lottery in Babylon" (*Ficciones*), for example, he describes a "vertiginous country" where citizens are governed by pure chance, taking part in a lottery that awards them fame or ignominy, riches or poverty, life or death, on a day-to-day basis. Interpretation is up to the reader, and in this case the story seems to suggest the fortuitous and unstable nature of what men call reality. In "The Sect of the Phoenix" (*Ficciones*) Borges rounds up the random characteristics of a secret rite which is never identified but could be any number of things. In the new fiction, the title story of *Doctor Brodie's Report* is of this enigmatic type. It is an outrageous description of an incredible tribe called the Mlch, or Yahoos (the latter is the name of the degenerate humans in *Gulliver's Travels*). As a narrative device, Borges lays before us the incomplete manuscript of a Scottish Protestant missionary, David Brodie, who lived among the Yahoos. It reminds us of many things: Gulliver, a story by H. G. Wells, Pío Baroja's *Paradox Rey*, and other accounts of bizarre peoples. But mostly it reminds us of the old Borges, particularly of his description of the mind of Ireneo Funes ("Funes the Memorious," *Ficciones*), who could not forget details and was unable to form abstractions, "to think Platonically"; or it suggests the imaginary planet Tlön ("Tlön, Uqbar, Orbis Tertius," *Ficciones*), which is made of purely ideal—i.e., mental—elements. The Yahoos suffer the opposite of Funes's affliction; they have a language of pure abstractions and cannot remember details. They cannot combine phenomena except of a homogeneous, Platonic type. Unlike the people of Tlön, who can concoct anything at will, the Yahoos cannot fabricate at all. In the story of Tlön, the imaginary planet begins to concretize—to impose itself materially on the planet Earth; in the Yahoos of "Doctor Brodie's Report" we may see the grotesque end-result of that imposition. The Yahoos cannot count above four, can hardly speak, and appear to have no discrimination of time. In a limited way, they can predict the events of the immediate future (these appear to be only extrapolations). They remember almost nothing, and if they do remember an event they cannot say whether it happened to them or their fathers, or whether they dreamed it. They live in the present, they eat in secret or close their eyes while eating, they execute their fellows for fun, and if one of them is a poet (if he puts a few words together unintelligibly, but with moving effect) he is considered a god and anyone may kill him. Their king is blinded, mutilated, gelded, and kept in a cavern, except in war, when he is taken to the battlefront and waved like a banner. Instead of declining into allegory, Borges's prose now tends to sharpen into satire, or even to move toward the intensive case of the modern novel, where the parable intersects with cultural anthropology, and whose characters obscure and overwhelm the symbols they encounter.

THE UNCHANGING BORGES

Borges's characters are still chessmen, however, and both character and action are subservient to situations of a chessboard kind. His settings are still indifferent; the *compadritos* could almost as easily be Chicago gangsters or western gunmen. Despite his return to the *arrabales*, Borges is not a portrayer of local color and customs; as somebody must have said before, his Buenos Aires is a situation, not a city. Many of his themes are still highbrow, esthetic, "irrelevant." References to systems of ideas, famous and arcane, are no longer profuse, but they have not vanished; we still find Spinoza, Euclid, Schopenhauer, the Kabbalah, Carlyle, Lugones, Carriego, Henry James, Hudson, and others. Still, these allusions seem to serve less purpose than formerly and to be more often literary than philosophical. Familiar Borgesian language crops up only here and there; in "The Intruder" we find "contentious alcohol" (*alcohol pendenciero*), a phrase he has used since the 1930s. Missing now are those very frequent words with which Borges used to point to the vast or infinite, such as "dizzying" (*vertiginoso*; this word used to do double duty, suggesting also the rise to an esthetic moment). Borges seldom plays with time and infinity, and instead turns to destiny, cosmic irony, and chance. Regrettably, we find no rich poetic images that suggest impossible intuitions like the plight of man before the chaotic universe: veiled men uttering blasphemous conjectures in the twilight ("The Lottery in Babylon") or old men hiding themselves in the latrines, with some metal disks in a prohibited dicebox, weakly imitating the divine disorder ("The Library of Babel," *Ficciones*).

Borges's language is still superbly laconic. It is less connotative, and conceits and etymological uses of words are no longer plentiful. Fantastic ideas still appeal to him, as we see in "The Meeting" and in "Juan Muraña," but they are no longer intended to rattle or astonish us; instead, they appeal to our esthetic sensibilities. There appears to be no significance, beyond Borges's personal whim, to the fact that the new stories are laden with Scotsmen (Brodie, Clara Glencairn, Glencoe, the Gutres), Germans (Zimmerman), and other North Europeans (the Nelsons or Nilsens of "The Intruder"). The prominence of red hair is consistent with all of these nationalities; all red things have symbolic meaning, I think, in Borges's work, and there may be a hidden significance here.

As before, Borges continues to throw in generalizations that are external to the narrative: "Carlyle says that men need heroes to worship" ("The Unworthy Friend"). Their effect is to give intellectual justification to a character's action, obviating a realistic or contextual explanation. This economy is fundamental to Borges's narration. He often inserts his own opinions; he tell us that the aged protagonist of "The Elder Lady" was gradually "growing dimmer and dimmer," and he justifies the metaphor by adding, "Common metaphors are the best because they are the only true ones" (*DBR*); and to explain Clara Glencairn's reason for taking up abstract instead of traditional art, he generalizes that "all esthetic revolutions put forth a temptation toward the irresponsible and the far too easy" (*DBR*). These asides almost always have the value of esthetic commentary. In "Guayaquil," for example, Borges remarks: "The successiveness of language . . . tends to exaggerate what we are saying" (*DBR*). This is given as a warning to the reader that Zimmerman's enumerated traits are "visual trivia," apparently not as important as the conclusion that he had lived an arduous life.

Borges has tallied, in the preface to *In Praise of Darkness*, a handful of his "*astucias*"—his stylistic and structural devices. The tabulation omits the majority of the subtleties that scholars have abstracted from his older works, and is obviously a declaration of present, not necessarily former, practice. Time, he says, has taught him to avoid synonyms, Hispanisms, Argentinisms, archaisms, and neologisms; to prefer habitual to astonishing words; to insert circumstantial details, "which the reader now demands"; to feign small uncertainties; to tell things as if he did not fully understand them; and to remember that former norms are not obligations. In the preface to *Doctor Brodie's Report* he says he has renounced "the surprises inherent in a baroque style" (*DBR*). He does not call his new, "straightforward" stories simple: "I do not dare state that they are simple; there isn't anywhere on earth a single page or single word that is, since each thing implies the universe, whose most obvious trait is complexity" (*DBR*).

Two of the devices he mentions are conspicuous because they preserve in Borges's new fiction an essential property of the old: namely, feigning small uncertainties and telling a story as if he did not fully understand it. Borges's chessmen—his people "seen through the wrong end of a telescope" (James Irby)—are not so much characters as props. Their faces are wiped off by Borges's aloof posture. He masks the activity of writing under the pretense of listening: "People say (but this is unlikely) that the story was first told by Eduardo" ("The Intruder," *DBR*); "Carlos Reyles . . . told me the story . . . out in Adrogué" ("The End of the Duel," *DBR*); "here is the story, with all the inevitable variations brought about by time" ("The Meeting," *DBR*). An occasional disclaimer, like "probably," keeps this objectivity in front of the reader: "She was unable to keep hidden a certain preference, probably for the younger man" ("The Intruder," *DBR*). The only new story in which he does not keep his distance is "Guayaquil," where he writes as the protagonist; but it is also in this story that he speaks of the necessity of objectifying and states the principle clearly: "I shall with all probity recount what happened, and this may enable me to understand it. Furthermore, to confess to a thing is to leave off being an actor in it and to become an onlooker—to become somebody who has seen it and tells it and is no longer the doer" (*DBR*). In contrast to the narrator of "Guayaquil," who is so involved that he purports to understand only dimly what has happened, his rival historian, Zimmerman, is noteworthy for his objective detachment from events and opinions; we feel that Zimmerman understands everything—even the things he cannot express but can only allude to.

THE ESTHETIC PHENOMENON

Borges's objectivity, his blurring of faces, is directly related to his esthetic. I have suggested that in his older fiction Borges carries his reader to a mythic awareness, an esthetic moment of near-revelation, and at the same time alludes to that moment symbolically through images of dizziness: vertigo, fever, alcohol, inebriation, exaltation, delirium. These images are part of a whole system of secondary symbolism (i.e., below the level of such overt symbols as mirrors and labyrinths) through which Borges used to create, in each narrative, a background drama—a play of allusions in which the overt action of the story is duplicated by symbolic forms as if these were the enlarged shadows of the characters. In Borges's system there are symbols of order and being (blood, tower, light, coin, tree, tiger, sword), symbols of chaos or nonbeing (circles, ashes, mud, dust, swamps, plains, night, water, wall), and symbols of purely ideal being and of world dissolution, made largely of combinations and interplays of the images of order and chaos. They comprise an archetypal, almost Olympian representation of the activity of the human consciousness as it creates, destroys, and re-creates reality. In this shadowy undulation there is a moment between the chaos of nonbeing (mere perception of meaningless things) and the lucidity of full being (complete, meaningful abstraction) when the consciousness hovers on the brink of a higher revelation. That revelation never comes; instead, what occurs is a kind of short-circuit resulting in "language," the abstraction of a bathetic reality small enough to be expressed. But that hovering instant when some kind of supernal truth seems imminent is the "vertiginous" moment to which Borges refers as the esthetic event.

We find far less evidence of this background drama of symbols in Borges's new fiction. Avowing his disbelief in esthetic *theories*, which he says are only occasional stimuli or instruments, Borges speaks continually of the esthetic *occurrence* or *fact*, "the imminence of a revelation." He built it allusively or allegorically into the fabric of such stories as "The End" (*Ficciones*); now it stares at us ingenuously from many of his new ones, and the forewords to the books he has published since 1960 are conspicuously concerned with the central point—the esthetic fact is not a collection of words on paper, but an experience: "A volume in itself is not an esthetic reality, but a physical object among others; the esthetic event can occur only when it is written or when it is read" (preface to *In Praise of Darkness*; translation mine).

Borges has shown that he is willing to judge literature good or bad using the *hecho estético* as a criterion. In the preface to his *Personal Anthology* (1961) he points to Croce's pronouncement that art is expression. To that idea, or to its deformation, he says, we owe some of the worst literature. He quotes verses from Valéry about a fruit whose form perishes in the mouth, giving delight by perishing, and other lines from Tennyson in which a boat fades into the distance and "vanishes into light." He doubts that anyone will finally include such verses among the best, saying that they represent a "mental process." We should infer that they carry an image or idea to its completion and that this is esthetically wrong. Borges adds: "At times, I too have sought expression; I know now that my gods grant me no more than allusion or mention" (translation mine). His comments do not finally cohere unless we understand that his "gods" are his ideas about how literature should be made. By opposing expression to suggestion he contrasts a finished mental process with one that is open-ended and indefinite, hovering over an unformulated idea. He seems to believe that allusion is not at all intellectual, hence the emphasis on event, on fact.

Borges likes the fruit image from Valéry. In another preface (to his *Obra poética* [1964]), he says he applies to poetry what Berkeley applied to reality: "The taste of the apple . . . lies in the contact of the fruit with the palate, not in the fruit itself. . . . What is essential is the esthetic act, the thrill, the almost physical emotion that comes with each reading." The bad writer, for Borges, is the one who *eats the fruit for us*, finishing the idea before we can savor its insinuations—or worse, letting his foregone conclusion shape the composition. Croce's "expression" is the complete verbal capture of a clear idea or feeling—the short-circuit that evaporates the pregnant myth. Borges points out in an essay on Nathaniel Hawthorne (*Other Inquisitions*) that Hawthorne's moralisms do not usually ruin his work, if only because they come in the last paragraph and because he did not fashion his characters to prove his conclusions. An "expressive" writer, an Aesop, builds a narrative that yields a simile between two realities (with the intention of giving one the color of the other), or between his fictitious events and the moral point or social theory he is trying to illustrate, while Borges himself wants only to distract his reader. Some quality held in common between two or more things links them secretly, and this is not something contrived by Borges but perceived by him. That perception, imparted to us, brings the momentary illusion that the chaotic world is somehow simplified or illuminated, and we are lifted toward a new insight or comprehension—which never solidifies.

Borges's esthetic idea is worked into his new fiction in at least two ways. In some stories he presents esthetically loaded situations, a "missing apex" type of suggestion which leaves the mystery incomplete. Usually this involves irony or paradox, and inevitably it raises the question of the character of God or of Destiny: an ironic competition between two dying rivals who had refused to kill each other in life; the redemptive crucifixion of an unbelieving, unsuspecting, unwilling "Christ"; a brother love that is no less admirable in itself (and perhaps is even more so) for having expressed itself in murder. The second way is that of the abstruse "allegory" (I now use the term inexactly, for lack of another) in which the esthetic event is pointed to by allusion as an objective idea. Only one of Borges's new stories is clearly of this kind, although others may be more subtly so; before turning to "Guayaquil," it will be helpful to look first at obvious allusions to the *hecho estético* in the short prose of *In Praise of Darkness*.

Borges uses, more often now, stories he has heard. Long ago he heard the one called "Pedro Salvadores," which is not really a story but a historical episode to which Borges adds his comments and shows his own esthetic reaction. Salvadores was an Argentine who, as an opponent of the dictator Juan Manuel de Rosas (deposed in 1852), was forced to hide in his cellar for nine years. This, plus the details, is his whole story. In the same way that Camus wondered, in *The Myth of Sisyphus*, what Sisyphus thought as he carried his eternal rock, Borges wonders at those nine years of dark isolation. (Internal elements lift the episode to a universal plane, and there is reason to suspect a parallel with Borges's blindness and his intellectual history). He conjectures about Salvadores's feelings, actions, thoughts, and very being—with no possibility of corroborating his intuitions. "As with so many things, the fate of Pedro Salvadores," he concludes, "strikes us as a symbol of something we are about to understand, but never quite do."

Very like that episode is the one called "The Anthropologist." Borges says he heard the story in Texas and he gives it to us without comment. Fred Murdock, a student of indigenous languages, goes into the desert to live with an Indian tribe and to discover the secrets behind its esoteric rites.

After a long time he returns to the university and informs his disappointed professor that he has learned the secret but cannot tell it—not because of a vow or the deficiencies of language; in fact, he could enunciate it a hundred ways. But the secret is less valuable than the steps that lead to it, and "Those steps have to be taken, not told."

"The Anthropologist" is brief and deceptively simple; it is not a story about an anthropologist but about a young man in chaos, uncommitted, who tried to reduce the world to a facet of itself, hoping to find in it the centripetal vortex of vision that would explain or justify the whole. It is the same story as "The Library of Babel" (*Ficciones*) in which the inmates of the library go blind looking for the compendious book. It is the story of a frustration, like "Averroes' Search" (*El aleph*), where Averroes is compared to the frustrated god "mentioned by Burton . . . [who] tried to create a bull and created a buffalo instead." It is the story told in Borges's poem "The Golem," where a rabbi tries to create a man and can only create a clumsy doll. Here we see vestiges of an allusive imagery that is much more evident in Borges's older work; it is not mere coincidence that the student dreamed of mustangs (in the Spanish, it is bison). He went into the desert to find a revelation and found only language. As he implies, the search was more valuable than the result, and the search has to be experienced, not told. The esthetic experience is in the contact of the fruit with the palate, not in the digestion of it.

Borges believes—I think it is clear—that the tales men tell and retell, the ones that comprise our myths, are all of the open kind. They respect and embody an esthetic of the unconsummated, rehearsing the cosmic mystery. All our science, philosophy, and explanations of the universe are buffaloes.

In a tiny poetic essay, "The Unending Gift," an artist promises Borges a painting but dies without sending it. If it had come, it would be a thing among things; but now it is limitless and unceasing, capable of any form or color. It somehow exists and will live and grow like music. "In a promise," Borges concludes, "there is something that does not die."

"GUAYAQUIL" AND *EL HECHO ESTÉTICO*

"Guayaquil," which I summarized earlier, is the story of a scholar who renounces intellectual fulfillment in order to preserve esthetic life. He sees more value in a myth than in an explanation, more virtue in an unformulated idea than in the language that purports to convey truth. The narrator of the story and his rival historian, Dr. Zimmerman, are contending for the privilege of appraising the newly found letter of Bolívar which will give Bolívar's answer to the renowned question of what happened in the interview with San Martín. We must remember that San Martín, after talking with Bolívar, withdrew from the revolutionary struggle; we might say that he, too, quit before his drama was done. Bolívar led his country's fortunes until his death, leaving his indelible stamp on the revolution and its aftermath. Transferred from the historical plane to the literary, San Martín's story is unconsummated and esthetic; but Bolívar's finished career (a completed "mental process") makes bad "literature." The conversation of the revolutionary heroes is somehow duplicated in that of the historians, who observe that it was no doubt Bolívar's will, not words, that determined the outcome at Guayaquil. The narrator finally concedes to Zimmerman the honor of publishing the letter in order not to repeat the action—the will—of Bolívar. To repeat Bolívar's error would be to turn an esthetically attractive historical event—a living myth—into mere short-circuiting language. The reason is this: there is mystery in the San Martín incident, and Zimmerman believes the letter cannot really clear it up because it gives only Bolívar's version, perhaps written in self-justification. If Zimmerman interprets the letter for the public, he will preserve the mythic ambiguity by weighing Bolívar's words in the proper perspective. But the biased narrator feels that if he publishes a commentary, the effect will be deadly; he is the descendant of revolutionists, very much involved in history and partial to San Martín, and his conjectural position on the matter is well known (although we are not told what it is). The public will link him with the letter, and the myth (the suggestive indeterminacy) will be destroyed by some miserable "explanation" which the public will suppose has been made by his conclusions on the subject. "The public at large," Zimmerman remarks, "will never bother to look into these subtleties" (*DBR*). If the narrator imposes his will, he will act, as Borges expressed a similar urge in *Dreamtigers*, from "no other law than fulfillment," and the result will be "the immediate indifference that ensues" ("The Maker").

To show Zimmerman that he has understood, the narrator recites two parables in which we can see a tension between simple correspondence and the esthetic fact. In the first parable, two kings play chess on a hilltop while their armies clash. One loses the game and his army loses the battle; the chess game was a mere duplication of the larger reality. In the second, two famous bards have a contest of song. The first sings from dawn until dusk and hands the harp to the other. The latter merely lays it aside and stands up, and the first confesses his defeat. We can take the second parable to mean that the best song remains unsung—limitless, unending, like a promise. The narrator makes statements at the beginning and end of "Guayaquil" which can be understood to mean that he will not destroy the esthetic indefiniteness surrounding San Martín's talk with the Liberator. At the beginning: "Now I shall not journey to the Estado Occidental [Western State]; now I shall not set eyes on snow-capped Higuerota mirrored in the water of the Golfo Plácido; now I shall not decipher Bolívar's manuscripts" (*DBR*). At the end the narrator, a man whose life has been dedicated to nailing down the definitive truths that explain history, seems to confess his conversion to an esthetic of the indefinite: "I have the feeling that I shall give up any future writing" (*DBR*). Borges fashioned the opening lines of this story from Conrad's *Nostromo*.

In the original Spanish, "manuscripts" is *letra*, which means handwriting or letter. *Letra* is one of Borges's old symbols for clear conception, visible reality, or abstraction, as in "The Secret Miracle" (*Ficciones*), where God is a tiny letter on a map. Among other symbols of ordered or abstract reality in Borges's older stories are mountains and other kinds of upward projections. The things the narrator of "Guayaquil" says he will not do are all symbolic, it seems, of the production of intelligible reality through expressive language; he will not see a mountain duplicated, behold a "letter," or write his definitive conclusions. As for the "western country," it seems enough to say that "western" is the opposite of "eastern" with its implication of mystery. This, too, is consistent with Borges's old symbolism, in which all things eastern and yellow suggest the chaotic, mythic, and esthetic.

Borges is still building into his fiction the occasional guide-images or omens that facilitate interpretations but certainly do not corroborate them. For example, when Zimmerman enters the narrator's house, he pauses to look at a patio tiled in black and white (an old image in Borges's work), prefiguring the parable of the chess game and perhaps suggesting that the events to follow will be a kind of duplication. Indeed, during the conversation it seemed to the two scholars "that we were already two other people"; their encounter occurs at twilight, which in Borges's familiar work is a frequent symbol of change or suspension of reality. When the first bard sings, he sings from morning twilight to evening; his song is a daylight song, a finished and patent thing, superseded by the unsung music that belongs to the dreaming hours as day recedes. And at one point Zimmerman remarks: " 'Everything is strange in Prague, or, if you prefer, nothing is strange. Anything may happen there. In London, on certain evenings, I have had the same feeling' " (*DBR*). Zimmerman is from Prague, the native city of Kafka, and of the ambitious rabbi of "The Golem," who tried to create a man but produced only a monster. Also in "Guayaquil" is a reference to *Der Golem*, a novel by Gustav Meyrink of Prague. In conversation Borges has said that the creation of the golem is "a parable of the nature of art."

One other important symbol deserves mention: blood. In Borges's older work, it is associated with fullness of being—with completeness, domination, victory, or will. The will in question in "Guayaquil" is not Zimmerman's, imposed upon the narrator; it is, rather, the narrator's, suppressed for a cause. Zimmerman observes that the narrator carries Argentine history in his blood, implying that he would treat Bolívar's letter with willful prejudgment. The narrator tells us that Zimmerman's words were "the expression of a will that made of the future something as irrevocable as the past" (*DBR*), but we must understand that Zimmerman's "expression" delineated the undesirable willfulness of the narrator, which the latter willfully subdued.

This interpretation of "Guayaquil" suggests taking another look at such stories as "The Gospel According to Mark"; instead of comparing the mentalities of Espinosa and the Gutres in terms of order and chaos—or, to use a term from Borges, order and *adventure* ("The Duel")—we might infer a contrast between the open, uncommitted, mythic-minded writer (Espinosa) and the closed-minded, compromised, or committed writers (the Gutres) who are guided by their determination (their "Calvinist fanaticism") to get a point across, to find their "beloved island." The work of such writers is predetermined; its meaning is as irrevocable as the preconceptions of the authors.

If we can judge by "The Maker," even his blindness is to Borges analogous to the abandonment of Aesopism, somewhere in his past, and to his espousal of the idea that literature should be written "blind"—for its own sake, not for an intellectual or practical purpose. Most of his stories are punctiliously contrived allusions to the idea of art for art's sake; in that sense they comprise art about art.

ETHICS

With the appearance of *In Praise of Darkness* (as Borges notes in the preface) two new themes are added to his work: old age and ethics. What he calls ethics goes beyond and embraces much of his philosophy and its esthetic foundations.

"Fragments of an Apocryphal Gospel" could be called poetry or prose; it is a collection of numbered apothegms and injunctions modeled in part on the Beatitudes. They alter many of the sayings of Jesus and other moral or theological axioms, often contradicting them or seeming to. They reflect a point of view which denies heaven and hell, reduces men to predestined beings who are ignorant of their destiny, rejects the idea of morality for the sake of reward, believes in pursuing justice for its own sake, and looks with kindly, humanistic eyes at the human species. These dicta strongly imply a pessimism overcome by courage—not stoicism, which suggests a dogged refusal to be affected, but blind, Tillichian faith, which has only rigor to justify it. Borges's ethic, as he seems to declare in "A Prayer" (discussed below), consists in a devotion to lucid reason and just action.

In his "Fragments" Borges is satirical, warm, wise, heretical, moralistic, sly, and often majestic. "Blessed are they who know," he says, "that suffering is not a crown of glory," and "Wretched are they that mourn, for they have fallen into the craven habit of tears." He has no use for the poor in spirit, who expect heaven to be better than earth, nor for those who comfort themselves with feelings of guilt; and the actions of men, he says, deserve neither heaven nor hell. You can't judge a tree by its fruit nor a man by his works; they can both be better or worse than they look. "Give that which is holy unto the dogs, cast your pearls before swine: for what matters is giving." To one who strikes you on the cheek you may turn the other, provided you are not moved by fear. To do good for your enemy is to give him justice; but to love him is a task for angels, not men. Happy are the lovers and the loved, and those who can do without love, and those who forgive others and themselves, and "Happy are the happy."

The latter pronouncement has an esthetic motive, expressed in "The Unworthy Friend": "The only thing without mystery is happiness, because happiness is an end in itself" (*DBR*). And there are other esthetic admonitions: "Swear not, for an oath may be only an emphasis." The moral and the esthetic are combined in: "Forgetting is the only vengeance and the only forgiveness." This idea is the theme of another new prose piece, "Legend," in which Cain asks Abel to forgive him. But Abel has forgotten who killed whom. Cain sees that Abel has truly forgiven, and says he will try to forget too. "Yes," Abel agrees, "as long as there's remorse, there's guilt." This idea is expressed also in "The Unworthy Friend."

"A Prayer" is perhaps the frankest and most intimate thing Borges has ever written and in my opinion the most magnificent. He begins by acknowledging that a personal prayer demands an almost superhuman sincerity. It is obvious, he says, that he cannot ask for anything. To ask that he not go blind (he is not entirely sightless) would be to ask for the suspension of cause and effect, and "Nobody is worthy of such a miracle." Neither can he ask pardon for his errors; forgiveness is an act of others, which purifies the offended, not the offender, and only Borges can save Borges. He can only give what he himself does not have: courage, hope, the urge to learn. He wants to be remembered less as a poet than as a friend; let someone recite a line from Dunbar or Frost and remember that he first heard it from Borges's lips. Faithful to his "gods" to the end, he combines the esthetic and the moral in a final observation: "The laws of the universe are unknown to us, but we are somehow sure that to reason clearly and to act righteously is to help those laws, which will never be revealed to us." When he dies, he wants to die wholly, "with this companion, my body."

The uncertain darkness of death and of blindness is the theme of *In Praise of Darkness*. In a piece called "His End and His Beginning," the two are united in superb metaphorical prose that subsumes all forms of transition into the unknown. Having died, and suffering the agony of being dead, Borges accepts death and it becomes heaven; blind, he accepts blindness and it becomes the beginning of an adventurous life in a new world. He praises his darkness, and in that praise there is a victory, as limitless as a promise, over all men's darkness. And somehow Borges extols the darkness of his own skepticism, his agnostic unknowingness, which is his philosophy; he translates it positively into an esthetic of conjectural expectancy. Borges's mind ranges over reality as the Vikings ranged over the world, plundering not for plunder but for adventure.

Reading this book, we are convinced of the sincerity of his apocryphal fragments, one of which says: "Let a candle be lighted though no man see it; God will see it."

Borges's "Immortal": The Ritual Experience of Literature

Sophia S. Morgan

Like several of the other short stories of Borges, "The Immortal" is a narrative within a narrative, built on a deceptively simple series of frames. The inner narrative—a story that may be characterized as fantastic or mythical—is found in manuscript, we are told, in the last of six volumes containing Pope's translation of the *Iliad*. This is a first, realistic and literal frame of sorts. The second, circumstantial and situational, is the occasion of the discovery of the manuscript: in 1929, the princess of Lucinge bought the six-volume set from a Jew of Smyrna and later found the said story in it.

There is nothing unusual or implausible about either of these two frames. And yet, finding a manuscript in a book (that is, a text within another text) is not quite like finding one in any other place—in a bottle, for example. The manuscript in the book becomes (as its counterpart in the bottle can never be) a connotative exemplification of the fact that this will be a story within a story. (It is also the first, subtle, and perhaps ironic instance of self-referentiality or reflexivity in the narrative.) This embeddedness, moreover, necessarily suggests the possibility of a relationship between the two texts. The story within the story may be a story about stories, or about the relationship between stories, or about what it means to tell or retell stories, and so on. After all, the six volumes are Pope's retelling of Homer's story, and therefore a reincarnation of the ancient myths. Is the Jew's addendum related to all this? If so, how? Can it be, coming as it does at the end of the first epic—the epic of war—an avatar of the second—the epic of homecoming? Is it a kind of *Odyssey* related to that of Homer in ways similar to the ways Pope's *Iliad* is related to Homer's?

From *Rite, Drama, Festival, Spectacle: Rehearsals toward a Theory of Cultural Performance*, edited by John J. MacAloon. © 1984 by the Institute for the Study of Human Issues.

25

Is it both similar to and different from them? Does it reaffirm the old story or negate it? Does it, above all, constitute a type of commentary on its predecessor, or does it use its predecessor as a set of footnotes to itself? To put this last question differently, Which of the two texts has the primacy here? Which of the two, if either, enfolds and contains the other? All of these questions and their possible answers begin now to take shape within the realm of reader expectation.

Similar considerations arise with respect to the second frame. The encounter of the Jew with the Princess, the place, date, and transaction are perfectly consonant with literary conventions designed to place a fantastic narrative within a realistic setting. But the encounter of the two has an additional and more important function. Although we are never told that the manuscript was either written or owned by him, the description of the antiquarian and the information concerning his death and burial indicate that, in the course of the story, a connection between him and the manuscript will become evident.

Laws governing textual coherence require that embedded elements (or, as in this case, narrative segments) fit an overall schema, structure, or significance: the manuscript found in a bottle, the map in code, the embedded story all have to connect to the fictional reality that surrounds them. Textual coherence is proportionate to the number of links between elements: the greatest coherence is the result of the greatest number of links between elements. The expectation that the antiquarian be connected to the manuscript in other than merely accidental and circumstantial ways is dictated by the demand for greater textual coherence. Thus the first frame promises that "The Immortal" will be a story about stories and about relationships between stories, and the second frame creates the anticipation that these stories will ultimately be related in turn to the significance of a specific biography—to a real life.

We are on promising ground: the problem of epics, myths, ritual passages perhaps; that of texts and how they relate to each other and to translations, annotations, footnotes, quotations, and repetition—all this will be connected to the life and death of a real individual who lived in many places and was buried in Ios. Here once more, as in most of his stories, Borges reopens the question of the relationship between life and its representations: between the book and the world. But even in this relatively unproblematic transaction between the Princess and the Jew, we already discern a strange disorder. This flesh-and-blood, book-selling mortal, this Jew, is not just any faceless and anonymous Smyrniot. He is Joseph Cartaphilus; he is Joseph the Lover of Texts; he is the Wandering Jew; he is a legend.

The symbolic space of the narrative is, thus, invaded by ghosts from the very start. For nothing is more ghostly than fictional, legendary, or mythical figures when encountered in the light of everyday reality. Next to our profound conviction concerning the identity of the self—that rational belief that "I" cannot be "another"—nothing is as certain as that the worlds of fiction and reality do not mix. Nothing constitutes a more radical trespassing of categories than that Don Quixote or Hamlet should be roaming our streets. Borges's story mixes these two domains—legend and reality—from the beginning. The book, the legend, penetrates "real life" in flesh and blood: not only does Cartaphilus sell books in Smyrna, he inserts his manuscript in a volume of Pope. The translator-poet might as well have had his labors annotated by Achilles himself.

There is nothing strange in someone's having inserted an autobiographical fiction between the pages of a volume of the *Iliad*. But that this someone may in fact be a figure from legend, that he may be no less than the magical old man who is destined never to die until the Second Coming, and that this legendary figure may be part and parcel of our contemporary historical reality (But isn't that what the legend precisely affirms: that he does circulate among us from time to time?) goes against all realistic conventions as well as against our common sense. The story trespasses against realism. Well and good. It still preserves the truth of the legend; we must take it, too, as a fiction.

But it also trespasses against the legend. For the legend tells us that Cartaphilus cannot die, but the story begins with the announcement of his death. Multiple categorical transgressions "celebrating paradox and welcoming ambiguity" place us squarely within that space out of which rituals and literature weave their cloth, and within that crisis which will lead to action and perhaps to resolution.

And with this it is time to turn to the inner narrative.

I

With the exception of the short editorial "preface" above and an equally brief postscript, the rest of the story—all five sections of it—is taken up by the first-person narrative of one Marcus Flaminius Rufus, military tribune of a Roman legion quartered at Berenice at the time of Diocletian.

This is the narrative of a quest. Rufus is met one day at dawn by an "*exhausted and bloody* horseman" from the East who has been seeking "the secret river that cleanses men of death"; before the man dies, he mentions the wondrous city of the Immortals, which rises on the far bank of the river. Like a runner receiving the torch from a fellow athlete, Rufus determines then to find the city and its river. He makes inquiries, converses with philosophers in Rome, and finally receives from Flavius, proconsul of Getulia, 200 soldiers for the undertaking. These, together with his mercenaries, and very like the prototypic companions of numerous other epic journeys, either succumb to the perilous journey or desert. Completely separated from civilized humanity, Marcus Flaminius then penetrates barbarous regions in which all is horror and everything presages death. Cut off from human society, and with the preliminary part (section one) of his journey over, Rufus can now enter the space of liminality, of danger and contradiction—the space proper of ritual.

His journey follows an initiatory schema of suffering, death, and resurrection—the archetypal pattern of all mysteries, be they of puberty or entry into a secret society. Here, too, one can say, Rufus dies unto himself to be reborn into another life. Eliade observes that "the man of the archaic societies strove to conquer death by according it such an importance that in the final reckoning, death ceased to present itself as a *cessation* and became a *rite of passage*." In this case, however, the rite is not ostensibly one that aims at integrating the subject into another state of greater wisdom or "of sacred and creative knowledge" but rather the very quest of immortality. Quest, rite, and the theme of the water of life are fused into one. Thus, what is at stake here is a myth. And not any myth at that, but a symbolic representation, or rather dramatization, of the ritual process itself. For if the function of all ritual is to bring the initiate or participant into contact either with the divinity or with a higher spiritual reality, the myth of the quest for immortality is in a sense a symbol of them all. If ritual is the negation of human finitude, this particular myth is a myth of ritual. As ritual goes, this is metaritual.

The narrative begins by situating Rufus historically and geographically, and also—most importantly—by defining his particular space-time as one of war and death. But he himself, not being given a chance to participate in the strife, is untouched by it all. And it is the pain of this "privation"— the pain of being unaffected by the pain of war, and not a desire to put an end to the pain of war—that sends him out on his quest for the city of the Immortals. This is probably the first Borgesian reversal in the story: Rufus, who would have liked to get "a glimpse of Mars' countenance," sets out on the quest for immortality begun by a man now dead—a man who was to die seeking the river, or who was seeking the river because he was dying. (Rufus also starts out as he might for war. The other was "probably" fleeing from it.)

The journey, in its broad outlines, follows familiar—one may say archetypal—patterns. The departure from Arsinoe constitutes the first separation from the quotidian, and once more the use of the actual place name, like that of Thebes Hekatompylos, marks unambiguously the opposition between the real, secular space of history and the desert—the timeless space of the monstrous or of the sacred. Opposed both to nature and culture, this desert is a space "where the earth is mother of monsters" and all custom the reverse of human law. Here "in the corrupted water of the cisterns some men drink madness and death." And it is here that Rufus thirsts, not for the water he originally set out to find, but for plain, natural water that sustains mortal life.

Since this is the reverse of the secular world he left behind, it is not surprising that life in this desert should be impossible. Cut off from the world of Diocletian as well as from the society of men, Rufus loses consciousness from thirst while dreaming of a jar of water in the center of a labyrinth. And with this almost literal but also primarily symbolic death, the first stage of his mythic journey comes to an end, at the very moment when he most resembles the bloody, thirsty horseman from the East. The first man's end, which is the second's beginning, replays itself in another beginning that is also an end.

II

The second stage of the journey is acted out among the troglodytes. Either because of the laws of narrative, which set everything into motion and turn all situations into their opposite, or because of the laws of ritual, which dictate that a "death" be followed by entry into an "other" condition, we may have expected Rufus to wake up in a world unlike the desert one. Symmetries, redundancies, and reversals of this sort are the hallmark of ritual journeys as much as they are of literary composition. The pattern of ascent/descent, loss/recovery, death/rebirth, defilement/cleansing—ancient formulas of storytelling as well as of living—prepare us to expect a reversal of fortunes and a shift in the register of so much darkness. But that is not the case here. On the contrary, the troglodytes among whom Rufus finds himself are of the same race as others encountered earlier in his career. They cannot speak and they devour serpents.

When, in this second phase of his adventures, Rufus regains consciousness, he is lying with his hands tied, "in an oblong stone niche no larger than a common grave." The symbol is a complex one: it stands for the ritual death of the hero (begun in section one with his loss of consciousness and the hallucinatory dream of the labyrinth); it signifies the end of his mortal existence (since he will emerge from it to drink of the water of immortality); and it points, ambiguously and paradoxically, in two directions at once: toward his life up until the present moment (which may be seen as only a kind of death compared to immortality), but also toward his new life as an Immortal, which, as the troglodyte Immortals demonstrate, may only be a kind of death compared to mortal life. Of course, in addition to these two, the stone grave may also be the emblem of the passage from one mode of existence to the other: among symbolic spaces, graves are rarely surpassed for liminal concentration and richness.

Rufus awakes at the very foot of the City of the Immortals; he drinks (though at the time he hardly suspects it) of the waters of the long sought River of Life, and even enters the city. It would seem, then, that this should constitute the highest point of the journey, the fulfillment of all desire, the justification of all previous suffering, the cessation of horror and dispossession, the healing and wholeness that come with the profound understanding born of the contemplation of the divinity and its signs. Here, if anywhere, is the place for the hierophany to happen. Structurally, too, the moment has been prepared as if it were going to happen: in that antechamber to the liminal among the troglodytes, Rufus has passed his "tests." Breaking the bindings, stealing the detested portion of serpent flesh, and dragging himself to the dirty water to drink are all acts qualifying him for the next stage, which, there is good reason to expect, will be nothing less than a tremendous mystery. Moreover, his hallucinatory itinerary through the labyrinthine city consists of both a descent and an ascent. The darkness and hopelessness of the descent lead the reader to expect a change. For one of the strongest laws of ritual and narrative journeys is that "everything happens for a good reason."

Borges, however, constantly defers the moment of illumination. Just as there was no relief from the monstrous spaces of section one to those of section two, here also the horror of the descent into the subterranean passages of the city is only a foretaste of what Rufus will experience when he comes out again. This part of the story, which is typical Borges and very beautiful, requires a careful reading. While describing his attempts to find a way to penetrate the city, Rufus says:

> Toward midnight, I set foot upon the black shadow of its walls, bristling out in idolatrous forms on the yellow sand. I was halted by a kind of sacred horror. Novelty and the desert are so abhorred by man that I was glad one of the troglodytes had followed me to the last.

Rufus then discovers a pit with a stairway, which takes him down into the foundations of the city:

> I went down; through a chaos of sordid galleries I reached a vast circular chamber scarcely visible. There were nine doors in this cellar; eight led to a labyrinth that treacherously returned to the same chamber; the ninth (through another labyrinth) led to a second circular chamber equal to the first. I do not know the total number of these chambers; my misfortune and anxiety multiplied them. The silence was hostile and almost perfect; there was no sound in this deep stone network save that of a subterranean wind, whose cause I did not discover; noiselessly, tiny streams of rusty water disappeared between the crevices. Horribly, I became habituated to this doubtful world; I found it incredible that there could be anything but cellars with nine doors and long branched-out cellars; I do not know how long I must have walked beneath the ground; I know that I once confused, in the same nostalgia, the atrocious village of the barbarians and my native city, amid the clusters.

What Rufus finds in this vestibule to the city is horrible—and doubtlessly no longer within the aura of sacred horror—because it consists of nothing but meaningless, purposeless repetition. Nothing means, nothing signifies, nothing speaks here. "The silence was hostile and almost perfect."

If novelty and the desert are abhorrent, as Rufus says, that is because they defy our powers to interpret them. Before them we are dispossessed of all the codes, structures, relationships, and blueprints with which we give meaning to the world. Before novelty (true and absolute novelty) the existing codes are not sufficient; before the desert they are too numerous or superfluous. Novelty and the desert are the two poles of the monstrous. Between them or beyond them, senseless, endless repetition—this treacherous return to the same or to another chamber equal to the first—is a monstrosity surpassing either of the other two because it combines their two fundamental properties: it is like novelty because, though manifestly articulated, it serves no signification and has no purpose; and it is like the desert because it is nothing but meaningless uniformity. Liminal spaces are those that bring together and mix contrary or incompatible but meaningful categories. But the foundations of this liminal edifice are built upon the conjunction of the two poles of the meaningless and the monstrous. Thus far, Rufus's journey has been the story of a series of losses: loss of companions, of memory, of the sense of time, of purity—of all that he had or was. And now he is witness to and affected by a loss so terrible that no words can express it. In this state all previous moments of desperate dispossession seem desirable: "I know that I once confused, in the same nostalgia, the atrocious village of the barbarians and my native city."

From this mute horror, Rufus emerges only to enter another variety of it equally divorced from rationality or the sacred. For when he finally succeeds in climbing up to the "resplendent City," he finds it to be so monstrously meaningless as to lack even the finality of labyrinths—structures compounded to confuse men. Not only is this not one of the labyrinths that have been used in myth and ritual to symbolize the passage from blindness to enlightenment, it is not even one meant to confuse. Before it, Rufus thinks, "This palace is the fabrication of the gods." And then, "The gods who built it have died." And finally, "The gods who built it were mad."

What then is this city? Judged by the place it occupies in the narrative and by the fact that it represents the ultimate object of desire, it ought to be at least the locus of a hierophany. But not only does the city have no truths and no mysteries to reveal, it constitutes merely by existing the ultimate derision and the ruin of all hierophanies: "As long as it lasts, no one in the world can be strong or happy." For the truth that it publishes, even from its secret desert, is the truth of the absence of Truth, of the absence of a Logos eternally present, though hidden, in all signs. And as long as the city lasts, its meaningless complexity "contaminates the past and the future and in some way even jeopardizes the stars." As long as it lasts, the city confronts all the other labyrinths constructed by men (or gods—the Immortals are precisely a juncture of the human with the divine), all the other attempts—from religion to science and philosophy—to build the model of the order of the world. For by its mere existence and per-

manence, it negates order, annihilates systems, ruins significance, and reduces to a pitiful heap of rubbish that "House Beautiful . . . which," in
Walter Pater's words, "the creative minds of all generations are always
building together." Novalis characterized philosophy as the longing for the
great homecoming: the longing to be everywhere at home. The city turns
this longing into a fool's dream and every other habitable "house" into an
illusion.

There is only one defense against its poison, and this Rufus uses: he
tries to dispossess himself of the city that has robbed him of every possibility
for significance: he tries to forget it:

> I do not remember the stages of my return, amid the dusty and
> damp hypogea. I only know I was not abandoned by the fear that,
> when I left the last labyrinth, I would again be surrounded by the
> nefarious City of the Immortals. I can remember nothing else. This
> oblivion, now insuperable, was perhaps voluntary; perhaps the
> circumstances of my escape were so unpleasant that, on some day
> no less forgotten as well, I swore to forget them.

So, too, the man of religious or scientific faith may choose to forget
both this city and the possibility of its existence. But whenever, as in essays
such as this, we reopen the question of whether structure and significance
abide in the object of our study or in our metalanguages, it is the possibility
of the city that casts its shadow on our words.

I spoke earlier of Borges's use of the pattern of ritual to create metaritual. One could add here that the first two parts of the story not only
constitute an implicit commentary on ritual strategies but also form a kind
of antiritual. For although some of the prototypic formulas of ritual are
meticulously followed through, the content of ritual as illumination, homecoming, reintegration, or recovery is negated. This is a nihilist's ritual:
beyond the thirst and the near death there was no truth, no harmony, and
no purpose—only chaos.

He who had sought the sacred fount of the water of life, and dreamed
of it at the heart of a labyrinth, finds at the end of his journey a dead and
sterile city, a space symbolic of the absolute absence of all meaning, as
poisonous as the corrupted cisterns in which one drank madness and death
in the beginning of the journey. The river and the city had been linked
together from the start. They are correlates of each other and are yoked
together as symbols of that other ubiquitous opposition: nature/culture. To
find the waters that cleanse men of the stigma of death would have as its
corollary finding a celestial city inhabited by perfect human beings. But the
city this time was death. The ritual dying that this military tribune had to
submit to did not lead him to an epiphany. Dante, who knew his ritual
patterns well, would have found this an incomprehensible error or a
blasphemy.

But the story is not yet finished. Borges, who may not be a nihilist at all, despite the claims of some critics, persistently defers the moment of illumination. Is not such deferment precisely the essence of a labyrinth?

III

No method of text analysis will ever be able to convey as well as do the original words the tension and the release from horror expressed in the opening sentence of the next section: "Those who have read the account of my labors with attention will recall that a man from the tribe followed me as a dog might up to the irregular shadow of the walls."

At the moment of the return, after the second crossing of the limits of the liminary, Rufus meets at the mouth of the cave the man who had followed him. The man traces rudimentary and indistinct signs, "like the letters in our dreams," which seem "on the verge of being understood and then dissolve." At the moment of reintegration, the initiate encounters once more two things: humanity and the word. Until now, all three stages of the journey have been marked by silence: the troglodytes, ignorant of verbal commerce; the labyrinth, with a hostile and almost perfect silence; the resplendent city, beyond nature or culture, silent in still another way—as the absence of all signification.

But what Rufus finds outside is merely a promise of humanity, merely a promise of language: the troglodyte's tracings on the sand are not real signs, and without language he can only subsist in "a world without memory and without time." The days that "go on dying, and with them the years," do so in monstrous undifferentiation and in a silence that the Roman tries to combat by bringing language to the savage (another test in which teacher and pupil are equally tested). But they both fail, until the miracle of the rain.

Like the color of the moon in the garden at Thebes, this rain must mean more than all the symbolism we can read into it. Certainly it is opposed to the symbolic river or the symbolic jar, and is more powerful than they simply because it is real and also, perhaps, because it is both a baptism and a communion. The tribe receives it in ecstasy and behaves "like Corybantes possessed by the divinity." Perhaps its power, for the reader, lies in the fact that it accomplishes what the ritual journey up to now has failed to accomplish: a true epiphany and a union (but with what? with man? with joy? with just water?). Perhaps there is also the feeling that this epiphany, which takes place not within the space of the sacred but in the everyday, natural world, is as untranslatable, as ineffable, as any of the other kind. Perhaps this "primordial" scene shows us precisely the birth of a divinity, the "translation" of a presence (which is also the object of a desire) into a Presence—a god.

One may see this downpour in the desert—this sudden gift of life from above—as a kind of miracle, the very embodiment of the unexpected, the extraordinary, and the sacred. One may also see it as an instance of what is endlessly repeated and experienced in quotidian space. And one may see it as both things at once: the eternal alternation of human want—of thirst, isolation, or loss—with the recurring moment of the rain—natural symbol of a manna that restores life to all things; miracle that always happens, here and now, within everyday space. It is the miracle of communion and communication, and of the recovery of a past now lost, but which memory, stammeringly, reshapes.

Again, the miracle is perhaps that this experience, which words cannot translate, is somehow, magically, captured in words. Once more, forgotten words are set into motion. The distance between the words stammered by Argos, the troglodyte who has followed, and the rain is both immense and infinitesimal. (What analytical rod can measure it? Only patterns are measurable.)

At this point one realizes that the incident of the rain retroactively restructures the pattern we have been reading. Rufus's encounter with what we had expected to be the sacred was a failure of enlightenment and an absence of signification. But now the downpour reveals the journey into the labyrinth to be only a preliminary stage leading up to the rain. Before we witnessed the descent/ascent into the sacred become a journey into horror without enlightenment and reintegration, but now we are given reintegration, community, and communion in enlightenment all at once.

> Argos, I cried, Argos.
>
> Then, with gentle admiration, as if he were discovering something lost and forgotten a long time ago, Argos stammered these words: "Argos, Ulysses' dog." And then, also without looking at me: "This dog lying in the manure."
>
> We accept reality easily, perhaps because we intuit that nothing is real. I asked him what he knew of the *Odyssey*. The exercise of Greek was painful for him; I had to repeat the question.
>
> "Very little," he said. "Less than the poorest rhapsodist. It must be a thousand and one hundred years since I invented it."

The search for a truth never before heard has led to the contemplation and recovery of a text everybody knows, and to the miracle of memory. Borges has retold in many ways that ancient tale (which one may read as an apologue of ritual journeys) of the man who goes on a long voyage in search of treasure. He learns from his jailer in a distant land that he (the guard) also has dreamed of a treasure in another land. The jailer describes this treasure as being buried next to a certain well, under a certain fig tree, in a certain garden. . . . The man recognizes the garden, the tree, the well as his very own at home, and returns to discover the treasure in his own back yard.

Ritual patterns are symmetrical; liminal spaces juxtapose irreconcilable or contrary pairs of concepts. The narrative or the ritual journey moves in a spiral: each successive step incorporates the previous ones in an ever widening curve of retroactive validation. The absence and loss of section two can now be seen as only the first "dark" station of a ritual progress toward an illumination that would be accomplished, not in the monstrous and sacred space of the city, but within the natural, the profane world of rain, joy, tears, and words. So, too, in many nonliterary rituals from many places, one finds horrifying masks whose purpose it is to mediate the initiate's return to the sacred in the profane, that is, to lead to the contemplation of the true nature of the profane, which is permeated by the divine. "Pro-fanum," after all, is the mode of existence before an epiphany.

The story, therefore, is no nihilist's antiritual. The ritual pattern is not complete before the end of section three, and it is here that the narrative proper comes to a halt. The opening sentence of the next section ("everything was elucidated for me that day") confirms this and leads us to expect only pure metacommentary in what follows.

IV

There are tricksters in rituals and there are tricksters in literature. But there are also trickster texts. Borges's story is not only a labyrinth that constantly displaces its own closure but also a genuine trickster that persistently shifts the locus of its own telling. What at first we thought was metacommentary at the end of a ritual cycle soon turns into another station, another liminal peninsula within the same journey toward illumination. This, too, was an illusion and a trick the text has played on us. The journey has not ended yet; the return not of Rufus among the troglodytes, nor of them all back to language, but of the Immortals to mortality and to life (or death) is still to come.

This does not negate the ritual pattern. If anything, it affirms it. But by displacing the point of the illumination outside the labyrinthine city, by letting the illumination take place not at the moment of confrontation with "the mystery" but in the exchange of a few ancient, fragmented words between Argos and the narrator as well as in their joint metacommentary, the narrative reveals a river of immortality very different from the one we had seen before. That river is the text itself. Rufus's exchange with Homer and the latter's teachings are the true communion, in which they both participate and within which each thing—the troglodytes, who are the Immortals, the rivulet, which is the river sought by the horseman—finds its true identity.

I believe it is here that Borges's story reaches its most lucid metaliterary as well as metaritual moment. Ritual quests provide the seeker with the treasure of which fables speak—the magical or sacred object, helper, knowledge, or power. Borges's story subsumes all of them and shows the "treasure" to be, not some arbitrary symbolic object, but rather the immersion into the river of repetition—the repetition of repetition. And *that* is ritual.

Looking at the hieratic procession of proper names from the beginning of the story, we find in the opening epigram Salomon, Plato, and Francis Bacon echoing one another; then Pope repeating Homer; Marcus Flaminius Rufus reenacting the journey of uncountable legendary heroes. The contours of fictions and realities blur and merge with each other: life cites and mirrors fables, to be cited and mirrored in turn by them. Rufus's story is a mythic journey that also faithfully repeats "The Monstrous Journey of Alexander" from *The Legend of Alexander of Macedonia*—that anonymous medieval epic which probably postdates Rufus's adventures. Borges has Rufus, in section three, briefly mention the return of a goldfish to the waters of a river. But this is the same fish that, in *The Legend,* indicates to Alexander that he has just crossed the river of immortality, the same fish that years later was to pass into the sacred pages of the Koran. "Real" life becomes legend. Legend merges with the reality of holy writ. The one "cites" the other, to be cited in turn. . . . Rufus's story is to the *Legend of Alexander* and to the Koran what in another register Francis Bacon is to Salomon and Plato. The river of immortality, to which the goldfish was returned, is the river of remembrance and commemoration. It is the river of citations. It is natural, then, that the narrative of Marcus Flaminius (this imaginary character created by a real-life author who is none other than the legendary Wandering Jew) has as its highest, most profound moment of revelation the moment when Argos remembers another remembering in Homer. And he who metaphorically is Odysseus's dog in a narrative many times removed from Homer's is also the Homer who invented, forgot, and once again remembered the story—in much the same way as Argos remembers his master. (Which text embraces which? Which has the nonchronological primacy over the other?) All these names, all these historical and imaginary figures that envelop and are enveloped by one another communicate—rather, "take communion"—within the text that speaks them: like shadows from the world of shades who need an offering of ritual blood to come to life once more, Argos, Rufus, but also Plato and Bacon come back to life (and to language—but the two are one) as they commune within the text, the way the tribe comes back to memory and its own humanity through the communion of the rain.

If the function of all ritual is to bring the participant into contact with a higher spiritual reality, the myth of the quest of immortality is in a sense a symbol of ritual itself. Further, if ritual is a negation of human finitude, this particular myth is a myth of ritual and, therefore, a kind of metaritual. Borges's story, however, not only constitutes a replay of the quest for immortality but raises this quest at least one meta-level up by shifting the focus from the particular content of such a myth (e.g., the river) to the vehicle of all myth and ritual: the river of language.

I used the word "text" earlier to refer to the abstract, archetypal pattern of the Great Journey, the primal formula of ritual (and perhaps all narrative) which dictates that darkness and ignorance always turn in the end to enlightenment. I was also referring to the fragmented and yet continuous patchwork of texts woven together by Borges, the composite of other journeys from ancient epics and legends which exemplify the formula. I said that the text restores to the troglodytes, to the river, to Rufus, their true identity. And it is the text, which is the house of being, that will restore even to the mad city of the gods what it had lacked at first: significance. Seen as the last symbol to which the Immortals had condescended before retreating into pure thought (a Platonic experiment certainly, but one whose Platonism will also be negated as it has been affirmed), the city loses its horror. It becomes no more than a joke on the part of the Immortals—a joke like Homer's when he sang of the mice and the frogs—a kind of parody or inversion and also temple of "the irrational gods who govern the world and of whom we know nothing, save that they do not resemble man." Homer's explanation restores to the edifice finality and a history, and at the same time turns it into carnival: parody, inversion, irrationality. It is in this trinity that man most resembles the gods.

Homer's commentary is the very opposite of mystery. It razes to the ground once more the monstrous city of the Immortals, just as the Immortals razed to the ground another city to build this one. We can see this, too, as a moment of ritual deconstruction. But as before, the deconstruction is only a preliminary step to yet another mystification. In the present instance, what is built in words after this demolition is no less monstrous than before. For the text—in which Homer's words mix and mingle with those of the narrator, and where we are given fragments of texts by others who have quoted others . . . and so on is no less confusing, frightening, and self-contradictory than the edifice it replaces. The word gives back to everything its being and identity, and in its plenitude alone presence is manifest. But at the same time, texts, and not just the text of carnival or horror, rob all things of what poor identity is theirs and change all things into their opposite.

Traditionally, ritual leads through ancient texts—through language—to a contemplation of ineffable mystery. Here the ineffable mystery itself leads us back to the contemplation of the mystery of language. And within that, the "vision" it shows us is language—the mother of order—spinning out of its infinite cocoon disorder and monstrosities of thought.

Like Homer, "like a god who might create the cosmos and then create a chaos," language and the text create an antitext for every text. At the next turn of the narrative spiral, precisely within the metacommentary that perhaps explains the monstrosity of the city, we shall find monstrosity reposited once more, but at a different level. A moment ago we were told that the city was a kind of parody or inversion: the carnival of the Immortals. As such, it occupied only a marginal position beside that other one they had razed, which is not described, and which Rufus never saw, but which we may imagine as the epitome of beauty, order, and rationality. Now, with the metaphor of the Hindustani cycles, the monstrous edifice reenters the stage, no longer the partial, carnivalesque image of the world, but as the model of all models: the only one that houses all possible models and the possibility of their negation as well. This time the city becomes, not just a space within which paradox and ambiguity forever find their true home, but the set of all sets, whether they contain themselves or not, whether they contradict themselves or others, or not. It houses and contains the world.

Naturally, this labyrinth has no exit. And here we may remember Rufus's premonition that when he left the last labyrinth, he would again be surrounded by the nefarious city of the Immortals. This is a true premonition. In this lawless space, the only law is the doctrine ("of small theoretical importance," we shall ironically be told—but then is the statement really ironic?) that says that for every law there is another law that negates it, for every text its antitext, and for the river "whose waters grant immortality another whose waters remove it." This law enables Rufus to return to mortal life. But by the same token, this law, while he moves within the river of the infinite text, deprives him of his own individuality: "Like Cornelius Agrippa, I am god, I am hero, I am demon and I am world, which is a tedious way of saying that I do not exist."

Religious rituals are processes that bestow being and identity to individuals and their world. They are, as many have said, solutions to ontological, existential problems. Section four shows the ritual movement of this narrative progressing toward a penultimate vision of a world in which everything eventually becomes all things—which means that identity or sameness is only illusion.

In going through a ritual the initiate changes both name and identity. He sheds one identity to acquire another, and his new name is the sign that such a transformation has taken place. The ritual Rufus goes through, namely, traversing not some symbolic space but the very space where symbolic spaces are created (the text), deprives him of whatever identity he had without giving him back another.

V

In section five are mentioned some of the numerous existences through which Rufus passes—existences that rob him of an identity by letting him have too many. At this point we could argue that the demolition of the ontological problem that Rufus's commentary performs may be valid for Immortals, or when one looks at the world sub specie aeternitatis, but that within finite time, and as far as mortal life is concerned, identity is no illusion at all. Only if we postulate an infinite period of time does "Rufus" turn into "Cornelius Agrippa."

But Rufus's account anticipates the objection and points out that something even graver than these successive immortal existences is the matter. In section four, he wrote a commentary on his adventures, consisting of Argos's explanations and his own addenda to them. Now he changes levels once more in order to create, on yet a higher level, a metacommentary of another kind: a critical examination of his own account as a document purporting to relate the truth. Rufus, who was the hero and narrator in his own narrative, now becomes its reader and critic. Here the anomaly becomes apparent through such a reversal of roles.

> After a year's time, I have inspected these pages. I am certain they reflect the truth, but in the first chapters, and even in certain paragraphs of the others, I seem to perceive something false. This is perhaps produced by the abuse of circumstantial details, a procedure I learned from the poets and which contaminates everything with falsity, since those details can abound in the realities but not in their recollection. . . . I believe, however, that I have discovered a more intimate reason. I shall write it; no matter if I am judged fantastic.
>
> *The story I have narrated seems unreal because in it are mixed the events of two different men.* In the first chapter, the horseman wants to know the name of the river bathing the walls of Thebes; Flaminius Rufus, who before has applied to the city the epithet of Hekatompylos, says that the river is the Egypt; none of these locutions is proper to him but rather to Homer, who makes express mention in the *Iliad* of Thebes Hekatompylos and who in the *Odyssey*, by way of Proteus and Ulysses, invariably says Egypt for Nile. In the second chapter, the Roman, upon drinking the immortal water, utters some words in Greek; these words are Homeric and may be sought at the end of the famous catalogue of the ships. . . . Such anomalies disquieted me; others, of an aesthetic order, permitted me to discover the truth. They are contained in the last chapter.

Ritual and the passage through liminal spaces entail a confrontation of the self with the other; of the "me" with the "not-me." They create a mixing of categories, which provides the ground for the identity crisis necessary for the eventual illumination of the subject, the integration in whose name the journey has been undertaken. But Rufus never seems to be existentially split in this manner during his sojourn in the land of the troglodytes. He sees there the whole world split and irrationally fragmented—words, gods, language, and history catastrophically fractured—but his own sense of identity is not disturbed. Even after having drunk the water of immortality, and still later when he finds its antidote, he remains an integral "I."

It is only in this last, metacommentarial and metatextual part of the story, when he reads his own words as a critic, that the catastrophic confrontation of the "I" with the "other," of the "me" with the "not-me" will take place. And in this case, in this final liminal station that involves neither ascent nor descent, and that plays itself out on no other space but the distance of the eye from the page of script, the "other" or the "not-me" will be discovered in the "I"—that "I" which has now become text. For the anomaly does not consist in a man's having lived many successive lives, nor does it concern the content of this monstrous biography. It has relatively little to do with what is being told, and is the direct result of something disturbing in the telling.

Until now there was one narrator, one "I" of the story. Now a voice, which "after a year's time" has "inspected these pages," tells us that in what he has narrated are mixed the events of two men: Flaminius Rufus and Homer. But how many men are these? Homer is at least double. Splitting amoebalike, masks multiply and identities explode. Homer, who is two—one of the *Iliad* and the other of the *Odyssey*—splits once again into Proteus and Ulysses. Just as the Roman has been said to be two men because his words repeat those of Homer, so too can Homer be said to be dual (at least) when through him speak the voices of two individuals. To call them individuals, however, is a philosophical error: Proteus and Ulysses are both symbolic loci within which the individual is negated. Between Ulysses' "no one" to Proteus' "everyone," the individual, in its philosophical unity, has no place to be. Graver still, when Homer receives his being from his own creations, not only identity but existence, too, becomes problematic.

In the new myth and the new ritual journey that Borges creates, none of the monstrosities encountered in the physical liminal spaces of the ritual passage compares with this: the split of the "I" and the "me," not in the face of the encounter with the "other," but at the moment when the "one" realizes the "other" (when the "I" encounters the "me") as utterance, as memory of an utterance, as fuzzy ghost vacillating between truth and lie. In this part of Rufus's (but is it still Rufus's?) narrative, the speaker splits into a multitude, changes position from the active to the passive pole, becomes spoken through the mere act of quoting himself.

> Such anomalies [those concerning the identity of the narrator] disquieted me; others, of an esthetic order, permitted me to discover the truth. [But were the anomalies of anything but an aesthetic order in the first place? Perhaps . . .] They are contained in the last chapter; there it is written [by whom? the first or the second speaker?] that I fought at Stamford Bridge, that I transcribed in Bulaq the travels of Sinbad the Sailor and that I subscribed in Aberdeen to the English *Iliad* of Pope. [But is the "I" that cites the same as the "I" that is cited? Is Rufus still writing this?] One reads *inter alia* [and *inter alia* the narrator-hero has in this sentence become "one": most impersonal of subjects, and here subject and object at the same time—reading and being read]: "In Bikaner I professed the science of astrology and also in Bohemia." None of these testimonies are false; what is significant is that they were stressed.

Is this a veridical document recounted by a liar, or one that lies while being scrutinized by a truth-telling man? Rufus's text recreates the paradox of the liar and echoes the confessions made by Don Quixote's narrator-translator/scribe about the veracity of his narrative. But if what motivated that impossible Cretan has been lost in the sands of time, here the speaker is explicit: what generates this impression of untruth is the "abuse of circumstantial details, a procedure . . . learned from the poets and which contaminates everything with falsity, since those details can abound in the realities but not in their recollection." In other words, (1) matters of an aesthetic nature contaminate everything with unreality; and (2) matters of an aesthetic nature allow one to discover the truth. We are thus back in the city. To speak, to write, to read what one has written—to engage in the most elementary form of "let me say what it was like"—engages one in the most complex labyrinth of all and in an endless "ritual" process from which the only exit, the only return, is the annihilation of identity. Language, which is the house of being, is also its tomb and executioner.

Just as other rituals aim at an experience of the sacred in the profane, Borges's story leads to that other vertiginous experience in which we contemplate experience in its representations; in which, through successive mirrorings, we no longer know which is the mirror and which the object; in which the frame and the framed constantly shift places until the latter embraces the former. The text has become the world.

Borges changes ritual pattern in two fundamental ways, relative to other uses of it in literature. The first and most important way is through the ritual pattern that structures the story. This is not merely a tripartite one that leads from a lack to the unambiguous fulfillment of that lack, in order unavoidably to come to a stasis and a closure at the end of the fulfillment. Here the displacement of the liminal and the consequent restructuring of the pattern result instead in a spiral and nonlinear progression that creates an infinite semiosis. Each stage of the journey, each illumination, in some way or another is negated, deconstructed by the next, which in turn . . . and so on. So that in spite of all repetitions—and they are indeed numerous and varied—the constantly changing, shifting context does not allow us ever to speak of the "same." "Like Cornelius Agrippa, I am god, I am hero, I am philosopher, I am demon and I am world, which is a tedious way of saying that I do not exist." But Cornelius Agrippa, who is not I and only like whom I am, who is he? For he is still Cornelius Agrippa, he who was. It is through the identity of the name that identity disperses itself into nonidentity.

The second way in which Borges changes ritual pattern is through the use of metacommentary to generate the displacements I have spoken of. This metacommentary operates in two ways: it occupies the very center of the ritual journey—it has usurped, in other words, the space of the function of unmediated spiritual illumination—and at the same time it frames both each individual narrative segment and the entire narrative as a whole. The story is placed between a double (perhaps triple) editorial preface and a double (perhaps multiple) editorial postscript. Thus, just as the hero of the story moves from identity to identity in order finally to become "no one," so too the ultimate voice of the telling becomes dispersed into an absolute and irrevocable anonymity.

The voice that generates the text—Rufus's voice—is only an illusion, since it is fictional. The true author of the journey we are reading is Joseph Cartaphilus, the man condemned to immortality by Christ, three hundred years before the time of Rufus and Diocletian. But Cartaphilus is in turn the name Rufus turned into after he became immortal, the "I" that writes section five and informs us that this "I" is double.

Both inside and outside the text—the way the metacommentary is both at the center and at the borders of the ritual—this speaking subject splits into two, into many, through metacommentary, just as it splits through ritual. And through or beyond all these named and anonymous subjects, between the names of the Bacon citation and the "no one" of the final footnote, the writer of this document disappears as an identity in order to leave instead a journey of transformations: from the desert to the monstrous, from the monstrous to the divine, from that to carnival, from carnival to a game, from game to text. And from text to footnote. All of which is a way of participating in the ritual journey of the text and as a symbol of the act of reading itself. Reading is both the journey and the river that Borges has symbolized.

That infinitely sad, poetic phrase that sums up the story (" 'When the end draws near,' wrote Cartaphilus, 'there no longer remain any remembered images; only words remain' ") is also the phrase that sums up the inexhaustible pleasure, the joy of being text becoming text.

It may be that Borges's story is, as some say, a demythicization of ritual and a deconstruction, and that it stands above all ritual and transcends it. And it may be that this incessant Heraclitan becoming, which is the reverse of the visible surface that his narrative gives us to read, is an illusion. In that case, the opening quote from Bacon should be read literally, and Borges's story becomes an authentic ritual experience in literature.

It may also be that the literal meaning of the quote from Bacon is not what the quote says (namely, that Plato and Salomon are saying very much the same thing). Once quoted, the meaning of those words is no longer to be found in their referent alone but is also found in the incessant movement between the "saith," the "is," the "had," the "remembrance," and the "oblivion," between the stasis that it speaks and the movement that speaks it—the infinite distance that no ritual journey, no incantation, and no exorcism can reduce to unity. There are many ways in which Borges's story could be seen as the representation of a performance. But this last—the movement from words to words—which it "dramatizes" and gives us to see in a most intense metaliterary experience, is a performance that can be enacted upon no other stage but mere paper.

Borges's story does not—as has been sometimes maintained about myths—resolve a fundamental contradiction. He merely presents the contradiction anew but in another intonation. The problem now becomes to define the difference in intonation between Ulysses's and Borges's "no one." And it may not be futile to try to remember the answer to that question at another place and another time.

"She Was Unable Not to Think": Borges's "Emma Zunz" and the Female Subject

Bella Brodzki

Celebrated by formalists, structuralists, and deconstructionists alike as a demystifier par excellence, Borges preempted many of the perturbing aspects about post-modernist literature and contemporary critical theory, aspects that still arouse suspicion for more traditionally-oriented readers. In his distinctive way of making literature its own commentary, he created his own precursors, modifying our conception of literary history and modifying its future. We identify him as a post-modernist writer and critic primarily by the utter gravity of his fictional cunning, by his relentless play with the idea of unlimited rhetorical possibilities, by the way he privileges form over content, structure over essence, event over character. He refined the art of paradox so that even as he subverts teleologies, he preserves mystery (or its formal equivalent, ambiguity). But as the modern critical emphasis has gradually shifted—from locating meaning within an originating author to a formalist text to a collaborative or, in some cases, resisting reader—the effects of such rhetorical gesturing may be less ambiguous than certain of Borges's theoretical proponents would have us believe.

"Emma Zunz," perhaps Borges's least characteristic work, is his only story whose protagonist is a woman. Since female characters are conspicuously absent throughout Borges's writings, the mere creation of an Emma Zunz is already an event in itself. This has been taken note of by critics of all persuasions, but for reasons other than my own in the following essay. Displacing the attention from why Borges chose to make a female character the centerpiece of his story (and one who is not a cipher, who is more than the sign of impersonality most often designated by his other characters) to the ideological implications of this choice is my concern here. The problem of authorial intention leads to a very thorny and more compelling

From *MLN* 100, no. 2 (March 1985). © 1985 by The Johns Hopkins University Press.

critical question: how do the meanings generated by this text pivot on the fact that the subject is a woman?

I say compelling because "Emma Zunz"—beyond its appeal as a formalist puzzle, an untypically realistic tale of revenge, or even as a parable of cosmic destruction and restitution—is a tragedy of restricted choices. As a female figure, whether within a "realistic" or "symbolic" fiction, Emma's possibilities are explicitly derived from a series of reductive dichotomies based on sexual analogy. Such a reading is immediately recognizable as a feminist one. Yet, the intimate interplay of the forces of identity and sexual difference, language and power, intentionality and indeterminacy makes a deconstructive approach the challenging consort to a feminist interpretation. Tracing this critical rapport will show why this narrative is a model one for examining some issues that are central to contemporary critical theory and to feminist theory, in particular.

The goals of feminism and deconstruction do not naturally proceed hand in hand, though the theoretical agendas of each have had radical effects upon the textual practices of the other. And, indeed, in a text like "Emma Zunz" the two strategies can be said to converge and diverge until a crucial point in the narrative when the reader must make a critical ideological move that either favors one position or the other. This point in the narrative is a performative moment of suspended revelation, when the implications of Emma's sex/speech act are grounded precisely in the interplay of forces I name above.

For both kinds of critics the notion of difference is supremely important, its significance turning on the ways in which the relation between textual and sexual difference is interpreted. Jacques Derrida's deliberately unsystematic presentation of *différance* is impossible to reduce to a word, concept or any positive definition. Articulated through this term are both its spatial and temporal aspects: to differ, to be unlike or dissimilar in quality, nature, or form; or to scatter and disperse; to defer, to delay, postpone.

> What we note as *différance* will thus be the movement or play that "produces" (and not by something that is simply an activity) these differences, these effects of difference. This does not mean that the *différance* which produces differences is before them in a simple and in itself unmodified and indifferent present. *Différance* is the nonfull, nonsimple "origin"; it is the structured and differing origin of differences.

Thus differance designates a passive difference already in existence as the condition that makes meaning possible, and an act of differing or deferring which produces difference. It cannot, however, be construed as the unadulterated alternative to sameness, or its negation, upon which could be based a new ontology perpetuating another metaphysical or ideological order.

It is not a being-present, however excellent, unique, principal or transcendent one makes it. It commands nothing, rules over nothing, and nowhere does it exercise any authority. It is not marked by a capital letter. Not only is there no realm of difference, but difference is even the subversion of every realm. This is obviously what makes it threatening and necessarily dreaded by everything in us that desires a realm, the past or future presence of a realm.

Michel Foucault alerts us as well to the difficulties that breaking down such conceptual categories poses:

The freeing of difference requires thought without contradiction, without dialectics, without negation; thought that accepts divergence; affirmative thought whose instrument is disjunction; thought of the multiple—of the nomadic and dispersed multiplicity that is not limited or confined by the constraints of similarity.

As a critical strategy, feminist theorists have had to declare a kind of allegiance to the notion of difference by reappropriating it and reconceptualizing it to women's advantage. Such a strategic decision suggests that the argument over whether subverting or transforming the binary mode of thought is desirable, or even possible, is in some circles, a moot one. For the purposes of this essay the argument is still a vital one, especially as it colludes with the deconstructionist project to break down the structuralist dependence on a dualistic model of thought and language. For the question remains: Is the Masculine/Feminine polarity perhaps the irreducible, the original opposition? And are then all the binary oppositions that follow therefrom implicitly valorized according to a system of sexual difference?

In a very lucid overview of the recent developments in feminist criticism, Catherine Stimpson describes the theoretical problem:

The very logic of feminist criticism, its concern with the syllogisms of female and male, entail[s] the tricky, theoretical exploration of sexual difference. . . . Feminist critics disagree about cause, permanence, signs, and significance. [Some reason] that sexual difference reveals both experience and organizing, organized structures—of the body, the conscious mind, the unconscious, and of language. The difference between female and male need not be oppositional. . . . It need not be hierarchical. . . . It might simply be difference, which language would quicken into complete being.

If what both deconstructionists and feminists are deriding is the kind of self-mystifying conceptual mastery that is masked by binary logic (Derrida's logo-centrism), they are only ascribing a critical procedure to what post-modernist writers like Borges have been doing in their critical fictions. A position that advances the engendering of differences suspends the idea of the self that as subject or consciousness serves as the source of meaning and as a principle of resolution or explanation. Rather this self is seen as a figurative construction, a linguistic effect, a specific category and product of discourse. The integral and integrated sovereign subject has been dethroned, whether in the role of author of authoritarian fictions or as character within them. This unitary subject can no longer be read as a unified representation of itself (i.e. Man), for what would that self be, least of all as mediated through language? The very notion of representation relies on and participates in the ontology of sameness—something stands for something else, speaks for, in the place of something else—and thus absorbs all difference into itself by creating a logic of generic, universal, unequivocal identity. The universal identity has traditionally been the masculine; that which is distinguished from and derived from that logically prior identity is the particular feminine. As the very condition that makes possible a relation based on the dichotomy of presence and absence (since language is never present to itself), representation is not merely logocentric, it is phallogocentric. Not only does it inevitably reduce woman to serving as man's mirror (even when the image she sees is not her own), but by denying her the duplicitous powers of self-representation, it reinforces masculine projections of a self that is no less fictive for being male.

Thus there is a strong impulse on the part of contemporary theory to conceive of a mode that fulfills the textual function of enunciating discourse while not maintaining the notion of a certain kind of subject, identity, or self that is intrinsic to both the logic and the romance of Western thought. The irony of such an endeavor at this moment in the history of feminist criticism when (for those schooled in the Anglo-American tradition, at least) its primary goal is precisely to restore, indeed establish, the subject of woman as a unified concept equal to man, cannot be overstated. It points to a current critical controversy, and reveals some of the ideological and strategic conflicts within feminist theory itself regarding the specific nature of women's writing and the implications of essentialism.

Having posited that the status of the subject in current critical terms is both complicated and precarious and that sexual difference does make a difference, let us return to that performative moment in the narrative when the feminist and the deconstructionist (note that I am not precluding the possibility that both might commingle within the same reader) must part company. The feminist reader, like the character Emma herself, will locate responsibility (collaborative) and attribute guilt (complicitous) and impose closure on what might otherwise continue towards an infinite play of meaning, arrest this movement and, in effect, suppress ambiguity and aesthetic pleasure for its own sake. Now concrete moral and social commitments will be demanded of the author who, on the one hand, is admired for a special brand of literary finesse and denounced on the other for not attending to the political value of literature and to the "real" referent outside the text.

By contrast, the deconstructionist will delight in the endless displacement of signification and will persistently stave off any perceptible tendency toward pinning the signifier to a/the signified. The ideological impulse (and there certainly is one) is precisely to mediate against any form of idealization, incarnation or hypostasization (Derrida's Transcendental Signifier)—to seek in the theologically ordained interpretive gesture only another detour, another deferral, further diffusion of meaning. Geoffrey Hartman aptly describes what marks this difference in approach in his preface to *Deconstruction and Criticism*. Using an expression from the preeminent deconstructionist, Nietzsche, that "the deepest pathos is still aesthetic play," he distinguishes those critics or readers for whom "the ethos of literature is not dissociable from its pathos. For deconstructionist criticism literature is precisely that use of language which can purge pathos, which shows that it too is figurative, ironic, or aesthetic." Such a distinction resonates strongly for a feminist reading which rejects the aestheticization of suffering and which regards pathos and play (in this text, at least) to be mutually exclusive.

This is all the more provocative because figuration and irony loom large in "Emma Zunz," as they do in all of Borges's writing. The story uncannily begins with the death of a father. Agonizing over his suicide, Emma seeks revenge against the embezzler who had covered up his crime by unjustly implicating her father. Aaron Loewenthal's accusation had forced Zunz to flee (from Argentina, we assume) to Brazil, where despondent that his name could not be cleared, he took his own life. Emma blames Loewenthal for the original injustice as well as for its ultimate result. Her wish is to guarantee the extinction of her and her father's enemy, but she decides that murder alone will not suffice. She elaborates a scheme to achieve both vengeance on her father's behalf and social justice, without impairing her own liberty or endangering her own life. Only a strategy assuring these ends would be satisfying and expiatory for Emma. Hence she plots the perfect crime, not as a criminal, but as the executor of divine justice.

In Borges's spare prose we etch out a portrait of this nineteen-year-old woman who "se declaró, como siempre contra toda violencia," and in whom men still inspired "un temor casi patológico." What complex constellation of motives, what unconscious structures could account for her choice of such carnally violent means to achieve such a pure and abstract end: divine justice?

The opening paragraph is replete with cunningly placed clues and with the depiction of those apparently significant and coherent extra-referential details that a realistic narrative requires and verifies—and whose code a Borgesian narrative always violates. On January 14, 1922, Emma Zunz, a worker in the textile factory of Tarbuch and Loewenthal, learns by letter of the death of her father. The message, written by a boardinghouse friend of Mr. Maier, relates the actual cause of death—accidental overdose of pills—and the name of the city in which he died. What follows is the description, at once both precise and abstract, of Emma's reaction to the news that she has become an orphan. Emma is the protagonist, but she is literally "without speech" until the finale when she tells her version of the story. Thus it is the narrator's account that constitutes one part of the double framework of the story, while Emma's constitutes the other. This adjudicating, interpreting voice renders and often imperceptibly merges with Emma's in a way that resembles a traditional, reliable third-person omniscient point of view, but whose perspective seems strangely askew. An elusive emotional ambience, pervaded by fatal mystery, is expressed by this mediating presence that hovers somewhere in the borders of Emma's consciousness as it becomes text.

And yet it is only the impression of interior depth that we are given, of that which constitutes subjecthood for a literary character. Emma may not be a cipher, but she doesn't quite qualify as a full-blown personality. This raises a question pertinent to our perception of all characters: where does a subject ever reside, if not "between the lines"? Two passages connected by allusion appear to be critical for the reader's understanding of Emma's character and for the entire narrative. And yet, despite or because of their crucial functions, little, except by extreme indirection, can be gleaned from them. The first passage, describing Emma's reactions to the letter, minutely registers a broad range of emotions that seem to be emblematic of a complex psychic state, but they remain cerebral abstractions. And it is from this ostensibly full rendering that the ominous inception of Emma's scheme emerges, the one whose linear or causal logic is undermined throughout the narrative.

> Su primera impresión fué de malestar en el vientre y en las rodillas; luego de ciega culpa, de irrealidad de frío, de temor; luego, quiso ya estar en el día siguiente. Acto continuo comprendió que esa voluntad era inútil porque, la muerte de su padre era lo único que había sucedido en el mundo, y seguiría sucediendo sin fin. Recogió el papel y se fué a su cuarto. Furtivamente lo guardó en un cajón, como si de algún modo ya conociera los hechos ulteriores. Ya había empezado a vislumbrarlos, tal vez; ya era la que sería.

By the time Emma has endangered and endured her desperate undertaking, the reader is accustomed to the remote but sympathetic narrative perspective, and has intuited what has been explicitly offered as Emma's emotional state. The scene as a whole is poignant, but the description still jars.

> Un acto de soberbia y en aquel día . . . El temor se perdió en la tristeza de su cuerpo, en al asco. El asco y la tristeza la encadenaban, pero Emma lentamente se levantó y procedió a vestirse.

Through this rhetoric of intimacy the reader is inclined to perceive herself as a witness to the radical transformation of a character. "Ya era la que sería" implicitly and provocatively contrasts with the person Emma used to be. But, who was Emma, who is she "already" and how does the reader discern between one image of her subjective personality and another? Her perception of her happy childhood is contrasted with her present wretchedness, her former timidity with her present self-assertiveness, and her past silence with her move into language. These indicate substantial character changes, not over time but in a symbolic moment that imitates the continuing but disruptive act of interpretation itself.

Thus the reader picks up the traces provided, and with Emma, actively searches through memory and dream-work to restore a fractured family romance to its pristine origins. The back and forth dialectic ("recordó") between idealized past and traumatic present has set up expectations for the reader: that what was obscure will come to light, that what was enigmatic will be explained, that what was undecided will be resolved. Such a sense is reinforced by the imagery that describes Emma's initial nocturnal resurrections of her submerged past and the dawning of her new consciousness as a process of painful, but progressive enlightenment.

> En la creciente oscuridad, Emma lloró hasta el fin de aquel día el suicidio de Manuel Maier, que en los antiguos días felices fué Emmanuel Zunz. Recordó veraneos en una chacra, cerca de Gualeguay, recordó (trató de recordar) a su madre . . . recordó los amarillos losanges de una ventana . . . No durmió aquella noche, y cuando la primera luz definió el rectángulo de la ventana, ya estaba perfecto su plan.

Emma, as lost child now become avenging angel, articulates her hatred of two systems of patriarchal oppression: an economic system whereby male bosses exploit male and female workers and a sexual system whereby men exploit women. Within this economy, the proper name is the mark of private ownership on a life, the only way to identify the owner who may in fact own little else. Daughter of Manuel Maier, who was forced to change his name from Emmanuel Zunz, Emma's name is a derivation of his past identity. She is, therefore, already stigmatized by his shame, and she lives in the secret shadow of his alleged crime. His suicide, the event which changes her status from daughter to orphan, and which marks her rise to female self-consciousness and her assumption of speech, is in her terms, not a single episode with tragic far-reaching implications, but the unifying thread of all past and future experience. "La muerte de su padre era lo único que había sucedido en el mundo, y seguiría sucediendo sin fin": the all-encompassing metaphorical sweep of such a statement has the rhetorical effect of becoming a privileged point of reference and of suppressing all other temporal and conceptual distinctions under its signifier "sin fin," in much the same way as the metaphorical pronouncement "ya era la que sería."

Playing on some of the notions of sexual and textual difference that have been described above, this text is a false story which is "substantially" true. Upon this paradox all the text's symmetrical oppositions and parallels, both literal and metaphorical, explicit and inferred, are constructed. As I have suggested, the pervasiveness of this binary system reflects the hierarchical nature of our own sexual politics. By simply formal means, Borges is attempting to fracture our assumptions about truth and falsity, the nature of the literary text and its fidelity to a real world outside the text, and in the process he points at the ideological structures which mirror those very deceptive constructs as well.

Such a technique Borges has certainly used elsewhere, but here the binary structure is so manifest that it is impossible to ignore. Organized as a series of metaphorical associations that are continually undercut by metonymical relations, the text exploits an implicit tension between the absolute and the contingent, between, for example, the imperative of Emma's design and the contingency of its execution, between what has been otherwise called motivated and arbitrary signification. Within this figurative interplay, metaphorizing speaks as/for the totalizing tendency of interpretation, if not as an act of closure asserting shared essences between the objects yoked in the comparison, then at least as a mode of suppressing paradox, contradiction, difference. To discuss metaphor in such terms is to stress not its creative or liberating dimensions or its valorization as the supremely poetic in language, but to call attention to its dominion over other figurative devices. Metaphor involves the perception of a similarity between two otherwise incompatible or unrelated objects of meaning, and in such a way that the sense of conceptual distance is preserved even as the leap of imagination or faith is being made. For the reader of this text these essences are perceived as overriding thematic resemblances, equivalences, substitutions and exchanges between ideas and things, the conceptual and the material, a projection and its actualization, between symbol and discourse.

For example, when Emma furtively hides the letter announcing her father's death (whose ulterior "knowledge" she already possessed) in a drawer, it has immediate metaphorical significance. She is attempting to repress its message by "putting it out of her mind." Later on, she tears it up before it can be used as the crucial shred of evidence that could potentially identify her act as premeditated murder, rather than self-defense, as she will claim. After her encounter with the sailor, the narrator describes Emma as tearing up the money he left her as before she had torn the letter, though the reasons for doing so are different. The act of tearing the letter (metonymically linked to the photo of one Milton Sills, under which it lies) is associated with tearing the money, which is likened to throwing away bread, both impieties and improprieties committed within the context of a greater "impiedad"—the loss of her innocence.

Of course, the positing of certain governing connections is necessary for narrative continuity of purpose. But to make ideas equal or like suggests a kind of theological design, one that links the order in nature with order in a text. To mediate against this transcendental temptation, Borges displaces the assumed meaning or puts it into question through the use of the contingent and the arbitrary. Metonymy is considered to be literal, referential, everyday language; it undercuts the grand pattern. Emma's narrative, as an effort to diffuse, differentiate, and contextualize meaning is the metonymic insertion of the uncanny and the incredible over and against the logical and the assimilable. The final, inconclusive ending announces the triumph of metonymy and what it stands for as a tool of (feminist?) subversion, as an ironic dissident voice in a chorus of predictable textual responses.

Another way to show the movement from metaphor to metonymy is through the father/daughter alliance. A convention or cultural construction which is based on substitution and analogy, it is posited as original and determining ("la muerte de su padre era lo único que había sucedido en el mundo, y seguiría sucediendo sin fin . . . 'He vengado a mi padre y no me podrán castigar' . . ."). But it is eventually effaced in favor of the natural mother/daughter relation, which is based on contiguity, though restored through analogy. ("Pensó [no pudo no pensar] que su padre le había hecho a su madre la cosa horrible que a ella ahora le hacían"). Carrying this thematic point further, metonymy is served at the expense of metaphor only to be metaphorized again in the following example. A profound childhood association is laboriously traced through the labyrinth of Emma's memory:

> Recordó (trató de recordar) a su madre . . . recordó la casita de Lanus que les remataron, recordó los amarillos losanges de una ventana . . . recordó (pero eso jamás lo olvidaba) que su padre . . .

This is later explicitly related to the "rape" scene:

> El hombre la condujo a una puerta y después a un turbio zaguán y después a una escalera tortuosa y después a un vestíbulo (en el que había una vidriera con losanges idénticos a los de la casa en Lanus).

The binary system is textually transformed by the co-existence of two discourses—the narrator's "true" story and Emma's subsequent narration of the same story, which is embodied in the first—and the engendering of a third multivalent, ambiguous non-synthesis. Neither mutually exclusive nor reducible one to the other, these discourses are perceived as equivalent, symbiotic, and interchangeable. The catalyst, the mediator of this transformation is Emma, who not only transforms the actual conditions of the narrative by taking a "merely" credible story and making it incredible, but who is in the end symbolically and actually transformed by it. Both author and character of her own psycho-drama, both perpetrator and victim in her sexual allegory of Crime and Punishment, Eros and Death, she strives to write a future that will redeem her past.

Within the story time of narrative past and future, where time and space are constantly juxtaposed, two contrasting conceptions of time and temporality are presented. One is in the judicial mode—a metonymic catalogue of characteristically Borgesian particulars—usually irrelevant, precise, repetitive details of location, proper names, dates, hours, and their causal connections, of the sort that Foucault claims is precisely the "distortion of classification":

> De vuelta, preparó una sopa de tapioca y unas legumbres, comió temprano, se acostó y se obligó a dormir. Así, laborioso y trivial, pasó el viernes quince, la víspera.

These details serve not as assurances of plausibility or verisimilitude, but as ironic subversion, in favor of the metaphorical non-time of memory, chaos, vertigo, of timelessness, of time outside of time.

> Los hechos graves están fuera del tiempo, ya porque en ellos el pasado inmediato queda como tronchado del porvenir, ya porque no parecen consecutivas las partes que los forman.
> ¿En aquel tiempo fuera del tiempo, en aquel desorden perplejo de sensaciones inconexas y atroces . . .

Borges undermines the concept of authoritarian fictions by establishing a narrator who is partially omniscient; but, he undermines that notion too, by the provocative and intrusive use of "perhaps" in contexts where ostensibly Emma's deepest psychological motivations are being described. The rhetorical force of repetition is not lost on the reader, who is seduced into deciphering the possible from the probable, and who then begins to realize that such distinctions aren't even useful.

> Referir *con alguna realidad los hechos* de esa tarde sería difícil y quizá improcedente. Un atributo de lo infernal es la *irrealidad,* un atributo que parece mitigar sus terrores y que los agrava *tal vez.* ¿Como hacer verosímil la acción en la que casi no creyó quien la ejecutaba, cómo recuperar ese breve caos que hoy la memoria de Emma Zunz repudia y confunde? Emma vivía por Almagro, en la calle Liniers; *nos consta* que esa tarde fue al puerto. Acaso en el infame Paseo de Julio se vió multiplicada en espejos, publicada por luces y desnudada por los ojos hambrientos, *pero más razonable es conjeturar* que al principio erró, inadvertida, por la indiferente recova. (my emphasis)

Each "perhaps" does not introduce or postulate an either/or choice, or one explanation or interpretation of events or phenomena; nor is this paradox for the sake of digression. Rather it serves the function of rendering an atmosphere of ambivalence that pervades and colors the entire narrative.

This ambivalence doesn't threaten the validity of the narrator, but instead guides the reader in integrating the two discourses by consistently posing alternatives, leaving their traces, and offering new interpretive strategies for these alternatives.

When the narrator says: "Pensó Emma Zunz 'una sola vez' en el muerto que motivaba el sacrificio?," and then responds with "Yo tengo para mi que pensó una vez," the reader is tempted to chuckle even in this most gruesome of situations. But, then we are immediately transported to the "primal scene" where, in a feminine revision of the child's search for lost origins, Emma does not witness but, in fact, re-enacts the moment of parental intercourse, and typically, denies and then represses that knowledge.

> Pensó (no pudo no pensar) que su padre le había hecho a su madre
> la cosa horrible que a ella ahora le hacían.

If, "en ese momento peligró su desesperado propósito," it is because she realizes the duplicity of her alliance with her father, and for the first time identifies with her mother as woman. Enervated by that revelation, she is yet empowered by her capacity to perform according to the law she despises:

> Fué una herramienta para Emma como ésta lo fué para él, pero
> ella sirvió para el goce y él para la justicia.

But, lest this abstract equivalence appear too pat even in such an ironic economy, the narrator recounts Emma's visceral response to the horror of her experience:

> El temor se perdió en la tristeza de su cuerpo, en el asco. El asco
> y la tristeza la encadenaban, pero Emma lentamente se levantó y
> procedió a vestirse. . . . Paradójicamente su fatiga venía a ser una
> fuerza, pues la obligaba a concentrarse en los pormenores de la
> aventura y le ocultaba el fondo y el fin.

Although the murder scene does not proceed either as quickly or as smoothly as planned, by a genial transformation, she inverts the hierarchy:

> Desde la madrugada anterior, ella se había soñado muchas veces,
> dirigiendo el firme revólver, forzando al miserable a confesar la
> miserable culpa y exponiendo la intrépida estratagema que per-
> mitiría a la Justicia de Dios triunfar de la justicia humana. (No por
> temor, sino por ser un instrumento de la Justicia, ella no queriá
> ser castigada.)

Now Emma holds the revolver and, therefore, manages to symbolize both phallic power and right, instituting a new order which encompasses both the human and the divine. And thus like the Method Actor who, in order to authentically express the emotions she is representing, looks inside her-self for a structurally analogous experience that can evoke or trigger that

desired emotional response, Emma realizes that the source and the nature
of her rage have been irrevocably transformed. She is no longer able to
represent her father; she can only represent herself:

> Ante Aaron Loewenthal, más que la urgencia de vengar a su padre,
> Emma sintió la de castigar el ultraje padecido por ello. No podía
> no matarlo, después de esa minuciosa deshonra.

The imagery of the murder scene *is* directly reminiscent of her own sexual
violation—"y una efusión de brusca sangre manó de los labios obscenos y
manchó la barba y la ropa," and she links the two events for the sake of
textual integrity. "He vengado a mi padre y no me podrán castigar."

> Luego tomó el teléfono y repitió lo que tantas veces repetiría, con
> esas y con otras palabras: *Ha ocurrido una cosa que es increíble . . .*
> *El señor Loewenthal me hizo venir con el pretexto de la huelga . . . Abusó*
> *de mi,* lo maté."

The following words of the narrator—"actually the story was true"—
achieve a double transformation of the two discourses, which are then
explicitly stated as equivalent. For the dramatic irony of Emma's discourse
is juxtaposed with the rhetorical irony of the narrator's marvelous subsequent explanation:

> La historia era increíble, en efecto, pero se impuso a todos, porque
> sustancialmente era cierta. Verdadero era el tono de Emma Zunz,
> verdadero el pudor, verdadero el odio. Verdadero también era el
> ultraje que había padecido; sólo eran falsas las circunstancias, la
> hora y uno o dos nombres propios.

Emma's story (false story) as incredible, impressed everyone, not as the
narrator says, because it was substantially *true,* but because it was more
credible.

What is true in symbol, if not in fact, determines the formal ending of
the story and reveals how fictions are made. The substantial account is that
Emma has been violated and that she shot Loewenthal dead. By arranging
these two episodes so that one follows from the other, she has, using the
Russian Formalist distinction between fabula and sujet, constructed the
causality of a fiction. The narrative is the fictive mediation between these
disjunctions. One represents justice in the normative or ideal world, the
other in the real.

Ideals like substance and justice and truth enable us to mediate the
disjunctions of life and text. Shame, hate, and outrage do metaphorically
and irrevocably link Emma's violation and Loewenthal's death. (In detective's terms, she has given us both motive and justification.) Emma's deconstructive coup, however, is to play one conception of truth against
another, to play the absolute against the contingent. And thus, despite our
desperate faith in the metaphorical absolute, in the transcendental sanctions
of signification, as mimetic interpreters we must, nonetheless, consider the

invocation of truth in such a context to be unacceptable. (It doesn't hold up as evidence.) Here the metonymical details count for everything, they make all the difference; they cannot be subsumed under abstract categories of resemblance. Emma's narrative demonstrates the complicity of language and deception, in particular self-deception.

For this is the point at which the feminist and the deconstructionist must diverge. Both will perceive the future of difference as being linked to the kinds of diffusion of meaning carried out by figures of metonymy. Both will support Borges's use of a female subversive. Emma, trying both to reconcile and differentiate the two realms of the absolute and the contingent, the ideal and the real, in a gesture of splendid self-possession, does transcend them. But, at what cost? She *has* written a new text—with her body, just as she has resisted being written into another text without changing the conditions that have governed its writing. But, the feminist will ask, doesn't she, ultimately, like all women, exist only as the possibility of mediation, transaction, and transference between man and himself? Isn't woman in turn metaphorized in this text?

The textual/sexual congruence breaks down because Emma's identity as a woman hinges on more than playing a role she believes she has constructed. Ultimately revealed through this non-congruence is the discontinuity between the text as project and the experience of the subject, the relation between a fractured subject and a divided text. No matter how radical a textual practice that strives to break out of the binary mode, given the constraints of language, it must remain a metaphorical formulation. Certainly a modernist can no longer defer (even in bad conscience) to isms which elegize the unitary or stop at the binary. We have already arrived at a new mode of signification. But, it too, as a figure of the mind, may be only a figure of speech. The mode itself has become a figure of multiple interpretation: out of its (closet) repertory of images comes Woman. She no longer represents herself or other selves, because we can no longer guarantee that such a notion of the self can be represented. And so she becomes a free-floating signifier of both specificity and difference when that furthers a theoretical strategy, and of multiplicity when another is at stake. And so the cycle of metaphorizing is not broken.

The provocative connections between "textuality and sexuality, genre and gender, psycho-sexual identity and cultural authority" are even made manifest in one of Borges's dense, enigmatic fictions. A deconstructive reading of "Emma Zunz" applauds her decision to assume the language of phallic discourse only to cast it aside with impunity after it has served her purpose. Certainly one part of the message or theme reinforces that. But, the *subject* is a woman; and Emma's virtuoso performance, though a victory, only reinscribes her (as she would say "sin fin") into the system of logic she so valiantly strives to transform. For the crucial question remains implicated in gender difference, not in symbol, but in fact. Could this story *be* if Emma were a man?

Myth as Time and Word

Ariel Dorfman

Although its origins fade into remote regions and its sociocultural coordinates are still a matter of debate, the present-day Hispanoamerican novel has a quite precise birthday. The year 1949 saw the publication of *The Kingdom of This World* by Alejo Carpentier and *Men of Maize* by Miguel Angel Asturias. This last work, both the fountainhead and the backbone of all that is being written on our continent today, has suffered a strange fate, like so many works which close a period and open up a new epoch.

Many essayists have judged the novel deficient, pointing to its lack of unity, its ungainly and evasive segmentation and its vacillation between genres, in contrast to that solid cathedral of dynamic coherence, that satanic church, *El señor presidente*, the most famous of Asturias's novels and the one which has enjoyed the greatest number of translations, prizes, and commentaries. Many critics dispose of *Men of Maize* in a couple of lines or ignore it altogether, irritated by this confusing, explosive offshoot which cannot be comfortably fit into the orderly evolution of the author toward the political themes of his banana trilogy. They are anxious to pass from his novels about tyranny within one country to his later works dealing with the external tyranny of imperialism. Readers must find the book tedious and difficult, judging from many conversations and, more conclusively, from the scanty three editions (1949, 1954, 1957) which it enjoyed until, after a delay of ten years, Ediciones Losada spurred by the Nobel Prize came out with a fourth.

A few critics have recognized the extraordinary quality of the novel, although they have not succeeded in refuting the arguments of its detractors, and they find themselves on the defensive, affirming its greatness in

From *Review* no. 15 (Fall 1975), translated by Paula Speck. © 1975 by the Center for Inter-American Relations, Inc.

spite of its defects. Giuseppe Bellini, who has given it the most fond and attentive study, attempts to justify the novel by declaring that its unity must be sought, not in its plot, but in its "climate," its atmosphere. He accepts the dispersed quality of the work as necessary to transmit the "spirit of Guatemala." Others, in support of the novel's singular structure, have excused it as "poetic," as a "symphonic poem," or have called attention to its fusion of the social and the mythic. The use of these vague and ineffectual terms symptomizes a basic misunderstanding of the text, for they are inadequate to describe a work which has contributed to founding a new dynasty of the real, a new way of seeing our America. The only way to understand the relation of *Men of Maize* to the future of which it is the seed, a way which will permit us, in passing, to solve the problem of its unity, is to analyze in detail each of its six parts, which some have criticized as discontinuous and others have tried to unify by invoking a poetic language which magically verbalizes nonexistent connections within something which has been defined by Juan Carlos Ghiano as "less than an epic, more than a novel."

GASPAR ILÓM

The first chapter tells how Gaspar Ilóm, the chief of the land of Ilóm, undertakes a war against those who sow corn for commercial ends. Señor Tomás Machojón, urged by his wife, Vaca Manuela, poisons the chief, who, abandoned by his own wife, La Piojosa Grande, drinks the river to calm his entrails and so saves himself. However, Colonel Chalo Godoy has taken advantage of the chief's absence to kill the Indian warriors; Gaspar throws himself into the river so as not to survive his followers.

These events must be decoded by the reader who plunges into the buzzing stream of words flowing dreamily between the real and the fictitious, into an atmosphere which develops and thickens, raining lights and shadows that struggle in thunderheads of words. He must interpret, undo the linguistic spells, unearth from this shifting cave the outline of a meaning. This narrative mode serves to indicate that we are confronted by a moment at the start of the book in which dream and reality cohabit, in which the mythological is still wholly embodied in man, in which the human and the natural are still conjugated together, still fused even to the extent of being designated by the same interchangeable terms.

Using certain repetitive, magical formulas, the "soil" tries to wake Gaspar Ilóm, who sleeps, buried, "unable to free himself from a serpent with six hundred thousand coils of mud, moon, forests, rainstorms, mountains, birds, and echoes he could feel around his body." The earth "falls dreaming from the stars," but it cannot continue sleeping, because there is no vegetation or shade: "awakens in what once were green mountains, now the barren peaks of Ilóm." The earth has been violated, wrenched out of its natural and sacred state; the magical union between man and nature has been destroyed, the primordial bond that was only possible in a pre-logical, unreal stage when the universe dreamed, not in a time like the present when the maize-growing earth is "bathed by rivers of water fetid from being so long awake." Provoked by the farmers who set fire to its vegetation in order to grow corn to sell, nature demands that Gaspar Ilóm exterminate the sowers, that he retaliate in kind and do to them as they have done to the earth. The earth calls for a purging of evil, a restoration of balance, vengeance against those who have separated man from nature, making exploitation inevitable. This alienation from the origin, a theme which runs through all of Asturias's work, always brings on oppression, whether that of a local dictator, of a Spanish conqueror, or of North American imperialism. Maize, "sown to be eaten," is "the sacred sustenance of the men who were made of maize. Sown to make money, it means famine for the men who were made of maize." There are two types of men of maize: those who live in the magic plenitude of sensual continuity with nature, a form of sleep or dreaming; and those who live in wakefulness, hunger, and death. These last are uprooted, for they have lost their roots, not only in a metaphorical sense, but also in a literal one: they have become vagabonds on the earth, deniers of the sacred growth of plants. For this reason, there is a hint of the picaresque in all of Asturias's works, and especially in this one: a senseless movement in search of food, absurd pilgrimages, a wind which devastates as it comes and goes. *Men of Maize* is a vision of both types of men, those who live in the exile of never-rest and those who root themselves in the myth.

In his struggle, Gaspar is aided by cosmic forces: the yellow rabbits for whom "there are no secrets, no dangers, no distances," born of the fire-spirit, fighting on even after the death of the chief, as an emanation of the natural order seeking to continue in existence. Everything related to Gaspar is seen through myth, through clouds of smoke from an apparent chaos where all things vibrate with the secret form of ritual. The exacerbated language; the baroque, serpentine syntax; the slithering advance of a world; the merging of dissimilar elements; their transfiguration through words that are sacred, solemn, and distant; brief glimpses of the action: everything recreates in the mind of the reader the encircling primitivism lived by the characters, forcibly equalizes dream and reality and mixes fiction and *factum* until the reader is not able to—does not wish to—separate them. The central theme of the novel, the relation between myth and reality, finds its narrative and linguistic correlative in this fusion, only fully realized in the first chapter, in which myth covers everything like a skin. The fact that legend and reality, word and event, are here the same experience for reader and character will contrast with the other chapters, in which the nearness and distance of these dimensions become problematic, preventing a manifestation of their union, such as the one given in the narration of Gaspar Ilóm's poisoning.

If we tried to place this moment in a chronological or merely logical order, we would find two successive or perhaps parallel sequences which share certain incidents (Gaspar is poisoned, the poison is made from two white roots, his wife flees), but whose interweaving does not allow the exact placement of each event nor the organization of this crowd of images, visions, and prefigurations. One of the two sequences (which of the two? both?) is a prophetic—or reminiscent—dream of Gaspar's wife. This repetition of events, once in a dream and again in reality without defining which is which, blurs our habitual way of seeing occurrences in the outside world. The reader must absorb and interpret what happens by himself; suddenly he has become, in his turn, a magician. That which is dreamed and that which is lived are inextricable and this means that any effort by the reader to order the world of the book will falsify it and end in failure. Just as his characters make war on civilization and everyday reality, so, in the rest of the book, Asturias will attempt to destroy the rational mentality, using, although less outrageously, any method he can to set the language seething: letting disorders slip into his chronology; weaving together personal and impersonal points of view; confounding popular rumors and the thoughts of the characters with the supposedly objective narration of events; silencing men and animating the world of plants and animals; dislocating points of reference; shattering the molds of academic conventions—so he carried out a great experiment, the birth of the future. Fire, one of the protagonists of the novel, is also its formal principle: its words are flames, they spark, they leap, they cannot be classified, they are like shining yellow rabbits, they rise and fall with the irrepressible rhythm of vengeance, the vengeance of fire, grandfather and son. And so we have come to the second chapter, which relates how the betrayers of Gaspar Ilóm were punished.

MACHOJÓN

When the chief died, the firefly wizards had prophesied the death of all the bringers of the poison and of their children, and foreseen that they would be sterile. The fulfillment of the curse begins in the second chapter, with the death of Señor Tomás, his son Machojón, and his wife, Vaca Manuela.

The first to disappear is Machojón, on his way to ask for the hand of his sweetheart, Candelaria Reinoso. No one knows what has happened to him; only we, the readers, directly witness his supernatural punishment: he is absorbed by the fireflies, by the fire which rises from the words of the wizards. Suddenly, a rumor arises that Machojón rides every time a field is set afire to prepare for the sowing of the corn. The story originates in a visit that a mysterious woman makes to Candelaria Reinoso. Everything indicates that she is a semi-imaginary creature: no one knows who she is nor where she comes from. What the visitor declares is also vague: ''Yes, child, the men who went out to burn saw don Macho riding through the flames. They say he was dressed all in gold, they say." Lost in the words of a stranger, anonymous, unfamiliar, taking the form given by the mysterious narrator, Machojón's legend is born. After hearing the story, "Candelaria Reinoso closed her eyes and dreamed, or saw, Machojón riding down from the mountain gullies . . . on his unbroken stallion." Whether she saw this, or dreamed it, is left unresolved.

In her turn Candelaria will transmit what she has heard or what she has wished to hear or what she has imagined to Señor Tomás, who will begin to give away his land to be cleared, so that he can see his son, who "appeared when the flames were highest, mounted on his stallion, all in gold . . . his spurs like stars and his eyes like suns." Señor Tomás consolidates the legend by trying to provoke the appearance of the supernatural, although he himself can see nothing. The peasants take advantage of his weakness, since it suits them to receive land to sow, and they feed his mania by pretending to see Machojón coming and going among the flames. So the legend spreads the fire farther and farther, until Señor Tomás, who learns, by listening to children and idiots, that the people have begun to mock the story and to turn his son into a scarecrow, decides one night to act out Machojón's ride just as it happens in the popular imagination. He disguises himself as his son and sets fire to a dry cornfield "in order to ride through the flames mounted on a stallion so they would believe he was Machojón." He wants this golden Machojón to exist (although he cannot see him, he knows he is real) and he wants the peasants (who claim to see him, but do not believe in his reality) to testify to this existence. As the fire spreads, the tone of the first chapter resumes and the fire lit by Señor Tomás becomes the mythic fire of the fireflies. First, the fire is said to be "like the ears of yellow rabbits, in twos, in hundreds, basketfuls of yellow rabbits fleeing from the fire, a round-shaped beast with nothing but a face, no neck, a face turned to the ground, rolling, a beast whose face looks like the swollen skin of an inflamed eye, among the thick eyebrows and beard of the smoke." The simile becomes metaphor and then the full and real presence, not just the narrated evocation, of the yellow rabbits, of the mythological element: "The ears of the yellow rabbits passed through sandy pools of deep water, unextinguished." Thus, in the same instant, men carry out one action (the burning of a clearing) and so provoke another (the vengeance of the yellow rabbits): they are the slaves of the fire and of the legend become reality. The fire and the myth originate in human actions, but they have their foundation, their *raison d'être*, in the magical fulfillment of a curse. Señor Tomás, the farmers and Vaca Manuela are consumed by the fire they themselves have lit, which is, at the same time, a cosmic fire sent to punish their betrayal of Gaspar. By provoking its own imitation, touching off its fire, the legend of Machojón finishes as truth.

It has been said that Asturias's basic theme is liberty. On the contrary, it seems to me that what preoccupies him most is tyranny, alienation, the monstrous threat of retribution in a fallen world. The political dictatorship of *El señor presidente* has become, in this book, a dictatorship of fire and words but both are tyrannies which man himself invokes, helps to construct and worships. As the Señor Presidente can rule because he is sustained by the fear and the conscious or involuntary support of others, so legend can impose itself on reality because man consents to live it out as a way of ransoming his humanity, and so the cosmic fire can break out because man lends his efforts to liberate it. Asturias's "tiny human shapes" end up destroying themselves, blasted to pieces by the forces that they have unleashed, or supplanted by the words that they have spoken. Social anthropologists have shown how the laws of a primitive community arise from the curse, how its system of justice is based on magic. I mention this fact to point out a possible parallel between the political and the magical worlds of Asturias. Although it could be argued that political tyranny is anti-natural and anti-human, while the tyranny of language and of the earth is essential to cosmic harmony, in any case there is no doubt that the spectre of inhuman powers ensnaring man runs through all of Asturias's work, from *The Bejeweled Boy* to *Mulata*, where man suffers victimization in the magical and Pantagruelish land of Tierrapaulita. Asturias leaves man with the consolation that he is responsible for his own condition.

And the vengeance continues.

THE DEER OF THE SEVENTH FIRE

The Tecún brothers kill all of the men of the Zacatón family. Ostensibly, they act to break the spell by which the Zacatón brothers have bewitched Señora Lucca, inserting a cricket in her navel; but in fact, they are punishing the brothers for being the pharmacists who sold the poison used against Gaspar, as we will learn in the last chapter. A folk-healer is called to direct the forces of the supernatural through human hands. In order to divine the source of the woman's pain, the healer needs a fire of living trees and we can guess that the Tecún brothers are the fire's spokesmen, that they are the instrument through which the forces of magic wreak their vengeance. The hiccoughs and the crickets that torment the mother of the Tecún brothers are part of nature, called up by the healer together with the yellow rabbits. And the severed heads of the Zacatón brothers will be burned, consumed by the words of the wizards, verbal flames: "As the flames smelled human blood they fell back, inching away, then crouched for the attack, like golden tigers."

The second part of the chapter narrates the death of the Deer of the Seventh Fire, who is, in reality, the healer. This section introduces the theme of animal and man as one being: "The curer and the deer were like you and your shadow, you and your soul, you and your lifebreath."

But there is another focus of interest in this short chapter. Seven years have passed since the death of Gaspar. Asturias has gradually distanced us from that moment, opening a gap in time that will permit the creation of a legend. The entire book is filled with dialogues in which characters dispute a past event, ritualizing it until it achieves a permanent linguistic form. At times this event, already witnessed by the reader, is retold word for word. At other times, the dialogue begins to deform the original event, to transform its meaning. In either case, the significance of these interchanges is clear: the legend is not entirely created in its first moment, the moment of human action, but continues to be formed in the process of transmission, in the rise and fall of that original instant, unforgettable and forgotten. As the pages pass by, mingled in the life of the men of maize, woven into the imperceptible movement of time, the myth is reduced to its essentials; it picks up momentum for the present and the future, it remakes itself, and it slips into the future along with man.

COLONEL CHALO GODOY

In this world crowded with sayings, with "according to according-to's of old times," with events becoming memories, the words of the wizards weigh more and more on the mind of the last bearer of the curse, Colonel Chalo Godoy. Throughout the ride he takes on the last day of his life, the light plays games with him, gradually surrounding him with signs of his imminent death which he cannot interpret—worms of fire, "the glare of chaos"—until he is burned alive.

His death is narrated in a peculiar manner which marks a new stage in the treatment of myth and reality. We never witness Godoy's agony as an objective fact; we are never certain how it occurs; the omniscient narrator refuses to help us by recounting this death. Instead, he surrenders the stage to one of his characters, Benito Ramos, who, because he has made a pact with the devil, enjoys the prophetic vision necessary to tell us how the colonel died (or how he is dying at this moment, far from where Benito gallops). This event, at least for us, has no being outside Ramos's words. The incident is a memory before it happens, an echo before it is a cry, a legend before it is a reality. The fabulous, moving farther away from its mythological axis as the years pass, fading in the glare of a post-Arcadian world, is made believable, an integral part of reality, when it springs from the viewpoint of a character. Submerged in daily life, exiled from the world of magic, but still capable of invoking its presence in legend made reality, the men of maize, in a process of continuous creation, engender the supernatural beings that keep them company.

With his narration, Benito becomes an accomplice of the vengeance, fixing forever the shape in which the events will remain in the popular imagination, confounding the form of their truth with the form of their transmission. These events can be rationally explained in many ways which are mentioned in passing, without insistence: Godoy forgot to put out his cigar; the Tecún brothers trapped him in the woods and set it afire. Many years—many pages—afterwards, we are told of the official report, the official lie: "The report sent to the government said only that Colonel Godoy and his detachment, on returning from a reconnaissance mission, perished in a forest that went up in flames."

And again, at the heart of the vengeance is fire, the element which unites the real and the fictitious: one of the circles that closes in on the colonel and kills him "looks like boiling cement, and it is formed by countless rings of dagger-trees with their daggers bloodied by a great fire. . . . Their bodies are formed by fireflies, and so, in winter they are everywhere, shining and putting out their lights and dying." It is the seventh field-clearing season, the time prophesied for the death of Godoy, and the avenging fire which arose from the death of the earth to become the death of the man who betrayed Gaspar. This death seems more ironic in light of the fact that the colonel enjoyed playing with fire: a few moments before dying he says that fighting guerrillas is like playing with fire and that he was able to finish off Gaspar Ilóm, it was because as a child he had learned to leap over bonfires on the nights before the Feast of the Conception and St. John's Day. Fire has become identified with time; it spreads everywhere and provides the unit for measuring out life: instead of years, clearings.

The first four chapters, then, show an obvious unity, developing around the death of Gaspar Ilóm and the vengeance wreaked on his executioners, a punishment carried out by human hands for superhuman reasons, a destruction which is reality and, at the same time, legend. The passage of time will allow each episode to be consolidated into a story, further mythified by each succeeding generation. The fifth chapter, however, seems to escape this unity. It has been called a jewel in itself, but it is repeatedly declared an episode independent from the others, without organic relation to the rest of the book.

MARÍA TECÚN

At first glance, it would seem that the critics are right. What relation could the preceding chapters have to the story of Goyo Yic, the blind man who recovers his sight in order to search for María Tecún, the wife who has abandoned him? Only tenuous threads of plot unite this episode to the first four, which seem to unfold in another time-period, almost in another geographic space.

Nevertheless, this story is essential to the subterranean development of the book. In essence, the chapter narrates the process of forgetting, the gradual disappearance of a woman down the roads of memory, due to the invisible passage of time.

An herb-doctor operates on Goyo Yic so that he can undertake the search for María Tecún; but when the blind man recovers colors and forms, light and distances, he realizes that his eyes are useless to him, because María is a "flower invisible to eyes that look outward instead of inward." The daily world, entering through his eyes, supplants the inner vision of his imagination, his original relation to the woman who abandoned him. He had created her inside himself, with the aid of all his senses; when he becomes like other men, he loses the experience that connected him to María. The chapter relates how Goyo Yic starts to betray this true image involuntarily; how, with the passing of the days, he loses contact with his first vision, the one he had when he was still blind, when he still created his own world as in a dream and made it into a phantasmal but secure image with a tangible invisibility. He seeks María Tecún, but in the depths of his consciousness he no longer seeks her. He has lost her.

One night he sees his own shadow in the moonlight. It is the shadow of an opossum, his *nagual*, his animal protector, but even more, his guardian essence, the fundamental being of his soul magnified and made visible as an animal. Like the deer for the curer, the opossum acts as Goyo Yic's double, the emblem of his dominant passion: "You know that man carries his children in a sack, like the 'possum." This little animal that accompanies him everywhere becomes the symbol of his need to find María Tecún and his children, so much so that "Goyo Yic was better known by the nickname of 'Possum' than by his own name." But when he has sexual relations with another woman, the possum disappears, taking with it the last hope of finding his wife. Afterwards, Goyo Yic wanders through many lands, falling into a forgetfulness sprinkled with memories, like doves seen through smoke. At the end of the chapter, he comes to confess to his *compadre*, Domingo Revolorio, who will go to jail with him, accused of smuggling: "But so much time has passed that I no longer feel anything. Before, *compadre*, I sought her in order to find her; now, in order not to find her."

Goyo Yic drifts away from his first identity just as the other characters have slowly separated themselves from the events that preceded them, the events which they have not witnessed personally but know by hearsay, which have come down to them in the form of words, of spoken memory. Goyo Yic takes leave of his first image of María Tecún; he loses his "flower," his blindness, his possum, and his archaic self; he ruminates on his past and vaguely remembers things that happened to another Goyo Yic, far-removed from himself. This inability to continue being himself, this dislocation of temporal continuity, creates a gap between the ex-blind man's life and the manner in which it took place and constitutes the first step toward its deformation and its reduction to essentials in the popular mind. What he does to the original Goyo Yic and María Tecún, the people will do to the story of his life: transform it into legend. The desire to recuperate some primeval, lost being through memory, through words, makes mythification possible and necessary.

Thus, Goyo Yic experiences the same process of the distancing and loss of a primary event which forms the theme of the rest of the novel, except that here the process is encarnated in an individual man, and the narration seeks out the psychological roots of what had appeared to be a purely social phenomenon. Goyo Yic lives out a specific process of forgetting, his subjectivity absorbed by the tricks of time. The same process unfolds in the other chapters of *Men of Maize*; throughout the novel things are done or suffered so that afterwards they may survive in the words of the future. Like a trick mirror, these words distance the original event as they reflect it but they capture its palpitating essence as legend, transcending the dismal truth of everyday life.

Of course, the psycho-biographical roots of fiction are not examined only in this chapter, but throughout the novel. Uperto, one of the Tecún brothers, undergoes a similar experience: "With the eyes of his imagination" he sees the deer killed by Gaudencio, in the forest, and "with the eyes of his face," the body of the curer spread out before him. This distinction between the eyes of the imagination and those of the face underlies every relation between the real and the imaginary, whether it be a relation of conflict or of cooperation. In Goyo Yic's case, the eyes of the face supplant those of the imagination; the substitution is necessary, the corruption of the original vision is inevitable, so that the future truth, the myth, can breathe itself into the vital center of every man. We can observe a similar phenomenon in Señor Tomás: he is unable to see Machojón with his physical eyes, but he can see him with the eyes of his fantasy. He sees the underlying truth of his guilt, he creates his own destiny—his death—according to this truth, and, in so doing, he breaks through the surface and wins an eternal place for his son in the trembling nucleus of daily conversation.

By individualizing the mythical phenomenon in the present chapter, by making it coincide with the life-cycle of every man, the irremediable weakening and loss of the self, Asturias has explored the creation of legend from another angle, the angle of the minute hand which hacks away at our life, which destroys its original once it has molded the myth into a series of events that stretches beyond us and allows us to touch others through mouths that reproduce us and tongues that repeat us.

COYOTE-POSTMAN

In order for these legends to acquire reality, it is essential that time pass, that men leave the past behind so that the actual event does not belie the words which transmit it. By the last chapter, many years have passed. One character remarks that his grandfather used to say long ago that he had actually seen a curer who could turn into a Deer of the Seventh Fire. In speaking of the past, the characters always give the impression that they are looking back over a vast, unbridgeable abyss created by the irreversible march of time. Because of the unresolvable confusion of its chronology and the distance of its points of reference, the transformation of the past into myth thrusts its characters into an eternal time. Normal duration is either unknown or nonexistent; limitless man cannot be measured with a clock. The story of Machojón, for example, not only passes from mouth to mouth, altered and autonomous, but it also becomes part of the vocabulary used by the people to interpret reality, a *cliché* that appears automatically whenever it is needed, a mental structure which men apply unconsciously. The events which the readers have witnessed survive only as folk sayings, as part of the dictionary of daily conversation: for example, something is said to become "a Machojón of hail-stones."

This incorporation of the past into the mythology of the present is underlined by the many dialogues in which a legend takes form in the midst of men's words. What had seemed past is relived and altered in order to escape from the prison of measurable time. This is the transformation of the impersonal by the individual human voice: the event, which before had existed only in the words of the narrator, now takes its being from the words of a character. The "objective" knowledge which the reader enjoyed while the characters suffered from the tyranny of facts, reintegrates itself into the world, digested by a thousand anonymous stomachs and sent out again so that it can continue its journey. It has become independent of its factual origin and lives only in its linguistic context; it has entered an atemporal world.

But in order that this other dimension, this communicative context which transcends the clock, may exist, time is necessary. In this sense, Asturias takes his place in the line of Proust, Mann, and Joyce, who demonstrated the presence of the eternal, of the mythical, in the corrosion of every moment, in the miniscule death of every object.

For this reason, it is no paradox that confronting this vague atemporality, this chaos of dates, there should also appear concrete references to measurable, regular time; just as we find, mixed with magical, associative language, the prosaic phrases of ordinary speech. It is in this great mosaic of growth and decay, among these unfolding lives, that the legend can appear and develop. Between the first and the last page of the novel stretch no more than fifty years but those pages are also separated by an eternity. Candelaria Reinoso, Machojón's sweetheart, is still at a marriageable age when the novel ends; Benito Ramos, who married María Tecún, is about to die; Musús, another associate of the colonel's, has married; María Tecún, who was one year old when the Zacatón brothers died, is a middle-aged woman with adult children at the end of the novel; the blind man, Goyo Yic, has served three years and seven months in prison. Many of these references contradict each other, and would even seem to prevent the consolidation of the legend (for example, María Tecún becomes almost proverbial before she is born), but they help to frame the characters within fluctuating, but definite, limits, in which the myth seems near and far at the same time. This contrast between the two types of time, this living in both dimensions, can also be observed in *El señor presidente* and in the rest of Asturias's work. The tension between eternity and subjection to time pulls the bonds between fiction and reality even tighter and duplicates on a temporal plane the fundamental structure of the novel.

On the other hand, this rocking prison in which the characters grow and decay is their punishment for having shattered the sleep in which the earth dreamed at one with man; it is the movement which crushes the men of maize who traffic in the grain that was once divine and is now the emblem of a degraded world, full of beggars, the sick, and the blind—characters which fascinate Asturias in all of his works. Thus, this deformation of the world in language, these vertiginous metaphors which twist objects until they are unrecognizable, this kingdom of the grotesque, this mirror in which time and the word sweat in monstrous copulation, is much more than a literary technique or an echo of European surrealism. It is an expression of horror at the loss of the magical, an attempt to expose the decadence of a world by using a baroque imagery of rotting flesh, to project a demonic reality through the twisted lens of the bestial. Perhaps, at bottom, it deals with the problem of that mysterious force which controls us and which we seek to exorcize with a spell that reproduces the image of the hell that it would banish.

How is it possible, then, that this myth, which shatters and rearranges what happened in the beginning, can become a treasury of human truth? Or, in other words, how can time and eternity meet in legend? The answer which Asturias gives to this question can be elucidated by an examination of the two most important episodes of the sixth chapter of *Men of Maize*.

The wife of Nicolás Aquino, the mail-courier of San Miguel, has abandoned him. Aquino, therefore, finds himself in the situation of Goyo Yic, whose story, now a legend, has suffered considerable alteration. Every woman who flees is called a "Tecuna" (as in the case of Machojón, the proper name has turned into a common noun), and every deserted husband is a "blind man." The popular imagination has pruned away the useless details, the surface which covered the essential human truth, and has left what will be remembered, although the final version (which, in its turn, will change with time) is far from corresponding exactly to the facts. Man himself remains trapped in the legend: he orients his behavior by the story he hears, until life begins to imitate fiction.

We can see the most typical example of this process in the survival of the wizards' curse. They had prophesied that those responsible for the death of Gaspar Ilóm would not be able to have children. But this curse is fulfilled in an interesting manner: if Benito Ramos's wife has a son, the only possible explanation is that she has deceived him; when Musús has a child, "it is his son by another." The legend cannot be put in question, for it has become so real that it determines the actions of men and their interpretation of these actions. By the mere fact of having been pronounced, the curse begins to work; when it is believed, it has achieved its goal. Everything that happens will become true or invalid according to the *a priori* beliefs of men. "Those people are sacrificed so the legend may live," says don Deferic, and his wife adds: "The victims aren't important . . . as long as they feed the monster of popular poetry." Springing from an almost insignificant individual situation, every archetype grows until it meets its justifying echo.

But this dictatorship is only possible because man has internalized the imaginative dimension, falling into the deepest, most universal regions of his beginnings: "[María Tecún's] cry disappeared in a storm of voices, together with her name, into the depths of his ears, down the canyons of his ears. He covered them with his hands, and he kept on hearing it. It didn't come from outside, but from within. The woman's name that all men shout in order to summon the María Tecún that they carry deep in their consciousness." The supposedly arbitrary evolution of the legend is, in reality, a development toward the everlasting human essence, man's should-be; and, as it shapes itself into this image, the legend casts off all forms which have not proved useful. At the end of the novel, after Nicho has gone down to meet his *nagual*, the coyote, in search of his wife, the curer (the Deer of the Seventh Fire) will explain that the rock of María Tecún is, in reality, María the Rain, La Piojosa Grande. Suddenly, we remember this other woman, the first one to flee from her husband, Gaspar Ilóm; the same train of events has circulated through the book three times, varying each time, disguising itself, but every time satisfying man's need to retell in an atemporal form the story of his separation from the past, in order to create a legend, to turn himself into a rock against time.

One character, however, does not believe in the "Tecunas," and so we come to the second sequence of the last chapter. Hilario Sacayón, the muleteer, has invented a legend which has become independent of its creator and grown on its own account, objectified by the people: "Who did not repeat that legend which he, Hilario Sacayón, had made up in his head, as if it had happened? Had he not been present at a Mass where they had prayed to God for peace and eternal rest for the soul of Miguelita of Acatán? Had they not been through the old ledgers of the parish register, searching for that miraculous child's birth certificate?" Here, for the first time, Asturias focuses on the problem of legend from the viewpoint of its inventor, whom he rescues from anonymity in order to confront him with the monstrous growth of his own lie, the product of drunken high spirits. This is yet another angle of the binomial myth-reality. Hilario Sacayón cannot accept the truth of the stories he hears because he knows that every legend (whether it tells of Machojón, a *nagual*, Gaspar Ilóm, María Tecún, or Miguelita) is founded on clouds of alcohol.

In vain the old woman Moncha explains to Hilario that "We think we've invented things that other people have forgotten. When you tell a story that no one else tells any more, you say, I invented this, it's mine. But what you're really doing is remembering—you, through your drunkenness, remembered what the memory of your forefathers left in your blood." Hilario refuses to be the speaking bridge that opens the road to a pre-existing past; he refuses to be merely the one who saved the story from forgetfulness so that it could "go on like a river." But one of the legends he doesn't believe will take over his being and force him to acknowledge the truth of some myths.

Nicho Aquino has left for the capital with the mail. Don Deferic, fearing that the courier will lose his footing in the legendary ravine of María Tecún, hires Hilario to overtake Aquino and accompany him through the dangerous passage. Hilario cannot find the courier but as he passes by the stone, he catches sight of a coyote, and the idea that it is Nicho whom he has seen begins to burrow into him like a parasite. Against his rational will, the possibility of magic takes possession of his mind and he grows obsessed with the thought that a man like himself could change into an animal. And so the man who invented a legend must recognize that there is truth in imagination and impossibility; in his heart, he must accept that he did not invent ''his own'' legend, but that it belongs to all men, and that no man can break the chains of magic that bind him to another world than that of daily existence, for history will recast the creation of the individual according to its sense of what is profound and authentic, and man will use it to explore his own destiny.

For Asturias, truth does not consist in the correspondence which can be established between a story and the factual events which gave rise to it; but a story becomes real when it transmutes these events profoundly, until they become unforgettable, when it rescues the myth from its circumstantial origin, although to do this it must obliterate part of what seemed to have happened. Human beings, blind and lost in a fallen world, have only their myths to help them find their way in the darkness, to gather up their essence, scattered through time. Reality begins to imitate legend, man becomes the instrument that plays for other ears, that perpetuates other beings. Thus, in the poetic acts of Asturias and of his characters, the individual merges with his social being, the real and the imaginary touch, time is eternalized and eternity becomes mortal, and the two types of men of maize make peace, for their struggle has finally been shown to be an intense solidarity, the two dimensions of one irreducible man. Myth and movement support each other, they need each other in order to survive: eternity feeds on the mobility of vagabond men, imperfect cross-currents in the veins of time; and man's endless motion sustains itself with the eternal company of his imagination.

The union of the men of corn finds its correlative in the unification of the text itself: what had seemed chaos is a deeper order, what was scorned as irregular narrative is the creation of a new cosmic vision, what had seemed disjointed expresses the temporal form of realities turning into words. Asturias narrated this experience (time, myth, reality, language, the internalization of social forces, America, our America) in the only way it could be narrated. Old woman Moncha never spoke so truly (and she was speaking to Asturias, who invented her just as Hilario invented Miguelita) as when she said: ''If it had not been you, it would have been another, but someone would have told it so it wouldn't be all lost and forgotten, because its existence, fictitious or real, is part of the life, of the landscape of these places, and life cannot be lost; it is an eternal risk, but it is never lost eternally."

On *Reasons of State*

Roberto González Echevarría

Carpentier's novels and stories are intricately constructed, symbolic machines that endeavor to manifest the ultimate coherence of historical event and artistic design. His narrative, especially during the 1940s, attempts to annul the presence of a self-conscious author by turning that agent into a sort of medium through whom the vast harmony of the universe flows. The project is, of course, as old as the imperialistic philosophy of Hegel and as new as Surrealism; it is, in the broadest context possible, part of Modernity's vast endeavor to replace theology with an all-encompassing world-view. Hegel's conception of the state as the fulcrum of all social and political activity, Marx's dialectical materialism, the biological imperative of *Naturphilosophie*, the tenuous constructs of late nineteenth-century Idealism, Breton's fantastic materialism, and, more recently, Structuralism are all variations of this all-out effort at world possession. Carpentier's fiction is characterized by one of the most tenacious and sustained efforts at bringing about such a closure. But his project is undermined—more so as his production reaches the fifties, sixties and seventies—by Modernity's critical passion: a passion that is manifest precisely in the consciousness of self. The irrevocable otherness of self vis-à-vis those constructs creates a radical doubt that leads to self-consciousness, irony, and finally to humor.

It is not by chance that the mature phase of Carpentier's work should have begun with both his most bitter critique of Surrealism and his first dictator-novel, *The Kingdom of This World* (1949). In the prologue to that novel, Carpentier denounced Surrealism for having become codified, a sort of Idealism to which he opposed a real/fantastic notion of "American marvelous reality." The fantastic lay there, he argued, in American reality, full as it was of unusual juxtapositions and startling coincidences. An example

From *Review* no. 18 (Fall 1976). © 1976 by the Center for Inter-American Relations, Inc.

of this was the rigorous set of coincidences to be found in the reiterations of certain dates and historical events in the story his novel narrated (roughly the history of the Haitian Revolution, particularly Henri Christophe's reign). Careful research indicates that, indeed, the novel faithfully follows history, and that this history contains a series of repetitions and coincidences. The mathematical relationship between Carpentier's chapter divisions and the numbers of the chapters underlines this order, as does the time-span covered by the plot, which divides into two mirroring halves at the center of the text—at the juncture, that is, of the two middle-subchapters. The metaphor binding historical incident with historical narrative is nature: in *The Kingdom of This World* history is presented as the product of natural cycles that are inscribed in an Eternal Calendar. But some of the reiterations are Carpentier's, not history's, so the faith in American marvelous reality that he demands in his prologue is still the bad faith of art, and the prologue, with its disclaimer of authorial intervention, becomes a part of the novel. Like the political order wrought by Christophe, depending on a theological metaphor fusing history and nature, the order to be found in the novel is an imposture. Both writer and politician fail as replacements for an absent god; and in the kingdom of this world, art and politics appear as the residue of man's will. Christophe's body is entombed in the damp cement of his still unfinished citadel, a Baroque emblem of his only final and enduring will, just as the prologue to the novel, representing the real Carpentier, has to be subsumed in the "flawed" text of the novel.

In *The Lost Steps* (1953), a complex autobiographical novel, Carpentier explored the relationship between the artist and his product which had been thrown into question by *The Kingdom of This World*. The most significant aspect of the novel is an error in the dating of the travel-journal that the narrator-protagonist writes as he travels through the jungle in search of a pure present. The error, which opens a gap between the self and the desired synchrony of nature and history, is the breach through which politics enters into Carpentier's work. After *The Lost Steps*, Carpentier's characters will be caught, not in the inexorable cycles of nature, but in the whirlwind of politics. History and the narrative will now be the product of error. In *Manhunt* (1956) the two protagonists are pursued by a history made up of all the errors of an implacable political order; it is the terror of the present as the inevitable nodal point where all the errancies of history converge. Writing is emblematically present in the stony labyrinth of the city (Havana) where the action takes place, threatening to petrify the self in a timeless order beyond its comprehension.

Explosion in a Cathedral (1962) dispels the tragic tone of *Manhunt* by dismantling the terror-inspiring cogency of the present and showing the more radical flaws of history. The title of the English translation alludes to a painting in the house of the protagonists that depicts a church at the moment it explodes. The painting is both an emblem of history and of the narrative in the novel. By capturing both the flash of the explosion and its effects, the painting undermines the notion of causality: as in our perception, cause and effect are one. The center or origin, the flash of the explosion, is not a source of order but, precisely, a void. That void is represented by the other important emblem in the novel, which alludes more directly to politics: the guillotine. The frame of the guillotine, through which Esteban contemplates the "shifting allegories" of the constellations, is also the page: the rectangular space in which signs, detached from their original codes (beheaded, as it were), shift meanings in a movement generated by the *décolage* between meaning and its material representation. Writing, art, and politics occupy the space of that dislocation. Victor Hugues, the revolutionary turned tyrant, succumbs, not to the order of nature as his predecessor in *The Kingdom of This World* did, but to the second and secondary nature of signs: he remains obstinately loyal to Robespierre long after the Incorruptible One has been beheaded. Humor in *Explosion in a Cathedral* issues from this lag that Victor Hugues and other characters are unable to perceive. The image of Billaud-Varenne imprisoned in Cayenne best conveys the humor created by that lag, showing in one glimpse the production of writing and its eventual, unexpected, use: "Billaud-Varenne was writing by the light of a candle in the next room, having taken off his shirt because of the heat. From time to time he would kill some insect which had settled on his shoulders or the back of his neck with a powerful smack. Beside him the young Brigitte lay naked on a bed, fanning her breasts and thighs with an old copy of *La Décade Philosophique*."

By going to the roots of Modernity in the period of transition between the Enlightenment and Romanticism in *Explosion in a Cathedral*, Carpentier self-consciously demonstrates the illusory nature of the modern desire to replace a theological worldview with a secular, all-encompassing theology. The novel displays not only the imperfect functioning of history, but also the limited apprehension of the world by men. In *Reasons of State* Carpentier turns to parody. The original title of the novel is *El recurso del método*, about which he has said: "It is Descartes's *Discourse on Method* turned upside down, for I believe that Latin America is the least Cartesian continent imaginable. And so *Le Discours de la Méthode* turns into *Le Recours de la Méthode*, *El discurso del método/El recurso del método*, for all the chapters— there are twenty-two—are linked in deadpan fashion, by Decartes's reflections taken from the *Discourse*, the *Philosophical Meditations* and the *Treatise on Passions*, which in spite of the rigidity of their thought, are the justification for totally delirious acts." If the critical passion of Modernity sprang from the consciousness of self, Carpentier's new novel corrodes the very notion of self through humor. For Descartes the first truth upon which to build a system of rational thought was that of the discoursing self: "I think, therefore I am." What Carpentier shows is the tautological nature of Descartes's enterprise; the recourse of method means the turning back of method onto itself.

This reduction of discourse to tautology is best observed in the novel when the Head of State mocks Colonel Hoffmann's classical military treatises: " 'Listen to this, listen!' he said, and in a portentously deep voice: 'Victory resulted from the fact that the battle had been won' (Scharnhorst)." The tautological character of discourse implies the dissolution of the discursive self as a source of truth and order—the constant and unsystematic shifts in point of view from the Head of State to other characters and to a third-person, free-indirect style underscore this. Discourse and the self are only apprehended "on the recourse": they emerge at the point when they turn onto themselves, not to manifest a rigorous cogency, but their radical discontinuity.

With the opposition discourse/recourse, Carpentier is not only undermining Descartes, or better yet, a certain mode of rationality represented by Descartes, but also pointing to the source of the inversion of Cartesian thought: Vico (*corsi* and *ricorsi*). If in Carpentier's fiction of the 1940s history appeared as a repetition of natural cycles, Vico offers an idea of return that does not constitute mere repetition and affirms historicity instead of denying it. History in Vico is a kind of second nature that begins when men begin to make history; a second beginning, as it were, that Vico places at the time of the Flood. One of Carpentier's recent stories, "The Chosen," uses as its theme the convergence of many arches, constructed by the many Noahs of different religious traditions who must remake the world after the Flood. "The Chosen" is a Viconian fable of origins: the story of the second beginning of history, the first recourse.

In *Reasons of State* the importance of this notion of second beginnings, of a second nature, is particularly relevant in the context of the Latin American tradition of the dictator novel. Carpentier's dictator is a *déspota ilustrado*, as opposed to Asturias's in *El señor presidente*, who appears as the personification of telluric forces in the tradition of Sarmiento's portrayal of Rosas, or Carpentier's own Henri Christophe in *The Kingdom of This World*. Carpentier's Head of State personifies the future of the Enlightenment, the product of the bourgeois revolution, like Victor Hugues. In the Head of State Carpentier has combined traits of Estrada Cabrera, Machado, Trujillo and other dictators in the worst Latin American tradition who, drunk on a liberal rhetoric, become entrapped in the ludicrous image of their own making. The Head of State is not only surrounded by coarse, obsequious goons, but also by academicians and writers: he can quote Renan from memory and order the best wines. If the Head of State is the center of power, he is a hollowed-out center, a *maniquín*, the mummy with which he is constantly equated. A Carnival mask of death, the Head of State is the end product of the swirl of history, of its various recourses, not the by-product of untamed nature. If in *The Kingdom of This World* the text crystallized into symmetrical parts, reflecting nature, the temporal disposition of *Reasons of State* is based on the erring that began with *The Lost Steps*.

Carpentier has said that *Reasons of State* "begins very precisely in the year 1913, but its action expands concretely by a synchronization of events and epochs until the year 1927, with allusions to various historical events. But later there is a period that takes my central character toward the thirties, forties, with a brief epilogue of two pages [one in the published version] that is titled '1972.' " This chronology can be easily corroborated by dating some of the historical events that are mentioned in the novel, such as the battle of the Marne, the entry of the U.S. into World War I and so forth. The year 1927 at the end is easily verified because the Student, who confronts the Dictator and is patterned after Rubén Martínez Villena and Julio Antonio Mella, is going to the Anti-Imperialist Conference in Brussels, which took place in that year. But this synchronization is far from creating symmetries. In fact, the most salient feature of the temporal and textual structure of *Reasons of State* is the presence of multiples of seven: there are seven chapters and twenty-one subchapters (plus the epilogue), and all important historical upheavals occur in subchapters seven, fourteen, and twenty-one. The rhythm of this temporal arrangement is not paralleled by the historical chronology. Up to subchapter thirteen the various dates and events do follow a historical sequence that takes us from 1913 to about 1918, a period of six years that constitutes one-half of the time-span discernible in the novel (1913–27). In subchapter thirteen we have the very Carpenterian Carnival scene, except that here, as opposed to the stories of the forties, it does not fall on the liturgical period assigned to the Carnival. It occurs instead as a result of the disturbance caused during a performance of *Aida* that sends Enrico Caruso in costume into the streets, where he is arrested for wearing "fancy dress when it was not Carnival time." Subchapter thirteen, however, does not end with just a Carnival, but with the beginnings of a popular revolt as the opposition takes advantage of the masquerade to attack the police (the revolt will reach full force in subchapter fourteen). The displaced Carnival becomes political Revolution.

A significant temporal displacement also takes place at the juncture of subchapters thirteen and fourteen. Now the allusions are to events that took place during Machado's dictatorship in Cuba; that is to say, there has been a chronological leap of seven years from 1918 to 1925. Subchapter fourteen contains another displacement, but on a liturgical level, as Christmas turns into the Epiphany (December 25 becomes January 6), a leap, as it were, over the thirteen days of Advent. (An error in the translation makes it read "three" instead of "thirteen.") The thematic motive for this shift is that, through U.S. influence, kids receive gifts from Santa Claus on Christmas Day, instead of from the Magi on Epiphany. The leap forward continues, however, for Epiphany soon turns into Holy Week. The first half of the liturgical year ends with the strikes that begin to erode the power of the Head of State. The textual and chronological centers do not coincide in *Reasons of State,* as they did in *The Kingdom of This World*; they constitute in their displacement, as in *Explosion in a Cathedral,* a chasm, the vortex of the historical whirlwind. The operatic Carnival was in the fall or winter while the Carnival that becomes a full-fledged Revolution occurred in the spring. All of the rituals conceived by the Head of State coincide, like the beginning of the novel, with the fall, and allude to the Day of the Dead. The leap is then from the Day of the Dead to the Resurrection.

The emblem of that displaced, moveable center is the mummy-fetus that appears as a double of the Head of State. The correlative is that enormous statue of the Motherland that the Dictator plans inside the newly-built Capitol, which is (as in Cuba, for instance) kilometer zero of all highways in the country. It is not by chance that when she is finally housed in the enormous (but not large enough) dome, we are in subchapter twenty-two; the mathematical center of the text, if the epilogue is counted. It is also at this point that, because the work on the Capitol will not be finished for the celebration of independence day, the central plaza of the city is decorated with painted palm trees and other theatrical props. The city becomes a stage set of monumental proportions. Like the mummy-fetus, this décor is both ruins and unfinished buildings, beginnings and ends lumped together by artifice: "And it then happens that in periods of inactivity the central zone of the capital was transformed into a sort of Roman forum, an esplanade from Baalbek, a terrace from Persepolis while the moon shone down on this strange chaotic landscape of marbles, half-finished metopes, truncated pillars, blocks of stone between cement and sand—the ruins, the dead remains, of what had never been." The dismantled, stony mother who arrives from Europe in various pieces (the greatest attraction being her one uncovered breast) is housed within a dome that is a permanent ruin. It is on this stage that the Head of State will deliver his translation of the *Prayers at the Acropolis:* discourse and its setting have become Opera, the amalgam of artifices drawn from various codes, the very image of *secondariness.*

In *The Eighteenth Brumaire of Louis Bonaparte* Marx writes: "Hegel remarks somewhere that all facts and personages of great importance in world history occur, as it were, twice. He forgot to add: the first time as tragedy, the second as farce." What *Reasons of State* seems to propose is that by its very secondariness writing can only aspire to represent history as farce.

A Return to Africa
with a Carpentier Tale

José Piedra

Caribbean portrayals of African traditions often translate on paper as co-lonialist acts. Even writers reclaiming Africa as their cultural backbone ex-press their claims in Western types of discourse. The fact is that, in deed or on paper, explorers are intruders. The development of native traditions in Africa is interrupted by the act of discovery and repressed by the act of recording. No modern attempt can undo the original takeover.

Caribbean texts exploring Africa shoulder responsibilities similar to those of chronicles of discovery—to relate two cultures within a frame of authority which inscribes the material discovered and, at the same time, justifies the act of takeover. Writing itself becomes an imperialist tool. The frame it provides forces European tradition upon the new territories. Not only is the exploitation of Africans considered a digression in the coloni-zation of America, but the concept of African culture becomes an addendum to the colonialist text.

A colonialist explorer approaches the target culture according to the frame of values of the control culture. The Caribbean literary explorer easily lapses into the same bias when claiming roots for his own culturally mixed domain. In both cases, the evaluation of his efforts and the authority of his results hinge on the timing and the spatial rendering of the discovery; that is, it all depends on who claims whom, when and how.

The question of timing serves as a suitable pretext for colonialism. Takeovers become less objectionable when disguised as reclaiming a space and a people which had been lost to history—the history of the colonial power, that is. Such a pretext served the Spanish colonial theory of the "just war" in the enslavement of Amerindians and Afro-Americans. The theory transformed Aristotle's dictum on natural slavery, by way of Thomas

From *MLN* 97, no. 2 (March 1982). © 1982 by The Johns Hopkins University Press.

Aquinas, into a political tool for Spanish expansionism. Aristotle's endorsement of hierarchies to maintain socio-historical harmony was interpreted by the Empire as a justification for the enslavement of people on the fringes of history. Ironically, the Spanish proposed to save the uncivilized from the neglect of history; otherwise they would be exterminated indiscriminately in the name of that very history. "Better to enslave than to ignore or to kill them" could have been the Spanish motto. The theory also endorsed the myth of the Indies as a lost part of the Known World needed in order to complete the harmonious unit of the Spanish Empire.

The spatial rendering of discovered cultures, the recording of found materials, constitutes another pretext for colonialism. Non-Western cultures are supposedly saved from obscurity by their cultural enslavement in the book format. Both the ruthless conqueror and the benevolent chronicler disguise their true aims as the saving of lost cultures. Cortés is just as guilty of fitting his experiences of the New World into the pages of the Old, as is the mestizo Peruvian Inca Garcilaso when explaining his Indian heritage to a European public. Even the efforts to record the American experience in native words require those words to follow a colonial syntax. And the most formidable syntactical frame available to the West is the book format.

The West regards the book as an authority-granting format, applicable to oral traditions or traditions otherwise recorded. Furthermore, the book serves to control communication, not only because few have access to its full potential, but because its sequential or linear syntax perpetuates the Western obsession with literacy and progress. As writers and readers confine themselves to the authority invested in a chain of books, they alienate themselves from a first-hand experience of culture. Even the most insignificant variables experienced first-hand have to be recorded reflecting the existing line of authority, and read by the standards of progress.

African methods of recording and reading are dramatically different. Individuals seek self-realization and social validation by fulfilling their duties and exercising their rights within tradition. They do not require the authority and progress inherent in the written texts of the West. Variables enrich African discourse to the extent that they cause it to grow off-center, by the apparently freewilling interpretations of the individual. Yet, individual interpretations do not lead to haphazard variability, but to a radial pattern of growth. Each individual takes a ritual center as a starting point; his behavior and his interpretations do not tend to stray far from the social core, precisely because he maintains first-hand contact with the needs of his society. The Western book format would never do full justice to African discourse since its view of reality encourages second-hand cultural experiences.

The introduction of the Bible into Africa offers an example of this dramatic cultural shortcoming. Biblical stories represent non-Western source materials which originally sought to codify individual beliefs as oral units with lasting socio-historic validity. Yet the ensuing written tradition has been used by the West to generate obsessively linear interpretations of belief. When the BaKongo were challenged by missionaries about their lack of culture, the Bible was presented to them as an example of literacy, the classic format of revealed authority. The BaKongo retaliated by treating the book as a source of divination. Divination cures the book format of its linear complex since individuals read according to their intentions rather than by abiding by the authority of the book. Yet the BaKongos' ingenious adaptation of Western values falls short of relieving the prejudice against the alleged non-literacy of African cultures.

The Afro-Hispanic cultures in the Caribbean have had to contend with a similar kind of literacy bias. Catholic dogma constituted their original frame of reference, an unfair but less linear format than the Bible's. Catholic dogma permitted more digressive interpretations to suit the changing interests of the establishment. Papal bulls and edicts of the Inquisition dictated the convenient scriptural readings. Those readings fed the *Leyes de Indias*, the Spanish legal account of the incorporation of America into the Empire. And although the end result does not reflect popular culture but rather an elitist view of history, the format permitted recording of multicultural values on American soil.

Alejo Carpentier, the late Cuban writer, partook in the Hispanic legacy of adjusting the authority of the book to accommodate revisionist readings. In novels such as *¡Ecue-Yamba-O!* (1933) and *El reino de este mundo* (1949), which symbolically open and close his Afro-Caribbean period, he uncovers details which set events outside of the enslaving line of authority. To do so, however, his texts establish the authority line as a model, both historically and aesthetically. In fact, in the author's white-ruled world, the official line is both underlined and underscored by the attempts of a black substratum to rise to the surface. Even when white authority is portrayed as inefficient, the popular black struggle to overcome it confirms the dependence of the oppressed on the oppressors' code. Thus the literary setting presents the full impact of the historical dilemma; the non-colonialist literary treatment predicates a bypassing and avoidance, or a mimicking and mocking of Western rules. Carpentier explores both alternatives.

In *¡Ecue-Yamba-O!* the liminal black society remains powerless and hence, much closer to the infra-structure of Cuban destiny than the ruling class. Black Cuban traditions are never gratuitously identified by Carpentier. They represent self-imposed obstacles for assimilation as well as socially-imposed aesthetic or historical prejudices. The enslaved black traditions portrayed by Carpentier are doomed to fail in white markets. *Ecue*'s blacks live in a culture of survival, as their only other alternative would be to legitimize their position by total compromise. The author's partial compromise avoids confrontation between Cuban and traditional Euro-American codes. If this restraint limits the native chances to achieve a white-worth victory, it also curtails the subjecting of Creole voices to a whitewashed defeat.

In *El reino de este mundo* the Creole's battle against the West is symbolically won. This triumph results in as much adaptation to the oppressors' code as if they had lost. In the revolutionary Haiti depicted, winners and losers, black or white, adapt to the whims of the *grande histoire*. Those are the textual rules for earth-bound Western kingdoms. The oppressed, as marginal figures, mock the oppressors by mimicking their code; as winners, they come dangerously close to mocking themselves by parodying such a code. Nevertheless, the doomed kingdom suggests a beyond. Haitians under Carpentier's rule can realize themselves through the *petite histoire* of an unfinished revolution. The popular ferment transcends the oppressive medium by which it is depicted. It does so by way of an African liberation myth—Yoruba-bred heroes literally bypass history by flying away to return at the right moment, beyond the reach of the text.

Both of the novels used as examples match the reach of Western history against the energy of African storytelling. Their plots outline events history considers nonevents because it is not prepared to deal with them. Carpentier's language as an obstacle to action, the intricate architectural reconstruction of events as remnants of a misunderstood past, create a distance between plot lines and recording methods. Such a distance epitomizes a wider cultural gap. The calculated obsolescence of recording methods marks the writer as an intruder in his own recorded material. His code is, in principle, unable to record the energy of transcendental acts trapped within the limited reach of their official wording. Any evidence of an admitted defeat against the colonial code enriches anticolonialist interpretations. The defeat designed by the writer opens a review cycle in the reading of the story and in the recording of history.

Carpentier's historical revisionism dominates his neglected tale "Histoire de lunes," first published in *Cahier du Sud*, 1937, and uncovered by Roberto González Echevarría in his 1977 book *Alejo Carpentier: The Pilgrim at Home*. The narrative synthesizes an official history line and an infra-official discourse. Both interact at a safe distance in a work conceived off-center: in French, for a European public, about the plight of racially mixed Cuban noble savages resisting the impersonal Euro-American encroachment. Language itself strays off-center, avoiding commitments. The text abounds in impersonal and reflexive constructions which hinder the reader in establishing syntactic relationships of sequence or of cause and effect.

Most of the action centers on the arrival of the express train in a remote Cuban town. An arrival full of the sad prospects of civilization: the politico, the captain, an animal trainer, music students and whores. Although the plot alludes to the linear passage of time—on that day, the next day, carnival time and patron saint's day, days of the week and hours of the day—a straight linear reading wavers under the puzzling evidence reinstating the train's arrival throughout the plot. Textual time is not gauged according to chronological progress, and rightly so, because most characters remain marginal to such progress. Instead, time is gauged according to the impact half-hidden details make on witnesses and interpreters of the ritual moment. As a consequence, a straight sequential reading must give way to a radial reading of events that do not lie quietly under the linear hold of history. Each reader attains a different radius of interpretation by exploring the self-limiting means furnished by Carpentier.

The writer sits precariously on the fence. Even the title of his work leaves options open. *Histoire* in the original French, as in the Spanish *Historia*, connotes both history and story. In my English translation I have settled for a compromise: *Tale of Moons*.

In Western terms, the plot hardly makes history, or for that matter, does an outline show the text to make much progress. *Tale* describes the events that led to Atilano's death, from his enigmatic placement in front of his shoeshine chair to the official report of his death as a Communist antihero. The protagonist's significance is trapped between two Western clichés: a low standing in Cuba's social hierarchy and the dubious honor of presenting an international menace. Early signs of deafness or absent-mindedness do not identify Atilano as a worthless outcast, but as a man marked by a ritual death. The police report towards the end is not a mere justification of his execution as a red provocateur, but the ritual death of the popular trust in the official line.

Once again Carpentier's text defies the enslaving official interpretation by turning a code against itself, by making evident the writer's limitations. On the one hand, the reader becomes an accomplice in Atilano's execution, burying him as a scapegoat for the sins attributed to the black slave: laziness, overt sexuality, love of the banal and the decorative, and loud, quarrelsome and generally uncivilized behavior. On the other hand, the reader becomes an acolyte in Atilano's ritual death. Black sins give way to the basic virtues of Africans under the yoke: endurance, search for outlets of love, hatred of hypocrisy and false authority, development of an inner life, imagination and self-realization.

From a Yoruba perspective, Atilano emerges as a multifaceted embodiment of human nature. He is an individual with a social duty, yet he never says a word. By voicing his plight he would bow to the oppressor's code; the text lets his silent presence irradiate the plot with the subjacent meaning of a secret code. It would be impossible to reduce his significance to the hierarchical or sequential values favored by the traditional literature of the West. Our tale shows the hero beyond the demarcations of word and action, good and evil, man and nature, now and then. He does not simply act like animals, plants, objects, forces and gods, he *is*, *becomes* or *is possessed* by them. In this context, words of explanation would establish superfluous linear links.

Certain characteristics used as metaphors in the plot are essential tools for an Afro-Cuban interpretation. For instance, the train represents the arrival of progress. The town's survival depends on the effects of such a progress, both because it expects the benefits of trade and the danger of betrayal from the outside world. Moreover, the train stands for Ogun in

Yorubaland, San Pedro or San Miguel Arcángel in Cuba. These manifestations of the Iron God relate to rites of passage—from circumcision, to awareness of sexual duties and the ritual fight for the advancement of humanity. Therefore the fight for survival takes an added dimension. Atilano's awakened phallic power, as interpreted by the townsfolk, acknowledges the hidden power of Ogun. Women, the traditional keepers of Yoruba-Cuban tradition, sense the full impact. Ogun sows the mythical seed; Atilano is his accidental means.

A Western interpretation alone cannot explain the plot line. Yet no Yoruba dictionary or timetable would readily translate the exact meaning and duration of the plot into Western terms. Dictionaries and timetables reflect an implicit Western bias. When applied to African cultures they become colonial tools as much as Bibles and history books. Carpentier avoids taking sides. He emulates the African radial format of inscription but makes it contingent to the Western historical tradition. According to the radial format, communication centers on a concrete nucleus which irradiates multiple interpretations. Spatio-temporal readings are discouraged because they are based on a hierarchical and sequential inscription of data. Yet, the text allows Western-trained readers to arrive at a limited spatio-temporal certainty after their radial exploration of Yoruba clues.

The ritual of Notre-Dame-des-petites-oreilles becomes the concrete nucleus of the metaphorical web. It leads two of the factions in town to confront each other, under the guise of debating Atilano's significance. The fictitious Catholic virgin has a Yoruba counterpart: Oba, one of Shango's wives, who cuts off her ear to regain conjugal bliss after her husband has strayed from their traditional union. Carpentier substitutes the feuding pair with two other Yoruba-born deities: Babalu-aye (San Lázaro) and Yemaya (Nuestra Señora de Regla).

The substitution itself is a lesson in survival techniques in the face of the colonizing efforts of history. In the presence of transculturation and adaptation to social oppression, Yoruba deities not only took the names of Catholic counterparts, but also traded attributes to become more compatible with Catholic dogma, Caribbean sensibilities and the strict writing rules of the Western book. The development of the two pairs in question serves as an illustration of such substitutions.

Shango is one of the most powerful and ambiguous of Yoruba deities. Its womanizing bouts are matched by states of subdued androgyny, its fury and deafness are matched by its kindness and understanding. Cubans venerate a milder, less ambivalent image of Shango in Santa Bárbara, the guardian of purity.

Oba's sacrifice of an ear was matched by Yemaya's lack of a breast. Oba's presence is rare in Cuban rites, although her attributes as well as Yemaya's are associated with Nuestra Señora de Regla. The polygamous relationship which Oba shares with two other wives of Shango, gave way to a more assertive, Amazon-like attitude during Cuba's colonial siege.

Babalu-aye's feared personality in the Yoruba cult mellowed to his revered status as the Cuban San Lázaro—the patron god of endurance since slave days. Yemaya's original carefree fecundity has been cautiously reinterpreted in Nuestra Señora de Regla as a symbol of nurturing motherhood.

Some processes of cultural adaptation are outlined by Carpentier in the plot. For instance, the character in *Tale* who impersonates San Lázaro is said to have once impersonated Santa Bárbara, following the historical evolution. The exchange of Oba for Yemaya as Nuestra Señora de Regla is more subtle. However, the ironic reference to Notre-Dame-des-petites-oreilles, by virtue of the name itself, encompasses the attributes of the two Yoruba deities on which it is based. Cultural adaptations either appear as explicit, but seemingly insignificant allusions in the text, or as implicit failures of the code to fix the African presence within Western words.

Carpentier's *Tale* illustrates the compounded problem of dealing with African cultures translated into a second-hand Cuban code. The domestic quarrels in the pantheon of Yoruba deities acquire poignancy as their traditions fight for survival in the text. Atilano is the messenger of such a battle. He is a literary disguise for the Santo Niño de Atocha. This Catholic figure represents the offspring of Elegba—the Yoruba trickster who questions tradition and ends up as the scapegoat. The reader who explores Atilano's cultural implications experiences the text as a scale model for cultural survival. Ironically, Atilano dies the cruel death of a forgotten martyr. He only survives the reading of the text.

Atilano's sacrifice irradiates meaning. It coincides with the waning crescent phase of the moon, when the moon is "dying." The eighth day of the slow celestial "death" marks the time for a *nganga,* "a pact with the dead." The most significant *nganga* occurs September 8th, during the celebration of the day of Nuestra Señora de Regla. Therefore, the African substratum supplies some spatio-temporal certainty to the plot; it places and dates the action as the readers learn to partake in the aforementioned beliefs.

Moreover, the African substratum follows closely the cycles of nature. The mysterious open ending of *Tale* reflects man's attempts to grasp the essence of space and time. The last sentence reads: "The bad influences of the moon vanished for it had entered a heavenly triangle dispelling its evil power over the skulls of men." The "heavenly triangle" in question consists of the other three quarters in which the moon is bound to show more benevolence, after the ritual sacrifice. During September, the benevolent period culminates with a celebration of purity regained, the blessings of nature, a rebirth. The new hope points toward three traditions: the Yoruba Obatala, the Catholic Nuestra Señora de las Mercedes, the pagan Harvest Moon. They embody the aspirations men of mixed heritage place on the passage from the twenty-third to the twenty-fourth of September.

The reader chooses among many interpretations implicit in, or suggested by, the cultural adaptations outlined in the text. However, Carpentier's readers share with him the responsibility of channeling such adaptations through the authority-frame ruling the book format. The situation compares to the colonial elite's use of the recording format of the Inquisition and the Papacy as models of authority covering their changing needs and aims in scriptural interpretations. The biased treatment of texts such as the Bible or the *Summa Theologica* never openly undermines the continuing line of authority. That is why the Conquistadors' Catholic dogma and the neo-Conquistadors' "magic realism" incorporate historical digressions and textual discrepancies into a legitimizing official code, without weakening its foundations. The voracious flexibility of the colonialist writing code allows two systems to coexist in the text: that of the oppressor and that of the oppressed. However, the ironic attitude implicit in such a compromise illustrates the frustrated efforts of a literature intent on recording traditions which history books remain reluctant or unprepared to assimilate, except in colonial terms. When the reader faces such a sad state of affairs, the text begins to yield the forced synthesis of hidden facts and glorified fiction characterizing Caribbean treatment of African materials.

In Carpentier's writing system, Yoruba culture challenges its submissive role. Instead, the text gives it a place of honor in the preservation of Cuban values within the frame of a colonizing history. This honor is warranted for, in general, Yoruba culture has survived well Western renderings. This is evident from a recent report of an Epa festival in Yorubaland reenacting the challenge of traditions and honoring the heroes who return hope or consolation to the group. In that festival, an Atilano-like trickster represents the individual whose ritual role is to question the interpretation of social destiny.

As the story claims and history verifies, Carpentier's *Tale of Moons* stands as a scale model for the ironic contradictions of Cuban discourse. Native variables put in doubt a Western control. But what appears as native variables are mostly cultural remnants adopted from African sources. Therefore, the colonized Cuban writer acts also as a colonizer. If African culture cannot win the textual battle, it can survive by default of the recording system.

The Picaroon in Power: Alejo Carpentier's *El recurso del método*

Julie Jones

In "El derecho de asilo" (1972) a political refugee uses his wiles to usurp the foreign ambassador who provides him asylum. The story, a mixture of "burlas y veras," first revealed Carpentier's interest in an idea fundamental to the novel that was published two years later—*El recurso del método* (1974)—the idea of "la picaresca del dictador." Carpentier explained what he meant by that phrase in an interview which coincided with the publication of the novel:

> Durante años soñé yo en escribir una novela que habría de titularse *Picaresca* y que sería la novela del personaje de Quevedo (Pablos en *La vida del buscón*), modernizado por tierras de América. Pero observando al pícaro trasladado a América, me dí cuenta un buen día que ese pícaro español . . . al pasar a América . . . cobraba apetencias nuevas y dejaba de ser aquel personajillo medio culto y gracioso—personaje de sainete—para transformarse primero en el político anunciador del politiquero. Después en el presidente de las elecciones amañadas, después en el general de los cuartelazos y, finalmente, civil o general, en el dictador.

Although numerous studies of *El recurso del método* have appeared, none deals with this aspect. The novel is not, of course, picaresque in the strict sense of the term. It lacks the framework of the pseudo-autobiography which most commentators agree is essential to the form, but it does reveal a number of picaresque motifs which create a pervasive atmosphere of roguery. What I intend to do in this [essay], then, is examine the picaresque elements which inform the character of the dictator and the novel as a

From *Revista Canadiense de Estudios Hispánicos* 7, no. 2 (Winter 1983). © 1983 by *Revista Canadiense de Estudios Hispánicos*.

whole. In doing so, I shall consider as important aspects of the picaroon his upward mobility, reliance on trickery, way with words, uneasy alliance with society, resort to role-playing, pragmatic world view and radical isolation, as well as the author's use of the first-person point of view.

During the sixteenth and seventeenth centuries, at a time in Spanish history when disorganization was rampant and the rigid social structure was being challenged, it was acknowledged, at least in some circles, that a man of lowly birth could ascend to an honorable position. Pero Mexía wrote in 1669 that "en cualquiera parte que nazca el hombre tiene licencia para procurar de ser muy grande y muy conocido, con tanto que sea un camino por las virtudes." Not surprisingly, however, many ambitious souls tended to aim for fame and position without being overly scrupulous about virtue. By condoning his wife's infidelity, Lazarillo attains a modest degree of comfort; Pablos tries, unsuccessfully it is true, to become a gentleman, and Yáñez's Alonso retires to a country retreat. Post-Spanish America, with its confused racial heritage, its tolerance for manifestly unqualified officials and widespread corruption, offers another such field of operation for the adventurer. Periquillo Sarniento, the first Latin American picaroon, does well, finally reforming his ways and ending up as a wealthy *hacendado*.

As *El recurso* opens, Carpentier's dictator is at the height of his power. The series of intrigues by which he has worked his way into this position are only hinted at, as is the humble background of his parents, so important to the picaroon. We do know that, as a young newspaperman, he had a hard time feeding his family, the offspring of an irregular union which was only solemnized when his improved condition made marriage expedient, that he has a touch of mixed blood (the equivalent to the *converso* strain in Pablos and other picaroons), that his generalship was not acquired through military training but rather auto-conferred. A self-made man, he has determined, like Lazarillo, that where *provecho* lies, *honra* will follow.

Yet, although he has become "muy grande y muy conocido," a man of distinction, equally at home in his mansion on the Rue du Tilsitt and the presidential palace in his country, the dictator continues to exercise many of the little ruses that facilitated his rise to power. Lauded for his abstinence from liquor, he is actually a heavy drinker who keeps rum and *aguardiente* in a pigskin case always near at hand. To hide the odor of drink, he sucks lozenges, douses himself with cologne, and

> siempre hablaba a las gentes—algo ladeada la cara, midiendo el alcance del resuello—con una mesa de por medio, o guardando una calculada distancia que acrecía, si cabe, la respetabilidad de su figura patriarcal.

He is a devoted reader of pornographic literature (as well as a frequent visitor at high-class brothels). When the Illustrious Academic finds him out, he simply attributes the books to his secretary Peralta. Envious of the tiny train which belongs to the long-established German colony in his country, he takes advantage of his government's declaration of war on the Axis Powers to seize the railroad and desport himself with the petite locomotive, a pastime he finds so diverting that for several days he forgets all about the war.

This festive quality, linked with the quick wit and great ingenuity that Carpentier attributes to the picaroon ("ocurrente, tramposo, fullero, mentiroso, grato en algunos momentos, ingenioso siempre"), makes the *Primer Magistrado* an extraordinarily *likeable* dictator, surely the first in Latin American fiction. The effect is disconcerting. The reader finds himself in the uncomfortable position of applauding, for example, the president's marvellous discovery that he can continue to suspend elections after the end of World War I because "aún estamos en guerra con Hungría. Y cuando hay guerra no hay elecciones. Celebrar elecciones ahora sería violar la Constitución."

Not all of his machinations are funny, of course. The trick with which he murders General Becerro and, worse, the false news of his death that lures crowds of people out into the streets only to be massacred by the presidential guards: these are recourses he uses with increasing frequency when his power is threatened. However, he does not revel in motiveless malignance as do Asturias's and García Márquez's dictators. He prefers to hoodwink his victims by gentler means. His favorite tool is, perhaps, his oratory.

In his book on the picaresque, Harry Sieber shows how important a gift for the gab is to Lazarillo, and other picaroons as well, in that it gives them a device for manipulating their world. Lázaro learns something new about language from each one of his masters; by a logical progression, he works his way up to town crier. Sieber argues that the entire *vida*, in fact, is an artful elaboration of language on Lazarillo's part, written with the intention of blackmailing the archpriest. Although Carpentier's dictator never gets around to writing the memoirs that would, presumably, justify his life, he does pride himself on his eloquent speechmaking.

His baroque rhetoric (a parody of Carpentier's own ornate style) is richly embroidered with

> espadas de Damocles, pasos del Rubicón, trompetas de Jericó, Cyranos, Tartarines y Clavileños, revueltos con altivas palmeras, señeros cóndores y onicrótalos alcatraces.

Although this use of the idiom furnishes the diplomatic community with no little amusement, it is most effective with the president's countrymen:

> sabía que con tales artificios de lenguaje había creado un estilo que ostentaba su cuño y que el empleo de palabras, adjetivos, epítetos inusitados, que mal entendían sus oyentes, lejos de perjudicarlo, halagaba, en ellos, un atávico culto a lo preciosista y floreado, cobrando, con esto, una fama de maestro del idioma cuyo tono

contrastaba con el de las machaconas, cuartelarias y mal redactadas
proclamas de su adversario.

As a speaker, the dictator has a keen sense of his audience. At the dedication
of the capitol, for example, he manages both to satisfy the expectations of
the ignorant and to pull the collective leg of the diplomatic corps, who are
mortified to learn that the unusually florid speech they have been covertly
chuckling about is actually Renan's *Oration sur l'Acropole*.

The president is equally aware of the effect of language in conversation.
He compares the speech that "según los casos y la condición del cliente,
pasaba del estilo Port-Royal al estilo Bruant" of Madame Yvonne, director
of his favorite brothel, to his own French, "mixto de Montesquieu y *Nini-
peau-de-chien*." The same observation applies to his Spanish. However adept
at manipulating the upper and lower registers of rhetoric, he is less than
successful at the middle reaches. In his interview with the Student, he
misses the mark because, although he is careful to avoid both the flowery
and the crude, he is unaware of the habitual use of the familiar *tú* among
the students, a failure which portends his downfall.

Since language means power and, in this case, very real power, the
dictator chooses his words with extreme care. However, there are occasional
slips. In the middle of an elevated discussion with his friend the Illustrious
Academic, he is set off by a remark about the difficulties of dealing with
the lower classes:

> se desencarriló de pronto el Primer Magistrado de su francés harto
> metido, harto cuidado de la pronunciación y de la justeza del
> vocablo, para lanzarse, impetuoso, por el disparadero de un alud
> de improperios criollos que el otro veía llegar, atónito, como una
> invasión verbal de idiogramas ajenos a su entendimiento, Indios,
> negros, sí; zambos, cholos, pelados, atorrantes, rotos, guajiros,
> leperos, jijos de la chingada, chusma y morralla.

The speech of his fashionable daughter Ofelia embraces the same range.

The disparity in his language reflects the deeper division in the president. He is passionately attached to the civilized circle of art and leisure
which Paris represents for him, an assiduous cultivator of the elite and the
near-elite (including a number of characters transposed from *Á la recherche
du temps perdu*). For him the phrase he uses so frequently—"hacerse
gente"—means not to become more humane, but to become more French.
He is nevertheless a barbarian, capable of none too refined cruelty should
it be necessary to retain power. Living in Parisian society, he is forced to
dissemble. The copious references to theatre all point to this role-playing.
In Paris the dictator, boulevardier and dilettante, both is and is not what
he seems.

Role-playing, as numerous writers on the picaresque have pointed out,
is a central motif in the genre. Lazarillo's is an apprenticeship in appearing
to be what he is not. This deception is necessary if he is to make his way

in the world. Pablos even takes to disguise, renting fancy apparel and fine horses and appropriating a false title in order to make a wealthy marriage. In *The Fiction of Satire*, Ronald Paulson describes the picaroon as "the man who pretended, appeared, or even believed himself to be part of society . . . while actually being an interloper from beyond the pale." The picaroon yearns for respectability, but he can only attain it through unrespectable means. He is for that reason what Claudio Guillén in *Literature as System* calls a "half-outsider," who never quite fits into the society which he aspires to become associated with. The ruthlessness which enables the dictator to achieve his position and, therefore, to cultivate the good life in Paris, eventually destroys him socially. The photographs of the massacre of Nueva Córdoba, for which he playfully posed, come out in the French press. Suddenly, as if by magic, all doors are closed, no one is at home to him. He mounts a costly campaign to regain his social standing, climaxed by the donation of a pre-Columbian mummy to the Trocadero Museum, but to no avail. He is washed up in the only place in the world where society matters to him.

In emphasizing the pathetic dimension of the dictator's Parisian role-playing, and the relative solitude into which it forces him (since dissembling involves a measure of secrecy), I should be wrong to overlook the fact that he is a man who *enjoys* theater and performs a number of other parts with great relish as well. At times he indulges in a taste for melodrama. When Peralta suggests that he take the money and run, leaving his troublesome country to fend for itself, he answers, echoing the words of Christ in an Easter pageant in which he himself played Pilate, "y si me quitara *aquello,* que sería yo, que me quedaría?" The factitious nature of the whole passage, reminiscent in tone of Wilde's *De Profundis,* is underlined by the president's shift in key. Suddenly abandoning his tragic voice rather than his country, he claps on a deerstalker and cape and announces, "Me parezco a Sherlock Holmes." At another point, meditating on his general's uniform, falsely assumed, "pensaba, burlándose de sí mismo, en el personaje de Molière que era cocinero cuando usaba gorro y cochero cuando se ponía librea."

Yet, despite his ability to laugh at himself, his self-understanding is actually rather modest. Its limits are most clearly revealed in the passage discussing his preparations for the impending operation against General Hoffman. Forced to make proclamations and admonitions as part of his counter-attack, aware that the populace hates him, he runs out of words:

Palabras, palabras, palabras. Siempre las mismas palabras. Y, sobre todo, nada de *Libertad*—con las cárceles llenas de presos políticos. Nada de *Honor Nacional* ni de *Deberes-para-con-la-Patria*—pues tales conceptos eran los que usaban siempre los militares alzados. Nada de *Misión Histórica* ni de *Cenizas de Héroes,* por la misma razón. Nada de *Independencia* que, en su caso, rimaba con *dependencia.* Nada de *Virtudes*—cuando se le sabía dueño de las mejores em-

presas del país. Nada de *Legítimos Derechos*—puesto que los ig-
noraba cuando chocaban con su personal jurisprudencia. El
vocabulario, decididamente, se le angostaba.

This dark night of the soul is brought to an end, not by a firm purpose of
amendment, but instead by the discovery of a new set of words, a new
slogan: "La Santa Cruzada de la Latinidad." Like most picaroons, the dictator has only as much self-knowledge as is expedient. He represents what
Paulson calls "a prudential awareness . . . joined to a moral obtuseness."
    His view of life is pragmatic. He greets the shot at Sarajevo with delight
since it diverts French awareness from the massacre at Nuevo Córdoba and
years later sees the armistice as a disaster because it signals the return to
free elections in his country (a contingency ingeniously avoided). Earlier,
in his chagrin over being snubbed by Parisian society, he pulls for a German
victory, bitterly regarding the Arch of Triumph, "cuya mole se le acrecía o
achicaba según quedarán satisfechos o frustrados sus anhelos derrotistas."
In *La novela picaresca y el punto de vista*, Francisco Rico argues that the picaroon sees himself as the only assurance of reality, the only standard of
value: "no hay valores sino referidos a la persona, y aún a título provisional." Given this bias, morality will always be self-serving. Once he realizes the connection between the black man who is his mother's lover and
their improved living conditions, for example, Lazarillo decides that he
likes him well enough. And once Carpentier's dictator makes the association
between General Hoffman, in revolt, and the German war effort, he is
forced to decide that "la causa walkiriosa era hoy, para él, una mala causa—
causa que 'no pagaba.' " Having abandoned his pro-French sympathies in
favor of Germany, he now turns around and drops the Germans in favor
of the French, as part of "La Santa Cruzada de la Latinidad."
    Since the picaroon is entirely self-centered, Rico insists that the first-
person narration is crucial to the elaboration of his world view: "el *yo* quien
da al mundo verdadera realidad." Carpentier chose not to use the device
of the pseudo-autobiography, instead opting for a combination of first-
person narrator, indirect free style and an anonymous, omniscient *nosotros*,
what Vargas Llosa calls in his book on *Madame Bovary* "un narrador-
personaje plural: el misterioso *nous*." Use of the first-person plural augments and offsets the president's reflections. Carpentier must have found
the exclusive use of the central character's consciousness too confining. In
the interview cited earlier, he emphasized that the Spanish picaresque was
"una novela realista que mostraba un ambiente resueltamente afincado en
lo circundante. Cuadro de costumbres, cuadro de época, visión de un
mundo en un momento determinado . . ." The mixed narration allows him
to present a broader view than that available to his president, and it also
allows him to suggest the presence of the *real* protagonist: the downtrodden
of the earth who suffer under the rule of such egocentrics. And yet, the
greater part of the novel is either presented through or colored by the

dictator's sensibility. He is as present in the work as the original picaroon in his *apologia pro vita sua.*

Finally, it is the dictator's inability to see beyond himself, to look farther than his own immediate profit, that does him in. He can deal with enemies of his own stamp, but cannot comprehend and, therefore, cannot control a disinterested opponent. His argument that history always repeats itself, only in part true as Frances Wyers Weber shows, offers him no handle for dealing with real change (not, of course, represented by the government that replaces him, but by the underground movement of the Student that overthrows him).

The motif of the "trickster-tricked" is a convention of the picaresque. Through the perspective of the dictator, Carpentier reveals corruption in society (Paris, too, emerges as fairly eager to sell out, but the force of the satire is directed at Latin America; in the interview, Carpentier pointed out that he had created "una galería de arquetipos, de personajes típicos de la historia contemporánea de América," a real rogues' gallery), but he also satirizes his central character, presenting his moral relativism, his societal consciousness and his limited cultural attainments with subtle irony. Perhaps the best example of this double perspective is the dictator's reaction when he learns of the innumerable, ingenious "con" schemes his subordinates have devised:

> Entre divertido y enojado—pero más divertido que enojado—contemplaba cada mañana, el Primer Magistrado, aquel panorama de fullerías y combinas, pensando que lo menos que podía hacer era premiar la fidelidad y el celo de los suyos con graciosa moneda de folklore. Porque él no era—ni había sido nunca—hombre de negocios pequeños.

Finally, when the country simply does not work anymore—consumed by corruption and plagued by strikes—the North Americans engineer the president's deposition.

Defeated, like Pablos, he goes off with a woman of easy virtue to seek his fortune on the other side of the Atlantic. Pablos sets sail for the New World and fares badly there. The Ex, as he now calls himself, heads off for the Old World, once his *Tierra de Promisión,* and fares badly as well. Betrayed by his associates, including his close friend Peralta, virtually disowned by his children, ignored by Parisian society, increasingly isolated, he finally abandons his pretensions. Holed up in the garret of his magnificent mansion on the Rue du Tilsitt while Ofelia dominates the lower rooms, he sees only the Mayorala Elmira and the Cholo Mendoza, reads only newspapers from *allá,* eats only American cooking; in short, he reverts to the simple life he must have known as a child. Old age has played the final joke on him. This trickster has been well and truly tricked. At the end, he has come full circle, but he has had some wonderful adventures on the way.

The Destruction of Realism in the Short Prose Fiction of João Guimarães Rosa

Allan Englekirk

To compose prose fiction is to create a world—a structure that portrays fantasy or reality by describing or interpreting an outer, physically defined setting and/or an inner, spiritually defined ambient. It is one person's world, whose parameters are determined by an artist with a given purpose, or purposes, directing the process of creation. The outsider, or reader, may accept these parameters or establish different contours or dimensions for this structure, depending upon perceptive capabilities and perspective. The end result is the evolution of a world that is many different worlds for many different readers, yet never nearly as complete or complex as life, for it is art, and art alone, that has been created.

The boundary separating the imaginary and the real in the novel and short story was generally well-delineated in the late nineteenth century. The imitation of life in art, the primary objective of the Realist, was not a revolutionary doctrine. What made Realism so unique was the spirit, the quest for "truth," which motivated the artists who chose to approach art from this perspective. Plot, characterization, language, and narrative technique in the Realist novel were all developed with the goal of objectivity as a fundamental concern. Sentimental, idealistic or fantastic distortion were generally eliminated by a writer dedicated to visualizing the exact appearance of character and ambience, for it was only through the most faithful portrayal of life that truth could be revealed. A "slice of life" was exposed to the reader, and the indiscriminate eye of a narrator attempted to present as thorough a portrait of life as had supposedly ever been depicted by art.

As the twentieth century progressed, however, the artist began to

From *South Atlantic Review* 47, no. 1 (January 1982). © 1982 by South Atlantic Modern Language Association.

question the meaning of reality, whether it was possible for art to capture it, and whether this goal should be the primary concern of the artist. The line between the fantastic and the real became imperceptible in many works of prose fiction as writers were less preoccupied with reflecting mere surface reality and more intent on creating, or suggesting, more profound or revolutionary images. Realism as it had come to be known in the pages of nineteenth-century fiction vanished into a fictional narrative in which recognizable objects, people, and situations were no longer necessary parts of the total construct. In the fictional world of many contemporary novelists or short story writers, "realism" is now a term whose nature is determined by the subjective rendition or interpretation of life emerging from the intellect of an imaginative artist.

The fictional world created by João Guimarães Rosa was quite unique to the pages of Brazilian literature. The immediate reaction to his first works of prose fiction was not unmitigated praise. *Sagarana, Corpo de Baile*, and especially *Grande Sertão:Veredas* were intricately conceived structures which stood in striking contrast to most other works of fiction in Brazilian literature. The author's perspective was quite often puzzling and unfamiliar. Even more confusing was the "quase mania do pensamento sentencioso" of various narrators or protagonists and the preference of the author for employing a plurisignificant language replete with obscure phrases and neologisms. Guimarães Rosa's fiction suffered in the eyes of many critics for failing to capture the world as it truly was but rather presenting "uma transcrição eminentemente literária da realidade"—the implication being that the author placed far too little emphasis on what was said and far too much emphasis on how it was said.

It was precisely because Guimarães Rosa's works were such an imaginative and artistic "literary transcription of reality," however, that they eventually attracted such national and international acclaim. Well before his death in 1967, the significance of Guimarães Rosa's contribution to Brazilian letters was recognized. For the German literary critic Gunter Lorenz, Guimarães Rosa was the "fundador de una nueva orientación literaria" in Brazil, thus placing him "entre los autores más importantes del siglo veinte." According to Assis Brasil, "a nova ficção brasileira" began with the narrative of this singular *mineiro* author. Luis Harss referred to Guimarães Rosa's sole novel, *Grande Sertão:Veredas*, as "una de las tres o cuatro novelas más acabadas de la literatura latinoamericana," and the Brazilian writer Augusto de Campos expressed a similar sentiment in stating "ninguém poderá construir qualquer coisa em prosa brasileira, pretendendo ignorar o *Grande Sertão:Veredas*." Guimarães Rosa's influence on Brazilian letters was considered to be so pervasive by many critics as to warrant dividing twentieth-century national prose fiction into those works published before and after the publication of his fiction.

The purpose of this paper will be to characterize the nature of realism in Guimarães Rosa's later works of prose fiction—namely in *Primeiras Es-*

tórias and *Tutaméia*. On a purely superficial level, Guimarães Rosa's first works depict worlds vaguely reminiscent of those defined by Afonso Arinos, Mário Palmério, and other writers of the regionalist tradition of Brazilian letters. A complex cultural phenomenon, regional literature in Brazil has ranged from idealized interpretations of picturesque rural scenes, to powerfully graphic visualizations of the confrontation between man and land, and Guimarães Rosa's works are an important part and product of this tradition. There is, however, in his prose literature, an apparent progression away from the mimetic reproduction of verisimilar characters and settings as the author destroys traditionally defined realism in many of his later works by transforming the nature of the fictional worlds in these narratives through his approach to characterization, plot, language, and narrative technique. In concentrating on *Primeiras Estórias* and *Tutaméia*, this paper will attempt to show how certain specific narratives of these works question the meaning of truth and reality and produce within their texts not so much an illusion, but more so the dissolution of reality—being less a presentation of the concrete and particular and more a perusal of the abstract and theoretical.

Most of the narratives of *Primeiras Estórias* and *Tutaméia* evolve fictional worlds relatively similar to those in previous volumes of prose fiction. In an interview with Gunter Lorenz, Guimarães Rosa acknowledged his profound ties to the *sertão* of Brazil and asserted that a spiritual identification with this specific area of the country was one of the most important factors determining the content, and very often the theme of his works of prose fiction. In commenting on the label given by Lorenz—"o homem do sertão"—Guimarães Rosa stated:

> Eu sou mesmo antes de tudo, este homem do sertão, e isto não é sòmente uma constatação biográfica, mas também . . . está presente como ponto de partida mais do que qualquer outra coisa . . . o pequeno mundo do sertão . . . é para mim o símbolo, diria mesmo o modelo de meu universo.

Vaqueiros, jagunços, fazendeiros, gypsies, simple country folk, beggars, prostitutes, blindmen, street urchins, crazed people, religious zealots, etc.—the full cast of regional characters evident in any of the author's previous works are still a prominent feature in the narratives of his final volumes. Typical conflicts identifiable with the regional setting, with regional literature in general, and with a vast majority of Guimarães Rosa's previous works likewise propel action: conflicts of man versus man, triggered by love, hate, greed, vanity, jealousy; conflicts of man versus self, arising from individual anxieties caused by psychological or physical factors; and conflicts of man versus nature, resulting from the oftentimes powerless position of man in confronting a potentially perilous and always unpredictable natural world. Expanding beyond the boundaries of the Brazilian *sertão*, the narratives of *Primeiras Estórias* and *Tutaméia* also reveal aspects of existence common to humanity in general—in these volumes, to a far greater extent than in his previous works. The illusion of reality presented in many of these tales transcends the immediate, being regional in detail and universal in perspective.

Not all the narratives of *Primeiras Estórias* and *Tutaméia*, however, present thoroughly recognizable or credible worlds. In certain instances, events portrayed in a narrative are verisimilar, but the author makes them seem fantasy-like in nature. A young lady in "Arroio-das-Antas" in *Tutaméia* is taken away from a depressing setting by a man on horseback. Both setting and action are plausible, but the surprise ending is definitely designed by the author to erase the line between the imaginary and the real, for the man who saves the girl is portrayed as a chivalrous knight, appearing from nowhere on a swift and large horse to gallantly claim a pure maiden and take her off to live and love happily ever after:

> E vinha de lá um cavalo grande, na ponta de uma flecha—entrante à estrada. Em galope curto, o Moço, que colheu rédea, recaracolando, desmontou-se, descobriu-se. Senhorizou-se: olhos de dar, de lado a mão feita a fazer carícia—sorria, dono. Nada; senão que a queria e amava, trespassava-se de sua vista a presença. Ela percebeu-o puramente; levantou a beleza do rosto, refloria. E disse altinho um segredo: "Sim."

With this ending, the illusion of reality is diminished by giving it an air of fantasy—a reality too perfect to be real.

In other narratives, the events themselves, rather than the manner in which they are portrayed by the author, lack verisimilitude. At times, unlikely occurrences are purely symbolic—such being the case in "A Terceira Margem do Rio" in *Primeiras Estórias*, where a man decides to spend the remainder of his life in a canoe in the middle of a river. In other instances, fantasy overpowers reality, as occurs in "Seqüencia" in *Primeiras Estórias*, where a cow with mystical powers leads an unexpecting lad a considerable distance to meet and immediately fall in love with his wife-to-be. Willi Bolle classifies "Seqüencia," "Luas de Mel," and "Substância" of *Primeiras Estórias* as "modernos contos de fadas," the first of the three labeled as such because a "magic helper"—the cow—plays an integral part in plot development and climax. Other narratives of the two volumes present a horse that drinks beer, a priest that momentarily becomes a pig, and "a very white boy," who, to the consternation of all in the story, disappears into thin air. In these tales, verisimilitude does not determine the coordinates for setting or action and, according to Paulo Rónai, "não funcionam nem as leis da casualidade nem as da lógica."

Many narratives of *Primeiras Estórias* and *Tutaméia* which could not be classified as fantasy possess protagonists who successfully construct their own imaginary worlds and live in them. Their perception of reality is quite distinct from the more "logical" or "rational" perspective of the characters who surround them and they are usually considered as laughing stock by these individuals. Jon Vincent labels the "irrational" protagonists of *Primeiras Estórias* and *Tutaméia* as liminal beings, with liminality defined as "an ontological state in which the reflective threshold being is expected to develop new perceptions of the relationships in his world." The man in "A Terceira Margem do Rio" who determines to pass his life in the middle of the river symbolizes the stance of many such liminal figures whose actions are apparently irrational and certainly not verisimilar, but whose conviction to seek a third bank to the river—to define truth and reality other than the way it is defined by most—sets them aside as heroes in the narratives in which they appear.

Three consecutive tales in *Tutaméia*—"João Porém, o Criador de Perus," "Grande Gedeão," and "Reminisção"—likewise possess such liminal characters. The importance of these tales is highlighted by the author in his setting them outside the alphabetical order according to title in which the other narratives are arranged. Appearing after "Intruge-se," the first letter of each of the three separate titles spells J.G.R.—the author's initials. Each protagonist in these narratives rejects "reality." In "Reminisção," for example, Romão, the shoemaker, falls in love with and marries a woman who is anything but attractive:

> Divulgue-se a Drá: cor de folha seca escura, estafermiça, abexigada, feia feito fritura queimada, ximbé-ximbeva; primeiro sinisga de magra, depois gorda de odre, sempre própria a figura do feio fora-da-lei. Medonha e má; não enganava pela cara.

Inexplicably, "Romão . . . gostou dela, audaz descobridor . . . pudesse achar melhor negócio. Mas ele tinha em si uma certa matemática." Despite her unattractiveness and unfaithfulness, Romão continues, seemingly blindly, to love Drá, though no one can understand why this is so until he is at the point of death. In his final hours, as Romão stares adoringly at his wife, for a fleeting moment, those people surrounding his bed see Drá as Romão has undoubtedly envisioned her from the beginning:

> Romão por derradeiro se soergueu, olhou e viu e sorriu, o sorriso mais verossímil. Os outros, otusos, imaginânimes, com olhos emprestados viam também, pedacinho de instante: o esboçoso, vislumbrança ou transparecência, o aflato! Da Drá, num estalar de claridade, nela se assumia toda a luminosidade, alva belíssima.

In almost all the stories with liminal figures, the world surrounding these figures is lifelike and verisimilar, yet the validity of truth or reality as presented in these worlds is brought into question when the author suggests the existence of other levels of reality and champions the cause of those characters able to penetrate to those levels.

With each new work of fiction, the question of illusion versus reality for Guimarães Rosa assumes increasing importance, becoming in *Grande*

Sertão:Veredas a preoccupation basic to the theme of the narrative. Riobaldo, the protagonist of this, the author's sole novel, is infinitely perplexed by the ambiguous nature of any "reality" perceived by man and constantly doubts his ability to distinguish, or the validity of his distinction, between truth and falsehood. He is concerned over the possibility of his being an unreliable narrator—a narrator whose perception of events might be overly influenced by his personal perspective and lead him to distort or interpret reality rather than re-create it as it occurred. Many of the narratives of *Primeiras Estórias* and *Tuteméia* call attention in similar fashion to the validity of "reality" as perceived by those telling the tales. "Antiperipléia," in *Tutaméia*, narrated in first person, relates the incidents surrounding the death of a blind man as told by the dead man's former guide. The narrator suggests several possible alternatives to explain the death of the blind man, defending the veracity of his story and denying any involvement in the death, but the reader realizes the dubious value of this "reality" as it is proposed by Prudencinhano, the narrator, for it seems all too possible that truth is being obscured. The narrator's eyes are no longer indiscriminate in perspective, but instead see reality from a purely subjective position. The narration ends with the mystery of the blind man's death unresolved and the reader must decide which version of the death to accept as reality, if in fact, any version is a true representation of actual events.

Formal aspects of Guimarães Rosa's later prose greatly affect the scope of vision or focus presented by the tales of these volumes—this being especially so in *Tutaméia*. Published in the journal *Pulso*, none of the forty narratives of the volume exceed three pages in length, a limitation which forced the author to severely condense exposition, virtually eliminate dialogue, and reduce character development and description of scene to a minimum while emphasizing the portrayal of action. The use of such techniques often results in an "abruptness" or "unpredictability" in certain narratives which produces a sense of incompleteness rather than synthesis. This sense of incompleteness is further induced by the tendency of the author to end many narratives without resolution of conflict. Events or actions critical to plot development are often left out, while tangential or insignificant actions are portrayed with unnecessary attention given to detail. Other techniques such as the abundant use of abstract neologisms, convoluted syntax, and a high frequency of narration or dialogue terminating in suspended points further complicate or confuse the version or vision of life emerging from these texts, with all the factors above-mentioned producing a "reality" less than coherent and intentionally partial. In characterizing the narratives of *Tutaméia*, Paulo Rónai states that plot "é mais entremisturado que contado; o autor dá a entender que conhece toda a história a fundo, mas só libera dela uma parte. Suas sentenças carregavam-se de um sentido excedente pelo que não diziam, num jogo de anacolutas, reticências, e subentendidos."

In comparing the prose of Euclides da Cunha to that of Guimarães

Rosa, Antônio Cândido notes a similar preoccupation with three basic elements—man, land, and struggle. How the authors employ these elements is completely different, however, for "a atitude euclidiana é constatar para explicar, e a de Guimarães Rosa, inventar para sugerir." Guimarães Rosa's first works might be classified as works that generally attempted to "constatar para explicar," for, basically similar to most traditional realist writers, he demonstrated a strong desire to fashion a fictional world both similar to the regional world it was modeled on, yet representative of the universe which surrounded it. The fundamental objective was one of re-creation, and the implication was that, though the exact events portrayed in the narratives might never have occurred, life, or reality, was very closely parallel to the image produced. The narratives published after *Grande Sertão:Veredas*, however, evidence a new attitude by the author toward the relationship of life and art. Though many narratives are still re-creations of verisimilar worlds, others are creations of new imaginative constructs. The author is no longer attempting to define life, or "truth," or "reality," in specific terms in these prose selections, but, rather, imply through various narrative techniques and themes that reality and truth are far too complex to be captured in other than tentative and speculative terms, and that, furthermore, in any case, the objective of literature might not be so much to—as Antônio Cândido has put it—"constatar para explicar" as "inventar para sugerir." The meaning of reality is questioned, and after Riobaldo determines how deceptive its nature truly is, Guimarães Rosa decides that his literature must seek new vistas from which to posit the complexity of this concept—searching for reality within illusion rather than trying to differentiate categorically between the two.

Eneida Maria de Souza believes that *Tutaméia* represents a "carnivalization of art"—with the author's literature no longer devoted to copying life or defining distinctions between opposites such as truth and falsehood, etc. To the contrary, in *Tutaméia*, Guimarães Rosa begins to mix opposites, and abolishes "distinctions between the sacred and the profane, the sublime and the insignificant"—producing a confused illusion of "reality" which is quite removed from the objective portrayal of life rendered by a traditional realist. In evolving such compact fictional worlds as those contained in *Primeiras Estórias* and *Tutaméia* and intentionally weaving partial and incomplete narratives that either have no end or admit gaps in the depiction of character and event, the author leaves to the reader the task of completing these images and creating his or her own vision of reality.

It must be reaffirmed, in conclusion, that the tendency remains strong throughout the literary production of Guimarães Rosa to evolve narratives that are intended to mirror life. In total, the author's literature spins a vast tapestry whose intricate patterns reflect a panoramic vision of existence on both particular and universal levels, repeatedly entering the realm of the metaphysical. Placed in opposition, or, perhaps better, complementing these narratives, is a set of tales whose texts do not produce a statement of "what reality is," but rather induce speculation on the question of "what is reality?" The prose fiction of Guimarães Rosa leaves its readers in the middle of a "whirlwind"—with God and the devil, or illusion and reality figuratively spinning in confusion to the point of being indistinguishable one from the other.

Anguish of the Ordinary

George Levine

By coincidence, I was in the midst of rereading *Madame Bovary* when I was given Juan Carlos Onetti's *A Brief Life*. Strikingly, the two novels began blurring into each other as I alternated between them: the century and the continent that separate them do not disguise their cousinship. Not that there is—or that it is necessary to imply—direct literary influence, but both novels occupy space in the Western tradition of literary realism that thickens with the paradoxes inevitably created by the attempt to speak truth about reality.

The discipline to which Flaubert subjected himself is closely analogous to the disciplines of Onetti's narrator. Flaubert's personal salvation seemed to depend on the most precise and particular notation of objects. Such notation was meant to purge both the hateful bourgeois reality it described and the catastrophic, romantic dreams of Emma Bovary. Ironically, however, the very intensity of Flaubert's notation begins to invest objects with significances that remove them from the ordinary world in which he desperately labors to place them. Object becomes symbol and resonates with new possibilities of feeling. The hiss of Emma's corset string or the beaded sweat on her bare shoulders is more passionately evocative than any of Emma's fantasies; we are in danger of substituting one dream for another. Flaubert imagined that his dream was better than Emma's, since it confronted what he imagined to be the worst and took shape in words so precise that they seemed to master the hideousness that always threatened to destroy him.

Juan María Brausen, Onetti's narrator, lives in a world of objects so intensely and profusely perceived that there is barely space for him. Unlike Emma Bovary, but like Flaubert, he begins disenchanted. The romantic

From *Review* no. 16 (Winter 1975). © 1975 by the Center for Inter-American Relations, Inc.

dream is reduced in him to the merest possibility that through the objects themselves it might be possible to enter a world and a self alternative to the hideous and repetitive bourgeois reality. But since the rules of Onetti's novel turn out to be pretty much the same as the rules within which Brausen's imagination must work (to reject the rules is to reject what Flaubert knew a century before), the alternative threatens to be pretty much the same as the original.

Onetti, that is, includes both Flaubert's subject *and* his attempted solution within his novel. If there be any solution to the ordinariness, the inevitable decay, the hard trivia and terrible sense of loss that make up the realist's "ordinary life," it seems to lie not in Flaubert's kind of imagination of objects, but in the imagination of that kind of imagination. We are threatened with a kind of infinite regress into an unattainable clarity of reality, as fiction becomes more and more self-conscious about its fictionality. Like Flaubert, we must see that the romantic and religious literature shaping Emma's consciousness is inadequate. Like Brausen, we must see that the kind of assertion of the ordinary towards which Flaubert moved is inadequate since it contains within itself a dream of control that contradicts its own impulses. Like Onetti, we must come to terms with the double inadequacy and perhaps return the hard way to a dream of freedom earned through that double recognition.

All of this is exquisitely tortured. So, too, *A Brief Life* is a book astonishingly rich in the anguish of the ordinary and in Chinese boxes of illusion. It contains almost three novels-worth of elaborations of these paradoxes—narratives that move in and out of each other, every one thick with particularities of life and decay. It is at once an exhaustingly intellectual novel, full of speculations about language and illusion and dreams of freedom, and an old-fashioned, heartbreakingly realistic rendering of loss and pain and isolation. It is both a naturalistic novel dwelling remorselessly on a slow descent into total loss and failure—like Emma's story, or Nana's—and a Beckett-like record of nothing happening. Part of the illusion is that we are made to feel that something is happening, but it is always and only Brausen's mind struggling to enact itself in action or in words.

Brausen is a neuraesthenic ventriloquist. We meet him first as he counterpoints two not-quite present realities as though they were present. Through the wall of his apartment he hears sounds from next door, where a woman has just moved in. But they become more than sounds: "I imagined her mouth moving in front of the refrigerator's cold vapor and vegetable odors as she faced the curtain of brown slats that hung rigidly between the afternoon sun and the bedroom, obscuring the disorder of recently arrived furniture." That imagined reality somehow participates in Brausen's hope "for a vague miracle that would bring springtime to me." But the girl next door is a "chippy," and the "vegetable odors"—the imagined decay—are juxtaposed against Brausen's imagination of his wife, who will soon be coming back from breast surgery: "A scar can be imagined as an irregular cut made on a rubber cup with thick walls, containing a motionless substance, pinkish, with bubbles on the surface, and that may give the impression of being liquid if we make the lamp that illuminates it sway back and forth."

The Brausen situated between these two women—Gertrudis, the wife whose breast amputation is a physical analogue to the death of their relationship that had preceded it, and La Queca, the chippy, whose chubby sexuality is a pathetic business substitute for the loves she will never have—begins inventing other worlds where "spring" may be possible. Indeed, the novel will end twice—just as Carnival ends—for at least two of Brausen's later incarnations, in an incipient spring with the masquerades over and the Brausen surrogates freed into the inevitable temporal failures, into "a final disenchantment without complexity."

But that disenchantment is only possible through the complexities of invented alternatives. To avoid the implications of the loss of his wife and of his job, he tries to write a screenplay that will bring him the success he has always missed. And he invents Díaz Grey of Santa María, who quickly becomes one of the novel's narrators; shortly after, as the two narratives proceed, Brausen turns himself into La Queca's "man," Arce, separates from his wife, and pretends to open his own office, rented to him by a man named Onetti, amiable and indifferent, at whose back he stares while he imagines Díaz's story.

Thus, in the life of the novel, and in the life of the mind, Brausen, a displacement of Onetti, is displaced continuously, though erratically. Díaz Grey's story begins clearly enough as Brausen's strenuous and conscious effort to invent it. He longs to achieve "the long initial sentence that would return me to life again." But Díaz Grey takes on his own life and possesses much of the narrative, except that his narrative falls into traps such that it must frequently be cancelled or altered. Brausen *can* alter the narrative, which comes to us with a kind of naturalistic fidelity that makes the manipulations shocking; Onetti cannot quite alter Brausen's narrative.

But the novel as a whole becomes a quest for a fiction that will, eventually, cancel itself out, will move outside the whoredom, the vegetable decay, the cancerous corruption, the personality defined by inadequate memories and impossible hopes. To be sure, the quest is doomed, and all the desperate turnings of the novel reflect something like Flaubert's romantic despair at the limitations of the quotidian. At one point, Brausen tells his wife that the problem is people's belief that "they're condemned to a single life until death. And they are only condemned to a soul, a manner of being."

Indeed, the ultimate coherence of the book depends upon this final limitation, Brausen's condemnation to a soul. (He, surely, is not condemned to a single life.) Although they are invented to overcome the deadly repetitiveness of domesticity, the narratives echo each other in ways that imply inescapable, psychological repetition. Like Díaz Grey, Brausen is attracted to a woman, Elena Sala, who is addicted to morphine and to a handsome young Englishman—in both of which addictions she is supported by her husband Lagos. Elena seems an alternative to Brausen's Gertrudis. Lagos seems another, more heroic version of Brausen's friend Stein—himself married to an ex-whore—who manages to be sentimental, successful, duplicitous and endearing. Arce, Brausen's surrogate with La Queca, moves into an alien world totally opposed to the middle-class world of Brausen next door. He treats La Queca as a pimp would, and settles easily into a brutal control, apparently waiting for the opportunity to kill a violent young friend, Ernesto, who had once beaten him. As Brausen himself, Brausen fails in his relationship with Gertrudis's sister, as he had failed with Gertrudis.

All the stories are of relationships thwarted, achievements forestalled, moments repeated. At one point, Brausen wonders at Díaz Grey's "growing tendency to wallow over and over again in the same event, at the need—which was affecting me—to suppress words and situations, to attain a single moment to express it all." Elena Sala is cast out of the story, returns, is killed, returns again. Neither Díaz Grey nor Brausen can control her. Arce plans to shoot La Queca. Ernesto does it. Brausen is resolved to suppress Díaz Grey, but he leads Ernesto to the real city he had imagined as Díaz Grey's home, and Díaz Grey returns. As Brausen attempts to protect Ernesto (hence to become master of the alien), so Lagos and Díaz Grey attempt to protect the Englishman who (not Díaz Grey) kills Elena. Both attempts fail.

Nothing can succeed, nothing but the extraordinarily imagined moments on the way to failure. In all of his incarnations, Brausen's "manner of being" persists. Nothing happens but what must. Brausen, Díaz Grey, Arce are all Flaubertian realists who somehow know that the objects participating in delay and occasioning failures are the only way out. The intractable reality that Flaubert imposed on his Emma is not merely, as Brausen knows, intractably out there.

The realist's "object," the artist's "word," the real world's "self" are all closely related. Lagos, like Brausen, looks for the saving sentence: "the spontaneous surrender to a moment we have always longed for. When we repeat the same sentence, and this sentence doesn't lose its novelty and serves to explain everything." The novel seeks the sentence, the word, that will pare away all conventions buffering us from the "object," from the experience, that protect us by ideas about past and future from ourselves. To transform himself into Arce, Brausen works through objects. "And I'm going to fondle them with such an intensity of love that one by one they won't be able to resist me." And we realize that from the first page, this is what Brausen and Onetti have been doing. The alien objects—dead leaves, hexagonal machine nuts—have been fondled, loved, penetrated, and through them the self is born. The realist ideal of recording commonly available reality becomes the means of transcendence into a new self.

In one of the most remarkable and beautiful passages in the novel, we are given a "part of the history of Díaz Grey [that] was never written." At a crucial point in an interview with a bishop, Brausen gives himself the option of imagining the bishop's talk as "amiable buffoonery" or, for Elena and Díaz Grey, "truth and revelation." The story branches off, depending for its movement on how a carving of a pensive angel behind the bishop is perceived. The angel seems to smile as the bishop forces Díaz Grey (and Brausen? and Onetti?) to see that "only God is eternal." A commonplace, to be sure, but crucial in the light of the book's effort to forestall time. "And," says the bishop, "the debased conscience that permits [us] to accept the capricious, dismembered, and complacent sensation that [we] call the past, that permits [us] to cast off lines of hope, and to correct mistakes that [we] call time and the future, is only, even admitting it, a personal consciousness." To this consciousness, eternity is not available. But, says our curiously existential and not altogether trustworthy bishop (the angel has winked), "I will kiss the feet of him who may comprehend that eternity is now, that he himself is the only end, that he must accept and strive to be himself, simply that, without need of reasons, at all times and against all opposition, living in abject poverty through passion, forsaking memory and imagination." The chapter ends with the only moment in which Díaz Grey and Elena are allowed compassion for each other. She "lay softly on the bed: nothing more than a precarious symbol of the world, of her relation with the world, unimprovable because of the circumstances, indispensable for the charitable act." But none of this was "written."

The terrible contradictions are all in this scene. Onetti had to write it and have Brausen tell us that it was not written. Elena, the imagined woman, is in her reality an alien object whose separation is a condition of the rare charity. Forsaking memory and imagination, the object is time-bound, alien, a condition of selfhood and eternity.

A Brief Life is, at last, an overwhelming and very beautiful book. It is not easy about that "eternity" of the bishop, but it knows how to love objects, how to feel loss and pain, how to confront the damaging limitations of mere personality. It is a drama of the creation of the unattainable sentence that Flaubert began writing a century before, that Faulkner (one of Onetti's favorites) could never quite finish. The disgust with the real which Flaubert had to overcome in order to exorcise his romantic self is transformed into a passionate acceptance of the ordinary and of the impossibility of writing it. The real, more intensely present, is perhaps less real than Flaubert dreamed he knew. The book's epigraph is from Walt Whitman, the American visionary realist, and it invokes "something escaped from the anchorage and driving free."

María Luisa Bombal's Poetic Novels of Female Estrangement

Phyllis Rodríguez-Peralta

Many women writers in Latin American literature have presented a feminine world overtly concerned with emotional responses which often carefully cover underlying repressive forces. In these works, man generates the impulses and reactions in the spatial corridors structured around him, whether or not his own space is focused at the center or at a distance. Baroque profusion enabled Sor Juana Inés de la Cruz to conceal her total personality. But Gertrudis Gómez de Avellaneda in the nineteenth century was openly dependent upon passionate relationships, and the twentieth century poetesses Mistral, Agustini, Storni, and Ibarbourou, although completely different in their responses, react to personal factors invariably designated as feminine concerns. (And only Juana de Ibarbourou clearly rejoices in her femininity.) In the line of developing female consciousness, the novels of María Luisa Bombal present the psyche of a young woman in the 1930s curiously poised between the attributes of the conventional, traditional woman of her era and the dissatisfactions of the contemporary woman. The structure and technique of these novels also position them in the antechambers of the New Narrative in Latin America.

Bombal's first novel, *La última niebla* (1935), flows from the personality of a nameless woman protagonist whose perception of reality comes from the dreaming states of her mind. Amado Alonso writes in his Prologue: "Todo lo que pasa en esta novela pasa dentro de la cabeza y el corazón de una mujer que sueña y ensueña." This woman is married to a man whose love belongs to his first wife, his beloved bride who died three months after their marriage. The protagonist, therefore, is an outsider, even an intruder in a second marriage. Without tenderness or understanding, she

From *Revista de Estudios Hispánicos* 14, no. 1 (January 1980). © 1980 by the University of Alabama Press.

sinks into great weariness until she is stirred by the blaze of emotion she witnesses between Reina, her husband's sister-in-law, and a lover. Hugging this borrowed warmth, she creates her own world: in the mist it is she who is found by a lover, and with him she experiences one night of rapture which enables her to dream and to imagine throughout the days and years that pass. She grows older, but it does not matter, for she can endure a long life of tedium cushioned by the memory of one beautiful adventure. She guards her precious hours alone so that she can dream and converse with her lover. Days of expectation drift by when she knows that he will come for her. And once, out of the fog that envelops the land, his carriage appears and he waves gravely to her before he is swallowed up in the mist. In time, when she and her husband resume their conjugal life, she begins to forget her lover's features, nor can she remember his voice, and this doubt of his existence brings the heaviness of mourning.

A telegram, with the news that Reina is dying after a suicide attempt, jolts her into actuality. They must go to the city. And there in the mist she sets out to find the house of her memory. But it has all been imagined. It is Reina who has experienced everything: love, emotion, abandonment. She takes a step toward throwing herself in front of a car, but her husband pushes her back. "Lo sigo para llevar a cabo una infinidad de pequeños menesteres, lo sigo para vivir correctamente, para morir correctamente, algún día. Alrededor nuestro, la niebla presta a las cosas un carácter de inmovilidad definitiva."

The unfulfilled and unfulfilling woman whose personality exists at the center of this novel can be reached only by surrender to the art forms chosen by the author. Thus, in her own way, Bombal has anticipated contemporary Latin American writers who consider narrative form as a creative entity in their work. Total subjectivity is achieved in *La última niebla*. A sense of a stream-of-consciousness comes about through the structural flow of the novel as a whole rather than in its stylistic segments (such as interior monologues which attempt to approximate the mind's switch from one thought to another). The spatial movement within the novel is consistently forward with only the barest indication of the passage of time. Hence without explanation, an immediate shift occurs from the emptiness of the wedding night to the protagonist's contemplation of a girl lying in her coffin, her face devoid of feeling. Silence, a great silence of years, of centuries, rises in that room given over to death, and, in panic, the protagonist rushes out into the mist which envelops her with a greater silence. She cannot even hear the leaves she is crushing in her flight because they are humid and decomposing. Losing a sense of reality, she feels that the mist is attacking her, and she cries out: "¡Yo existo, yo existo . . . y soy bella y feliz! Sí ¡Felíz! La felicidad no es más que tener un cuerpo joven y esbelto y ágil." The entire frenetic scene becomes a metaphor of the impression created by the young girl's dead body, indicative in itself of her own insensible marriage.

To accompany this structural flow, Bombal adds the stylistic technique of inserting external details which subsequently will be taken into the protagonist's mind and converted to emotions. Inadvertently seeing Reina's hair tangled in her lover's vest, she thinks of her own hair now kept within the rigid confines of a braid in imitation of the first wife. Later, before her mirror, she remembers when her hair was loose and flowing, then that it is losing its luster, then, with anguish, that there will be no one to appreciate her own beauty. More complex is a later scene where the original detail is prolonged into a series of poetic images. In their bedroom, lulled by the sound of rain, her husband offers her a cooling drink. The bedroom becomes submerged in the lilac twilight, and the mirrors, shining like compressed waters, make her think of the trickling of clear pools. She imagines dusty highways, cities chastised by the implacable sun, and then the rain falls again. A feeling of well-being comes over her. She seems to feel the water slipping sweetly over her feverish temples and over her breast replete with sobs.

In reverse procedure, while sitting in front of the fire and searching for her lover's eyes, she tries consciously to evoke his image by removing the ashes of her memory so that a spark can leap up. Suddenly a great wind comes which blows down three oaks. The wind, the trees, and the mother-in-law crossing herself in fear are all real, but it is this great wind which returns her lover to her.

M. Ian Adams deals with Bombal's use of poetic imagery in expressing alienation, particularly imagery associated with the mist which shrouds both countryside and city scenes and fragments reality in the mind of the protagonist. As her withdrawal deepens, so does the mist, which prevents direct vision and induces an isolation within herself. It filters into the house, into her room, through her hair, effacing everything. (Only the face of Reina, beloved, adored, remains intact.) Erasing the corners and muting the sounds, the fog seems to choke her. But safe with her lover, the mist beats its wings in vain against the windowpanes and cannot infuse a single atom of death into their room. (Here the mist does not necessarily symbolize physical death, but the death of feeling, which is akin to death.) In the end, everything disappears in the mist—her lover's house, her love, and her adventure, to be taken up by the final imagery of "definitive immobility."

Although the personality of the woman protagonist is psychologically convincing, Bombal avoids the probing analysis of a psychological novel and remains constant in her presentation of the woman through impressionistic techniques. Living within herself, she reflects her sensual perception of subtle fragrances and sifted sounds. Her death wish is projected through autumnal imagery: she feels nostalgia for abandoned parks and wants the autumn leaves left on the grass until the humidity turns them into silence. To parallel her own joylessness, there are no natural rhythms of nature, no joyful awakenings of a blossoming springtime. Unable to escape the monotony and boredom of her life, she escapes into her mind. A constant fatigue accompanies her in this flight, which at times also acts as her defense against an unwelcome reality. A sweet sadness brings a tired smile to her lips as she drifts in a dreamlike state, interspersed with an occasional resolve to dedicate herself to daily household tasks in order to bring peace of mind. The dirty, sad light of dawn filters into her room to interrupt the reality of her dreaming. As her depression increases, there is a peculiar loss of identity together with a loss of will, and she seems faceless as well as nameless. Her self-perception is indistinct, like the mist.

In *La amortajada* (1938) the death wish of the first novel has been accomplished. Encircled by silence, Ana María lies in death. But she sees and she feels, and an immense happiness invades her being because those who surround her can admire her beauty, pale and smooth-skinned again, without a sign of care or worry. As each mourner approaches to gaze on her for the last time, the dead woman's thoughts flow through those portions of her life which each has shared.

The first to come is Ricardo, the love of her early youth. His presence annuls the long years and takes her back to their childhood. Even as a child, she had felt the force of his attraction, and later, with overwhelming emotion, she had given herself to him. His desertion and her pregnancy and miscarriage had been bewildering. Her father comes to her gently, her father who used to ask if she remembered her mother. She knows he will suffer alone, barring any entrance to his grief. She notices her sister praying next to her, and she talks to her, mentally, of their differing concepts of God. Her sons look upon her quickly, those sons who did not want to recognize her right to remain young and yet were secretly pleased when friends praised their youthful mother. The cry of grief from her daughter surprises her, her daughter so proud of her twenty years, who smiled indulgently when her mother showed photographs to prove that she, also, had been charming and attractive at twenty.

Fernando's visit disconcerts her with memories of their self-destructive relationship. Confidant of her marital misery, she looked to him to deny her complaints of her husband's neglect; but envy and egotism always sealed his lips. She hated the desire that shone in his eyes, and yet that daily, unswerving homage flattered her. Indifferent to his feelings, she was sometimes rude and belittling, but "Oh, Fernando, para sentirme vivir, necesité desde entonces a mi lado ese constante sufrimiento tuyo."

At last the principal figure in her life arrives: Antonio, her husband, adored, hated, unreachable. Her thoughts return to their early married life, to his ardor and her lack of response, her desire to return to her father's house, his delay in coming for her, and his courteous indifference from then on. Even the birth of their first son did not bring back his love. She remembers her schemes to re-interest him, her reliance on her legitimate position, her ire at his infidelities. Irritation and rancor permeated her suffering, which over the years turned into a sustaining hatred. She contemplates his bowed head. She is amazed that he is crying, and from her vantage point of death, she knows that now he will always feel a strange sensation of loneliness which will never allow him to enjoy anything completely. Her hatred evaporates. How can she hate a being destined for sadness and old age?

In neither loving nor hating him, she feels that the last knot of her life structure has been undone. Putting her cheek against the hollow shoulder of death, she floats out beyond herself. A current—someone, something—pushes her through tropical vegetation, under pale foliage, into the watery pulp of nature. She returns. They are putting her in her coffin, and they carry her through the house, down the steps, out through the forest and the swamp. It is infinitely sweet to be transported, with her hands folded on her breast, like something fragile and very beloved. They reach the cemetery and enter the chapel. Father Carlos's thoughts accompany the final blessing. And then begins her descent, slowly, slowly, avoiding strange beings, colliding with human skeletons whose knees are pulled up as though again in the womb of their mothers. She reaches the bed of an ancient sea and reposes there among the millenary snails. From her body she feels an infinity of roots sinking and spreading in the earth like a powerful cobweb through which the constant palpitation of the universe ascends to her: "Había sufrido la muerte de los vivos. Ahora anhelaba la inmersión total, la segunda muerte: la muerte de los muertos."

Creativity of concept in *La amortajada* is matched by creativity of technique. While the residue from surrealist currents remains, the structure and style flow toward the techniques of the contemporary novel. With complete mastery, Bombal has blended the supernatural with reality. In commenting on the novel, Jorge Luis Borges says that he had advised Bombal of the impossibility of writing such a work, among other reasons because the magical zone would invalidate the psychological, and vice versa. Yet when she presented him with the manuscript, he saw that the dilemma and the risks that he had predicted had been overcome to the extent that the reader was not even aware of their existence.

Although the dead woman's memories and thoughts remain at the center of the work, Bombal moves toward an interchange of narrative perspectives. This is particularly true in the segment between Ana María and Fernando. Each speaks mentally to the other, using "tú" directly, but without attempting to cross the barrier of death that separates them. Thus the reader enters the thoughts of each one concerning the other. At the same time within this segment sections appear in the third person which fluctuate between the dreaming state of Ana María and a traditional exterior narration:

> ¡Este hombre! ¡Por qué aún amortajada le impone su amor!
> Es raro que un amor humille, no consiga sino humillar.
> El amor de Fernando la humilló siempre. La hacía sentirse más

pobre. No era la enfermedad que le manchaba la piel y le agriaba
el carácter . . .
Lo despreciaba porque no era feliz, porque no tenía suerte.

In contrast, the segments with Ricardo and with her husband have
only the perspective of her thoughts and her comments, a stylistic approach
which underlines their failure of communication in life. The segment with
her father is presented in the third person, while the closer relationship
with her sister is evident by her soft mental conversation framed in "tú."
When the casket is placed before Father Carlos, the narration comes from
his memories of her, conveying the impression that her consciousness has
left her body momentarily in order to exist within those memories.

Throughout the novel there is the constant marking of "I remember,"
or "She remembers," or directly to the person, "Do you remember?" An
added dimension enters these memories when Ana María incorporates
conversations once spoken to her by others. She does not always move in
chronological order in her reminiscences. Thus when her husband appears
in the long segment belonging to him, the reader has already met him
through the mental conversations of Ana María and Fernando and the
confidences which she has shared with the latter.

A "leitmotiv," "El día quema horas, minutos, segundos," indicates
the passage of time (and is associated with the candles flickering around
her as she lies in state). The passing hours are also shown by the slow
disintegration of her body, which she herself notes. The consciousness
beyond death which floats through the novel is centralized in the psyche
of one woman; nevertheless, the evocation of this essence can be called a
prelude to the collective consciousness present in Juan Rulfo's *Pedro Páramo*
(1955).

Imagery formed from nature is part of the poetic texture of both Bombal's novels, even though the focus and the emphasis differ between *La
última niebla* and *La amortajada*. The symbolic quality of the fog, together
with other attributes of nature, is clearly evident in the first novel. At times
in this novel creatures may relate symbolically to the woman (the hunter's
trophy of the wild pigeon, still warm and bleeding, which Reina's lover
tosses in her lap, takes the place of the woman victim). Or with symbolist-
surrealist technique, a nature object can be carried from one scene to another
(an unfeeling tree which the woman embraces in a gesture of longing
appears later as her support which she is leaning against, weakly, when
her imagined lover comes for her out of the mist). In *La última niebla*, Bombal
often uses aspects of nature to accompany the mood she is projecting: a
dismal rain dripping through the broken tiles of the old country house
greets the bride on her sad wedding night, while on other occasions light
rain brings consolation. Bombal's sensitivity enables her to escape an obvious use of nature in the sense of the romantics, although a rare brush
stroke in this novel comes perilously close to romantic stylization. The

sensual richness of nature is an integral part of *La amortajada*, always present in the thoughts and memories of the dead woman, as well as in the perceptions and sensations she continues to possess. But the relationship between nature and the woman is lyric more than symbolic. And in the end, she merges into nature to become part of the oneness of the universe.

Poetic similes and metaphors, characteristic of Bombal's style, enhance the lyric quality of both novels. She speaks of a silence so absolute that it creates a desire "de removerlo como a un agua demasiado espesa" (*La amortajada*). In this same novel Ana María's hands, crossed over her breast and clasping a crucifix, have acquired "la delicadeza frívola de dos palomas sosegadas." In *La última niebla* the rain withdraws slowly, "como una bandada de pájaros húmedos." The woman protagonist in this novel must move about as the only way to impose a certain rhythm on her dreams, widening them, making them describe a perfect curve. "Cuando estoy quieta, todos ellos se quiebran las alas sin poderlas abrir."

As part of the poetic process in her novels, Bombal conveys an exquisite sensation of motion. This is always presented through the perception and sensitivity of the central character. For the nameless woman in *La última niebla*, the sound of barking constantly approaches and withdraws. A nocturne, scattering the grains of its notes, doubles and multiplies in the air. She listens. The frogs stop their song. Then, in the distance, from the heart of the night, she hears his steps. They press down the moss, they stir the dry leaves, they advance to the gate. And then there is silence. The keenest sensation of motion (paralleling the stillness of death) is achieved in *La amortajada* as Ana María is taken from her home to the cemetery. Lying in her casket, the dead woman sees the ceiling above her swinging back and forth as they turn through the rooms, the halls, the front door. She feels the narrowness of the vestibule, the jolting of the steps, the sway of her coffin on its journey. From this perspective, she sees the undulating reflections of the tall trees, she hears the wind lifting the dry leaves that strike the casket, and as they pass into the forest, she breathes the acrid perfume of plants that envelops her with another shroud.

The relationship of the real and the unreal in these novels has a peculiar opposition. In one, there is the unreality of a dead woman projecting the reality of remembered actions. In the other, the unreality of fantasized actions functions against reality. But the narrative world of both novels emanates from the mind of the respective protagonist. Therefore, beneath the poetic texture and the imaginative techniques lies the personality of a woman whose character reflects both personal and contemporary social factors.

The narcissism of the two women protagonists is their most salient characteristic. Neither ever loses sight of the fundamental importance of her physical beauty. Almost the first thought that Ana María expresses in death is to rejoice that her dark hair looks lovely as it cascades around her in her coffin. The nameless woman of the first novel constantly thinks with horror of losing her beauty in old age and of having to hide a body that will no longer deserve love and desire. Concerned only with herself, each woman relates exclusively to her own personal world, and the dreamlike flow of the narration makes it possible for each to become surfeited with herself without exterior considerations. The self-insight that each possesses is pitifully limited, particularly in the case of the unnamed woman. Wrapped up in herself, it is equally impossible for the latter to achieve any insight into the indistinct beings who surround her. In the second novel, and from the perspective of death, Ana María gains some knowledge of qualities in other persons which she had not perceived during her contacts with them in life. However, both women remain singularly superficial in their self-knowledge and in their dealings with others.

Ana María has many more facets to her nature than the dreaming protagonist of *La última niebla*. Nevertheless, both live in spiritual and mental estrangement, particularly from their husbands, and they suffer from loneliness and rejection. This isolation seems symptomatic of the area often reserved for women, even if their own inertia, lack of perception, and inability to communicate have helped to build the barriers that hedge them in. They use feminine defenses, both weak and strong, against this crippling aloneness. The first woman, increasingly neurotic and exhausted, occasionally goads herself from her dreaming retreat into spurts of domestic activity. Ana María also busies herself with daily household tasks, and she learns to take refuge in her family and to combat her anguish by surrounding herself with her children. Her concern for feminine details of domesticity is never far from the surface: even while the pallbearers are carrying her through the house to her tomb, she is upset because they have put her blue rug in the hall, where it will soon fade.

The character of Ana María is more fully developed than that of the nameless woman, partially because she touches many more lives and partially because the shift of perspectives in the second novel allows the reader to view her occasionally through the eyes of others. Like the first woman, Ana María often feels fatigued; she finds it difficult to comb her hair, to take responsibilities, to smile; she cries frequently. But in an atmosphere of indifference, she adapts her own vehement love to what she considers to be the mediocre and limited love of others. She learns to restrain herself from throwing her arms around her husband or her children, feigning frivolity in order not to frighten away the little love coming toward her. Ana María also incorporates vengeful streaks into her character, particularly in her dominant role with the ever-attentive Fernando which she flaunts in front of a husband who merely tolerates her. Her ideas of revenge enable her to conjure up great plans which almost always end in petty acts.

Bombal's novels deal openly with a woman's sensuality and sexuality. In *La última niebla* the protagonist's repressed desires produce various sexually oriented scenes. Fleeing from the passion that she senses swirling around Reina and her lover, she runs from the house into a mist pierced with sun rays. Throwing herself against the insensitive bark of a tree, she feels a strange lassitude, and in the floating sunlight she removes her clothes and sinks into a pond. She had never dared look at herself like this: the waters lengthen her body into unreal proportions, the currents caress her, and her breasts, small and round, seem diminutive corollas suspended over the water. The vivid sexual scene with her lover is presented from the viewpoint of a woman, heightened because it takes place with an imagined lover and therefore is comprised entirely of a woman's longings. With abandon she rejoices in his adoration of her physical beauty, and with all her senses she follows him into complete fulfillment. The sexual scenes in *La amortajada* are revealing of a woman's initial psychological problems with sex. In spite of Ricardo's great attraction, Ana María knows that he found her to be cold since she was unable to share his ecstasy and desired only his kisses. With her husband she tries to remain passive in order to discourage his constant desire, and she describes her unwilling pleasure as a union in the same shame. It is significant to note that the *detailed* sexual scenes, appearing only once in each novel, occur between an imagined lover in the first novel, and the husband in the second. The identities of the men, plus the poetic texture of the descriptions, keep the scenes from straying very far beyond the confines of contemporary convention in the 1930s. Other details, such as Ana María's reactions, also reflect the mores of that era.

A strong maternal instinct does not appear as a corollary to the sexuality of the two women. The childless protagonist of *La última niebla* never includes any aspect of motherhood in her dream fulfillments. Ana María, the mother of three grown children who seem distant and uninvolved, does not direct any memories to the days when they were babies and she their nurturing force. Even though she remembers happy family scenes as she is being carried from her home for the last time—and although the reader knows that Fred is her favorite—the relationship between parent and children is not structured as part of the center space. On the other hand, Ana María does turn her thoughts to her first pregnancy, which ended in miscarriage. These memories flow from the impressions of a pregnant woman, in combination with conventional descriptions of whims and cravings. Although she reflects on being "confinada en mi mundo físico," the memories encompass a sense of wonder, and they are free of complaints.

In Bombal's novels, where the woman exists at the center, the male characters are projected through a female consciousness. From this perspective, all men are seen as incomplete figures, distant and unreachable. In the opening scenes of *La última niebla*, the husband, momentarily focused from a short distance, is aggressively sarcastic and totally unfeeling toward his wife, with wounding words that seem designed to cover a suppressed rage. Never again is he focused in close proximity, and from a distance he lives withdrawn and disinterested, existing in a world incomprehensible to her. Even when they resume their physical relations after several years, he remains an estranged, indistinct figure. Her lover is totally nebulous. In their wordless love scene he is the dominant one, but the circumstances and the surroundings hazily waver and float around them. Years later, when her retreat from reality has deepened, he comes again, and the dream-like quality attached to him is much more evident. She sees his carriage appearing out of the mist; the horses do not make the slightest sound as they pass over the dead leaves, and when they lower their heads to drink, they do not open a single circle in the polished surface of the water. In anguish she tries to call his name—unknown—but there is no answer. Focusing both the husband and the lover from a perspective of great distance not only keeps them distant from the reader but illustrates the distance between the male characters and the protagonist. Incapable of going beyond herself, her lack of comprehension makes both men seem like hollow shells to the reader, as indeed they are to her.

The men in *La amortajada* are varied in their relationships to Ana María, including sons, father, admirer (all marginal figures); but the lover and the husband retain most of the attributes of their counterparts in the first novel. Ricardo's actions remain an enigma to Ana María. With veiled contempt, her husband treats her like a foolish creature who bores him. Their failure of communication was solidified early in their marriage when Antonio, still ardently enamored, was unable to understand her nostalgic desire to return to her father's house, and she, without space to become accustomed to the city and time to mature, was incapable of expressing her feelings. A stunted marriage of alienation and mutual discontent resulted.

While it is evident that neither woman establishes mature bonds with men, it is equally clear that their goals and aspirations revolve entirely around their relationships with the principal men in their lives. The first woman dreams of being given over completely to the will of a man who adores her. Ana María believed that she had this relationship with her youthful lover, and belatedly she seeks the same thing with her husband. With the perception that death has added, she ponders: "¿Por qué, por qué la naturaleza de la mujer ha de ser tal que tenga que ser siempre un hombre el eje de su vida? Los hombres, ellos, logran poner su pasión en otras cosas. Pero el destino de las mujeres es remover una pena de amor en una casa ordenada, ante una tapicería inconclusa."

The nameless woman who spins out the workings of her mind, or the dead woman who spins out her memories, came into view just before the New Narrative in Latin America, which dates from the Second World War. The "boom" writers are men. In general, their concept of woman varies from earth-mother, to goddess, to sex-object, to willing dispenser of comfort and well-being, to destroyer-force; but regardless of her functions, she remains outside their principal concerns. In Bombal's novels, the woman's concept of herself embodies some but not all the roles assigned to her by these writers. She is not earth-mother, procreator, goddess, or destroyer. On the other hand, she is dependent, subservient, passive, and yielding.

She obeys docilely, yet without any apparent wish to please or to serve. Certainly she does not conceive of herself as bringing comfort and healing, nor is she the "heart of the home" in either a maternal or a religious sense. Her dreams of fulfillment concern only her own gratification which comes from adoration by the male.

The imagery applied to males in the New Narrative is associated with hard, stony earth, cutting implements, cruel, shining knives. This is contrasted in Bombal's novels with the softer imagery of mist, light rain, wind— subtle images that float or drift, that are formless, shapeless, insubstantial, like water that molds itself to the vessel that holds it. The tenuous fiber of these novels reflects inner needs and unconsciously reveals the tensions of transitional currents.

In both technique and in content, Bombal has reached the crossroads of the old and the new. The woman in her novels is caught in the confusion of her roles. She reflects present-day themes of futility and alienation and she appears as a marginal figure, an outcast like the contemporary authors' version of her. She is, therefore, far from the stereotyped woman of Latin American literature before this era, and she does not reflect the traditional Hispanic concepts of femininity. At the same time she herself offers little or no positive rebellion against her diminished humanity, and, instead, longs for the romantic role once assigned to her. She feels her human estrangement, but she has nothing to substitute for the old ideals.

An Approach to Lezama Lima

Julio Cortázar

> *Then after, in the sands, silken intermediate pauses,*
> *between the submerged unreal and the dense, irresistible apparition,*
> *was created the metric accordance, and the navel of the earth*
> *overcame the promiscuous horizon which confounded man with a repetition*
> *of trees.*
>
> —JOSÉ LEZAMA LIMA, "The Approach to Montego Bay"

Well, then, are we both crazy? Where can I break the surface to breathe, frantic for air, after that deep dive of six hundred and seventeen pages, *Paradiso*? And why, suddenly, Jules Verne, in a book where nothing would seem to evoke him? But yes, of course it evokes him. To begin with, doesn't Lezama himself speak of oblique influences, hasn't he said somewhere that they act "as if a man, without knowing it of course, switching on the light in his room should start up a water fall in Ontario," a Vernian metaphor if there ever was one? Doesn't he introduce us to this tangential causality when he recalls that when Saint George thrusts his lance into the dragon, the first to fall dead is his horse, just as at times, a bolt of lightning will descend through the trunk of an oak and pass harmlessly through thirteen seminarians absorbed in Swiss cheese and the worship of the ace of clubs, before carbonizing a canary which was twittering in a cage fifty yards away? Well then, yes, Jules Verne, then; certainly, to approach Montego Bay one must pass through the center of the earth. Not just certainly, but literally, and the proof is this: rare reader of *Paradiso* (I picture, with some vanity, a very exclusive club, comprised of the few who, like you, have read *Der Mann ohne Eigenschaften, Der Tod des Vergils,* and *Paradiso*; only in this—I mean in the club—do I resemble Phineas Fogg), did you realize that the actual reference to Verne is . . . demoniacally provoked by an erotic episode analogous to one which a few decorous researchers have begun to reveal in the creator of the Nautilus? Leregas the oarsman, of phallic propensities, is about to receive a visit from the hitherto-unsuspected athlete Baena Albornoz, who descends into the inferno of a Havana gymnasium to receive, compliant Adonis, the boar's tusk which will penetrate him until he bites

From *Review* no. 12 (Fall 1974), translated by Paula Speck. © 1974 by the Center for Inter-American Relations, Inc.

the bedstead in an ecstasy of pleasure. Leregas awaits the humbled visit of the Hercules who, after so much diurnal labor, by night spins at the womanly wheel of his true condition. And then, in that tense waiting, ''The memory of the crater of Iasshole went down to the basement, the shadows of Scataris also reached there. The ringed shadow of Scataris over the crater of Sneffels.'' Diabolically, the resonance of the innocent Icelandic orography becomes a lascivious erotic suggestion, and the message of Arne Saknus-semm, wonder of our childhood (Descends dans le cratère du Yocul de Sneffels que l'ombre du Scataris vient caresser avant les calendes de Juillet, voyageur audacieux, et tu parviendras au centre de la Terre) propounds, through its sound and images, a lubricious revelation. Iasshole, ringed shadow (''il a perdu ses trente deux plis,'' a Jean Genet character will say, referring to another Baena Albornoz), Sneffels, reminiscent of *the sniffles*, Scataris, which in this context evokes the scrotum, and the images of descent into the crater, of caresses, of dark regions. . . . Oh, Phineas Fogg, oh Professor Lidenbrock, what are we doing with your progenitor?

Peace on the hermit of Nantes and his speleologists, but first I will filch another passage from him on my own account, a passage just as significant as if it had been extracted by Lezama himself, and I will place it, so that it may serve us as a guiding laser, at the head of everything which follows:

> Enfin, mon oncle me tirant par le collet, j'arrivai près de la boule. ''Regarde, me dit-il, et regarde bien! il faut prendre des leçons d'abîme.''

> Jules Verne, *Voyage au centre de la terre.*

In ten days, interrupting myself long enough to breathe and to give my cat Theodore W. Adorno his milk, I have read *Paradiso,* completing (completing?) an itinerary which I started many years ago with the reading of several chapters slipped into the review *Orígenes* like so many objects from Tlön or Uqbar. I am not a critic; some day, I suspect distant, this prodigious total will find its Maurice Blanchot, for from this breed must come the man who would intern himself in its fabulous larvary. I only propose to point out a shameful ignorance, and to tilt in advance against the misunderstandings which will succeed it when America finally listens to the voice of José Lezama Lima. I am not surprised at the ignorance; I myself was unaware of Lezama twelve years ago, and it was necessary for Ricardo Vigón, in Paris, to tell me of *Oppiano Licario*, which had just been published in *Orígenes*, and which now closes (if anything can close) *Paradiso*. I doubt if, in those twelve years, Lezama's work has attained the active presence which, in an equivalent period, was achieved by the work of a Jorge Luis Borges or an Octavio Paz, in whose class he belongs, beyond the slightest doubt. Instrumental and essential difficulties are the first reasons for this ignorance: to read Lezama is one of the most arduous and often irritating tasks which can be undertaken. The perseverance demanded by pioneering writers such as Raymond Roussel, Hermann Broch or the Cuban master is rare even among "specialists," and thus the club has many empty armchairs. Borges and Paz (I cite them again in order to hang my target from the very top of the Latin American literary tree) have the advantage on Lezama in that they are translucent writers, almost Apollonian in their perfect adjustment of expression, in the coherent system of their spirit. Their difficulties, and even their obscurities (Apollo can also be nocturnal, descend to the abyss to kill the Python) answer to the dialectic evoked by "Le cimetière marin":

> Mais rendre la lumière
> Suppose d'ombre une morne moitié.

Keystones of an arch rooted in the Mediterranean, they exert their greatest force without the three preliminary enigmas which turn the reader of Lezama into a perpetual Oedipus. And if I say that this constitutes an advantage for the former over the latter, I am referring, in an almost ethical sense, to those readers who detest the labor of Oedipus, who opt for the greatest harvest at the least risk. In Argentina at least, there is a tendency to dodge hermeticism, and Lezama is not only hermetic in the literal sense, in so far as the best of his work propounds an apprehension of essences by way of the mythic and the esoteric in all of their historic, psychic and literary forms vertiginously combined within a poetic system in which a Louis XV armchair often serves to seat the god Anubis, but is also formally hermetic, as much in the candour which leads him to assume that the most heterogeneous of his metaphorical series will be perfectly comprehensible to others, as in the originality of his *barroquismo* (by origin, in opposition to a baroque lucidly *mise en page*, like that of Alejo Carpentier). One sees, then, the difficulty of entering the club when so many obstacles accumulate against the pleasure of a reading, unless the pleasure begins with the obstacles themselves; and so I began reading Lezama as if trying to crack the code of *messunkaSebrA.icefdok.segnittamurtn*, etc., which finally resolves into: "Descends dans le cratère du Yocul de Sneffels." It would seem that the feelings of haste and guilt excited by bibliographic proliferation lead the contemporary reader to reject, often with an ironic comment, any *trovar clus*. To this is added a false estheticism and the solemn blinders of badly understood specialization, now at last under attack by attitudes like the structuralist one. Goethe still managed to fuse the philosopher and the poet, already in his century at odds, within an overwhelming unitary intuition; up to Thomas Mann (I speak now of novelists) it seemed that this partnership had maintained itself alive in authors and readers, but already the work of a Robert Musil, to keep to the field of Germanic literature, failed to encounter the universal echo which it deserved. The same reader, today tends to adopt a specialist's attitude according to what he is reading, at times subconsciously resisting any work which presents him with mingled waters, novels which shade into poems, metaphysics which are born with one elbow resting on the counter of a bar or upon a mattress devoted to amorous chores. He accepts, with moderation, extraliterary cargo in a novel, as long as the genre conserves its basic prerogatives (which, incidentally, nobody knows, but that's another question). *Paradiso*, a novel which is also a hermetic treatise, a poetics and the resulting poetry, will find its readers with difficulty; where does the novel begin, where does the poem stop, what is the meaning of this anthropology overlapping a mantra which is also tropical folklore, which is also a family chronicle? One often hears these days of diagonal sciences, but the *diagonal reader* will take his time in arriving, and *Paradiso*, cross section of essences and presences, will feel the resistance in the grain of received ideas. But the cut has been made; as in the Chinese story of the perfect executioner, the victim stands without knowing that as soon as he sneezes, his head will roll across the floor.

If instrumental difficulty is the first reason that so little is known of Lezama, the circumstances of our political and historical underdevelopment are the second. Since 1960, fear, hypocrisy, and guilt have allied to separate Cuba and its artists and intellectuals from the rest of Latin America. Those who were already recognized, Guillén, Carpentier, Wilfredo Lam, cleared and still clear the barrier by means of an international prestige antedating the revolution, a prestige which guarantees them continuing attention. Lezama, already pushed to the margin in the value-schemes of Peruvian, Mexican, or Argentine critics, has remained on the other side of the barrier, to the point that even those who have heard his name and would like to read *Tratados en la Habana, Analecta del reloj, La fijeza, La expresión americana,* or *Paradiso,* cannot and will not be able to obtain copies. He, along with many other poets and artists of Cuba, find themselves forced to live and work in an isolation of which the best that can be said is that it is disgusting and shameful. Of course, the important thing is to stop the spread of totalitarian communism. *Paradiso?* Nothing meriting that name could come from such a hell. Sleep softly, the OAS watches over you.

THE SCHOOLMASTER IN US ALL

There remains a third, and perhaps more carefully concealed reason for the fierce silence which surrounds Lezama's work; I will speak of it without reticence precisely because the few Cuban critiques of that work with which I am acquainted have not wished to mention it, and yet I know its destructive force in the hands of our literary pharisees. I refer to the formal errors which abound in his prose, and which, by contrast with the subtlety and profundity of its content, provoke in the superficially refined reader a reaction of shock and impatience which he is almost never able to overcome. Furthermore, since the editions of Lezama's works often contain careless typographical errors, and *Paradiso* is far from being an exception, it isn't surprising that the difficulties of the material are multiplied by an impatience produced by orthographic and grammatical extravagances which trip up the gaze of the schoolmaster within all of us. Years ago, when I began to show or read passages from Lezama to people unacquainted with his work, the wonder provoked by his vision of reality and by the daring of the images which communicated it was almost always mitigated by a condescending irony, by a superior smile. I soon realized that a rapid defensive mechanism began to operate here, and that those threatened with the absolute hastened to magnify formal flaws as a perhaps unconscious excuse for remaining outside Lezama, for not following him in his unrelenting penetration of deep waters. The undeniable fact that he seems determined never to write an English, French, or Russian name correctly, and that his quotations in foreign languages are studded with orthographic fantasies, would induce a typical intellectual from the Río de la Plata to see in Lezama a no-less-typical autodidact from the underdeveloped world, which is correct, and to find this a justification for not recognizing his true dimensions, which is very lamentable. Of course, among the idiosyncratic Argentines, correctness of form, in writing as in dress, has always been a guarantee of seriousness, and anyone who announces that the earth is round in an acceptable voice will earn more respect than a cronopio with a frog in his throat but much to say behind the frog. I speak of Argentina because I know a little about it, but in Cuba I also found young intellectuals who smiled ironically to themselves on recalling how capriciously Lezama pronounces the name of a certain foreign poet; the difference was exposed when those young people, proposing to say something about the poet in question, could get no farther than their impeccable phonetics, while Lezama, in five minutes, left them far behind. One of the indices of our underdevelopment is our fastidiousness about anything which touches the cultural rind, appearances, the veneer on the door of culture. We know that Dylan is pronounced Dilan and not Dailan, as we said at first (and they looked at us ironically, or they corrected us, and we knew something was wrong); we know exactly how to say Caen and Loan and Sean O'Casey and Gloucester. Everything's fine, just like having clean fingernails or using a deodorant. The rest comes afterwards, or doesn't come at all. For many of those who excuse Lezama with a smile, it never comes, before or afterwards, but their fingernails, I'll swear, are perfect.

To a defensive irony which feeds on superficial faults is added that often provoked by the odd ingenuousness cropping out in so many moments of Lezama's narrative. At bottom, it is for love of this ingenuousness that I speak of him here: beyond any scholarly canon, I know of its penetrating force; while many seek, Percival finds, while many speak, Mishkin knows. The many-rooted baroque which is producing in Latin America work as dissimilar and yet akin as that of Vallejo, Neruda, Asturias and Carpentier (we are dealing not with genres but with foundations), in the special case of Lezama is colored by a breath of what I can only call tentatively: naïveté. An American naïveté, insular in the direct and open sense, an American innocence. A naïve American innocence opening its eyes Eleatically, Orphically, at the beginning of creation, Lezama-Adam before the fall, Lezama-Noah like the one who diligently attends the parade of animals in Flemish paintings: two butterflies, two horses, two leopards, two ants, two dolphins. . . . A primitive who knows everything, a proper *Sorbonnard*, but American in the sense that the stuffed albatrosses of *Ecclesiastic*-al wisdom have not made him a "wiser and a sadder man"; his science is a palingenesis, his knowledge is original, jubilant, it is newborn, as water was with Thales and fire with Empedocles. Between the knowledge of Lezama and that of a European (or of his equivalents from the Río de la Plata, much less American in this sense) stretches the distance from innocence to guilt. Every European writer is "the slave of his baptism," to paraphrase Rimbaud; whether he wishes it or not, his decision to write entails carrying on an immense and almost terrifying tradition; if he accepts it, if he struggles against it, this tradition inhabits him, it is his familiar or his incubus. Why write, if everything has been written down in some form already? Gide remarked sardonically that since no one is listening, everything must be said over again, but a fear of guilt or of superficiality moves the European intellectual to the most extreme vigilance over his calling and methods, the only way to avoid returning to paths too well-trodden. Hence the enthusiasm produced by novelties, the mass assault on each new slice of the invisible which someone has managed to materialize in a book; it is enough to mention symbolism, surrealism, the *"nouveau roman"*: at last something really new, unsuspected by Ronsard, by Stendhal, by Proust. For a while guilt feelings can be allowed to sleep; even the epigones come to believe that they are doing something new. Then, slowly, they become European again, and each writer awakes with his albatross hanging from his neck.

A HANDFUL OF CULTURE

Meanwhile, Lezama wakes up on his island with the joy of a pre-Adamite without a bow tie, and he does not feel guilty of any direct tradition. He appropriates them all, from the adivinatory Etruscan livers to Leopold Bloom blowing his nose on a dirty handkerchief, but without historical commitment, without becoming a French or Austrian writer. He is a Cuban bearing a mere handful of his own culture on his back, and the rest is knowledge pure and free, not the baton in a relay race. He can write what he likes, without reminding himself that Rabelais, that Martial. . . . He is not a link in a chain, he is not obligated to do more, or better, or differently, he does not need to justify himself as a writer. His incredible overabundance as well as his deficiencies proceed from this innocent freedom, from this free innocence. At times, reading *Paradiso*, one feels inside another universe. How is it possible to ignore or defy to such an extent the taboos of the intellect, the *thou shalt not write*'s of our shamefaced professional commandments? When the innocent American presents himself, the good savage who treasures the beads without suspecting that they are worthless or out of style, then two things can happen with Lezama. The first, the one that counts: his genius bursts forth without the inferiority complex which overburdens us in Latin America, with the primordial force of the thief of fire. The other, which receives a smile from the ones with the complex, the impeccably cultivated ones, is his *Douanier* Rousseau side, the bluffing side, *à la* Mishkin, of the man who, in *Paradiso*, after writing an extraordinary passage, begins a new paragraph in the most absolute tranquillity: "And what was Ricardo Fronesis doing while his family history was being recounted?"

If I am writing these pages, it is because I *know* that paragraphs like the one just quoted will weigh more in the judgment of the schoolmasters than the prodigious inventiveness with which *Paradiso* creates the world over again. And if I quote the sentence about Ricardo Fronesis, it is because this and many other barbarisms disturb me as well, but only to the extent that I am disturbed by a fly resting on a Picasso, or a meow from my cat Theodore when I am listening to music by Xenakis. Incapacity, confronted with intricacy in a work, disguises its retreat with the most superficial pretexts—since it has not passed beyond the superficial. Thus, I once knew a gentleman who never listened to recordings of classical music, because, according to him, the scratching of the needle prevented him from enjoying the work in its complete perfection; after setting such an exacting standard, he spent the day listening to a frightful recording of tangos and boleros. Every time that I quote a passage from Lezama and reap a smile and a change of subject, I think of that gentleman. Those incapable of accepting *Paradiso* will always defend themselves in this way, and for them everything will be scratching of the needle, fly, and meow. In *Hopscotch*, I defined and attacked the "female reader," the one incapable of a truly loving wrestle with the work, like that of Jacob with the angel. If anyone should doubt the legitimacy of my offensive, this example will be enough: reputable critics in Buenos Aires began by not understanding the double system of possible readings of the novel, and from there they passed to the opposite extreme, asserting pathetically that they had read it "in the two ways indicated by the author," when the unhappy author had only proposed an option, and had never pretended that in our times the same book should be read twice. What then can we expect from the "female reader" confronted with *Paradiso*, which, as a character of Lewis Carroll's would say, could try the patience of an oyster? But there can be no patience where there is not first humility and hope, where a conditioned, prefabricated culture, overpraised by writers whom I can only call functional, with rebellions and heresies carefully delimited by the Marquis-of-Queensberries of the profession, rejects any work which truly goes against the grain. Capable of facing any literary difficulty on the intellectual or sentimental plane as long as it conforms to the rules of the Occidental game, prepared to play the most arduous Proustian or Joycean chess with familiar pieces and predictable strategies, it retreats with indignation and ridicule when invited to explore territory outside the genres, to struggle with a language and a plot corresponding to a narrative system which springs, not from books, but from long *lessons of the abyss*; and here at last I have been able to slip in the reason for my epigraph, and it is time to go on to other things.

A Cuban Proust

Severo Sarduy

One may consider *Paradiso*—which in a sense also postulates itself as a poem, indeed claims this type of reading—as the non-historical biography of José Cemí, a writer living in Havana, in the heyday of the Republic, strongly influenced by his own mother's exile during the time of the Spanish colony as well as by her somber Christmases in Jacksonville, involved in the university scuffles of his own youth but all the same a forerunning reader of Sartre who is destined to confound any attempts at chronological reconstruction. The sole truth behind the narrative lies in its being a *Bildungsroman*. A biography laid out between two moments of revelation: the asthma attack of a child on the verge of suffocation, inhaling and exhaling "as though he would have to make considerable efforts at achieving a natural rhythm," and the discovery made by the poet, as an adult, while tinkling a glass with a teaspoon—he tastes his coffee with milk while he smokes—of a *hesycast rhythm* in a phrase heard elsewhere, long before, but which ultimately becomes clarified and modified by his own recollection.

The process that goes from suffocation and breathlessness to complete possession of breath in meter, the life of José Cemí and the non-linear text that envelops it (insofar as this is the character's own nautical journal under its own cultural weight), are all factors in the construction of this, the most proliferating of literary architectures to come to light after Góngora's.

The text: if according to Lezama, the novel is nothing but the final outcome of poetry, the image, the only support of the poetic process—an image whose descriptive fitness and whose unforeseeable, stupefying terms cannot be recreated in the reader without some sort of vertigo—leads the novel, then, in its own endless transformation, toward a generating center, a "secret logos":

From *Review* no. 12 (Fall 1974), translated by Enrico-Mario Santí. © 1974 by the Center for Inter-American Relations, Inc.

131

At a given time, the poet begins to recognize the steps of his own visions and the poem turns itself into a dance hall, into a magical pageantry. Labyrinths and connections are verified and the poem, organized like a resistance in face of time, is changed into an ark that floats on the water with all the secrets of nature. The ark gets to a deserted island; there it finds a shipwrecked admiral who is sustaining an endless dialogue with a glass-eyed hen: that is, with a novel.

The story: Cemí's life is traversed by another discourse, his mother's, who, as though she herself were seated upon a throne, soberly dictates her own sentences, charged with poetic and mythological passages: a Marian majesty in which Catholic tradition, of which *Paradiso* is a part, becomes fused with Creole eloquence, exemplified in the novel's humor as well as in its flagrantly hyperbolic tone. And it is precisely within the realm of such a maternal verb, within the type of destiny which Rialta's discourse lays out for her son, where the two complementary poles make their appearance. Here the two polar characters who meet Cemí in his adolescence are revealed in all their defining traits. She tells her son:

> a secret will to go with you all through your life, and for you always to have a determination that would bring you to seek what can be seen and what is hidden. A determination that would never destroy, but that would look for the hidden in the visible, and find in the secret what will rise up for the light to give it form.

Rialta's wish thus prefigures a quest for day within night and for night within the heart of day, a search for reciprocal refractions, much like adjacent squares on a checkerboard, which Cemí manages to accommodate in between two characters—poles in a magnetic field that equally determine his own gnostic space: Foción, Cemí's descent to Hades, whose Neronian sign determines his madness; Fronesis, his ascent to the visible world, who is marked by the "Goethian sign."

After finishing a day of classes at Upsalón—the University of Havana, according to the novel—the three find themselves in the midst of a demonstration, where the police

> were wearing rat-colored brown capes, shining with a damp iridescence like the shells of cockroaches. They rattled their swords in the air, a scorpion leaping through the blood that passed over to the steel.

In the midst of such chaos, something resembling "an Arab market, a Toulousian square or the Bagdad fair," Cemí, Fronesis and Foción, the Pythagorean triad, pursue a debate, or rather, they choose to undertake a summing up of things while indulging in Macaronic philology, overburdened with bibliography and copious documentation: all knowledge bound up to the laws of geometry, according to the rules of numbers:

If only they would teach us to count, merely from one to seven, according to the Pythagorean numerical symbols, we'd have the enchantment of proportion and the columns of Greek temples, and medieval cathedrals. Thus, in Apollo begins the One, *a* is *absence of*, *polys* is *many*: the exclusion of multiplicity. The coin, the diversity, the sun.

Thus, the numbers parade around the center of the student circle: "the spell of numbers laden with symbols."

Their debates, delightful in themselves for their invention and verbal truculence, dazzling in their rhetorical tone as well as in the offhandedness of their many cultural references, are pursued across the whole span of the book in a complex discussion about homosexuality, which is especially developed in chapter 9 and then summarized in chapter 11, which accounts for the androgynous origins of man and the human embryo's first and foremost sexless stage of life.

What is important about such a rhetorical triangle is that the discussions about eroticism always resolve themselves in an ideology of writing (*écriture*). The devouring substance of the word, which constitutes the raw material of the novel-image, finds an exacting correspondent in the androgynous substratum of creation, which in turn is brought about within a totalizing, homogeneous eroticism whose contrary is non-existent. The Augustinian concept of the *logos spermatikós*, dear to Lezama himself, determines such a causality. All this is confirmed by the book's plan: after the threesome's *Convivium* about sexuality, there comes a chapter in which four narrative sequences—which, because of the characteristic constants of its style and notwithstanding their apparent disparity, are interpretable as literary exercises of the narrator himself—alternate and ultimately fuse together at chapter's end. The story of Atrius Flaminius, a captain of the legions that belong to the time when

> the Augustan peace had spread throughout the world in Vergilian hexameters and in Horace's rustic pleasantries.

A child's inspection of some scenes etched upon the surface of a Danish vase:

> small ships like the silver ones displayed in shop windows, on a bay like something in an oversimplified schoolboy's painting. The city walls surrounding the plazas and the royal palace, with the mayor receiving a delegation of Chinese students, who show him a print collection picturing the China of mountains and lakes.

The confessions of an insomniac who is tormented by [a]

> very commonplace horselaugh, typical of Russian bass in a popular song, or perhaps one of Shakespeare's characters, greasy, employing the diaphragm in a highly mannered way.

The fantastic adventure of Juan Longo, a seventy-year-old music critic with pre-Raphaelite manners, who will achieve an artificial life beyond his own death and who dies a second time in his coffin upon becoming a Roman soldier.

The appearance of Oppiano Licario, Cemí's mentor and the signifier for writing, is the subject of the last chapters of the book, in which his *Poetic Syllogistic* is deployed, described in language studded with quotations from Góngora.

I have already mentioned that a secret, poetic logos supports Lezama's system. It is essential to note that the story's progression is not determined by mere accident; neither is it due to pure metonymic connection. Rather, it follows an anti-Aristotelian "methodology," the best example of which is its own formulation. The following are the four basic points of this methodology:

The *occupatio*, much discussed by the Stoics, is the complete occupation of a body: here it is the image that occupies the poem (the novel), allowing for the recovery of its own substance and the penetration of its own space.

The *oblique experience:* "It is as though a man, without being aware of anything himself, of course, would cause a waterfall in Ontario by turning the light switch in his own room. We could mention a striking example: when Saint George thrusts his lance against the dragon, his horse is the one that falls dead."

The *surprise:* "If someone who knows German well enough, finds the word *vogel* (bird), then the word *vogelbauer* (bird cage) and later finds in the end the word *vogelon* (the sexual act in *Zarathustra*), suddenly, in a flash similar to the strike of a match, the meeting of the bird with the cage gives away the word *vogelon*, a word born without any cause whatever and which elicits the word that means this: the entry of the bird within the cage, that is, copulation."

The *hypertelic method:* "An example: for a long time it was thought that intestinal worms receded with the tide. But it's been observed that even when there was no tide, they receded all the same. There are certain insects that kill off the male during copulation. Such a hypertelic way, which always goes beyond its own end as in this case, has poetic roots."

The difficulties inherent to an article that attempts at a summarizing review of *Paradiso* are evident here, especially since this is precisely one of those "world-books" in which a given writer may find everything that could furnish him with an entire grammar of creation. At least, my purpose was to cast some light upon the tension found in *Paradiso* between the verbal, iconic proliferation and exuberance, whose sapience is almost without precedence, and the rigor of method in which poetry is the procedure by which all things become organized and scanned.

Pursuers

Saúl Sosnowski

They are marked by a kind of need, by signs of searching. They are marked by manias of persecution and the desire to imbricate themselves into an ever more rough and elusive filigree. They are marked by the desire for an encounter or the illusion of an encounter. They are Cortázar's characters, and they keep battering against doors which will not open up to thrusts, pleas or violent ejaculations. Every traveler generates a space that may or may not be spanned. Every narrator has the desire to name what eludes him, what holds him back from his fine ending, another passage undone. There is also a certain kind of reader whose escape is the use of carefully aligned spots. Yet flight could also be an extrapolation, a possible confrontation with a mirror: a clash that may send him from his reading back to that inescapable position of viewer, viewing what others are seeing, what they themselves are viewing.

A certain kind of character, and also a certain kind of reader, accedes to the proposition set forth by the narrator, paving the narrator's way. It is bits and pieces in chapters displaying what they will later conceal; bits and pieces, marking the return trip as well, by way of tables of instructions, numbers at the top and at the bottom of the page; a deceptive ease found in titillation, a titillation that anticipates variations of all sorts, openings to passages unknown: darkness within but the flashlight very firmly in hand. Besides, there is always the certainty that the whole thing may not be so bad after all. If it could be a reading that did more than linger in order to fondle the words, then it could—and why not?—get closer, get *us* closer to exploring other territories outside and within the text. To say that a text "se deja leer" (here we clearly enter into what is proposed by *Rayuela's*

From *The Final Island: The Fiction of Julio Cortázar,* edited by Jaime Alazraki and Ivan Ivask. © 1976, 1978 by the University of Oklahoma Press.

Table of Instructions) is no assurance of the easy surrender by the one who is actually charging us for that very momentary spasm and all the analogous echoes of its false counterresponse. A text which is not read but which rather "submits itself to the reader" is inviting an (apparently) easy seduction, opening itself, as it were, to recommendation by those already initiated by the provocative *sobrador*.

This, then, is a seduction to an order whose members are thus pledged as addicts: "So please do come; this text abandons itself to you. I am different, yes, and my 635 pages, my fluctuations, my queasiness, may well frighten you. But just a moment; keep an eye out. I'm letting you decide: why not come a little closer?" The make-up is on just right, and the one about to be seduced seems on the point of falling into the trap. "And if you like it—well, if you dare, and how can you dare not to, as *macho* as you are!—then we'll go deeper, to the limit, no signs that say stop, no looks that hesitate at further penetrations. The book will let itself be read. You may enter confidently, for this is an expert old tongue, not limited to mere adolescent maneuvers."

This book indicates paths, it frames the way, it shows signs, it makes signs on the cards of him who enters trustingly as he accepts the warmly extended hand. The reader is curious, naïve. He can be seduced by a presentable, exotic façade. That particular mechanism leaves out other elements, but these he does not manage to see. He is already caught in the "babas del diablo," the devil's spittle, already submitting himself to be possessed, as a virgin would be, by so much "hangustia hexistencial." Now he begins, first fondling forms, then learning new ways, repeating those variations; and yet when he's finished, he still has the voids, the same ones felt before between so many other sheets. No, this partnership will not do. Having submitted is degrading, it is belittling, he is just some makeshift kind of seduced male-female. He starts over again. This time the narrator and the reader are in perfect harmony, their tools warmly joined. They begin new searchings, they fill up other gaps, gaps requiring other mechanisms, other games, games signaling other types of frameworks, other dimensions and perhaps other ways out. The crests, the ebbs between desire and encounter, fall in and out. The encounter, the rejection and seeking, the seeking out and possessing: it is a dynamics that demands and forces constant movement, even though its price be the abandonment of partial solutions, of the small joys, of the choices which really are not choices, of the oscillating between cobblestones and threads, of such pains as the warmth of a bed or the satisfaction of a "well-written" page that will no longer soothe. No time here for the pause that refreshes and the resultant satisfied smile coming from the other side of the sheet. If here you are faced with an onslaught of cobwebs, brush them off and return to penetrate from other angles, or from the same angle but as if for the very first time. Evidently it is all a question of going backward, the farther back the better. That way the romantic little marker will move up another compartment with each new shove, each time closer to heaven, that heaven that survives in the imagination, boxed in by desire.

Sax and sex and drugs: none of these is an end; each is a possible means of access to what cannot be articulated. Each demands the presence of someone who is not a victim of self-abuse, the one with the polka-dotted tie, the one to translate this language—if that's what it is—into something accessible to others—if it is indeed possible. Any experiment, hallucination or inner vision is a luminous interstice between the blocks that guarantee that there is no way out, that any encounter (with what? with whom?) need take place on this ground-level world of ours, need be reduced to a language which the Contax 1.1.2 would not transmit beyond the initial dry plate, which the Lettera 22 would not tap out unless a reasoning hand dictated the mediatization. This mediatization is the obstacle to and the impossibility of direct access. Once again it is a demented logic which secures the path, the same path to be left for certain experiments, the same path to which one will eventually return. There you will fall down once and then again, to see it waiting there: peacefully, smug, knowing the only escape is to that form of order which I use even now to find the understanding wink of my *paredros*. Logic is a mischievous witch that knows about an escape from which one returns only to slide on his own slippery stick. So? One may not know how to tell something, but yet one must try. Some sequences will get broken up, some will interpolate spaces that the distant reader must bear for there to be a bridge, for him to be integrated into "the zone" and be seated confidently on "the island," knowing he is all right: he hasn't gone too far alone; there's a return ticket still ready for those waiting.

There is someone waiting while the other goes to recover what he feels to be lost echoes, but it is he who waits who is actually "the man of the species": the poor dentist who gambles away all he has left; the one at the port who knows the newcomer will bring multicolored vociferousness and an end to domestic tranquility; the biographer too, ever mediocre, who permits a certain access to the pursuer's workshop. There is no reason to question the writer's sympathy for certain characters' desires to abandon what alienates them from the West, to imbricate them into a world whose components do not demand a constant alienation from what is outside man's world. It is obvious that for the writer the quest must begin with a serious questioning of the tools of his trade. It is understandable, moreover, that such a questioning and desire should be translated into multiple debates between his characters, and that these disquisitions—with or without Morelli, but definitely with Johnny-Bruno, Persio-Medrano, Oliveira and the ones we shall see later on—may be the ones to signal, I believe, a sort of resignation to remain on this side, to specify even more the immediate goals that can be achieved with the limited equipment with which our daily alienation provides us.

Let me specify: if in fact Johnny's quest can really arouse our emotions, can induce us to empathize with him to the point of identifying ourselves with what he does not quite manage to say, it is Bruno who stirs up all these reactions through his narration, through his confession in the eyes of Johnny's challenge. Johnny's biography, as transmitted through the omissions he himself and Bruno make, is a mask, a false face for the consumer (literally: he who consumes; and therein lies the director of "Las ménades"), a criticism whose point of departure is deception; for not only are the images desired by the public false, they are subserviently acceded to. In spite of this, Johnny himself accepts it all the while ("Está bien tu libro, Bruno"), perhaps in anticipation of the final request, the one asking to replace his fidelity to his quest with a mask as well. There is no trace of criticism—which is precisely what is open to criticism—in Bruno. His Johnny is a product tailored to the taste of those who wish their images and illusions reinforced by the (apparent) authority of the printed word. The function of unmasking—if the scheme "life and works" is to be adopted—is replaced with the obliging bestseller recipe and the expected translation, with his wife's satisfaction amid the growing good news. The possibility of acting like a critic capable of confronting what Johnny suggests and joining him in his quest is abandoned for the sake of bourgeois complaisance. Johnny is canned and placed on a shelf with a fancy label; Bruno is wrapped in the satisfaction of having got out a new edition with its very apropos appendix about the subject's death.

This is a version of writing which denounces its very self in the simultaneous opening of two channels of reception, showing by means of Bruno's language his own critical inability and affirming the negation of the biographer, not of the instrument he uses. If Johnny attacks the bourgeois concepts of time and order, he does so through words which register them as being of Bruno's world; there is no denouncement, again, of the tool. This same instrument is the one which condemns its user, thus showing its other critical capacity: that of emerging from itself, from its own condemnation and destruction, to recover its original meaning.

And so it is inevitable that one revert to terms like "capacidad poética" and "lenguaje analógico," already analyzed elsewhere. But it is necessary to persevere with a language used not as a mere object for fondling the objects named, leaving them on the periphery, but rather as an instrument which could leave off with the caressing in order to take a virgin look at each of the elements. The result would be an account that would slowly undress the object and face it with the necessity of being uncovered. It would be conventional language, but it would abhor conventional expressions and use them only to attest to that abhorrence: obsolete expressions, the worn-out thoughts of members of sybilline clubs which serve to accentuate their obsolescence and strive for a more advantageous plane. This would redeem certain primal acts, certain types of contact which do not need so much intermediary verbiage just to come together. It means looking for primary colors before looking for intricate configurations, looking for friendly unions for the sheer, although not simple, desire for love. It means La Maga before so much vain disquisition about the reality that Oliveira let slip through his fingers, Berthe Trépat and the punishment of the prodigal son who for so many decades of hypocritical learning refused pity, and it means sorrow and friendship too when faced with so many threads and water basins. It means, then, a primary language as well, not a return to the innocence of a nonexistent twentieth-century Adam, but rather an opening up to a language of moderation, utilized with no more clownish antics of cuff links and tie. It would certainly mean an honest look at our present moment, at history and at such improvements as are possible for us to realize. No, it is not a question of negating a "literary" or "everyday" language, but rather of the "caricature" by which it is so heavily weighted down; it is not a question of denying the history these very words attest to, but rather of examining their potential in a projection toward the future.

These terms, the ones I have just used, are rigorously examined from a viewpoint that would like to deny the very separation they promulgate. Thus they are replaced with notions of "continuous flux" and "abolition of binary systems," new words as old as the past ones, but words which in their impact suggest possible solutions as yet unelaborated and unaccomplished. These possibilities fork out toward other models which thousands of letters serve to coagulate in the rose of the kaleidoscope; they fork out toward the types of traversings that found cities, which through the sobriety of humor establish zones in which there can also be bridges, in which someone simply named Juan can add himself to a growing chain of pursuers. And these models that seek to be must first lapse into words and worn-out patterns, again to be mistreated by so much abuse. It is left for them to readjust, omit the nexuses, drown out all comfort, arouse once again the storehouse of words belonging to the reader-possessor, the reader who must go back to an adult childhood with its puzzles and erotic dolls, the reader-viewer of explicit situations, ones which underline that eroticism and its translations into physical conduct and are not just a road that leads to being (or to the beginning of being), but a language as well, with its own claim on the city.

What is left is rescue, then, through multiple modes of access, gliglical states of coitus, suggestions from "La Señorita Cora," the echoes of pederasts, lesbian encounters (fern/lakes/hills), exaltations and defenses of onanism, all joining Cortázar's central scheme: how can we talk about a new man (new woman?) while this one keeps hiding behind the proverbial fig leaf, while he still believes in a decency defined in terms of what remains hidden. The nostalgic trip back to Eden acquires a double sonority: a return to the moment of embarking upon what Cortázar considers the wrongly-chosen road; a return as well to the moment just before the first bit of shame was felt about the body. A natal beginning, the joy of discovering a world to be possessed without all the cloaks and conventions. Permission granted—by not having asked for it—to utilize verbs and conjugations in their original meanings, to extend bridges toward others, to be a bridge with others. It is also expected that this eliminates the egocentric viewpoint, that it overcomes the *I* and replaces it with the *we*. There is hope for such a view, not based on negating others, not based on oppressing their being in order to advance to a certain position on a gameboard, a gameboard drawn up according to an alien table of instructions.

Each one of Cortázar's pursuers has to follow a certain plan, not always drawn up by him, in order to get closer to his vision of a possible solution. For some of them failure is the final sign; for others the truncated, inconclusive search. Thus we go back to what "El perseguidor" proposes: so many metaphysical goings-on hovering around Oliveira, so many desires for an encounter that he doesn't quite manage to see his discovery until it is lost. At any rate, love and contact with other people would have seemed too superficial to him. Madness? No. Suicide? No again. Rather the useless lucidity of before; once more to seesaw between Ovejero's "Ahá" and "Death to the dog." It is science, it is deceit, it is "el gran hengaño," the great deception. It is also Persio, who is so much the astral poet that even if he does see what is going on in his world he does not participate. It is Medrano, who does participate and so dies. Personal purification, yes, but what did he contribute to Claudia's time or to the others'? They are already resigned to just one more day, just one more beer, and to forgetting. It is Juan, who seeks access and the opening to Hélène, who repeats, however, certain patterns already drawn by Oliveira. But now a fundamental difference is added: we are no longer facing a Club de la Serpiente which does and undoes itself according to certain internal rules fomented by the mediocrity of some of its participants. Now all the lines are extended toward "the zone," toward a total participation in others, of others, toward a coagulation where beings no longer figure as individual entities, but rather are all projected in a single thrust toward the rest. This human coagulation is translated onto a narrative plane in the first thirty-nine pages of a novel, a narrative coagulation from which we will derive all explicative lines, from which we respond to the oneness of the character's city—a look into the kaleidoscope. If the maximum beauty of these "patterns" is not to be found there, then certainly there is at least the possibility of that one encounter in which it is no longer just one "I" magnified over and beyond the others. Another difference, and certainly not an insignificant one, is a greater, more human responsibility toward the desired woman and a corresponding augmentation of the obstacles which put off the encounter.

I don't want to suggest what is commonly known as "the author's trajectory." I do wish to suggest that a greater opening up to others and a greater corresponding recognition of others' presence are shown. It is a recognition of their participation in oneself and one's own conformation as a result of that participation. That is why in the world of "La Joda" Lonstein's refinements can also have a place. This group—with the reservations already formulated elsewhere—develops the will of every member who will be integrated, *from* his participation in communal interests, *with* the presence of the others. Let us note that Lonstein's solitary pleasure is important because it does not stay shut in, because it obliges the "el que te dije" and those who read about it to participate in his opening up. It is not a matter of convincing; it is a matter of accepting—accepting behavior no less esoteric than that of a luminous mushroom's fortunes or that of a Parisian penguin.

If we continue to classify pursuers, the label obviously corresponds to Andrés. His search would appear to pick up where the others' left off, to depart from an encounter of the *I*, from a partial reconciliation with that *I* toward actions with others. It is no longer a question of passive acceptance, but rather of concrete, physical action, though it may remain on a low level of importance. Here it must be pointed out, however, that Andrés will inherit the function of the "el que te dije." The latter being dead, it is Andrés who must continue with "el libro de Manuel." Once again we have a collage that serves to document the moment it is hoped will one day be prehistoric. I say "once again" because it is the same with *Rayuela,* a collage, in part, of the cliché of all those intellectuals who are so well read but so slow to act. In the cases of both *Rayuela* and *Libro de Manuel* it is not so much the collages of Western ideas, of daily acts of terrorism, which linger after having read them, but the overlapping of these notions into a language which denounces them and which allows, or awaits, their destruction.

Again we have a dual reading of the text: a fact and its inscription into a framework denouncing its presence. This results in a single effect: the impact of the fact already denounced, sending the reader back to his previous passive position. A hope may arise: to accentuate indignation. We already know that such a text will convince neither the incredulous nor those who support or tolerate these acts. It will only accentuate the indignation of one already indignant. In any case, it means a nexus between reader and narrator by means of a text, part of whose extrinsic reality they must both share, the reading of a shared language that unites those who empathize with the proposal, the extension of a bridge where one already exists, hope where perhaps it already awaits. Once again: *challenge* and hope for that *response* which starts up the mechanism, a critical reading which requires a pursuer who would act and which proposes an author who assumes language to be an instrument of denunciation, if no longer one of combat.

But it is not only the searching as action which one gets out of Cortázar. There must also necessarily follow a preoccupation with the function, or multiple functions, which language can and must perform. In *Octaedro* these problems reinstate themselves with a fundamental variation in one special instance. In "Liliana llorando" the sick person writes at first to distract himself, but later notices that he is living the written-imagined parts more than his concrete reality, which is what frees him from his death. "Professional deformation" of reality—is he a writer? a journalist?—allows him these luxuries. The words that fill up the void also establish another reality, the one that forces itself upon his will. Here we could drive home the motif of the power of the word as an instrument of creation, as one unleashing other worlds (e.g., the mention of Nico in "Cartas de mamá"), but I prefer to underline for now the distraction aspect and the replacement of one reality by another (neither of which is desired).

In "Manuscrito hallado en un bolsillo" to write is a way of objectifying, of trying to understand something that is not logical, of pushing it onto the written page. If this writing truly does lay down certain arrangements, certain differentiations that to one's initial apprehension were not necessary (cf. "Las babas del diablo"), then to explain what was done is simpler than living it, even if sometimes there is no way to articulate it. The notebook, just like the Métro map (a variant of the module Persio used, a map of Portuguese trains), imposes an order, invents a time outside of the game to which he is bound and which strange forces prevent him from violating, even at the risk of once again having it said that "no se culpe a nadie."

It is "Los pasos en las huellas" which allows us to elaborate another angle of what was suggested by "El perseguidor" about biography as translation. The title itself underlines the other side of the exercise, as indicated in the initial note: "Crónica algo tediosa, estilo de ejercicio más que ejercicio de estilo de un, digamos, Henry James que hubiera tomado mate en cualquier patio porteño o platense de los años veinte." The narrator develops the new steps that will fill up the tracks by using his text against the grain. This will be the mark of the biographer, registered in the figure of the one he studies. Thus there are new cutouts of the double, through analogy, through entry into a world where one very rationally goes to live, with the minor variations of an avatar, what will be denounced by a book and by a discourse (instead of "una flor amarilla").

New also is the change in the poet = pursuer/critic = follower relationship; the critic redeems the deeper meanings of and the reasons for his subject's poetry from beneath the transitory fame where they are buried. There is a redemption, likewise, from a mediocre academic position by means of a "bestseller"—that institution which transforms everyday lives by sanctioning them for acceptance with the use of rubber stamps and ministerial recognition. From the very beginning, then, we have a re-creation by the critic of the miserable life of his subject. This is a double vengeance, to be achieved when the book forces its way onto the popular market.

The text can then become a mirror, the critical text can become a dissembled autobiography, an exorcism of recognized transgressions in the choice of subject studied. A radical difference is drawn between Bruno, the mere follower of a pursuer, and Fraga, who transforms the study of Romero's life into an examination of his own attitudes in the presence of that greatest of literary frauds. A single approximation turns out in opposite directions. The popular image of Johnny is consumed by the public, thus gratifying his critic. His truth is measured in the number of editions printed, the number of contracts for translations. The recipe has had the desired effect. Bruno and his wife are delighted. They will stay in the game. The possible omens that surface when he is confronted with Johnny dissipate upon leaving the vitiated air of his poorly formulated questions, of his non-methodical questing. In spite of all this, the critic accepts Johnny's superiority, recognizing that his road does not allow for both sanity and coexistence with the parasites of the species. Johnny's remarks when faced with his literary image (image: a glossy surface that hides the true model) alter neither the order nor the reception of Bruno's Johnny. No other exists except the one pressed out between the journalistic sheets, written to assure triumph and international contracts. The choice of subject matter suggests no analogies, no likenesses, no common projects; it responds to the needs of the market, to the necessity of pacifying the reader by assuring him that the artist is what he was expected to be. It is a nice easy chair, with no danger of someone's coming up behind with a dagger or with a version that would change everything around.

There is criticism of what in turn sees itself as a critical text (and there is no text that does not do so); there is layer upon layer of powder over the make-up that is already on. It is a text which refers to the scaffolding behind the critique and its reception—a text like "El perseguidor" transmitting criticism through arousal—an entry, in other words, into the critic's workshop, analogous to its multiple productions with the use of marked cards. Writing here is not the instrument of a search or even the search itself, but a way of enveloping it, of organizing it for worldwide acclaim, for fashion's dictates, to affirm it as one more product to be acquired—Rocamadour boutiques, Macondo restaurants. Everything is obtained, digested and expelled in the direction of yet another consumer.

At some point during this process the collision can occur: the gaze that comes peeking out of the looking-glass, the sign demanding a response, the necessity of opting for the continuation of the hallowed deception, or its rejection and thus its payment, with a return to those uncomfortable positions already overcome once. The dissembled biography has assured what was expected. The *arribismo* of the poet is repeated in the *arribismo* of his critic: the same pattern is drawn, the same hallowing result is obtained. It is simply not convenient to alter proven formulas. Every narrated fact is aimed at those who will devour it, those who will translate it into other equally digestible media. Thus criticism alters its own sign: the research, the files, the wording are all mere steps which reiterate the desired result. There is no critical reading, no critical writing. The critic is the beloved lackey of those who read what they would love to have written, and their applause is of a one-handed variety.

At the moment when success does arrive, however, a sincere questioning may occur: it is a gaze without pretexts upon the mirror, reflecting a falsely revered image; it is the official version, the one that will not allow any idols with clay feet to stand. This is the moment for an obeisant smile, or the smile of him who is preparing to make the leap that will annihilate him along with the philistines. Once again desire for authenticity (Medrano), for faithfulness until death (the first Johnny), of at least not tumbling again into the double infamy of repeating alien deceptions. A double glance, too, toward the *I* and toward those who refuse to tolerate the reduction of something newly enlarged to its vile, rapscallion truth. The new image is the one assimilated, and deception by a truth which has already deceived once will not be tolerated. The acceptance/refusal speech for the prize can only be a product of "indisposition," of a bad moment to be later excused.

The temptation is now mine to go back to theories that might bore some, even though they themselves use them. "Me aburren las hipótesis tempoespaciales, las *n* dimensiones, sin hablar de la jerga ocultista, la vida astral y Gustav Meyrink." It is "contactos tempo-espaciales," "uniones posesivas" and faraway but still visited bestiaries. It is approximations through words that exorcise after having hidden other objects, and beings no longer accepting the forces imposed on them. Of course, it is the farce of the poet himself, that succubus possessor who perhaps also desires to arrive at an ending. There is the possibility of definitively falling from an exalted scenario into bed with Susana/Ofelia, an honest acceptance of limitations, an oh so flogged-about inner peace and a small joy—knowing that even from this side, from the side of true simulation, fidelity was possible— the rejection of decisions, terminating in insane laughter (or hunting the pistol so near at hand in the desk drawer).

To read one's favorite writers and stroll through their new books could be a visit to spots which recognize each other in a friendly way, thanks to other frameworks, a visit to figures who point toward unalterable goals, ones which must be confronted because not to do so would be to remain silent forever. Affirming this is in itself a search for some bridge which extends from opposite points toward the middle. Solitary writing and solitary reading have been (theoretically) progressively abandoned in order to move toward a communal encounter—the trip being nothing more than a stage leading back to the others—a direct appeal to the very one now facing these letters.

It is no longer a question of narrating what can be catalogued by a perpetually self-adhering label (nor is it possible to prevent it from sticking of its own accord at times) in order to entertain, to document certain phenomena attributable to diverse causes within and outside of logical paradigms, to write and to leave what is written to the unwitting disposition of the texts. Conscious of the limits imposed by any narrative framework, one appeals directly to the reader, conscious of the fact that a single graphic plane is not enough to explain—isn't that a main part of what it's all about underneath the multiple ludic drawings?—what has been imposed, along with the very imposition, without the intervention of one's will in these encounters. It is necessary to continue finding and testing approximations that would form a bond between participant and the one who lived it all, on a common analogous plane.

From the very first submission to these means of communication we know there will be insurmountable obstacles unless we denounce those means, unless we resort to their very negation, unless we make explicit their insufficiency before those facts demanding clarification in the face of the "ahí pero dónde, cómo." It is here that silence fits in, or a perpetual quest for a formula, the one closest to a faithful translation of what has been accepted, but without so much mediation. Now, and more so each time in Cortázar's works, one must freely receive those signs, which are each time no longer mere paper words, in order to arrive at an immediate contact with the one who, from his side, draws closer and closer to his own version of the encounter, to the sparrow's pecking. Thus one must seek, it seems, total participation, in which writing and the reading of it are no longer two separate exercises, but rather a simultaneous action of translating and assimilating a desired reality.

Rayuela: Chapter 55 as Take-(away)

Barbara L. Hussey

In his "Tablero de Dirección" for the reading of *Rayuela*, Julio Cortázar informs the reader that he can approach the novel in many ways, but mainly two. The first possibility, designed for the "traditional" or passive reader, allows a sequential perusal of the fifty-six chapters pertaining to the first two sections, "Del lado de allá" (Paris) and "Del lado de aquí" (Buenos Aires). The active, participating reader, on the other hand, will follow the alternate format suggested by the author—a reading that would insert chapters of a third section ("De otros lados") in apparently random order between the chapters comprising the first book, which retains its original configuration. There is, however, one notable exception: Chapter 55 is conspicuously absent from the second book. Generally critics of the novel have either disregarded this omission or noted it without further comment. However, it is my contention that elision constitutes an affirmative gesture. What Cortázar leaves out of the second book reveals as much about his philosophy of art as what he inserts, and asserts, through the *Morelliana* of the third section. Absence is, in fact, a kind of presence, like the silences of John Cage's "experimental" music: "For in this new music nothing takes place but sounds: those that are notated and those that are not." If anti-literature represents, as Ihab Hassan would have it, "will and energy turned inside out" [*The Literature of Silence*], silence becomes, as in Cage, both an aperture and a form of expression. I would first like to explore here what Cortázar may very well have expressed through the exclusion, which I believe to be intentional, of chapter 55 from the second book of *Rayuela*. I will then attempt to clarify the often problematical relationship between the two books in light of the interdependence of "something and nothing"

From *International Fiction Review* 8, no. 1 (Winter 1981). © 1981 by the York Press.

(chapter 55 and the lack thereof), graphically illustrated by Cage in his "Lecture on Nothing":

			But
now		there are silences	and the
words	make	help make	the
silences			

It has been argued that silence is that perfect state beyond language and form toward which all literature strives. In *Le Degré zéro de l'écriture*, Roland Barthes insists that modernity begins with the search for an impossible literature. At one extreme of this search, the artist employs ancient and classical forms which he believes transcend History. At the other, he mines literary language and creates a chaos of form in order to deny History. Although Barthes suggests the possibility of a neutral state between these poles, the rationale of the latter school, to which Cortázar appears to belong, is of most interest here. According to Barthes, those writers who would free language from order, end by creating their own laws and defining new conventions for literary language. Their final recourse, as they flee this ever newly-created order, is silence. Thus, theirs is a language of suicide, of literature led to the gates of the promised land, defined by Barthes as "un monde sans littérature." Silence not only frees us from the restrictions of language and the burden of History but implies the existence of a world that has ceased to need literature. Ihab Hassan, who holds that art is a form of action, suggests that "perhaps the function of literature, after all, is not to clarify the world but to help create a world in which literature becomes superfluous." Bustrófedon, the voice of absence in Guillermo Cabrera Infante's *Tres tristes tigres*, embodies this future state of literature in his memoirs, "Algunas revelaciones," consisting of four blank pages—presumably the ultimate revelation.

Such silences at the center of the novel may signal optimism, the anticipation of a world in which language will no longer define the limits of imagination and form will no longer circumscribe art. Nonetheless, the literature of silence remains quite audible, sustaining itself at a mortal margin, according to Barthes, "pour mieux chanter sa nécessité de mourir." Blank pages and a world without literature aside, Cabrera Infante offers the following compromise through Bustrófedon: "si quieres alguna clase de posteridad . . . la grabas, así, y luego la borras, así (haciendo las dos cosas ese día, menos con las muestras pasadas) y todos contentos. ¿Todos? Yo no sé." This literature on the brink of silence, taped and immediately erased, seems to be a more viable alternative than total silence. In *Rayuela*, the absence of chapter 55 opens an abyss at the center of the second book, a promise or a threat of sustained silence. However, more important at present than the possibility of absolute silence is Cortázar's "salto hacia el silencio," which Octavio Paz identifies in *Corriente alterna*. Cortázar's handling of the omission of chapter 55 induces a metaphorical silence characteristic of a literature on the verge of abdication. In an effort toward understanding the mechanics of this omission, I would first like to examine the attitudes and the tendencies toward silence which lie at its roots.

In *The Literature of Silence,* Ihab Hassan identifies a specific current of negation at the heart of anti-literature: "The point is this: silence develops as a metaphor of a new attitude that literature has chosen to adopt toward itself. This attitude puts to question the peculiar power, the ancient excellence of literary discourse—and challenges the assumptions of our civilization." Accordingly, in response to some questions posed by Rita Guibert for *Life* magazine, Cortázar attacked the sanctity of History and the venerability of art. He discredited reverence for the presumed sacred and enduring qualities of the work of art, finding that as a form for preserving the past and as an object of preservation art reflects only the necessary deadness of tradition:

> By the way, for how long must we go on clinging to libraries? With every day that passes I realize more that those apparently obsolete ivory towers have all their floors right up to the roof occupied by a race of scholars who are horrified by any extraliterary invasion of literature, which they think of as the product of man's conformism, rather than the free gesture of Prometheus when he stole fire from the gorillas of his day. This brings me back again by analogy to the problem of a writer's "commitment" to his subjects, because the occupants of ivory towers turn as pale as death at the very idea of making a novel from situations or figures in contemporary history, their idea of literature being basically aseptic and uchronic, stretching out pathetically toward eternity and absolute and permanent values. *H*as for *h*instance the *Odyssey, h*as for *h*instance *Madame Bovary,* et cetera. Many writers, painters and musicians have stopped believing in such permanence, that books and art should be made to endure; although they go on writing or composing as well as they possibly can, they have given up any superstitious belief in a lasting object, which is really a bourgeois relic that is being liquidated by the increasingly vertiginous speed of history.

Cortázar stresses here the same necessity the surrealists felt for a revitalization of literary forms and language—only possible to the extent that a work is created to *not* endure. As a response to "spasmodic antics aimed at an increasingly improbable permanence," he constructs a novel opposed to permanence and rigid form, a novel which, like those works Barthes calls the great works of modernity, stops on the threshold of Literature. For, "Le Roman est une Mort; il fait de la vie un destin, du souvenir un act utile, et de la durée un temps dirigé et significatif." In order that the novel not be a death, it must become provisional, a tenuous human expression that stands at the brink of History. Cortázar therefore cultivates in

Rayuela a form that, like the game of hopscotch which the reading of the second book approximates, represents a constant process of improvisation and adaptation; the novel is an activity and not an end. It survives the speed of history by its refusal of History—its ability to mobilize its form and thereby continually accommodate itself to the demands of the moment. ("Difícil explicarle que cuanto más frágil y perecedero el armazón, más libertad para hacerlo y deshacerlo.")

Cortázar tells us through Morelli in the "capítulos prescindibles" that "sólo vale la materia en gestación." His statement will echo in Ihab Hassan's description of the use of improvisation as a metaphor for silence in the novel: "Finally, literature strives for silence by accepting chance and improvisation; its principle becomes indeterminacy. By refusing order, order imposed or discovered, this kind of literature refuses purpose. Its forms are non-telic; its world is the eternal present." Cortázar creates this eternal present in *Rayuela* by refusing to transmit a message or impose another well-wrought urn upon tradition. Because the novel exhibits a reverse entropy, ever tending toward order, the novelist may conscientiously reject order by focusing on the gestation of the novel, its ongoing creation and self-apprehension. Through its ability to generate new relationships between its elements and realize forms which are materially unachieved, *Rayuela* projects itself into the future. Its protean evasion of History is a form of silence. To further defeat the forces of Order, Cortázar demands a reader-accomplice who, in the act of reading, will create, through his transitory and unrepeatable experience of it, a new work at each moment. *Rayuela* therefore indicates the threshold to a maze of nearly unlimited combinations of meanings and potential personal interventions in the text and encourages the reader to "esperar lo inesperado." Emphasizing what may be possible rather than what the text actualizes, the novel functions through its ability to evolve instead of through its inherent rigidity of form.

Rayuela's capacity for improvisation and self-generation, manifested in its use of the game of hopscotch as a structural model, finds a revealing parallel in Cortázar's interest in music, and particularly jazz—a recurrent theme in the novel. Insofar as music operates in an essentially atemporal dimension, a *durée* which suspends external time to mark its own time, each note is an unrecoverable moment from which each successive note departs in an unforeseen direction. Writing on Cortázar, Malva Filer characterized jazz as not admitting definitive forms: "se da en él, por el contrario, la coincidencia de la creación y la ejecución en un solo momento de expresión libre e irrepetible" [*Homenaje a Julio Cortázar*]. Cortázar, like those writers described by Barthes who would deny History, strives for such a coincidence of creation and execution in an unrepeatable sequence. This underscores the fact that the novel, as Cortázar regards it, is neither sacred nor eternal, but a fugitive moment of conception which replaces historical time with a continual present on the verge of the future. Moreover, the work only endures to the extent that future readers particpate in this moment of simultaneous creation and expression. I offer the following to facilitate that complicity.

In a section of *La vuelta al día en ochenta mundos* called "Take it or leave it," Cortázar elaborates on the correspondence between jazz and his view of the ideal literature:

> Diferencia entre "ensayo" y *take*. El ensayo va llevando paulatinamente a la perfección, no cuenta como producto, es presente en función de futuro. En el *take* la creación incluye su propia crítica y por eso se interrumpe muchas veces para recomenzar; la insuficiencia o el fracaso de un *take* vale como un ensayo para el siguiente, pero el siguiente no es nunca el anterior en mejor, sino que es siempre otra cosa si realmente es bueno.
>
> Lo mejor de la literatura es siempre *take*, riesgo implícito en la ejecución, margen de peligro que hace el placer del volante, del amor, con lo que entraña de pérdida sensible pero a la vez con ese compromiso total que en otro plano da al teatro su inconquistable imperfección frente a perfecto cine.
>
> Yo no quisiera escribir más que *takes*.

Cortázar denies permanence and perfection here to emphasize performance and the necessary transcience of the literary vision. He further explains how, when a great jazzman dies, a record company will frequently produce, from its archives, a recording of several "takes" of one theme. Commenting on the implications of listening to a work in multiple variations of itself and, as it were, eavesdropping on the artist's interruptions and recommencements, Cortázar remarks on the power of the disc "que puede abrirnos la puerta del taller del artista, dejarnos asistir a sus avances, a sus caídas." This opening of the door on the artist's activity is comparable to what Cortázar attempts with chapter 55, which, while it may be purely coincidental, ends with this same word "caída." With this chapter, he offers the reader a sense of participating in the immediate creative process of the author, encouraging him to experience the novel as a performance and, as such, temporary rather than timeless. In the novel, all order is, as Barthes indicates, "un meurtre intentionnel." The eternal present and the margin of danger which are Cortázar's response to order represent a necessary step in the direction of silence.

In the first book of *Rayuela*, chapter 55 relates Traveler's insomnia on the night of Oliveira's descent with Talita to the morgue of the mental institution. Talita subsequently returns to discuss with Traveler Oliveira's imagined recovery, through her, of his missing Maga. In the second book, Cortázar omits the chapter itself but reconstructs it in chapters 129 and 133, which supply an additional detail from this same sleepless night in Traveler's reading of a plan by Ceferino Piriz for a society of nations. The first two sentences of chapter 55 are reproduced verbatim in the corresponding sentences of chapter 129. The second version of the third sentence ("El sillón de mimbre parecía más fresco que la cama y era una buena noche para seguir estudiando a Ceferino Piriz"), however, slightly amplifies the original ("El sillón de mimbre parecía más fresco que la cama y era una buena noche para quedarse leyendo"). Cortázar continues to make apparently arbitrary substitutions ("Talita se habría ido a trabajar a la farmacia" becomes "Talita se habría vuelto a su farmacia"), deletions ("De todas maneras era raro que Talita no hubiera vuelto de la farmacia" becomes " 'es raro que Talita no vuelva' "), and revisions (" 'Está tan contento de tener miedo esta noche, yo sé que está contento' " becomes " 'Está tan contento de tener miedo esta noche, yo sé que está contento en el fondo' "). While these otherwise unaccountable modifications do not appear to improve upon the prose, they do provide the reader with a sense of spying upon the creative activity of the author. The work no longer pretends to present a selected and definitive version but several variations on a theme designed to stress the project rather than the result. In keeping with the character of the "take," Cortázar does not alter the sequential order of the phrases as they appear in the first book. Moreover, every sentence of chapter 55 finds some form of representation in these "replacement" chapters: Chapter 129 includes the first three sentences of chapter 55, and the remainder appear in chapter 133. Ostensibly, the chapter from the first book figured as one possible performance of a piece of fiction, which Cortázar "replays" later with elaborations to demonstrate the plasticity of the novel, its capacity for improvisation and the marginality it would like to share with jazz. The embellishments of the second performance, notably the added material from Ceferino's paper, may be equivalent to the ad-lib of the jazz musician, or perhaps an intervening solo from a guest performer. In accordance with Cortázar's insistence that if a "take" is really good, it is not an improvement on the preceding execution but something different, these later chapters are not mere echoes of chapter 55 or critics of the novel, such as David William Foster who remarked without further explanation on the absence of chapter 55 from the table of directions, might have noted its duplication. As it stands, each succeeding chapter, like each "take," is at once a new experience and a repetition.

The same philosophy which inspired Cortázar's treatment of chapter 55 prompted, I believe, his publication in the *Revista Iberoamericana* of a suppressed chapter of *Rayuela* (originally 126) which he says essentially generated the first two sections. When he found upon completion of the novel that this "piedra fundamental" prematurely crystallized the process to which it subsequently gave birth, he attempted to remedy the situation by deleting the names of the characters, thus rendering the chapter ambiguous. When this proved unsuccessful, he reluctantly omitted it (replacing it with a citation that begins " 'Por qué, con tus encantamientos infernales, me has arrancado a la tranquilidad de mi primera vida . . .' "). He later offered it to the journal with the gaps remaining where the names of the characters had been erased and a note containing the following statement: "Hoy que *Rayuela* acaba de cumplir un decenio, y que Alfredo Roggiano y su admirable revista nos hacen a ella y a mí un tan generoso regalo de cumpleaños, me ha parecido justo agradecer con estas páginas, que nada pueden agregar (ni quitar, espero) a un libro que me contiene tal como fuí en ese tiempo de ruptura, de búsqueda, de pájaros." Cortázar's desire to thank his readers with an unedited manuscript, a key to the process of the novel's composition, shows to what extent he stresses the importance of the reader's ability to reconstruct the author's creative activity ("Así el lector podría llegar a ser copartícipe y copadeciente de la experiencia por la que pasa el novelista, *en el mismo momento y en la misma forma*") and provides a parallel to what he intended to accomplish within *Rayuela* through his treatment of chapter 55. He in fact insists on this opening of the door on the artist's activity as a means of rupturing the closed order toward which the novel tends.

I believe I have shown here that Cortázar's exclusion of chapter 55 constitutes an intentional and significant gesture. It opens a silence at the center of the novel and at the same time contributes toward the novel's leap in that direction by creating the improvisational and eternal present essential to its denial of History and repudiation of abiding values in the work of art. An acknowledgment of the importance of this omission must conduce to a reexamination of the relationship between the "two books" of *Rayuela*, to which it provides a valuable and perhaps intended key. Referring again to Cage's "Lecture on Nothing," we find that words make silences. Obviously chapter 55's absence in book two derives from its presence in the first book. Without its appearance, we have neither a discernible silence nor a privileged insight into the improvisational nature of the second book. This would indicate a necessary symbiosis of novel and antinovel.

A view of chapter 55 as a "take" and as an affirmative omission must lead, then, to an unequivocal conclusion about the interdependence of *Rayuela's* two books. However, in an article, "Notas sobre el 'Tablero de Dirección' en *Rayuela* de Julio Cortázar," which appeared in the abovementioned issue of the *Revista Iberoamericana* dedicated to Cortázar, Ken Holsten rightfully called attention to the fact that many critics of the novel have assumed that the author proposed a double reading of *Rayuela* when he had, quite emphatically in fact, indicated a choice between two approaches to the book. Holsten verified this by citing both the "Tablero de Dirección" and *La vuelta*, in which Cortázar makes the following statement:

En *Rayuela* definí y ataqué al lector-hembra, al incapaz de la verdadera batalla amorosa con una obra que sea como el ángel para Jacob. Si se dudara de la legitimidad de mi ofensiva, baste este ejemplo: críticos reputados con sede en Buenos Aires empezaron por no entender el doble sistema posible de lectura de la novela, y de ahí pasaron al *pollice verso* después de asegurar patéticamente

que la habían leído "de las dos maneras que indica el autor,"
cuando lo que proponía el pobre autor era una opción y jamás
hubiera tenido la vanidad de pretender que en nuestros tiempos
se leyera dos veces un mismo libro.

If the reader were to ignore the blatant irony of the last sentence and take
Cortázar's option literally, he would have to consider a single book within
whose limits he could not derive the desired effect from the reciprocal
relationship between chapter 55 and chapters 129 and 133 nor appreciate
the palpable silence at the heart of the second book. The silences of the
antinovel, both real and metaphorical, rely on the tradition of the novel.
Just as he labels essential chapters "prescindibles," Cortázar often proclaims
the opposite of what he means. Although he clearly states in the table of
directions and insists in *La vuelta* that he intends a choice between two
possible readings, he repeatedly draws the lessons of the second book from
the presence of the first, and a reexamination of the "option" offered to
the reader will demonstrate the absurdity of any choice between the two.

Cortázar in fact proposes in his table of instructions only the illusion
of an option, which for the active, or participating, reader grants less freedom than he otherwise may have felt. He offers this "choice" for the sole
purpose (as he admits) of singling out and attacking the passive reader,
whom such an unconventional proposition as the table of instructions will
already have discouraged from reading this novel. The female reader, as
the object of Cortázar's attack, is rather a component of the traditional
novel than an actual reader possibility. While Ken Holsten argues effica-
ciously for the merits of the second book, no self-respecting reader could
"choose" the first book with its "tres vistosas estrellitas que equivalen a la
palabra *Fin*" and the dispensable chapters which the author assures him
he can ignore with a clear conscience. Consequently, Cortázar has effectively eliminated rather than suggested an option. The logical result of the
fact that the first book never counted as an option is that it cannot then be
disregarded as such. Its purpose is not, as the author ironically claims in
his instructions, to provide an alternative for the traditional reader ("que
por lo demás no pasará de las primeras páginas, rudamente perdido y
escandalizado, maldiciendo lo que le costó el libro"), but rather to provide
the novel Cortázar's antinovel contains and to offer the assumptions about
literary orders that it cancels. The second book relies on the first book for
its condemnation of conventional plots, passive readers and numerically-
ordered systems as well as for its illustration of Cortázar's contention that
the best literature is always "take." The first book posits an order that the
second book ruptures, a plot that the second book makes irrelevant, and
a permanence that the second book undermines by altering its figurations
and exposing them as subject to the caprice of their creator.

Rayuela contains clues in addition to chapter 55 as to the indispensa-
bility of both books. As soon as the participating reader makes what must

be the obvious choice between the two systems offered by the author and begins the second book with chapter 73, he confronts the following argument, which he may apply to his act of selection: "El solo hecho de interrogarse sobre la posible elección vicia y enturbia lo eligible. . . . Parecería que una elección no puede ser dialéctica, que su planteo la empobrece, es decir la falsea, es decir la transforma en otra cosa." At this point, the reader, if he has taken the author at his word, has already made such a dialectical election between the two methods of reading and thereby impoverished the possibilities of his options. Nonetheless, based upon the system Cortázar has established, he cannot "choose" the first book in the manner in which it has been offered to the passive reader. His situation has become impossible: the author has extended him a non-option disguised as a choice and subsequently reproached him, in effect, for the act of selecting the inevitable. Only by transcending the either/or principle of Western rationalism which Cortázar criticizes throughout *Rayuela* can he solve his dilemma. While electing to disregard the first book, he must simultaneously read it, thus extricating himself from the dialectics of what Octavio Paz has called the Western world of " 'esto o aquello' " and entering the Eastern world of " 'esto y aquello' y aun de 'esto es aquello.' " *Rayuela* and the antinovel operate within this seemingly self-contradictory world in which art sings of its necessity to die. Anti-literature is literature nevertheless, but it is radically ironic in that it attacks the form and the language it employs. The reader must therefore, like the antinovel, live with conflict and read the first book in order to understand the novel which he must "elect" to not read.

A consideration of the premises of the antinovel and its relationship to the novel will further testify to the impossibility of an option between the two as they are represented in book two and book one, respectively. Jean-Paul Sartre first formulated a definition of the antinovel in a preface to Nathalie Sarraute's *Portrait d'un inconnu:* "Les anti-romans conservent l'apparence et les contours du roman; ce sont des ouvrages d'imagination qui nous présentent des personnages fictifs et nous racontent leur histoire. Mais c'est pour mieux décevoir: il s'agit de contester le roman par lui-même, de le détruire sous nos yeux dans le temps qu'on semble l'édifier, d'écrire le roman d'un roman qui ne se fait pas, qui ne peut pas se faire." Insofar as it does conserve the appearance of the novel, the antinovel does not constitute a true alternative to the traditional novel. As Roland Barthes points out in *Le Degré zéro de l'écriture*, literature of negation comes to define its own tradition. Literature as well as anti-literature are forms of order. The alternative to art is consequently not anti-art, but silence, and to promote its own eventual absence, the novel must contest and cancel *itself* ("¿Para qué sirve un escritor si no para destruir la literatura?"). For this reason book two both contains book one and stands in relation to it; the first book is the object of an activity for which it provides the components. Unless one selects the former, there is no choice between novel and antinovel: the second book is written in terms *of* and *in* the terms of the first. The antinovel is a novel engaged in a particular activity—deconstruction carried on as a form of composition ("Sé el volumen o el tono de la obra pueden llevar a creer que el autor intentó una suma, apresurarse a señalarle que está ante la tentativa contraria, la de una resta implacable"). Book one is the quantity from which book two "subtracts as it pursues a process that adds to its volume while undermining the foundations of Art." The goal of this subtraction is a silence and an openness beyond the reach of literature, briefly glimpsed in the absence of chapter 55.

Movement and Stasis, Film and Photo: Temporal Structures in the Recent Fiction of Julio Cortázar

Lois Parkinson Zamora

Ah, art
is fro
zen Zen.
—JONATHAN WILLIAMS

Argentine novelist and short-story writer Julio Cortázar constantly employs visual media to test and measure his own verbal medium. Unlike many of his Latin American contemporaries—for example, Borges, Fuentes, Vargas Llosa—whose aesthetic context is primarily literary and whose work is often self-consciously and conspicuously related to particular verbal traditions, whether fictional or metaphysical, Cortázar's fiction is oriented by an optic aesthetic. His fiction often not only alludes to the visual arts but also strives to reiterate their visual structures on the printed page. It is therefore fitting, perhaps, that the best known of Cortázar's short stories, "Las babas del diablo" ("Blow-Up"), is so by virtue of the film inspired by it, and fitting as well that few fiction/film relations have received more academic attention, from critics of both film and literature. "Blow-Up" is the story of a static image that becomes irrationally mobile: the arrested past of photograph is converted into the moving present of film in the mind's eye of the narrator, and the syntactic structure and tempo of the narration reflect the change. The shift from photo to film, Cortázar implies, allows the narrator to approach, at least temporarily, a medium flexible enough to express a constantly changing and hence unstable world. A more recent story, "Apocalipsis en Solentiname" ("Apocalypse at Solentiname"), reiterates this transformation of a static image into a moving progression of images and again suggests the narrator's essential perception of the mobility latent in all form. In the discussion that follows, however, it is *not* this transformation of the fixed into the mobile, of photo into film, which I wish to consider, but what might be said to be its contrary. In several recent works, Cortázar interrupts or terminates a serial movement of images with a fixed

From *The Review of Contemporary Fiction* 3, no. 3 (1983). © 1983 by *The Review of Contemporary Fiction*.

image, a still shot, in order to manipulate the temporal structure of the work and comment upon the nature of time itself.

In "Fin de etapa" ("Stopping Place") and "Deshoras" ("Bad Timing"), from Cortázar's most recent collection of short fiction, *Deshoras* (1983), what I will call the narrative technique of arrested serial movement serves to define the characters' relation to their own historicity, to their own mortality (to the inevitable image of the immobile self, the still shot which waits at the end of the moving temporal medium called life). Both stories use static images which may be understood in terms of photography, especially in terms of the aesthetics of photography proposed by the late Roland Barthes in his last work, *Camera Lucida.* Cortázar creates verbal analogies of film and photograph which define the movement of the narration and bear in particular on the closural devices of each story. Whereas the author uses the arrested image for purposes of psychological revelation in "Fin de etapa" and "Deshoras," it becomes a means of conveying political significance in "Queremos tanto a Glenda" ("We Love Glenda So Much," in the collection of the same title, 1983), and the novel *Libro de Manuel* (*A Manual for Manuel*, 1973). In this second pair of works, I will suggest that Cortázar uses film and photograph not only to structure his narration but his political vision as well.

In "Fin de etapa" (literally the end of a stage or leg of a journey, a job, a life, more freely translated as "Stopping Place"), Cortázar explores the contradiction inherent in the term "still life." The phrase in Spanish— *naturaleza muerta,* "dead nature"—portrays that contradiction from a slightly different point of view, but in both languages, the tension between movement and stasis, continuation and termination, is evident, as it is in Cortázar's story. A woman on a car trip who has planned the trip and her life in symmetrical *etapas,* stages, stops for lunch in a town along her route. To kill time, she enters a museum where she sees exhibited large still lifes of empty rooms, or rooms with bare tables or a single male figure, his back turned to the viewer. At first the woman, whose name is Diana, thinks that they are photographs, so realistic are the paintings. The character dismisses her vague uneasiness at their uncanny realism by telling herself: "al fin y al cabo había tantos artistas que copiaban exactamente sus modelos, tantas mesas de este mundo habían acabado en el Louvre o en el Metropolitan duplicando realidades vueltas polvo y olvido" ("after all there were so many artists who copied exactly their models, so many tables of this world had ended up in the Louvre or the Metropolitan, duplicating realities which had long since turned to dust and had been forgotten"). The statement is revealing, for we will see that her attraction to these still lifes lies precisely in their stillness: the implicit contrast between her reality, lived in stages which move serially in time and space on the one hand, and the immobilized world of the paintings on the other, becomes explicit as the plot develops.

The relationship of reality to this "hyper-realistic" art, as the woman labels it, is increasingly the focus of narrative attention. When the museum closes for the lunch hour, the character leaves behind the pictures of the house, only to come upon the house itself. The woman senses her double perspective as she approaches the house which she recognizes so clearly: she seems to be on both sides of the canvas at once, approaching the real house from outside and standing inside the rooms in the paintings. She is both observer and participant, as is Andrés in *Libro de Manuel,* whom I will discuss subsequently in similar terms. She enters the house and sits at a bare table: only the smoke rising from her cigarette separates the scene in the room from the still lifes in the museum. After lunch, she returns almost compulsively to the museum to see one last painting which she had not seen in the morning. At this point, the immobile world of the still life and the reality of the woman merge beyond all doubt or coincidence. In the painting, at the table where Diana has just sat, now sits a painted female figure, "su inmovilidad inexplicablemente más intensa que la fijación de las cosas y los seres en los otros cuadros" ("her immobility inexplicably more intense than the fixity of the things and people in the other paintings"). The woman in the painting appears to be dead. Although Diana tries to reestablish her own mobility, speeding out of town in her car, she feels an undeniable compulsion to turn around and go back. As she reenters the house, which now *is* the still life, her own life is also stilled: the story ends, as she sits with a lit cigarette in the empty house, with the words: "la luz inmóvil como todo el resto, como ella y como el humo inmóviles" ("the light immobile like everything else, immobile like her and the smoke"). So her visit to the museum does in fact kill time: we know there will be no more stages.

That Cortázar embodies his character's desire to escape time's movement, by making her a part of a static visual image described as photographic, links this story in obvious ways to Roland Barthes' *Camera Lucida.* Barthes insists that the primary characteristic of any photograph is the immobility of its temporal content; the photograph interposes itself in history's flow, snatching people and objects out of time, serving as unmediated proof of a past without apparent relation to any future. The photograph states quite simply, *"That-has-been."* Barthes says that there is no future in the photograph, a fact which lends to every photograph an air of pathos, melancholy. In Cortázar's story, the woman seems impelled by a similar perception: she is attracted to, and ultimately embraces, the death which she intuits in the pictures. For this character, as for Barthes, photographic images are our modern substitute for monuments to the dead.

Although Barthes may emphasize the static quality, the *memento mori* element of the photo, almost to the exclusion of other characteristics (*Camera Lucida* was written as the author contemplated photos of his beloved mother, who had recently died), there are famous photographers whose emphasis is strikingly similar. Lewis Hine speaks of photographs as the "human document to keep the present in touch with the past," a statement more political and social than aesthetic; Danny Lyon says, "There is something so dead about a photograph, something so akin to a record in a file cabinet, however beautiful, that if I did not keep making new ones, I could hardly stand looking at them. I want them to speak, to smell, to live and die as we must do." If Hine's statement is polemical, Lyon's is personal, but both nonetheless reflect and support Roland Barthes' observations, and support as well the illusion of truncated time which Cortázar conveys in his story by means of the photographic still lifes.

Cortázar's narrative style in "Fin de etapa" seems itself to aspire to that of still life. The tone and spatial descriptions of the third-person narration are as bare as the paintings, and as motionless. The lines and angles of the rooms, the rectangular shadows on the floor, and the symmetrical placement of the few isolated objects seem inspired by a very solid geometry. Even the rays of yellow light are described as a solid substance which weighs upon the surfaces where it falls. What movement there is in the story is devoid of volition, hypnotic, floating in slow motion: the woman slips along the sidewalk as if on a conveyor belt, explanations "without handles" slip away from her (in both cases, the verb is *resbalar*, to slip), and when she tries to drive away from the town, "el cuerpo se tendía hacia atrás como resistiendo al avance" ("her body leaned backward as if to resist advancing"). Like the other stories and the novel with which I am concerned here, the narrative ending of "Fin de etapa" reinforces the temporal end which it describes. The final sentence of the story, like Barthes' photographs, instantly transforms a living person into a melancholy image, motionless and futureless.

In his review of a book of photographs of psychiatric patients by photographers Sara Facio and Alicia D'Amico, Cortázar writes that "la locura es un sueño que se fija" ("madness is a dream that becomes fixed"), and he finds the photographic medium perfect for recording that fixity. Again, Barthes' vision is consonant with Cortázar's, for Barthes too proposes a link between photography and madness. The paradoxical temporality of the photograph, the seeming presence of the now absent person, the illusory vitality of the non-existent moment, plus the fixed, hence hallucinatory, gaze of the photographed subject, lead Barthes to conclude that the photograph is a "mad image, chafed by reality." Cortázar, concluding his discussion with similar language, cites a line from the poetry of Homero Manzi: the photos, Cortázar writes, are "el último gesto frente al paisaje final e instantáneo de la demencia" ("the ultimate gesture before the final and instantaneous landscape of dementia"). The phrase may well describe as well the photographic landscape of "Fin de etapa," into which the character slips and stays.

The title story in Cortázar's most recent collection also contemplates the possibility of immobility in life and art. In "Deshoras," film and photo are not explicitly mentioned, but these visual media are nonetheless present, structurally and thematically. This is a story of the temporal dislocation which results when the static images of memory intrude upon and eventually blot out the phenomenological flux of the experiencing eye. The narrator begins by asking himself a series of questions: Are the images of the remembered past, which he will subsequently recount, in fact worth remembering and recounting? How will he translate those images into words? And why should he want to anyway? In the first few sentences, the narrator refers to his desire for *continuity* between past and present, and yet he seems to contradict himself, for he also speaks of *immobilizing* the images of memory in words: "las ponía en palabras para fijarlas a mi manera" ("I was putting them into words to fix them in my own way"). The contradiction becomes acute as he looks back to his past, regrets its unrealized possibilities and retrospectively imputes a future to that past which never was, nor ever can be. In particular, Sara, the object of his adolescent fantasy, occupies his mind's eye. His static images of her are less remembered than invented by the narrator, then framed with words like a faded daguerreotype. His narration of recurring childhood experiences resolves itself into a single, timeless image of sexual culmination, "una noche que las palabras irían llenando de sábanas y caricias" ("a night that words would continue to fill with sheets and caresses"), the image of his unfulfilled desire. It is, to use Roland Barthes' phrase about photography, "prophecy in reverse," a complex and troublesome mixture of hindsight and projection. Although it seems likely that only in images can the past be captured and held, it is the obsessive focus of the narrator which is at issue. This static image from an imaginary past imposes itself on the moving present and in some sense obviates future potentiality: when his wife Felisa and his children invade his fantasy, bringing him back to the present, the narrator asks himself desperately, "pero cómo seguir ya?" ("but how can I go on?"). The question is not rhetorical: like "Fin de etapa," this story ends with the cessation of the character's temporal movement. Thus fixity engenders fixation, and vice versa: the character is immobilized in the past, by and with his image of Sara.

The narrator's account of his childhood in the provincial town of Bánfield is not all static; in fact the immobility of the images of Sara is what sets them apart from the rest of the remembered scenes. The blissfully schedule-free holidays, the seemingly endless days of boyhood activity, the perennial activities with his friend, Doro, Sara's brother, are recounted in the imperfect tense and are interspersed with the word *siempre* (always):

> Y el verano, siempre, el verano de las vacaciones, la libertad de los juegos, el tiempo solamente de ellos, para ellos, sin horario ni campana para entrar a clase, el olor del verano en el aire caliente de las tardes y las noches, en las caras sudadas después de ganar o perder o pelearse o correr, de reírse y a veces de llorar pero siempre juntos, siempre libres. . . .

> (And summer, always, summer vacation, the freedom of their games, time belonging to them, existing for them alone, without schedule or bells to call them to class, the smell of summer on the

warm air of the afternoons and evenings, on the sweaty faces after
winning or losing or fighting or running, laughing and sometimes
crying but always together, always free. . . .)

Although it might be argued that the passage creates the effect of a single,
unchanging image by virtue of the repetition of the described activities, in
fact the overriding impression is not of stasis but of continuance, of predictable temporal movement. But, the narrator tells us at the outset of the
story, the continuous companionship of Doro is only a pretext for his fixed
focus on "the image of his older sister, the image of Sara."

The iterative series of the narrator's summer activities is interrupted
and eventually halted by the singulative image of Sara. The narrator specifically uses the word "image" to refer to his memories of her, and he
describes them as if they were separate objects, glasslike, blindingly bright,
"de una precisión cortante bajo el sol del verano de Bánfield" ("of cutting
precision beneath the summer sun of Bánfield"). They are sharp enough
to hurt him, he tells his reader, and powerful enough to stop time—the
sun of Bánfield—itself. I will mention in my subsequent discussion of *Libro
de Manuel* that one of the narrators in that novel expresses his desire to
manipulate narrative and temporal movement by "stopping the film"; in
this story too we sense that narrative impulse. Roland Barthes, in his discussion of the special temporality of the photograph, compares the *passé
composé* of the photograph to the present progressive of film: whereas the
movies carry the inherent presumption that the human experience surrounding the cinematic world continues, even extends, that world in a
constitutive fashion, a photograph proposes not the continuation of the
image into its surrounding context but its isolation, its inherent self-
containment. For Barthes, the photographic image is complete, framed, as
the movies are not. The characters who walk off the screen continue to
live, according to Barthes, whereas the people in photographs cannot leave
their enclosure: "They are anaesthetized and fastened down, like butterflies." Barthes' comments bear upon the activity of Cortázar's narrator in
"Deshoras," for the character wants to stop visual movement, to "fasten
down" his immobile image of Sara. We see that his description of the
temporal unfolding of his activities in Bánfield contrasts sharply with what
he refers to as his "isolated image" of Sara. He wants to verify and confirm
his memory—his love—by removing the image of his beloved from the
flow of his past, by stopping time altogether. The narrator conforms to
Barthes' description: by depriving Sara's images of successiveness, he hopes
to prevent her life from extending beyond those summers in Bánfield when
he knew her. So he fosters the illusion that he possesses her completely,
that she neither has, nor has ever had, any life outside of his mental image
of her.

Of course this narrator is translating the visual into the verbal, images
into sentences, a fact which complicates considerably his relationship to

the remembered past. Like the movies, narration is necessarily a serial process, words like cinematic frames following one another in a progression which is both temporal and spatial. It is perhaps for this reason that the narrator must work so feverishly to authenticate his static image of Sara, and why he fails to do so. Barthes points to the contradiction between the written text and the photographic image: "In the image . . . the object yields itself wholly, and our vision of it is *certain*—contrary to the text or to other perceptions which give me the object in a vague, arguable manner." He continues that, whereas the photograph does not invent but is rather "authentification itself," language is by nature fictional, and attempts to render it unfictional require apparatus of measurement, such as logic or sworn oath. (It is in this context of authentification, in fact, that Barthes invokes *Blow-Up*.) So the polymorphous and polysemic nature of language, as well as the very seriality of its form, inevitably betrays the static image into which the narrator hopes to frame the world.

If the two stories I have just discussed use film and photo implicitly, the next two works use them quite explicitly. "Queremos tanto a Glenda" ("We Love Glenda So Much") is a story about cinematic movement and its forced cessation, and in *Libro de Manuel* there are explicit references to movies which provide both thematic and structural models within the novel. In "Queremos tanto a Glenda," Cortázar's first-person narrator describes a group of admirers of the films of the movie actress Glenda Garson. So devoted are they to her work that when she retires, they quietly go about the business of collecting all the copies of all her films and editing them to conform to their conception of Glenda's art. They cut scenes which they consider to be inferior, substitute sequences, change their order. Through these activities, which the narrator refers to as their "mission," the fans achieve the contradictory end they desire: static perfection in a mobile medium. Like the narrator of "Deshoras," they wish to possess completely the object of their desire, so they, like he, impose on a moving series their own unchanging image, to arrive at "la última imagen de Glenda en la última escena de la última película" ("Glenda's last image in the last scene of the last movie"). So Glenda's fans reject the inherent variations in her movies in favor of the static image behind those variations that will be free from the vagaries of temporal transformation. They seek, in other words, to deny the most basic aspect of film: its temporal unfolding, its *moving* pictures. They are lured by the illusory promise of cinematic perfection, of a changeless and hence controllable ideal.

The finality of their image of Glenda is threatened, however, when Glenda announces that she will come out of retirement to make more films. The narrator, one of her most devout fans, sighs, "un poeta había dicho bajo los mismos cielos de Glenda que la eternidad está enamorada de las obras del tiempo" ("a poet had said under Glenda's same skies that eternity is in love with the works of time"). Although murder is never mentioned, the reader is given to understand that her disciples will not tolerate any disruption of the static image which they have created. Their only means of assuring perfection is to stop time, or at least the lifetime of Glenda: "Queríamos tanto a Glenda que le ofreceríamos una última perfección inviolable" ("We loved Glenda so much that we would offer her one last inviolable perfection"). So movie star becomes motionless icon. The story concludes with an appropriately medieval devotional tone: "En la altura intangible donde la habíamos exaltado, la preservaríamos de la caída, sus fieles podrían seguir adorándola sin mengua; no se baja vivo de una cruz" ("On the untouchable heights to which we had raised her in exaltation, we would save her from the fall, her faithful could go on adoring her without any decrease; one does not come down from a cross alive").

Because of their desire to suppress divergences from their own unanimously held ideal, the group and their spokesman (who narrates in the first-person plural) inevitably appear to assume an ideological stance. Their ideology is most apparent in the narrator's attitude toward movement and stasis, and in the images he uses to embody that attitude. In referring both to Glenda's acting and the group's actions, he uses the word "rhythm": Glenda's films are revised in order to provide her with "el ritmo perfecto" and their own common activity is described in terms of a heart or an airplane, "ritmando una coherencia perfecta." It is clear that for the narrator and the group he represents, movement does not imply variety or innovation but rather *regular repetition*: the unexpected, the idiosyncratic, or individualistic are *not* to be permitted. The narrator's careless mixture of the human and the mechanical to describe the group's movement—a heart or an airplane—leads to another almost predictable image, that of mechanical movement gone awry. If Glenda makes more movies, the group's machine will break: "el horror estaba en la máquina rota, en la realidad de cifras y prestigios y Oscares entrando como una fisura solapada en la esfera de nuestro cielo tan duramente ganado" ("The horror was in the ruptured mechanism, in the reality of figures and awards and Oscars entering our so hard-won heaven like a hidden fissure"). The predictable unison of the group's falsification (stylistically embodied in the rhythmic repetition of the phrase, "queremos tanto a Glenda") cannot coexist with the unpredictability of individualized reality: resumption of movement on Glenda's part implies cessation of theirs. So, they tell themselves, they have no choice: though the narrator's insinuation that they will eliminate their opposition is insidiously indirect, it is clear enough. The distinction between "fan" and "fanatic" begins to blur: the implications of blind devotion, uncritical commitment, are necessarily social and political as well as aesthetic.

Cortázar is well known for his creation of fictional atmosphere laden with unspecific but nonetheless palpable terror. If such atmosphere was created in his early stories by probing the deepest layers of the unconscious, in his more recent fiction, political tyranny and social injustice are often the sources of the fear and violence latent beneath life's surface. In a recent interview, Cortázar referred to a personal turning point caused by his awareness of the Cuban Revolution, a turning point which is clearly reflected in the increased political content of his fiction. In the stories written since the early seventies, personal and psychological elements often carry social and political significance. Indeed, it is often the sheer imbalance between the vulnerability of the individual and the power of the political machinery which creates the atmosphere of terror to which I have referred. Thus, stories which can be fruitfully read on a psychological or aesthetic level may yield political insights when submitted to scrutiny: in Cortázar's recent fiction, private life may well unmask the metaphysics of politics, and vice versa. Such is the case in "Queremos tanto a Glenda."

The insistence of Glenda's fans on a single, unchanging aesthetic is implicitly related to social and political repression. The narrator speaks derisively of differences of opinion, of moral objections within the group itself ("analytical voices contaminated by political philosophies"), but he assures the reader that such "heresy" has been eradicated. And when certain moviegoers protest that they remember Glenda's films differently, the narrator dismisses public memory as fickle and transitory: "la gente es frívola y olvida o acepta o está a la caza de lo nuevo, el mundo del cine es fugitivo como la actualidad histórica, salvo para los que queremos tanto a Glenda" ("people are fickle and forget or accept or are in search of what's new, the movie world is ephemeral, like the historical present, except for those of us who love Glenda so much"). Once more, a seemingly careless narrative juxtaposition—the movie world and historical reality—is highly significant, for the relationship between the group's cinematic revisionism and the historical revisionism practiced by repressive political regimes in our century thus becomes apparent. The group's manipulation of the public memory of Glenda's art, and hence their manipulation of its very existence in the past, has strong political resonance. As the fans modify cinematic images to conform to their requirements, so dictatorship often has attempted to revise reality by depriving people of their relationship to the remembered past and to the "ephemeral" temporal continuum of human history, whether individual or collective. The group's editing suggests governmental censorship, and their vision of aesthetic totality suggests totalitarianism.

Cortázar has lived for thirty years in France, an exile at first by choice but in the past decade, without choice, because of his opposition to the military regime in Argentina. It is interesting that another exiled artist, the Czech writer Milan Kundera, indicts political repression with a photographic image similar to Cortázar's in this story. Although Kundera's political stance is more explicit than Cortázar's, as is his assignment of political significance to the images of memory, his insights bear cogently on the identity and activity of Glenda's fans.

Kundera begins his brilliant work of literary and political dissidence, *The Book of Laughter and Forgetting,* with the description of a photograph from which the figure of a discredited Czech leader has been airbrushed into oblivion by the revisionist historians of the Communist Party. Of the agents of this revisionism, Kundera's narrator says, "They are fighting for access to the laboratories where photographs are retouched and biographies and histories re-written." Despite what would seem to be their different positions on the political spectrum, both Cortázar and Kundera describe political repression in terms of the imposition of a static image of retouched reality upon the vertiginous movement of history.

For Kundera, the images of memory are the essence of individual and national identity, reference points in the flow of time which differentiate among human beings and cultures. The self is everything we remember, so when the past is intentionally distorted or destroyed, the distinctions among people and nations are necessarily obliterated. Kundera writes that the prophet of a world without memory was Franz Kafka. In his novels, Prague is a city with no memory, Joseph K. a man with no previous life: "Time in Kafka's novel is the time of a humanity that has lost all continuity with humanity, of a humanity that no longer knows anything nor remembers anything, that lives in nameless cities with nameless streets or streets with names different from the ones they had yesterday, because a name means continuity with past and people without a past are people without a name." It is in a similar context—the discussion of the uniqueness of the human face—that another exiled Slavic novelist [Vladimir Nabokov] has his artist-character say, "What the artist perceives is, primarily, the *difference* between things. It is the vulgar who note their resemblance." The forced homogenization, the imposed unanimity—aesthetic, political, personal— of the repressive regimes which he experienced was for Vladimir Nabokov the basis of all other abuses and the frequent object of his subtle novelistic satire.

Cortázar's characters in "Queremos tanto a Glenda" are nameless and faceless: their lack of individualized features and specific names suggests both the stereotyping effects of their goal of absolute unanimity and their methods of attaining that goal. Of course one might argue that the characters in Cortázar's stories are often nameless; so cerebral and psychological is the fictive interaction among many of them that the sociological name tag is irrelevant. Here, however, the characters seem to have willfully assumed masks without features in order to dissemble their insidious activity. The characters' anonymity is a principal source of the atmosphere of vaguely defined malignity that pervades the story.

The retouched image of reality which Glenda's fans create is of course called by quite another name in the story: the narrator refers repeatedly to the "perfection" which the group seeks. Revision, falsification, intolerance, even murder, are justified in the present for the sake of future "perfection." The narrator explains that "queríamos tanto a Glenda que por encima y más allá de las discrepancias éticas o históricas imperaba el sentimiento que siempre nos uniría, la certidumbre de que el perfeccionamiento de Glenda nos perfeccionaba y perfeccionaba el mundo" ("we loved Glenda so much that above and beyond ethical or historical disagreements the feeling that would always unite us remained, the certainty that perfecting Glenda was perfecting us and perfecting the world"). What event or idea or person cannot be dismissed as an "ethical or historical discrepancy" if it should happen to conflict with the group's definition of perfection? If it should happen to jostle their static ideal? Again, Milan Kundera's literary vision bears resemblance to Cortázar's, for Kundera describes the abuses spawned by inflexible idealism, dogmatic utopianism, in similar terms: "Totalitarianism is not only hell, but also the dream of paradise—the age-old dream of where everybody would live in harmony, united by a single common will and faith. . . . If totalitarianism did not exploit these archetypes [of paradise] which are deep inside us all and rooted deep in all religions, it could never attract so many people, especially during the early phases of its existence." Whether it is the "rulers of paradise," as Kundera ironically calls the contemporary Czech leaders about whom he writes, or Glenda's fans who attempt to impose iconic perfection onto the past or the future, they do violence to the multiplicity and variability—the "fissures" and "discrepancies"—of temporal reality.

The word "perfection" by definition contains the notion of unanimity and temporal stasis. Words which suggest change over a period of time— progress, growth, development, decay—are in some sense its opposite. Such definition is rooted in Judeo-Christian myth, which proposes that perfect worlds are necessarily outside of time altogether: on either side of history lie the eternal realms of Eden and the New Jerusalem. ("Eternal" does not mean "endless" or "forever," as we often misuse it, but rather "atemporal," "timeless.") Christian history moves toward a point where "time shall cease," according to St. John of Patmos in his apocalyptic vision of the end of time. Because temporal and spatial immobility inhere in such versions of perfection, those who would embody perfection in political or aesthetic form are particularly interested in the nature of ends and endings, in the consummation of their ideal, in the terminal point of time or form. Cortázar's narrator emphasizes "la obra cumplida" ("the completed, accomplished work"), the "última perfección inviolable" ("the last, inviolable perfection"), and the narrative structure supports that emphasis.

In the last phrase of the story, ending and end, form and content seem to coincide, for the finality of the image, placed in the final structural position of the narration, reinforces the group's search for timeless ultimacy: "no se baja vivo de una cruz" ("one does not come down from a cross alive"). The image justifies the Christian interpretive context in which I have placed the group's fanatic idealism: that the crucifixion image is applied to a contemporary movie star emphasizes the inversions and perversions of such fanaticism; that it is used to conclude the story serves as ironic reinforcement of the finality of the group's intentions and of the story itself, for the crucifixion is, in its usual Christian context, a symbol of the negation of death, of the subversion of finality. If the cross traditionally represents an end which is also and more importantly a beginning, here Cortázar skillfully manipulates the meaning of the symbol to imply its opposite. The forceful closure of the narrative structure, like the group's activity, seems calculated to deny any illusion of temporal continuance, either within the fictional world or beyond it. It is for this reason that the epilogue to the story, published in *Deshoras* three years after the story itself, comes as something of a surprise.

"Epilogo a un cuento" ("Epilogue to a Story") takes the form of a letter to Glenda Jackson, the avowed model for Glenda Garson, and is labeled with place and date, Berkeley, California, September 29, 1980, where in fact Cortázar was teaching at the time. The writer of the letter, purportedly Cortázar himself, sits in the same position as the narrator of "Blow-Up," in front of his window, his hands poised above the keys of his typewriter. And like the narrator of "Blow-Up," this narrator, in an ironic assault on his own story, considers the problematic enterprise of detaining a moving medium, whether film, narration, or human history.

In his letter, the narrator recounts his story to Glenda Jackson, emphasizing the dialectic between movement and stasis which I have discussed. He reiterates his character's retirement in terms of the group's ideal of arrested movement, her retirement "clausurando y perfeccionando sin saberlo una labor que la reiteración y el tiempo hubieran terminado por mancillar" ("bringing to a close and perfecting without knowing it a labor which repetition and time had ultimately sullied"). He describes the group's opposition to Glenda's return in similar terms, explaining that the group is determined to maintain the image which they have created, "clausurado, definitivo." But, writes Cortázar to Glenda Jackson, the continuity of life undermines the finality of fiction. A film called *Hopscotch*, in which she stars, has appeared just after the publication of "Queremos tanto a Glenda," as if to defy the absolute end which the story proposes: that the new film should have the same title as his most highly regarded novel seems to Cortázar to add force to the defiance. As Glenda Jackson's film undoes the fictional seal on Glenda Garson's art, so Cortázar's epilogue reverses the finality of his story, calling into question the desirability—indeed, the possibility—of fixity in any art form, of complete closure in any aesthetic structure. The epilogue ends with a reference to Glenda's next movie.

The narrative uses to which Cortázar puts film and photo in his extended novelistic structure, *Libro de Manuel*, are more varied and complex than in the short stories that I have discussed so far. For example, these visual media are allusive in ways they are not in the stories. Repeated reference is made to a movie by German director Fritz Lang, and though the movie is not named, the description of the plot given by the principal character, Andrés, suggests Lang's 1931 masterpiece, *M*. Whereas Cortázar's reference to Glenda Jackson carries little allusive weight (any movie star, male or female, would have served the purposes of his plot), his reference to Fritz Lang's art is particularly suggestive in this most avowedly political of Cortázar's novels. For reasons of political context as well as aesthetic structure, Andrés cannot stop dreaming Lang's movie.

The films of Fritz Lang may be considered representative of the political and social orientation of art during the Weimar period in Germany, from 1919 to 1933. If the French avant-garde movement before 1914 established the aesthetic values and forms which predominate even up to our own times, it was Germany in the 1920s that experimented with the social applications of that avant-garde aesthetic. Concern for the social relevance and purposeful economic application of the arts was typical of artists and intellectuals during the Weimar period, and politics was often closely, if not always felicitously, linked to the arts. In the relatively new, technological media of photography and film, there was much visual experimentation which carried political implications. Photography was providing entirely new images of reality, the camera an instrument of social criticism available even to the oppressed classes of society who were also its frequent object. And silent film, perhaps the most international of contemporary media, affected more people than any other art form. Of inestimable documentary and propaganda importance, films often treated specific political and social situations. Bertolt Brecht, to whom I will return, deals in his one authentic film, *Kuhle Wampe* (1932), with an immediately topical subject, the Berlin unemployed, and in his plays, of course, with a variety of current material. Fritz Lang, in his autobiography, summarizes the generally held attitude of the time toward the proper relationship of art and reality: "I believe in artistic rebellion. I think new approaches, new forms are needed to reflect the changed world we live in." And yet the artistic rebellion of Weimar culture can never be dissociated from its terrible sequel of repression. It was in part the impending disaster of Nazism which gave impetus to artistic experimentation, with its social and political orientation, and it was also Nazism which brutally halted such experiments. *Libro de Manuel,* like much Weimar art, was produced in response to a particular situation of political and social repression. By alluding to Lang, Cortázar allies his novel to a tradition of formally experimental *and* politically committed art (in his preface, he dismisses social realism as a viable possibility for his political fiction). He also allies his work to a highly problematic historical and national context in which artistic commitment was both difficult and essential, as Cortázar feels it to be in contemporary Latin America as well.

Andrés is an Argentine, and supposedly a member of a Latin American revolutionary group operating in Paris. His relationship to the group is in fact highly ambiguous, for he is both inside and outside the group, an observer and a participant, withholding commitment yet committed despite himself. His Fritz Lang dream suggests Bertolt Brecht's concept of alienation. For Brecht, art must be structured to provide an objective external viewpoint on the action; it must prevent, by formal means, the emotional identification of the viewer or reader (i.e., it must alienate him) in order to engage his intellect and ultimately inspire political and social commitment.

Andrés tells a friend about the experience of the dream: "estoy actuando a la vez como por dentro y por fuera del film de Fritz Lang . . . soy doble, alguien que fue al cine y alguien que está metido en un lío típicamente cinematográfico" ("I'm acting simultaneously inside and outside the Fritz Lang movie . . . I'm double, someone who went to the movies and someone caught up in a typical movie plot"). With the heavy-handed symbolism more typical of dreams than of Cortázar's fiction, a Cuban man waits purposefully and patiently for the dreaming Andrés. It is only on the night of the violent encounter between government forces and the revolutionary group, when Andrés finally and fully commits himself to political action, that his dream and reality converge:

> veo una cara, oigo una voz, todo lo que soñé Fritz Lang recuerdo, como una sábana que se desgarra en mitad. . . . Miro al hombre que me mira desde el sillón hamacándose despacio, veo mi sueño como soñándolo por fin de veras y tan sencillo, tan idiota, tan claro, tan evidente, era tan perfectamente previsible que esta noche y aquí yo me acordara de golpe que al sueño consistía nada más que en eso, en el cubano que me miraba y me decía solamente una palabra: *Despertate.*

> (I see a face, I hear a voice, everything that I dreamed Fritz Lang I remember, like a sheet that's torn in half. . . . I look at the man who looks at me from the chair slowly rocking, I see my dream as if I'm finally dreaming it and so simple, so idiotic, so clear, so obvious, it was so perfectly foreseeable that tonight and here I should remember all of a sudden that the dream was nothing more than that, that the Cuban was looking at me and saying only two words to me: *Wake up.*)

Again, as in "Deshoras" and "Queremos tanto a Glenda," we are reminded that the recuperation of the images of memory is indispensable in the process of establishing individual and political selfhood. His dream allows Andrés to integrate the images of past and present, and thus to make an authentic political commitment to the future. The dream is the objective correlative of Andrés' political vacillation and of his ultimate political action: it mirrors and frames the Brechtian conclusion of Cortázar's plot. Andrés, the detached observer, is led to political engagement through the critical contemplation of his Fritz Lang dream.

If Cortázar illustrates the effects of Brechtian artistic alienation in Andrés' political awakening, he also embodies a Brechtian aesthetic in the difficult narrative structure of his novel. *Libro de Manuel* is composed of a multitude of defiantly discontinuous short chapters, among which are interspersed, at random, newspaper clippings, graphs, charts, governmental reports. This inserted "information" is given in its original typographic form; the idiosyncratic typography of the composite calls attention to the verbal surface of the narrative, reminding the reader that he is just that. Further alienating formal elements are the lack of transition among the narrative fragments, a constantly shifting narrative perspective, a problematic narrator, "él que te dije" ("the one I told you"), who is not only a character but also the alter ego of several others, and, one senses, of the author himself. These and other narrative devices impose a complexity which impedes any simple emotional identification on the part of the reader. Like Andrés viewing his dream, the reader is at once drawn emotionally to the action of the novel and alienated from it by the intellectual challenge of the fictional form itself. However, Cortázar's interpolation toward the end of the novel of official accounts of the torture of citizens by the Argentine military regime is calculated to reverse the reader's alienation, to engage his emotions (horror, repugnance, sympathy, anger), and inspire political commitment based on his visceral reactions as well as his rational judgment.

Andrés' dream and Cortázar's novel are comparable not only in their Brechtian orientation but also in their structural movement and stasis. Andrés says that the visual experience of his dream is "a perfect montage right out of the movies," the "hardest part" of which is to translate it into words, into the "little honey combs of our damned verbal hive." That may be, but unlike the narrator of "Deshoras," who wishes to stop time with his static image of Sara, Andrés' concern is to relate his moving, cinematic dream to a moving, historical situation. In that sense, it seems to me that the fragmented narrative structure of the novel might in fact be considered analogous to the frames of a strip of celluloid, each a kind of arrested temporal image which contains its own significance but which is essentially suspended in time, waiting to be endowed with its full meaning by the progressive movement of the images from one to the next as the movie is viewed or the novel read.

This tension between the momentarily static fragments and the moving continuum of the whole is strongly felt in the films of the Weimar era, as it is in *Libro de Manuel*. Because photography in the twenties in Germany was more advanced than film, it lent its theories and its techniques to the movies. The films of the time were often very photographic, with shots depending on the static formality of spatial composition rather than serialized movement through time, as the fascinating collection, *Great Film Stills of the German Silent Era*, attests. Lang, for example, creates seemingly static images by emphasizing intersecting vertical and horizontal lines; *Metropolis* (1925–26) is full of such composed shots, where the only movement in the visual grid is the rhythmic repetition of machinery or of mechanized human beings (a vision consonant with that of the narrator of "Queremos tanto a Glenda"). Cortázar also creates tension between static scenes and the necessary narrative movement of the novel with what he calls in his preface vertical and horizontal elements, that is, the psychological conflicts of his characters and the temporal unfolding of the historical context. Though his use of these terms is metaphoric, they nevertheless may describe the structural composition of the narrative. For example, the "vertical" set scene from Andrés' childhood—the Buenos Aires garden in early evening, with tablecloths, jasmine, a lamp dotting the immobile landscape of memory—immediately precedes a "horizontal" fragment—a newspaper clipping from the twenty-eighth of May in Clermont-Ferrand, France, in which an event, without preface or sequel, is isolated and immobilized in its narrow column of newsprint. So the vertical and horizontal may be said to intersect innumerable times as the fragments of the novel are juxtaposed along its course.

Of the many kinds of static narrative fragments in the novel, it is the newspaper clippings that most vividly convey the impression of time's stoppage, of the isolation of the instant of past time, the sense of *"that-has-been"* which Roland Barthes attributes to photographs. The lack of explicit connection or transition among the narrative fragments heightens one's sense that the novel is a series of still shots to be contemplated and connected by the reader's efforts, rather than a moving camera which sweeps the reader along. Literary structure should awaken the reader, not lull him into complacency: the photographic images become a cinematic continuum only as the reader relates those images to one another and animates them with his own perceiving eye.

In the climactic scene of the revolutionaries' violent confrontation with government forces, when in fact the narrative pace begins to move as rapidly as the events themselves, the narrator, as if to slow both the events and the narration, uses a cinematic metaphor. In a long sentence which enumerates the shots, tear-gas grenades, and the general confusion, the narrator inserts "una pausa como de película accidentada" ("a pause like the ones in a broken film"), then develops the analogy:

> . . . para que pretender decir algo que imposiblemente había sucedido, decir lo imposible de que todavía estuviera sucediendo, tanto que *no podía dejar de pensar que esa detención de la película* que de un segundo a otro provocaría los silbidos de la platea, esa pausa de las tres huestes antes del final podía ser también su propia pausa en la escalera, *su notoria incapacidad para lo simultáneo e incluso lo consecutivo cuando iba demasiado rápido.* (my emphasis)

> . . . why pretend to say something that impossibly had happened, to say the impossible that it still should be happening, so much so that *he couldn't stop thinking about that stopping of the film* which from one second to the next would bring on the hoots of the audience, that pause of the three hosts before the finale might also be his own pause on the stairs, *his notorious incapacity for the simultaneous and even the consecutive when it was going too fast.* [my emphasis])

The reference to the mobile medium of the movies reinforces the historical movement, the terrible pressure of time, felt by the revolutionary group. Again an actor and a spectator, but now in a historical drama rather than a dream, Andrés' vision of stopping the movie, of stopping time itself, emphasizes his sense of the overpowering onrush of political circumstance and his sure knowledge of the cost of the political commitment which he has made.

Roland Barthes contrasts the speed of the movies to the immobility of the photograph in terms which suggest Andrés in the scene I have just cited. Barthes finds that the speed of the cinematic images prevents imaginative contemplation of the kind that the photograph provokes. When watching a movie, Barthes argues, he cannot close his eyes, for when he opens them, the image that he was holding in his mind's eye has disappeared, has been obliterated, has been replaced; so one is subject to the "continuous voracity" of the movies. The photograph, on the contrary, encourages Barthes to close his eyes and "make the image speak in silence." It would seem that Andrés does manage to "stop the film" and the narration: a few fragments follow the passage quoted above, then the rapid movement crystallizes into photographic stasis. The final image of the novel does in fact seem to speak in the silence.

That image is of a corpse in a morgue, presumably the body of one of the revolutionaries. The description of the scene—another kind of still life— recalls the famous photograph of Ché Guevara lying in a stark room in the Bolivian jungle where he was killed by government forces. If the indirect reference to a corpse at the end of "Queremos tanto a Glenda" negates the very possibility of a future, here the corpse, alluding as it does to Ché Guevara, suggests a far more complex relation to historical movement. Of course a dead body is an obvious and irrevocable terminal point: we are told that in the morgue "all marks of history" will be washed away. However, there are also suggestions that the ending of the novel is not the closed temporal structure that the corpse would seem to imply. The member of the revolutionary group who attends the body says, "Seguí tranquilo, hay tiempo" ("Rest easy, there's time"), as if to assure his companion (and himself) that he hasn't died for nothing, that the revolutionary struggle will continue. The photo of Ché has of course become an icon among social and political activists in Latin America, but unlike the icon that the fans of Glenda would create, this one implies a future of radical political change. Unlike the inverted Christian image at the end of "Queremos tanto a Glenda," this still shot of individual death implies collective continuance. The journalistic photograph of Ché Guevara, like the movies of Fritz Lang, provides not only a visual analogue by which to structure the narrative movement of the novel, but also an image of political hope.

Of course, the reader has known all along that the novel he is reading implies another: Cortázar's *Libro de Manuel* is, among other things, a book about the preparation of a book which is just being undertaken as this one ends. So the temporal context of the novel extends beyond its own ending, into both a political and a literary future. The book which Andrés begins at the end of Cortázar's novel is intended to preserve a record of the past for the baby Manuel in the future, and is thus a gesture of affirmation which is at once metaphysical and historical. Much as a family photo album fixes on its pages the visual images of moments of the familiar past, so Andrés will fix in words historical moments of a more public sort. Indeed, Andrés seems to want his images of the past as fixed as possible, perhaps to impede the kind of revisionism, the retouching of history, practiced by Glenda's fans and Kundera's rulers of paradise. The newspaper clippings and government reports which will make up his book are meant to be authoritative, objective, extracted from a moving temporal medium in the same manner as photographs. They are meant to remind us—and to condemn—*"what-has-been."* This stasis is, however, polemical rather than aesthetic: political and social abuses must be remembered and recorded precisely. Hence the documentary nature of Andrés' verbal record.

Despite the fixity of the images which might ally Andrés' record of revolutionary activity to a photo album, I think that it is possible to consider it instead an inversion of the photographic process which Roland Barthes describes as "prophecy in reverse." Andrés' revolutionary commitment, as we have already seen in his interpretation of his Fritz Lang dream, must be understood in terms of the etymological root of the word "revolution." For Andrés, revolution implies cyclical movement, return to the past as well as movement toward the future. Although we commonly use the word to mean a radical break with the past, Andrés' dedication to his historical record (as well as his dedication to the images of his own personal past) suggests his conviction that revolutionary change in the future depends not upon leaving the past behind but rather upon recuperating it, at least partially, in words. Regard for the past and progress toward the future fuse in the revolutionary order, an order symbolized for Andrés by the book he will yet create. So Andrés' historical fragments, however much they resemble photographs in their temporal fixity, do not merely look backward, do not merely prophesy in reverse. While they conform to Barthes' formula by showing that *"that-has-been,"* they also point toward what will be: Andrés' "album" in fact attains what Italo Calvino calls "the true total photograph." Referring to Calvino's rubric of "the true total photograph," Barthes at the end of *Camera Lucida* explains that such a photograph

> accomplishes the unheard-of identification of reality (*"that-has-been"*) with truth (*"there-she-is!"*); it becomes at once evidential and exclamative; it bears the effigy to that crazy point where affect (love, compassion, grief, enthusiasm, desire) is a guarantee of Being. It then approaches, to all intents, madness; it joins what Kristeva calls "la verité folle."

In Andrés' dedication to his project, we sense this "guarantee of Being": Andrés in his book, as well as Cortázar in his, sees in the images of the past a projection of the future, "la verité folle" of human commitment.

In these four works by Cortázar which I have chosen to link together, movement clearly takes on metaphysical, psychological, and aesthetic importance, particularly when it is explicitly opposed to non-movement; and the visual media of film and photo become the symbolic and structural means of embodying that movement or lack of it. As I have shown in the four works I have discussed, Cortázar uses these media to achieve different though related effects. Whereas the static images in the three short stories are basically negative, suggesting untimely death (the still lifes in "Fin de etapa"), psychological paralysis (the arrested image of Sara in "Deshoras"), and aesthetic and political totalitarianism (the fans' dogmatic revisionism in "Queremos tanto a Glenda"), the still shots in *Libro de Manuel* (the documentary slices of history, the narrative fragments, the final implicit allusion to the photo of Ché), have a positive effect. Because they are imbued with revolutionary commitment to the future, they seem to escape their temporal frames and continue into the surrounding world in the constitutive fashion which Barthes attributes only to the movies.

These four works propose, it seems to me, another major area of inquiry which I have touched upon but have not developed specifically or completely, and which I want to conclude by mentioning. That area of inquiry is concerned with the nature of memory and of cognition itself. How does the mind grasp and remember reality through images? What is the relation between image and imagination? Of course theories of visual perception and mental images have long occupied philosophers. Giordano Bruno, mystic philosopher who was burned at the stake in 1600 for his heretical ideas, wrote that "to think is to speculate with images," and numerous philosophers from the seventeenth and eighteenth centuries developed theories of imagistic perception, among them Locke, Hartley, Hume, Berkeley, and Newton. Cortázar raises, though certainly never resolves, the question of the place of the fixed mental image in memory and artistic creation, a question which has specifically and continually preoccupied modern writers from Proust to Robbe-Grillet and García Márquez. It is a question which future criticism will want to address, perhaps in the terms of film and photography that I have traced here. These visual media provide Cortázar with both themes and techniques for exploring his aesthetic and political concerns and for creating, in his verbal medium, first-rate literary fictions.

Three Versions of *Pedro Páramo*

Paul B. Dixon

One of the most often mentioned cases of visual ambiguity concerns the question: "Which is the figure in a particular representation and which is its background?" Edgar Rubin's "reversible goblet" is a familiar specimen of this phenomenon, called "figure-ground reversal." When we see a goblet in the figure, the space surrounding the goblet is without structure and serves only as a background. But when we perceive the figure as two human profiles facing each other the goblet melts away and becomes but a space between structures.

This [essay] will discuss an analogous phenomenon in Juan Rulfo's novel, *Pedro Páramo*. [The edition of *Pedro Páramo* referred to in this chapter is copyright © 1964 by Fondo de Cultura Económica.] Involved in this "figure-ground reversal" are not two, but three competing structures. Each one motivates its own interrelationship among elements in the novel. The perception of one of these structures seems to require the disappearance of the others, just as with Rubin's figure seeing the profiles requires the disintegration of the goblet, and vice versa.

Ambiguity matters most in a work when tension is created between the opposing propositions. Before beginning a description of these structures in *Pedro Páramo*, we will briefly discuss such a tension-producing factor in the novel, which is usually present in ambiguous texts—what we might call a solution-finding mode. Ambiguous works thrive on the impression that a solution is both possible and necessary. It is the promise of a solution that draws the reader into the text, makes him weigh evidence and encourages him to linger cautiously over the work's language.

Juan Rulfo's novel is the sort of work that encourages resolution, but at the same time seems insoluble. The very first sentence of the novel, uttered by Juan Preciado, is "Vine a Comala porque me dijeron que acá vivía mi padre, un tal Pedro Páramo." With this statement we become aware that the novel involves a quest for someone or something. The sentence also establishes the importance of language and testimony in that search, with the words "porque me dijeron." Right away the epistemological difficulties are made evident. Abundio, the muleteer who accompanies Juan Preciado into Comala, asks, "—¿Y a qué va usted a Comala, si se puede saber?" The phrase "si se puede saber" is on the one hand a polite expression, equivalent to "if I might ask." On the other hand, however, it exposes the essential problem of the quest, with the more literal meaning "if it is possible to know (or find out)." The search will be a challenge, for it involves illusions, dreams, and false hopes. Juan indicates this as he promises his dying mother he will seek out his father, and continues,

> . . . no pensé cumplir mi promesa. Hasta ahora pronto que commencé a llenarme de sueños, a darle vuelo a las ilusiones. Y de este modo se me fue formando un mundo alrededor de la esperanza que era aquel señor llamado Pedro Páramo, el marido de mi madre. Por eso vine a Comala.

The role of equivocation in the quest, especially as it reflects on the unreliability of language, is highlighted in the encounter between Juan Preciado and Abundio. In the following interchange, Abundio is the first to speak:

> —¡Váyase mucho al carajo!
> —¿Qué dice usted?
> —Que ya estamos llegando, señor.
> —Sí, ya lo veo. ¿Qué pasó por aquí?
> —Un correcaminos, señor. Así les nombran a esos pájaros.
> —No, yo preguntaba por el pueblo, que se ve tan solo, como si estuviera abandonado. Parece que no lo habitara nadie.
> —No es que lo parezca. Así es. Aquí no vive nadie.

Twice in the passage, Abundio and Juan fail to "connect" semantically. Abundio's first utterance seems to Juan to be a curse, something like "Go to hell!" When asked to explain, however, Abundio says something about going not to hell, but to Comala. Abundio has previously remarked that Comala is "en la mera boca del infierno," so there is a vague pejorative connection between seemingly unrelated utterances. Juan asks "¿Qué pasó por aquí?" meaning "What happened here?" and Abundio instead answers the question "What passed by here?" a more literal interpretation of the same words. Even Abundio's final remark, "No es que parezca. Así es," calls attention to the fundamental question of appearance versus essence.

Such equivocations and questions about knowing are essential considerations in an ambiguous work. The first few pages of *Pedro Páramo* set the tone for the novel, and in effect instruct the reader what to expect and how to react (Juan Preciado is a kind of prototype for the novel's implied reader). The beginning establishes that the work will involve a search for under-standing, and that it will be a difficult search full of mistaken judgments, illusions, failures of communication, and exaggerated hopes. The rest of the novel fulfills the expectations encouraged by the opening scene, by means of ambiguity appearing in many places and on different levels.

THE NEAR-SOLID NARRATIVE STRUCTURE

The first structure we will discuss—the most obvious one—is the story of the protagonist Pedro Páramo. This is the novel's most evident structure not necessarily because it is the most accessible one, but because by con-vention novels have a narrative element, and we tend to look for that one first. Actually, the novel's underlying story requires considerable effort to uncover, because of the numerous artistic transformations, including achronological ordering, digressions, and deletions, which produce the surface representation. Even so, we may discover a relatively stable story. As Luis Leal has stated, at first glance the novel "da la impresión de tener una estructura bastante desorganizada, por no decir caótica. . . . Una lec-tura cuidadosa, sin embargo revela que, dentro de esa aparente confusión, hay una ingeniosa estructura, bien organizada y con una rígida lógica interna."

For Leal, the story line of the tale is "más que sencillo." Close exam-ination reveals, however, that in certain parts the story is actually "menos que sencillo." At numerous specific points, *Pedro Páramo* has an ambiguous story. This ambiguity has the same features as those which we described [elsewhere] in [Machado de Assis's] *Dom Casmurro*. It involves the coex-istence of two or more mutually exclusive propositions, but differs with respect to its location. In Machado's novel, we saw that conflicting hy-potheses were central, suggesting substantially different interpretations of the story as a whole. In Rulfo's work, ambiguity is not so central to the narrative; there is really only one story or underlying structure. However, within that relatively univocal story there are pockets of ambiguity that defy resolution.

Several of these pockets of ambiguity center around individual char-acters. Our discussion of the matter begins with the question of who is dead and who is alive in the novel. The conventional, worldly means for separating the dead from the living of course do not apply in the work, because people who are dead by definition, such as Juan Preciado's mother, Dolores, can continue talking and moving about. The reader is first faced with the problem of deciding who is dead or alive. Then the point in time at which characters die becomes an open question. Here we will analyze the mechanism used to create this ambiguity, starting with Juan Preciado, and what Kent Lioret calls the "case of multiple possibilities" concerning his death.

The first explicit indication of Juan's status comes at the point when after a day and a night in Comala he tells Dorotea that he has died from lack of air:

> No había aire. Tuve que sorber el mismo aire que salía de mi boca, deteniéndolo con las manos antes de que se fuera. Lo sentía ir y venir, cada vez menos; hasta que se hizo tan delgado que se filtró entre mis dedos para siempre.

Life and death can have their own definitions in fiction; it is especially evident from *Pedro Páramo* that the state of death is a matter defined internally by the novel. It is also internally defined that there is a *distinction* between life and death. The fact that Juan Preciado talks about dying at a particular moment implies that he passes from state A to state B, and that there is an essential difference between the two. On other occasions, characters stress the necessary distinction between life and death. For example, upon arriving at Comala, Juan Preciado asks Abundio about finding lodging, and the latter suggests, "Busque a doña Eduviges, si es que todavía vive." The implication is that Juan may stay at Eduviges's place only if she is alive, and that if she is dead he will have to look elsewhere. Juan indeed finds Eduviges. She later tries to ascertain whether the Abundio Juan met on his way to Comala is the Abundio she knows. Because the one she knows is deaf and the one Juan spoke with seems to have heard well, she determines that Juan's acquaintance must not be the same person, and concludes "No debe ser él. Además, Abundio ya murió." One might well ask why Eduviges is asking about Abundio if he is dead, but there is still with the last statement a definite distinction made between life and death. Juan Preciado could not have spoken to the Abundio Eduviges knows, for he is no longer alive. The obvious implication is that Juan is alive. Eduviges tells Juan about receiving a visit from Miguel Páramo some time earlier, in which the youth thought he must be insane because he could not find his girlfriend's village. Her reply, "No. Loco no, Miguel. Debes estar muerto," shows the same rigid thinking oriented toward life and death as distinct and separate worlds. Miguel cannot find the village because he now lives in another world. Life and death are exclusive: that is the hypothesis encouraged by these distinction-drawing passages. Following such a hypothesis, we can assume that Dorotea, Donis, and his sister/lover are alive, because they are the ones who bury Juan Preciado. Dorotea is only able to join Juan in the grave by dying as she helps to bury him. Eduviges must be alive, because Juan finds her at home, talks to her, and she offers him lodging. And Juan is alive up until his suffocation.

But while this solid life/death dichotomy seems necessary according to certain textual clues, upon consideration of others it seems quite impossible. Eduviges, the one most instrumental in establishing the hypothesis of distinctions, is also the one who most places it in doubt. If Miguel Páramo is dead, if he can see her, and if she can talk to him, then she must be dead also. Damiana Cisneros suggests to Juan Preciado that Eduviges *is* dead: "—¿Eduviges Dyada? —Ella. —Pobre Eduviges. Debe de andar penando todavía." Following the criteria established, where the dead and the living may communicate, but only with their own kind, then Juan Preciado, who has talked to Eduviges, has been dead at least since meeting her. Abundio may also have been dead, and therefore been the one Eduviges knew (although we still have to wonder about his deafness). Information from the third-person narrator, which Juan Preciado has no knowledge of, establishes the fact that Eduviges truly is dead, that she has committed suicide. Juan would then seem definitely to have been dead long before he thinks he died. But what about Dorotea and the others, who were witness to his death and burial? Perhaps they are dead along with everyone else. But that would present us with the strange case of the dead burying the dead, which might be an acceptable hypothetical teaching device in the New Testament but hardly fits into the rigid distinctive system the novel seems to call for.

The dichotomy between life and death and the incongruous arrangement of textual evidence put the reader in a quandary. Who is dead and who is alive? If they are all dead, at what point did they die? One possible reaction on the part of the reader is to come to regard the distinctions as meaningless, to maintain that the rigid logic of the life/death dichotomy does not exist. On the one hand, the novel with its impossible interface between life and death seems to lead us in this direction. But on the other, it induces us to sustain rigid logic and seek a solution. We have seen that from the beginning of the work, the theme of the quest for knowledge is established. In a first-person narrative involving this theme, because the reader has only as much knowledge as the protagonist he is practically obliged to become a participant in the search for knowledge. *Pedro Páramo* has a mixture of first-person, third-person, and objective points of view. Perhaps the reader's impulse to take part in the quest is ambivalent because of this mixture. But it seems that as long as Juan Preciado is actively involved in the effort to know about the status (alive or dead) of his acquaintances, of himself, and of his father, we as readers tend to be searching also. Juan goes about his quest with a high degree of seriousness and intensity: "¿Está usted viva, Damiana? ¡Dígame, Damiana!" The intensity of this search seems to rub off onto the reader, so that instead of seeing the textual situation as a set of hopeless contradictions, he sees them as a set of clues apparently incongruous, but quite possibly soluble. As he weighs certain possibilities he momentarily forgets their corresponding impossibilities. Characters seem to move back and forth between the world of the dead and that of the living.

In matters other than life or death, we find characters in other pockets of ambiguity. One of these is Susana San Juan, the woman whom Pedro

Páramo has loved since childhood. There is a suggestion that Susana has an incestuous relationship with her father. Fulgor Sedano, Páramo's fore-man, mentions seeing them after an extended absence from Comala, and Pedro asks:

> —¿Han venido los dos?
> —Sí él y su mujer. ¿Pero cómo lo sabe?
> —¿No será su hija?
> —Pues por el modo como la trata más bien parece su mujer.
> —Vete a dormir, Fulgor.

The conversation between Susana San Juan and her father, Bartolomé, in which Bartolomé tells her Pedro wants to live with her, is a rich specimen of ambiguity:

> —¿De manera que estás dispuesta a acostarte con él?
> —Sí, Bartolomé.
> —¿No sabes que es casado y que ha tenido infinidad de mujeres?
> —Sí, Bartolomé.
> —No me digas Bartolomé. ¡Soy tu padre! . . . Le he dicho que tú, aunque viuda, sigues viviendo con tu marido, o al menos así te comportas; he tratado de disuadirlo, pero se le hace torva la mirada cuando le hablo, y en cuanto sale a relucir tu nombre, cierra los ojos. Es, según yo sé, la pura maldad. Eso es Pedro Páramo.
> —¿Y yo quién soy?
> —Tú eres mi hija. Mía. Hija de Bartolomé San Juan.
> En la mente de Susana San Juan comenzaron a caminar las ideas, primero lentamente, luego se detuvieron, para después echar a correr de tal modo que no alcanzó sino a decir:
> —No es cierto. No es cierto.

Obviously Bartolomé does not approve of Susana's living with Pedro Páramo. But why? Is it because Pedro Páramo is "la pura maldad," or because Susana is a sort of wife to Bartolomé? The words, "Le he dicho que tú aunque viuda, sigues viviendo con tu marido, o al menos así te comportas," are equivocal. They might mean that Susana lives with her husband in the sense of maintaining loyalty to him and being unavailable to others. But it also might suggest that Susana is living in a quasimarital relationship, that her father is her "marido." Susana's calling her father by his first name might suggest more of a husband-wife relationship than a father-daughter one. Surely Bartolomé is sensitive about her addressing him in such a familiar way. Bartolomé tries to use his parental authority to get her to stay with him: "Tú eres mi hija. Mía. Hija de Bartolomé San Juan," and after some time Susana says, "No es cierto." Is she reflecting upon her role as a "wife" to Bartolomé when she says this? Is she going crazy? Is she correcting her father's judgment of Pedro Páramo? Different contexts seem to shift back and forth from prominence to unimportance, figure to ground.

There is a suggestion that Bartolomé abuses his daughter physically as well as sexually. Again describing his conversation with Pedro Páramo, Bartolomé says,

> Así que te quiere a tí, Susana. Dice que jugabas con él cuando eran niños. Que ya te conoce. Que llegaron a bañarse juntos en el río cuando eran niños. Yo no lo supe; de haberlo sabido te habría matado a cintarazos.
> —No lo dudo.
> ¿Fuiste tú la que dijiste: no lo dudo?
> —Yo lo dije.

To what does Susana's comment "No lo dudo" refer? If it has reference to Bartolomé's "te habría matado a cintarazos," then Susana seems practically to be calling her father a child beater. However, it might also refer to Pedro Páramo's statement that he and Susana swam together in the river as children, and carry no suggestion of abuse.

This passage makes us wonder if there is not an ambiguous suggestion of physical abuse a few pages later, when a flashback depicts Bartolomé lowering Susana by a rope into what seems to be a mine shaft: Susana "Estaba colgada de aquella soga que le lastimaba la cintura, que le sangraba sus manos." Bartolomé insists that there is money and gold at the bottom of the shaft, but instead Susana finds a skeleton:

> Entonces ella no supo de ella [la calavera], sino muchos días después entre el hielo, entre las miradas llenas de hielo de su padre.
> Por eso reía ahora.
> —Supe que eras tú, Bartolomé.

At the point in the novel when Susana says, "Supe que eras tú, Bartolomé," she seems to have already gone insane. So the most obvious interpretation of the remark is that it is a demented one: Susana has confused the cadaver at the bottom of the shaft with her father, who is holding the rope at the other end. But might there be some lucidity in the remark after all? Might she be realizing that there was no treasure to be found, but rather that she was simply being played with by her father? His "miradas llenas de hielo" suggest something sinister. Might he even be responsible for the skeleton? The text supplies data to suggest alternative hypotheses, but not enough to substantiate any hypothesis satisfactorily.

A further bit of ambiguity surrounding Susana concerns her obsession with Florencio. Because every reference to Florencio within the novel is filtered through Susana San Juan (part of her monologue from the grave, her dreams, or her interior monologue while alive), and because we know that Susana has gone insane, it is impossible to establish definitely even if Florencio exists. There are a number of propositions that suggest themselves. Surely as far as Susana is concerned, Florencio has been her lover and has died. One possible hypothesis is that Florencio was Susana's husband. We have already seen that Susana's father refers to her as a widow.

However, we have also seen that because of the suggestion of incest between Bartolomé and Susana there is reason for wondering if she really is a widow. Bartolomé might be obliquely referring to himself as her "husband"—"sigues viviendo con tu marido." A second possibility, then, is that Florencio is in Susana's mind a purified version of her father. We know that Bartolomé dies at about the time Susana moves in with Pedro Páramo. Páramo orders Fulgor Sedano to "desaparecer al viejo en . . . regiones adonde nadie va nunca," and Justina, a servant at Páramo's, announces Bartolomé's death to Susana. When upon receiving a visit of consolation from Padre Rentería, Susana thinks, "Ya sé que vienes a contarme que murió Florencio." It seems quite possible that she is considering Florencio and her father to be one and the same.

Still another possibility is that Florencio is a purified, idealized conception of Pedro Páramo, held by Susana since childhood, who perhaps "dies" when Susana is forced to face the real Pedro. We hear a monologue by Susana in her grave, recounting her bathing naked in the sea with an unidentified man. The tone is consistent with her sensual, idyllic evocations of Florencio, so we assume she is referring to him. But this monologue reminds us of Pedro Páramo's having told Bartolomé "Que . . . ya conoce a Susana. Que llegaron a bañarse juntos en el río cuando eran niños." Therefore, through the motif of the "baño" there is a connection suggested between Pedro and Florencio as well. Susana's deceased husband? An idealized representation of Bartolomé or Pedro Páramo? Perhaps an entirely nonexistent being based on scraps of remembered experience with various individuals? The reader seems encouraged by the work's coincidental motifs to advance conjectures. But the incompatibility of suggested propositions, plus the paucity of additional detail, makes any sort of well-founded conclusion impossible.

The character Abundio, who appears at the beginning and end of the novel, provides yet another locus of ambiguity within the narrative structure. One question that must be asked in his case is: "Is Abundio one character, or are there two Abundios?" The Abundio who demands money from Pedro Páramo at the end of the work is clearly named Abundio Martínez. The one who accompanies Juan Preciado into Comala at the beginning might be named Abundio Martínez, but then again might not. "—¿Y cómo se llama usted? —Abundio —me contestó. Pero ya no alcancé a oír el appellido." Here a distinction on the basis of last names is made to seem possible, but at the same time, no distinction can be made. Likewise, we are encouraged to make a distinction on the basis of deafness or hardness of hearing. The Abundio at the end of the work is supposed to be hard of hearing. Doña Inés, who gives Abundio liquor at her son's bar, speaks to Abundio shouting, because "Abundio era sordo." The Abundio with whom

Juan Preciado speaks seems to have had no problem hearing. On that basis, it would seem that there are two different Abundios. However, it is not quite that simple. The question becomes not only whether there are two different Abundios, but whether either is really hard of hearing. Doña Inés' conversation with Abundio illustrates:

> ¿Qué es lo que te trae por aquí tan de mañana?
> Se lo dijo a gritos, porque Abundio era sordo.
> —Pos nada más un cuartillo de alcohol del que estoy necesitado.
> —¿Se te volvió a desmayar la Refugio?
> —Se me murió ya, madre Villa. Anoche mismito, muy cerca de las once. Y conque hasta vendí mis burros. Hasta eso vendí porque se me aliviara.
> —¡No oigo lo que estás diciendo! ¿O no estás diciendo nada? ¿Qué es lo que dices?

On the basis of this passage, if anyone seems hard of hearing it is Doña Inés, just as Juan Preciado is the one who has problems hearing when he talks with Abundio. Abundio seems to hear well. But then, Doña Inés *is* shouting so she can be heard. Perhaps she can only hear herself, or is hard of hearing as well. When Abundio Martínez arrives at the Media Luna, he seems to have no trouble hearing Damiana Cisneros, but then, she is shouting also:

> . . . los gritos de Damiana se oían salir más repetidos, atravesando los campos: "¡Están matando a don Pedro!"
> Abundio Martínez oía que aquella mujer gritaba. No sabía que hacer para acabar esos gritos. No les encontraba la punta a sus pensamientos. Sentía que los gritos de la vieja se debían estar oyendo muy lejos. Quizá hasta su mujer los estuviera oyendo, porque a él le taladraban las orejas, aunque no entendía lo que decía.

This passage gives the impression both that he hears and that he is deaf. He hears the shouts, feels that even the dead must hear them (his wife is dead), but at the same time does not understand what the shouts are saying. One or two Abundios? Deaf or not deaf? Once again we see that the text provides us with indices for making a determination, but that the data that is to help us decide is equivocal, so we can make no determination.

Critics who have commented on the matter have generally agreed that Abundio kills Pedro Páramo. We know that Abundio stabs someone, but are we sure it is Páramo? Here is the crucial passage:

> —¡Ayúdenme! —[Abundio] dijo—. Denme algo.
> Pero ni siquiera él se oyó. Los gritos de aquella mujer lo dejaban sordo.
> Por el camino de Comala se movieron unos puntitos negros. De

pronto los puntitos se convirtieron en hombres y luego estuvieron aquí, cerca de él.

Damiana Cisneros dejó de gritar. Deshizo su cruz. Ahora se había caído y abría la boca como si bostezara.

Los hombres que habían venido la levantaron del suelo y la llevaron al interior de la casa.

—¿No le ha pasado nada a usted, patrón? —preguntaron.

Apareció la cara de Pedro Páramo, que sólo movió la cabeza.

Desarmaron a Abundio, que aún tenía el cuchillo lleno de sangre en la mano:

—Vente con nosotros —le dijeron—. En buen lío te has metido.

Here we see the image of Abundio's bloody knife. Surely he has stabbed someone. But there are apparently two persons he might have stabbed. Abundio is obviously distraught by Damiana's yells, and gropes for "qué hacer para acabar con esos gritos." Suddenly her shouting stops, she drops to the ground and has to be carried into the house. Abundio might well have stabbed Damiana. But how about Pedro Páramo? His men try to find out about his safety, and all the text gives us on the matter is the marvelously vague "Apareció la cara de Pedro Páramo, que sólo movió la cabeza." At other moments, Damiana screams, "¡Están matando a don Pedro!" and Páramo says to himself, "Sé que . . . vendrá Abundio con sus manos ensangrentadas a pedirme la ayuda que le negué." These comments, while perhaps suggesting that Abundio kills Páramo, are by no means unequivocal. Why would Damiana say "están" if she were referring to Abundio alone? Pedro Páramo's comment seems like a premonition, but can it be taken as evidence of an accomplished fact?

All of these ambiguities—Florencio's identity, Abundio's crime, the existence of one or two Abundios, Susana San Juan's relationship to her father, etc.—are like cracks in an aged sculptured monument that efface an area here, create a dubious form there, but leave the more general representation intact. Generally speaking, the ambiguities belong to the more dispensable and superficial *free motifs*, rather than to the *bound motifs* that make up the essential underlying structure of the narrative. How Pedro Páramo dies may be equivocal, but the more important fact, that he dies as the culmination of a gradual self-induced corruption, remains unambiguous. This narrative structure, tracing the rise and decline of the *cacique* Pedro Páramo, and the generally tragic effect his life has on others, is stable, and readers can readily agree on the general story and themes of the work. The portion of the novel concerning Juan Preciado's search for his father, which occupies a rather large part of the concrete, surface structure of the novel and is one of the most ambiguous parts, is rather marginal as far as the deep structure or abstract story is concerned. Again, if one is concerned only with the fact that Juan Preciado dies, all the ambiguity concerning when, where, and how is of little importance. But the work seems designed to direct our attention to these details, these small fissures and gaps that come into view as we take a closer look at the monument. We weigh possibilities in the choice of words. We consider both literal and figurative meanings of statements. We find alternative referents for certain statements. And, when our initial attempts to solve the enigmas are frustrated, we tend to return to the text for another try.

THE EXPRESSIONISTIC READING

While noting the applicability of some general notions of linguistic theory to the study of the novel, I mentioned that a novel and a sentence can be considered analogous in certain respects. One of these is that both the novel and the sentence have a form of syntax. Just as we can consider the connections among phonemes, morphemes, and words in the formation of a sentence, we can analyze the connections between units of narrative in a novel, and thereby gain some notion of a syntactic structure for the work.

The idea of breaking a work down into minimal narrative units is not a hard one to grasp when we consider *Pedro Páramo*, for graphically the job has already been accomplished. The narrative consists of about sixty-five short segments, separated by white spaces. We need not go into whether these sections qualify as minimal narrative units by the various rather technical definitions developed by specialists in the morphology of narrative. For our purposes, each block may simply be considered as one unit, which might be compared to a word for purposes of discussing syntax.

Syntax involves the concatenation of elements. In grammar, subjects are connected to verbs, verbs to objects, modifiers to nouns or verbs, etc. The chief syntactic forces acting in a novel are causality and chronology (pratically always acting harmoniously). *Pedro Páramo*, like other narrative works, has a syntax based on these forces. But its narrative syntax does not correspond with the segments' syntax in the concrete medium of the novel. For example, consider the essential narrative material of the novel's first four segments: (1) Juan Preciado meets Abundio on his way to Comala; (2) Juan, now in Comala, is invited into a woman's house; (3) Juan arrives at Comala and takes leave of Abundio; and (4) Juan learns the woman is Eduviges and enters her house. The narrative syntax of these segments is one, three, two and then four, rather than the order in which they are artistically presented. Considering the work's chronology of events, these segments actually belong near the end rather than at the beginning. The work's underlying story has a syntax determined by causality and order in time, but through a series of artistic transformations its representation has frequent inversions in this order. Reading the novel involves reworking its surface syntax—mentally putting the segments of narrative back into their causal sequence. Hugo Rodríguez-Alcalá compares the novel's structure to that of a mosaic, "un mosaico de numerosísimas teselas. Y estas teselas debe el lector mismo ordenar, o, mejor, reordenar, a fin de componer las figuras musivas en forma completa e inteligible." This narrative-based ordering, which emphasizes Pedro Páramo's drama and deemphasizes Juan Preciado's, is one version of the novel's syntax. However, it is not the only one. In competition with this ordering, a series of repeating elements constructs a network among the narrative segments that tends to be equally as persuasive as a syntactical system, but not always compatible with the causal, temporal linking. Specifically, we refer to the technique of tying contiguous segments together by means of a common word, phrase, image or motif. Following are several examples of this type of concatenation, all occurring not within, but rather between segments. Usually, but not always, the concatenated elements occur near the end of one segment and the beginning of the next:

1. "—Iré. Iré después" (p. 15), and "Ya voy, mamá. Ya voy" (p. 17).
2. "Y tu madre se fue" (p. 23), and "El día que te fuiste" (p. 24).
3. "Había estrellas fugaces" (p. 33), and "Había estrellas fugaces" (p. 34).
4. "En este cuarto ahorcaron a Toribio Aldrete" (p. 37), and "levantó el acta contra actos de Toribio Aldrete" (p. 37).
5. ¡Vaya!" (p. 38), and "¡Vaya!" (p. 39).
6. "me respondió mi propia voz" (p. 47), and "Y las voces" (p. 47).
7. "salió la estrella de la tarde, y más tarde la luna" (p. 57), and "Volví a ver la estrella junto a la luna" (p. 58).
8. "nubes ya desmenuzadas por el viento" (p. 57), and "Las nubes deshaciéndose" (p. 58).
9. "el golpear de la lluvia" (p. 65), and "gruesas gotas de lluvia cayeron" (p. 65).
10. "a una le cierran una puerta" (p. 70), and "Llamaron a su puerta" (p. 70).
11. "Vete a descansar" (p. 79), and "Estoy acostada" (p. 79).
12. "¿No lo sabías?" (p. 88), and "¿Sabías, Fulgor . . .?" (p. 89).
13. "la lluvia sobre las hojas de los plátanos" (p. 93), and "la lluvia, . . . rodando sobre las hojas de los plátanos" (p. 93).
14. "Comala seguía anegándose en lluvia" (p. 95), and "La lluvia" (p. 95).
15. "eres tú, Bartolomé" (p. 95), and "¿Eres tú, padre?" (p. 96).

These repeated motifs provide another basis for the connection of segments. We are urged to link segments because of their concatenating words, images, or phrases, rather than because of their causal relationship. Approximately half of the time, there is no conflict between story-based syntax and the chains of elements we have mentioned. There are several groups of segments in the surface representation of the novel that belong together, insofar as the story is concerned. In these cases, both syntactical systems act together. Example number seven, featuring the words "había estrellas fugaces," links a segment in which several men converse during the night of Miguel Páramo's burial, and a segment in which Padre Rentería recriminates himself for "selling out" to those who support him financially. The padre's meditations are also related to Miguel Páramo's burial. In example number thirteen, the words about rain falling "sobre las hojas de los plátanos" link segments that are also chronologically linked, because both have to do with Susana San Juan's bedridden delirium.

In several other cases, however, the syntax of repetitive elements is in direct opposition to the syntax of causality and chronology. Example number one links Juan Preciado's meeting with Eduviges and Pedro Páramo's bathroom reverie about Susana San Juan. Number two creates a link between Eduviges' account of Dolores' leaving Pedro Páramo, and a conversation between Pedro and his grandmother. And number ten involves the connection of a dialogue between Juan Preciado and Dorotea in their graves, and the arrival of Miguel Páramo's body to the Media Luna estate.

These two syntactical systems—the system of narrative causality and the system of element concatenation—urge two incompatible readings of the novel. Both accentuate the duality between the novel's surface texture and its underlying content or story. On the one hand, *Pedro Páramo* urges us, through a sort of reader's quest, to piece together the narrative elements so as to arrive at a comprehension of the narrative content. It is possible to apprehend the work's story, but only through a reordering of the narrative units as they appear on the surface. In order to perceive the story as a solid, firmly comprehensible structure, one must impute a certain fluidity to the artistic discourse so that it can be reordered. The novel thus lends itself to a representational reading. When we follow the representational urge we perceive the novel's deep structure as being solid, rigid, and demanding, while of necessity the novel's surface structure must be malleable and accommodating, perhaps even transparent, more like a liquid than a solid.

But the surface structure makes demands of its own. The system of concatenating elements, both when it harmonizes with the syntax of the story and when it acts against it, provides strong motivation *not* to reorder the segments, but rather to apprehend them in the order presented in the novel itself. When one is oriented towards this highly formal syntax, he perceives the *surface* of the novel as the more rigid and demanding side of the dichotomy. The requirements of causality and temporality must lose something; the deep structure becomes the more fluid, transparent, accommodating structure. With this sort of reading the representational aspect of the novel becomes faded and distorted. Rather than a sharply defined representation, what emerges is the *expression* of a much more subjective sort of reality.

An expressionistic reading does not necessarily refer to expressionism as a school or movement, although in many respects *Pedro Páramo* conforms to the norms of the movement. For our purposes, an expressionistic reading is one that takes account of literary discourse as expression per se, rather than as a depiction of something else. Concentrating on the expression means giving legitimacy to the novel "as is," as an individual communicative act. It means ignoring that "otherness" which the expression is about.

The story-centered reading and the expression-centered reading are in a kind of figure-ground relationship. As with Rubin's goblet/profiles figure, we cannot perceive both at once. While all narratives feature the duality of surface structure and deep structure, of story and expression, not nearly so many force this sort of ambiguity between the two. Most feature a more or less transparent expression that does not call attention to itself. But *Pedro Páramo*, particularly because of its conflicting syntactical systems, is different. Story and discourse each call attention to themselves, and each distracts from the other.

It is interesting that *Pedro Páramo* at one time had another provisional title—*Los murmullos*. The difference between these titles suggests the dichotomy between the novel's expressionistic and representational readings. Rulfo was perhaps himself ambivalent about whether his novel was a story about Pedro Páramo, or rather a collection of poetically expressed impressions of some scarcely definable subjective reality. Convention dictates one title for one work; obviously Rulfo chose his. But perhaps it was an arbitrary choice. The novel might just as appropriately been called *Los murmullos*. Both titles stand for something essential to the work, and both perhaps fail to be entirely satisfactory as labels for the totality of the work.

To recapitulate our discussion of ambiguous syntax and the opposing readings it engenders, we may pretend that there are actually two different novels—one called *Pedro Páramo* and one called *Los murmullos*. Contrasting these two novels will give us an idea of the mutually exclusives that are somehow coexistent in one novel.

Pedro Páramo	*Los murmullos*
1. Represents objective conditions.	1. Expresses subjective impressions.
2. Reader must reorder narrative segments.	2. Reader need not reorder narrative segments.
3. Has a syntax based on causality, chronology.	3. Has a syntax based on a chain of formal elements.
4. Surface structure is fluid, giving way to the demands of the story.	4. Surface structure is solid, demanding attention to its form.
5. Deep structure is solid, because of the rigid demands of the story.	5. Deep structure is fluid, because the story gives way to the demands of formal discourse.

Rulfo's novel is somewhere in between *Pedro Páramo* and *Los murmullos*. The experience of reading the work seems to be one of hesitation, of going and coming, between the two. Both are demanding, but neither is completely satisfying. For example, just when we feel we are succeeding in piecing together the story, we come across the mysterious narrative segment wherein a mother announces to her son, "Han matado a tu padre." We learn several pages later that the episode involves Pedro Páramo and his mother, but at this point we cannot tell who the son and mother are, because, as is typical, no names appear. For lack of character identification, and because so many men are killed in the novel, our story-based syntax breaks down. It at first seems that the segment might connect to any number of segments, or that it might connect to none. The final line of the segment, "¿Y a ti quién te mató, madre?" is a nonsequitur. It has little to do with what is represented, but does contain evocative power. This unworldly question jars us loose from perceiving predominantly the story, and makes us savor its anguished, nonsensical expressiveness. *Pedro Páramo* disintegrates at such moments, and we begin reading *Los murmullos*. At other times, however, *Los murmullos* disintegrates as well. We follow the repetitive cadence of images, words, and phrases. The concatenation of discursive elements carries us along through one segment after another, but at critical points, the concatenation terminates. In these gaps, the persuasive force of the story is allowed to take over, and as it does so, the rocklike surface structure turns to liquid.

The image just employed ought to remind us of an arresting image in the novel, where Juan Preciado finds himself in bed with Donis' sister/lover: "El cuerpo de aquella mujer, hecho de tierra, envuelto en costras de tierra, se desbarataba como si estuviera derritiéndose en un charco de lodo." This is only one of numerous images sprinkled throughout the novel in which a relatively rigid structure disintegrates into something nondescript, less-rigid, or even nonexistent: "Y [los hombres] se disolvieron como sombras"; "mis manos tenían que haberse hecho pedazos estrujando su desesperación"; "El cadáver se deshizo en canillas; la quijada se desprendió como si fuera de azúcar"; and Pedro Páramo "dio un golpe seco contra la tierra y se fue desmoronando como si fuera un montón de piedras."

On the other hand there are several images where a soft or formless structure acquires rigidity. For example: "La voz sacude los hombros. Hace enderezar el cuerpo"; "Aclaraba el día. El día desbarata las sombras. Las deshace"; and "Por el camino de Comala se movieron unos puntitos negros. De pronto los puntitos se convirtieron en hombres." These frequent images of disintegration and integration harmonize with the competing structures of the novel shifting between exigent rigidity and lax fluidity. Likewise, they suggest the waxing and waning of the reader's will as he grapples with conflicting propositions, alternately experiencing the promise of solution and the frustration of irresolution.

Chiasmatic Motifs

Page

7	30	50	70	90	110	129
1a						1b
2a					2b	
3a					3b	
4a						4b
5a				5b		
	6a				6b	
	7a				7b	
	8a			8b		
	9a				9b	
		10a			10b	
		11a		11b		
		12a		12b		
		13a		13b		
			14a 14b			

Motifs

THE STRUCTURE OF CHIASMUS

As if these two rival modes of apprehending the novel were not enough, there appears to be yet a third structure that demands our perceptive attention. *Pedro Páramo* seems to be structured upon a system of dual motifs that causes the first half of the novel to mirror the second half, in reverse. Consider the above table; each number in the table appears twice, and refers to a pair of textual details that will be outlined shortly. The numbers are distributed horizontally according to the page numbers upon which the signified motifs occur. The vertical distribution is an arbitrary, equal spacing between numbers, which facilitates our seeing the chiasmus. Following are descriptions of the textual details represented by the numbers:

1a. Dorotea advises Juan Preciado to make Pedro Páramo pay for his paternal neglect: "exígele lo nuestro. Lo que estuvo obligado a darme y nunca me dio . . . El olvido en que nos tuvo, mi hijo, cóbraselo caro" (p. 7). Juan begins to seek out his father after his mother's death.

1b. After his wife's death, Abundio, apparently another of Pedro's neglected sons, seeks out his father and demands financial help (pp. 125–27). He is in effect "cobrando el olvido en que Pedro lo tuvo."

2a. Abundio remarks, "Bonita fiesta le va a armar" (p. 8), when Juan says he is going to see his father.

2b. The people of Comala literally "arman una fiesta" after Susana San Juan dies (pp. 120–21).

3a. Abundio appears briefly at the novel's beginning (pp. 7–12).

3b. Abundio (perhaps a different one) appears briefly at the novel's end (pp. 123–27).

4a. Eduviges invites Juan Preciado to eat, and he responds, "—Iré. Iré después" (p. 15).

4b. Damiana Cisneros offers to bring Pedro Páramo his lunch, and he says, "Voy para allá. Ya voy" (p. 129).

5a. Susana San Juan is depicted at the bottom end of an "hilo," flying a kite (p. 16).

5b. Susana appears at the bottom end of an "hilo," lowered by her father into a mine shaft (pp. 94–95).

6a. Pedro Páramo mentally evokes the departure of a loved one, supposedly Susana, with the words, "El día que te fuiste entendí que no te volvería a ver" (p. 24).

6b. Pedro Páramo says to himself, "Hace mucho tiempo que te fuiste, Susana" (p. 122), and mentally evokes the moment of her departure.

7a. Eduviges converses with Miguel Páramo, her secret lover, through a window. Later Eduviges says, "Y cerré la ventana" (p. 26).

7b. Damiana sees Pedro Páramo climbing through a window to Margarita, his secret lover. Then Damiana "Cerró la ventana" (p. 110).

8a. In bed, Pedro awakens, and "Hace endurezar el cuerpo" (p. 27). He learns that his father has been killed (p. 28).

8b. Susana gets out of bed, "Endurezó el cuerpo" (p. 93), and receives word that her father has died.

9a. Padre Rentería resists giving the final blessing to Miguel Páramo's soul at his funeral mass; finally, he gives the blessing (pp. 29–30).

9b. Padre Rentería tries to give last rites to Susana, but she resists; the padre does not pronounce the final blessing (p. 119).

10a. Several men, walking home to retire for the night, discuss Miguel Páramo's death (pp. 32–33).

10b. Two women, walking home to retire for the night, discuss Susana San Juan's approaching death (pp. 115–17).

11a. Pedro Páramo has Fulgor Sedano arrange for his marriage to Dolores Preciado, so as to be rid of debts (pp. 40–41).

11b. Pedro Páramo has Fulgor Sedano arrange for Bartolomé's "disappearance" so that Pedro can live with Susana San Juan (p. 89).

12a. A young man tries to persuade a woman named Chona to run away with him. Chona resists, saying her father needs her (p. 49).

12b. Susana San Juan and her father discuss Pedro Páramo's proposal to live with Susana. Her father resists (pp. 87–88).

13a. An incestuous relationship is depicted between Donis and his sister (p. 54).

13b. An incestuous relationship is suggested between Susana and her father (p. 85).

14a. Juan Preciado lies down with Donis' sister (p. 61).

14b. Dorotea lies down (in the grave) with Juan Preciado (p. 65).

The motifs in the first part of the table appear in the order they are introduced in the novel. It will be observed that the order of their counterparts is not in precise reversal. However, their approximate conformity to the pattern of chiasmatic reversal is visible. What seems clear enough is that there is an echoing pattern involving certain actions by characters, in which the first and second halves of the novel duplicate each other. The point of division for the pattern is the moment at which Juan Preciado becomes conscious of his death—the same point generally acknowledged by critics as a structural halfway mark for the novel. The paired motifs mentioned are probably not all of those involved in this pattern. In most cases, the pairs are notable for their differences as well as for their similarities. For example, the point of equivalence between 1a and 1b is "requiring Pedro Páramo (as father) to pay." Points of difference are that in one case, Juan Preciado seeks out Pedro at his mother's death, while in the other, Abundio seeks him out at his wife's death. The complementary nature of these differences is often apparent. By virtue of these pairs of similarities and differences, various characters at these points act as doubles of each other.

Some ambiguity is endemic to the pattern of chiasmus. Its halves are equivalent to each other, yet they are also nonequivalent, because their order is reversed. The perception of chiasmus requires the mind to go in opposing directions. The reader proceeds without hesitation to the crux, but then he must read forwards and backwards at the same time—forwards to take in each new motif, and backwards to compare that motif with its earlier counterpart. All of this works against the traditional linear reading of the work, and in addition calls into question whether the second half duplicates the first, or whether it is the first half that duplicates the second.

Chiasmus as a structure involves a return to the point of origin. In *Pedro Páramo*, this structure harmonizes with the frequently expressed theme of return—Juan Preciado's and Abundio's return to their father, Susana San Juan's return to Comala, man's return to the earth through death, etc., and highlights the liberal sprinkling of verbs like "volver" and "regresar" one finds in the novel.

In many other respects, however, the chiasmatic structure is in dis-

harmony with the other structures. The weighing of differences and similarities that is required with nearly every set of paired motifs causes the
reader to perform a reduction that discards irrelevant differences. We find
emerging from this analysis not so much the *qualities* that characterize the
individuals and context of each single motif, as we find the *quantities* that
are held in common after these differences have been peeled away. The
pattern emerges only by virtue of these quantitative cores. Appropriately,
the term "chiasmus" itself derives from the word *chi*, the symbol "χ" which
is so often used to stand for a mathematical quantity. A reading of *Pedro
Páramo* in which characters and situations are but part of a χ-like form is
one that emphasizes the abstract, almost mathematical pattern at the expense of other more concrete considerations.

This third reading of the novel has a figure-ground reversibility with
the other two. The chiastic pattern takes elements from Juan Preciado's
frustrated search as well as elements from Pedro Páramo's story, and causes
the multitude of other elements in the novel not directly related to the
pattern to drop into the background. Thus, most of the narrative details,
as well as most of the texture of the transformed expression, are consigned
to nonstructured background status. The narrative reading is essentially
linear and chronological as is the expressionistic reading with its concatenation of elements. The chiastic reading is also linear, because it proceeds
in a fixed order from one motif to the next. But at the same time it appears
to be nonlinear and achronological, because it ends up where it started. To
the extent that it is nonlinear, the chiastic reading excludes the other two
readings of the novel.

Like the narrative and expressive structures we have examined, the
structure of chiasmus is not completely convincing. We need only look at
its graphic representation to see that it is an imperfect, slightly vague form.
Towards it vertex and its ends it is relatively solid, but in the middle regions
it seems to begin melting away. The question of whether a particular motif
belongs to the pattern must frequently be posed, because in addition to
the repetitive pattern of chiasmus and that of concatenation, there are more
random repetitions and leitmotifs that echo through the novel.

The reader who looks for possibilities in *Pedro Páramo* will find at least
three attractive readings that can be alternately postulated. But the careful
reader who seeks a satisfying solution to the novel's ambiguity will be
frustrated. As we mentioned earlier, there appears to be an implied definition of the reader within the novel, and that reader (as a counterpart of
the character Juan Preciado) is a searcher for such solutions. On the one
hand we are encouraged to join in the search, and on the other, we are
frustrated. Just as Juan Preciado tries to knock on a door but winds up
knocking "en falso," the reader is often given to expect that he is about to
hit upon some solid structure, only to find because of the imperfection of
the structure itself and because of other competing structures, that there
might be nothing solid there after all.

Juan Preciado's search ends in frustration; he never finds his father.

It might be noted as well that frustration is a common denominator for a good many of the novel's characters. Pedro Páramo is frustrated in his desire to possess Susana San Juan, Dorotea in her need for a child, Padre Rentería in his quest for integrity, Bartolomé in his search for gold and silver, and so on. As with the main characters, so it is with the reader.

Another common denominator among most, if not all, of the characters is that they are dead. Perhaps the reader must also succumb, in the sense that reading is defined as solving something, but there can be no positive solution. He might waver between possible solutions, as if to linger somewhere between life and death. Insisting on the validity of a partial reading, the reader might make it appear from a limited perspective that he is alive and well. But if the structures to be resolved are truly ambiguous, the concept of a reader as a solution-finder must eventually falter and crumble.

Authority and Identity in Rulfo's
El llano en llamas

Steven Boldy

There is a point in most of the stories of *El llano en llamas* where an individual comes up against the discourse of others, in the form of an accusation or declaration, and is annulled by it. His memory, knowledge, consciousness, sanity or even identity is destroyed. My first task is to describe the mechanism of that loss of consciousness. Though the alien discourse originates in a clearly identifiable figure of authority (*cacique*, parent, priest, government, army, the law), it is usually mediated by an unidentifiable impersonal or plural voice. The second question is thus why the voice of authority has become so fragmented, impersonal and empty. Three factors recur constantly: violence, transgression of structure, often family structure, its most basic form, and the death of the father. I have found it difficult to establish any strict hierarchy between these factors, any clear process of cause and effect. Rather they seem to be linked in an ever degenerating vicious circle.

"En la madrugada" provides a labyrinthine example of the mediation of the annihilating word, when the cowherd Esteban is accused of killing his land-owner employer: "Me llegaron con ese aviso. Y que dizque yo lo había matado, dijeron los díceres. Bien pudo ser; pero yo no me acuerdo." In "Macario," the repetition by the authoritarian figure of the *madrina* of the plural accusation that the boy had attacked a woman turns the report into an absolute truth for him, again to the detriment of his knowledge and memory: "Yo no sé por qué me amarrará las manos; pero dice que porque dizque luego hago locuras. Un día inventaron que yo andaba ahorcando a alguien; que le apreté el pescuezo a una señora nada más por nomás. Yo no me acuerdo. Pero, a todo esto, es mi madrina la que dice lo que yo hago y ella nunca anda con mentiras." In "Diles que no me maten," the accusing voice of the colonel comes from inside a building, and is

From *MLN* 101, no. 2 (1986). © 1986 by The Johns Hopkins University Press.

relayed through subalterns. The subsequent punishment not only kills, but makes the accused unrecognizable: "Tu nuera y tus nietos te extrañarán . . . Te mirarán a la cara y creerán que no eres tú."

A further grade of mediation is reached when the accusation is presented only in the discourse of the accused. In "El hombre," the accusations made by the "señor licenciado" which arbitrarily turn the shepherd who has just reported a crime into an accomplice are reported only in the replies of the accused, who is reduced to bewilderment and ignorance: "De haberlo sabido" is all he can repeat. "Pero yo qué sabía?"; "Soy borreguero y no sé de otras cosas." The absorption of the other's words, however, finally produces an unjustified guilt, and thus a partial acceptance of the crime: "Eso que me cuenta . . . no me lo perdono." In "Es que somos muy pobres," the guilt of the mother at her daughters' becoming prostitutes is also expressed in terms of not knowing and forgetfulness: "Mi mamá no sabe por qué Dios la ha castigado tanto. . . . Quién sabe de dónde les vendría . . . aquel mal ejemplo. Ella no se acuerda." There is nothing for her to remember, unless it be original sin: everything, including the title, shows that it is poverty and socio-geographical determinism which produce the prostitution. The alien discourse which gives her the feeling of having forgotten a crime is totally internalized, and is clearly that of the Church: "Todos fueron criados en el temor de Dios," she muses.

An unfounded accusation may create not only guilt but an actual repetition of the crime. In "La Cuesta de las Comadres," the tyrannical authority of the Torricos cancels out in the consciousness of their neighbours what the latter know to be true. The narrator says that the land distribution programme had only given the Torricos a small plot, but that "a pesar de eso, La Cuesta de las Comadres era de los Torricos. . . . No había por qué averiguar nada. Todo el mundo sabía que así era." The accusation by Remigio Torrico that the narrator had killed his brother does not immediately expunge the memory that he had not done so: "Me acuerdo bien de que yo no lo maté." The accused rules out any dialogue with the accuser, and kills him. He now has another memory: "Así que cuando yo maté a Remigio Torrico . . . Me acuerdo que había una luna muy grande"; "Me acuerdo que eso pasó allá por octubre. . . . De eso me acuerdo." The accusation and the memory of the crime, with the difference of a Christian name, becomes true.

"Nos han dado la tierra" and "El día del derrumbe" depict government authority and show it to be purely linguistic. Its word is totally empty and despite or rather because of its emptiness, its effects are devastating. In the first story it takes the form of the decree of the peasants' ownership of a barren wasteland, and the refusal of their words of protest: "Pero no nos dejaron decir nuestras cosas"; "Pero él no nos quiso oír." The result is literally a drying up of their words, described in a manically repetitive paragraph: "No decimos lo que pensamos. Hace ya tiempo que se nos acabaron las ganas de hablar. . . . Uno platicaría muy a gusto en otra parte, pero aquí cuesta trabajo. Uno platica aquí y las palabras se calientan en la boca con el calor de afuera, y se le resecan a uno en la lengua hasta que acaban con el resuello. Aquí así son las cosas. Por eso a nadie le da por platicar." When one character does talk, it is to repeat as his own the word of authority: "Esta es la tierra que nos han dado." Very rightly, the others consider this a sign of madness: "Yo no digo nada. Yo pienso: 'Melitón no tiene la cabeza en su lugar. . . . Y si no, ¿por qué dice lo que dice?' " Lacan defines madness as being spoken by language rather than speaking it. The destruction of language as communication reduces the initial solidarity of the four characters to deafness, a deafness which perpetuates and generalizes that practiced by the official: "Yo ya no oigo lo que sigue diciendo Esteban." In "El día del derrumbe," the word of authority similarly swamps the individual consciousness, dislodging his most personal interests. It is the account of an incredible feat of memory by a second character called Melitón, who repeats verbatim the words of another: the speech by the governor who comes to make a lengthy but vacuous promise of aid after an earthquake. The failure to help is again perpetuated in the listeners when the narrator *forgets* to call a midwife for the birth of his son. Not knowing as well as memory/forgetfulness also reappears in the song which duplicates the story's content: "No sabes de alma las horas de luto."

A further insight into the process is provided by "Talpa" and "En la madrugada." They illustrate well the discontinuity between the exercisers of force and authority (the brother and wife of Tanilo, and don Justo) and the resultant fragmented and empty word which is presented as imposing death and unconsciousness. In "Talpa," the desire of the killers and of the victim is formally the same: the pilgrimage. The content of their desire is opposite: Talino seeks a miraculous cure for his illness, while the others calculate that the trip will kill him so that they will be left free to enjoy their adultery. When he does die after they oblige him to complete the journey, they are separated by guilt and cannot forget his corpse, while their positive memory is obliterated: "Y Natalia se olvidó de mí desde entonces." At the moment of his death, moreover, their desire and consciousness are replaced by a plural and impersonal discourse. While Tanilo is praying, a tear drops from his eye and puts his candle out, yet the light from a multitude of other candles in the church prevents him from realizing this. Parallel to this extinction, the prayers of the congregation cancel out his own, so that he has to shout to realize that he is praying: "Pero no se dio cuenta de esto; la luminaria de tantas velas prendidas que allí había le cortó esa cosa con la que uno se sabe dar cuenta de lo que pasa junto a uno. Siguió . . . rezando a gritos para saber que rezaba." When the candle as consciousness ("aquella cosa con la que uno se sabe dar cuenta"), and the discourse of desire (intercession with the Virgin for a cure) goes out, so he dies. In "En la madrugada," Esteban's amnesia and loss of consciousness also coincide with the extinction of light: "Esa noche no encendieron las luces, de luto, pues don Justo era dueño de la luz." The ominously named *cacique*, don Justo, is the owner of light, of life and consciousness, yet when that power is exercised, he is dead. The word which extinguishes the light of consciousness becomes impersonal and plural: "Y que dizque yo lo había matado, dicen los díceres. Bien pudo ser; pero yo no me acuerdo." The father figure, the giver of language and identity, is absent and yet his force is present: he is both dead and alive. As Rulfo says of the faith of the characters of *Pedro Páramo*, his word is "uninhabited": "Aunque siguen siendo creyentes, su fe está deshabitada. No tienen un asidero, una cosa de donde aferrarse." This uninhabited word kills. The death of the father-figure thus seems to bring about a loss of identity. But, as we shall see, there is also a radical loss of consciousness and identity in the story before his death, which suggests either a previous death, or a chain of deaths.

The normal pattern, which could be adduced here, of the murder of the father and his return in the superego does not seem to operate, not least because the superego imposes prohibitions, structure, difference and thus identity, whereas all these things collapse in the stories. There is clearly a more complex and wider crisis in the role of the father and authority. "No oyes ladrar los perros" contains a typical inversion of the expected patterns. Ignacio has killed his *padrino*, a substitute father, and is thus the guilty party. Rulfo frequently describes guilt as a weight to be carried on one's back. Yet it is the father who carries the son on his back, and not vice versa, as might be expected given the relation of guilt with the paternal structures of the superego.

The loss of consciousness and identity on the part of Esteban and don Justo before the latter's death foregrounds two more terms in the equation of the stories: violence and transgression against family structure. The two men, master and servant, are made identical, and thus lose their individual identities, by their transgressive actions during the early morning, which form a curious but well-developed parallel. Esteban returns to the ranch with the cows; he finds the gate closed and, on receiving no answer, climbs in and opens up from inside. On glimpsing don Justo, he hides, fearing he will be rebuked: "Yo me escondí hasta hacerme perdedizo arrejolándome contra la pared, y de seguro no me vio. Al menos eso creí." He decides to separate a cow from its calf ("Ora te van a desahijar, motilona"), but re-unites them out of pity. Don Justo also enters a prohibited area and separates a mother from a child: his niece Margarita, with whom he sleeps, from his invalid sister. Aware of the condemnation their relationship would bring from the priest, he decides to keep it secret: "Dirá que es un incesto y nos excomulgará a los dos. Más vale dejar las cosas en secreto." Both men thus hide from authority after breaking a family structure. Like Esteban, don Justo returns the daughter to the mother at dawn. In both cases, this precedes an explosion of verbal violence: Margarita is called "prostituta," and the calf "hijo de res," before being kicked for sucking too hard. Both men, *amo* and *criado*, are made equal by the transgression of an internalized prohibition: their breaking that structure annuls the structural difference between them. While in fear of father figures, both men are in turn nominal fathers themselves: Esteban of the calf and don Justo of the daughter of a widowed sister. They renege on that role and leave it empty, bequeathing it in a debilitated state for others.

It is after these events that the violence takes place: don Justo beats Esteban for kicking the calf, and is later found dead, either from a blow by Esteban, which is unlikely, or from "coraje." Violence is itself a contagious force in society, dissolving of structure and identity. Whether because of this violence or the previous identification between the two men, don Justo's words are drained of meaning: "gritándole cosas de las que él nunca conoció su alcance." Within the concept of light as consciousness developed earlier, it is significant that neither can open his eyes during the fight: in the case of don Justo, "una nublazón negra le cubrió la mirada cuando quiso abrir los ojos"; and of Esteban, "no se supo cómo llegó a su casa, llevando los ojos cerrados." It is blindness, the extinction of the faculty which enables one to distinguish, to perceive differences, which confirms the loss of difference between them: "Quizá los dos estábamos ciegos y no nos dimos cuenta de que nos matábamos uno al otro."

The internalized authority of the priest and employer which was unable to check the transgression and violence, and contributes to alienate the subject from his own consciousness, becomes even more phantasmal, but more deadly, in the final extinction of Esteban's awareness of self, action, and reality: "Dicen que maté a don Justo. Bien pudo ser, pero no me acuerdo." The logic of cause and effect between the death of the father, transgression and violence is either cumulative, inverted, or circular. Circularity is suggested by the fact that at the beginning of the story Esteban's belly-button is cold: a strangely precise zone to be cold, but perhaps significantly the place where the umbilical cord is severed. It is cold after a fright from a *lechuza*, perhaps an "ánima en pena" like those which are encouraged to come out in the prayer which closes the story. The most likely "ánima en pena" is don Justo, who has not yet literally died. That previous, phantasmal death of the father-figure again produces loss of memory: "Yo tenía el ombligo frío de traerlo al aire. Ya no me acuerdo por qué."

The act of violence which is at least partially an effect in "En la madrugada" is the cause and starting point of the drama in "El hombre" and "Diles que no me maten." Violence generates reciprocal violence, and the reciprocity has the effect of linking the antagonists to the extent that they lose their individual identity. In "El hombre," the reader experiences serious doubts as to whether the pursued and the pursuer are not one and the same, one a projection of the other's guilt, a doubt only dispelled when the pursued is found with various bullets in the back of his head. Loss of consciousness and identity is clearly shown here to be contagious: the phantasmal voice at the end accuses not one of the antagonists, but a witness, the shepherd in whom the stability of subject, truth and innocence is undermined nearly as fundamentally as in Esteban. In "Diles que no me maten," a parallel situation is established between two fathers and two sons, one family in authority, a landowner and a colonel, and the other powerless. The violence of Juvencio Nava against his *compadre* Guadalupe Terrero is reciprocated on him by the latter's son, with the result that his face, his identity, is destroyed by the bullets. The "tiros de gracia" which put him out of his thirty-year-long agony suggest that, like his victim, he had been virtually dead for that time. The voice which accuses him is the victim's son, the reciprocity of the violence being disguised by the impersonality of the son's official military role. The official discourse overlays the personal in the same way the opposing desires of the characters of "Talpa" are subsumed in their common participation in the mass pilgrimage. Given the links suggested earlier between the death of the father and the emptiness of language, it is significant that the official is an orphan. His formulation is echoed throughout Rulfo's tests: "Es algo difícil crecer sabiendo que la cosa de donde podemos agarrarnos para enraizar está muerta." This rootlessness causes and is reflected in the rootlessness of language: when the accused approaches the building where the colonel is waiting, "[estaba] esperando ver salir a alguien. Pero sólo salió la voz." The emptiness of his language annihilates the individuality of the accused, turning him into merely a body occupying a space: "No podría perdonar a ése, aunque no lo conozco; pero el hecho de que se haya puesto en el lugar donde yo sé que está, me da ánimos para acabar con él." This linguistic death foreshadows the literal destruction of the subject's face. The pattern is repeated in *Pedro Páramo*: the death of the father (Lucas Páramo) creates the annihilating discourse of the son (Pedro Páramo), which destroys the consciousness and individuality of others, reducing them to the uninhabited "murmullos" which are the truest expression of his tyranny.

In a few cases, we see the individual hit back with a counter-discourse. In "La herencia de Matilde Arcángel," Euremio Cedillo's mother is dead, and his father, who considers him so little of an individual that he fails to give him a name different from his own, further attempts to annul him by consuming his inheritance, "con el único fin de que el muchacho no encontrara cuando creciera de donde agarrarse para vivir." The son's counter-discourse is the music of his flute, and for once the death of the tyrannical father seems to cause little trauma: "Venía en ancas con la mano izquierda dándole duro a la flauta, mientras que con la derecha sostenía, atravesado sobre la silla, el cuerpo de su padre muerto." Music is significantly not, however, the normal medium of the intersubjective communication which makes the individual an individual by meshing him dialectically with the discourse of others. And a more representative counter-discourse is the isolated delirium of madness, explored in the first story of the collection, "Macario," and in the case of Susana San Juan in *Pedro Páramo*. After the death in life of her father in the mine-shaft, Susana loses her sanity, but gains a mad discourse of metonymical associations which is impervious to the word of Pedro Páramo and his lackey padre Rentería.

"Macario" contains all the elements of the constellation we have examined so far: the "condenaciones del señor cura," the negative authority of a substitute parent figure, *la madrina*, transgressive and basically incestuous sex between the young Macario and the maid, Felipa, the impersonal accusation of an act of violence which is not remembered. The death of parents is also present as the first element of the *histoire*, though it is characteristically placed last in the text: "sin pasar ni siquiera por el purgatorio, y yo no podré ver entonces ni a mi mamá ni a mi papá, que es allí donde están."

The text is articulated around a set of strict oppositions, starkly positive and negative. The father has been described as having a double role in the transmission of language and identity: he gives a name and a "no," an identity and the prohibitions which conform the structures within which identity is formed and developed. Though the duality of the role is inseparable in normality, when on the other hand the presence of the father is perceived as being empty, the duality increases and the "no" predominates. In various stories, after the collapse of the fullness of the father, his word polarizes into something approaching schizophrenia. In "No oyes ladrar los perros," for example, the father carrying his son addresses him alternately as *tú* and *usted*; while the condemnatory *usted* voice is perceived as carrying the son sadistically to his death, the paternal *tú* carries him towards medical aid and possible recovery. Dolores Preciado similarly sends her son both to heaven and hell in Comala. In "Macario," the originally whole presence of the mother is split into two opposite maternal figures: the kind and sensual maid Felipa, and the authoritarian *madrina*. Associated with this split are the oppositions between heaven and hell (where the two women pray respectively that he should go); frogs and toads (edible versus inedible); day and night; crickets and scorpions (beneficent versus maleficent). Such differences are simply exacerbations of normal conceptual and linguistic structures normally held in check by a healthy discourse.

The insanity of the protagonist, Macario, is defined only once, and a curious definition it is; he is mad because he is constantly hungry: "Dicen en la calle que yo estoy loco porque jamás se me acaba el hambre." His hunger is mad because it does not respect the oppositions described earlier as structuring the story: he eats not only frogs, but toads, "aunque no se coman"; the milk from Felipa's breasts though she is not his mother; "leche de chiva y también de puerca recién parida," both goat's milk which is normal and pig's milk which is not; "el garbanzo remojado que le doy a los puercos gordos y el maíz seco que le doy a los puercos flacos," food destined for animals not humans, and *both* strictly codified types without distinction. The curious equivalence between *comer* and *platicar* in a parallel sequence confirms that eating, like everything else in the story, becomes discourse: if he stops eating, he muses, he will die and go to hell; if he stops chatting to the listener-reader, he will fall asleep, not kill the frogs, and be taken to hell by the devils his aunt will invoke. If he does not want to go straight to hell, it is mainly because he would miss the chance of seeing his parents. His discourse is thus his only possibility of maintaining some of their vital presence. The connection between eating and thus talking and the recovery of the maternal presence is further suggested by the fact that by far his favourite food is the milk from Felipa's breasts, "los bultos esos que ella tiene donde tenemos solamente las costillas," reflected in a far less positive manner in the "dos montoncitos" of food offered by the *madrina*.

Like his eating, the metonymic chains of Macario's *plática* are transgressive of normal difference: discrete objects become rootless signifiers which turn everything into a phantasm of the mother. The story opens with Macario out killing frogs. Abstracting phrases from the first page, we read: "Las ranas son verdes de todo a todo, menos en la panza. . . . Las ranas son buenas para hacer de comer con ellas. . . . Felipa tiene los ojos verdes como los ojos de los gatos [he means of course green like frogs]." Frogs are green; frogs are good to eat; Felipa's eyes are green . . . "Felipa is good to eat" is surely the conclusion of the sophism. And Felipa's food is the maternal milk. Macario's insatiable hunger ("Yo sé bien que no me lleno por más que coma todo lo que me den") is clearly equivalent to the absence and emptiness of the mother: this gap is a hungry vortex into which the whole of language is sucked until it signifies nothing but absence.

The story is almost entirely composed of warring discourses, one trying to cancel out the other, and corresponding to the two halves of the word of the mother embodied by the *madrina* and Felipa. The crickets drown out the screams from Purgatory: "Felipa dice que los grillos hacen ruido siempre . . . para que no se oigan los gritos de las ánimas que están penando en el purgatorio." The drum stifles the condemnations of the priest: "aquel tambor se oye de tan lejos, hasta lo hondo de la iglesia y por encima de las condenaciones del señor cura." The croaking of the frogs prevents the *madrina* from sleeping: "la gritería de las ranas le espantó el sueño."

The counter-discourse of Macario's *plática* is destined to lose out. Felipa does not want him to harm the frogs, the frogs which are good to eat and lead him to the positive mother. But the language of the frogs keeps the negative godmother awake, and Macario is ordered to kill them. The reason why he must obey the *madrina* is overwhelmingly final: "Es mi madrina la que saca el dinero de su bolsa para que Felipa compre todo lo de la comedera." As the possessor of money, she is, like the "dueño de la luz" don Justo, the ultimate controller of discourse, consciousness and identity. It is also the *madrina* who decrees that Macario will go to hell for knocking his head against the floor. He beats his head because it sounds like a drum: the drum which cancelled out the "condenaciones del señor cura." To beat his head is thus equivalent to the self-destructive discourse of madness against the guilt imposed by the authoritarian father-figure. There is a typical Rulfo inversion or vicious circle here: the drumming of beating his head cancels out the condemnations, but he is condemned for it. The condemnation is previous to the guilty discourse which brings it about; as elsewhere, it is the condemnation which creates the crime. Guilt, obviously related here to the death of the parents, is previous, original, or at least inherited and self-perpetuating: hence presumably his acceptance of the accusation that he had attempted to throttle "una señora nada más por nomás."

The pattern, in this story at least, seems to be that the absence or death of the parents produces a rootlessness of language in the son, a splitting of the paternal word into positive and negative discourses, and guilt. The guilt embodied in the condemnatory paternal discourse is countered by the discourse of madness designed to recover the full presence of the mother. Because of its transgression of the categories of thought and difference, the meshing of the two languages is broken, and the individual isolated. The discourse of the other becomes fragmented and phantasmal. The "no" of the father, successively embodied in the "condenaciones del señor cura" and the financially backed injunctions of the *madrina*, is finally articulated in the annihilating accusation of an anonymous and plural other, in which all notion of self is irreversibly lost: "Yo no sé por qué me amarrará mis manos; pero dice que porque luego hago locuras. . . . Yo no me acuerdo. Pero, a todo esto, es mi madrina la que dice lo que yo hago y ella nunca anda con mentiras."

Rulfo's own orphanhood, like that of César Vallejo, the loss of a centred, meaningful and beneficent domestic discourse, leads him to a painful but privileged consciousness of the emptiness of the language of society and authority which replaces it. All Mexicans become orphans with him, pawns in the vacuous discourse of a political power which likes to present itself as paternal. The characters of "Luvina" know better: "Pelaron sus dientes molenques y me dijeron que no, que el Gobierno no tenía madre." It may be overoptimistic to suggest that the awareness provoked in the reader of the extinction of the consciousness and word of the individual is in Vallejo's words "potente de orfandad."

Form and Content in Elena Garro's
Los recuerdos del porvenir

Harry Enrique Rosser

The literature of Latin America has long been recognized as social in its orientation. This is not surprising in view of the fact that so many Latin American nations have continually faced an enormity of socioeconomic and political problems in their efforts to establish national identity. As Alfonso Reyes once put it, "la verdadera historia literaria de nuestros pueblos queda un poco más vinculada con su historia política y social de lo que ha podido acontecer en pueblos más viejos." The interest in presenting social concerns in the form of a novel is attributed by some critics, Uriel Ospina among them, to the human make-up of the area, "la misma estructura humana del continente, inmenso laboratorio de razas, de carácteres y de personalidades."

As a vehicle for communicating and interpreting social norms and human values the novel is the genre which best serves Latin American writers in their artistic treatment of social reality at a given time and place. Manuel Pedro González emphasized the point in one of his studies, saying: "De todas las formas literarias la novela es la que más enraizada está en la vida y en la realidad económica y social que aspira a reflejar y resulta absurdo—particularmente trantándose de la novela—pretender explicarla en el vacío y sin relacionarla con el ambiente social, político, religioso y cultural en que se gestó." Particularly applicable to the majority of those Latin American writers who have cultivated the genre is Leo Lowenthal's view that a novel is especially illuminating not only for its direct social observations and its portraits of representative human types but also for "those larger portrayals of human reaction and expectation that give greater depth to the study of social influences and allow us to discern the inse-

From *Revista Canadiense de Estudios Hispánicos* 11, no. 3 (Spring 1978). © 1978 by Asociación Canadiense de Hispanitas, Carleton University.

curities and frustrations, or the securities and satisfactions, experienced by men in a given society" [*Literature, Popular Culture and Society*].

Recent generations of novelists in Latin America have shown a continued concern for the individual and the problems of human destiny, while paying special attention to unifying aesthetic and formal elements with this social commitment. This attitude is shared today by such writers as Alejo Carpentier, Julio Cortázar, Carlos Fuentes, Gabriel García Márquez, Mario Vargas Llosa and Agustín Yáñez, to mention some of the more prominent. They believe that the artist is a kind of guiding conscience with special responsibility for circulating ideas, truths and images through an artistic form in hopes of avoiding the loss of human perspective during difficult and threatening times. Carpentier speaks for many of his fellow writers when he declares that the function of the novel "consiste en violar constantemente el principio ingenuo de ser relato destinado a causar 'placer estético a los lectores, 'para hacerse un instrumento de indagación, un modo de conocimiento de hombres y de épocas—modo de conocimiento que rebasa, en muchos casos, las intenciones de su autor." Carlos Fuentes has emphasized the difficult mission of the novelist in his metaphor of the writer straddling two horses—one aesthetic and the other political. He suggests, however, that perhaps in the long run they are really one and the same horse because, after all, "toda obra literaria, fiel a sus premisas, y lograda en su realización, en su expresión, tiene un grado primario de significación social. No de un programa, impuesto desde afuera . . . sino de una convicción. Hablamos no de escritores comprometidos, sino de escritores que se comprometen: hay una gran diferencia entre los dos." At any rate, these by now established writers have all made important contributions to the new Latin American novel through their efforts to resolve an ongoing literary dilemma in their part of the world: to what extent should a novel represent or reveal objective socio-historical conditions and how valid is it to go beyond these conditions to fashion an artistic concentration of reality by means of techniques and stylistics that are practiced in more fully developed areas of the world?

While she has not shared the limelight with the more renowned novelists of Latin America, Elena Garro is a writer who has also made a valuable contribution in confronting the issue of the dynamics between form and content in her work *Los recuerdos del porvenir*, published for the first time in 1963. As do some of the more publicized Latin American literary figures, Elena Garro shows in her novel that life, history—the context—is closely bound up with the particular artistic work itself. She bears out the view offered by her compatriot Emmanuel Carballo that "el subdesarrollo económico y político no tiene que desembocar necesariamente en una novela conformista técnicamente ni en una novela que se desentienda del contexto histórico." In *Los recuerdos del porvenir* she has made a concerted effort to present a close relationship between form and content in a tightly-knit artistic whole. Her novel is proof that the two are logically inseparable. If the form of a work transmits and is in turn determined by the content, it follows that the former does not really exist without the latter. Garro has created a text that may be viewed as what Carlos Blanco Aguinaga has referred to as "una resolución dialéctica del conflicto vida-literatura." In other words, as a significant work of art, the novel is essentially the creation of Garro's own world. She depicts her characters as complete human individuals who live in a circumscribed, self-contained context in which social relations, as in life itself, are in constant flux. *Los recuerdos del porvenir* is an ordered whole which conveys the truth about the world represented therein, and the relations within the world. She has succeeded in fashioning what Lukács would call "an intensive artistic totality," which is the result of "the circumscribed and self-contained ordering of those factors which objectively are of decisive significance for the portion of life depicted, which determines its existence and motion, its specific quality and its place in the total life process" [*Writer and Critic and Other Essays*].

Basing her novel on the period of social unrest in Mexico known as the Cristero Wars, which raged in the 1920s following the first armed phase of the Revolution, Garro makes a masterful evocation of the spiritual and psychological anguish experienced by many people when the regime of Plutarco Elías Calles resorted to a campaign of violence in its attempts to curb the power of the Roman Catholic Church. On occasion she blurs the distinction between appearance and reality in order to dramatize a sense of human alienation, a procedure which coincides with Lukács's view of art as a process in which man's spirit or inner being is projected as "significant form." By focusing on the multi-faceted human reaction to the external world, Garro has fulfilled what to Lukács's way of thinking is an essential requirement for successfully making an artistic reflection of reality: "to provide a picture of reality in which the contradictions between appearance and reality, the particular and the general, the immediate and the conceptual, etc., is so resolved that the two converge into a spontaneous integrity in the direct impression of the work of art and provide a sense of inseparable integrity." In her treatment of life in a small town that becomes caught in the strife arising from the revolutionary government's hardline interpretation of the new Constitution of 1917, Garro constantly shifts between individual and collective planes. She manages to maintain an intricate, intimate relationship with what John Rutherford describes as "all the other structures and systems into which we can divide existence, that is, the economic and social structures of the group, the physiological and psychological structures of the individual." And indeed, by doing this Garro dramatizes such personal conflicts as General Francisco Rosas's unrequited love and his subjective interpretation of power and authority. On the more overt, collective level, attention is brought to various social forces at work in the town before the arrival of the outsider for whom the hermetic townspeople's hatred knows few bounds. Mutual destruction ensues in one form or another. When Rosas finally departs, what is left of the town remains in a kind of suspended animation. The impossibility of self-realization under oppression in any guise emerges as a principal characteristic of the human condition.

Garro's success in revealing the concrete and abstract potentialities of individual people and their connection with social and historical forces is dependent, of course, on the literary techniques she employs and the characterization she achieves through them. For the most part, she relies on the presentation of typical characters with qualities and tendencies which gradually emerge out of the whole, a complex interaction of a variety of people and their social institutions (i.e., the legal system, the military, the Church, the government bureaucracy at the national and local levels). Her characters are enduring human types, complete within themselves. Without losing their individuality they convey the essence of a particular period, living within the complex stratification of their social reality. By creating characters who are a unity of the universal and particular—the typical and the individual—she is able to present, again in Lukács's terms, "the greatest possible richness of the objective conditions of life as the particular attributes of individual people and situations." Underlying Garro's overall portrayal of society and its constituents, moreover, is the view that the historical process, like the life of the individual, involves an interaction between the past and the future. The very title of the novel reflects this. The author's conception of the present condition in her work, generally pessimistic and critical, is that it has come to be as a result of the way in which society's problems have been dealt with at some point in the past. The social realities of tomorrow depend in large part on how men confront those realities that take place today.

Turning to the matter of techniques or literary methods in more specific terms, the primary narrative responsibility of *Los recuerdos del porvenir* is assigned to the town of Ixtepec itself. Concerned with evoking emotion, the author makes full use of a lyrical, subjective-objective approach to reality by personifying the town through a dual role of narrator and protagonist. Garro alternates narrative attitudes by shifting from first person singular to first person plural to omniscient third person singular and plural. She thereby translates tangible reality into an introspective range of feelings by this emphasis on personal involvement. On occasion a situation is temporarily objectified by adopting a narrative distance that interrupts the intimate association of the reader with the principal narrator.

The sort of narrative transposition employed by Garro has drawn some negative criticism. Walter Langford feels that the technique of personifying the town is "not completely convincing." John Brushwood has remarked that the narrative procedure is "the only really disturbing aspect of the novel." While Garro's technique may initially come across as contrived, it soon establishes a rhythmic pattern of shifting from one narrative proximity to another, and it becomes clear that Garro's method not only provides several levels of perspective but also intensifies the points of view themselves. The subjective-objective approach to reality practiced here is one that is encouraged by the new romanticists whose particular aspiration is to combine realism with romanticism. The former allows for a focus on man's social development while the latter finds its inspiration in the more noble human ideals. The result is an artistic method which, as José Díaz Fernández explains, "ajusta sus nuevas formas de expresión a las nuevas inquietudes del pensamiento."

Another function of the narrative technique in this novel is to blur the line between objective reality and the kind of unreal or dreamlike dimension to life that some people experience. The characters in *Los recuerdos del porvenir* are disoriented, alienated and deprived of hope for the future. They exist in a kind of psychic limbo. In this state, the spectre of finality, or death, eliminates conventional conceptions of time and chronological sequence. The traditional, orderly progression from past to present to future is distorted by the novelist to dramatize the frustration and uncertainty that are part of universal experience. A unique quality of this work, then, stems from what Joseph Sommers sees as "the prism of time through which the narrator views the microcosm of Ixtepec." Garro has succeeded in depicting a timeless existence in which the consciousness of death is ever-present.

The characters who inhabit the town of Ixtepec are aware that they experience their lives in recurring patterns of *déjá vu*. In their imperfection and impotence, the people are condemned to live in a kind of "prestructured trap of existence." On occasion they express their feeling that time is out of their control. The future is essentially a recurrence of the past. The present is a point at which the past and the future converge. Because of this, the human memory cannot distinguish between the conventional, chronological divisions by which man attempts to order his existence. Thus a principal character, Isabel, is led to remark: "Francisco, tenemos dos memorias. . . . Yo antes vivía en las dos y ahora sólo vivo en la que me recuerda lo que va a suceder." There is little hope of self-realization for people who suffer from a self-imposed and/or other-imposed repression. The town-narrator draws attention to this, lamenting:

> Una generación sucede a la otra, y cada una repite los actos de la anterior. Sólo un instante antes de morir descubren que era posible soñar y dibujar el mundo a su manera, para luego despertar y empezar un dibujo diferente. . . . Y vienen otras generaciones a repetir sus mismos gestos y su mismo asombro final.

The narratives of *Los recuerdos del porvenir* jump forward and backward in time to show the unimportance of chronological sequence when life is a form of death in a meaningless, stagnant set of circumstances. At the same time the technique of detailing an event long after the outcome has been established heightens the impact of that event. An air of mystery is given an incident such as the suspicious death of a local priest. General

Rosas cannot find the body and begins to doubt that the clergyman ever lived in the first place, believing that the townspeople are only attempting to escalate the tensions in Ixtepec. Long after the fact of the priest's death comes to light, the narrator looks back to the events leading up to his murder. Another method used by Garro to highlight an event involves jumping ahead in order to show how a prediction or premonition is fulfilled. In addition, she uses random flashbacks, smoothly integrating them into the text. They further contribute to the delineation of the characters. The retrospective views are presented largely in the form of memories directly introduced by the narrator.

By stressing the impact of a particular event upon a character the author communicates the idea that there is often no clear line dividing that which is experienced from that which is imagined. Each event is subject to a highly individualized interpretation of reality but is presented as though there were absolutely nothing extraordinary about it. It involves capturing the mysterious air that may envelop an event or a situation in a world in which there are many shades of meaning, many interpretations, many forms and facets of reality. The use of unusual associations and juxtapositions serves to convey the subjective involvement of Garro's characters. Everyday reality is transformed into something extraordinary because the particular emotional state of the individual induces him or her to perceive the event as unusual. In the passage that follows, Garro emphasizes the tired and depressed state of one of the characters, describing in an objective narrative fashion the uncontrollable sensations experienced by the physically and emotionally vulnerable Isabel:

> —Yo no quepo en este cuerpo!—exclamó Nicolás, vencido, y se tapó la cara con las manos como si fuera a llorar.
> —Estamos cansados—dijo Félix desde su escabel. Durante unos segundos la casa entera viajó por los cielos, se integró en la Vía Láctea y luego cayó sin ruido en el mismo punto en el que se encuentra ahora. Isabel recibió el choque de la caída, saltó de su asiento, miró a sus hermanos y se sintió segura; recordó que estaba en Ixtepec y que un gesto inesperado podía reintegrarnos al orden perdido.

This intense subjective involvement of Garro's characters in experiencing people and situations produces distinct imagery. For example, the lack of people's response to the eccentric Tomás Segovia's efforts to communicate is deeply felt, and is expressed by the narrator as follows: "Tomás Segovia se esforzó por ensartar frases brillantes como cuentas, pero ante el silencio de sus amigos perdió el hilo y las vio rodar melancólico por el suelo y perderse entre las pastas de las sillas." Finally, Garro's subjective-objective approach to reality serves to intensify an event, as when the cry of "¡Viva Cristo Rey!" echoes through the streets of Ixtepec:

El grito se prolongaba en los portales. Sonaron disparos persi-
guiendo aquel grito que dio la vuelta al pueblo. A oscuras lo co-
rreteaban los soldados y él surgía de todos los rincones de la noche.
A veces corría delante de sus perseguidores, luego los perseguía
por la espalda. Ellos lo buscaban a ciegas, avanzando, retroce-
diendo, cada vez más enojados. Después, durante noches y
noches, se repitió el baile del grito y de los soldados que zig-
zagueaban por mis vericuetos y mis calles.

Such "magic realist" perceptions not only heighten a sense of surprise
and suspense but also contribute to the overall delineation of the characters.
While the voice of Ixtepec functions in the aforementioned dual role of
narrator-protagonist, the information offered directly about the characters
is kept to a minimum. Garro favors providing glimpses into the lives of
the townspeople. She allows them to delineate themselves partially through
revelation of their inner reality. Memories of the past blend with intimations
about the future while the characters exist in an unrecognizable present.

At the center of the novel is General Francisco Rosas, who, after Ixtepec
itself, the collective protagonist, is the most fully developed individual
character. He is a man of violence, delineated on a dual plane that exposes
the tensions between his exterior ruthlessness and his inner life of illusion.
He is a character of tragic dimension who, reminiscent of Rulfo's Pedro
Páramo, struggles with his obsession for a woman, the aloof and enigmatic
Julia Andrade. Suffering from unrequited love, the General is driven to
acts of terror against the people of Ixtepec in a futile effort to overcome his
personal pain. Rosas persecutes the townspeople largely through emotional
need rather than ideological or constitutional principle. The church-state
conflict in Ixtepec is made all the more tragic and hopeless.

In contrast to Rosas is the beautiful and solitary Julia Andrade. She is
depicted in a somewhat sketchy fashion in order to portray her as ethereal
and unattainable. She lives in a world of her own, constructed upon her
memories of other places and other men. The opposite natures of Julia and
Rosas are underscored by the way in which they react to each other and
to their existence. Rosas seeks refuge in the present, hoping to fully possess
Julia just as he is possessed by her. She retreats to the past and blocks him
out of her inner life. Rosas cannot understand her. Indeed, no one can,
for she has erected an impenetrable barrier between herself and those
around her. Julia's languid nature is in sharp contrast to Rosas's outbursts
of emotion and energetic activity. She is essentially an abstraction—the
image of love for all Ixtepec.

A host of other characters appear in *Los recuerdos del porvenir*. Garro
presents them clearly in a few broad brush strokes. She introduces a number
of officers and their women living in the same hotel where General Rosas
and Julia reside. There is a view of a "house of ill repute" run by the

dynamic La Luchi and occupied by Juan Cariño, a demented soul who extols the value of rationality and fancies himself the president of the town. The author introduces the reader to an upper class social circle through the personages of Don Joaquín Menéndez and his wife Matilde who gather with others of their ilk in a time of crisis to engage in idle and fatuous conversation. Garro traces the way in which the wealthy Goríbar family's greed and self-interest drive them to accumulate capital through land-grabbing schemes and outright theft. The resistance to General Rosas is led by the Moncadas, a family of integrity and enlightenment who is supported by such strong and humble servants as Félix, Gregoria and Cástulo. The clergymen of the village, about whom no descriptive information is provided, appear as figures supported by the townspeople and persecuted by Rosas and his men during the escalation of the conflict between Ixtepec's conservative inhabitants and the military force of the federal government. In addition an anonymous, faceless mass of Indians and other outcasts lurks in the shadows of the social scenario, serving as targets of verbal abuse and providing the bodies for General Rosas's lynching rampages.

All of the characters, the secondary as well as the primary, become in themselves like memories in a world in which time has lost its meaning. Their separate recollections come to be the only thing that differentiates them from one another during the period of terror. The town's "future" never really comes. The presence of love is not felt strongly enough to be of any consolation to Ixtepec's people, and a lack of communication leads to solitude, anonymity and nihilism. The characters all face, in their own way, the meaning of life in a stagnant, oppressive environment which fosters a living form of death—an existence which is possibly worse than death itself.

In her flowing style Garro relies largely upon sensory imagery. To convey the nature of the external world and impressions of human activity, she favors descriptions of pungent smells, bright colors and the noises of life, as evidenced in the passage that follows:

> Los sábados el atrio de la iglesia, sembrado de almendros, se llena de compradores y mercaderes. Brillan al sol los refrescos pintados, las cintas de colores, las cuentas de oro y las telas rosas y azules. El aire se impregna de vapores de fritangas, de sacos de carbón oloroso todavía a madera, de bocas babeando alcohol y de majadas de burros. Por las noches estallan los cohetes y las riñas: relucen los machetes junto a las pilas de maíz y los mecheros de petróleo. Los lunes, muy de mañana, se retiran los ruidosos invasores de-jándome algunos muertos que el Ayuntamiento recoge. Y esto pasa desde que yo tengo memoria.

Her writing is characterized by a flexible, poetic language. There is a sensitivity to the sound of words and their syntactical rhythms, apparent in a passage like the following in which she describes Julia's appearance at the public plaza:

> Olvidamos todo por verla entrar en la plaza. Venía con uno de aquellos trajes suyos de tonos rosa pálido escarchado de pequeños cristales, translúcidos, centelleante como una gota de agua, con sus joyas enroscadas al cuello y los cabellos ahumados meciéndose como plumas ligeras sobre la nuca. Dio varias vueltas, apenas apoyada en el brazo de su amante que avanzaba con ella con respeto, como si llevara junto a él a toda la belleza indecible de la noche.

The author's descriptive powers are also evident on the interior, lyrical plane which serves to reveal the inner essence of her characters' contrastive moods and feelings:

> Isabel estaba en el centro del día como una roca en mitad del campo. De su corazón brotaban piedras que corrían por su cuerpo y lo volvían inmovible. "¡A las estatuas de marfil, una, dos, tres . . . !" La frase de juego infantil le llegaba sonora y repetida como una campana. Ella y sus hermanos se quedaban fijos al decirla, hasta que alguien a quien habían señalado en secreto pasaba por allí, los tocaba y rompía el encantamiento. Ahora nadie vendría a desencantarla; sus hermanos también estaban fijos para siempre. "¡A las estatuas de marfil, una dos tres . . . !" Las palabras mágicas se repetían una y otra vez y el día también estaba fijo como una estatua de luz. Gregoria le hablaba desde un mundo ligero y móvil que ella ya no compartía. La miró sin pestañear.

Garro's characters exchange words in brief dialogues that have a natural, easy-flowing tone to them. A conversation between General Rosas and some of the ladies of Ixtepec about the planning of a party that would facilitate a truce goes as follows:

> —¿En que puedo servirlas?—insistió Rosas con amabilidad.
> —¡General, vinimos a ofrecerle un ramito de oliva!—lanzó Doña Elvira con aire pomposo y contenta al descubrir la juventud y el buen parecer de su adversario.
> Los ojos amarillos del general la miraron sin entender el significado de su frase.
> —Hay que aligerar el aire. . . . No podemos vivir en esta violencia. Queremos ofrecerle nuestra amistad para acabar con esta guerra civil tan perjudicial para todos nosotros.

There is no attempt to convey class origins or social status through the use of speech with the result that the characters sound much the same throughout the novel. On the few occasions in which the author calls attention to the particular speech patterns of a character, it is done through a brief description on the part of the narrator rather than through punctuational devices or word contractions. Garro indicates that General Rosas is a northern officer occupying a southern town, saying that he "arrastró sus palabras, alargándolas sobre las vocales y luego cortando brúscamente el final, como todos los norteños."

Particular attention is given to language *per se*, however, through the memorable Juan Cariño, a strange character who is fascinated with words and their proper usage:

> . . . las palabras eran peligrosas porque existían por ellas mismas y la defensa de los diccionarios evitaba castástrofes inimaginables. Las palabras debían permanecer secretas. Si los hombres conocían su existencia, llevados por su maldad las dirían y harían saltar al mundo. Ya eran demasiadas las que conocían los ignorantes y se valían de ellas para provocar sufrimientos.

Cariño is impressed by the power of words and makes it his business to collect all the "palabras malignas" that he hears pronounced during the day. Upon returning home he takes the words apart, letter by letter, and puts them back into the dictionary where he feels they never should have left in the first place. The light touch in handling this subject provides respite from the generally melancholy tone that pervades the novel.

Elena Garro's criticism of the Mexican Revolution as a whole is more bitter than the view of a number of her fellow novelists who deal with recent Mexican history in their works. The thrust of *Los recuerdos del porvenir*, written some fifty years after the national upheaval, is a pessimistic one with regard to the accomplishments of the "revolutionary" regime. It is made clear in Garro's novel that for many Mexicans the policies of the new government meant invasion of their privacy, military occupation of their town, disruption of their religious and social life, severe economic loss and, for a number of them, death itself. Garro expresses cynicism for the way in which the government functions. At the same time she raises a question regarding the human condition. Is life under circumstances in which there is no avenue for self-realization really anything more than a living death?

The personal tragedy of General Rosas, ordered to govern Ixtepec during the period of terror, lies in his inability to communicate with the townspeople. His own posture is a reflection of the national government's:

> Los pistoleros eran la nueva clase surgida del matrimonio de la Revolución traidora con el porfirismo. Enfundados en trajes caros de gabardina, con los ojos cubiertos por gafas oscuras y las cabezas protegidas por fieltros flexibles, ejercían el macabro trabajo de escamotear hombres y devolver cadáveres mutilados. A este acto de prestidigitación, los generales le llamaban "Hacer Patria" y los porfiristas "Justicia Divina." Las dos expresiones significaban negocios sucios y despojos brutales.

Garro's interpretation of the recent history of her nation is that the Revolutionary efforts were betrayed by many generals who allied themselves with staunch supporters of the old Porfiriato. The central narrator of her novel minces no words on the subject:

> Hubo un momento, cuando Venustiano Carranza traicionó a la Revolución triunfante y tomó el poder, en que las clases adineradas tuvieron un alivio. Después, con el asesinato de Emiliano Zapata, de Francisco Villa y de Felipe Angeles, se sintieron seguras. Pero los generales traidores a la Revolución instalaron un gobierno tiránico y voraz que sólo compartía las riquezas y los privilegios con sus antiguos enemigos y cómplices en la traición: los grandes terratenientes del porfirismo.

The benefits of the Revolution, then, have gone mainly to those opportunists who have manipulated it to their own ends. Being a member of a particular class is not necessarily an advantage. One character in the novel, in addressing fellow elitists, points out: "La Revolución no la hicieron ustedes. Es natural que ahora no les toque nada del botín."

One of Garro's more interesting views lies in her perception of a connection between the Cristero Wars and the government's policy on agrarian reform. The church-state conflict of the 1920s was revived and exacerbated in part to enable those in power to conveniently gloss over the real issue at hand:

> En aquellos días empezaba una nueva calamidad política; las relaciones entre el Gobierno y la Iglesia se habían vuelto tirantes. Había intereses encontrados y las dos facciones en el poder se disponían a lanzarse en una lucha que ofrecía la ventaja de distraer al pueblo del único punto que había que oscurecer: la repartición de las tierras.
>
> Los periódicos hablaban de la "fe cristiana" y los "derechos revolucionarios." Entre los porfiristas católicos y los revolucionarios ateos preparaban la tumba del agrarismo.

Besides diverting the course of agrarian reform, the church-state conflict brought on years of terror in which the Church was unable to function in any capacity. A result of this, particularly in the towns of rural Mexico, was a stark feeling of loss of identity. The Revolution may have served to open the doors of the provincial town, and in some cases, to jolt the people out of their isolation and inertia, but it was apparently temporary. Moreover, what they had to face immediately after in the form of repressive military rule and religious persecution, all in the name of the Revolution, made many people question whether or not it had been advantageous to have a revolution in the first place. This insecurity and doubt on the part of inhabitants of towns like Ixtepec exacerbates their feelings of alienation and hostility, not only toward the government, but toward one another as well.

Los recuerdos del porvenir is a pessimistic protest integrated into an artistic portrayal of provincial Mexico in the 1920s. The critical thrust of Elena Garro goes beyond that stage in the Mexican historical process. While she calls attention to the injustices of the early decades of the Revolution, her novel has implicit meaning for contemporary Mexico as well. Today there are new problems which must be dealt with. But a number of old ones that Garro has set forth in her novel carry over to the present day. Beyond the context of the Cristero Wars, *Los recuerdos del porvenir* has a universal projection, for the novelist has focused on the question of whether the human condition can ever really be identified as life rather than death, where today is yesterday's tomorrow.

Writing/Transvestism

Severo Sarduy

Although it is perforce restrained, a hint of ridicule is apparent in Goya's reverent and polished portraits. The absurd, the compulsive force of the ridiculous, as if it were tearing the canvas to shreds, eats away at those ladies of the Spanish court until they are transformed into placid monstrosities.

If we see, simultaneously, respect and derision, piety and mockery, in those figures it is because there is something in the royal entourage which suggests that it is all *false*. I am thinking of Queen María Luisa in *The Family of Carlos IV*, jewel-encrusted and plump, with a diamond arrow piercing her coiffure, and, above all, of the Marquesa de la Solana, crowned with a huge flower made of pink felt.

The subliminally false in these examples—*without having to alter a single element of their basic form*—changes the jewels into paste, the gowns into disguises, the smiles into grimaces.

I make these references to Goya because they all seem related to, and ultimately explained by, the character Manuela in José Donoso's *Hell Has No Limits*. In Manuela, queen and scarecrow, we see falsity, we see the abomination of the *postiche*. The portrait becomes a blot and the outline a blur because we are dealing here with a transvestite, with someone who has carried inversion to its limits.

The goyesque in Manuela appears when, on the level of gestures and sentences cast in the feminine gender, we suddenly realize that they all refer—*without having to alter a single element of their basic form* (grammatical form)—to Manuel González Astica, the dancer who came to town one day to brighten up a party at La Japonesa's bordello. He was "as skinny as a

From *Review* no. 9 (Fall 1973), translated by Alfred MacAdam. © 1973 by the Center for Inter-American Relations, Inc.

broom stick, with long hair and with his eyes as heavily made-up as those of the Farías sisters [obese harpists]" and the execution of a *tableau vivant* along with the madame made him a father.

The central inversion, Manuel's, provokes a chain reaction of inversions, and these make up the novel's basic structure. In this sense, *Hell Has No Limits* continues the mythical tradition of "the world turned upside down" so assiduously cultivated by the Surrealists. The novel's meaning— more than simple transvestism (the outward expression of sexual inversion)—is inversion itself. The progress of the narrative is dominated by a metonymic chain of "upsets," of displaced *dénouements*.

Manuela, who novelistically (grammatically) is defined as a woman— initial inversion—*functions* as a man, since it is as a man that he attracts La Japonesa. It is this attraction which induces the curious madame to execute the *tableau vivant*; her ambition (the village bourgeois promises her a house if she can excite the apocryphal dancer) is nothing more than a pretext, one in which money justifies all transgressions.

Inside this inversion there arises another: in the sexual act, Manuela's role—he having been termed masculine by the narrative—is passive. Not that it is feminine—we are dealing with an inversion within an inversion and not with a simple return to the initial transvestism—but rather that it is of a passive man, one who engenders *malgré lui*. La Japonesa possesses him by having herself possessed by him. She is the active element in the *act* (also to be taken in its theatrical sense: a single glance is enough to create the space of the show, to crystalize the Other, the scene). The succession of adaptations, the metaphor of the Russian doll, could be diagrammed.
Inversions:

1st.   A man dresses up as a woman

2nd.   who attracts because of whatever there is in her which is masculine

3rd.   which is *passive* in the sexual act.

This formal chain, which gives shape to narrative space as it marks out its coordinates, is "reflected" thematically on the level of emotional attraction: Pancho Vega, the official *macho* of the hamlet, besieges Manuela, fascinated, in spite (or because) of scandal, of the mask or of the goyesque imposture. The final sadistic act, which Pancho and his follower Octavio perpetrate, is a substitute for an act of possession. The *macho*—that reverse form of transvestism—incapable of confronting his own desire, of assuming the image of himself which his desire wills he assume, becomes an inquisitor, an executioner.

Donoso skillfully disguises his sentence, he masks it in order to locate it symbolically at Manuela's emotional level. He does this to delegate the "responsibility" of the tale to her (the third person narrator seems to be just another means of hiding the facts), to an ego which is lurking, dissimulated, the real subject of the sentence: the entire *he/she* structure is a cover-up; a latent "I" threatens it, undermines it, cracks it. As in that other place without limits, dreams, everything here says "I."

Verbs with an aggressive meaning (*kick, punch*) are often "dubbed" with others which have sexual connotations (*pant*), with metaphors of desire (*men are hungry*), of penetration (*their drooling and hard bodies wounding his*), of pleasure (*their hot bodies twisting around*). One sentence, finally, as if the subterranean discourse relaxed for a second, makes the sadistic joy explicit: "delighted to the depth of their painful confusion."

Another inversion may be seen on the level of social functions: the present madam of the bordello (La Japonesita) is a virgin, and as if to underline the fact that in this inverted world the only possible attraction is that which is governed by disguise, no one desires her.

This game of "upsets" which I have outlined may be extended to the entire narrative: Donoso substitutes for the tale-within-a-tale an inversion-within-an-inversion. If this system of twists, one within another, never straightens out into an image analogous to that of the "right-side-up world," but goes on spinning further and further, it is because the thing inverted in each case is not the totality of the surface—economics, politics, class tensions, none of these is changed in the upsets, and they always correspond to "reality"—but only its constantly changing erotic signifiers, certain verbal levels, the topology which certain words delineate.

APPEARANCES DECEIVE

We are deceived by those things which constitute the supposed "exterior" of literature: the page, the blank spaces, all that comes out of those spaces to appear between the lines, the horizontality of writing, the writing itself, etc. This appearance, this display of visual signifiers—and through them (the visual aspects) those which are phonetic—and the relationships which are created in that privileged place in the association that is the *plane* of the page, the *volume* of the book. These are the things that a persistent prejudice has considered the exterior face, the obverse of something which must be what that face *expresses:* content, ideas, messages, even a "fiction," an imaginary world, etc.

That prejudice, manifest or not, sweetened with various vocabularies, taken up in various dialectics, is that of realism. Everything in it, in its vast grammar, backed up by culture, the guarantee of its ideology, supposes a reality outside the text, outside the "literalness" of writing. That reality, which the author should limit himself to expressing, to translating, should direct the movements of the page, its body, its languages, the material quality of writing. The most ingenuous people suppose that it is the reality of the "world around us," the reality of events; the wisest displace that fallacy in order to present us with an imaginary entity, something ficticious, a "fantastic world." But it's all the same: pure realists—socialist or not—and magic realists promulgate and have recourse to the same myth. It is a myth rooted in aristotelian, logocentric knowledge, knowledge about a "source," about something primitive and *true* which the author brings to the blank page. And it is to this kind of thinking that we may relate the *fetishization* of this new singer, this demiurge recovered by Romanticism.

The progress of certain theoretical studies, the complete turnabout those studies have brought about in literary criticism, have made us re-evaluate all of what had been considered as an outside, an appearance:

(1) the unconscious considered as a language subject to its own rhetorical laws, its own codes and transgressions; the attention given to signifiers, which create an *effect* which is the sense, the attention given to the manifest substance of dream. (Lacan)

(2) the "content" of a work considered as an absence, metaphor as a sign without content and it is "that distance from meaning which the symbolic process designates." (Barthes)

The apparent exteriority of the text, the surface, that "mask" which fools us, "since if there is a mask there is nothing behind it; a surface which doesn't hide anything but itself; a surface which, because it makes us suppose that there is something behind it, stops us from thinking it a surface. The mask makes us believe that there is a depth, but what the mask covers is itself: the mask feigns dissimulation to dissimulate that it is nothing more than a simulation."

Transvestism, as Donoso's novel practices it, is probably the best metaphor for what writing really is: what Manuela makes us see is not a woman *under whose outward appearance* a man must be hiding, a cosmetic mask which, when it falls will reveal a beard, a rough, hard face, but rather *the very fact of transvestism itself*. No one cannot know, and it would be impossible not to know it, given the obvious falsity of the disguise, that Manuela is a tired out dancer, a dissimulated man, a goyesque *capricho*. What Manuela reveals is the coexistence, in a single body, of masculine and feminine signifiers: the tension, the repulsion, the antagonism which is created between them.

By means of a symbolic language this character comes to signify a painting-over, a concealment, a hiding of something. Painted eyebrows and beard: that mask would enmask its being a mask. That is the "reality" (limitless, since everything is contaminated by it) which Donoso's hero enunciates.

Those planes of intersexuality are analogous to the planes of intertextuality which make up the literary object. They are planes which communicate on the same exterior, which answer each other and complete each other and define each other. That interaction of linguistic textures, of discourses, that dance, that parody, is writing.

José Donoso: Endgame

Alfred J. MacAdam

Both in their titles and in their *mise en scène, La vida breve* and *Paradiso* demonstrate that the *locus* of writing is language, literary language, and that all "new" texts are reflections and echoes of extant models. The writing of a narrative is an exercise in interpolation: just as a narrative "opens" to allow the insertion of an interpolated tale, just as the narrator of *La invención de Morel* enters Morel's film, the literary tradition constantly opens to allow variation. But all variation, all novelty, is perforce limited. Recombination may be infinite, but the elements recombined inevitably show family traits. This sense of literature as a "family affair" may go far as a metaphor useful for understanding Latin American narrative, a literature which, as we have seen, often chooses as its framework the history of families or of familial combinations such as brothers or doubles. Throughout the texts under consideration here there is the idea of repetition and variation, of text-begetting-text, of family rivalry, of incest, and of persistence through time: survival. Like many of Beckett's narrators, like vast families of orphans, these works all try to reach a goal, a point, yet they are at the same time reluctant to reach it because of the ominous connotations of closure. The family, the text, is born to die, to be unable to "go on," but to be incapable of anything else.

This paradoxical will-to-survive coupled with a will-to-conclude draws attention once again to the linguistic aspects of the literary text. The forces of metaphor and metonymy, manifest in Bioy Casares, Sarduy, Lezama, and Onetti—but just as clearly present in Cortázar and Puig, whose texts oscillate between alternative endings or return to the beginning at the end—have a symbiotic yet antagonistic relationship. Metonymy is oriented to-

From *Latin American Narratives: The Dreams of Reason.* © 1977 by The University of Chicago. University of Chicago Press, 1977.

ward keeping things moving, while metaphor is oriented toward finality, just as the instinct of self-preservation is in obvious conflict with the idea of suicide. Narrative may indeed be said to resemble the ego in the id-ego-superego configuration. Instead, however, of being a monolithic totality, it is made up of conflicting elements which may ultimately fall out of harmony and into chaos. A text's "natural death" occurs when its final metaphor is forged, when the only possible prolongation would be verbatim repetition.

The concept of plot is the reduction of these oppositions to a deceptively harmonic concept of order: a beginning automatically postulates an end; a middle represents the holding in abeyance of these two poles, the illusory time in which both are repressed. The fragmentary or fragmented text, *Tres tristes tigres* or *Rayuela*, for example, raises the act of repression to its highest point. In the same way, a sung epic would suppress the whole (the entire song) in order to concentrate on the scene, and it would create thereby the illusion of a text without boundaries. The poignancy of Gertrude Stein's "rose is a rose is a rose" or Beckett's "Ping" is that the moment the first printed word is reflected by the reader's eyes, the text enters into combat with itself: how long can it keep going before it swallows itself up in its own metaphor?

It is precisely this idea of metaphor versus metonymy, of continuance versus closure, that is enacted in José Donoso's *El obsceno pájaro de la noche* (1974). The narrative is concerned in this case with itself, with keeping itself moving, keeping alive despite its own tendency to end. Donoso's text, for our purposes, combines elements from Sarduy, Onetti, and Lezama: the idea that the characters are nothing more than permutations of the poles of narrative, metaphor and metonymy, the idea that these poles are in opposition, and the idea that the only possible subject of the narrative is the narrative itself, that the text is a self-consuming, self-generating verbal object.

Such a text is, of course, monstrous, but we should recall that the Latin American texts examined is this essay are all monstrous in their way. Monstrosity is an essential part of satire, monstrosity understood as an exaggeration of any kind which renders the distorted object grotesque. But this distortion transcends the comic, the parodic, and the satiric (in the sense of that which pokes fun at something else) because it erases the relationship between the real (the normal) and the grotesque (the distorted version of the real). Satire, as we have been observing it, seems to be saying, "You may see or be tempted to see a relationship between the real and the unreal here, but you must forget that relationship, forget the idea of mimesis or representation." Satire may have begun as vituperation and may have been used as a moralizing tool, but these are not its limits: satire is the drama of idea in conflict with idea, of Coleridgean fancy freed from the ordering constraints of imagination. Like the reality of dreams, satire utilizes elements similar to things in the "real" world but organized in a form, a language, different from that of reality. To see satire exclusively in terms of carnival inversions or as a means whereby we see behind everyday reality is to simplify it, reduce it. Perhaps this is our only means of controlling a potentially destructive, antisocial force: satire, as Petronius, Quevedo, and Swift practice it, is one step from madness, from the devaluation of all our fictions of order, *misura*, and reason.

It is not unthinkable that the author of a monstrous text might himself be a monster—it is difficult to find readers who think Céline, for example, is anything other than a fiend. Wayne Booth's moralistic statement about Céline might stand as a judgment on all satirists: "Though Céline has attempted the traditional excuse—remember, it is my character speaking and not I—we cannot excuse him for writing a book which, if taken seriously by the reader, must corrupt him." Booth, writing in a tradition of literary criticism that runs from Arnold to Plato, is certain that he knows what is moral, what corrupts, what should and should not be allowed to be printed. He also assumes that the reader of Céline will read only Céline, that he will be swept away by Céline. This surely flies in the face of the entire literary tradition, particularly that part which sees the artist as a kind of outlaw, the kind of author Cervantes imagined in Ginés de Pasamonte or Shakespeare in Autolycus. A. Bartlett Giamatti has carefully delineated this figure in Renaissance literature as that of Proteus, and Proteus is certainly the name one would be inclined to ascribe to the satirist, who, as verbal *magus*, weaves a labyrinth of words to make us aware of the horror of order, the very order consecrated by the divinely inspired *vates*. That the satirist's vision is ironic or dark is certainly often true; but without darkness, light is insignificant or blinding.

Proteus, the demonic element in language, its powers to seduce, to fool, is at the center of *El obsceno pájaro de la noche*, where once again art, artist, and text are fused. The ironic Arcadia of literature Borges figures forth in so many of his texts, and explicitly describes in "Borges and I," is one in which the immortality conferred by the text changes the author into an involuntary Proteus, changed in meaning by every reader who takes up the book. This proliferation of shape-shifters may seem dizzying, yet it helps to define the status of the literary text, particularly the satire, because it points out the fundamental ambiguity of any verbal work of art—the loss of significance that occurs when the text leaves the author's hand, mixed paradoxically with the text's apparent possession of meaning. Donoso depicts in his satire the literary work of art in action, a grotesque work-in-progress that fights to stay alive as it seeks to destroy itself.

In addition to Proteus, two other literary metaphors may serve as aids to reflect on *El obsceno pájaro de la noche*, the Ptolemaic cosmology and Mary Shelley's Dr. Frankenstein. The Ptolemaic cosmology, as Dante used it, saw the universe as a series of concentric spheres: to this world-within-world concept Donoso adds, in the cosmology of his text, the ideas of the microcosm and reversibility. The idea of the microcosm, related to synecdoche, suggests that the fragment constitutes a minute recapitulation of the whole. (In the Renaissance, man was often spoken of as a microcosm because he seemed to be the entire universe in miniature.) *El obsceno pájaro de la noche* is composed of successive story layers (as is *La vida breve*), each one a version or metaphor of the next, an arrangement which suggests that the reader will eventually reach a center that will give him a perspective on the rest, a vantage point from which the relationship of all the parts may be seen. But this idea is replaced by that of reversibility, the idea that the peeling off of the successive layers brings the reader no closer to the center and that at a certain point the process reverses itself. Instead of getting to the center, the reader finds himself again at the beginning.

The Ptolemaic system is repeated throughout the text by the idea of enclosure. The first scene of the book takes place in the Casa de Ejercicios Espirituales de la Encarnación de la Chimba, a combination convent and old-age asylum. The old women in the convent are continuously putting things into packages, tucking the packages away, just as they themselves have been tucked away in the cloister, just as a dead body is put inside a coffin, as bad memories are repressed. The pattern established here makes all acts of enclosure—the sexual act, the gestation of a baby, wearing clothes, binding a text within covers—metaphors for each other. The narrator, who speaks to us from within various *personae* or masks, encloses himself within various identities, each one breeding another: the book encloses the pages, the words are enclosures we fill with meaning, the totality is enclosed within an interpretation. The closer we come to the text the further away from us it moves; at best we can see the layers as the narrative's own desperate attempt to create the illusion of infinite space, to keep on moving despite the fact that it is doomed, limited by its own nature, that of any book.

The kind of artist-creator depicted in Mary Shelley's *Frankenstein, or The Modern Prometheus* (1816) prefigures in many ways the narrator in *El obsceno pájaro de la noche*. Frankenstein, like Donoso's narrator, is a sick creator: he is in love with himself or with versions of himself, thereby compounding narcissism with incest; he creates out of season, in the fall, and he despises what he creates. The body that Frankenstein (the ultimate *bricoleur*) creates out of pieces taken from corpses seems to him beautiful as he creates it, yet becomes hideous when alive. Frankenstein at first flees it (represses its existence) when it comes to life and then spends the rest of his own life trying to destroy it. This antagonism between the creator and his creation may seem quite typical of romanticism, but it has further reaching ramifications. In Donoso's text, as in *Morel*, the conventional distinction between art and artist (the monster and Frankenstein) disappears, and the narrative itself is seen as a monstrous creator, incapable of doing anything except narrating, creating stories in its own image.

What the narrator (he has several names, but we see him first as the convent janitor, Mudito, the mute) says is in effect irrelevant. What matters most is the telling itself, the imposition of order (grammar) on arbitrarily chosen things (signs), and the equally arbitrary identification of certain segments of the discourse with certain names, and other parts with other names. The teller here is what he tells; the constant shifts of identity, of enclosure, are therefore nothing more or less than the ebb and flow of the discourse itself. It is always *in medias res*, wherever it happens to be, and it always ends with a death, a loss of voice. The final scene of *El obsceno pájaro de la noche* is one of total dispersion: a crone (a witch? a sybil?) empties over a fire, which consumes everything, the sack in which the narrator (by now nothing more than a disembodied voice) has been sewn: "In a few minutes nothing remains under the bridge. Only the black spot the fire left on the rocks and a blackened tin can with a wire handle. The wind knocks it over, it rolls along the rocks and falls into the river." The speaking mute (the text) is destroyed, just as it is in *Cien años de soledad*, but here there is no idea that a prophecy has been fulfilled, only the notion that the only death of the text, of the narrator/narrative, is silence.

To tell "what happens" in *El obsceno pájaro de la noche* is virtually impossible, and here again the text's huge size (some 530 pages in the original) and lack of a single unifying plot are signs of its monstrous nature. But a number of its stories may be listed: First (in reading, not chronological sequence) there is the story of the funeral of an old serving woman (Brígida) who lived in the Casa. This tale, narrated by Mudito, introduces the theme of death both as a starting point and as an end point for a narrative, the death-to-life of the author, his passing into the Arcadian immortality of literature, the theme of class relationships (especially between masters and servants), and the theme of enclosure (the convent, coffin, and vehicles). A second story, also set in the convent, is that of a perverse Immaculate Conception. One of the orphan girls in the convent has sexual relations with the narrator, who must wear a gigantic papier-mâché head to arouse her, and the old crones immediately define her pregnancy as a miracle. By verbal magic, the narrator becomes the miraculous child, becomes his own father.

The world inside the convent might have been described to provide an ironic contrast with the "real" world (like the contrast between hierarchies inside and outside of the military school in Mario Vargas Llosa's *La ciudad y los perros*), but this is not so. The world outside the convent is no less an enclosure than the convent itself; there the enclosures are social classes, history, sexual roles, and education. Outside the convent (in an earlier period), the narrator becomes Humberto Peñaloza, sometime writer and factotum for the aristocratic Jerónimo de Azcoitía. Just as Mudito must wear a giant head in order to possess the orphan girl, Humberto can only possess his master's wife (Inés) by pretending to be his master. The product of that union is a monster, Boy, for whom his putative father, Jerónimo, builds a hidden world, populated only by monsters. Just as the narrative voice blends with the "miraculous" child in the convent, only to be engulfed by that world (in the form of the final crone), Jerónimo too is murdered by the world of freaks he creates, murdered by his own monstrous son. World-within-world, sphere-within-sphere, inside and outside: these pairs and oppositions are all states in which the narrative happens to find itself as it attempts to proliferate and survive. But none constitutes "reality" as such. They are all metaphors one for another, repetitions strung together until the fates (the convent crones?) cut the cord and nothing is left but a burned-out, empty can (enclosure) which falls into the river.

Any description of *El obsceno pájaro de la noche* is partial and therefore misleading, but it may also be stated that any one scene or story may be seen as a metaphor for any other scene or story, recalling once again the Ptolemaic system. Perhaps the one image that gives a kind of unity to the entire text (along with the package or enclosure motif) is the idea of the book itself. A book is a repository, an enclosure, in which signs, the doubly metaphoric marks which represent the oral signs, are deployed in a certain way. In Donoso's book the signs are arranged in the manner of the Ptolemaic system or, to use another analogy, a color wheel. We know that the color wheel represents the visible spectrum, the colors evoked in the eye by light stimulation. We do not see light in itself, but we do see its variations. The narrative in Donoso's text might be the equivalent of light: we experience it as a series of stories, some of which comment on the totality. The life of the narrative depends on the weaving of more and more variations, or on the repetition of those variations.

But built into the proliferation is the idea of death or ending. And this knowledge pervades the entire narrative. To write is to die, to continue to write is to draw nearer and nearer to the fatal moment, but to cease to write is also to die. It is for this reason the narrator is a crazed Proteus; he changes shape to prolong his life. He creates and discards names (his own and others) as he sees fit, but there is the maddening awareness in him that he will be appropriated, his identity taken by another, as he takes the identities of others. The narrative engenders the monsters which populate the text and which are the narrative, but those stories have their own order. The narrative is always threatened by one of its parts; the subplot may swallow up the main plot. In the same way, the act of publishing a book makes the author's name public property (as it is in "Borges and I"), and that act may constitute a loss of identity, a death. This problem is taken up in chapter 9, where Mudito/Humberto is caught trying to steal his own book from Jerónimo de Azcoitía's library, a vain attempt to recover his lost name.

The importance ascribed to names—the author's, the narrator's, the characters'—is of course illusory. Just as the reader suspects that the secret power in the text is actually the old women in the convent, who are nameless and who may very well be the outward manifestations of language, the signs, so also he wonders how a narrative voice as weak and fallible as that of Mudito/Humberto can really be generating the various stories.

The end of the text would seem to bear this out because the crone who destroys the narrative voice by fire and leaves the blackened container for the wind to blow into the river is like a devil, like Mephistopheles come to claim Faust's soul. The narrative must be effaced, the deployed words returned to the lexicon, the narrative voice wiped out.

In no other of the satires considered in [*Latin American Narratives: The Dreams of Reason*] is the satirist so roundly satirized. To attempt to make oneself the master of language, to make oneself into the all-powerful Proteus, is impossible. The author is at best a partial Proteus, predestined like Kafka's hunger artist to do that which constitutes a slow sort of suicide; yet he cannot do otherwise. Donoso's text dramatizes the problem of the artist as only satire can: the artist is not a personality but a function, not a human being but an activity. It is not who but what the narrator is that is at stake here, just as it is in virtually all the works we have been examining. Machado's mad narrators leave texts that justify their meaningless lives; Bioy's anonymous diarist shows how the literary character becomes a text; Cortázar's Oliveira is nothing more than a plot seeking its resolution; Cabrera Infante's figures are nothing more than the pale transcriptions of an author/character, and so on. It is from language these texts come and to it they return. It fell to Donoso to delineate that trajectory in full, in its most tortuous and monstrous gyrations.

Reading Clarice Lispector's "Sunday before Going to Sleep"

Hélène Cixous

The story is about a family's Sunday outings. The family used to go to the port where the father stared at the oily waters in such a way that if he "were still alive he would perhaps still have before his eyes the oily water." His look disquieted the daughters. At nightfall, the youngest daughter who enjoys the father's special favors, climbs on a high swivelling stool in one of the city's numerous bars. This, the father found amusing:

> And this was gay. She then acted more charming and already this was not so gay. To drink, she chose something that was not dear, although the swivelling stool made everything dearer. The family stood, waiting. Timid and voracious curiosity with regard to joy. That was when she knew bar *ovomaltine*, never before such a great luxury in a tall glass, heightened more by the foam, the high and uncertain stool, *the top of the world*. Everyone waiting. She fought from the first against the nausea but went on to the end, the perplexing responsibility of the unhappy choice, forcing herself to like what must be liked from then on mixing, with the astonished distrust that *ovomaltine* is good, the one who is not worth anything is me. She lied that it was the best because standing there they were witnessing the experience of dear felicity: did it depend on her that they believed or not in a better world?

It all takes place within the small sphere of the family and under the law of the father. The strength of this text is in making us feel that the work is done completely on the phonic level; however, the syntax is also fascinating. There is a center in the center of this text, as there is a tree in the center of paradise, which is the top of the world. And there is the

---

From *Boundary 2* 12, no. 2 (Winter 1984), translated by Betsy Wing. © 1984 by *Boundary 2*.

moment in which there is the personal subject "who" in the Brazilian construction ("who is worth nothing is I"), where we have this throwing of the subject back to the end of the sentence. The lexicon also is very important as much in its choice as in the system long-short. For example, if I see "The daughters worried obscurely," the "worried obscurely" ("se inquietavam obscuramente" is long as it is written in the text, whereas in the French "s'inquiétaient obscurément" that aspect disappears. There is a whole phonic and graphic reading.

I return to the question of the primary scene. This text, though very small, is immense. The time questions are particularly complex. Fairy tales begin with: once upon a time there was, once upon a time there was and it began long since. On the contrary, the stories of originary scenes are stories of rupture, which is after once upon a time, which is a since, which is ever since this moment. This text is a story of since. There is some "there was," because one could say: once upon a time there was the father, and once upon a time maybe there was no father, the question of the strange survival, or of the possibility of the father is posed in the text. From the beginning we are very surprised by the phrase: if the father were still alive, which is an extremely violent phrase. What is very shrewd of Clarice Lispector, is that this plays in a double-dealing manner on childhood and its opposite. One can take it as something naive, like a narrative, a childhood memory. There are some naive phrases, phrases falsely naive, everything is, on the contrary, perfectly cunning. If you take the beginning of *Portrait of an Artist*, it imitates the style of early childhood, whereas here that isn't true. There are occasional mimetic outbursts, but as a whole it is a mixture, the supreme *mélange* of absolute innocence and absolute knowledge, pointed out to us in the first phrase which is "On Sundays the family . . . leaned against the low wall, and if the father were still alive," and there is the violence in the writing, and because it is perfectly calm, it is so much the more violent. That's Clarice; you go somewhere with the family, including the father, and in the following sentence the father is dead, whereas they are telling a story in the father's lifetime, whereas there is something permanently undecidable about the death and life of the father, something which means both at once, that "if the father were still alive," which means he is not alive and that he lives always. It is death that is in question. It is not: if he were not dead, to say if he were still alive, it is recalling him, one is never free of the father here. Everything plays out in the tricks of tense. There is a value of repetition. It is at play on the level of addition, but not only on the level of addition, it is at play on both levels.

The singular-plural system is incredibly rich, not only singular plural, because there are also collectives and the collective noun is a singular-plural. There are Sundays in the plural, while one has Sunday, there are going to work on one Sunday, on Sundays, on Sunday. It plays out there like a series. There is also a shaping of the single and the plural of the subject, since one begins with: "the family" which is a collective whose components one doesn't know, and from which the father and the littlest daughter will detach themselves. There are some daughters, one doesn't know how many there are; as for the mother, perhaps she is just the sea, the water, towards which the father is looking and who is absent.

The questions of value are important, the questions of economy are astonishing. There is "dear" (expensive) "not dear," but it should not be restricted to the simple equivalence of the financial value of that economy. It goes much farther than that. It is a question of symbolic values, and also narcissistic value.

Sunday is the Lord's day, is the father's day, what one may miss at first reading is the enormity of this story which is entirely within the father. If one succeeds in figuring out this text, it delineates something, it outlines inclusion, inscription, (no incorporation) in the father.

The text as a whole delineates perhaps an egg, or a spiral, it turns while turning inwards; and the general scheme is picked up again and splendidly reinscribed in the last sentence.

The text is caught between Sundays and Sunday, between the series with its frequentative side—to say Sundays gives a sort of continuous time, as if time were made of Sundays. The time which is striking is the series of Sundays, but they are also days, units of time—and then Sunday, which is a proper noun. The heroes of this text are the little girl (Cordelia) and the father and there is Sunday. What Clarice lets herself do is this: "On Sundays the family used to go to the quay," but in the last sentence we have: "Sundays was always that (immense) night," whereas when the family goes to the quay to look at ships, it is not yet nighttime. Therefore there is a slippage, which puts itself back together in the last sentence, which equates: Sunday, domingo, night, and we see, we are told, that it is the original night, which engendered, which engendered: Sunday, which is masculine, this immense night, which is feminine, I could translate: it is the father who is the mother. At the origin, in the mythologies, in the ancient cosmogonies and I suppose the same in the Brazilian cosmogonies, and surely Clarice Lispector was ignorant of none of that, there is the universal mother about whom one always asks questions, and in general she is the night, night which brings the day to light, etc. The same as here: the father was always this immense mother who engendered all the other fathers, who engendered cargo ships, water, milk with foam, etc., and in this fascinating type of hatch-like engendering, a multiple engendering, because everything comes out of this Sunday. Sunday engenders a quantity of things, like God, whereas one knows that in mythology when a woman engenders she makes twins at the most, but here it is a question of a masculine genesis. And some egg of the *ovomaltine* variety is inscribed in this system. I don't want to do more than evoke the question of the egg and the hen, because it is not impossible that it is the egg and the rooster/shell (*coq*[*ue*]) that should be discussed.

At the level of the structure of filiation and of genealogy, this is a story of father and daughter, of father's daughter. It is related to writing. *Near the Wild Heart* begins between the father and daughter. It is Clarice Lispector's story, the father-daughter story, and what that could mean.

The question of the look is there from the beginning, "the father would have before his eyes," can be interpreted in terms of a screen; "he would have oily water before his eyes," or in his terms of an offering: the oily water stays before his eyes, the before is very important. In other respects one sets off with this idea of watching, spying, if one keeps looking at the look, one has a key to the reading of the text, it is going to pass through a level of evaluation that passes through the look, evaluating the look passes through narcissism. There is a look which works in two different ways: one sees the father looking, the daughters were worried and were bringing the father's look back to themselves, back to the interior. They are trying to control the father's look, I want to control your look that is the child's cry. Everything is going to play itself out there. I want to look at what I myself consider better, which can be anything at all; one sees what is at stake in the father's look—it is the father's look which as always is going to be the valuation bearer, the value giver.

Then we have the story of access to the father's look and the ascent of the littlest one who is obviously the favorite, etc. We are taken into the city "When it got dark . . . each bar," it is the false childish sentence, and at the same time it is the true one. The city is this thing full of lights and full of stools. It is a structure: stools, high and turning, in each bar. It is also the father's place. "The youngest daughter wanted to sit on one of the stools," and there, there is a sudden breaking into the system of tenses, a past tense, one has the childhood memory, whereas one was in the frequentative. It's the famous Sunday, its the originary scene, but what scene? It begins with "the first time she wanted to sit on one of the stools, the father found it amusing." The first moment, she pleases the father. It is a narcissistic, simple moment, and immediately we have this little phrase "and it was gay," which is entirely biblical, it was right, it was good, and it was gay, and it was joy. It was gay and it came to an end "she then acted more charming and already this was not so gay." It seems to be nothing, and yet all is lost. (This recalls the marionette scene in Kleist. There is a scene of narcissism recounted by the narrator. It is the story of a sixteen-year-old boy, and is also a fall from grace. It is lost grace. This boy lives in a sort of absolute happiness. He has all the charms, and one day his friend says to him that he makes him think of the sculpture of an adolescent with a thorn in his foot—at which he receives the *coup de grâce*, he has a violent and negative fit of narcissism, and spends his time trying to reproduce this famous work of art, and, Kleist cruelly recounts, the boy becomes absolutely grotesque. He is surprised by his friend in the act of trying to reproduce it, his friend bursts out laughing, and this boy who was sublime, becomes a wreck, a poor idiot forever.) The text's secret is there, and the other is the *ovomaltine*, but they go together. That secret is this: the story of grace and the loss of grace. But how and why? The little girl wanted to sit on one of the stools. She wanted to. She had a desire. It is her desire. It is spontaneous. The father finds it amusing. It is sanctioned by the father who at the same time legitimates the spontaneous grace and in making it legitimate deprives it of spontaneity, recuperates it, approves it; upon which the little girl starts all over again to please the father. In other words, I am pushing things as far as I can, she prostitutes herself. She sells her desire to the father. She no longer does the thing because it pleases her, she is no longer eating her apple, but she is acting charming to please the father; there is not the least commentary by Clarice Lispector, "and that was already not so gay." And that is the fall. That touches on what I have called the two knowledges, a knowledge which would merge with bliss (*jouissance*) which would not separate itself from the very necessity for bodily *jouissance*; and the reproductive knowledge, which is not part of the body, but which plasters itself to the body, this type of doing-on-purpose, and instead of there being a living scene, we are at the theatre. That is tied in very quickly beneath the simplest guise of a childhood memory. "To drink, she chose," now we are in the series of tests, "something that wasn't dear . . . everything." We don't know who chose, the daughter is confused with the father. She is now caught in the value discourse of the father, who will say on returning: "we did nothing and yet it cost so much." We are the paternal economy. She takes something which isn't expensive. Doubtlessly the father must have said something, but it isn't said. That is the great discretion of this text. But luckily she keeps something, she keeps the stool. She is on the pinnacle apparently despite everything.

What gives value? We are going to see now all the systems of symbolic value. "The family stood waiting," it is going to be awful. Even if one doesn't notice it right away, this is the test. "Timid and voracious curiosity with regard to joy": one is inside the mirrors, from the moment in which the father looked, and in which the daughter saw herself, seen, one is inside the mirrors. One can say to oneself that "the timid and voracious curiosity with regard to joy," is rather what is going to happen later with the family, how the family looks at bliss (*jouissance*). There are systems of voyeurism, at the level of perversity, but it is delegation as well. It is awful because the little girl perceives that she is now the guardian of the family's *jouissance*, hence of all *jouissance*. She feels it because they make it known to her, since they are all around her to see what she is going to feel, and if she is going to take pleasure (*jouir*). It is vaguely like this also because the family, which cannot take pleasure, which is already at a distance from *ovomaltine*, delegates its possibility to take pleasure to her. It is she who is going to delight and, they will take pleasure in her joy, "timid and voracious curiosity," because they are going to eat, to drink her joy for her. At the same time she also has something of this timid and voracious curiosity, that is playing on the level of absorptions.

One cannot not see that *ovomaltine* is the center, since it is italicized, it calls attention to itself. In other respects, *ovomaltine* goes with the *top of the world*, on the graphic level, not only is it in italics, but it is full of "o's" and there are foreign words, they inscribe strangeness. It is the relationship of *jouissance*-strangeness which is multiple. The apple is strange, it is that which one has not yet tasted which is desirable, and for the moment it is still a question of desire. Afterwards, when she tastes distance, difference, the strangeness is going to go in through her mouth, that is going to be another matter, and one can only say that *jouissance* is not of this world. It is from another world, from another tongue. There is a magnificent sentence there: "that was when she knew bar *ovomaltine*," which may be a childhood phrase and at the same time it may be an extremely skillful sentence; "that was when," it's the big event, it's the production. Afterwards there is the question of knowing, which is explicit. Afterwards there is "bar *ovomaltine*," it's not just *ovomaltine*, it is noble *ovomaltine*, from the bar, from the paternal place. "Never before such a great luxury": there is something there which gathers itself together from the childhood memory and which is very intense. It is the structuring of childhood *jouissance*. It is this condensation of luxury "such a great luxury in a tall glass." All the signifiers cross-check in this manner, one multiplies the other, more and more, more and more, the glass which is high and heightened by foam, and one moves towards the scene of shivers of gaiety or of joy, "the high stool," and there is a little warning, "uncertain," because it moves, and one knows in what direction, as we well know, one doesn't stay "on the top of the world." "Everyone waiting," with the Brazilian word which is stronger: everyone hoping. And there is the drama, we recommence the story of lost grace "she fought against nausea," because while they are waiting, she is struggling, and we set out on this violent sentence "and she went on to the end," that is where it is so intense, she felt the delegation of *jouissance*; "she has the perplexing responsibility of the unhappy choice, forcing herself to like what must be liked." "What must be liked" is obviously the law, it is thou shalt like, thou shalt not like, thou shalt, thou shalt not, etc., thou shalt like what thou dost not like, and what she is in the process of doing, what she is in the process of absorbing, with this foam, is literally the juice of the law. At the time she resists, she is someone who leans towards *jouissance*. Her resistance is going to be marked by mixture. She does not entirely make one body with the law. At the same time she is going to resolve to do it or to conform with it because of the others. One might believe that she is only reproducing a classic structure, but it isn't true. There are specific traits, particularly this very beautiful thing, this sentence which says "did it depend on her whether they believed in a better world?" that has always been her question. It is the origin of Clarice Lispector's moral, whether in general, or specifically her own, but with a very precise mark which is "did it depend on her whether they believed or not in a better world?" It is just a question, she doesn't know anything about it, and she will not know. It is starting from this question, starting with the possibility that belief in a better world depends on her, that she is going to make a pretence, that she is going to draw back into pretence, in which she does not believe. It is out of love, a love one can wonder about.

I return to this little scene, this scene of mixture: "the astonished distrust that *ovomaltine* is good," may not be good, "the one who isn't worth anything is me," because if *ovomaltine* is good and I think it is bad, then I have two possibilities, either I am right contrary to the whole world, or even if, contrary to the whole world, I am right, I cannot even think it, and I choose the world against myself. At that moment, I am obliged to say, since I think it is bad then it is I who isn't worth anything; a classic exchange, but it is certainly the way the law functions. "The one who isn't worth anything is me" it is the moment of this apparently greatest downfall which is also the sublime moment. It is the moment of sublimation, there she is obliged to abandon her own demand, her own erotic claims. She is obliged to believe her body has lied about them, and therefore she is going to lie. She belies her own body. She lied that it was very good, but she is lying to herself. The lie is always conscious. She lies. She lies to herself. She doesn't lie to them, on the contrary, she gives them back their truth, their false truth, but that doesn't matter, it is her body which she belies.

Look at the positions, the little girl is seated on her turning stool at the top of the world, and everyone is standing around her. "She lied that it was good, because they were witnessing the experience of dear felicity." That is the conflict, if she said it was bad, *their* universe would completely collapse. All the more so because it is in relation to the father that it is playing itself out, all the more so because they told her that this bliss cost dearly, although they told her also that it was not dear. As the father paid with money, she herself had to pay with her pleasure. She pays for the father, she pays for the family. The dear felicity costs her dearly as well, on all levels, it plays in the ambivalence.

The phrase "did it depend on her that they believed or not in a better world," is the ethics of the one who will become the writer. Will it depend on her or not that they believe in a better world? And how? She chooses to say "it's good." She chooses not to vomit all the while dying to vomit. She chooses not to say what she has just discovered, since she was on the top of the world, it means there isn't any better world. She chooses not to say it, and from this moment on, we pass into the "better world," and the better world is a world that is going to be marked in a very interesting way by shadows.

There is no answer to "did it depend on her that they believed or not in a better world," but all of that was surrounded by the father. We return to the father and we return into the father's supposedly better world, "and she was comfortable within this small world." Hence we aren't going to touch this little world which is in the father's hand. Then we are caught in a sort of return path, backtracking, "On returning the father said: even without having done anything," while she did so very much, she did, undid, traversed, knew, etc., "we spent so much."

"Before falling asleep, in bed, in the darkness,"—this phrase marks the last phase of retreat, of reflection, now we are going to have this vision, that the whole story leads up to, the vision of the "better world." It is "out of the window, on the white wall." There is a screen, "the shadow" of something that doesn't exist. We have returned to the world of the shadows of things that don't exist, and what she has done, what she is in the process of doing, is to serve the apprenticeship of the shadow, of appearances. What is more, she's no fool. Appearances are much larger, much more beautiful than reality. For example this gigantic shadow of a small and sparse tree, about which we might say—it is the father and the daughter.

Then, the daughter is about to fall asleep, in bed, in darkness. She sees, out of the window, the shadow of the boughs, enormous at night: "Sunday was always that immense night that engendered all of the other Sundays and engendered cargo ships and engendered oily water and engendered milk with foam and engendered the moon and engendered the giant shadow of a little tree." That is how we arrive at this Sunday "Sunday was always that immense night." We have been in the once, in that episode of discovery which kept it silent. She said nothing. She swallowed everything she could discover, think, etc. That is where we can question the fact that Sunday was this complete day. With the evening, suddenly it becomes "that immense night," as if this silence, this burying spread out, as if it was a symbolic night, not just a real night, as if this Sunday not only always was but had to remain in this night, not the day which engenders things with their appearance in the shadow. And things with their appearance, that is the addition. It is the water plus the oil, the oil that floats on the water. It is the milk plus the foam, the *ovomaltine* plus the name *ovomaltine*, the tiny tree plus its gigantic shadow, with this violent thing that "engendering the moon" is and we travel this ascent again, which is a joyous trip because she set out in a terrific ascent of pleasure up to the top of the world. Then we speak again of the water, the milk, we go up to the moon, we arrive at a "gigantic tree," and we arrive at the "little tree," and we come to the end on "little," the little girl.

Family Ties: Female Development

Marta Peixoto

Since the publication of her first novel *Perto do Coração Selvagem* (Close to the Savage Heart) in 1944, when she was only nineteen years old, Lispector has been recognized as one of the small number of true innovators in Brazilian modernism, the only woman to attain a place within that canon. Critics agree that her distinctive contribution lies in her original, often strange language, dense with paradoxes, unusual metaphors, and abstract formulations that at times elude the rational intelligence. João Guimarães Rosa, an acknowledged master of twentieth-century Brazilian fiction and a Joycean innovator in language himself, told an interviewer that "every time he read one of her novels he learned many new words and rediscovered new uses for the ones he already knew." As a woman writer, Lispector did not have the benefit of a tradition in Brazil of important female authors. One could say that Lispector, along with her older and far less innovative contemporary, the poet Cecília Meireles (1901–1964), are the founding members of that tradition, writers whom all younger women writers somehow take into account. Although Lispector mentions her early discovery of Katherine Mansfield and several critics have found in her fiction a kinship to Virginia Woolf's, Lispector preferred to think of herself as a writer unmodified by the adjective "female." Yet her numerous female protagonists testify to her fascination with the experience of women and the shape of female lives.

In Lispector's eight novels, seven of the protagonists are female, as are most of the main characters in her five collections of short stories. Yet criticism on her work has neglected to inquire into the specifically female

From *The Voyage In: Fictions of Female Development*, edited by Elizabeth Abel, Marianne Hirsch, and Elizabeth Langland. © 1983 by the Trustees of Dartmouth College. University Press of New England, 1983.

dimension of her characters. Lispector's critics, frequently concerned with tracing the affinities between the philosophical ideas present in her fiction and those of Heidegger, Kierkegaard, Camus, and Sartre, discuss repeatedly "man's" nature and existence, and "his" plight in a world doomed to absurdity. Other critics have analyzed her style: her use of the epiphany, internal monologue, and certain rhetorical devices. Beyond an occasional reference to her "feminine sensibility," no mention is made of the fact that the author is a woman and her fictive world preponderantly female. Those critics' blindness to the male/female opposition in her work leads to a blurring of meaningful differences. One critic, for instance, in an otherwise valuable analysis of her short stories, discusses *father* as an important recurring motif, adding that "many times it is referred to as *father*, at others as *mother*." Even if *father/mother* in Lispector's fiction stood for an identical role, *mother* would still be the most frequent term of the pair. Revisionist readings of Lispector, which include Hélène Cixous's enthusiastic presentation of the Brazilian author as a practitioner of "écriture féminine," have begun to appear in France and in the United States. Further critical readings from a feminist perspective will no doubt enrich Lispector's work with the discovery of previously unrecognized dimensions.

Family Ties (*Laços de Família*, 1960), Lispector's most studied and anthologized collection of short stories and the only one available in English, offers a good starting point for investigating symbolic functions assigned to women in her fiction and for examining her models of female development. Appearing at the beginning of her third and perhaps most fertile decade of publication (Lispector died in 1977), *Family Ties* contains well-made stories, less idiosyncratic and difficult than most of her later work. In addition to the accessibility of these stories, it is perhaps its critical evaluation of family relationships and female life from youth to old age that has gained for this collection its readership.

In only three of the thirteen stories of *Family Ties* are the central characters male. The female protagonists, middle-class women in an urban setting, range in age from fifteen to eighty-nine. The stories in which they appear can be read as versions of a single developmental tale that provides patterns of female possibilities, vulnerability, and power in Lispector's world. The author assigns traditional female roles to her protagonists: adolescents confronting the fantasy or reality of sex, mature women relating to men and children, and a great-grandmother presiding over her birthday party. Through the plots of the stories and the inner conflicts of the heroines, Lispector challenges conventional roles, showing that the allegiances to others those roles demand lead to a loss of selfhood. The protagonists' efforts toward recuperating the self emerge as dissatisfaction, rage, or even madness. The stories present the dark side of family ties, where bonds of affection become cages and prison bars.

All the stories in the collection turn on an epiphany, a moment of crucial self-awareness. In the midst of trivial events, or in response to a chance encounter, Lispector's characters suddenly become conscious of repressed desires or unsuspected dimensions of their psyches. These women experience the reverse of their accepted selves and social roles as mother, daughter, wife, as gentle pardoning, giving females. In their moments of changed awareness, they may realize not only their imprisonment but also their own function as jailers of women and men. Their epiphanies, mysterious and transgressive, bring to consciousness repressed material with potentially subversive power. The negative terms which often describe these moments—"crisis," "nausea," "hell," "murder," "anger," "crime,"—convey the guilt and fear that accompany the questioning of conventional roles. Internal monologues shaped by antithesis, paradox, and hyperbole display a wealth of opposing moral and emotional forces. After these characters' crises, when by recognizing their restrictions they glimpse the possibility of a freer self, they more or less ambiguously pull back, returning to a confinement they can't or won't change. The intensity of their conflicts may be enlightening for the reader, but the protagonists return to their previous situations after questioning them for only a moment.

Of the three tales of adolescent initiation in *Family Ties*, two have women protagonists. It is instructive to compare the male and female patterns. In "The Beginnings of a Fortune," a young boy suddenly fascinated with money grasps its connection with power and its usefulness in attracting girls. Yet he also sees the vulnerability to the greed of others that the possession of "a fortune" would entail. "Preciousness" and "Mystery in São Cristovão" have parallel plots on a symbolic level. Both hinge on the intrusion by several young men into a young woman's private domain. In "Preciousness," the protagonist on her way to school undergoes a violent sexual initiation when two young men, strangers passing by, reach out and briefly touch her body. She accepts and turns to advantage this negative experience, darkly intuiting it as a lesson about her fragile individuality in a world of powerful men. Unlike the young boy, who realizes that acquiring his fortune requires purposeful activity, the young girl feels within herself "something precious." Something which "did not compromise itself, nor contaminate itself. Which was intense like a jewel. Herself." But she is "precious" also in her new status as a coveted object, able to arouse men's lust. And this second kind of preciousness undercuts, compromises, contaminates her preciousness to herself. Immediately after the attack she retreats into a profound passivity:

> Until this moment she had kept quiet, standing in the middle of the sidewalk. Then, as if there were several phases of this same immobility, she remained still. . . . She then slowly retreated back toward a wall, hunched up, moving very slowly as if she had a broken arm, until she was leaning against the wall, where she remained inscribed. And there she remained quite still.

As a lesson drawn from this incident, she keeps repeating to herself that she is all alone in the world. Sex and its concomitants, intrusion and violence, lead her to isolation instead of relationship. Yet she also learns the necessity of protecting herself. She confronts her parents with a request for new shoes: "Mine make a lot of noise, a woman can't walk on wooden heels, it attracts too much attention! No one gives me anything! No one gives me anything!" She demands to be given things, possessions to compensate for her deeper dispossession, for her broken confidence in herself and in her relationship to others. And her assertiveness in demanding new shoes serves, paradoxically, her need for self-effacement, for camouflage, as a way of protecting herself.

"Mystery in São Cristovão" reworks in parable form a similar version of female sexual initiation. At the epiphanic moment, three young men on their way to a party, dressed up as Rooster, Bull, and Devil, trespass to steal hyacinths in "the forbidden ground of the garden" at a young girl's house, as she looks on from her window. The moment when the four participants stare at each other seems to touch "deep recesses" in all of them. The young men guiltily slip away leaving behind a "hyacinth—still alive but with its stalk broken"; the young girl screams, waking up her family. Like the protagonist of "Preciousness," she too becomes passive and cannot explain anything beyond her scream. She suddenly seems to age: "to the horror of her family, a white strand had appeared among the hairs of her forehead."

The male and female initiation tales offer, then, a number of contrasts: activity versus passivity; a young boy who seeks wealth and power versus young girls who are "precious" themselves, metaphorically identified with jewels and flowers; preoccupation with acquisition versus concern with self-protection; entrance into the world of economic and social exchange versus retreat in fear into oneself. Development, for the young girls, clearly will not proceed according to the male model.

It is in a context of attachment and affiliation with others that the women characters develop. After initiation into the vulnerability to which their female sexuality exposes them, they find protection and a measure of satisfaction in family ties. We see in other stories several of Lispector's women safely ensconced in a domestic life. The stories reflect the matrifocal organization of Brazilian society where the extended family still prevails, so much so that the word *família* usually refers not only to the small nuclear family but to a numerous network of relatives. The title story shows most clearly the ambivalent function of the family in the whole collection. In "Family Ties," the power a woman wields within the family has a negative, constricting side: deprived of the chance to develop herself beyond the scope of the family, she attempts to control those close to her.

"Family Ties" opens as Catherine says goodby to her elderly mother at the train station, feeling an awkward tenderness and relief. With this scene between the two women, as well as with flashbacks and the narration of the emotional consequences of the mother's visit, the story touches on several types of family relationships: mother-daughter, mother-in-law-son-in-law, grandmother-grandson, husband-wife, and mother-son, all presented as subtle or not so subtle struggles for power. Catherine's memories of childhood include a friendly alliance with her father against her mother's domestic rule: "When her mother used to fill their plates, forcing them to eat too much, the two of them used to wink at each other in complicity without her mother even noticing." As she looks at her mother through the train window, Catherine becomes aware of the strong though ambivalent bonds they share:

> "No one else can love you except me," thought the woman, smiling with her eyes, and the weight of this responsibility put the taste of blood in her mouth. As if "mother and daughter" meant life and repugnance.

Relieved of her mother's company, the daughter recovered "her steady manner of walking—alone, it was much easier." But that tie to her mother also facilitates in her an emotional availability: "she seemed ready to take advantage of the largesse of the whole world—a path her mother had opened and that was burning in her breast." This very openness to others leads Catherine, it seems, to attempt to bind her son to her in the same way she was bound to her mother. The last third or so of the story is told from the point of view of the husband who feels left out and jealous as he watches Catherine and their small son from a window, perceiving an intense interaction between them:

> At what moment is it that a mother, hugging her child, gave him this prison of love that would descend forever upon the future man. Later, her child, already a man, alone, would stand before this same window, drumming his fingers on the windowpane: imprisoned. . . . Who would ever know at what moment the mother transferred her inheritance to her child. And with what dark pleasure.

Here, the metaphorical prison entraps all members of the family: the father, who also speaks about his own predicament, sees the male as victim of the imprisoned and imprisoning female, the mother, who transmits this family tie to the next generation. The male power, deriving from his role in the world outside the home, does not prevail in the domestic world of intimate relationships, where his wife has a power at least equal to his own:

> This is what he had given her. The apartment of an engineer. And he knew that if his wife took advantage of his situation as a young husband with a promising future, she also looked down on the situation, with those sly eyes, running off with her thin, nervous child. The man became uneasy. Because he could only go on giving her more success. And because he knew that she would help him to achieve it and would hate whatever they achieved.

He takes revenge for her disdain by subjecting her to small humiliations: "he had gotten used to making her feminine in this way." Despite these dissatisfactions, it seems clear that at least the husband wishes to preserve the status quo: "When Catherine returned they would have dinner, shooing away the moths. . . . 'After dinner we'll go to the movies,' the man decided. Because after the movies it would be night at last, and this day would break up like the waves on the rocks of Arpoador." For the husband, then, the events of the day, like waves breaking on the rocks, seem to be minor, if recurrent, crises within the sustaining institution of the family.

The family as context for female development in Lispector's stories is, then, both positive and negative. It allows women the satisfaction of affirming ties to others but confines them to the subordinate role of ministering to other's needs, depriving them of themselves. The narrator of "Love" measures the rewards of a domestic life for the protagonist Anna, and hints at her sacrifices:

> Through indirect paths, she had happened upon a woman's destiny, with the surprise of fitting into it as if she had invented that destiny herself. The man whom she had married was a real man, the children she mothered were real children. Her previous youth now seemed strange, like an illness of life. She had gradually emerged to discover that one could also live without happiness: by abolishing it she had found a legion of persons, previously invisible to her, who lived their lives as if they were working— with persistence, continuity, and cheerfulness.

From perspectives similar to this one, several protagonists face their crises. Women devoted to love, marriage, and children discover within themselves allegiances subversive to those roles. These stories follow the generic model that Susan J. Rosowski proposes in her article "The Novel of Awakening." Lispector's characters also attempt to find value "in a world that expects a woman to define herself by love, marriage, and motherhood." For each protagonist, "an inner imaginative sense of personal value conflicts with her public role: an awakening occurs when she confronts the disparity between her two lives." Lispector's protagonists also follow Rosowski's model in awakening to conflict and limitations. Their social world and even their own selves cannot accommodate new allegiances. They discover that their loyalty to others excluded possibilities for themselves. As Lispector puts it in a story from another collection, "To be loyal is not a clean thing. To be loyal is to be disloyal to everything else." Four stories from *Family Ties*—"Love," "The Imitation of the Rose," "The Buffalo," and "Happy Birthday"—are Lispector's versions of this kind of awakening.

In "Love," plant imagery conveys Anna's everyday awareness of herself in her thriving domesticity: "Like a farmer. She had planted the seeds she held in her hand, no others, but only those. And they were growing into trees." Although "at a certain hour of the afternoon the trees she had planted laughed at her," Anna feels steady in her chosen course. A casual encounter upsets her equilibrium. From a tram, she sees a blind man standing on the street, calmly chewing gum. His mechanical, indifferent acceptance of his fate perhaps mirrors for Anna her own blindness and restriction. The blind man is also a victim of the brutality of nature, which maims some of its creatures, a threat Anna usually forgets. When Anna continues her meditation in the botanical garden—a place that confines natural growth, making it follow a prearranged plan—a nausea analogous to Sartre's *nausée* overtakes her: "a vague feeling of revulsion which the approach of truth provoked." The initial tranquillity she perceives in this enclosed garden gives way to a disquieting vision of a secret activity taking place in the plants, as decay encroaches upon ripeness:

> On the trees the fruits were black and sweet as honey. On the ground there lay dry fruit stones full of circumvolutions like small rotted cerebrums. The bench was stained purple with sap. . . . The rawness of the world was peaceful. The murder was deep. And death was not what one had imagined.

The lesson she learns in the garden unsettles Anna's sureness about her immanent family world, the seeds she had planted and which grow into trees. At home, guilt-ridden for her transgressive thoughts, Anna feels both threatened and dangerous: "the slightest movement on her part and she would trample one of her children." In her final considerations about the afternoon, Anna sees the blind man "hanging among the fruits in the botanical garden." The blind man as Anna's double provides a frightening vision of her own destiny: death among the rotting fruit as the consequence of her stunted capacity for transcendence and the lack of personal freedom in the life she has chosen. Yet after a reassuringly ordinary evening at home, Anna seems content to forget her disturbing afternoon: "Before getting into bed, as if she were snuffing a candle, she blew out the day's small flame." Anna puts out the light of her confused enlightenment, a flame that could threaten her domestic life if it were allowed to burn.

"The Imitation of the Rose" contains a similar configuration of opposing forces: a familiar, domestic world threatened and undercut by the laws of another realm. For Laura, who has just returned from a mental hospital, images of light represent her powerful attraction to madness, suggesting that in madness she finds insights otherwise unavailable to her. Laura's dutiful relief at being "well" again, her drab descriptions of herself and her activities, contrast with her luminous, lively account of her mad self. Sleepiness, fatigue, obsession with method, cleanliness, and detail, a certain slowness of body and mind, boring to others as to herself—all signal that Laura is "well." An alert lack of fatigue, clarity of mind, a sense of independence, of possessing extraordinary powers, accompany her returning madness. In the encounter that sets off the struggle between sanity and madness, Laura admires the wild roses in her living room. The conflict between the impulse to send the roses to a friend and the desire to keep them for herself reflects Laura's lifelong struggle between selflessness and selfhood. She can only satisfy herself and what she perceives as society's demands by an exaggerated rendition of the role of a giving, submissive woman. When "sane," she succeeds in keeping down any impulse toward clear self-definition. "Chestnut-haired as she obscurely felt a wife ought to be. To have black or blond hair was an exaggeration which, in her desire to make the right choice, she had never wanted." The roses, in their beauty, exemplify a distinct, glorious selfhood that Laura denies herself: "something nice was either for giving or receiving, not only for possessing. And, above all, never for one to *be*. . . . A lovely thing lacked the gesture of giving." Yet as soon as Laura decides to give away the roses, her madness begins to return: "With parched lips she tried for an instant to imitate the roses inside herself. It was not even difficult." Tranquillity, self-sufficiency, and clarity signal Laura's changed state; she sits "with the serenity of the firefly that has its light." The story ends with the husband's view of Laura, whom he watches with a fear and respect that only her madness can elicit: "From the open door he saw his wife sitting upright on the couch, once more alert and tranquil as if on a train. A train that had already departed." This final image implies that only in madness can Laura give herself permission to have an independent self. She departs in the metaphorical train of madness, since other departures are beyond her capability.

The role of woman in love limits severely the protagonist of "The Buffalo." She only senses her deficiencies when her husband or lover abandons her and she is deprived of her source of identity. She then feels mutilated, incomplete, because she cannot experience anger and hatred toward him. She visits a zoo in a conscious search:

> But where, where could she find the animal that might teach her to have her own hatred? That hatred which belonged to her by right but which she could not attain in grief? . . . To imagine that perhaps she would never experience the hatred her forgiving had always been made of.

She senses that she is the one who is caged, "a female in captivity," while a free animal watches her from the other side. She focuses on the buffalo in her effort to free herself from her own compulsion to be the loving and pardoning female. She looks to the buffalo, with its narrow haunches and hard muscles, as a masculine presence, the embodiment of her hatred and her strength "still imprisoned behind bars." The buffalo seems to overwhelm her. She becomes terrified by the hatred which she projects upon the animal and which he in turn releases in her. As the encounter between the woman and the animal continues, it is couched in terms of a deadly struggle:

> Innocent, curious, entering deeper and deeper into those eyes that stared at her slowly, . . . without wanting or being able to escape,

she was caught in a mutual murder. Caught as if her hand were stuck forever to the dagger she herself had thrust.

Perhaps not ready to allow herself to hate, the woman faints in the final scene: "before her body thudded gently on the ground, the woman saw the whole sky and a buffalo." Fainting signals, no doubt, her failure of nerve: a traditionally feminine strategy of withdrawal, it obliterates from consciousness her involvement and insights. Yet the open spaces of the sky, ambiguous as this image becomes in conjunction with the fainting, seems to offer, in a story cluttered with cages, the possibility of release.

In "Happy Birthday," the protagonist belatedly rejects her family, implicitly questioning her own role as a prototypical matriarch. On her eighty-ninth birthday, when her power and the bonds of love have already been eroded, her family gathers to mimic the appearances of closeness. The narrative method—a mosaic of internal monologues interspersed with dialogues and the narrator's remote, at times ironic commentary—shows the resentment and hostility among members of the family and presents the protagonist from the outside as well as from the inside, what she is to others and what she is to herself. In a Kafkaesque progression reminiscent of "The Judgment," the old woman at first appears decrepit and later demonstrates a surprising, malevolent vigor. At the start, she is propped up, ready for the party:

> The muscles of the old woman's face no longer betrayed any expression, so that no one could tell if she was feeling happy. There she was, stationed at the head of the table—an imposing old woman, large, gaunt, and dark. She looked hollow.

She remains aloof and passive until urged to cut the cake: "And unexpectedly, the old lady grabbed the knife. And without hesitation, as if by hesitating for a second she might fall on her face, she dealt the first stroke with the grip of a murderess." Cutting the cake rouses the old woman from passivity; she goes on to shatter her image as dignified and respected mother. The metaphoric association cutting/killing continues, linking the birthday gestures with those of a funeral: "The first cut having been made, as if the first shovel of earth had been thrown." As the matriarch surveys her family "with her old woman's rage," Lispector resorts again to the recurring images of female imprisonment and powerlessness:

> She was the mother of them all. And, as her collar was choking her, she was the mother of them all, and powerless in her chair, she despised them. She looked at them, blinking. . . . How could she, who had been so strong, have given birth to those drab creatures with their limp arms and anxious faces? . . . The tree had been good. Yet it had rendered those bitter and unhappy fruits.

Her scorn and anger mount, and the old woman spits on the floor. At a solicitous remark from a granddaughter, she curses them all and demands a glass of wine. The imagery and elements of the plot with sources in primitive and contemporary ritual—birthday party, funeral, spitting, cursing, wine—seem to assimilate the old woman's revolt into the very institutions she challenges, suggesting that her anger and its ritual-like expression can be encompassed within their framework.

The old woman rails against the loss of her power; in a sense she is a victim of old age. Her dominance stemmed from her personal capacity to play the most powerful role traditional Brazilian society allows women, that of mother in a mother-dominated extended family. Her ability to command attention is eerily revived when she cuts the cake, spits, and curses. These actions serve as a crude demonstration of the willfulness which in her prime she would have manifested in more subtle and socially sanctioned ways. Yet this old woman, like Lispector's other protagonists, is also ultimately a victim of her social role. Her power issued from a control of others that is neither healthy nor enduring. One of her sons, observing that "she had not forgotten that same steady and direct gaze with which she had always looked at her . . . children, forcing them to look away," thinks that "a mother's love was difficult to bear." Since she cannot rule the life of her progeny, she despises them. By showing the lovelessness and will-to-power of this mother's love, Lispector suggests that the role of matriarch affords a false power that entraps women as well as their families.

After the old woman's outburst, the narrative method shifts back to external presentation. She relapses into an enigmatic passivity, clutching the ghost of her power: "seated at the head of that messy table, with one hand clenched on the tablecloth as if holding a scepter, and with that silence which was her final word." Like so many of Lispector's female protagonists, she returns at the end to her initial situation. As they move from youth to old age, the protagonists of *Family Ties* also trace a circular path, beginning and ending in passivity—from the withdrawal of a frightened young girl to the abstraction of an old woman, her power over her family, repressive in itself, all spent.

Through the plots and internal monologues of her characters, Lispector questions, as we have seen, the conventional roles she assigns to her protagonists. A tendency similar to the subversion of stereotypes in characters and plot recurs on the level of language. Lispector destroys and recreates the meanings of certain ordinary words, redefining them through paradoxical formulations. In "Love," the title word acquires multiple and contradictory meanings as the protagonist attempts to align her confused yearnings with the *eros* and *caritas* she had always believed gave direction to her life. In "The Imitation of the Rose," madness takes on a positive value, signifying the expansion of Laura's independence and self-esteem—at the end of the story Laura is "serene and in full bloom"—without of course losing its acceptation of illness, the delusion of power. Anger in "The Buffalo" becomes the elusive object of a quest, while pardon is defined as covert hatred. A reversal of values also occurs in the imagery: the thriving plants, metaphorical analogues of Anna's domesticity, reappear on the literal level as the lush and rotting vegetation in the botanical garden: the birthday party is described in terms of a funeral; family ties appear as chains and cages. The tendency to redefine words and concepts, to reverse traditional metaphoric associations or draw images from negative and antithetical realms supports and furthers Lispector's questioning of "a woman's destiny."

Lispector's protagonists, as they shift from one set of specific circumstances to another, repeatedly find themselves in metaphoric prisons, formed by their eager compliance with confining social roles. Their potential development—the ability to integrate into their everyday selves the greater autonomy they desire in their moments of insight—again and again falters and stops short. For the youngest protagonists, the prison is their own fearful passivity in a society that accepts as normal intrusions by men such as the ones they experience. Anna's attachment to domestic routines blocks her from participating in a wider social and moral world, both frightening and exhilarating to her, the outlines of which she only obscurely intuits. For Laura, living according to others' expectations and suppressing her own desires leads to madness, an illusory escape into another prison. The woman in "The Buffalo" is caged in her inability to recover emotions she had long repressed, and in "Happy Birthday" and "Family Ties," mother-love itself imprisons. These women start out and remain in spiritual isolation. Locked in desired yet limiting relationships to husbands and children, they find no allies in other women—mothers, friends, or daughters—who appear if at all as rivals and antagonists. Their only power lies in passing on an imprisoning motherly love to their children.

Carolyn G. Heilbrun and other feminist critics have pointed out that with few exceptions women writers have "failed to imagine autonomous characters," denying them even the autonomy they as authors have achieved, reserving for male characters their more assertive roles. This holds true for Lispector in *Family Ties*. In "A Chicken," the limitations of the female role take on the sharpness of caricature. This story repeats the plot of failed escape from the confining roles of nurturing and submission. The protagonist, a chicken about to be killed for Sunday dinner, escapes her fate by setting off on a mad flight across the rooftops. Pursued and brought back by the man of the house, the flustered chicken lays an egg. The little girl who witnesses this surprising outcome persuades her mother to spare the chicken's life and adopts her as a pet. She seems to intuit a similarity between the chicken's predicament and the possibilities her own future may hold. (Another girl has the same understanding of chickens in a story from another collection which begins: "Once upon a time there was a little girl who observed chickens so closely that she knew their soul and their intimate desires.") Gender determines the meaning of the chicken's adventure. During her escape the chicken is described as "stupid, timid, and free. Not victorious as a cock would be in flight." In her attempt to cast off the passivity expected of her and to assert her independence, the chicken echoes the central action of several other stories. Acquiring a "family tie" ends the chicken's adventure. It literally saves her life, but does not provide her with enduring dignity or even safety. Her reprieve lasts many years but not forever: "Until one day they killed her and ate her, and the years rolled on." Like the women she represents, the chicken's dilemma takes the form of an opposition between independence and nurturing: women may choose one role but not both and Lispector's women end up settling for the latter. After her "epiphany" the chicken returns to a timid life. Occasionally she recalls her "great escape":

> Once in a while, but ever more infrequently, she again remem-
> bered how she had stood out against the sky on the roof edge
> ready to cry out. At such moments, she filled her lungs with the
> stuffy air of the kitchen and, had females been given the power
> to crow, she would not have crowed but would have felt much
> happier.

Ellen Moers analyzes ways in which women authors use birds "to stand in, metaphorically, for their own sex." The chicken in this and other stories written later is Lispector's comically distorted image of the selfless, nurturing female incapable of sustained self-determination. The perspective implicit in this choice of metaphor includes compassion but also conde-scension, an attitude that carries over to Lispector's presentation of women in other stories of *Family Ties*. Most of the stories end with the female protagonist silent and described from an external vantage point, perhaps another sign of the author's desire for distance between herself and her characters. It is tempting to suppose that for her these stories may have functioned as a kind of exorcism. She presents in excruciating detail pro-tagonists bound in "women's destinies" and measures the extent of their disadvantage. Through this repeated exercise, Lispector could perhaps free herself—and her future characters—for richer, more varied roles. Indeed, Lispector's imagination seems to require repeated incursions into the same themes. As one of her narrators puts it, "How many times will I have to live the same things in different situations." Lispector allows her later female protagonists greater independence. Among them are several writ-ers, a painter, and women engaged in spiritual quests that are not invariably cut short by their return to confining feminine roles.

Within the predominantly bleak view of female possibilities in *Family Ties*, there is a curious exception, represented by the grotesque, almost fantastic protagonist of "The Smallest Woman in the World." This story elaborates on a supposedly documentary anecdote: a bewildered explorer meets the smallest member of the smallest tribe of African pygmies—a tiny pregnant woman, measuring a foot and a half—and names her Little Flower. Readers of the Sunday newspaper react to her story and see her life-size picture. She herself does not experience an epiphany but instead causes moments of insight in other characters. Women of all ages seem fascinated by this hyperbolic representative of the fragility and powerlessness associated with their sex. One woman fights against an involuntary identification with Little Flower: "looking in the bathroom mirror, the mother smiled, intentionally refined and polite, placing between her own face of abstract lines and the primitive face of Little Flower, the insuperable distance of millennia." While those considering Little Flower turn to her amazing smallness and supposed vulnerability with a greedy interest, wanting to possess the miracle and even use her as a pet, the small creature herself feels powerful and contented. Living constantly with the danger of being devoured by animals and members of other tribes, she experiences the triumph of having so far endured:

> And suddenly she was smiling. . . . A smile that the uncomfortable explorer did not succeed in classifying. And she went on enjoying her own gentle smile, she who was not being devoured. Not to be devoured was the most perfect feeling.

Even her incipient motherhood will not lead her to confining bonds, for among the Likoualas a dubious practice prevails: "when a child is born, he is given his freedom almost at once." In answer to a question put to her by the explorer, Little Flower says that it is "very nice to have a tree to live in that was hers, really hers. Because—and this she did not say but her eyes became so dark that they said it for her—because it is nice to possess, so nice to possess."

With the story of Little Flower, Lispector creates a comic parable of a native female power, sustained against all odds. The jungle inhabitant manages to retain the tranquil independence sought eagerly by city-bred women in their civilized world of enclosed spaces, prescribed behavior, and family ties. Lispector heaps on her protagonist multiple signs of powerlessness and oppression: membership in a black African tribe reminiscent of slavery and colonialism, the female sex, minute size, and the special dependence that pregnancy entails. She places her in opposition to a white male explorer (*explorador* in Portuguese means both "explorer" and "exploiter"). Yet the most vulnerable of women is not a victim. Unlike Laura, who cannot keep the roses, and unlike Lispector's other protagonists, who cannot hold on to and use their insights to change the forces that bind them, the smallest woman in the world, alone in her tree house, possesses herself—Lispector's wry symbol of a successful development, though not of the means to attain it.

Voices of Patriarchy:
Gabriel García Márquez's
One Hundred Years of Solitude

Susanne Kappeler

Praise of Márquez's novel is almost unanimous. Its sales records and multiple translation attest to the worldwide gratitude for a modern masterpiece, one that satisfies not just the refined tastes of academic *jouisseurs*, but equally the broader desire for the pleasure of reading. It may be *lisible* in comparison to the *nouveau roman*, but it does not for that reason fall within the category below the very best. On the contrary, its "readability" is employed in the service of its keener pleasure, bursting the binary opposition between readable pleasure and the ecstasy of writing-reading.

The novel's delightful readability is its ploy of seduction; not the wily seduction of the innocent, but the conscious seduction between consenting partners who know where it is leading. In literary historical terms the seductive factor is epic. Yet the twentieth-century reader knows that this is not the era of epics; and Márquez knows it too.

Epic features are unmistakably present in *One Hundred Years of Solitude*, and most uncontestably, I would argue, in the first part of the book. There, the word is absolutely the Word, in a brazen assertiveness that allows no self-consciousness of a subject: it is the bona fide word of storytelling. The question, "Who is speaking?" is beside the point in the presence of such authority of representation. We can hardly even speak of a voice in the singular, just as there is no "viewpoint." "Representation" bespeaks post-epic awareness of a gap, a possible tension between *histoire* and *récit*. The truly epic word, however, does not represent: it speaks what *is*, and only that is which is spoken. Presenting, the epic is its own and only present, albeit in the narrative past tense; and even when it shifts into the past, we find ourselves once more in the present of that past, as in the cinematic

From *Teaching the Text,* edited by Susanne Kappeler and Norman Bryson. © 1983 by Susanne Kappeler. Routledge & Kegan Paul, 1983.

cut to a flashback. Auerbach has made such a flashback in the *Odyssey* famous, sharply distinguishing the interpolated account of how Odysseus came by his scar from the psychological perspective of a memory. No one actively recalls this story, neither Odysseus himself, nor the nurse Euryclea who recognises him by the scar: it is the epic voice itself which shifts into the present of that past event, with no linking through perspective, no view other than to what is in the focus of its present.

Characteristically, the epic mode strikes the modern reader as in a certain measure naive; though the term need not be pejorative. Rather, that *naïveté* is charming and endearing in its simplicity—the very voice of the childhood of literature. As with the child, time and space exist only within its own presence. But the epic word takes the utmost liberty in choosing its focus, taking the large grand view of the world at its beginning, or zooming in on to the minutiae of a specific afternoon in Macondo, Casa Buendía. "The world was so recent that many things lacked names, and in order to indicate them it was necessary to point." From the childhood of the world to the routine of years: "Every year during the month of March a family of ragged gypsies would set up their tents, and with a great uproar of pipes and kettledrums they would display new inventions." Zooming in still further to the very afternoon in March of the year when "they brought the magnet." And on it goes on an even plane in the full present and presence of the entire scene of dialogue between Melquíades and José Arcadio Buendía, and the transaction which makes the magnet José Arcadio's. An occasional "flash-forward" defines the present from the other side: "Many years later, as he faced the firing squad, Colonel Aureliano Buendía was to remember that distant afternoon." The narrative voice dwells on the lives and deaths of its favourite characters, or sums up the lives of less favoured ones in a single sentence, with the goal orientation characteristic of early narrative. Its voice is life, and it bestows it only on those of whom it speaks, and who come to life only at its wilful call.

Amaranta, that shadow figure in the Buendía household and almost step-great-great-grandmother of Gabriel García Márquez, is an obvious victim of epic arbitration. She exists only sparingly, in glimpses: we see her fleetingly "lying in a wicker basket," abandoned by her mother who left her in search of her runaway son. Then the care of her and of her coeval nephew is "relegated to a secondary level," and having been left in the charge of the Guajiro Indian woman Visitación, the two are raised on lizard broth and spider eggs and the Guajiro language. Amaranta is briefly brought to the fore on the arrival of her companion-to-be Rebeca, with whom, now as a twosome, she sinks back again into narrative oblivion. Until one day when Úrsula looks up from her busy manufacture of candy animals: "She looked distractedly towards the courtyard . . . and she saw two unknown and beautiful adolescent girls doing frame embroidery in the light of the sunset." Úrsula's vision turns into her recognition of the girls' approaching nubility, which in turn leads first of all to her feverish enlargement of the house to accommodate future children's children. This in turn leads to the discovery of the residence in Macondo of a magistrate sent by the government. These events at once take over the narrative, or the narrative takes over these events and abandons again the lives of the two glimpsed girls.

Yet this arbitrary omnipotence of the epic is distinct from the omniscience of the nineteenth-century realist author. *His* or *her* view is the large and all-encompassing wisdom of the Creator of a universe, a gaze full of responsibility, control and order. The epic voice by contrast has the exaltation of youth, and if it is not exactly irresponsible (a characteristic perhaps more of post-realism), it is capricious and unashamed of its own ignorance and omissions. "Epic is life, immanence, and the empirical," says Lukács in *Die Theorie des Romans:* it need not strive for the transcendence to God's view of the universe. Epic is life chronicled, rather than historicised, if we understand chronicle as "a conjunction of non-causal singular statements which expressly mention [the] subject," and history as explanatory interpretation of events. Such definitions are difficult, since even the chronicle, and certainly the epic, contain a rudimentary causality, though one that would not satisfy the "objective" criteria of history. The epic chronicler in fact enjoys the privilege of assertion without having to supply his sources.

Thus the chronicling voice of *One Hundred Years of Solitude* may assert that "Actually, Remedios the Beauty was not a creature of this world," and that "Actually, [the muttering Aureliano Segundo] was talking to Melquíades." Actually Melquíades is dead; he has already died twice, and was buried as the first deceased in Macondo. Again, the epic voice may introduce its report with the boldness of "That was what happened," and yet fail to give an account of who "actually" sent that spurious letter announcing the death of Pietro Crespi's mother on the eve of his wedding to Rebeca. This voice may carry the aplomb of the General Truth, as in "Then [Aureliano Segundo] married, as all sons marry sooner or later." On the other hand, the chronicle may side with the opinion of its protagonist of the moment, drifting temporarily in the third-person form of his or her consciousness. Frequently, the chronicler leans on Úrsula's opinion, without always having to judge or correct it with what was "actually" the case. It is Úrsula's suspicion that the twins (Aureliano Segundo and José Arcadio Segundo) "had been shuffled like a deck of cards since childhood" and, when they finally settled into their respective identities, had got it exactly wrong. At least, Úrsula in her blind and visionary old age "reexamined her old memories and confirmed the belief that at some moment in childhood [José Arcadio] had changed places with his twin brother, because it was he and not the other one who should have been called Aureliano." No need for the chronicler to settle the question.

Similarly, comment and judgment can be withheld at convenience, and events be listed with the characteristic indifference of chronicle:

When calm was restored [after the bloody carnival], not one of the false bedouins remained in town and there were many dead and wounded lying on the square: nine clowns, four Columbines, seventeen playing-card kings, one devil, three minstrels, two peers of France, and three Japanese empresses.

No stance, just an inventory. Describing the merry goings-on in the Street of the Turks, "gambling tables, shooting galleries," sooth-saying and "tables of fried food and drinks" are effortlessly followed by the "Sunday mornings [when] there were scattered on the ground bodies that were sometimes those of happy drunkards and more often those of onlookers felled by shots, fists, knives and bottles during the brawls." But from these dead the narrative voice returns quickly and unperturbedly to the living, for its business is life. Life includes, moreover, the categories of magic or the supernatural, which the chronicler exercises his right of asserting. The faithful ghost of Prudencio Aguilar *is there*, in the Buendías' courtyard or bathroom, "with his sad expression," just as towards the end of José Arcadio Buendía's life he is, "actually, the only person with whom [José Arcadio] was able to have contact." José Arcadio Buendía has long become susceptible to the *"status quartus materiae,"* the fourth dimension, which he enters as easily as the Latin language he has never learnt. José Arcadio Buendía himself will remain, in *stato quarto*, under the chestnut tree after his death, perceived by everyone except his obstinate and solitary son, the old Colonel Aureliano, who urinates in primal fashion exactly under that chestnut tree. Aureliano was born with a sense of premonition, but premonitions and omens "abandoned him" after that last inspiration to demand that his death sentence be carried out in Macondo, where indeed he survives it. But the supernatural does not exclusively concern death and the lonely dead who seek the company of the living, but is also preeminently a part of life. It manifests itself most ebulliently in Petra Cotes's "supernatural proliferation," in her fecundity so powerful as to generate progeny in her lover's cattle and multitude in his money chest, yet not, surprisingly, in herself.

Premonitions, omens and superstitions are often mentioned, yet without the clarity of distinction from the "real" or "true" that the modern reader would expect. Of Úrsula it is said: "It was a supposition that was so neat, so convincing that she identified it as a premonition." A sentence spoken by a fluctuating subject, one that first identifies her idea as a supposition and then, as if convinced, as a premonition proper. The reservation of the first part is not sustained to the end of the sentence, where, for consistency, it would have to read "that she took it, or mistook it, for a premonition." To identify is a cognitive performative, feasible only if, by definition, the identification is correct.

Consistency and non-contradiction are not, however, among the goals or standards of the epic voice, whose only truth is that of "life," of "what happened," and whose order is the empirical rather than the structuration imposed on the empirical by a unitary subject. Indeed, the pattern of the sentence just quoted repeats itself on a larger scale, most crucially, for instance, in the episode of the three thousand workers and unionists at the station. Among them a Buendía, José Arcadio Segundo, is present, who thus provides a suitable locus for the epic narrative voice. Leaning imperceptibly on his consciousness, we learn of the gradual build-up of the strike, of the tensions and confrontations, and of the intervention by the army. And we share in the depiction of those soldiers who "were all identical, sons of the same bitch," and who "with the same stolidity . . . all bore the weight of their packs and canteens, the shame of their rifles with fixed bayonets, and the chancre of blind obedience and a sense of honour." And we live through the horror of the massacre at the station from within, always close to José Arcadio Segundo, who is "the only survivor." But then the chronicle returns to its impartial business and voices as conscientiously "the official version": "there was no dead [sic], the satisfied workers had gone back to their families, and the banana company was suspending all activity until the rains stopped." " 'You must have been dreaming,' the officers insisted. 'Nothing has happened in Macondo, nothing has ever happened, and nothing will ever happen. This is a happy town.' " Such is the power of the official word, as it was dispensed from the higher courts already earlier, when "it was established and set down in solemn decrees that the workers [who were the plaintiffs] did not exist." We recognise this voice of political dictatorship and terrorism, as we recognise the silence of fear and acquiescence in its citizens and victims. The epic voice, however, is devoid of such recognition. It turns against its own earlier account, gainsaying it with "the official version" and refusing to arbitrate with its elsewhere available "actually, that was what happened." José Arcadio Segundo is transposed into the hiding place of the fourth dimension, where the "supernatural light" of Melquíades's room protects him from the sight of the searching military, although he is plainly seen by his trembling mother Santa Sofía de la Piedad and his twin brother Aureliano Segundo. The only narrative remnant of the massacre is José Arcadio Segundo's persistent memory, the subjective knowledge of the sole survivor. For the narrative voice is that of chronicle, and not that of an investigative journalist or an omniscient Author, who would have questioned the workers' families or counted the inhabitants of Macondo. The banana company is said to have suspended all activity "until the rains stopped," and not, one notes, because there might not have been any workers left to take up such activity. As it happens, the rains go on for "four years, eleven months and two days," after which the banana company packs up and disappears for ever.

In terms of a proper epic we should not, of course, ask after what is omitted, since all there is, and all that matters, is the narrative itself. Yet the open conflict of these self-contradictory voices pressingly raises the question of "epic *naïveté*." Adorno traces the roots of the epic *naïveté* and follows its transformation in the later descendant of the epic, the bourgeois novel. *Mythos* and narrative are in fundamental opposition, the former the embodiment of the ever-same, the latter, the *telos*, the dimension of difference and of the abstraction of rational discourse. Epic narrative, in Adorno's view, is the irresolvable attempt to capture the singular and concrete in the conceptual medium of generalisation. The reflection of this conflict in style makes it appear as silly, naive, unaware, and as clinging to the particular where it is already dissolving into the general—summed up by Adorno as *Urdummheit*. What traditionally is regarded as a bonus, the *naïveté* of the epic, becomes in his analysis the price. With the accuracy of description the epic tries to compensate for the falseness and untruth of discourse: the tricks of verisimilitude, "history-likeness" (Kermode), "reality effects" (Barthes).

Failure is thus immanent in the epic intention itself. The modern reader, moreover, no longer believes in the possibility of the project "chronicle," the neutral and transparent presentation of "things as they are." Even the chronicle itself is necessarily historical, structuring, ordering, explaining its material in representation, although one might call this an involuntary historiography. Above all, the epic chronicle contains the implicit assumption that the world makes sense, sense that is shared by its inhabitants and especially by its readers. The particular sense that the world of Macondo makes is the order of its unchallenged patriarchy. We have seen it innocently manifest in the general truth that "all sons marry sooner or later," building the lines of children's children that are known "by the house of their fathers" (Numbers 1:18). It is the sons, too, who forge history, or at least events; who, in other words, together with their genealogies, make for epic narrative material. The women, in Macondo society as in the narrative, live in the kitchen, servicing and providing for their men of action. Amaranta, not even a bearer of children, appears only periodically to confirm an event, or to receive into her care the child of one of the Buendía sons. The widowed Santa Sofía de la Piedad, "the silent one, the condescending one, the one who never contradicted anyone, not even her own children," "had that rare virtue of never existing completely except at the opportune moment." It is Úrsula, the matriarch, who holds a unique female position in that patriarchal texture. Her function in the narrative is primary, and not just the simple complement to that of her husband, the founding father José Arcadio Buendía. They may together stand at the apex of the family tree, yet while José Arcadio finds proliferating succession in his sons and grandsons, Úrsula is more like the stem which runs down that entire tree, supporting all its branches. Not until the advent of her great-great-granddaughter Amaranta Úrsula does she find even a partial heir to her name. The patriarchal line is defined by succession, by the chain of the houses of fathers, while the matriarchal function, it seems, is not so easily handed on, is possibly even unique. Hence, perhaps, Úrsula stays alive for well over a hundred years and for the greater part of the book, until the moment when her faith in the function and necessity of the matriarch begins to fade, and when her principal interest, to keep the family line going, begins to appear to her as dubious.

Curiously enough, it is Fernanda among the daughters-in-law who turns into the partial matriarchal successor as she takes over the rule of the house. Yet Fernanda's interpretation of that role introduces also a regime which is incompatible with, and indeed a travesty of, Úrsula's matriarchal values. Fernanda brings into the house the chilly breath of her bourgeois upbringing in the city, the funeral air of her rigorous etiquette and the prohibitive codex of her Saints' calendar. As domestic bursar and moral superintendent of the house she fulfils a fraction only of Úrsula's previous prodigious role.

It would lead too far to explore the full scope of Úrsula's matriarchal power and support, but we should consider the circumstances and implications of her abdication. Úrsula started out with the unquestioned values of patriarchy, focusing all her energy and attention on that prime patriarchal emblem, the House. She runs and maintains it, periodically rejuvenates and enlarges it, and effectively also provides the money, be it with her lucrative candy business or by burying assorted treasures in the garden for future necessities. Yet despite her own crucial function, her sense of rightness makes her fixate her hope on the men in her family. "Head of the House" is a patriarchal title, to be filled, even if only nominally, by a male. Her own husband was early lost to the mundanities of domestic husbandry, squandering his time and the (first) family fortune in alchemical experiments. Her first son runs away with the gypsies, her second goes out to fight thirty-two futile civil wars. José Arcadio gets himself shot by a firing squad; Aureliano José, as well as the seventeen Aurelianos engendered during the thirty-two wars, incur the vengeance due to their father. Aureliano Segundo leaves the House to live with his mistress and spends his life feasting and drinking; José Arcadio Segundo becomes a worker at the banana company and a union leader soon bereft of workers and union. Those of the male Buendías who survive their abortive history-making end up retiring into the silver workshop or Melquíades's four-dimensional room, both shacks at the back of the House. It is about this time in the family history that something happens to Úrsula's unfailing good faith.

Intermittently she had been troubled by her repeated bad luck with her sons and their sons, as for instance when José Arcadio Segundo set out to build canals to cross the region by navigation which José Arcadio Buendía had tried to cross on foot. " 'I know all this by heart,' Úrsula would shout. 'It's as if time had turned around and we were back at the beginning.' " In her "staggering old age," when she applies herself to turning her great-great-grandson José Arcadio into a future pope, her previous suspicion of the cyclical nature of time turns into the conviction of "a progressive breakdown of time." The epic voice, however, adds a corrective to Úrsula's view: "something that she herself could not really define and that she conceived confusedly as a progressive breakdown of time";

and further on: "The truth was that Úrsula resisted growing old even when she had already lost count of her age."

The original kind of time, the time of happy patriarchy and of happy epic narrative, was like a kind of space, the space of the eternal present. The passage of time would only flow through it evenly and calmly, as the ever-changing water through the river which remains the same. To Fernanda, "one day seemed so much like another that one could not feel them pass." Characteristically, José Arcadio Buendía eventually falls into a trap of perpetual Mondays. "He spent six hours examining things, trying to find a difference from their appearance on the previous day in the hope of discovering in them some change that would reveal the passage of time." But the space of time is left intact, untouched by any passage of time-flow. Many years later, his children's children gazing at Melquíades in the fourth dimension realise that it is

> always March there and always Monday, and then they under-
> stood that José Arcadio Buendía was not as crazy as the family
> said, but that he was the only one who had enough lucidity to
> sense the truth of the fact that time also stumbled and had acci-
> dents and could therefore splinter and leave an eternalized frag-
> ment in a room.

The time-flow may be dammed, or solidified and splintered like ice, that magic substance of José Arcadio Buendía's obsession and dreams. The young Aureliano, abandoned to his silversmith work, "seemed to be taking refuge in some other time" as if it were another room.

The floods of rain bring a deluge of time—"unbroken time . . . , relentless time, because it was useless to divide it into months and years, and the days into hours, when one could do nothing but contemplate the rain." Macondo is swamped by a pool of stagnant time, in which action, which is in need of moving time, becomes impossible. Waiting, the verb of duration, is the only one available to the subjects in this non-temporal discourse of activity. Aureliano Segundo and Petra Cotes cease to make love, and Úrsula is "only waiting for the rain to stop in order to die." Even the transition to death is too active to be accomplished in this viscous medium of time.

The spatial, patriarchal time, like the present of the epic, is symmetrically abutted by the past and the future on either side. Memories and premonitions are the looking-glasses through which they may both be glimpsed from the position of the present. When Macondo is stricken with the plague of insomnia, followed by the collective loss of memory, Pilar Ternera adapts her gift of cartomancy and reads "the past in cards as she had read the future before."

Úrsula's first suspicion of something amiss with the common order of time is less a fundamental questioning of the spatial or patriarchal conception of time than a shifting of her attention towards the flowing element traversing the space of the present. Somewhere behind their backs, some-one is redirecting the same old flow and letting it pass through their space again. Once, she had feared that that flow might dry up: " 'What's hap-pening,' she sighed, 'is that the world is slowly coming to an end and those things [the annual visits of the gypsies] don't come here any more.' " Hence Úrsula, now in charge of the "apprentice Supreme Pontiff" and suspecting a progressive breakdown of time, expresses her annoyance with "this bad kind of time" in terms of her ingrained spatial conception of time, though complemented by her new awareness of the trick of the recycled flow. Time wears off, it seems, in this process of recycling, and the "pro-gressive breakdown" indicates a deterioration in the quality. Or even in the quantity, which, in a flow, is the same thing: "When God did not make the same traps out of the months and years that the Turks used when they measured a yard of percale, things were different." " 'The years nowadays don't pass the way the old ones used to,' she would say, feeling that everyday reality was slipping through her hands." What is wrong with this "bad kind of time" is that it has lost its spaciousness, for you cannot fit as much into it as before. In the old days, "after spending the whole day making candy animals, she had more than enough time for the children"; now, with nothing much to do and walking about all day with the little pope on her arm, she is compelled "to leave things half done." Or remember the "dying Colonel Aureliano Buendía, who after so much war and so much suffering from it [and after so many pages and chapters] was still not fifty years of age."

The subjects living in the expansive space of the continuous present relate in a curious manner to the flow of time that passes through it. Above all, growing old is something they do within that space, and has nothing or little to do with the passage of flowing time. Or it is something they don't do, as Úrsula, who resists growing old despite her hundred-odd years. Or Pilar Ternera, that deputy matriarch who is annexed to the House of Buendía like the stables or the granary in which she reads the cards of the first-generation sons, and who is "also almost a hundred years old, but fit and agile in spite of her inconceivable fatness." Coping effortlessly with her blindness, Úrsula is merely annoyed and indignant at her clumsiness, deciding that it is "not the first victory of decrepitude and darkness but a sentence passed by time"—another trick of the "bad" time.

Úrsula is the only one to view the space time with the suspicion of the recycled flow. The other members of her family lose themselves in different corners of static time, in the "attic of bad memories," in "times reserved for oblivion, in labyrinths of disappointment," "a trap of nostalgia," or in Melquíades's room of Mondays. With this new shift from the space of the present to the flow of passing time, however, Úrsula has taken the first step towards the discovery of history. The patriarchal order knows no history. It conceives itself as timeless, unchanging, ever-present. Its du-ration is filled with the anecdotes of events, with the episodes it celebrates in epics. We have seen the epic voice itself politely dissociate itself from Úrsula's subversive vision of time. The order of patriarchy has no history, it has a past represented in the present in ghosts and memories. For José Arcadio Buendía, the repetition of days or seasons or gypsies' visits only leads eventually to the solidification of his static conception of patriarchal time, a time that gets frozen into a perpetual Monday in March. For Úrsula, on the other hand, repetition becomes the trigger of suspicion:

> the insistent repetition of names had made her draw some conclusions that seemed to be certain. While the Aurelianos were withdrawn, but with lucid minds, the José Arcadios were impulsive and enterprising, but they were marked with a tragic sign. The only cases that were impossible to classify were those of José Arcadio Segundo and Aureliano Segundo.

—the ones she thought must have been shuffled like a deck of cards. Drawing a lesson from history, "she decided that no one again would be called Aureliano or José Arcadio." Yet she is overruled and the next child, son of Aureliano Segundo (who should have been José Arcadio Segundo), is named José Arcadio. Úrsula then draws the second lesson from history and decrees that he shall become "a man who would never have heard talk of war, fighting cocks, bad women, or wild undertakings, four calamities that, according to what Úrsula thought, had determined the downfall of her line."

It was finally with her blindness that Úrsula acquired "such clairvoyance as she examined the most insignificant happenings in the family that for the first time she saw clearly the truths that her busy life in former times had prevented her from seeing." She "made a detailed recapitulation of life in the house since the founding of Macondo and . . . completely changed the opinion that she had always held of her descendants." There follows a whole page of Úrsula's revaluations (a page well worth quoting if space permitted) which shows these revaluations as *interpretations*. It is motivation for action, rather than deeds and effects, that now makes the new history of the Buendías. Thus it is pride rather than idealism that made Colonel Aureliano fight thirty-two wars, as it was pride rather than fatigue that made him lose them. Nor was it the suffering of the wars that made him withdraw from the family, but rather his fundamental "incapacity for love." "Amaranta, however, whose hardness of heart frightened her, whose concentrated bitterness made her bitter, suddenly became clear to her in the final analysis as the most tender woman who had ever existed," in whom the "fear . . . of her own tormented heart had triumphed [in the] mortal struggle between a measureless love and an invincible cowardice." Comparison of repetition and a rebellious courage of interpretation turn Úrsula into the first historian in this book, an historian who overtakes even the epic chronicler who notes her findings down. It is not too surprising that the epic chronicler lags behind, chronicles her views without committing himself or approving them. For her history is also the history of patriarchy, and as such necessarily the critique of patriarchal order and the epic which it engenders. As the successive failures of the bearers of patriarchy are recorded, the values of their motivations are exposed. All that propelled them into action and out into the world, in turn rendered them incapable of love towards the family which is their very pride. Amaranta, the shadow figure of the House and of the narrative, is partially redeemed through the assessment of the vice of impossibility into which the patriarchal order condemned her. "Rebeca, the one who had never fed on her milk . . . , the one who did not carry the blood of her veins in hers . . . Rebeca, the one with an impatient heart, the one with a fierce womb, was the only one who had the unbridled courage that Úrsula had wanted for her line." Rebeca, the unknown stranger dragging a bag with the bones of her parents, embodies the final verdict on patriarchy. And with it, for Úrsula, the judgment on her complementary matriarchal role and her ambition to nurture that line.

With history, the old past of patriarchy acquires a new dimension, as the desire to derive laws from the past to predict the future is the archetypal motivation of history. Memories are like the eidectic skills of Freud's *Dekkerinnerungen,* static images that cover up what historical interpretation reveals, and they are "devoid of lessons." On the other side of the present, history is complemented by prophecy, as the patriarchal memories are matched by glimpses of premonition. Prophecy is not the future, but the history of the future, the future perfect. Melquíades's parchments are the counterpart for the future to Úrsula's history of the past. "No one must know their meaning until he has reached one hundred years of age," just as Úrsula had to become a centenarian before she began to know the meaning of history. And as her visionary sight came with blindness, so it is said of the parchments that "the last man who read these books must have been Isaac the Blindman."

It is Aureliano, the "Moses" who had been delivered in a basket from the nunnery, and who with his aunt Amaranta Úrsula engendered the last of the line, Aureliano with the tail of a pig, who will be the first and the last to read Melquíades's documents. When his pig-tailed son and cousin is devoured by the ants Úrsula had fought for over a hundred years, "Melquíades's final keys were revealed to him and he saw the epigraph of the parchments perfectly placed in the order of man's time and space: *The first of the line is tied to a tree and the last is being eaten by the ants.*" So he takes up his ordained task of deciphering the documents, which he can read without any difficulty although they are written in Melquíades's mother-tongue Sanskrit, and complicatedly encoded.

However, his desire to read "his fate" and future is inseparable from his curiosity for his "origin." His "final protection," in the face of the imminent revelation of his fate, lies in "the fact that Melquíades had not put events in the order of man's conventional time, but had concentrated a century of daily episodes, in such a way that they coexisted in one instant." He is protected, in other words, from the teleological linearity of ordinary narrative which could precipitate him prematurely into the abyss of his disclosed end. Thus he proceeds to read "the chanted encyclicals" of Melquíades, not noticing the "cyclonic" storm which uproots the House. "He began to decipher the instant that he was living, deciphering it as he lived it, prophesying himself in the act of deciphering the last page." Before reaching the last line, however, he has understood that he will never leave this room, since it was foreseen the Macondo would be "wiped out by the wind and exiled from the memory of men at the precise moment when Aureliano Babilonia would finish deciphering the parchments." The interpretation of the past and the history of the future conflate in that instance of the present where living and reading, historical being and its interpretation, merge together in an insoluble hermeneutical circle. Prophecy has joined history, squeezing out any tenable present for the subject Aureliano, shrinking the moment to the degree zero of total comprehension which can have no extension. For "everything written . . . was unrepeatable since time immemorial and forever more, because races condemned to one hundred years of solitude did not have a second opportunity on earth."

Aureliano Babilonia, with the gift of tongues and of deciphering, the first to be linked to the House of Buendía not through the house of his father but through his mother, is not one hundred years of age at the moment of this apocalypse. But with him as its last scion the Buendía patriarchy has come of age.

The Autumn of the Signifier:
The Deconstructionist Moment
of García Márquez

Patricia Tobin

One Hundred Years of Solitude arrived as a boon to the North American heart. So captivated were we with our first introduction to an exotic world, wider and wackier than our own, that we did not inquire of the genie out of the bottle whether the superabundance was due to the innocence of Latin-American consciousness or the sophistication of Latin-American art. Much of our elation was due to the imperturbability with which Gabriel García Márquez fashioned a fictional universe unfettered by the laws which, the new structuralism had taught us, governed our language, thought, behavior, disciplines, and institutions—the rules of identity and opposition, hierarchy, cause and effect, substitution and combination. And just as people were becoming thoroughly sick of daddies, Jacques Lacan had disclosed, as the origin and stabilizer of all representation, the Biggest Daddy of them all: the Phallus—Signifier of signifiers, Authorizer of the Word, Law, Truth, and the Symbolic order. How giddy we felt, then, as we witnessed the dynastic rut and romp of seven generations of Buendías, with not a Symbolic patriarch among them, but riddled with incestuous, alchemic, bastardly, celibate and pig-tailed sons escaping the system and exceeding the Father! We cheered for the lawless mesh of "*mágico realismo*" and "*lo real maravilloso,*" laughing our heartiest at the wholesale erasure of the boundaries that sustained our own precise categories of difference. It is the moment in which the laughter bursts from Michel Foucault, in his preface to *The Order of Things,* as he sees Western logic shattered by the unthinkable classifications of Borges's Chinese encyclopedia. It was the last moment of pure glee we were to enjoy before literary theory turned unholy and *unheimlich* on us. It is the moment when rule-constrained structuralism is brought low by rule-breaking deconstruction.

From *Latin American Literary Review* no. 25 (January–June 1985). © 1985 by *Latin American Literary Review.*

The Autumn of the Patriarch is a book for the head, a book that allows us to think the thought of our times. It is the great contemporary novel written from the place of the Big Stud, the site from which García Márquez perpetuates a creative outrageousness fully compatible in its decentering effects with the systematic deviancy of post-structuralist deconstruction. It is the book that *Cien años* would have been, had its author crossed the ten-foot chalk circle drawn around Colonel Aureliano Buendía and punctured the solitude and craziness at the empty seat of power. *The Autumn of the Patriarch* is grounded in Foucault's second moment directly following the laughter when, gazing at the *Las Meninas* of Velásquez, Foucault suddenly becomes very serious and springs his uncanny codicil: Representation works, only when/because the Sovereign Signifier is absent. The Sovereign—he who is sitting for the painting within a painting, around whom it is all centered—must be invisible, inaccessible, exterior to it, faintly present merely in the mirror and in the directed gazes of the others. Only when the very site of representation, the point of all perspectives, is nowhere to be found, can representation inaugurate and sustain itself lawfully. Thus originates the unequal reciprocity between word and image: He who sees cannot signify, and he who signifies cannot see. To become Sovereign, the Signifier must disappear; for the Symbolic Father to authorize our discourses, the Real father must fade from view. What King Philip IV felt about this exile we do not know, but there is no mistaking the protest of the patriarch in his autumn when he cries out, "Who the hell am I because I feel as if the reflection in the mirror is reversed?"

Now there is nothing *unheimlich*, either scary or familiar, about the structuralist Signifier removed to extraterritorial space. The Symbolic Father, after all, is the dead father, the Phallus is not a penis, and everything circulates in an orderly system of exchange. However, when the deconstructionists deterritorialize the founding center into the locus of indeterminacy, inconsistency, and noise; or when García Márquez locates there a Señor Signifier, metamorphosed as a wild card, alive and well and thriving on catastrophe—then we suffer the awesome discomposure of the *unheimlich* third moment. If the Center does not hold, is the Symbolic order which it upholds then a fiction? Is it the crackbrained Center itself that looses anarchy upon world and word? What kind of grotesque Sublime grounds our linguistic and social orders? It is the Patriarch, in His autumn, who forces on us these disconcerting intuitions of the uncanny, and it is his history that maps the anatomy of these three moments.

Structuralism tells us that the world of discourse is an orderly space, stabilized by perpendicular distinctions between sameness and difference, which regulate our metaphorical substitutions and metonymical combinations, our grammar and our syntax. Everything circulates in a system of mutually exclusive and reciprocal exchange, because the Center that holds the poles apart is fixed and immobile. We begin by noting that this Signifier of signifiers enjoys the traditional attributes of godhead—omnipotence, eternality, invisibility. So also does the "undoer of dawn, commander of time, repository of light" of García Márquez. Our patriarch is "the one who can do everything . . . the one who gives the orders," and his indestructibility is the star that guides the lesser lives of his children: "The only thing that gave us security on earth was the certainty that he was there, invulnerable to plague and hurricane, invulnerable to Manuela Sánchez's trick, invulnerable to time, dedicated to the messianic happiness of thinking for us, knowing that we knew that he would not take any decision for us that did not have our measure." Of an age so ancient that it can be computed only within a range of error of a hundred years, the Patriarch has killed death once, has risen on the third day, and if he dies again, who is not to believe that he will rise again? During the long reign of the Patriarch one gets used to repetition without variation, and temporal difference begins to look like eternal sameness. Everything returns in the commemorative calendar of the Patriarch—the year of the plague, the time of the comet, the anniversary of August 12, the victory of January 14, the rebirth of March 13. Emptied of its dialectical content, its unique and real events, history may come to seem like no history at all, like myth in fact. In the kingdom of the Patriarch, "time passes—but not so much."

Omnipotent and eternal, the Patriarch is also invisible, rarely seen, and then on a palace balcony distantly, through a touring-car darkly. To his people, "general sir . . . you yourself were only an uncertain vision of pitiful eyes through the dusty peepholes of the window of a train, only the tremor of some taciturn lips, the fugitive wave of a velvet glove on the no man's hand of an old man with no destiny with our never knowing who he was, or what he was like, or even if he was only a figment of the imagination." Having already refused to die the literal death demanded by the Symbolic order, this patriarch also disallows any literal representation of himself. No words can be matched to such an elusive object, no mimesis pertain with any reliability. Indeed, only faked images of this disembodied god are allowed to circulate. What makes the rounds are counterfeited portraits, fabricated newscasts, false medals of imaginary victories, and even an "official impostor," Patricio Aragonés, who mimes the master just well enough to die his death for him.

Later on, many of his people will more or less cynically agree that these official images are untrustworthy, yet earlier these were the same folk who began to fabricate a sublime discourse around him: "All he had to do was point at trees for them to bear fruit and at animals for them to grow and at men for them to prosper, and he had ordered them to take the rain away from places where it disturbed the harvest and take it to drought-stricken lands, and that was the way it had been, sir, I saw it, because his legend had begun much earlier than he believed himself master of all his power." An unseen, absent Father apparently presents no obstacle to belief as it is elaborated in language; to the contrary, a vacuum, void, empty set seems to some to exist only to be filled back in with the fertile stuff of legend. When the whole man is unavailable for literal representation—when he is known only through his parts, a hand, his lips, his eyes—then this metonymical incompletion leads to metaphorical escalation. How rapid and absolute that escalation can become is seen in this wholly mythical description of the Patriarch at the height of his power: "Official schoolboy texts referred to him as a patriarch of huge size who never left his house because he could not fit through the doors, who loved children and swallows, who knew the language of certain animals, who had the virtue of being able to anticipate the designs of nature, who could guess a person's thoughts by one look in the eye, and who had a secret of salt with the virtue of curing lepers' sores and making cripples walk." For he who appears from nowhere, there is provided the origin myth of the son-of-no-father; and for he who is everywhere, there is the predictable apocalypse associated with his imagined demise "that the mud from the swamps would go back up river to its source, that it would rain blood, that hens would lay pentagonal eggs, and that silence and darkness would cover the universe once more because he was the end of creation." In such an economy, where visual representation and verbal imitation are all but impossible, words are worth a thousand images; and discourse, without the negative feedback of the Real, becomes destabilized, on runaway. Although such unauthorized mythologizing authorizes the Father and legitimates the Center, from a meta-perspective it also allows us to understand that Father as a generator of excess as well as a stabilizer of order. His very absence from reality dictates his ascent into myth.

We have heard what his people say, but what would they see if—like the reader or the deconstructionist—they invaded the space of the Patriarch? A silly, sullied, senile Sublime. A deaf and amnesiac Phallus dragging around a gigantic herniated testicle. The Signifier stripped down to a portable latrine, a pallet on the floor, and a common soldier's uniform *sans* insignia. The Emperor, shouts the irreverent post-structuralist, has no clothes! An illusory monarch, this poor, imperfectly forked animal is also a captive monarch, a slave to the power of which he should be master. García Márquez intends this minimalist emphasis, I think, to define the seat of power as a limbo, as a claustrophobia-inducing prisonhouse that suffocates its vassal. The suggestion is that the patriarch, caged up and cast away, maintains a certain site of innocence and gains courage from an endured victimage. This captive of power, nonetheless, is also a vicious wielder of power whenever he extends himself beyond his cage. The old bison suffering in his solitude, the locus of his nation's lives and legends, is likewise a volcano-god whose hot lava erupts over the land, flooding it to the peripheries. Our patriarch is a Papa Stalin, keeping his lonely vigil in the Kremlin out of concern for his children; but whether he chooses to confer parades or purges, shifts or gulags, whenever he reaches out, he is a devastating destabilizer. It seems clear that García Márquez is also insisting, significantly, that the safely exiled Signifier is but a consoling structuralist fiction.

This is a man who carries disorder in his bones and leaves a trail of devastation in his wake, even within his own privileged space. In his palace, at the heart of power, there are cripples on the stairs, whores in the laundry rooms, cows on the carpet, lepers in the rosebushes, hens pecking away at the government files. Into the house of power has seeped a folk-flood, eroding spatial orders and hierarchal proprieties. Outside the palace, the patriarch's most clearly intended reforms are deformations, as when the sweeping schools, instituted to provide employment and clean up national litter, issue in the Sisyphean practice of trundling a nation's rubbish from province to province; or when the massive urban renewal of the Dogfight District results in thousands of displaced refugees. The site of power begins to look like a carnival presided over by a clownish, captious lord of misrule, who upturns and overturns the rectilinear distinctions of his extensive domain.

If order leaks out of space, time fares no better in the kingdom of the patriarch. Temporality loses the serial punctuation that would permit gradualism and regularity, and is made instead to submit to the exclamatory mark of the catastrophe. We begin to realize what the world must have been like when gods were taken seriously. Our invisible patriarch has a sudden, brutal way of being noticed, of making a large, abrupt difference. The Catholic Church refuses to confer sainthood upon my dead mother? Herd every nun and priest out of the country, naked as the day of their infamous births, expropriate the Church properties, beat up the Papal Anuncio, and declare war on the Holy See! My old friend, the minister of defense, is plotting against me? Stuff him with herbs and pine nuts, and serve him for dinner to the other potentially traitorous Cabinet members! The children who draw for the national lottery threaten a very profitable swindle? Ship all 2000 of them out to sea, and dynamite the raft into silence!

Not only is the patriarch a disruptive child at play and a victimizer of his people, but any strategy he chooses to insure order inevitably issues in increasing disorder; any attempt at correction simply exacerbates the noise and escalates the static in the system. The lottery-drawing children are a case in point. Instructed to pick from the bag only the billiard ball that is iced, the children must be removed from their families after each drawing to insure their silence. Protesting parents begin to fill up the nation's jails, and the children to overpopulate the dungeon beneath the harbor. As public indignation spreads, an international commission is sent to investigate. Now the children must be shuffled back and forth in boxcars to the uninhabited swamps, mountains, and rainforests until the investigators depart in defeat. With their departure the patriarch is free to massacre the children, but then the population must be decimated in the general insurrection that follows. And all for the lack of an honest lottery. For the want of a Symbolic Father, the Symbolic order is lost.

Excess is in fact mandated in the Signifier that refuses to die a literal death. With no one to say no, no off-button to stop him, no negative feedback to halt the snowball effect—the patriarch puts any system on runaway. Soon enough, his secret wishes and commands will be carried out before he can utter them: A nun will be kidnapped for his future wife, the soap operas on television will be rewritten to afford him happy endings, waterfront whores will be passed off as innocent schoolgirls to serve his aged lust. When silence authorizes definitively, copying errors increase, chance may become necessity and mistakes law, as when one diplomat's waving, white handkerchief becomes everyone else's protocol for attracting the attentions of the deaf patriarch. In or out of his bottle, the patriarch is an imp of catastrophe, a perverse clown, a sorting demon gone wild, a lightning rod for violence and excess.

Traditionally, the hero has been conceived in a condition of mediation, the third party between us and the gods, our official stand-in for those difficult negotiations. Yet this Daddy, unfit as a Center and emphatically disqualified for rational mediation, cannot be the fated hero of tragedy. If he is an Oedipus at all, he is the Oedipus of farce. Full of bluff and bluster, given to the immorality of ruinous waste, he is the criminal-as-detective who initiates national witch-hunts for the perpetuators of the crimes against humanity he himself has committed. When their jobs are done, his hired assassins are hunted down and shot, quartered, beheaded, electrocuted. Confronted with an atrocity apparently not his own, the patriarch typically escalates his feverish search for an arbitrary scapegoat into a national reign of terror. To discover who commanded the pack of dogs that tore apart his wife and son in the marketplace, he establishes a secret police force and thereafter, each time more cynically and wearily, signs individual receipts for the 918 severed heads that are delivered to the palace. Like Oedipus— who will accuse Creon, the Tiresias, then the messenger, and finally his shepherd foster-father—the patriarch may have initially thought he was seeking out the Truth. You must speak out, he tells his children, when the apostolic representative begins his investigation into the miraculous powers reputed to his dead mother, Bendición Alvarado. And speak out they do, dutifully and for pay, through seven volumes of testimony taken from the dropsy victims cured and the dead men raised—by the mother lying in state who "had been stuffed according to the worst skills of taxidermy" to provide relics for enterprising dealers. For such a grotesque national conspiracy against the Truth, whose is the ultimate responsibility? "Everything had been a farce . . . a carnival apparatus that he himself had put together without really thinking about it when he decided that the corpse of his mother should be displayed for public veneration on a catafalque of ice long before anyone thought about the merits of her sainthood." In the country where the lie is king, the Oedipus of farce lets the lie live (civil sainthood for Bendición), banishes the Church and the Truth, and he himself and his eyes stay put.

Near the end of his eternal reign, the only truth surviving in the country of the patriarch is the anonymous graffiti scrawled on the walls of the palace toilets. As one for whom virtue and love are impossible, the "general of the universe" has come to the determination that "a lie is more comfortable than doubt, more useful than love, more lasting than truth." He has arrived, this Signifier of signifiers, at "the ignominious fiction of commanding without power, being exalted without glory, being obeyed without authority." Yet even though the Center has been eroded, emptied out, dilapidated—the absolutes of command, exaltation, and obedience remain. How is it that nothing has stayed pure—that absolutes are grounded in the shakiest relativisms, the sublime in grotesqueries, Truth in farce?

According to Michel Serres, steps were taken very early in Western culture to insure that it couldn't happen here. In the first stunning volume of his *Hermes*, Serres engages in two brilliant pieces of theoretical speculation concerning a relation of similarity between the dialogues of Plato and the geometry of Parmenides. Customarily, the two interlocutors in a Socratic dialogue are supposed to be opposing each other in a dialectical search for the Truth. In the newer view of communication theory, they are on the same side, tied together by a mutual interest: the elimination of the noise that threatens to interrupt the communication. Mathematics likewise presents itself as a successful communication, in firm command of a code that is maximally purged of any interference. Serres calls this common enemy "the third man." The third man may be background noise, static, the chronic transformations of language-as-Babel, irrational numbers—in short, the entire empirical domain that can overwhelm any formal system. With Plato and the geometers Western thought begins its massive, concerted campaign to render an ideal form independent of its empirical realizations, to isolate it from the noise of the world, to eliminate everything that hides form. The structuralist Signifier is a contemporary manifestation of this hard-fought Western battle against noise and for formalization. The empirical domain, Lacan's Real, must be eliminated if a formal system, such as language, is to be born; the Real father must die, in order to inaugurate the Symbolic domain of the Signifier of signifiers. It is only in this exclusionary, restricted, formalized space that we conduct our searches and support their results as Truth.

Kurt Gödel in his famous Theorem tried to warn us that we couldn't win. In refuting the symbolic logic of Whitehead and Russell, he demonstrated mathematically the impossible coexistence of consistency and completeness within any formal system. If a system of thought is consistent, then it is so because it is incomplete; if it is complete, it will necessarily be inconsistent. Or, in Serres's formulation: If you successfully exclude the third man, you will have a neat formal lie; if you allow the background static in for the sake of completeness, you will have a tiger by the tail. The West has almost always opted for the first alternative, faking completeness in order to maintain consistency. Consistency has been as important to our thinking as unity to our sense of self, as continuity to our sense of time, as order to our sense of space. Remove one brick from that edifice, the house that Plato and Parmenides built, and you have a system in ruins.

García Márquez has removed all four—consistency, unity, continuity, and order. He has taken the second, infrequent way out of Gödel's Theorem, deciding to go for the completeness and let the consistency go. He chooses not to exorcise the demon of noise, but rather to show how it is the necessary origin and end of all our systemizations. In *The Autumn of the Patriarch* he has taken us to the kingdom of the third man who refuses to be excluded. His patriarch is the empirical fact of contradiction that threatens the consistency of formal systems, at the same time that it grounds such systems as the background noise. In Serres's memorable metaphor, the patriarch is a spinning top: "The top spins, even if we demonstrate that, for impregnable reasons, it is, undecidably, both mobile and fixed. That's the way it is." Fixed, *i.e.*, dead, the Symbolic Signifier thus establishes a boundary that doesn't shift, a bottom-line to representation, an ultimate sticking-place for referentiality. Captive of his power, the Patriarch enables the orderly circulation of words and goods, the proper distribution of functions, the stability of structuration—all because he doesn't move. But, like Galileo's earth, he *does* move, and catastrophically, undoing his own ordering powers and promoting the uneasy suspicion of a ground-that-shifts at the center of things, a ground itself decentered and decentering. Not to observe the boundaries is to erode the ground of representation, is to make verification and falsification impossible, is to destroy Truth and literality at the same blow. By taking the patriarch out of the mimetic portrait for which he is supposedly sitting firm, García Márquez measures the potential for havoc in the Signifier, exposing it in a mirror of the Real where contradiction and undecidability within Symbolic systems are escalated from formal inconsistencies to the empirical wilderness of "that's the way it is."

The imaginative intelligence of our author is decidedly post-Einsteinian. After Einstein, that perpetuator of relativity, God is the third man, a joker "of invisible power whose dice decided the fate of a nation." Márquez's patriarch is the demon of noise that actively works to disrupt successful communications. He knew "the secret of maintaining parallel services to stir up distractive rivalries among the military . . . identical organisms that he made look different in order to rule with more relaxation in the midst of the storm making them believe that some were being watched by others, mixing beach sand in with the gunpowder in the barracks and confusing the truth of his intentions with images of the opposite truth." The patriarch is that *unheimlich* vortex where contraries whirl, mix, and displace one another, where the only Symbolic laws that pertain are Planck's randomness, Heisenberg's uncertainty, and Schrödinger's undecidability. It is this vortex—where Señor Signifier shits as he fucks—that is the ultimate focus of the deconstructionists. Probing and prodding only those nodes of a text where the Center shifts from stasis to static, the deconstructionist critics, appalled by its indeterminacy, themselves prolong the rigorous task of the text almost infinitely, steadfastly refusing to recuperate for system and theory the various entropies of the Real. Like García Márquez, they are suspicious of premature closures, embarrassed by any complacent conviction of completeness, and bored by the convention of consistency.

Against those who would argue for the interpretive Truth of a text, the deconstructionists employ their most radical strategy: the literalization of metaphor, and the metaphorization of the literal word. With this move, they effectively reduce to absurdity the notion of a ground. And where there is no ground, there can be neither mimesis nor antithesis, but merely figure after figure after figure, each one a surface without a depth. This, in Serres's phrase, is the "chronic transformation" that prevents the completion of communication and casts suspicion upon the existence of Truth. The patriarch's people learn this mistrust early, which García Márquez explicitly connects to his death which was a non-death, suffered only by his double, the official impostor: "We knew that no evidence of his death was final, because there was always another truth behind the truth."

Not only does García Márquez adopt the literalizing/metaphorizing tactics of deconstruction, as we shall presently see, but he also makes his patriarch's life a literalization of one of deconstruction's own central metaphors. I refer here to the trade-off between insemination and dissemination, as elaborated in the thought of Jacques Derrida. The inseminating Father is the reliable Signifier of the structuralists, he who respects the past as a legacy, guarantees the legitimacy of his progeny, and stands securely for a calculable future. The patriarch of García Márquez neither inherits nor confers such dynastic credentials. The origin myth affirms that "a wandering birdwoman at the beginning of time had given difficult birth to a no man's son who became king." Further testimony about Saint Bendición reveals that she "was languid, went about dressed in rags, barefoot, and had to use her lower parts in order to eat, but she was beautiful, father, and she was so innocent that she fitted out the cheapest lory parrots with tails from the finest cocks to make them pass for macaws, she repaired crippled hens with turkey-feather fans and sold them as birds of paradise." The bastard son of an impoverished, possibly retarded con-woman who survives by disseminating confusion, the patriarch is himself a scatterer of his seed, wasting it on the large number of illegitimate seven-month runts he fathers. The herniated testicle that causes him continual pain and shame concretizes the anti-structuralist metaphor of deconstruction's crippled Phallus, and accounts in the narrative of his life for the kind of furious impotency that propels his "rooster love" with the unending train of females he summons to his presence. His is an impotency realized empirically in the political sphere, where his absolute power is converted to absolute powerlessness, as when his *Doppelgänger* taunts the patriarch with "You're president of nobody," and his executioner reminds him impassively, "You aren't the government, general, you're the power." The disseminating father so scatters and squanders his seed that neither appearance nor reality, neither cause nor effect can be legitimated within the formalizations that Western Truth demands.

Throughout *The Autumn of the Patriarch* there are authorial techniques that deconstructionists would recognize as their own. For instance, there are the abrupt shiftings of pronouns that revise and add to the truth-tale of the farcical Oedipus, the foreign perspective of the third man that causes orderly narrative to leap its tracks and follow after local surprises. Still, deconstructionists have never followed their structuralist predecessors in their exclusive fascination with syntax. Much more challenging to them are the devious ways of metaphor, particularly in its folding-back into the literal, and vice versa, where the weaving of the symbolic and mimetic most resembles the double helix or golden braid which contains simultaneously all possibilities, every interpretation.

If we follow to the end one of these woven strands in the patriarch's history, we can readily see how it turns back on itself, so that "end" and "beginning" lose their significance as terminal points in a biography. Already we know that, in the moment of inauguration, eternity was conferred upon the Signifier simultaneously with his entrance into profane temporality. We might well suspect, then, that with whatever temporal journeying his life offers him, he will never move from where he is. We are now prepared to notice how García Márquez has through the play of rhetoric implemented the following formulations, which would create static in any formalized system: The end is in the beginning; secular temporality is all the eternity we have; the waters of undifferentiation are from whence we spring and whither we go; the feminine principle is but the female anatomy, the "oceanic feeling" and the womb merging in the indeterminacy of metaphorical and literal inscription.

"I did it all so that I could get to know the sea," confesses this old man from the backlands, who has sold the seacoast of his landlocked country to foreign exploiters, to ease the huge national debt. The ultimatum from his creditors is, "Either the marines land or we take the sea." What follows is this incredible writing, no deciding its identification as either metaphor or literalness, that runs away with the "take" metaphor/literality, twining the sublime with the grotesque: "So they took away the Caribbean in April, Ambassador Ewing's nautical engineers carried it off in numbered pieces to plant it in the blood-red dawns of Arizona, they took it away with everything it had inside, general sir, with the reflection of our cities, our timid drowned people, our demented dragons." Almost every word gives us cause for pause. The linguistic signs that point to precise, unambivalent signification—the proper names, the details of agency, time, and place— are evenly countered and cancelled by the enumeration of the mythical contents of the patriarch's sea. This is the ultimate dispossession of the Signifier. The Center is revealed as the primal soup; at the source of all circulation is not a male center of differentiation, but a female reservoir of undifferentiation; and the sea-womb is a tomb, the resting-place of both the pre- and post-individual. We are, already and always, where we are going to. Bracketing, as we must, the absurdity of this language, we can see that it encompasses both completeness and consistency. There is the consistency of the human condition within time and its accompanying lament for "this meatbeating life that goes only in one direction"; and there is completeness in the before/after symmetry of timelessness with which the temporal consistency is braided, tracked, and traced.

The patriarch of mythical birth, moreover, has been given the prophecy of a death that sounds very literal—he will die as "a solitary drowned man"—until we begin to extrapolate metaphorically by saying that this apparently means the embryonic waters will return to reclaim him. This is a rather comforting notion when pitched at the sublime level of the archetype, but the literalizing account of the patriarch's death in Ambassador Kipling's memoirs is a distinct downgrading to the grotesque: "He told how he had found him soaked in an incessant and salty matter which flowed from his skin, that he had acquired the huge size of a drowned man and he had opened his shirt to show me the tight and lucid body of a dry-land drowned man in whose crooks and crannies parasites from the reefs at the bottom of the sea were proliferating, he had a ship remora on his back, polyps and microscopic crustaceans in his armpits." Undecidability is multiplied here with almost every phrase. Might the salty matter be sweat rather than seawater? Huge on the outside and tight on the inside is both for and against a literal drowning. There aren't any crustaceans that are microscopic, are there? And perhaps, "a dry-land drowned man" is a metaphor for the power-victimized patriarch? Faithful readers of García Márquez will recognize this typical play on deconstructionist territory, where Truth can be neither confirmed nor disconfirmed. I myself like the quiet thud of the sentence Márquez writes for the minister of health's examination of the dead patriarch: "(It) revealed that his arteries had turned to glass, he had beachsand sediment in his kidneys, and his heart was cracked from a lack of love." It is the "lack" at the source of things—the repressed castration-wound whose first cut becomes our first boundary-limit—that makes of our lives a rehearsing over and over of the birth trauma. Perhaps the wisest intuition of the patriarch is that we can do nothing else but go home again. He voices it in the circular metaphor that his life has literalized: "Seas are like cats, he said, they always come home."

If it is womb/woman from whom and to whom we journey without moving, she is surely not one of Jung's archetypes, all of whom circulate within, not prior to, the economy of lack. Available to rational thought because they follow inauguration, the archetypes have no place outside of human consciousness and the neuroses of temporality. By their very differentiation into types, the virgin and the whore, wise crone and witch, madonna and matron are tainted with the marks of human longing and desire. If we seek the pre-embodiment woman, we are more likely to find her through Jacques Derrida's meditation upon Nietzsche's meditation on woman, as "one name for the untruth of truth." There, one finds Derrida strenuously opposing both philosophical and hermeneutical recovery of the text, through their devaluation of metaphor as the lying art that disrupts both logical thought and literary representation. There is nothing verifiable, of course, about Derrida's and Nietzsche's equivalency of woman and the swerve away from logic that is figurative language, of sexuality and non-truth. However, with the equation as a model for reading, he would have us adopt a tangential, and therefore perverse, relation to our texts, one that cuts across the normal conventions and dissolves our categorical languages along the slope of the diagonal. Put simply, the challenge is whether or not we can conceive the truth as skepticism, whether we can accept a ground that shifts beneath our stable foundations.

Originally, that stability was guaranteed by the purity of the concept, basic to philosophic thought, the Platonic idea. But in the fallen, ontological world the concept becomes contaminated with images of undecidability, evoked through the incessant human oscillations between the spiritualization and sensualization of love and hostility. The Platonic idea becomes woman; the becoming-female is a "process of the idea" (*Fortschritt der Idee*). Derrida's text is Nietzsche's *Twilight of the Idols*, specifically that section called "History of an Error" which immediately precedes his story of truth. There, Nietzsche says of the idea that "it becomes female . . . Christian," a statement which Derrida transposes as "she castrates (herself)," noting the Christian Church's preference for the excision and extirpation of passion, for "curing" through castratism, for seizing consistency through exclusion. Hostile to life, the Church and the concept are hostile to its invasion of their purity through woman, who is life. In the reactive position, either as truth or non-truth, woman is debased, censured. She eludes her conceptualized identity as sexual antagonist only when, as Derrida says, "she affirms herself, in and of herself, in man" as the Dionysiac and artist, whose multiple styles render the idea "subtle, insidious, incomprehensible" and suspend "the decidable opposition of true and non-true." Hence, the heterogeneity of the womanly text, the entropy within sexual differentiation.

Now let us return to the patriarch of García Márquez. In all *his* castrated delusions of virility, in *his* dangerous delight in playing the thunder-god, in *her* seductive distance and captivating inaccessibility, in *her* tantalizing promise of transcendence—our *his/her* patriarch enacts the becoming-female of the Platonic idea, of the structuralist Signifier. Indeed, in his advanced age, he bears a striking resemblance to the eternal, sceptical Úrsula Buendía. His life given over entirely to domestic duties, he moves through his household with the lurching gait and the slovenly appearance of a slattern, counting the hens, covering the birds in their cages, burning the cow plops, turning out the lights, locking up for the night—without eliminating the disorder that disrupts, but also without arranging anything that will not be undone once again in the morning light. In accommodating the mess of his palace, the patriarch-as-Úrsula evinces a style, as passive as it might appear, that nonetheless makes the meshings of sexual difference intractable to hard-and-fast coding.

Whether his stylistic manifestations are active or passive, in the funhouse mirror of the deconstructionists, the Sovereign is this man-dressed-as-a-woman. His inaugural appearance must surely have been early, quite possibly in *The Bacchae* of Euripides. In that Greek tragedy we see the two genders in their active and passive orientations, uncastrated and castrated—as power, powerful impotence, impotent power, and impotence. There the already dilapidated Signifier appears through a principle of doubling, in the two-in-one of Pentheus, the sacrificial victim, and Dionysus, the god of misrule and intoxication. Arrayed in curls and gown, eager for his debut as a voyeur, Pentheus the king acts out the prelude of dedifferentiation that is necessary for the Dionysian rites of undifferentiation. The catastrophe occurs in the midst of carnival, with the dismemberment of Pentheus by his unseeing mother and the other women empowered and crazed through their shared communality of excess. The final scene features—not a responsible *deus ex machina* come to purge the city of its Dionysiac impurities—but rather a monstrous bull-man-god, smiling down from the top of the temple at the noise he has literalized at the hearts and hearths of the Greeks. With this supplement, tragedy is born.

Tragedy (here we might substitute Western history, logic, narrative) has always been the story of our resistance to an entropic heterogeneity that leaks out order through an inscription tangential to its own declamations of thesis and antithesis. It is not smart to choose sides within a nonorganic totality. It is much better to find a style that undoes the fetishes and reifications of rationalized representation. My own choice among the Greek models of style-setters is not the Dionysus/Pentheus of Euripides, but rather the Hermes of Michel Serres. I like this jokester, this forever mobile, fleet-footed messenger of the gods. I like the seductiveness of his tricks, feints, ruses, and disguises. I like the way he keeps turning up as the god of commerce and exchange, of the crossroads, of thieves and secrets, of comedy. I like the zero-degree of reductionism implied by his caduceus rod, which looks so much like the double helix of DNA. Without being terrorized by the Dionysius who is Nietzsche's father of tragedy, we can appreciate Hermes as the background noise that precedes and founds our differentiations and individuation. To confront Hermes is to imagine at the Center the uncastrated woman, the (wo)man of the universe. In taking the structuralist Signifier straight, we were futilely countering the cosmic drift of entropy, trying once more to command nature without first obeying her. Now, in the autumn of the Patriarch, we should be prepared cheerfully to embark upon our unstable practices, assured that we are moving—and not moving—with the universe.

The Heir Must Die: *One Hundred Years of Solitude* as a Gothic Novel

Claudette Kemper Columbus

A brief survey of the salient conventions that distinguish the Gothic novel may convince readers of Gabriel García Márquez's *One Hundred Years of Solitude* that the book suits the genre. Reading *Solitude* as a Gothic novel not only yields a comprehensive interpretation but also heightens appreciation of its wit and craftsmanship. If the reader bears in mind the Gothic conventions dear to devotees of Bram Stoker's *Dracula*, Mary Shelley's *Frankenstein*, the Edgar Allan Poe canon, Emily Brontë's *Wuthering Heights*, and Alejo Carpentier's *Explosion in a Cathedral*, the reader will see how ably the Gothic conventions in any one of them can also pump the pedals of Pietro Crespi's pianola though the birds of magic realism sing other songs.

Gothic novels began in romances, sentimental novels, and Oriental tales, notably *The Thousand and One Nights*. Edmund Burke's theory of the sublime added the most distant geographical reaches to the influence of Gothic architecture that in itself accentuated effects of spatial stress through contrasting light and dark, height and depth, succession and variation. After Burke, the Gothic novel raised exotic literature, satanic architecture, and polarized nature to a new pitch in that nature, seen through Burke's views on the sublime and his construction of an aesthetics of terror, provided no explanation for natural devastation. Neither religious nor marital resolutions redressed the imbalances of massive environmental distress that Burke conjoined with the vast, awful, obscure, identity-disturbing nature of nature and of aesthetic pleasure.

The Gothic novel united torturous terrain in the outside world with intemperate and tormented interior terrain. What Burke considered "sublime" in geography—its vastness and illimitability, the astonishment of its

---

From *Modern Fiction Studies* 32, no. 3 (Autumn 1986). © 1986 by the Purdue Research Foundation, West Lafayette, Indiana.

effects, its power, the obscurity of its meaning—was seen as indistinguishable from the ravages of fear and desire. Add to this combustible mixture of bizarre tales, strained architecture, an unsettling aesthetics of nature, and an unstable psychic life one simple notion, and you achieve an "A" in the awful. The one, additional notion on the part of characters within the Gothic novel was that protection from all that lies out of bounds could be had through possessions, through power and property, in which property consists of what one owns, of what one knows or might know, and of owning or being owned by bodies, including one's own. Bodies, unabashedly represented as objects in the Gothic novel, are properties, commodities. Flesh is territory, property, commodity, text.

To mistake property for a defense against the terrors of the unknown activates a devastating machinery in which those material buffers designed for protection against the unknown become in themselves insurmountable barriers against knowing. In their attempt to possess themselves and others, to possess the body of knowledge, to control the world's body, Gothic characters go beyond unintelligibility. Having confused property with power and authority, having confused property with control of consciousness, Gothic characters find themselves and their possessions locked behind skin or stone façades that are overpriced, overwritten, and misunderstood.

Through pathetic fallacy, writers show geography itself in the Gothic novel suffering Sybilline psychosexual vicissitudes. That is, the writers attribute human passion to the landscape, and sublime nature becomes psychotic. The climatic fuses with the climactic in a tangle of miasmic guilt and the world's worst weather.

Although to explore/possess territory seems to offer emotional, financial, intellectual escape from the mechanics of enslavement, neither the psyche nor its territorial double can be possessed and understood. Territory claimed, culturally imprinted, individually stamped or inscribed, remains ominously free, obscure, and, though much-lettered, inscrutable. For, like the psyche, territory is ours and not ours. The property we inherit as we inherit our bodies and our drives and desires has been encoded by nature and imprinted by culture and imprisons us. Intricately implicated, the world outside and the world of the interior remain sublime: grand, miniscule, repetitive, variable, astonishing, obscure.

Appetites from the libido that Gothic characters cannot confess or control inscribe the territory they inhabit and write upon their bodies, faces, clothing, houses that which they would conceal. The more Gothic interiors are denied, the more markings, scars, inscriptions, epistles, missing volumes, entire libraries appear to denounce them. Nubile girls and devoted scholars are particularly prone to evasive tactics such as obsessive absorption in the digging out and deciphering of texts that purport to tell the whole story . . . about the perfidious behavior of other people.

For no matter the apparent clarity of goodness, nor in what matte nor brilliant blacks evil is represented, in the Gothic vision, deity conspires with demon, the gorgeous with the grotesque in a duplicity or doubling beyond deciphering, and gargoyles are no less a part of a single whole than the icons of an unknown God. (*Gott* is encoded in savage "Gothic." In *One Hundred Years of Solitude*, when the awful insomnia plague strikes, the mystifying inscription "GOD EXISTS" is displayed on a reassuringly immense sign on the main street of Macondo.) Good and evil disguise and transform one another until the conclusion seems inescapable: human reason is insufficiently sharp to cope with their changeability.

"Good" characters do not perceive the depths to which they are disguised to themselves. For instance, heroines of the Gothic novel are habitually exposed as strangers to themselves. In their relationships to men, Jane Eyre, Catherine Earnshaw, Ursula Buendía remain dangerously confused, doing harm without meaning to, "unconsciously"; whereas Manfred, Dracula, Colonel Buendía bring a beguiling magnetic energy to evil more genuine than the striking of righteous and acceptable social attitudes on the part of the ladies—or for that matter, on the part of gentlemen as frigid and obtuse as Mr. Lockwood or as slavishly self-restrained as Pietro Crespi. Indeed, the presumption of goodness is a salient component of the disguise motif, one convention of the genre that persists in all of its manifestations. In the Gothic novel a character's delusions of "goodness" provide a marvelous even if unintended disguise. (García Márquez has said that Remedios the Beauty was modeled on a nymphomaniac who did not ascend to paradise on the wings of sheets being laundered but disappeared from her family more conventionally and conveniently.) One-dimensional, "flat" goodness is never dulled by overuse because the disguise suggests fundamental fears at heart: the fear that human beings may not be able to understand ourselves, that we do not really recognize the difference between supposedly polar opposites—good/evil, white/black, love/hate, life/death, hot/cold, mine/thine—and that we may not actually exist, that we are in some indefinable way critically absent.

In a Gothic world fatally deficient, indiscriminate human beings seem uneducable until it is too late. They seem unable to interpret what lies behind the double messages inscribed in dreams, inscriptions, landscapes, faces, scenes. As with the Gothic line in architecture, "a spaghettilike interlace whose puzzle asks to be unraveled," the plot line in the Gothic novel remains obdurately convoluted, its motion always turning back on itself so that it never faces where it is going (Linda Bayer-Berenbaum). The lengths and distances to which, and the speed with which characters attempt to locate and/or interpret crucial texts, sometimes written in foreign languages or hidden in enormous(ly) strange places, or in stories-within-stories-within-stories, reflect the Gothic as preeminently the art of encoding incomplete messages with minimally double meanings that interminably defer interpretation while hopeful interpreters discover themselves haplessly entrapped in riddles and doublebinds.

A list of some Gothic machinery and some stock characters of the genre should set off little shocks of recognition in admirers of *One Hundred Years of Solitude*. The list begins, of course, with the castle, mansion, or family home and its cognates: torture chambers, labyrinthine dungeons, prisons, bedrooms, boxes, closets, beds, coffins, and the locks and keys that pertain to these: images simultaneously of presence and absence, of the concrete and contained, and of the transient and lost. Señor del Carpio, a singular example of paternal and grandparental repression, having mailed off his entire inheritance to his offspring, forwards his corpse for Christmas, a Gothic gift. A cutaway of the floor plan of a cathedral exposes the transept and chancel-nave, the route to eternal life, as two coffins crossed, or one man crucified, or a deathlike corridor with many doors and no exits. Other cognates for doors that connect life and death are mirrors, ancestral paintings, miniatures, daguerreotypes, eyes. All reflect figures disguised or veiled, or whose identities are mistaken, or who have twins or doubles or alter egos, or who share family names or family resemblances. The twins, Arcadio Segundo and Aureliano Segundo, play intricate games "like two synchronized machines"; they exchange appearances, displace appearances, confound questions of identification. There are those who otherwise fail to look wholly "themselves" and so are related in oblique ways to a mysterious stranger or a gypsy, perhaps, or a foundling who appears out of nowhere, who may be related to anyone, and who raises the twin specters of insurrection and incest, as does Amaranta, who murmurs at one point, "I'm your aunt. . . . It's almost as if I were your mother." Openly libidinous appetites range from cannibalism to exhibitionism. José Arcadio Buendía, son of José Arcadio Buendía, possessed a magnificent, imperious, inscribed penis decorated with words in several languages tattooed in red and blue. After long absence from Macondo, he returned wearing a medal of Our Lady of Help around his bison neck and "exhibited his unusual masculinity on the bar completely covered with tattooes [the Gothic secret text in a novel guise]." Such is normal Gothic fare, as are professional persons such as doctors and lawyers (the terrorist, Dr. Alirio Noguera) and their counterparts, monsters of rectitude, grossly aggressive teachers and priests and nuns and wives (Fernanda spirits away her daughter, the unmarried and unrepentant Meme, in a carriage that looks "like an enormous bat," to immure her in a nunnery), the monk gone mad (the pederast José Arcadio of the "papal air"), and the—sine qua non—monomaniacal dad, a figure so potent that he is omnipotent even when absent. Inherited guilt is attended by a mystifying prophecy that, fulfilled, ruins or restores the line or the house. Recall Úrsula's pro-leptic and epi-leptic fear of the birth of a child with a curly tail of a pig that corresponds to cycles of time, recurrence, heredity (inherited guilt), memory, and fatality. These examples provide no more than a broad-brush assemblage.

One difficulty in criticizing a Gothic novel methodically is that 1) a number of themes intersect at every major image; 2) every major image is doubled or paired with an image ostensibly other; 3) all the major images are homologous. Like castle/territory, fire/ice depicts the relationship of power to isolation; of acquisitiveness to isolation; of lust to solitude; of solitude to death. Moreover, fire/ice, *casa*/territory also depict the family drama, family ties 1) fixed, 2) fought, 3) sought. In an endless cycle family ties are fought to the point of solitude and found to the point of incest and always by characters all but oblivious to context, until finally the twenty-second Aureliano, born with a swinishly curly tail, dies from neglect, the utterly self-contradictory image of a fatal lust for love/death.

Where the theme is evasion, substitution is continuous. A character who does little else but seek knowledge is usually actively in flight from its immediate application. As the infinitely receding, perishable vistas of a dreamed village made of mirrors is an image of José Arcadio Buendía's egotism and his avoidance of insight, so also is the obsession with interpreting a text homologous to egotism, an assertiveness ever threatened by illiminable meanings. The meaning of a text keeps receding into other texts. The walls of the house prove perishable. The estate is only too transferable property. Ice, mirror, castle, reading, metaphors of the conscious mind's image of itself, also image those aspects of the mind that the mind most seeks to evade; hence the subterranean connection of inheritance (freeing us from dependency) and enslavement. The flight-and-pursuit patterns, the territorial imperative, voyages into remote places, interminable stories-within-stories-within-stories are all unread indications that we cannot have what we desire: privileged stability. Yet what we cannot have not only enslaves us but destroys. The infinite internal needles of insecurity puncture comprehension, destroy family life, shatter political life on a national, on an international, on a global scale. So it is that the themes of flight-and-pursuit and of oppression and obsession find homologues in a still centerpiece, the castle or inherited home, and in ice brought by colonization to the tropics, and in unexamined, incestuous relationships that, entangling heart and head, condemn us to solitude.

The figure-in-the-landscape and the landscape-in-the-figure also represent territorial conquest as a traumatic component of the psychoeconomics of inheritance (of property, of the body itself). The possessors are the possessed, heirs inevitably in error. The sliding signifier of the name of disinherited Jane Eyre is a clear instance of shifty possessiveness: heir, *aire* in French (*Jane Eyre*), air, err, are, R, slide into the lettered animus of the masculine: Jane St. Rivers's saintly suitor and cousin, John St. Rivers; Jane Eyre's cousin and (potentially incestuous) assailant, John Reed, precursor of Rochester, Jane's rough beloved. Heathcliff's name also exemplifies the territorial theme, the slippery connectedness of letters to psychic trauma and of psychic trauma to terrain. Dark, gypsyish, an impoverished changeling, Heathcliff compensates for injury to his ego by forcing his way into a Wuthering "inheritance" through mysteriously acquired "means." And yet he fails to come into his own, clearly inscribed on his name: Heathcliff, "borrowed" from Catherine's deceased brother. Figuratively and literally, the heath and the cliff of Penistone Crag are his inherent being, his sexuality, his "earth-body," crucially *outside* of his possessing. He, the Gothic heir, the outcast, cannot escape the consequences of a past that excluded him. The more he dominates, the more the past possesses him; the more it possesses him, the more ferocious his ambivalent urgencies: to possess and to be emptied out into a landscape he does not possess but that possesses/is Heathcliff. Heathcliff typifies the Gothic dilemma of inherited guilt and concomitant territoriality, along with Poe's Pym; Maturin's Melmoth; several Manfreds-manafraids; and García Márquez's Rebeca, who, as an abandoned waif, arrives in Macondo with an insatiable appetite for eating earth and ends with her absolute isolation in the property her husband has illicitly amassed. Her living room becomes her tomb. And then of course there is the patriarch, José Arcadio Buendía. In the midst of his home(text) that grows like a tapeworm, José Arcadio becomes a mad stranger who speaks gibberish (Latin) and who must then, to the day he is carried to his bed, perhaps to die, be bound to a chestnut tree. "A smell of tender mushrooms, of wood-flower fungus, of old and concentrated outdoors impregnated the bedroom as it was breathed by the colossal old man weatherbeaten by the sun and the rain." The scenery of José Arcadio's death recurs at his son Aureliano's death:

> he went to the chestnut tree, thinking about the circus, and while he urinated, he tried to keep on thinking about the circus, but he could no longer find the memory. He pulled his head in between his shoulders like a baby chick and remained motionless with his forehead against the trunk of the chestnut tree.

Morbid, manic territoriality becomes contiguous with physical and psychological appetite, and the inverse also: psychological necessity is spread out over the countryside. Dracula's interloping and locked castle, his queer family history and genetic peculiarity, his psychological aberrations are all of a too-loose (mysterious) and yet of a locked piece: what the count lusts for is congress with himself, but that he cannot have, unless he gives himself away. Therefore bearing his earth-filled coffins from port to port, Dracula and his terrain become literally one, the flight-and-pursuit pattern openly presented as fused to territoriality, conquest, as is Rebeca's carrying with her the bones of her unknown parents, cloc-clocking in a bag. She eats earth to "find" herself.

The velocity and the violence with which plot developments take place fragment and refract personalities and perceptual fields, dispossessing characters of their names, of their lives, even as they seek to ground themselves, as it were. The pace of the action conjures life in Bedlam, a sensation deepened by characters who in this context madly pursue "the sacred riddles and ciphers of the self" (Robert Martin Adams). In traumatic and repercussive situations a character may resort to anything, alphabetization, say, as a cover up against fragmentation and interpretational impotence.

We—characters and readers—see more awfulness and emptiness than we can say we know we have seen, and the refusal to accept what we have seen splits us into infinite, internal needles, freezes us into parts of beings. Women become spinsters or sluts or domestic angels, all forms of disguise and escape, as the mating of "born" spinsters with demon outcasts suggests. Endless incongruity, endless fragmentation—perceptual, psychological, moral—effected through high speed plot development disperses identity or integrity into duplicate or proliferative or curiously indecipherable existences. It becomes impossible to detect who, if anyone, is sane or reliable; who is guilty, or who is dead; who victim, who victimized; or even who is who. The names of characters encode their perplexity. In Poe's "The Cask of Amontillado," Fortunato is *un*fortunate. His counterpart—victimizer, murderer, other self, echo—is Montresor, who possesses a name as paradoxically "crossed," confused, as illegible as *Gott* embedded in Gothic, or "I" in "ice," *yo* in *hielo*, or *amar* in Amaranta, signaling a double-bind message to the suitors she does not love: she loves. She burns for love.

Not only do individual characters rely on castles and icy mirrors and enslavement to prove that they really, containably exist; not only do they acquire property, inherit estates, or globally encompass the very poles; even that will not suffice to find a way to understand themselves because what they desire *au fond* is to deny what they know. No incredible feat exerts sufficient power to prove that individuals matter and can influence the helter-skelter course of events. No writing—letters, journals, diaries, notes, logs, narratives—provides "definitive" evidence. Nor does the voyeuristic reading of these "documents" release us from "hermeneutical delirium" (*One Hundred Years*). No means are found to quell Gothic anxiety concerning our reality when we do not inhabit our texts, our names. Our skins likewise become as cryptogrammatic as José Arcadio Buendía's penis or Amaranta's skin. Poe's A. B. C. Smith in "The Man That Was Used Up" is doubly alphabetized, into and out of existence, metonymically reduced to spectral words, syllables, initials as he undergoes a process Kristeva describes as "pulverization" into "fragmented elements." Every soul in a Gothic society suffers dis-memberment; each becomes, in the words of John Ruskin, "the syllable of a stammerer."

Therefore, to validate our doubted reality, the formulas of science and technology, of geometry and arithmetic are invoked as more in fact than we are. But, as manias mystical and magical do nothing to establish the boundaries of reality, so also do mathematics and mercenary means fail. The cloistered exactitudes of ratio and price become annexes of the rude, mad, unrestrained, and distended: propriety/impropriety, reality/unreality, sanity/insanity. Ursula's sense of herself becomes inextricably and oddly confused with the candy fauna she concocts in her kitchen and sells. The hermetic gold (*au*) fish Aureliano manufactures become dubious proof of his continuing existence, envoyed articles of faith after he has become a colonel in trouble, everywhere at once. With some of the same propensity for disappearing from his family that Aureliano exhibits, Frankenstein, that self-deceived monster of emotional ineptitude, tries magic, medicine, magnetism, mathematics and manufactures a monster who must murder to matter and who therefore must be murdered, in the name of morality, by his maker, who, as his name states, though he denies it, is frankly a monolith of solitude. The hard sciences only inflame a painful Gothic double-bind: reasoned means invoked to demonstrate the reality of the human situation reify the possibility that human beings are abstractions, departures, repetitive relational geometries, mystifyingly encoded commodities. The irrational unconscious is nothing but a calculating machine, a workshop, a factory (Gilles Deleuze and Felix Guattari).

The question of the credibility of fragmented beings—our credibility, Frankenstein's, the Aurelianos'—raises the spooked issue of authorial intent. Did García Márquez really intend *La Casa* (*Solitude's* working title) to be a Gothic novel? His interviews suggest Gothic influences. "I left Fidel Castro a copy of Bram Stoker's *Dracula*, which is an absolutely fantastic book but one that intellectuals consider unworthy." Stoker says Dracula's castle "seemed to have in it the whole history of a country." But the country is and is not foreign; strange Transylvania is strangely connected to the fortunes and future of England. So also the predestined Buendía family with its psychosexual peculiarities (ordinary though they may be) and the fortunes of its house, prefigured at the beginning of the novel and fulfilled at the end, are not only consubstantial with the fortunes of Colombian history but as well with biblical history, with universal history. In *Dracula* as in *Solitude* as in history, the fated is also accidental, the inevitable eerily laced with chance and error.

It was chance that gave Macondo its name, according to García Márquez, who says he glimpsed a ranch named Macondo as he rode by (interview in *Paris Review*). And yet the "chance" word contains the power of an "overheard" reality. It becomes "invention," the Gothic village of Macondo in which Colombian readers locate and identify personal possessions and family members. Macondo, warp (fact) and woof (fiction), territory and text, interweaves the meanings and values of texts historical and fictional with territories. García Márquez uses other Gothic writers in his quintessentially Colombian text. So the central action of *Solitude*, the rise into glory and the fall into ruin of the Buendía establishment, village, territorial holdings, swamp, is a text and a territory that is also Faulkner's invented/real Gothic Yoknapatawpha County and Poe's Edgarton. Through Arthur Gordon Pym, Edgar Allan Poe encrypts himself in his enciphered name and his grandfather's body as inherited text and territory and flight and pursuit (the ship on which Poe, or that part relettered as Pym, flies is named the *Grampus*; Poe does not leave home). Poe credits Walpole's *The Castle of Otranto* for Gothic influence and so continues the Gothic riddle of where the territorial quest ends, where the text ends, where another begins. For Gothic texts are strange, simultaneously missing and omnipresent; Gothic territory, anybody's.

In the Gothic novel names that begin with "M" reoccur with notable frequency (Morel, Mentoni, Metzengerstein, Melquíades) and indicate, insofar as I can determine, the wellspring of language, the initial, archaic, primal, mumbling effort to respond meaningfully to a critically stimulating situation (primal scene) with a sound that instantly passes beyond conscious recall and becomes critically lost, secret, an Ur-text. García Márquez's Meme is such a "forbidden" mother of meaning, another, ill-fated, Ma(c)ondo, greedy (me, me) ma-ma, matrix both physically and metaphysically of the "missing," that is, the inadmissible word of which we have only the trace, the "M," or its close kin, "H" and "A." Walpole's Manfred likewise indicates a buried text when he, "in artful guise" "sounds" "the Marquis on the subject of [forbidden] Matilda." And yet "M" names also suggest metatexts, magnitudes of meaning not infrarational but suprarational. Like Medieval Merlin, Melquíades is a possessor of strange powers, a clairvoyant, perhaps a magician, who brings science and technology in his wake (magnifying glasses, magnetism, mining, manufacturing, and infinitely more). Then, again, García Márquez's relation to his own text typifies Gothic equivocation concerning author-ity. As skin (physiognomy, family, resemblance) is inscribed with indecipherable messages, so is paper inscribed. Because the Gothic genre suggests that we are written upon by culture and its cruel corrections and biology and its drives, original authorship is patently at several removes from the texts that we, cultural and biological ventriloquists, believe to be our own products. García Márquez makes this Gothic point by transposing himself as author of the text to minor character appearing late and marginally within the text. He is enclosed by, rather than in control of, the text. He is inscribed by his family in text and context. *García Márquez* and his great, great-grandfather *Gerinaldo Márquez* share membership in biological, familial, cultural presses printed by demons unknown. The laws of biology engineer genetic codes and mechanical reproductions, stage Gothic genetic melodramas in and out of texts, trigger literal invasions of the body snatchers.

The connection between *Solitude*'s action and its ice is made at the start: "Many years later, as he faced the firing squad, Colonel Aureliano Buendía was to remember that distant afternoon when his father took him to discover ice." Colonel Aureliano Buendía is not executed by that firing squad nor by any other. Nor does he die in the field nor when he fires a bullet through an iodine circle painted over his supposed heart. His initiatory facing of a firing squad, the book's leitmotif opening scene, comes to represent the contagion of awareness of death, suppressed and therefore proliferate. Facing the *pelotón de fusilamiento* brings the intercessive memory of ice to mind and innumerable other events at a rate sufficiently rapid to disguise the presence of death.

Colonel Aureliano's memory instantaneously transports the reader to some indeterminate time in the past when gypsies were visiting Macondo, that is, to the end of the first chapter. The gypsies have brought the Buendías news of the archgypsy Melquíades's death (the return of the repressed). Because Melquíades did not enjoy death, he returns to life. When the reader first meets Melquíades, it is some time before the first time that Melquíades dies, although not the last. The reader has been straightaway set in the midst of many lives and deaths in a novel that begins in many medias res and tempi. From the opening chapter, time travels to multiple velocities, depths, and directions: the future perfect, the future infinitive, the future indicative; in Melquíades's case, the future optative, because, as the reader reads this chapter, Melquíades presumably has already set about wishing his return from death.

The action of the novel sweeps along in several pasts: the simple past, say, of one hundred and fifty some years pseudochronologically ticked off. The reader views the past century and a half or so mirrored in an indefinite number of recollections. The first exposure to memory, Colonel Aureliano's, is an exposure also to the memory of the omniscient narrator. Both of their memories lie within Melquíades's memory. For Melquíades has foreseen and inscribed on parchments in a language unknown to the Buendías (Howdy Doody newcomers) prerecorded actions that the narrator recovers. Clearly time is not linear, diachronic, or synchronic but Gothic: infinitely and obscurely refracted. And as it is with time, so it is with texts. Melquíades's parchments are obscurely refracted and multilingual and polyvocal. These odd documents, "intact" and "with pages missing," lift the missing letters of the Gothic novel to the nth degree of opacity and importance, a doomsday book on holdings and houses and lots in life, stored: in a chamber in the text of the novel, as the text of the novel, as outside the fictive in the contexts of history, personal experiences, and other literature, Nostradamus's prophetic writings, folktales, stories repeated over centuries of solitude. There are innumerable analogies among Melquíades's parchments of other texts: García Márquez's (*Innocent Eréndira*); Carlos Fuentes's (*Death of Artemio Cruz*); Borges's labyrinths; Alejo Carpentier's; but, most importantly, to that touchtext of the Gothic that unites storying to double-dealing, dominance, enslavement, sex, violence, licentiousness, treachery: *The Thousand and One Nights,* where the homologous action of holding death at bay and telling tales, of inscribing on parchment and on the living skin of experience is made explicit by the firing squad relationship between the shah and Scheherazade. Being inscribed/ inscribing means subjection/rebellion, means fragmenting an individual infinitely into (i)(mages) shedding distinctions that might identify when, why, what, where. The thousand distracting, diverting, embedded tales disguise the ice of death, warmed though it may be by recounting tales. García Márquez found the warmth necessary by using the homely tones of his grandmother's remembered voice, as she recounted, among others, episodes from his grandfather's life in his struggle with Colombia's Conservative party, referred to as Goths in fact (Regina James) and in fiction.

The elaboration of Gothic elements at the end of the first chapter is worth extensive citation. The discovery of ice that Colonel Aureliano remembers as he faces the firing squad many years later occurs during one of many amazing exhibitions put on by visiting gypsies.

> There was a giant with . . . a heavy iron chain on his ankle, watching over a pirate chest. When it was opened by the giant, the chest gave off glacial exhalation. Inside there was only an enormous, transparent block with infinite internal needles in which the light of the sunset was broken up into colored stars. Disconcerted, knowing that the children were waiting for an immediate explanation, José Arcadio Buendía ventured a murmur:
> "It's the largest diamond in the world."
> "No," the gypsy countered, "It's ice."
> . . . José Arcadio Buendía . . . put his hand on the ice and held it there for several minutes as his heart filled with fear and jubilation at the contact with mystery. . . . Aureliano . . . put his hand on it, withdrawing it immediately. "It's boiling!" he exclaimed, startled. But his father paid no attention to him. Intoxicated by the evidence of the miracle, he forgot at the moment about the frustration of his delirious undertakings and Melquíades' body, abandoned to the appetite of the squids. He paid another five reales and with his hand on the cake, as if giving testimony on the holy scriptures, he exclaimed:
> "This is the great invention of our time."

Ice, indistinguishable from its opposite, the heat of fire, is implicated in the piracy and enchainment of greed and commerce (the largest diamond in the world). Mystery and miracle are indistinguishable from technology. Ice spreads fear and jubilation over the senses and invades incredulous consciousness and seizes the heart and soul of José Arcadio Buendía with the sparkling sunset of solitude. With its infinite, internal needles, life-ice, lust-ice, death-ice sweeps in like the snowstorm of a gypsy sideshow, like a whoring gypsy girl.

The Colonel, who does not die remembering ice before that or any firing squad, is not a simple man. He has long before been refracted and fragmented by ice. Although the Colonel may still look like his Byronic and Don Juanish self, that is, like pictures of high-cheekboned Tartar warlords, he is no longer himself but fragmented within himself. Also he is reported as being simultaneously here and there in the world as in his seventeen sons named Aureliano. Eve Kosofsky Sedgwick notes of the Gothic novel that there seem to be no "noncoded differences between persons that could not also occur in any one person over time." Moreover, "hieroglyphic faces multiply and confront one another, and multiply *by* confrontation . . . tyrannically and uncontrollably." The Colonel's mother Ursula later remarks that he no longer looks like himself, whereas others report him everywhere, a fragmentation analogous to the consequences of the act of writing. Writing about the world breaks up "its individual, contingent, and superficial representations and makes of them an *inorganic nature,* a pulverization of fragmented elements" (Julia Kristeva). The fragmentation follows "formulas of disguise" that also dissolve the authorial self into the hieroglyphic crystallizations of writing, the "I" dying into the negative, into the peripheral and the polyvalent, broken up into hundreds of contagious characters (letters and individuals). But not only is writing a form of death; it is also a form of undeath. Just as ice does not literally symbolize death but laterally invokes death's many disguised relatives, so is the author, as are Melquíades and Aureliano and Dracula and Count Alfonso and Scheherazade, all—undead.

Only if a stake is driven through the discovered heart, only if a woman can truly love, only then can Scheherazade fall silent or Dracula die and bring to an end the night of the living dead, of the bloodsuckers, among whom must be numbered people located in microtexts, in texts, in macrotexts; in brief, everyone. Culture as inscribing macrotext colonizes the skins and psyches of its people by stereotyping them, by manufacturing tyrants and spellbinding technocrats who heartlessly continue printing inscriptions in the doomsday book of house "holds." The situation does not change with time. Although the machinery of technology replaces the Gothic cathedral, "Medieval" Gothic architecture remains expressive in train stations and lift-off pads. "The cathedral was created by men of divine effrontery as a house for God—not for a god of darkness and forest magic, not for a god of random, arbitrary power, but for a god of perfect geometry" (Lawrence Lee), a God of stone, a God of nails, hauled into place by contraptions, a technocrat's God, celebrated in every metropolis ("M").

Ice may seem as unnatural in tropical Latin Macondo as Mina, dear girl-wife, assiduously recording Dracula's movements on her typewriter or dictating her diary onto a phonograph. Ice invokes symmetry, rigidity, a keyboard of set characters, a soundtrack. Ice is natural to Macondo, a Medieval village that represents the impossible Gothic marriage of absolute ratio to total mystery, the marriage of dream to machine:

> José Arcadio Buendía dreamed that night that right there a noisy city having mirror walls rose up. He asked what city it was and they answered him with a name that he had never heard, that had no meaning at all, but that had a supernatural echo in his dream: Macondo. . . . José Arcadio Buendía did not succeed in deciphering the dream of houses with mirror walls until the day he discovered ice.

Ma(c)*ondo:* it is deep, that ice that keeps us on the surface, ice possibly an originary matrix, a transhistorical ice, deeper than the past of our grandfathers, deeper than our collective guilt for the destruction of feudal fidelities and the feudal happy families we imagine to have existed, ice deep as prehistoric eggs, as the fear we will give birth to a child with the curly tail of a pig, the heir of the Buendía/Maldía line, the heir predestined to recapitulate the precursor mutant of its past, the heir that must die because of deformity, because of negligence, because we mirror.

The ice of Macondo is homologous to the symmetrical structure, the crystalline plot of a Gothic novel. For instance, *Dracula* begins and ends with cold and blowing snow. Icescapes parenthesize convoluted accounts of Dracula's bloodlust. *Dracula*'s structure invokes the symmetry of the plot of *Frankenstein,* which also begins and ends with fire-ice imagery. The (missing) heart or center of *Frankenstein* is also enclosed but not contained by the parenthesis of Arctic scenes, polar cold. *Frankenstein*'s climactic scene occurs on Mont Blanc's Mer de Glâce (the meanings in *mer/mère* and *glâce,* ice, glass, mirror, slide). The scene appears midway between Walton's opening Promethean push to the North Pole and the ostensible terminal scene, the double death: the monster's funeral pyre on the ice cap, Frankenstein's burial among the floes. Another counterpart for infinite ice in *Solitude* is the "holy scriptures" of the ice citation. The deaths dealt life's energies by the church, particularly to Fernanda's, invoke the iciness of *Frankenstein*'s letters; the epistle sent from Archangel bears witness. None knows whether the letters sent from these polar regions were ever received or, if received, read. Has anyone ever, even Ms. M. S. (Margaret Seville, Mary Shelley, another ms.), taken *Frankenstein*'s warning personally, even though ice is embedded in any and all of its symmetrically placed stories-within-stories-within-stories, these stories reflecting outside the story of *Frankenstein* in the infinity created by a Chinese box structure, a framing device that fails to contain the contagion of incomprehension? The letter motif is a critical one in *Solitude* and culminates in an unread letter that, if it contained news of the relationship of the last pair of Buendía lovers, has in any event arrived too late.

> The stranger's letter, which no one read, was left to the mercy of the moths on the shelf where Fernanda had forgotten her wedding ring on occasion and there it remained, consuming itself in the inner fire of its bad news as the solitary lovers sailed against the tide of those days of the last stages.

Like hereditary memory, like infinite internal needles, the structure of the multiple, symmetrically framed stories-within-stories is repeated in, among other Gothic classics, *Zadig, Melmoth, Wuthering Heights, One Hundred Years of Solitude.* The ice of Solitude is that marvel, technology's ice-nine. See the same ice here in 1848 in a text, *Bewick's Birds,* within the text of *Jane Eyre:* " 'the vast sweep of the Arctic Zone, and those forlorn regions of dreary space—that reservoir of frost and snow, where firm fields of ice, the accumulation of centuries of winters, glazed in Alpine heights above heights.' " Jane comments, "I cannot tell what sentiment haunted the quite solitary churchyard, with its inscribed headstone; its gate. . . ." Icescapes parenthesize Jane's reflections and her search for herself. And *Jane Eyre* opens and closes with as-if-machine-set scenes of fire and ice. At its symmetric heart, " 'Fire rises out of lunar mountains: when she is cold, I'll carry her up to a peak and lay her down on the edge of a crater.' " And the same pattern again, ice-hard, in 1838 in *The Narrative of Arthur Gordon Pym*. On a cold night, Augustus and Arthur and their author and the author of their author set sail to escape authority and end approaching a figure in the South Pole with skin of the perfect whiteness of snow: an ice/death deity, a white mythologist, isomorphic with, indistinguishable from a God of love, a deity that uses the earth as a wax tablet for inscription. Yet he cannot be approached. His writing, the figures in the landscape, are characters of an alphabet that contain figures *in* the landscape. Some of the characters are buried alive in chasms formed by letters inscribed on the earth by an unknown, savage deity: the territorial imperative of the Gothic, the desire to dominate meaning and the desire to dominate the earth show themselves again to be one.

Like mirrors held before mirrors, endlessly reflecting, Gothic stories function like the relentless story within *One Hundred Years of Solitude*:

> They would gather together to converse endlessly, to tell over and over for hours on end the same jokes, to complicate to the limits of exasperation the story about the capon, which was an endless game in which the narrator asked if they wanted him to tell them the story about the capon, and when they answered yes, the narrator would say that he had not asked them to say yes, but whether they wanted him to tell them the story about the capon, and when they answered no, the narrator told them that he had not asked them to say no, but whether they wanted him to tell them the story about the capon, and when they remained silent the narrator told them that he had not asked them to remain silent but whether they wanted him to tell them the story about the capon, and no one could leave.

One stands before the firing squad always—that is to say, for a bare second in front of one's own fate before memory interferes and evades confrontation through another (but associated) story about the vicissitudes of family and political life: revolution, civilization, colonization. *Solitude* presents Sir Francis Drake, the pirate and precursor conquistador, hunting crocodiles with cannon and returns on its last page to Sir Francis Drake, whose story has not been told. For if the story is understood, we may understand ourselves and that would be awful. The vastness and savagery in this repetitive writing correlates to committing incest; correlates to the Ur-Gothic monk Ambrose raping and murdering the beautiful Antonia, his sister; correlates to Aureliano, the penultimate, generating in his frolicking with Amaranta Ursula, who is his aunt, the child with the curly tail. (Run-on sentences are appropriate to the subject matter.) Finally—I should say terminally, but that would be difficult to substantiate—Aureliano discovers these dreadful relations, discovers he has been committing incest when "he began to decipher the instant that he was living, deciphering it as he lived it, prophesying himself in the act of deciphering the last page of the parchments, as if he were looking into a speaking mirror." Lines from A. R. Ammons's poem "The Put-Down Come On" come to mind: rather marvel at the ice than finish the story; rather enjoy the "empty-headed / contemplation," "still where the ideas of permanence / and transience fuse in a single body, ice, for example . . . " (ll. 4-6).

Ice is the burning muse of the Gothic: silver-backed eyes, glass, mirrors, microscopes, telescopes: enslavement. To date, only children, innocents, and the mad believe we can free ourselves from the distortions of power and consciousness. For them, perhaps, the resolution of Hans Christian Andersen's "The Snow Queen" holds some credibility.

> Look you, now we're going to begin. When we are at the end of the story we shall know more than we do now, for he was a bad goblin . . . [binary consciousness at work]. One day he was in very good spirits, for he had made a mirror which had this pe-culiarity, that everything good and beautiful that was reflected in it shrank together into almost nothing, but that whatever was worthless and looked ugly became prominent and looked worse than ever. [The scholars of the Goblin school let the mirror] fall out of their hands to the earth, where it was shattered into a hundred million million and more fragments. And now this mirror occasioned much more unhappiness than before.

Fragments in people's eyes stick; fragments stick in their hearts; some fragments are large enough to become windowpanes. When a fragment entered little Kay's heart, "He dragged a few sharp flat pieces of ice to and fro, joining them together in all kinds of ways, for he wanted to achieve something with them. It was just like when we have little tablets of wood, and lay them together to form figures—what we call the Chinese game. Kay also went and laid figures, and, indeed, very artistic ones. That was the icy game of reason" and Kay's autistic art much like José Arcadio Buendía's fascination with alchemy, an alchemy as fascist as demonic mir-ror-vision:

> mirrors were associated for a long time with witchcraft, or the aberrations of the senses. A Christian distrust of optics, besides, as a vain devotion to appearances, would be formulated in nu-merous . . . comparisons or metaphors based on perspectives— as, for example, in the characteristic words found in William Drum-mond. . . . "All we can set our eyes upon in these intricate mazes of Life is but Alchimie, vain Perspective, and deceiving Shadows, appearing far other ways afar off."

mazes in which José Arcadio Buendía loses himself and his family.

It was Prudencio Aguilar [the ghost of the man José Arcadio had slain] who cleaned him, fed him, and brought him splendid news of an unknown person called Aureliano who was a colonel in the war. When he was alone, José Arcadio Buendía consoled himself with the dream of the infinite rooms. He dreamed that he was getting out of bed, opening the door and going into an identical room with the same bed with a wrought-iron head. . . . He liked to go from room to room. As in a gallery of parallel mirrors, until Prudencio Aguilar would touch him on the shoulder. Then he would go back from room to room, walking in reverse, going back over his trail, and he would find Prudencio Aguilar in the room of reality. But one night, two weeks after they took him to his bed, Prudencio Aguilar touched his shoulder in an intermediate room and he stayed there forever, thinking that it was the real room.

José Arcadio is not deliberately wicked, demonic; his cold-heartedness comes from absent-heartedness, in the style of the Gothic cathedral that points to God and reality as elsewhere, in the style of cool scientific principles. Because reality goes on without him, he need not confront the actual stoppage of time, the ice of entropy, adult ice. When he does become conscious, he becomes insane. " 'This is a disaster,' he said. 'Look at the air, listen to the buzzing of the sun, the same as yesterday and the day before. Today is Monday too.' "

If there is an escape from typeset lives, from lives that feed on the blood of others, from Gothic lives that will end as foreseen, homologously in the reproduction and conclusion of the human family with heirs born with the curly tail of pigs, tails curled by the intensities of incestuous and narcissistic self-interest, maybe it will be through the interchange of letters, through taking letters to heart if and when we receive them, and seeing their meaning clearly enough to take them personally, if the no one writing the colonel becomes someone writing about life on the other side of dictation.

Terra Nostra:
Coming to Grips with History

Jaime Alazraki

I shall begin by anticipating that my observations are concerned less with the text of *Terra Nostra* than with its context. This is a deliberate choice. I believe that before entering into the vast and dense forest of the novel, one must traverse its perimeter, and that before examining the workings of its invention, one must understand some of the thrusts of its motivation. *Terra Nostra* is a novel woven with contexts, hypertexts and intertexts. It is fitting, therefore, to begin with a reading that focuses on the strong, deep roots of the novel before reaching the thick, rich foliage at its top—a reading, however, not of its sources but of the forces that precipitate and give meaning to its text. I do not pretend to explain *Terra Nostra* by simply providing some of its contexts. But if the novel is, as I believe, Carlos Fuentes's reply to the history of Hispanic America, then it makes sense to begin by examining the question to which he responds.

The theme of *Terra Nostra* is History, the history of Spain and Hispanic America, Rome and Mexico, Christianity and Quetzalcóatl. *Terra Nostra*, however, is not a history book but a work of fiction. The novel's story, its plot, deals with the fate of three brothers, bastard sons of El Señor, who bear the mark of a cross on their back and six toes on each foot. Here fiction is sustained by history while, at the same time, history is turned into fiction. In becoming fiction, history fulfills a purpose prohibited to this discipline: that of making the present speak through the past and of compelling the past to signal a direction for the future. Fiction speaks where history is silent. The novel thus becomes a dramatization of history so that it may reveal what the chronicles refuse to tell. This has always been the purpose of the best art: to reshape our versions of reality—even those of a modest

From *World Literature Today* 57, no. 4 (Autumn 1983), translated by David Draper Clark. © 1983 by the University of Oklahoma Press.

still life—so that the reordering of the materials might elicit a meaning that is missing in the original version. Compare, for example, Picasso's *Guernica* with the actual massacre in that Spanish town, Shakespeare's *Hamlet* with Saxo Grammaticus's Amelthus from the *Danish History*, the Gospels' versions of the Passion with Bach's choral Passions. Fuentes himself has said that "every novel, by necessity, is born out of history, has its seat in history, but at the same time transcends it." In *Terra Nostra*, fiction is born out of history, and to transcend history, the novel must struggle with it as Jacob did with the angel, as Oedipus did with Laius and as every son has done with his father. History and fiction participate in the same circular, ascendant and conflictive course to arrive at a reencounter with the first link that put them in motion, not by becoming enclosed in the circle of the past but by breaking out of that circle and opening it up to the future. Pollo Phoibee descends to the eschatological destiny of the three bastard sons in order to ascend again, purged, to his present-future. "He was a man," we read, "who would not accept a past that had not been nourished in the present or a present that did not comprehend the past."

The theme of history is not new to Hispanic American literature. Quite the opposite. History is, beyond all doubt, its dominant course: from the chronicles of the Conquest to the biographies of Facundo, El Chacho and Aldao written by Sarmiento; from Ricardo Palma's historical sketches to Mármol's *Amalia;* from the great novelistic cycle of the Mexican Revolution to the contemporary novel of the Hispanic American dictator. If the earliest novels of Carlos Fuentes—*Where the Air Is Clear* (1958), *The Good Conscience* (1959) and *The Death of Artemio Cruz* (1962)—form part of the narrative cycle of the Mexican Revolution, bringing it to a close, *Terra Nostra* (1975) adds one more icon to the gallery of dictators produced by Latin American history and portrayed in the region's most counted. The past represented shame and chaos; the future, on the other hand, gleamed with hopes and promises. The ships finally had to be destroyed. The father had to be killed. This is what our first encyclopedists and liberals tried to do.

Sarmiento's outbursts are very well known, "Do not laugh, oh, people of Hispanic America, at seeing so much degradation! Remember that you are Spanish, and the Inquisition educated Spain in that manner! We carry this disease in our blood!" And in another place he states even more caustically that the intelligence of the Spanish people "became atrophied by a kind of mutilation cauterized with fire. . . . [The Spanish] have lost the habit of exercising the brain as an organ." If the exercise of intelligence enlarges the brain, then "one can well believe that the Spaniard's has not increased any since the fourteenth century, before the Inquisition began to function. . . . Phillip II was the embodiment of the Mohammedan-Spanish principle of the unity of beliefs. He, and not the Pope, established the Inquisition. . . . The Pope kept the Inquisition alive without fire. But only in Spain . . . could they build altars to cannibalism." And finally this conclusion, which in its sarcasm expresses much of the abused son's hatred toward his repressive father: "The Spaniards, and more so the South Americans, are born enervated by this atrophy of governmental faculties already acquired by the human race. . . . A Spaniard or an American of the sixteenth century should have said, 'I exist, therefore I do not think.' "

All or almost all of Sarmiento's ideas have become outdated and today sound like anachronisms. At the time that he formulated them, however, they expressed the shame, frustration, abuse and resentment that brewed throughout the course of three centuries of Spanish colonization and that the men of the second generation since Independence were, finally, able to verbalize. Esteban Echeverría, who had lived in Paris from 1826 to 1830, returned to Buenos Aires with his suitcases full of books on the Enlightenment and romanticism that were to mold the members of his generation. Echeverría was an eyewitness to that modern Europe which had nothing to do with the old Europe that had been transplanted to the New World. He wrote: "Spain had resisted the Reformation and the Renaissance, the sixteenth-century philosophical manifestation of the struggle, with the spirit of absolutism and with the Inquisition. . . . Spain, 'ruling and conquering by arms, but without a comprehensive intelligence, had been unable to establish anything either beautiful or robust, nothing for herself, and nothing for the other peoples, since the force that destroys does not create anything.' . . . America 'was infinitely more backward than Spain. . . . Separated from Europe by an ocean and walled in by a prohibitive system, with the Inquisition in its midst, Hispanic America vegetated in darkness.' " Spain has been the domineering mother, the witch, and the authoritarian father, the tyrant. The son, the victim who "breaks the chains," needed to explain his deformities and aberrations. Alberdi, a member of Echeverría's generation, confronted the father with parricidal rage: "The kings of Europe taught us to hate as foreign anything that was not Spanish." He spoke of Spain, but he was also speaking of her heir in America, Rosas, who saw a threat in everything foreign. "The fatherland," continued Alberdi, "is not the land. We have had the land for three centuries, but we have only had a fatherland since 1810." The son does not recognize himself in the father. The son is born only upon the death of the father, and since the biological father did not count—being undesirable and abhorred—the son adopts the father that he would like to have had. "We," says Alberdi, "who call ourselves Americans are but Europeans born in America. . . . We could define civilized America by saying that it is Europe established in America." And since Spain was not Europe, the Europe that the Americans admired and emulated, the adoptive father had nothing in common with the biological father.

In a different way, these ideas have been formulated by the most brilliant minds of the Hispanic American generation that followed the generation of Independence. The previous generation had achieved political emancipation; this generation would fight for psychical emancipation. The first generation had killed the father; the second generation would find the adoptive father. "The body has been emancipated," Echeverría says, "but not its mind. . . . The arms of Spain no longer oppress us, but its traditions still weigh us down. The revolution marches on, but with shackles." There is "a political emancipation" and there is "a social emancipation": "The American social emancipation can only be attained by repudiating the heritage that Spain left us." The Chilean Lastarria recommended a similar solution: "Society had the duty of correcting the experience of its ancestors in order to assure its future. Is it not necessary then to correct the civilization that Spain has given us?" The despotism of the kings had fallen, and the despotism of the past remained alive with all its vigor. Another Chilean, Francisco Bilbao, raised the problem in terms of a dichotomy comprised of religion and rationalism: "Either Catholicism triumphs," he says, "and monarchy and theocracy rule America, or republicanism triumphs, with free reason and the religion of law dominating the conscience of every man. . . . Either Catholic dogma builds its political world, a monarchy, or the republican principle rises and affirms its dogma, rationalism." The Mexican José María Luis Mora restated the dilemma from his national perspective: "Even though the basis of Mexican character is entirely Spanish, since it could not be anything else, the mutual motives of anger which for twenty years have been fomented between both peoples by barbarism and prolongation of the struggle for independence have caused the Mexicans to show the greatest zeal in renouncing everything that is Spanish. For they do not consider themselves completely independent if, after having shaken off the political yoke, they find themselves subject to habits and customs of the former mother country."

In all of them the past weighs as a burden that perpetuates the chains of the colony in the present. Lastarria stated, "The Spaniards conquered America, soaking its soil in blood, not to colonize it, but rather to take possession of the precious metals that it produced so abundantly." When they attempted to colonize her, they transplanted into Hispanic America "all the vices of her absurd system of government, vices that multiplied infinitely as a result of causes that had their origin in the system itself." Bilbao wrote: "Our past is the Spain of the Middle Ages." "The body and soul of the Middle Ages," Leopoldo Zea adds, was "Catholicism and feudalism. We have 'emerged from the Middle Ages of Spain.' " Sarmiento finally came to say, naïvely, that the fate of Hispanic America would have been different had the region been colonized by England. The perception of Spain as a hateful forebear was as deeply rooted as possible, and the flat rejection of the past amounted to parricide.

But alongside the rebellious and parricidal sons, Hispanic America had other sons who zealously and loyally clung to their Hispanic father. They were the heirs of authority, the followers of that autocratic system of hierarchies under whose aegis the new owners received the lands, serfs and wealth from their Hispanic fathers; they were the caudillos and patriarchs who defended their fiefs, their recalcitrant Catholicism and the old social, economic and political structures of the Colonial Era. "All Hispanic America," writes Zea, "was divided into two great camps: those who sought to make it a modern land and those who believed that the time for this had not yet come and that only a government similar to the Spanish government could save it. Unitarians against Federalists in Argentina, *pelucones* against *pipiolos* in Chile, Federals and Centralists in Mexico, Colombia, Venezuela, and other countries. Nevertheless, no matter who won, the spirit inherited from Spain soon reappeared. Some wanted only to re-establish Spanish order, but without Spain, while others, now in power, considered that it was first necessary to prepare the Hispanic Americans for liberty and that dictatorships were a necessary preparation." Feudal despotism on the one hand, enlightened despotism on the other. Those who clung tooth and nail to the past went down with it; they reproduced on endemic levels the evils that they had inherited from their fathers. Those who rejected the past, lured by the liberal future which Spain had resisted, ended up denying that part of their being which was made from the same past they condemned. By commission on the one hand and omission on the other, both groups remained tied to the burden of the past. Octavio Paz has best summed up this vicious dualism. With the history of Mexico in mind, but alluding equally to the rest of Hispanic America, he writes:

> The Mexican nation was created by a minority that succeeded in imposing its scheme on the rest of the people, against the wishes of another minority that was actively traditional.
>
> Like colonial Catholicism, the Reform was a movement inspired by a universal philosophy. The similarities and differences between them are significant. Catholicism was imposed by a minority of strangers after a military conquest; liberalism was imposed by a native minority, though its intellectual formation was French, after a civil war. The former was the reverse face of the Conquest: the Indians, with their own theocracy destroyed, their gods dead or exiled, and without lands to develop or other regions to which they could emigrate, embraced the Christian religion as a mother. . . . Liberalism was a critique of the old order and a projected social pact. It was not a religion but a utopian ideology; it fought rather than consoled; it replaced the notion of an other world with that of a terrestrial future. It championed man but it ignored a half of his nature, that which is expressed in communion, myths, festivals, dreams, eroticism.

(The Labyrinth of Solitude)

One party embraced the past; the other, by denying the past, also denied that part of history that had made them what they were; they denied, as Paz says, a part of their very being.

Sarmiento suspected this, inasmuch as he accepted with a smile the title of "Dr. Montonero" with which some of his contemporaries sardonically addressed him. He was a man of ideas, a liberal and a champion of that civilizing dream that obsessed him all his life, but he did not hesitate in employing the same arms, the same violence,the same hunger for power that he criticized in his enemies. He justified violence and despotism in the name of civilization and progress; the others, in the name of tradition, religion and what they knew best, the Spanish heritage. The past left its imprint on both: on the latter because they refused to leave the past; on the former because they refused to deal with it. Historians have said time and again that the nations who ignore their history are destined to repeat it. They have also said that one condition for leaving the past behind is to assimilate it to the present. "Modern man," says Zea, "refuses to accept a past that he has not made as if it were his own, but he accepts it in the form of what has allowed him to become what he is. The Latin American, on the other hand, feels as if he cannot escape his past; his ancestors, his dead, are still alive, imposing conditions upon him, limiting his possibilities and passing on to him their blame. Burdened with a history he has inherited, the Latin American is unable to begin his own history."

The past manifested itself and continues to manifest itself in the figure of the dictator. Hispanic American dictators are ghosts of the past who carry with them the curses of the same feudal system which engendered them and which they perpetuate. From the very beginning of Hispanic American political independence it could be augured that the satrapies of Santa Ana in Mexico, Dr. Francia in Paraguay and Rosas in Argentina were not the exception but the norm. They were mere replicas of the only form of government the New World knew and was accustomed to. During the tyrannical government of Rosas, when his mobs of torturers and murderers raided the streets of Buenos Aires beheading dissidents, Alberdi could already warn in 1847: "Everywhere when an orange tree reaches a certain age, it produces oranges. Wherever there are Spanish republics formed out of former colonies, there will be dictators. . . . Many states of America will have their Rosases. . . . Not in vain was Rosas called 'a man of America.' He is, in truth, the man of America, because he is a political type that will be seen throughout America as a logical product of what produced him in Buenos Aires and of what exists in other Spanish American countries." Rosas and those who followed him reinstitutionalized the violence, obscurantism and other excesses of the Spanish Conquest. With him the so-called *Conquista del desierto* (Conquest of the desert) began in Argentina, a sequence of events which was nothing more than the usurpation and genocide of the Indians, just as the conquistadors of earlier years had dispossessed and sacked the Indians who resisted their expansion. The past destroyed both those who viewed it as their tradition and those who condemned it. The dictator is thus defined as the personification of the past and its metaphor: the past turned into man, dead history personified, the belated offspring of Phillip II, who in America prolonged his decadence, solitude and agony.

The novels about the Hispanic American dictator that have appeared in recent years permit a better look at the true face of Latin America, a face free of masks and makeup, a ferocious and simultaneously anemic face touched up at times with constitutional cosmetics which only add pathos to the prevailing corruption, terror and crime. But in order to understand the son, it is also necessary to understand the father; in order to know the small dictator, one also has to know the great dictator, and in order to understand the present, it is imperative to understand the past—not by negating it, as our liberals did, or by glorifying it, as the dictators did and still do, but by knowing it thoroughly, in its truth, and by understanding it in all its various dimensions to accept it at last and be able to leave it behind. This is what *Terra Nostra* does: the novel of the father, the novel of the great dictator, the novel of our past. As with every novel that responds to an overwhelming reality and then is turned into our myth and becomes a face of our identity—*Pedro Páramo, Hopscotch, One Hundred Years of Solitude*—with *Terra Nostra* too, we wonder, not without perplexity, why this novel, which was already part of our Latin American perception, was not written before. Spain had been the object of curses or adulation, of rejection or submission. One had to approach Spain neither as a parricidal son nor as a sacrificial son, neither as a victim nor as a victimizer, but rather as an adult son who, having reached maturity, could understand and accept his father, and who was able to distinguish—as Fuentes says—"the cruel father, Cortés, from the generous father, Las Casas." There were two Spains, just as in every father there are two fathers; it was necessary to rescue both fathers, both Spains.

History was not just the wrecks of the Conquest; it was also the legacies of the language. History represented more than just the abuses of the colonial system; it also brought to the New World thinkers, humanists and writers, as much as the Inquisition had gagged or banished them. One cannot erase or perhaps forget the other. Not at all. All acceptance entails negations and affirmations, and only from that admission is it possible to exorcise the monsters of the past and to assimilate the Spanish heritage, to which Hispanic America owes a great deal of what it is. Fuentes himself has explained, however, that "in order to re-encounter Spain, Mexico first had to re-encounter itself. . . . Mexico, in rediscovering itself, ended up rediscovering its authentic Spanish heritage and defending it with the passion of one who has regained his father from misunderstanding and hate." To regain the father was to reencounter the history of Spain, to recapture it, in order finally to integrate it with the present so that the future can take off. "The future will respond to the enigmas of the past," states the narrator of *Terra Nostra*. The axial character around which the entire novel pivots, Felipe El Señor, is not only Phillip II but all the kings who, from 1492 onward, caused Spain to lose the course of its history. If to reencounter Spain, Mexico had first to reencounter itself, as Fuentes says, to reencounter itself, Mexico (and all of Hispanic America) first had to reencounter history.

Mexico's history did not begin with Cortés or Santa Ana or Porfirio Díaz; it began with the Spain of the greedy specters that procreated them. When Ludovico presents himself before El Señor, who has recently returned from the New World, the King addresses him saying, "Then you triumphed. Your dream was realized." To which Ludovico responds:

> "No Felipe, you triumphed: the dream was a nightmare. . . . The same order you desired for Spain was transported to New Spain: the same rigid, vertical hierarchies; the same style of government: for the powerful, all the rights and no obligations; for the weak, no rights and all obligations; the new world has been populated with Spaniards enervated by unexpected luxury, the climate, the mixing of bloods, and the temptations of unpunished injustice."

To understand the order that was transplanted to New Spain, one had to understand the order that ruled Spain—that is, its history at the time of the Conquest. How is it possible to reduce such a vast and complex order to the pages of a novel? Such is the challenge which faced Fuentes in *Terra Nostra*. To repeat history as the textbooks tell it would be a redundancy; it would also be fastidiously prolix. Besides, history is history and fiction is fiction, and even though history is a form of fiction—Lévi-Strauss *dixit*—its methods are different from those of fiction proper. The line of inquiry in history is documentation; the method of fiction is imagination; and although the historian uses imagination and the novelist also relies on documentation, there are clear degrees of difference. The historian strives to view the past from the past; the writer seeks to understand the past from the present. The order of history is chronology; the order of fiction is a simultaneous time that seeks to reveal a face denied to chronology. It is, therefore, a myth because it is the product of the documents of history; but above all, it is the product of the traces that those documents leave, like palimpsests, underneath the works of art. Furthermore, the works of art tell, between the lines and through their metaphors, what the documents do not, since they record the asides of history, those truths that tyrants silence and that the inquisitors destroy by fire. Fuentes states this eloquently in *Don Quixote, or The Critique of Reading*.

> Because the history of Spain has been what it has been, its art has been what history has denied Spain. . . . Art gives life to what history killed. Art gives voice to what history denied, silenced or persecuted. Art brings truth to the lies of history.

Hence *Terra Nostra* incorporates in its version of the history of Spain those faces that have been disfigured by its tyrants but kept in vivo by its works of fiction: *La Celestina, Don Juan* and *Don Quixote*. This is why in *Terra Nostra* la Celestina is as powerful a character as Felipe El Señor; the chroniclers of the court cross paths with the great chronicler, Cervantes.

This is why the official, deformed and sterile moral standards of the Church are debauched by the vital and fertile attitudes of Fernando de Rojas and by the other face of the official morality, Don Juan. There were two separate Spains, and both of them had to be rescued. If the Quixote is, as Fuentes says, "an unparalleled critical operation to save the best of Spain from the worst of Spain," *Terra Nostra* seeks to save both Spains, the worst and the best: the worst of Spain in order to understand the worst of Hispanic America and to leave it behind like a dead body; and the best of Spain, that side which, as Paz has said, "in Spain itself has been looked on with suspicion or contempt," because it is an intrinsic part of the Hispanic American soul.

How does one amalgamate these two faces of Spain without falling into the incoherence of an impossible discourse? How does one redeem history by means of the imagination without turning it into a riddle? *Terra Nostra* responds with a comment by Julián to the Chronicler: "Give no attention or credence to what others tell you, . . . nor hold any faith in the simple and deceitful chronologies that are written about this epoch in an attempt to establish the logic of a perishable and linear history; true history is circular and eternal." Not the mutilated history which Felipe, like his own Procrustes, dictates from his tomb or the official history that the chroniclers write to honor the "illustrious" dead, but—as Ludovico explains to Felipe—"the single instant which is all times, and . . . the one space which contains all spaces, . . . a single source of wisdom that unifies everything without sacrificing the unity of any part . . . , all things being converted into all men, all men into all things, . . . simultaneously and eternally." The Aleph, yes; not an abstract Aleph glimpsed in the depths of a frozen imagination, but rather the Aleph of History, because just as History, as recorded in the history books, never existed, the only History that can approximate reality is that one that—as *Terra Nostra* points out—incorporates "today's epic, yesterday's myth, and tomorrow's freedom." A history that combines document and imagination, the versions of the chronicle and the versions of art, the parts with the whole, because, as Fuentes recalls by way of Nicholas of Cusa, "totality is in every singular thing, . . . each thing is a diverse point of view on the universe."

"The world," Felipe tells Ludovico "is contained here within my palace; that is why I constructed it: a replica of stone to forever isolate and protect me against the snares of everything that multiplies, corrodes, and conquers." The world was just that, a tomb for the worst of Spain; but the world was also the revolt of the *comuneros* in 1520, the sallies of Don Quixote, the Spain of Las Casas and Fernando de Rojas, of Luis Vives, of Fray Luis de León and Quevedo. Of the many sides of the past, only one becomes the official version; of the many forces that interact in history, only one thrusts its power on the others; of the many bloodlines that mix in the Spanish people, only one proclaims itself pure and self-righteous to suppress the others; of the many social strata that form its society, only one rules and subjugates the others. It was necessary to recover the other versions of the past, to vindicate the other forces of history, to restore the rights of the other bloods and to provide a voice for the other strata of Spanish society. Such is, I believe, the purpose of *Terra Nostra:* a reencounter with the other versions of history that form part of that total memory alluded to in the novel, a memory including "what could have been and was not," a "memory as total knowledge of a total past." The Theatre of Memory of Valerio Camillo, the Theatre of Memory of Spain and Hispanic America, the memory of "what could have been and was not," of "all the possibilities of the past." "History," says Valerio and says Fuentes, "repeats itself only because we are unaware of the alternate possibility for each historic event: what that event could have been but was not. Knowing, we can insure that history does not repeat itself; that the alternate possibility is the one that occurs for the first time. The universe would achieve true equilibrium." Only when the (history) book becomes the history not of a tyrant but of all people will the reality also be for all. Only when the History of Spain becomes the history of all Spains can the past be present and future. The tyranny of the past would end, because the past will not only be the history of a tyranny but also the history of those suppressed and strangled by tyranny, the other Spain, "an ancient, new, and varied Spain, the work of many cultures, multiple aspirations, and different readings of a single book."

"Without Sin, and with Pleasure": The Erotic Dimensions of Fuentes's Fiction

Wendy B. Faris

> *Dream of total union: everyone says this dream is impossible, and yet it persists. I do not abandon it.*
> —ROLAND BARTHES, *A Lover's Discourse: Fragments*

From the ecstatic embrace of Federico Robles and Hortensia Chacón on Independence Day in *Where the Air Is Clear* to the mysterious and sensual fusion of Pollo and Celestina at the end of *Terra Nostra*, erotic couplings recur throughout the novels of Carlos Fuentes. These scenes appear regularly and yet rarely, too powerful for indiscriminate use. In these embraces, to varying degrees, the lovemaking of a man and a woman takes on telluric significance, and in some cases their sexual union achieves a kind of cosmic eroticism, implicitly rejuvenating the world around it—the world of the referent and the world of the prose. For Fuentes then, as for the surrealists, eroticism serves as an opening to a reality beyond the everyday, not so much to the individual unconscious as to supra-individual forces in the universe. The words of another descendant of surrealist thought, Georges Bataille, suggest that in this Fuentes captures a universal erotic principle: "in individual love as well as in impersonal eroticism, a man is immediately in the universe."

The scenes from Fuentes's texts that I will discuss constitute a vital force within a highly conceptual discourse. Such scenes take place in a defined symbolic space, generally an enclosure, but one that, like many of the houses Gaston Bachelard finds in modern French poetry, is open to the elements, in communication with cosmic forces. Not surprisingly, these hierogamies are celebrated with appealing natural images and colors. It is also significant that these embraces are most numerous in *Terra Nostra*, Fuentes's most explicit rewriting of Hispanic history, and in *Where the Air Is Clear*, his first novel. They constitute one particular aspect of the general idealistic imperative behind much of Fuentes's work, providing tantalizing glimpses of utopia as he might envision it, for "life in the new millennium

From *Novel: A Forum on Fiction* 20, no. 1 (Fall 1986). © 1986 by Novel Corp.

must eradicate all notions of sacrifice, work and property in order to instill one single principle: that of pleasure." This imperative joins the experimental writer to the political man in a kind of sexual Zapatism, a desire for the return to paradise in the new world.

In discussing the erotic scenes in Fuentes's fiction I have found the formulations of Bataille useful. Fuentes cites Bataille's monumental study *La Part maudite* in his list of books that contributed both to *Don Quixote, or The Critique of Reading* and *Terra Nostra*, though the 1967 edition in Fuentes's list only includes the first part of Bataille's work, on the economy of luxury, not the successive volumes dealing with eroticism. However, given Fuentes's familiarity with French culture and criticism, and his presence in Paris at a time when Bataille's ideas were popular, I think it likely that Fuentes was familiar with the entire range of Bataille's thought, so that in the case of *Terra Nostra* we might posit a case of influence. But more importantly, Bataille's philosophy, based on an analysis of the ways in which excesses in human activity are expended, is particularly suited to shed light on Fuentes's works, which often deal with excessive forms of behavior. In introducing her recent study of Bataille's thought, Michele Richman tells us that "Bataille characterizes his enemy as the economizing person whose individualistic ethos is consonant with the pursuit of random ends determined by the criteria of utilitarianism." Fuentes often inveighs against utilitarianism in his essays; it is a mentality that offends him. Furthermore, both writers uphold in different ways the extravagant expenditure of sexual energy as an antidote to the prevalent mentality of increasingly utilitarian societies, an expenditure of energy which they both perceive to go against the often rather niggardly tone of much contemporary life.

The key scenes that form the erotic pulse in Fuentes's texts are the following. In *Where the Air Is Clear* Hortensia Chacón's room shelters a primordial time; she waits for Federico Robles there, "as naked in darkness as at the beginning." As Federico recalls their embraces, his language clearly carries the signs of cosmic significance: "the attenuated moment of unrepeatable meeting when every movement endangered the stability of all creation; then one could reach for air and grasp it, shoulder the crust-earth and carry it to another region, liquid and incandescent, among stars. . . . With Hortensia, it was time, the unmeasured hours." In their final embrace, as elemental "man and woman," they affirm their total union in the language of bodily interchange of one as two and two as one that will reappear again at the end of *Terra Nostra:* "Desire drew near. Blind, in the darkness of the room, both sought it with tact and direct breathing and without words. It was not as if they were alone, nor as if they were one; nor was it as if they were two. They were two, yes; but each was the other." Again, the cosmic dimension appears, for as Federico sleeps and Hortensia watches over him, we hear that she is the first thing he will see on awakening, "and in her he would see the world," rejuvenated, restored to him anew. The world they will share—when they return to the land and raise their son—will be an indigenous world; significantly, just as Hortensia and Federico start to make love, we are reminded of "Hortensia's delicate Indian features," and of their "brown skinned" bodies, which sense "a common sweetness [which] anticipated a recognition." Federico Robles's wife Norma is not granted the same erotic rejuvenation as her husband, but we sense that she does approach it momentarily as she makes love with Ixca Cienfuegos on the beach:

> She looked at his tracks in the sand and loosened the knot of her consciousness and let herself be enclosed by his body, which claimed everything and took all her flesh, to annihilate it and drain it in a spasm like that of death; . . . And wasn't that what she wanted, just what he offered? Their bodies bound together on a wet beach, his spume and salt exciting her dry and sun, stopping time and the future, here, here and now was everything, the sun paralyzed, waves held forever in the instant before their breaking.

One problem here, of course, is that Ixca has a program which Norma ignores, for on one level he intends to sacrifice her to his mother's ancient sun god. But for the moment, their timeless embrace in the salty spume of the sea affords them contact with cosmic forces, respite from the social and historical impulses that typically structure their interaction.

In the brief embraces of Artemio Cruz and his young lover Regina between battles during the revolution in *The Death of Artemio Cruz* we recognize the strong bodily union, the rejuvenating force, the wordlessness, the room with special light that expands outward towards the world, the nearness of death, and the presence of nature—even the sea—which will become increasingly familar:

> The mosquito net isolated them and they were together within it. . . . Darkness was not enough to prevent her long eyes from shining, half-open. . . . The heat of their thighs melted into a single flame. . . . And beside him, the sea scent of a woman moistened and soft. . . . Her lips sought his neck. . . . Without tongue, without eyes, only the mute flesh abandoned to its own pleasure.

After they make love, "Regina went to the window and opened it wide. . . . The circle of brown mountains advanced with the sun. . . . She wanted to grasp the day by the shoulders and drag it inside to the bed." Time stops, for they agree that their love should not "be measured as any time is measured." And as often, we hear that "they were two, but really one." In his dying memories, the old Artemio Cruz returns again and again to Regina and their love.

In *A Change of Skin*, as in *Artemio Cruz*, the lines of battle between the sexes are pretty constantly drawn, and even the scant scenes of love are filtered through heavy irony. We witness only one cosmic embrace, between Elizabeth and Javier, during an idyllic summer they spent on the beach at Rhodes during their youth. It momentarily erases their habitual recriminations and abolishes time, collapsing their present and past love-making. In this scene, they are the elemental couple, expanding into all humanity, creating a timeless, wordless rhythm that flows from one to the other, even nearing death:

> You fell with him, on him, unable to separate from him, above him in his position imitating him, . . . time counted its own seconds and minutes, words spoke themselves in an effort to prolong the dark and vibrating sensations of your intercourse, he transformed into your woman and you into his man in shared desire that was a fruit falling from but still hanging to a single tree; . . . you and Javier, Javier and you, . . . you and he, father and mother, mother and son, . . . two women, two men, you and he making love now. . . . You want it never to end: to die in this moment renouncing life if the pleasure can only go on.

We return several times to the scene of this embrace as to a lost paradise, recognizing the characteristic elements of rejuvenating eroticism: elemental surroundings, natural beauty, wordlessness, the enclosed space opening out, the sexual rhythm:

> You felt that you were at the center of everything and that the words you spoke would spread in ever widening circles through all being. . . . Words were not for night when you lay together very simply in the plain white room with the white beams. . . . Each embrace longer, everything unnecessary suspended, everything alien to the hours of your love removed. . . . Together and apart in a dark arc that pulsated from the sexual hair to the seeking lips. You by your life gave life to the earth.

Finally, *Aura* ends with the well known union which transfigures Felipe and Consuelo/Aura, and *Terra Nostra* with the long erotic coupling of Pollo and Celestina. The fusion of Pollo and Celestina in *Terra Nostra* may be seen as a resolution of unsatisfied desires in the other novels, which prefigure it in part. Compare it for a moment with the temporary erotic fusion of Ixca and Norma in *Where the Air Is Clear*. Both scenes evoke the erotic potential of the new world, free from paternal cultural pressure. The natural world, particularly the beach—place of discovery—contrasts with the civilization surrounding it in *Where the Air Is Clear*. In *Terra Nostra*, Pollo and Celestina are in his room, not outside, but the room is permeated with a sea-like green light—and here there is no corrupt peach-colored house perched on a hill overlooking the scene as there is in *Where the Air Is Clear*. In between these two scenes, Fuentes's works trace a constant battle between separation and fusion, a pattern that defines the texture of many relationships. Early on, Catalina and Artemio Cruz exemplify this dialectic in their rational daytime separation punctuated by their erotic nighttime unions.

The final transfiguring couplings in *Aura* and *Terra Nostra* are the fullest expressions of the cosmic embrace. Like Federico and Hortensia's union, they are completely erotic in that they describe sexual union in ecstatic terms which imply more than momentary physical pleasure, while at the same time celebrating that pleasure. The two scenes both take place under special light, though the silvery moonlight in *Aura* indicates a less complete rejuvenation, a less utopian vision at the moment of coupling than the "warm luminosity . . . like ground emeralds" in *Terra Nostra*. They also include the donning and lowering of masks, which suggest the archetypal status of the participants. This is clear in *Terra Nostra*: "[Celestina's face] is covered by another mask of feathers, dead spiders, darts. . . . 'Put on your mask, and I mine.' . . . You look at Celestina, masked. She approaches, . . . she embraces you with passion. . . . The masks fall." In *Aura* it is less obvious because masks and faces are curiously layered and symbolic. Consuelo first puts on the mask of Aura, so to speak, to attract Felipe, who at the end, face to face with Consuelo, discovers that his own youthful face has been a mask for that of the general: "You fall exhausted on the bed, touching your cheeks, your eyes, your nose, as if you were afraid that some invisible hand had ripped off the mask you've been wearing for twenty-seven years, the cardboard features that hid your true face." In each instance we are reminded of the intersection of time and eternity by clocks which are no longer relevant. And both scenes focus on the physical properties involved in a symbolic merging of figures. In comparison with the coupling in *Aura*, in *Terra Nostra* these properties increase, and the sexual excitement is stepped up as well, recreating a Lawrentian rhythm of intercourse. In *Aura*, Felipe describes principally his own actions in the future: "You [will] bring your lips close to the head that's lying next to yours. You [will] stroke Aura's long black hair. You [will] grasp that fragile woman. . . . You [will] tear off her taffeta robe, [will] embrace her, [will] feel her small and lost." In *Terra Nostra* the language generates a more reciprocal pattern, one which we have seen prefigured in the earlier passages, particularly in *A Change of Skin*: "You kiss one another, slowly, caress one another, she kisses your whole body, you kiss her whole body, you tell yourself you are recreating one another with your touch, she with her two hands, you with your one, you kiss one another's lips, eyes, ears, her breath moistens the hair of your pubis, yours the young perfume of her armpits." The reader is drawn into the embrace to a greater extent here. And, as Gloria Durán has pointed out, the physical elements temporarily seem to submerge the spiritual, though, we might note, not the literary, for Pollo cites Dante (through Pound)—"ed eran due in uno, ed uno in due"—to postpone his own orgasm and thus to achieve just what the words express, complete union. Nevertheless, by the end, we have the biblical language of a rewriting of Genesis, fusing the erotic and the religious (a subject to which I will return shortly). In a sense, then, the embrace in *Terra Nostra* begins where *Aura* leaves off; in *Aura* the duality of past and present is abolished in an eternal time of love, but the two sexes remain separate, though joined in an embrace. In *Terra Nostra*, as everyone knows, the two sexes are magically fused in one perpetually copulating androgynous being. These embraces attempt to go beyond, or rather to return to a time before the complex dynamics of separate selves, mirrors, and masks begins, to go forward, once again, by going back, to remember the future. In them we might discern a desire to silence the battle of opposing dualities that traverse Fuentes's texts: male/female, myth/"reality," rich/poor, Indian/Spaniard, American/European, past/present, individual/communal.

In *Terra Nostra*, erotic scenes throughout the novel prefigure the final embrace. First, we have La Señora and Juan the youthful pilgrim, whom she even calls "my young androgynous god" and who is at first "unconscious of time or place or even the identity of the woman who was adoring him." El Señor, who, like Ixca Cienfuegos, habitually operates under the sign of death, and the young novitiate Inés, are momentarily transfigured in an embrace. El Señor's reflections on his coupling with Inés emphasize the unique, self-sufficient, liberating, and idyllic nature of these sexually charged moments. The language of erotic interchange here heralds that at the end of the novel:

> I am lying here beside you, and you beside me, alone, . . . the only relationship our own, yours and mine, you I and I you . . . a man and a woman alone, together, their only offering to each other the draining coming together, sufficient, swift, eternal, gratuitous, . . . its own pleasure, its own misfortune: Heaven and Hell. . . . Enclosed in a circle of delectable flames, . . . and nevertheless the greatest pleasure and the greatest worth.

The same is true of Juan and La Señora: "I am she, and if I am she, as I love her I love myself, and as I make love to her I make love to myself, and eventually I shall not be able to answer the question: Who am I?" In the chapter entitled "The Last Couple," Celestina speaks of "A love in which one loses forever, without hope of redemption, one's soul, and gains, without hope of resurrection, eternal pleasure." Shortly thereafter, erotic pleasure here, as it was in *Where the Air Is Clear*, is mysteriously linked to a specifically indigenous American reality, to visions of the new world. Celestina recounts that as she and the pilgrim embraced, "we were, perhaps, both possessed by the news my own body received as we made love, . . . for in love-making the youth's memory returned and what he remembered is this: there is another land, far beyond the ocean, . . . he knows the new world." Furthermore, the pilgrim in "the new world" receives directions for its exploration from the lips of a goddess-like woman as they make love. In this scene we easily recognize the signs of cosmic union: compelling natural images, encompassing sensual pleasure, conflation of selves, unity with the universe, the proximity of death, intimations of eternity. The "being I call woman," is haloed by butterflies, her mouth made of multicolored snakes. The pilgrim describes the embrace as "coupling with the black jungle; I was one with everything about me. . . . I felt I was melting into the woman's flesh and she into mine, and we were one. . . . All my being told me I must never be parted from this union . . . I was about to die in the hands of the woman who made love to me at the foot of the burning temple—who was I, as I was she."

The question of whether or not the final embrace and the often rather gruesome couplings in *Terra Nostra* are intended to shock the reader is a complex one. And perhaps it necessarily elicits the question of *which* reader. We know already that Fuentes advocates a healthy lack of respect for *soi-disant* good taste in literature. The answer is probably that yes, he would just as soon shake up the traditionally "genteel" reader a bit, and in this he would see himself as following in the wake of illustrious predecessors, for the first thing Fuentes says of *La Celestina*, for example, is that it constitutes a "discourtesy" in the strict sense of the word, "a decided lack of respect for the courtly style." On the other hand, we ungenteel readers of contemporary fiction are accustomed to such fare. Nevertheless, our un-shockability should not blind us to the fact that Fuentes is writing with earlier traditions in mind, and in that context some force of disrespect still obtains. So that in the end we are provoked but not outraged.

These, then, are the major instances of Fuentes's cosmic erotic vision; but there are also a number of other scenes that move in the same direction and further document the perennial nature of this mode in Fuentes's texts. In *The Hydra Head* Félix Maldonado seeks relief from his international spy intrigues in the bed of Mary Benjamin. Mary's repeatedly mentioned "violet eyes flecked with gold" are a spot of color in an otherwise rather gray Mexico City, where, just after the scene with Mary, "Félix had difficulty locating the Director General in the vast, deliberately murky penumbra of the windowless office." Theirs is not a full-scale cosmic union, as Fuentes indicates when he informs us that Félix's "physical relation with Mary could not tolerate either the time of dream or the space of separation. It could not tolerate desire." Nevertheless, their lovemaking is a welcome respite from a wearying world for both of them. That it might be a small step on the road to a more perfect existence is suggested by Félix's fleeting vision as he waits for Mary in a sleazy motel room: "for a moment he imagined how it would be to be at the shore, away from the altitude of Mexico City, by the sea, digesting his food normally in an unattainable paradise of simple, short meals served at fixed hours." As Félix finally makes love to Mary (their union having been delayed by circumstances),

> on Mary's body Félix avenged with fury the death of Sara Klein, . . . and his humiliating impotence before Ayub and the Director General, . . . and with Mary's body he liberated himself of the

desire he had felt for Sara's dead body and Angelica's unconscious body beside the swimming pool. . . . And they came together . . . and she said, Félix, Félix, Félix, and he said Sara, Mary, Ruth, Mary, Sara.

They meet in a sense as elemental man and woman, satisfying a mutual hunger, as Mary implicitly recognizes when she tells Félix that what she enjoyed about their adventure was that she didn't know whether she went to bed "with an imposter or a ghost." An even more striking instance where a burst of physical passion brings momentary relief from a stifling social world is the fierce embrace of Mercedes Zamacona and Federico Robles in *Where the Air Is Clear*; they seek each other "by pure sensual inspiration, without voices . . . their eyes dilated." And even for Catalina Cruz, who, while succumbing to his raw sexual force—and her own pleasure—by night, hates her husband by day, it is true that in the darkness of passion, "things happen before one can give them a name."

I am primarily concerned here with heterosexual union, but two further scenes, where the couples are of the same sex, merit a moment's pause. Near the end of *A Change of Skin*, just before the earthquake that recalls ancient and mysterious cosmic powers, Javier and Franz begin by wrestling and end in an embrace, "a violent embrace of hatred transforming itself, as the two women looked on, into desire. . . . A sensual, excited embrace between two men . . . locked together at the loins in a way that neither had expected, neither had foreseen, . . . beside the frieze of darkness and mystery." Similarly, at the end of *Distant Relations*, we see "two bodies, embraced, two fetuses curled upon themselves . . . joined by their umbilicus." This time, however, the bodies are dead; they are a final perverted version of an "angel" that the father of one of the boys has been trying to fashion—a failure because it is motivated by exclusive rather than communal ideals. We have a premonition of this final vision in an earlier scene where the two boys embrace mysteriously; the embrace fuses not only their two bodies but also two halves of a puzzling shiny object, one half of which one of the boys found in a ruin in Mexico. (Both angel and spherical object recall the classical idea of an original complete androgynous being as well as the globe.) In both *A Change of Skin* and *Distant Relations* the union of live bodies is incomplete and temporary, but it momentarily abolishes the habitual solitude of the figures involved. The two scenes further confirm the cosmic nature of these embraces. And even here, in these fusions of two males, the sexual element is not entirely absent, so that the embraces provide another intermediate stage in the achievement of total erotic union.

The question of just how these erotic scenes in Fuentes's fiction fit into a more general literary discourse of love is illuminated by a brief comparison with Roland Barthes. In the pieces that constitute *A Lover's Discourse: Fragments*, Barthes is concerned with recording elements of a code, where we recognize certain familiar figures as true. In the erotic scenes in Fuentes's texts, this is not usually the case, for these scenes seem to be iconoclastic. The sense of recognition is largely absent; we experience them as moments that attempt to go beyond ordinary sexuality, beyond a system, beyond coherent discourse. Just as he often tends to rewrite history, in these encounters Fuentes rewrites all our love scenes, as it were, proposing his lover's discourse as an alternative to the familiar ones we hear around us. Barthes is, of course, charting instants in earthly loves; Fuentes is imagining cosmic unions taking place outside time. In describing the composition of his book, however, Barthes defines an aspect of his erotic texts that sheds light on Fuentes's as well. Barthes maintains that the figures he is recording are "non-syntagmatic, non-narrative. . . . The lover speaks in bundles of sentences, but does not integrate these sentences on a higher level, into a work." Hence he chooses an arbitrary alphabetical listing for the moments of discourse recorded in his book. The momentary visions of cosmic love in Fuentes's texts reveal the same disjunctive quality as Barthes's fragments in their disruption of story—or history—flashing out from their narrative contexts, with which they often contrast.

The theoretical implications of these key scenes in Fuentes's novels fall under the headings of the erotic and the religious, death and eroticism, and erotic union as a form of utopia. In discussing these areas, we shall observe Fuentes's erotic scenes as components or interruptions of other kinds of discourse.

Aura provides a striking initial example of the fusion of erotic and religious domains when "Aura opens up like an altar." Denis de Rougemont, who has reflected at length on the erotic myths of Western culture, maintains that an "oscillation between the religious and the erotic . . . is one of the conclusive secrets of the Western psyche." Fuentes's moments of cosmic erotic union attempt to overcome that dialectic by encompassing both terms. Even with their explicit sexuality, the couplings I have mentioned are described with a high seriousness akin to traditional religious passion. They lift the reader out of the everyday world of the prose that surrounds them, to a mysterious and ecstatic plane. Even more specifically, Mercedes Zamacona and Federico Robles make love in the crypt of a church; Consuelo's room contains an altar; Franz and Javier's embrace takes place at the ceremonial heart of an ancient sanctuary; *Terra Nostra*'s version of Don Juan impersonates Christ and couples with a mother superior; the pilgrim and the butterfly goddess make love in front of a burning temple. Thus Fuentes's texts may form part of what de Rougemont considers a contemporary erotic upheaval akin to the one that produced the troubadours of the twelfth century: "lyricism, eroticism, and mysticism unleashed over all of Europe." Those three qualities are just what we have found in Fuentes's erotic scenes.

In his discussion of love, de Rougemont contrasts the figures of Don Juan and Tristan. For him, "Don Juan presupposes a society encumbered with exact rules which it prefers to infringe rather than throw off," transgression, we might say, being nine tenths of his law. Don Juan represents "pure immanence"; he is a prisoner of the world's appearances, "the martyr of increasingly disappointing and contemptible sensation, while Tristan is the prisoner of timelessness—beyond day and night—the martyr of a rapture which is transformed into pure joy upon death." In brief: "Tristan, woeful time, joyful eternity—Don Juan, joyous moments, an eternity of hell." Fuentes illustrates—really parodies—de Rougemont's dialectic in *Terra Nostra* with the courtly posture of El Señor who refuses to sleep with his wife for fear of defiling the purity of his love, and Don Juan who plays himself in all his seducing variety. In contrast, Fuentes's most powerful erotic unions combine aspects of these two poles, tempering the temporal with the eternal, the profane with the sacred.

The presence of death in scenes of love also reflects a long tradition. *Aura* is of course the most striking example of this conflation in Fuentes's work. As Jaime Alazraki has recently pointed out, Octavio Paz characterized this aspect of *Aura* early on: "Through love Fuentes perceives death; through death, he perceives that zone we once called sacred or poetic. . . . The eroticism is inseparable from the horror." In his portrayal of wild activities in the Escorial as well, Fuentes touches on the mysterious connections between eroticism and death, as the old La Señora reconstitutes her dead husband and travels around the country with him in a closed carriage—the ultimate in deathly erotic possession, as Barbarica and a pilgrim make love among cadavers, as Juan and La Señora "died together, . . . two souls inhabiting the same body died only for an instant." These scenes suggest that (as Bataille says) "inevitably linked with the moment of climax there is a minor rupture suggestive of death; and conversely the idea of death may play a part in setting sensuality in motion. This mostly adds up to a sense of transgression dangerous to general stability." Though the experience is not a rational one, the reasoning here is that if death is the loss of the self, then losing oneself in another resembles dying. Presumably this feeling is dangerous to general stability because the lovers are not subject to normal social rules—often reinforced by the implicit threat of death, a threat that is for them momentarily meaningless. Certainly the sensual winds of passion that blow through the Escorial threaten to disrupt El Señor's fanatically guarded stability. Fuentes's and Bataille's portraits of this dance of love and death make explicit what we have absorbed from centuries of love poetry, which regularly couples love and death. For Fuentes, the central tradition here is that of Quevedo and Góngora—and his compatriot Sor Juana. But once again, Fuentes is *rewriting* literary history in his cosmic embraces, making fictionally possible everyone's desired reversal of the *carpe diem* refrain.

The whole question of the possible and the impossible is central to the notion of utopia, which Fuentes himself has defined as "there is no such place and there is such a place." Fuentes's portrayal of erotic unions momentarily creates such a place, though we sense that they are the scene of an encounter between the possible and the impossible, dependent on the fictional world for their existence. As the ancient says in *Terra Nostra*: "Never again will there be the absolute freedom we knew before the first death. But there will be freedom in spite of death. It can be named. And sung. And loved. And dreamed. And desired." Bataille begins his study of eroticism in a similar vein, with a miniature fiction implying the imaginary nature of complete erotic fusion: "soon we shall be permanently united. I will lie down with open arms, I will encircle you, I will cavort with you in the midst of the great secrets. We will lose each other and find each other again. There will no longer be anything to separate us. What a shame that you can't participate in this happiness!" Barthes confirms Fuentes and Bataille in simultaneously asserting the possibility and the impossibility of "a lover's discourse," which "is spoken, perhaps, by thousands of subjects (who knows?), but warranted by no one. . . . Driven by its own momentum into the backwater of the 'unreal,' " it becomes the site of "an affirmation," if not a reality. Because of their relative infrequency, their spatial isolation, and their occasional magical properties, in the "backwater of the unreal" is just where Fuentes's unions seem to take place; they are only possibilities, and yet he affirms them nevertheless.

Still pursuing the dream of total union, Barthes reports spending an afternoon trying to draw Aristophanes's hermaphrodite: "I persist, but get nowhere, being a poor draughtsman or an even poorer utopianist. The hermaphrodite, or the androgyne, figure of that 'ancient unity of which the desire and the pursuit constitute what we call love,' is beyond my figuration; or at least all I could achieve is a monstrous, grotesque, improbable body." Fuentes may be a somewhat better draughtsman than Barthes, but even so, in *Aura*, in *Terra Nostra*, and especially in *Distant Relations*, we are confronted with quite improbable bodies. Fuentes is also an imperfect utopianist, mainly because he is too good a historian. Full erotic love is a dream, a counterpart to the real nightmares of history from which we are wishing to awake. But except in *Aura*, where ancient walls protect the private space of love, in Fuentes's novels we are not allowed to persist in that dream, to remain surrounded by "the wall of private life," which "particularly if it protects individual love, encloses a space outside history," according to Bataille. For Fuentes, man dreams in a space outside history, but lives within it.

In their treatment of sexuality, both Bataille and Fuentes formulate their ideas in the domain where the political and the erotic intersect, implying a utopian desire that the two realms might just possibly approach one another some day. Sexual union from *Where the Air Is Clear* to *Terra Nostra* is a sign of hope in the face of other forms of oppression. Particularly in *Terra Nostra*, Fuentes opposes the erotic to the despotic. Like Bataille, he allies eroticism with cosmic rather than societal forces, thus pointing up Bataille's "fundamental opposition between individual love and the state" with the official and decidedly unerotic marriage of El Señor and La Señora.

Fuentes's cosmic lovers generally allow themselves to be consumed by passion in opposition to the acquisitive society around them. Much is made, for example, in *Where the Air Is Clear* of the unworldly simplicity of Hortensia's room in comparison to the gilded and mirrored splendor of Norma's. Fuentes's lovers prove Bataille's contention that the society of lovers is one of consummation while the state is a society of acquisition. As I have suggested, both writers prefer the extravagant expenditure of potlatch in "primitive" societies to the stockpiling tendencies of modern capitalism.

All of these considerations show clearly that these moments of erotic explosion in Fuentes's texts form part of the dynamics of Mexican character and culture that Octavio Paz traces in *The Labyrinth of Solitude*. In the perennial oscillation from solitude to communion, erotic moments, like fiestas, represent the latter term; they are part of the "impossible fiesta" that we hear of in the epigraph to *A Change of Skin*. As Paz and others have pointed out, the festive raising of masks and lowering of barriers between individuals serves as an important release valve in Mexican society and is consequently a central component of its literature. Speaking in more general terms, Barthes confirms the same idea: "the amorous subject experiences every meeting with the loved being as a festival." In a sense, then, we can read Pollo and Celestina's union at the end of *Terra Nostra*, Federico's lovemaking with Hortensia in *Where the Air Is Clear*, and Consuelo and Felipe's transformation at the end of *Aura* as Fuentes's desire to turn the inhabitants of civilization and its discontents into dwellers in paradise; in more Mexican terms, to replay and thus to heal the original *chingadura*, the violation of the conquest. While we are thinking of the possibility of impossible dreams, and of history and politics, we might also argue that for twentieth century Mexicans, the Revolution is still the most important moment in the life of the community. Many of Fuentes's texts are set implicitly against this historical backdrop. In the tradition of Paz, who sees the Revolution as yet another manifestation of the explosive fiesta, the cosmic embraces in Fuentes's fiction can be seen as reverberating private repetitions of that central public event, replays of that other primal cultural scene with hopes of achieving a more complete success.

A generalized sense of transgression, of the breaking of boundaries and patterns, is what these cosmic unions suggest. They are Fuentes's sign to his readers that utopia is unlikely yet not entirely impossible on earth. The move into the symbolically non-verbal domain of eroticism, particularly in the case of the extended description of lovemaking at the end of *Terra Nostra*, indicates the enormity of the change that these scenes propose, and that the rest of the novels at once desire and deny. At this revolutionary moment, at the decisive instant when the stirrings of transgression take over from the discursive account of transgression, descriptive language becomes meaningless, at least in theory. As Bataille recognizes, though, this very formulation contains its own contradiction, for how can we even "speak" of such silence-bound moments; "language . . . alone can show us the sovereign moment at the farthest point of being where it can no longer act as currency." As is often observed, however, the overwhelming and generally positive eroticism of the last two pages of *Terra Nostra* serves to counterbalance the preceding several hundred, thus achieving a totality of the erotic and the cerebral. Once again, Bataille confirms Fuentes's practice, asserting that "the world of eroticism and the world of thought complement each other; and without their agreement totality is not achieved."

It is interesting to note, however, that even Fuentes's most complete unions—in *Aura* and *Terra Nostra*—harbor ambiguities. On one level, Felipe represents the rejuvenation of General Llorente by Consuelo's love, his and Consuelo's—and our—desires coinciding: to be forever young and to be loved forever, even when one is old. On another, Felipe is simply trapped by an old witch. Pollo and Celestina exit into the fresh green light of a new Eden, but we readers—and presumably the rest of Europe— watch a post millennial diminished sun rise at the very end of the book. Furthermore, unlike the concluding transformation of Felipe and Consuelo, Pollo and Celestina's embrace thus comes very near though not precisely at the end of the text. Fuentes cannot quite let their union have the very last words, indicating its status as an imaginative possibility rather than a practical program. Like the perennially unfinished story of *Distant Relations*, which the narrator and his readers are condemned to carry on, the end of *Terra Nostra* suggests a fear of perfect closure. This is because, as Fuentes suggests in *Distant Relations*, a perfectly closed story leaves no room for the rest of us, for narrative to go on. It is a balloon with no string, so to speak, with no possibilities for future threads of story. For, as Nietzsche (quoted by Barthes) has said, " 'Joy has no need of heirs or of children. Joy wants itself, wants eternity, the repetition of the same things, wants everything to remain eternally the same.' The fulfilled lover [adds Barthes] has no need to write, to transmit, to reproduce."

The erotic unions I have been discussing, essential and yet ephemeral, contending with the relentless historical flux of the texts that contain them, necessarily plead the importance of the present moment as a passport to eternity, as Joyce put it. (All utopian projects, of course, while learning from history, wish to abolish it and start from scratch.) In his discussion of the changes that occurred during the Renaissance, Fuentes articulates the new importance of the here and now by citing a metaphorical description of an embrace, O. B. Hardison's reading of Petrarch: "this particular moment and this particular woman, framed in this particular mixture of light and shadow, are important." Even more important for his own fiction, Fuentes identifies Petrarch as epitomizing another duality—a tension between the concrete and the abstract, between the earlier tendency to explain everything by references to symbols graded in virtue of their distance from or proximity to the supreme being and the tendency, which Petrarch inaugurates, to substitute explication with immediate apprehension of things and people. Clearly, in portraying cosmic embraces, Fuentes encompasses both traditions, endowing the participants with immediate sensual presence and significant allegorical meaning. Fuentes continues speaking of Petrarch as "the first modern poet because what he writes doesn't illustrate allegorically, anagogically, morally, or literally truths previous to his experience, but rather he returns time and time again to personal experience and takes off again from that, recreating it, revising it, defending it from the temptation of abstraction." Fuentes himself, by contrast, is not entirely a "modern" in this context, for the allegorical, the presence of truths previous to his experience, has always loomed large in his texts. In fact, Fuentes recognizes this same dichotomy in Petrarch, whose Laura is constantly "on the point of becoming an allegorical figure." For him, "Petrarch's vision is the vision of reality besieged by abstractions and defeating them time and time again through a sweet, tormented, and profane return to that year, that month, that day, that place, that hour, when he first saw Laura. The concrete woman doesn't predate, allegorically, the direct vision of the beloved." In his own texts, on the other hand, when abstractions lay siege to reality, they often hold their own.

A recent piece by Fuentes on how he wrote *Aura* occupies an intriguing place in this oscillation and a concluding example in this discussion of the erotic dimensions of Fuentes's fiction. It almost seems intended to counteract the tendency toward abstraction I have just attributed to his texts. It also provides a rare glimpse—albeit fictionalized—of a personal erotic moment in Fuentes's own life. And possibly even a biographical equivalent of the fictional cosmic embraces, though since it was written later, I cannot in all fairness claim it as their precursor, except, in Borgesian fashion, after the fact. It shares characteristic elements with them: the spatial isolation of an enclosed space (like Pollo and Celestina's, in Paris), which expands outward through "abundant mirrors" which reflect *"another* time, time past, time yet to be," the abolition of linear time, the sense of the lovers that they are somehow other than only themselves, the special quality of the light, and the proximity of death:

> That light—I remember it—. . . transformed itself into a luminous pearl encased in a shell of clouds. . . .
>
> She was another, she had been another, not she who was going to be but she who, always, was being.
>
> The light possessed the girl, the light made love to the girl before I could, and I was only, that afternoon, "a strange guest in the kingdom of love" . . . and knew that the eyes of love can also see us with—once more I quote Quevedo—"a beautiful Death."
>
> The next morning I started writing *Aura.*

This essay, called "On Reading and Writing Myself: How I Wrote *Aura*," begins very specifically, almost as Fuentes's version of the way Petrarch returns to his meeting with Laura: "ONE, yes, ONE GIRL, twenty years of age, in the summer of '61, over twenty-two years ago, crossed the threshold between the small drawing room of an apartment on the Boulevard Raspail and entered the bedroom where I was waiting for her." It is as if Fuentes wishes to give a personal and direct dimension to a text and its woman who have for the most part been regarded as allegorical repetitions of earlier texts. We quickly move on to those other "witches who consciously mothered Aura," but at the end we return to the original figure, to "that year, . . . that place," to concrete life—and eventual death: "I published *Aura* in Spanish in 1962. The girl I had met as a child in Mexico and seen re-created by the light of Paris in 1961 when she was twenty, died by her own hand, two years ago, in Mexico, at age forty." The way Fuentes has chosen to end this anecdote poignantly illustrates the attraction of the cosmic embraces in his fiction by its deviation from them. In contrast to this piece, where a woman dies by her own hand at the beginning of middle age, they satisfy our desire that the historical realities of death and separation be counterbalanced by imaginative embodiments of utopian unity, our unwillingness to abandon dreams of total union, even while admitting their virtual impossibility, our wish that the linear onslaught of history be momentarily halted by the circle of an embrace.

Though very much a modernist in his techniques, in these visionary fictional moments, Fuentes reveals a characteristic strain of Promethean romanticism. These utopian scenes may well constitute one of the differences between Fuentes, who has not yet, as Roberto González Echevarría claims, "abandoned the novel of cultural knowledge," and some of his successors who have, and whose fictions often embrace repetition and "indeterminacy" rather than searching for "any sort of primitivistic ideal." At crucial moments throughout his work, moments which even recently are imbued with a desire for cultural knowledge, Fuentes affirms regarding the indeed rather primitivistic "dream of total union," that even though "everyone says this dream is impossible, . . . I do not abandon it."

A Secret Idiom: The Grammar and Role of Language in *Tres tristes tigres*

Stephanie Merrim

Tú, que me lees, ¿estás seguro de entender mi lenguaje?
    —JORGE LUIS BORGES, "La biblioteca de Babel"

Since even before entering the text proper, the reader of *Tres tristes tigres* (*Three Trapped Tigers*) is warned (in the "Advertencia") that the whole novel is written in an "idioma secreto," the nocturnal jargon of Havana, it comes as no surprise to find critics saying that "a new language is created in the space of the text itself." This kind of statement, however, tells us nothing in particular: all literary works create private languages; a text is as much a linguistic as a fictional universe. Instead, we should ask what is different and "secret" about the language of *Tres tristes tigres*? How does it surpass the mere recording of a dialect? What are its rules and grammar? These questions have been difficult to answer because *Tres tristes tigres* is so disjointed a text, a collage of so many styles and genres that there seems to be no binding force. I believe, however, that there can be found a consistency and development of style which would justify calling this odd pastiche of materials a cohesive language or, indeed, a metalanguage—a comment on the workings of language itself.

Bearing in mind this continuity, I should like to investigate the *role* of language in the text as a whole by examining the novel section by section in serial fashion, to show that since the theme of language so totally pervades the novel and ties in with diverse themes, each section either captures or further elucidates a different aspect of Cabrera's literary sign or his concept of language and thereby progressively builds—on the scale of the novel—a secret language.

Unlikely as it may seem, the loosely jointed features of *Tres tristes tigres* do respond to a generic impulse, that of the carnivalesque novel or menippean satire, for since the text's two most direct models, Petronius' *Sa-*

From *Latin American Literary Review* no. 16 (Spring–Summer 1980). © 1980 by *Latin American Literary Review*.

tyricon ("*Tres tristes tigres* es una traducción fallida del *Satiricon*") ["*Three Trapped Tigers* is an unsuccessful translation of the *Satyricon*"] and Lewis Carroll's *Alice* novels participate in this genre, one can expect to find carnivalesque traits in Cabrera's novel. It is well known that the structure of a carnivalesque work is characterized by an extraordinary freedom of composition which manifests itself in a multi-generic or collage texture, by the lack of a finalizing authorial presence which allows characters to evolve their own truth in a Socratic conversation of divergent voices, and by an apparent shattering of the customary novelesque logic of narrative, although "the appearance of carelessness that results reflects only the carelessness of the reader or his tendency to judge by a novel-centered concept of fiction." By debunking traditional narrative plot and character development and pushing them into the background, menippean satire permits intellectual freeplay—or in our case, intellectual wordplay—to come to the foreground. We shall explore these structural features in the course of this study; for now, I should like to focus on the characteristics of carnivalesque language.

M. Bakhtin, who first elaborated the concept of the carnivalesque as such, believes that the language of the carnival work—characterized by *skaz*, stylization and parody—falls outside the bounds of linguistics, being a metalinguistic phenomenon, double-edged or dialogical: "A single trait is common to all of these phenomena, despite their essential differences: in all of them the word has a double-directedness—it is directed both toward the object of speech, like an ordinary word, and toward *another* word, toward *another person's speech*" [*Problems of Dostoevsky's Poetics*]. In other words, the prime feature of the dialogical word is that it is *never equal to itself*. Each type of carnival discourse stands in a different relationship to the 'other' word hidden inside it. *Skaz*, from the Russian *skazat* (to say, to tell), indicates an orientation towards another person's spoken language: when the author reproduces someone else's speech, not his or her own, this is double-edged *skaz*. Stylization extends another person's style by means of exaggeration. Faithful to the tones and intentions of another author's style, stylization merely makes that style double-edged by inserting it into a foreign body of work. Parody, on the other hand, "introduces a semantic direction into that word which is diametrically opposed to its original direction." If in stylization the two voices merge, parody sets them against one another in hostile conflict. Considering the wide range of double-edged discourse, Bakhtin concludes that dialogical language lies at the foundation of prose, as versus poetic, language: "The possibility of employing within a single work words of various types in their extreme expressions without reducing them to a common denominator is one of the most essential characteristics of prose. Herein lies the most profound distinction between prose style and poetic style." In effect, Bakhtin is saying that prose language is essentially intertextual, bearing the traces of the other literary contexts through which it has passed.

Monological or single-voiced language is virtually absent from *Tres tristes tigres*. In order to convert spoken into literary language, Cabrera states, he transferred speech from the horizontal to the vertical plane, increasing the resonances of the word:

> uno de mis experimentos . . . era tratar de llevar este lenguaje básico, convertir este lenguaje oral en un lenguaje literario válido. Es decir, llevar este lenguaje si tú quieres horizontal, absolutamente hablado, a un plano vertical, a un plano artístico, a un plano literario.

> (one of my experiments . . . was to try to turn this basic language— to convert this oral language—into a valid literary language. In other words, to take this, if you will, horizontal, absolutely spoken, language, onto an artistic plane, a literary plane.)

The end product of the transfer was to replace monological language by dialogical *skaz*, intertextuality, parody, and a further double-edged form, translation, making Cabrera's language eminently self-conscious—literary—referring less to a real context than to an intertext.

It is no accident that while *Tres tristes tigres* starts off with a barrage of oratorical rhetoric in its prologue, Petronius' *Satyricon* commences with a fierce diatribe against exactly this same rhetoric. Thinking anachronistically, one might consider the opening chapter of the *Satyricon* as an implicit response to, and criticism of, the high-blown rhetoric of Cabrera's emcee, which grossly distorts the image of Cuba it sets forth. His is a rhetoric of the old Spanish school—sonorous, romantic, clichéd, with little meaningful connection to the underlying reality. However, when the lights fail to go on, the emcee forgets himself and says "coño": here, then, we encounter the first debunking of canonized culture, an attack on its language which illustrates *Tres tristes tigres*'s anti-rhetorical stance.

There are various kinds of translation in the prologue, and all are betrayals. The greatest distortion takes place in the translation of Cuban reality into language, for the announcer filters Cuba not only through rhetoric but also through stereotypes, the result being a version of Cuba whose only reality is found in the glossy blurbs of travel brochures. Brazil suffers the same misrepresentation, transformed into a Hollywood paradise, the "*Brazil* de Carmen Miranda y de José Carioca." These are actually intercultural translations which shape foreign realities to accord with tourists' preconceptions, or rather, misconceptions. Whenever the narrator provides an instantaneous translation from English to Spanish, or vice versa, he perpetuates the fraud. Passing from one class of false discourse to another, with each 'literary,' and thus non-literal, translation he adds new rhetorical flourishes. At the same time, he is guilty of serious translational boners, through mispronunciation ("Brazuil terra dye nostra felichidade"), misrepresentation (William Campbell, we learn later, is not the heir to the soup fortune), and mistranslation ("Discriminatory public"). Oral neologisms, reproducing the announcer's speech patterns, heighten the absurdity of his translations ("Amableypacientepublicocubanoes MisterCambellelfamosomillionarioherederodeunafortunadesopas"). Yet auguring the change in language which follows the prologue, the narrator concludes by nullifying his own language: "Sin traducción . . . *without translation* . . . sin palabras pero con música y sana alegria y esparcimiento."

The emcee has presented the reader with an entirely verbal reality, one which exists only in his words. Accordingly, if not conversely, what assumes great importance is the negative space, what is *not* said, but will be said later. For behind the eloquent rhetorical facade lies the true language of Cuba, the spontaneous oral speech which dominates the rest of the novel, beginning with "Los debutantes."

Because the narrations of "Los debutantes" appear to be straight monologues with no wordplays or literary allusions, and because, after all, much of "Los debutantes" represents the characters' first steps *towards* the night-world, one might be tempted to equate these monologues (and here I am referring primarily to the women's voices, because the men's have more 'literary' features) with monological language. From the very first, however, the language of *Tres tristes tigres* is dialogical, characterized by polyphony and *skaz*.

In the carnivalesque novel, the author abdicates to the characters the right to a definitive word or style. Each character becomes a voice articulating one point of view, and in his words coexist two voices: the voice or *skaz* of the character, and the voice of the author which tries to reproduce the character's voice and which always stands at a certain remove—different with each character—from its object. Similarly, the wide range of verbal textures in *Tres tristes tigres*, more noticeable in "Los debutantes" than in any other section (since the male narrators of the remaining chapters tend to speak something of a common language), evinces the author's surrender of his voice to other voices as he attempts to faithfully record the oral *skaz* of each character. Far from monological then, each seeming monologue contains a hidden dialogue between the voice of the author and that of the speaker.

"Los debutantes" most explicitly contributes to the *idioma secreto* by capturing "los diferentes dialectos del español que se hablan en Cuba" ("the different dialects of Spanish spoken in Cuba"), the whole range of Cuban speech. One barometer of its striking assortment of voices is the presence of oral neologisms, created to simulate the characters' oral pronunciation or dialect. Already in the Prologue oral neologisms were employed to produce an ironic perspective on the announcer's rhetoric; here, appearing in greater abundance and variety, they serve to distinguish between the several, often unidentified voices. If, as has been said, *Tres tristes tigres* combines the detective story with semiology, then these special signs, the neologisms, provide an important clue to (or sign of) the speaker's identity.

For example, although Delia Doce's letter to her friend Estelvina is written, its neologisms derive from oral pronunciation. Most of her neologisms are either simple spelling mistakes playing on the few non-sound/symbol correspondences of Spanish (i.e. interchanging v and b; s, c, and z; ll and y; omitting h's); mispellings based on pronunciation ("rialidá," "yegârá"); or the conjoinings of words according to pronunciation ("Mariasantísima"). In the narrative about Magalena Cruz we find the highest incidence of neologisms. While the speech of its mysterious narrator (is it Beba Longorio, who later is seen in Magalena's company and has some peculiar hold over her?) may appear to be the most lower-class or unregenerated, it is nevertheless the most uniquely Cuban, displaying several traits characteristic of Cuban Spanish: exchange of the liquid consonants *r* and *l* ("hablal," "coldel"); apocope of the final syllable ("na ma" for "nada más"); suppression or aspiration of *S*'s ("así mimo," "etás"); dropping of the intervocalic consonants ("vestia" for "vestida"), and so on. If indeed Beba Longorio is the narrator of this monologue, her next monologue reveals a language in the process of transformation. Characterized by the same features of Cuban Spanish just mentioned, her speech has now gravitated towards a more sophisticated tone, acquiring the mannerisms of what she believes to be upper-class speech: a 'feminine' emphasis on words, indicated by italics ("Bueno, *menos* en eso, *Creo*"), or their elongation ("ma-ra-bi-llo-sa"); creation of high-sounding neologisms ("la visconversa"); use of foreign words ("trusó," "senkiu"), and so on. Here, as earlier in the Prologue, the use of *skaz* borders on parody, with the author using the character's voice to hostile purposes.

Oral neologisms entail a making strange of language and as such signify the first step towards wordplay. Unfamiliar to the eye and mind, but not to the ear, the distortion of a word's orthographical representation constitutes, in essence, a separation of the signifier from the signified in order to accentuate the word's sound. Unlike the wordplays and allusions which begin to emerge in seminal form with the male narrators' monologues, oral neologisms are pure sound. Their signifiers neither hide nor create unsuspected signifieds; they are self-reflexive, referring back only to the oral dimensions of the word. Orality, therefore, is at the root of all of *Tres tristes tigres*'s neologisms, but in wordplay the neologisms acquire a metaphorical depth, an intra- or inter-textual dimension. In sum, this making strange of language indicates the path that the novel will take: by substituting the oral for the written and emphasizing sound over meaning, *Tres tristes tigres* defines itself as a large-scale tongue twister.

In many ways, Laura's story represents the "other" of *Tres tristes tigres*, both in terms of point of view—hers is another, outside perspective on the tigers' nightworld—and in terms of its implications for language. Thematically, Laura's story, told through her monologue in "Los debutantes" and through the eleven sessions with a psychiatrist interpolated throughout the novel, supplies both the woman's point of view on the male-dominated novel, and a different temporal perspective, for her first monologue takes place before she has entered the nightworld, and the sessions occur after she has married Silvestre, thereby bringing to a close both their participation in the nightworld. Consequently, her monologues are our only outside view of the nightworld and, importantly, its aftermath, and they form another novel in miniature, a whole other series within this polyphonic novel.

Significantly enough, the novel proper commences with Laura's statement: "Lo que no le dijimos *nunca* a nadie fue que nosotras también hacíamos cositas debajo del camión" ["But what we *never* told anyone was that we too used to play with each other's things under the truck"]. What she never told, simply put, was the truth, because the truth was too shameful for Laura and her friend Aurelita to tell. Instead, they displace what was too shameful to tell, the homosexual nature of their activities, onto a more acceptable form, their story exposing the (heterosexual) activities of Petra and her lover. And further, with each performance of their tale, the two children enlarge upon the details of the story, distorting even that truth. Their translation is thus a betrayal, both of the event and of themselves, and the avoidance of the truth engenders a series of periphrastic lies, lies which come to represent not only a false language, but repression itself. Normal discourse, the truth, is replaced by an "other" language, one with negative connotations.

When we next meet Laura in the first session, the game has become life and the need to tell all that she has repressed is overwhelming. Faced with a stifling lack of communication with her husband, Laura describes herself as "la esfinge ajita de secretos" ["the sphinx that had its bellyful of secrets"] and turns to the psychiatrist in the attempt finally to unburden herself. Yet she has no words to impart her feelings: nothing that Laura says in the first session is her own; she speaks with her husband's words. The inability to speak the truth has installed itself as the center of Laura's life, making her an inveterate liar who translates her life into a series of falsehoods. Only by the seventh appointment does Laura endeavour to undo the lies she has told the psychiatrist ("El viernes le dije una mentira, doctor. Grandísima" ["I told you a lie on Friday, doctor. A really big lie"]). Peeling away the layers of falsehood, Laura grasps for a mode of genuine communication, but in the last, eleventh, session, she is on the verge of total breakdown.

"Seseribó" and "Casa de los espejos" further develop the counterpoint between men and women in *Tres tristes tigres*. While *Tres tristes tigres*'s male characters find an outlet for political and sexual frustration in verbal humor, its female characters are denied that outlet and thereby condemned to madness and artificiality, forced to play Ophelia to the men's Hamlets. Women are seen as dangerous and taboo ("Seseribó") and exposed as fakes of monstrous proportions when they pass through the "cámara del detector de mentiras" ["lie detector"] which strips them of their disguises ("casa de los espejos"). At the same time, in both chapters whenever women are present, we note a surge of wordplay or "masturhablarse" on the men's part, in defense against the women. This curious attraction and repulsion that the female characters exercise over the males can, on the one hand, be attributed to the fact that the female characters in *Tres tristes tigres* represent the baser plane of sensuality while the males strive for a higher, intellectual plane. In other words, whereas the closely-knit circle of "tigers" postulate the nightworld, largely a mental construct, as a pure space removed from time, their women, who operate on a physical and sensual level, resort to grotesque extremes of makeup and disguises to ward off the ravages of time. Derided and scorned by the male characters (consider, in this regard, also the episode in "Bachata" with Beba and Magalena), the women—disallowed the gift of humor—serve as victims who must be sacrificed in order to preserve the intellectual purity of the nightworld. On the other hand, but analogously, the true surrender of oneself to a woman (as in the case of Silvestre) would bring an end to the nightworld, hence the tigers' insistence on their masturbatory verbal continence which precludes the need for (the opposite) sex.

It is thought that macaronic or polyglot literature, with its monstrous verbal exuberance, may originally have been developed to celebrate the crowning of those real monsters, the carnival king and queen. Be that as it may, there is certainly a carnival impulse in the polyglot nature of *Tres tristes tigres*, which transforms the normally unilingual stylistic surface of a text into a polyphonic Babel of languages. This plurality of languages echoes the plurality of styles which make of *Tres tristes tigres* a collage of heterogeneous materials.

Not only different languages, but different kinds of languages—negative and positive—coincide in the novel. The polyglot conversation in English and French of the third section of "Seseribó" where Cué and his girlfriend show off their sophistication is ridiculed: "Ellos dos parecían muy preocupados en demostrar que podian hablar franglés y besarse al mismo tiempo" ["They were both deeply absorbed in showing they could speak French and kiss at the same time"]. Eribó complains that the two of them "quieren convertir al español en una lengua muerta" ["want to turn Spanish into a dead language"]: the use of foreign languages is one negative product of Cuba's cultural "barroquismo" and hence receives a parodic treatment in *Tres tristes tigres*. At the same time, there figure in the text specialized languages or professional jargons, which fulfill a positive function as alternative languages. Already in *Un Officio del Siglo XX*, the *mundo al inverso* of movies is equated with its specialized languages, as in the section entitled "La lengua de Caín es el lenguaje del cine" ["Cain's language is the language of the movies"]. Here, each tiger chooses a particular art upon which to base his private *mundo al inverso*, a gateway to the absolute, and each field has its own jargon. Eribó speaks the language of music (in "Seseribó"), Silvestre the language of the movies, Códac of photography and Cué, whose conversation is a weave of quotations, of the theatre. Beginning with

"Seseribó," then, and extending throughout the text, we encounter a variety of alternative languages giving voice to the several underground worlds which converge in the nightworld.

To the eye, "Ella cantaba boleros" and the other narrative sections present a smooth narrative surface, unbroken by dialogue, short paragraphs or typographic play. But although the surface may look homogeneous, like all else in *Tres tristes tigres* it is woven of a heterogeneous body of stuff, encompassing many layers. Códac's narratives avail themselves of the technique, used by Beat Generation writers such as Jack Kerouac, of framing massively long sentences—often the length of a paragraph—into which are drawn many thoughts, sentences, points of view and voices, Dialogue enters only indirectly, without quotation marks, creating, almost imperceptibly, a tissue of alternating voices, such as the following:

> y al poco rato el griego que me dice ¿Por qué no saca a bailar a mi mujer? y yo le digo que no bailo y él me dice que cómo es posible que haya un cubano que no baile y Magalena que le dice, No hay uno, hay dos, porque yo tampoco bailo . . .

> (and soon the Greek is saying to me, Why don't you ask my wife for a dance? and I tell him I don't dance and he says, It's not possible, a Cuban who doesn't dance? and Magalena says, There's two of them because I can't dance either . . .)

Ostensibly a monologue, in reality Códac's narratives are a melting pot of voices, a polyphonic dialogue. Cué's contribution to "casa de los espejos" also partakes of these twisting polyphonic sentences, supplementing the dialogical interplay of characters' voices with literary allusions or quotations. Once again, as with the *skaz* of "Los debutantes," but in a different way, the monologue proves to enclose a dialogue.

While in "Ella cantaba boleros" there is a little verbal distortion through wordplays, we do find innovative distortion in terms of the sentence. The polyphonic phrases of *Tres tristes tigres* represent an opening up of language, for certain techniques allow the sentences to continue almost indefinitely. Cabrera employs existing linguistic means such as parataxis, hypotaxis, semicolons and colons to extend the sentence, while adding a technique of his own—slashes ("un si es no es falsa/trabajada/viril").

However, within this framework it is through a more far-reaching means of reorganization that the sentences succeed in perpetuating themselves at such great length. Metaphorical construction is the important and all-pervasive structuring technique of Cabrera's prose and usually takes the form of paradigmatic overlapping—repetition with change:

> y alargaba una pierna sepia, tierra ahora, chocolate ahora, café ahora, tabaco ahora, azúcar, prieto ahora . . .

> (and she stretched out a leg sepia one moment, then earth-brown, then chocolate, tobacco, sugar-colored, black . . .)

ella puso sus cinco chorizos sobre mi muslo, casi sus cinco salami que adornan un jamón sobre mi muslo, su mano sobre mi muslo.

(she put her 5 *chorizos,* five sausages, on my thigh, almost like five salamis garnishing a ham on my thigh, she put her hand on my thigh.)

The omnipresent devices of repetition, slash constructions and anaphora also create metaphorical planes of equivalence:

nunca la vi más hermosa que en aquella penumbra—excepto desnuda excepto desnuda excepto desnuda.

(I have never seen her more beautiful than she was that evening—except naked except naked except naked.)

fabricó la gana/el ansia/la necesidad de que la viera desnuda.

(/Livia/was manufacturing the desire, the anxiety, the necessity for me to see her naked.)

Es la salvaje belleza de la vida, sin que me oyera naturalmente, sin que me entendiera si me había oido, naturalmente . . .

(She's the savage beauty of life, without Irenita hearing me, naturally, not that she would have understood if she had heard me, naturally . . .)

(my translation)

Most often, several of these metaphorical techniques will appear in conjunction, converting the sentence into a syntactically orchestrated instrumental solo which generates its own varying rhythm of repetitions.

Carrying our investigation beyond stylistic analysis to the narrative organization of the text as a whole, we can point out certain similarities between style and narrative structure which reveal *Tres tristes tigres* to be what might be called an "aphasic" text. All of its narrative structure obeys a non-traditional, non-linear logic and development. Each section is situated in a time/space different and discontinuous from the next: for example, . . . the reader is surprised to learn that Bustrófedon had already died by the time the opening scene of the novel takes place, a fact which implies that the majority of the text deals with the last sparks of the nightworld. Further, as stated earlier, *Tres tristes tigres* features a collage-like construction, binding together generically heterogeneous materials and obliterating the linear development of a plot. These multi-generic elements (such as "Los visitantes," "La muerte de Trotsky," etc.) are linked to the more narrative sections only through association, for they extend and often define the novel's major themes. In fact, the narrative sections themselves are organized associatively and not linearly, following cinematic techniques of flashback and montage. The end product is a nonlinear text which works on a new associative logic, and whose structure reflects Bustrófedon's particular kind of aphasia: a contiguity disorder that impedes the metonymic organization of discourse.

The story on which "Los visitantes" is based is purposely banal and cliché-ridden. Therefore, with the subject matter so trivial, the reader's attention is automatically shifted to *how* the story is told or presented. And since the story is presented through a series of translations which become travesties of an (absent) original text, it is the process of translation that comes to the fore. Translation, as we shall see, gives rise to a new kind of double-edged word, one in which the translated word struggles to remain faithful to the original voice inside it, but often falls, inadvertently, into parody.

"Los visitantes" explicity illustrates the problematics of translation with several cases in point in which, at every stage, the *traduttore* is a *tradittori* who betrays both reality and language. As in the "Prólogo," there are two kinds of translation to be found here—intercultural and intralingual; as the first is quite obvious, let us turn to the second.

Upon first reading, Silvestre's appears to be a "good" translation; it reads well, the Spanish is colloquial; in sum, the translation seems to stand up as well as an original might. But only when we read Rine's "pésima" ["awful"] translation do we realize what has happened. This second translation, and, obviously, the original story, abound with cultural references, wordplays, and foreign languages, many of which Rine finds untranslatable and resorts to footnotes to explain. (Perhaps this is a comment on the untranslatability of the text itself, which features the same traits.) Then, returning to Silvestre's version, we find that he has merely left out the untranslatable elements, flattening the polyphonic texture into a single dimension. Silvestre thereby sacrifices accuracy for style, achieving a "readable" text by betraying the original.

However, it is a toss-up which translation, Silvestre's or Rine's, is the greater betrayal, for they illustrate the two possible extremes of translation. While Silvestre's version undermines its double-edgedness, being good Spanish, by disregarding the original, Rine's is patently double-edged, a literal translation. In a literal translation the original language shines through, determining the lexicon and syntax of the new product; such translations in effect are little more than a linguistic pony to aid the reader whose knowledge of the foreign language is insufficient, but who nevertheless wishes to sample the original flavor. The paradox, then, is that a literal translation, while faithful to the original language, is a betrayal of the original text and its stylistic integrity. In other words, the most faithful double betrays its own image, as Cué makes clear: "O estabas pensando en la traición o tradición o traducción de Rine, siempre leal, al pie de la letra así?" ["Or were you thinking of the treason or tradition or translation of Rine Leal, always loyal, to the letter of the law?"] (my translation).

Built into the story itself is another kind of translation, a critique taking the form of Mrs. Campbell's "Reparos" or "Correcciones." Mrs. Campbell criticizes both her husband's style and his portrayal of the events; demanding realism or journalistic accuracy, she unmasks the fictional character of her husband's narrative. However, at the same time as she adopts the stance of a literary critic finding fault with the inaccuracy of his style, she endows her own narrative with a recognizably "literary" style in phrases such as: "Navegamos por entre edificios de espejos, reverberos que comían los ojos. . . . Un muelle se acercó lenta, inexorablemente." ["We sailed between buildings that were more mirrors than buildings, reflections that could swallow the eyes of those who gazed at them. . . . Slowly, inevitably, a pier moved toward us."] By positing this contradiction, Cabrera seems to suggest that any written form is a style—that there is no "zero" degree style—and that objectivity is simply an illusion. Yet the greatest illusion of all is Mrs. Campbell's mere existence. At the end of the novel we learn that there is no real Mrs. Campbell, that the paper tiger wife of "Los visitantes" is only a fictional projection of the author's personality onto a different persona, as are all characters. In this case, language gives rise to an illusion which betrays not only reality, but also the reader.

Although "Rompecabeza," with its subordination of the narrative to wordplay, seems to stand apart from the body of the novel, it actually comprises a key or *scholium* as vital to the text as "Bachata." When read word by word, to paraphrase Gertrude Stein, this writing that is anything becomes something—more specifically, wordplay reveals itself as the matrix for *Tres tristes tigres*'s *idioma secreto*. We shall examine, as space permits, certain salient characteristics of wordplay.

Throughout this elegiac text, as we repeatedly see, much is made of the fact that all translation is a betrayal and that any language proves insufficient to carry out *Tres tristes tigres*'s ecological task of recapturing the nightworld lost. Viewed in this light, wordplay appears as a substitute or *anti*-language evolved in the face of the betrayal of conventional language. As a result of the failure of language to successfully translate reality or a given message, wordplay de-emphasizes the signifier, centering its discourse on the actual physical properties of the sign—its plastic and musical dimensions—and not, as one critic [Nicolás Rosa] aptly notes, on the conveying of a message:

> La comunicación ha sido no sólo pospuesto sino inexorablemente conmutada por una devaluación del carácter racional del lenguaje en una exaltación de la palabra como signos musicales o plásticos.

> (Communication has not only been postponed, but inexorably switched, by means of a devaluation of the rational character of language, into an exaltation of words as musical or plastic signs.)

By taking recourse to the signifier and the phonically determined associations of signifiers, this new oral idiom attains to what can be seen as an autonomous, non-referential language, giving (at least) the *illusion* of an absolute structure, independent of reality and complete in and of itself. Under these conditions, language can no longer be accused of betraying reality or even meaning, since it is faithful only to its own origins—the linguistic code—and any 'meaning' it produces will be found in the relationship between signifiers.

Cabrera's special wordplays most often combine the characteristics of the anagram and pun, for a single sign (such as "Dádiva") proves anagramatically to harbour a series of signifiers (Dádiva—ávida, vida, ida, David) related by sound and not by meaning. Carlos Fuentes has praised Cabrera for destroying "la fatal tradición de univocidad de nuestra prosa" ["the lethal tradition in our prose of univocality"] and for revealing the word as "un nudo de significados" ["a knot of meanings"]. Such an opening up of language, in which one word engenders many, results in an excess of signifiers, an "intratextuality" of the word. And this intratextuality, in turn, reveals wordplay as an eminently *dialogical* form.

Now one of the most serious objections levied against the word-within-wordplay series is that they rupture the metonymic storytelling flow of the narrative. However, a closer look at the relationship between signifiers reveals another structuring principle at work as binding as metonymy. As in the narrative sections, here we encounter the *metaphorical* technique of paradigmatic overlapping, repetition with change. A good illustration of this technique is the following wordplay progression where the paradigm (Bustro- or Bus-) is added to a (syntagmatic) series of qualifiers:

> y nosotros en el más acá muertos de risa en la orilla del mantel, con este pregonero increíble, el heraldo, Bustrófeno, éste, gritando, BustrofenóNemo chico eres un Bustrófonbraun, gritando bustrórriba marina, gritando, Bustifón, Bustrosimún, Busmonzón, gritando, Viento Bustrófenomenal, gritando a diestro y siniestro y ambidiestro.

> (and we're still there in the hereafter drowning of laughter on the shores of the tablecloth . . . with this unbelievable public proclaimer BustrophenoNemo, a Bustrofonbraum, crying out loud, Bustyphoon, Bustornado, Bustrombone, out-crying himself, Bustrombamarina, crying to left and right.)

The concatenation of names is paratactic and metaphorical, relating disparate terms not through conjunctions but by the prefixation of Bus- or bustro-.

The various properties of wordplay suggested here, which make of it an anti-language, have been criticized as purposeless and self-indulgent. Yet how can they be purposeless when Cabrera has stated that "the book's sense and sound is the book's language and the book's language is the book's meaning?" Given the unsuspected continuity between wordplay and the *idioma secreto* of the text, might not these self-indulgences be said to comprise a pure core or model of the linguistic axis of the text? If *Tres tristes tigres*'s protagonists are indeed the nightworld and language, the correspondence is exact: world and language/anti-world and anti-language.

Whereas in "Los visitantes," the devaluation of the story's content brought matters of translation to the fore, the fact that "La muerte de Trotsky" repeats the same story in several versions allows questions of parody and style to surface. There are two possible ways of looking at "La muerte de Trotsky": we can consider each story separately as a parody of a particular author, or we can take all the stories globally as a fan of stylistic permutations or translations of a single ideal (and thus absent) story, as an excess of signifiers for one signified. From the first standpoint we shall see that parody functions as a translation of style, to which is added an explicit measure of irony (in translation proper, we repeat, the ironic or parodic element is unintentional, though perhaps inevitable), irony which links up with iconoclasm. With regard to the second standpoint, I believe that Cabrera aspired to include the whole gamut of Cuban literary culture, showing how Cuban writers might adapt themselves to the demands of socialist literature. The result is a series of diverse styles in which each literary language entails another modulation of Cuba's polyglot voice.

While it is truly remarkable that one country should have produced the many, disparate literary voices we find when we take each piece separately, one further tie besides Cuba unites them: representatives of sanctioned culture, they are all debunked by Cabrera's parodies. Parody joins with iconoclasm on more than one front to dethrone the powerful. The task of parody is ridicule and reform, an ironic literary criticism. By attaching this "song sung beside" to the works of all major Cuban writers, Cabrera aims a blow not only at the writers but at the Cuban establishment which sanctions them. Another important factor in "La muerte de Trotsky," this time a thematic one, is that of generational conflict, in which a second generation of revolutionaries kills off the first, symbolized by Trotsky himself. Much the same conflict comprises a defining characteristic of parody: one generation of writers figuratively kills off the previous generation or generations, their parodies furnishing an antithetical completion of the previous writers' works. Lastly, this parodying of a political action, Trotsky's murder, not only mocks but also neutralizes that action. Anything threatening that enters the nightworld must be deactivated, often through humor. Here political action, history, is first transformed into literature and then neutralized by parody: a monological form is rendered impotent by a dialogical form.

There is further irony in the fact that these examples of Socialist literature, a genre so committed to the transparent representation of reality, should here produce so great a variety of styles. That the infinite variety of style represents one of Cabrera's central concerns is reflected in *Exorcismos de esti(l)o*, "La muerte de Trotsky," and, indeed, in the collage-like structure of *Tres tristes tigres*. As the similarity in titles indicates, *Exorcismos* obviously takes its cue from Raymond Queneau's *tour de force*, *Exercises de Style*, a unique "essay" on style in which a single, unexceptional anecdote is told ninety-nine different ways. As in "La muerte de Trotsky," in Queneau's text the content of the story remains unchanged while the style permutes itself around a central axis, thereby giving rise, in both texts, to a large-scale configuration of paradigmatic overlapping.

However, there is a cardinal difference between Queneau's exercises and those of Cabrera: while Queneau's work is constructive, forming a unique dictionary of literary styles, Cabrera's is destructive, an exorcism of style. Both authors utilize a process of deconstruction (of discourse into its various components) and hyperbolic accumulation (of a single technique, or techniques in the case of Cabrera) to create a product which is recognizable as a style or *écriture*. But whereas Queneau's exercises tend more to stylization, i.e. simple exaggeration, Cabrera's fall squarely in the realm of parody. Through parody, like is turned on like as style destroys—or exorcises style. "La muerte de Trotsky" thus mirrors a prime intention of this whole text, which elevates oral language and parodically debunks literary style.

> —No puedes oir cómo el viejo Bach juega en la tonalidad en re, cómo construye sus imitaciones, cómo hace las variaciones imprevisiblemente pero donde el tema lo permite y lo sugiere y no antes, nunca después, y a pesar de ello logra sorprender? No te parece un esclavo con toda la libertad?

> (—Can't you hear how old Bach plays on the tonality in D, how he builds up his imitations, how he makes his variations always unpredictable but only when the theme allows and suggests it and never before, never after, and how despite that he always manages to take you by surprise? Doesn't he seem like a slave with all the freedom in the world?)

This remark, a key within a key, tells us certain crucial things about "Bachata," the self-styled scholia and longest section of *Tres tristes tigres*. Its first sentence refers to Bach's serial compositions, "The Art of the Fugue," along the lines of which "Bachata" is structured. Defining a fugue as,

> A polyphonic composition constructed on one or more short subjects, or themes, which are harmonized according to the laws of counterpoint, and introduced from time to time with various contrapuntal devices,

we can see how polyphony informs the structure of "Bachata," with its discussions and variations of several philosophical themes. Indeed, polyphony stands out as the foremost characteristic of "Bachata," and especially of its language, for here is found the culmination of the dialogical word, in concentrations of wordplay (intratextual and intertextual) denser even than those of "Rompecabeza." The second sentence of the quote evokes the concept of game, in which the fixing of rules affords the player a special kind of freedom. A key to those special games, the text and the nightworld, "Bachata" clarifies their rules. But, as we shall see with particular respect to language, the principles of the game assert themselves only to fall apart as the nightworld dissolves, because "the center cannot hold."

In "Bachata," where the dialogical word reaches its peak, we encounter the whole range of oral and paragrammatic forms previously discussed. Silvestre, Bustro's most dedicated disciple, carries on his friend's wordplays in homage to him. And a rival "Rompecabeza," Cué's "Confesiones de un comedor de gofio cubano," features number puzzles, projects for aleatory literature and typographical games. Parody plays as important a role as before: Silvestre stylizes Borges's "Tema del traidor y del héroe," and Cué's poem, "Si te llamaras Babel y no Beba Martínez" parodies Neruda's "Bacarola." Cué's specialty as an actor, however, is to speak in quotations. All manner of quotations, be they direct ("Yo soy yo y mi circumstancia"); deformed (the vast majority, e.g. "El joder corrompe, el joder total corrompe totalmente"); or disguised ("Pero no quiero conocerla, que no quiero verla"), figure in his speech, endowing it with a paragrammatic, or plagiaristic texture. Since what Cué plagiarizes are cultural commonplaces, his paragrams acquire a parodic edge through two techniques. First, like puns, they are non-contextual: quoted out of context, the phrases form a kind of *bricolage*, bits and pieces gathered without regard to their specific function. Second, they are almost invariably distorted, turned into parodic doubles of themselves. If, as Lautréamont said, "Le plagiat est nécessaire," then Cué's speech represents that intertextual dialogue latent in every literary word.

A feast of dialogical language, "Bachata" celebrates the nightworld on all levels, affirming it one final time in the face of ever-encroaching reality. "Bachata," which along with the reference to Bach means "spree," is exactly that, an afternoon-through-morning of carousing, drinking, eating, driving, attempted womanizing and, most of all, conversation. Since in Bustro's "Geometrías del espíritu" a circle symbolizes perfect happiness, the concentric construction of "Bachata"—variations and returns to a theme all the while encircling the Malecón in the car—suggest the characters' desire to keep their happiness intact. But even in the neutralized space of the nightworld there enter threats, both negative and positive, to its existence. Fierce negative images, such as references to death, Silvestre's horror movie fantasies, nightmares of apocalyptic visions, and so on, abound in "Bachata." More and more the nightworld is invaded by a reality of dark, menacing aspect: Silvestre may be going blind, he is unable to write, Cué's artificial posturing alienates his friend, Magalena is either mad or being tortured by Beba, Bustro is dead. On the other hand, betrayal of the nightworld and of each other is imminent as Cué and Silvestre prepare to abandon their Hamlet-like passivity and take positive action, Silvestre by marrying Laura, and Cué by joining Fidel. Its existence rendered extremely precarious by these invasions on either side, the nightworld asserts itself one last time in full force, exposing its true nature as a defense against reality.

As the threat of reality causes the nightworld to affirm itself, so, on the level of language, do the presence of truth and danger give rise to wordplay as a defense. Like Laura, Silvestre is unable to tell the truth and avoids doing so with a series of periphrastic substitutions—not with lies, but with allusions and wordplay. Many of Silvestre's allusions (to Shakespeare, horror movies, literature) are ruled by Laura, with the hidden meaning implied but not stated. Yet allusions do not suffice, for Cué will avoid understanding Silvestre's confession at all costs; unable to convey his message obliquely, Silvestre breaks into compensatory wordplay:

> No entendió o no quiso entender. Al entendedor renuente no le bastan las palabras. Hay que hacerle cifras, mostrarle los numeritos. Lástima, podía haberle hablado ahora. Lo haré para mí. Masturhablarme. Solución que es polución. La solution d'un sage n'est que la polution d'un page . . .

> (He didn't hear or he didn't want to hear. Words are not enough for the Pythagorean listener. It needs figures. I'd have to show him some prime numbers. A pity. I could have spoken to him just now. Well, I'll talk to myself instead. To masturdebate. . . . Make a solution of pollution. The solution of a sage is to pollute a page . . .)

At other points in the text dense wordplay, either by one character or in a dialogue between characters, is set off by dangerous elements: Silvestre alternates between wordplay and narrative in his meditations on death; watching Cué look at himself in the mirror after his confession about going to the Sierra reminds Silvestre of the theme of the betrayal of doubles and incites wordplay; the presence of women, now particularly threatening because it recalls Laura, spurs a long exchange of wordplay between the men, to the exclusion of Beba and Magalena. Here, more than ever, we are given to understand wordplay as an alternate or compensatory language, explicitly called an "anti-lenguaje" [anti-language] by Silvestre.

When, at these points, wordplay does take over, it comprises a fully self-sufficient language with its own structure and logic. In "Bachata" we can see the full-scale workings of *Tres tristes tigres*'s dialogical language in dense pages of wordplay such as those of Silvestre, which are motivated by Beba and Magalena's entrance. Here any pretensions to a narrative, storytelling logic are abandoned as the discourse moves onto an associative plane ruled entirely by sound rather than meaning. The separation of the signified from the signifier, along with refuge in the signifier found in wordplay, once again manifests itself as the central organizing principle of *Tres tristes tigres*'s language. Effacing, at once, the pole of the signified and the monological word, all the forms of dialogical language which have appeared separately until now, from the intratextual to the intertextual, converge and work together to the exclusion of non-carnivalesque elements. Related by sound, any one dialogical form can induce another or others, for they bounce off each other as well as combine to work together. Though apparently the most "self-indulgent," such pages as this nevertheless represent the culmination and conquest of the text's *idioma secreto*, its defeat of monological discourse.

Yet, ironically, this culmination of dialogical language at the same time bespeaks its downfall; deforming a quote from Yeats, Cué remarks, "The *Beast* lacks all convictions, while the words are full of passive insanity." Cué's and Silvestre's words are indeed suffused with a "passive insanity" which derives from the desperate, ultimately futile, attempt to avoid truth and ward off threats to the nightworld. If before, as in "Rompecabeza," the nightworld and language held strong, here they are crumbling, with the infiltration of reality transforming wordplay into a pathetic avoidance of the truth. To ward off danger (in the form of the two women), Cué and Silvestre contrive to speak a language unknown to the women, thereby purposely alienating them; the men and the women are in effect speaking two different languages, and the Babelic breakdown of communication precludes any seduction of the women. Trapped between two conflicting impulses, of attraction and repulsion, Cué and Silvestre lose command of themselves, uncontrollably persisting in their solipsistic game:

> Creo que fue entonces cuando nos preguntamos, tácitamente . . . por qué hacerlas reír. ¿Qué éramos? ¿Clowns, el primero y el segundo, enterradores entre risas o seres humanos, personas corrientes y molidas, gente? ¿No era más fácil enamorarlas?

> (I think it was at this point that we began wondering tacitly . . . whether it was worth making them laugh. What were we? Clowns, 1st and 2nd gravediggers when we weren't laughing or human beings, common and garded persons, people? Wouldn't it be easier to make love to them?)

Rather than succumbing to madness, Cué and Silvestre commence their re-entry of reality on positive, though divergent courses. Cué's theory of *contradictorios*, based on Ortega y Gasset's theory of tragedy, heralds their abandonment of the nightworld. In Cué's conception, *contradictorios*, who historically were warriors so brave that they were allowed to break all tribal rules in times of peace, are people with the courage to challenge society's norms, or, according to Ortega y Gasset, people who carry their ideal project into the world and defend that project. At first, after exhaustively listing figures whom they believe were *contradictorios*, Cué and Silvestre confess that they themselves are not. Later, however, Cué admits that Silvestre is indeed: "Un contradictorio. ¿Del cine, de la literatura o de la vida real? O hay que esperar todavía . . . el último capítulo? Titulado como, Desenmascarado o Evilly the Kid Strikes Back?" ["A contradictory. Of movies, literature or real life? Or do we have to wait for the final episode, like in those old Monogrammed serials? Unmasked or Evilly the Kid Strikes Back?"] An unmasking, a striking back which would allow Cué and Silvestre to become *contradictorios,* entails assuming a course of positive action which would carry the utopian core of the nightworld into the outside reality. And while the last chapter falls outside *Tres tristes tigres* (though perhaps in the realm of *Vista del Amanecer en el Trópico*), each character's choice represents one pole of a possible ideal project: Silvestre's, personal fulfillment, and Cué's, social fulfillment through political action.

The reentry into reality also entails an annihilation of the secret language. When at last Silvestre discloses the truth about Laura, he is forced to cut his way through the ruins of the game language:

> Me quedé callado. Traté de encontrar algo más que refranes y frases hechas, una frase por hacer, palabras, alguna oración regada por aqui y por allá. No era ni pelota ni ajedrez, era armar un rompecabezas.

> (I fell silent. I tried looking for something better than the usual pat sayings and catchphrases. A phrase to catch. Words and sentences scattered here and there. It wasn't either baseball or chess, it was a seesaw puzzle. Crisscrosswords.)

Eschewing all double entendres, he finally states quite simply, *"Me voy a casarconella"* ["*I'm going to marry her*"] thereby nullifying the periphrases and signalling his re-entry into monological discourse. And although Silvestre's crucial remark, "una frase por hacer" ["a phrase to catch"], symbolizes a search for the word to be carried over into the absent "ultimo capitulo" ["last chapter"] perhaps language's double, silence, will replace the much-sought word: at the end of "Bachata" "en silencio" is obsessively interpolated between the pieces of Silvestre's discourse. Here, as throughout the novel, when language cedes to silence, talk cedes to action.

That madness which Silvestre and Cué must needs avoid, but whose presence lurks in their words and in the nightworld, gains a voice in the Epilogue. Like Laura's psychoanalytic sessions, the Epilogue takes us, for one final moment, beyond the sphere of the text proper; both inside and outside the novel, it provides a picture of the madness and the language of madness which hover at the extremities of the nightworld. *La loca* sits in the park and talks to herself; running uncontrollably through the same monologue each time, endlessly, like a pianola score, she is unable to translate the world except into broken scatological images. Fragmented, oral, repetitive, metaphorically structured, ruled by a hermetic and unfathomable logic and thus robbed of its communicative function, her language resembles a crude distillation of wordplay carried to its ultimate extremes—the game become life. A Dorian Gray portrait of wordplay turned to ruin, the Epilogue draws the fine line between anti-language and the language of madness.

With this cruel touch, the Epilogue adds one final dimension to *Tres tristes tigres*'s secret language. In the course of our discussion we have witnessed the development of a new language: its inception in the *skaz* of "Los debutantes," its infiltration of style and syntax, its assuming of various dialogical shapes (parody, translation and *bricolage*) and progressive acquisition of paragrammatic depth, its culmination and takeover of the verbal space in "Bachata," and finally, the secret idiom's annihilation when threatened by its analogue, the language of madness. Polyphony, emphatic dialogism and metaphorical logic, among other techniques, bind this idiom to the text's grammar, making of the work a cohesive language and of *Tres tristes tigres* an orderly, if otherly, textual universe.

Manuel Puig at the Movies

Frances Wyers (Weber)

Movies have a powerful effect on us because the photographic reproduction of the material world is put at the service of wishes and fantasies. The impression of reality is much greater in film than in novels, plays, or figurative painting because we are plunged directly into the imaginary. A writer might have recourse to this experience of a paradoxically dreamlike reality or realistic dream by incorporating the devices of cinematographic narrative. By relying on our memories of film, a text might almost make us forget that we are reading instead of seeing. The written page might call for the projection of a visualized story complete with sound track. This particular kind of doubleness, moving back and forth between reading a book and watching an imaginary film, would contribute to and compound the duality that the esthetic experience invariably involves. The special attention that art requires means a bracketing from "non-art." As Jurij Lotman says, "art requires a two-fold experience—simultaneously forgetting that you are confronted by an imaginary event and not forgetting it." E. H. Gombrich has shown us how our pleasure in illusion rests precisely on the mind's effort in bridging the difference between art and reality, in the oscillation between two series of associations.

Manuel Puig's *El beso de la mujer araña* is built up on a series of representational and narrative dualities: the characters create—or rather reproduce, modify, embellish—in short, recreate stories, filmed stories, so that the entire circuit of artistic creation and reception is played out before us. The novel has two principal characters (a third one is very marginal): Molina, a homosexual convicted of corrupting minors, shares a prison cell with Valentín, a political activist in Buenos Aires. To pass the time, Molina

From *The Hispanic Review* 49, no. 2 (Spring 1981). © 1981 by the Trustees of the University of Pennsylvania.

recounts movies and Valentín offers comments and analyses, political and psychoanalytical. Through this sharing of ready-made dreams we come to know the characters and see them change. In the foreground, then, are two humble fabricators, and beyond them, enriched by the reader's own visual and affective memories of film, the luminous myths and stars of Hollywood.

We remember other weavers of tales. Velázquez's "The Spinners" is an elaboration on the theme of reality and representation as intricate in its composition as "Las Meninas." In the foreground, large-figured, ordinary women spin, fabricate; behind them, in another room that is also another world, where the figures are fainter, lighter, and painted in a more illusionistic manner, another spinner, Arachne, is about to meet her destruction at the hands of Athena. Velázquez, who painted ordinary scenes and people with great seriousness, here combines the everyday world and the mythical one showing how "representation as such, the imitative or descriptive side of art" can serve as "the basis of the elevated fiction of art."

One does not have to suppose that Puig had Velázquez in mind, but he too is interested in the problems of representation. He has modestly said that what gives him most pleasure is copying. "Crear no, no me interesaba para nada. Lo que me interesaba era rehacer cosas de otra época, cosas ya vistas. Recrear el momento de la infancia en que me había sentido refugiado en la sala oscura." Crucial to his art is memory, primarily the memory of dreams and fantasies turned out by the producers and marketers of a highly commercialized art. But copying, as this novel eloquently demonstrates, is by no means a mere passive recording. Gombrich tells us that copying is a process of proposing schemata that are "corrected" against the real object or objects portrayed. To attempt a "truthful record of an individual form," the artist must begin with an idea or concept. Reproduction displays a constructive or reconstructive character. The artist combines and matches. Molina's copies, of course, are representations of other representations, though the films he tells are in no way realistic; he loves whatever is far from daily life: movies about panther women and zombies, improbable adventures, melodramatic stories of love and self-sacrifice, musical comedies, even a Nazi propaganda film whose beauty, he says, must be seen to be believed. At the center of the novel's production, then, is a character, both audience and creator, who uses language to refashion works that are seen and heard. As in "The Spinners" we watch the fabricator(s) mediate between the mythical and the ordinary, illusion and reality, while shifting or "translating" from one medium to another. Ovid's tales become tapestry and then paint; movies become a spoken narrative that is one strand in a novelistic web.

Puig's statement also underlines the protective or consoling function of art, even in its mass-commodity form. It offers respite from a rigid and deadened world; in his case, from an authoritarian and "machista" culture that disdains weakness and sensitivity. The real world is displaced by something more gratifying and more humane. "Poco a poco fui cambiando los términos: lo que era la realidad pasó a ser una película clase Z en la que yo me había metido por equivocación. La realidad eran las películas, las superproducciones que llegaban de Hollywood." And within this novel, remembered movies provide Molina and Valentín with a temporary escape from the narrow limits of their prison cell. Puig's narrative impulse is born of the fertile opposition of two realms, a degraded reality and a sentimentalized fiction. The reader is made constantly aware of this duality.

Within the text the doubleness of life and art is set before us through the age-old device of the story within the story. Molina tells stories. But *Beso* is quite different from other narratives that use this technique because Molina is not the traditional first-person narrator-witness who appears in the story yet tells it. He does not address the reader but Valentín. Nor is the situation one in which a speaker and a listener are seen from the outside by a third-person narrator who allows the reader to listen in (Conrad's *Lord Jim*). The novel begins "—A ella se le ve que algo raro tiene, que no es una mujer como todas. Parece muy joven, de unos venticinco años cuanto más, una carita un poco de gata, la nariz chica, respingada." "—¿Y los ojos?" This sets the pattern of Molina's telling and Valentín's questioning and commenting. Certain other kinds of speech are, however, inserted into this pattern, and I shall discuss their function shortly.

The story-within-the-story intrigues us, not as some critics would have us believe because we are interested in the artifice itself, but because, captivated by the framing narrative, we sense that the inner one must be at least as fascinating, because we see that it intrigues our new acquaintances, the novel's characters. If Don Quijote and Sancho want to hear about Marcela and Grisóstomo, or the "curioso impertinente," we do too. But in this case the planes are reversed; the book opens directly onto one of the film stories and only later, and gradually, does the frame story piece itself together. From the very start the two speakers are turned almost entirely towards the fictions that Molina recounts. No narrator interrupts their dialogue. No third person ever intrudes his judgments, his distance, his Olympian knowledge. From what Puig has said about his first novel we know that he mistrusted the use of the Spanish language except in the form of the reproduced dialogues or interior monologues of people he knew very well ("a mí el castellano puro me hacía temblar. A lo único que me animaba era a registrar voces"). In his second and third novels (*Boquitas pintadas* and *The Buenos Aires Affair*) he used the third person. Since, however, "el carácter omnisciente de esa técnica me seguía resultando sospechoso," he limited it to an inventory of external actions. In *El beso de la mujer araña* the film stories absorb our attention so completely that we are almost put off when the two men talk about their own lives and concerns. Christian Metz tells us that "films release a mechanism of affective and perceptual participation in the spectator" much more convincing than in any of the other representational arts. Here the conjunction of the told film and the imaginary one that seems to be projected "behind" Molina's words heightens the impression of reality.

In film it is impossible to separate narration and description. The distinction can be made only in written narratives. "Cinema is," according to Metz, "the 'phenomenological' art *par excellence*, the signifier is coextensive with the whole of the significate, the spectacle its own signification." Puig manages to approximate this in a literary text. The book is full of descriptions; the details of dress and locale are lovingly recorded, but recorded by Molina, not by some extraneous narrator. We know that from Flaubert on, the novel has increasingly relied on the evocation of purely visual information, on what Alan Spiegel calls "concretized form" or "seemingly unmediated visual language" (he refers to Conrad's saying that before all else he wanted to make the reader *see*, and to Flaubert's declaration that he derived "almost voluptuous sensations from the mere act of seeing").

Puig creates a special kind of visualized form. Instead of attempting to suppress the voice of the narrator in order to present us with the flat, neutral sound of documentation, he gives us a storyteller whose tales are so enchanting that we concentrate fully on both the speaker and what he tells us, on both visual texture and the perception or interpretation of that texture. We are sucked into imaginary worlds and yet we remain aware of the process of fabulation. We glide back and forth between two kinds of representation. Molina's cinematographic editing strengthens the illusion that we are witnessing a movie and not a written narrative. Hollywood films of the thirties were designed to present events so that the spectator's mind would naturally understand. "The American film makers in this era found that if space were broken up according to the logic of the narrative, it would pass unnoticed as integral or real space. Editors learned to cut a scene into its narrative components and thus follow the line of curiosity of the audience. The film thereby mirrors the perceptual process of the spectator to such a degree that he barely notices that time and space are being fragmented, because he is concerned with the relationships between events not with the intrinsic value of the events themselves." Two examples of Molina's use of such shifts in focus:

> Él sale sin darle el gusto de decirle adónde va. Ella queda triste pero no deja que nadie se dé cuenta y se enfrasca en el trabajo para no deprimirse más. Ya en el zoológico no ha empezado todavía a hacerse de noche, ha sido un día con luz de invierno muy rara, todo parece que se destaca con más nitidez que nunca, las rejas son negras, las paredes de las jaulas de mosaico blanco, el pedregullo blanco también, y grises los árboles deshojados. Y los ojos rojo sangre de las fieras. Pero la muchacha, que se llamaba Irene, no está. Pasan los días y el muchacho no la puede olvidar, hasta que un día caminando por una avenida lujosa algo le llama la atención en la vidriera de una galería de arte.

la otra se vuelve a la casa, que es como un hotel de mujeres muy
grande, un club de mujeres, donde viven, con una pileta grande
de natación en el subsuelo. La arquitecta está muy nerviosa, por
todo lo que pasó, y esa noche al volver a su hotel donde está
prohibido que entren hombres piensa que para calmar los nervios
que tiene tan alterados lo mejor es bajar a nadar un rato. Ya es
tarde de noche y no hay absolutamente nadie en la pileta. Ahí
abajo hay vestuarios y tiene un casillero donde cuelga la ropa y
se pone la malla y salida de baño. Mientras tanto en el hotel se
abre la puerta de calle y aparece Irene.

These passages illustrate not only a filmlike editing but also the contributions of the speaker such as "ha sido un día con luz de invierno muy
rara" and the color notations for what is surely a black and white movie.
Certain kinds of information also suggest the intrusion of the speaker: "ella
queda triste pero no deja que nadie se dé cuenta." Molina's accounts almost
always contain extratextual explanations that make us aware of two simultaneous series, the story and the intervention of the storyteller. He
introduces material whose source is not specified. On the novel's first page
we are told about a woman drawing a panther in the zoo. Suddenly the
animal sees her and growls. Valentín asks if he couldn't smell her before
and Molina answers "No, porque en la jaula tiene un enorme pedazo de
carne, es lo único que puede oler." Is this "fact" established in the film by
camera close-ups or does Molina make a sensory whole on the basis of
visual memory and his own "naturalizing" strategies? Another example:

Y ella es como si le pasara una nube por los ojos, toda la expresión
de la cara se le oscurece, y dice que no es de una ciudad, ella viene
de las montañas, por ahí por Transilvania.
    —¿De dónde es Drácula?
    —Sí, esas montañas tienen bosques oscuros, donde viven las
fieras que en invierno se enloquecen de hambre y tienen que bajar
a las aldeas, a matar. Y la gente se muere de miedo, y les pone
ovejas y otros animales muertos en las puertas y hacen promesas,
para salvarse. A todo esto el muchacho quiere volver a verla.

We do not know if the "information" about the mountains, the wild animals, and the ways people try to protect themselves comes from this movie
or from other movies or from some general mythology transmitted through
"popular culture."

Through such laminations the text welds narration and description.
Molina's accounts reveal his own desires, wishes, fantasies, and consola-
tions. Indeed, at one point Valentín accuses him of inventing half of the
picture and Molina protests, "no, yo no me invento, te lo juro, pero hay
cosas que para redondearlas, que las veas como las estoy viendo yo, bueno,
de algún modo te las tengo que explicar. La casa, por ejemplo." Valentín:

"Confesá que es la casa en que te gustaría vivir a vos." Molina immediately senses that Valentín will now formulate some theory about the origin of his homosexuality ("Y ahora tengo que aguantar que me digas lo que dicen todos").

In this way Molina's personality emerges from his narratives. The reader comes to recognize the characteristics of his verbal style and the kinds of interpretations he is apt to make; he is much more present to us than the so-called "autonomous characters" in Unamuno's novels or than other storytellers in more recent works. Molina, however, insists that his accounts are accurate; he assumes that what he describes would be evident to any other viewer: "A ella se le ve que algo raro tiene" presupposes agreement. But constantly he infuses his descriptions with his own esthetic values as well as his sense of history made concrete through the changes of fashion or dress.

> Bueno, de golpe se ve un teatro bárbaro de París, de lujo, todo tapizado de terciopelo oscuro, con barrotes cromados en los palcos y escalera y barandas también siempre cromadas. Es de music-hall y hay un número musical con coristas nada más, de un cuerpo divino todas, y nunca me voy a olvidar porque de un lado están embetunadas de negro y cuando bailan tomándose de la cintura y las enfoca la cámara parecen negras, con una pollerita hecha toda de bananas, nada más, y cuando los platillos dan un golpe muestran el otro lado, y son todas rubias, y en vez de las bananas tienen unas tiritas de strass, y nada más, como un arabesco de strass.
> —¿Qué es el strass?
> —No te creo que no sepas.
> —No sé qué es.
> —Ahora está otra vez de moda, es como los brillantes, nada más que sin valor, pedacitos de vidrio que brillan, y con eso se hacen tiras, y cualquier tipo de joya falsa.

At this point the impatient listener says "no pierdas tiempo, contáme la película." Eager to get on with the story, Valentín sometimes finds Molina's descriptions too profuse. But we, the readers of the novel, see his digressions as part of the whole work; they characterize him. Characterization and plot are two sides of the same coin.

In his *Theory of the Film*, Béla Bálazs talked about microphysiognomy and microdrama, about a realm of surfaces, dramatic gestures, emotional expressions revealed not through words but directly in a world immediately accessible to visual perception. The autonomy of the senses that distinguishes modern art finds natural expression in cinema where sights and sound (musical score, for example) orchestrate meaning. In film our eyes constantly interpret. We are reminded of this by certain of Molina's statements like "ella miente," "él se da cuenta que es extranjera por el acento," or "él la trata como amiga pero se nota que en el fondo ella está enamorada de él, aunque lo disimula." These are "readings" of a visual script. At first glance Molina looks and sounds something like an omniscient narrator, but he is rather a narrator-interpreter who conveys his personal version of the story and its motivating factors.

Molina's rather naïve style points to film's affinity to folk art and to the teller's roots in a popular culture which we all share. The text opens before us a wide range of perception, interpretation, and recreation, thus heightening the illusion of a reality too rich to be contained in words, a reality that stretches beyond our descriptive powers. As Michael Polanyi says, we always can know more than we can tell. "We recognize the moods of the human face without being able to tell, except quite vaguely, by what signs we know it." So any describing or naming requires the sympathetic co-operation of the receiver. "Our message has left something behind that we could not tell, and its reception must rely on it that the person addressed will discover that which we have not been able to communicate." The text shows us the workings of this collaboration in Molina's storytelling and Valentín's questions.

Valentín is an active listener, eager to comment and theorize. At first Molina is put off by this but Valentín justifies himself: "Me gusta la película, pero es que vos te divertís contándola y por ahí también yo quiero intervenir un poco. No soy un tipo que sepa escuchar demasiado . . . y de golpe me tengo que estarte escuchando callado horas." Knowing full well that the pleasure of art is always active, he proposes that they talk about the films together. "Si te parece bien me gustaría que fuéramos comentando un poco la cosa, a medida que vos avanzas, así yo puedo descargarme un poco con algo." They discuss characters as if they were real persons and speculate about others who do not even appear in the movie. Imagination supplies a missing cast. "A mí me gustaría preguntarte como te la imaginás a la madre del tipo." Sometimes Molina corrects or modifies his own view to agree with Valentín: "Él entonces se ablanda de nuevo, y la toma en los brazos, tenías razón vos, que para él es como una nena." In other words Molina and Valentín do exactly what our teachers and literary critics always used to tell us not to do. They abstract the character from the film in order to analyze psychological features that are only hinted at and to construct a past history which would explain the feelings and actions portrayed. Valentín's psychoanalytical and political commentaries constitute a personal reality beyond the film. Characters exist in the free space of speculation.

As readers we attend both to the story and to a mode of presentation that activates a particular kind of receptive behavior. Gombrich refers us to Philostratus's biography of Apollonius of Tyana in which the hero claims that "those who look at works of painting and drawing must have the imitative faculty." Listening to Molina and Valentín we insert ourselves in the same conversation and thus participate in a game of the imagination between readers and text. This book calls for the reader's collaboration more effectively than a novel like Cortázar's *Rayuela* which makes such a point of it. Psychologists have told us that the movies individualize and isolate us; they contrast this supposed lonely anonymity to the sense of community created in a theater audience. But moviegoers know otherwise; we know how we shape the film in our conversations about it (television allows us to do this more immediately, without the restraints of the silent audience). The movie thus becomes a shared spectacle that can take on the quality of a dream told to others. In a scene in Buñuel's "The Discreet Charm of the Bourgeoisie" an army officer asks a private to recount his dream to the guests at a dinner party; the soldier's dream enthralls both the characters in the movie and the spectators watching it. A similar exchange of telling and picturing links Molina, Valentín, and the novel's readers. To the doubleness of the narrative material Puig adds the dialectics of the communicative circuit.

Since the written text refers us to another medium, its images and techniques, we might make a comparison with the so-called "transposiciones artísticas" of the Hispanic Modernist writers who evoked other texts, sculpture, paintings, myths of other times and places in order to situate their works in a museum without walls. The device, whether employed seriously or ironically (as often by Valle-Inclán), distances the figured world of the text by making apparent its constructed, secondary quality. The repeated references to this imaginary museum keep the reader from being absorbed by the story. But we do not lose ourselves in the museum either because the narrator's insistent display of similarities and divergences between his productions and the ready-made ones puts all of them in a cultural deep freeze. In such texts the narrative stance almost destroys the mimetic illusion; instead of a story we find ourselves reading a literary essay on the relations between the arts. We are scarely concerned with "what happens next?" as we follow the play of artistic allusions.

In Puig, however, everything is at the service of plot. "A mí me interesa el espectáculo, la comunicación directa con el público. El cine es inmediatamente accesible. Imagen; interés narrativo." If Molina tells movies so well it is because for Puig, as for many of us, the most captivating narrative art is film. As Metz says, film is "the supreme storyteller . . . its narrativity . . . endowed with the nine lives of a cat." So film is not a new kind of "transposición artística" but a signal to the reader that we are in the realm of pure storytelling. (Pop art in the sixties was the most recent avatar of this device. The blow-ups of comics show us the dots of the printing process and not the allure of the comic-book fantasy. The technique is at once demystifying and utilitarian; it appropriates isolated images from a different medium in order to use them as raw materials for a new work of art. Pop art is cannibalistic and ironic. Puig's is integrative and his use of film is anything but tongue in cheek.)

Because what most interests him is "the image, narrative interest," Puig recreates for us the compelling narrativity of movies. Far from being distanced from the fictions we are drawn into them. Some critics find in the author's use of popular forms an alienating effect. For example, Alicia Borinsky, writing about *La traición de Rita Hayworth*, says that "alienation is the structuring principle of the novel," not a theme but an effect. Such a view goes along with moral and esthetic judgments about the writer's materials: "Trash appears in the novel as the effect of a complex system of artifices." But "bad taste" and "trash" may also be in the eye of the beholder and in the hierarchies of a given social-economic order. Puig is simpler, more direct. "Yo no creo que el folletín y la novela policial sean géneros menores, porque son los que me gustan, por eso trato de demostrar su validez." Their tales and images are as valid as any and they are a part of the cultural heritage of most of us. It takes only the sensitive recreation of the artist to activate the reader's esthetic response. Robert Escarpit reminds us that it is not absurd to think that "las historietas de dibujos tan despreciadas, tan criticadas, merecerían un día la consideración de género literario, cuando los que hacen de ellas su lectura habitual posean los medios intelectuales y materiales necesarios, por una parte, para formular un juicio estético sobre ellas, y por otra, para lograr que este juicio se tenga en cuenta, pudiendo participar así en la vida literaria." Popular culture ("mass" culture) is the very kernel of Puig's literary works. By absorbing the moving pictures, *El beso de la mujer araña* takes on their sheen. Throughout its history, the novel has drawn on so-called "extra-literary" forms, and we see here the continuation of that tradition. Not alienation but reintegration.

Although Molina's telling of movies constitutes the bulk of the book, other forms of discourse appear. Some are variations of the principal one. Molina imagines or remembers a film he evidently does not recount; it appears in italics, interrupted by a brief dialogue between Molina and Valentín on the usefulness or uselessness of political action; it ends with the only segment in which we can read Molina's thoughts about Valentín, angry thoughts which explain the silencing of the film ("a mamá le gustó con locura y a mí también, por suerte no se la conté a este hijo de puta . . . hijo de puta y su puta mierda de revolución"). A second movie-like fiction, also in italics, appears a bit later; it seems to be a daydream in the mind of Valentín; the style, quite different from Molina's spoken style, builds on obsessively repeated nominal phrases ("una mujer europea, una mujer inteligente, una mujer hermosa, una mujer con conocimientos de política internacional, una mujer con conocimientos de marxismo"). Anaphora is the organizing principle which alternately advances the "plot" and holds together a sequence of shifting modifiers that enact the gradations of intense ambivalence: "un padre que fué ajusticiado como criminal, un padre que fue tal vez un criminal, un padre que cubre de ignominia a su hijo, un padre cuya sangre criminal corre en las venas de su hijo." The divided feelings that emerge in this pictured fantasy have to do with the hero's mother and father, Europe vs. America, racial mixing (an embodied sexual ambivalence), and, repeating and encompassing those relations, with the inevitable betrayals called forth by the class struggle in a dependent Latin America. Valentín's fantasies are compulsive and speechless, addressed to no neighbor, locked in an inner world that can only reflect, without telling, the impotence of his class ("un muchacho que abre fuego contra su propia casa, un muchacho que abre fuego contra su propia sangre").

Other kinds of discourse stand against the telling or dreaming of movies—the bureaucratic prose of the prison records and two dialogues, in play-format, between the warden and Molina. The speakers are identified only by their function in the penal system, "director" and "procesado." The reader learns that Molina has been "planted" with Valentín in order to extract information about his political activities and associates, but also that Molina has secretly reneged on this agreement. The objectivity of the theatrical form makes us sensitive to the duplicities of both warden and prisoner. But what lies behind their speech is not the depth and multiplicity of fiction or fantasy but the simple reversal of deceit.

On a different level of doubled consciousness are the fragments of stories or images in the minds of both Molina and Valentín inserted in italics throughout the second half of the novel; these private stories or thoughts never surface in dialogue. The book closes with two brief sections, the police report on Molina's release and death at the hands of Valentín's associates (we are told that Molina seemed to be prepared for this), and Valentín's feverish monologue in which fantasy mingles with film scenes and imaginary dialogue.

Still another kind of language is found in the long excerpt from the publicity service of the Tobis-Berlin studios. Whereas Molina's speech is both self-reflective ("me imagino") and attuned to the other's understanding ("¿verdad?" "¿me entendés?"), the prose of the studio advertising release is authoritarian, bent on filling up any porosity and on inhibiting interpretation or intervention. It over-explains and never invites the reader to conjure up pictures and give free reign to associations: "Leni se recuesta en el pasto y mira los ojos azul límpido de Werner, ojos de mirar plácido, confiado, puesto que están puestos en la Verdad." Value judgments are imposed through the supreme self-confidence of the anonymous writer. Good and evil are clearly identified in a prose which would have us believe that the movie camera records the "truth" of history—the evil of the Jews ("hebreos errantes portadores de la muerte. Todo ello puntualmente registrado por las cámaras"). Myth rules supreme in "documentary" film.

A long running footnote, interspersed at different moments throughout the text, presents in objective, discursive prose a survey of various theories on homosexuality, pre-Freudian and Freudian. It ends with the views of Marcuse and Norman O. Brown on sexual repression and the work of Anneli Taube on sexuality and revolution and the revolutionary non-conformism of homosexuality. Puig apparently saw no way of incorporating the theoretical material into the text itself; whatever the author's reasons, the device reinforces the sense of divergent perspectives on human behavior, counterposing different psychological interpretations to a fiction in which homosexuality is particularized and dramatized in the life of a character who, though in no way a revolutionary, comes to love his revolutionary cell-mate.

The split between drama and theory also shows up in the contrast between Molina's taste for "illusion" and Valentín's attempts to explicate the constructions of fantasy. "¿Por qué cortarme la ilusión, a mí y a vos también?" asks Molina, and Valentín answers that he must lead his companion to "un planteo más claro." When Valentín himself succumbs to illusion, when he identifies emotionally with a character or expresses his fondness for an invented person, he attributes it to "cosas raras de la imaginación." Yet for Molina, his friend's psychoanalytic analysis is "todo imaginación tuya." Valentín counters that "si vos también ponés de tu cosecha, ¿por qué no yo?" Fiction and its exegesis are equally products of the imagination. Molina tells stories; Valentín tries to fit them into the ideal scheme of his political beliefs, a scheme that makes sharp distinctions between duty and pleasure, between the future world and the present ("Está lo importante, que es la revolución social, y lo secundario que son los placeres de los sentidos"). But the two men, the "dreamer" and the "reasoner," draw closer together, they come to care for each other and to make love; two different kinds of fantasy give way to affection and sexual expression. (Early on Valentín had said "es curioso que uno no puede estar sin encariñarse con algo . . . Es . . . como si la mente segregara sentimiento, sin parar"). Near the novel's end Valentín describes Molina as the spider woman, "la mujer araña que atrapa a los hombres en su tela" ("—¡Qué lindo!" says Molina, "Eso sí me gusta"), but it is Molina who is finally caught and lets himself be killed in the web of Valentín's revolutionary dreams.

Almost throughout we find only the present tense. The fragments of imagined or remembered film are in the present tense. Valentín's scenario for a political movie is in the present. The two dialogues between warden and prisoner are in play-format, necessarily present although, since those passages refer to Molina as "el procesado," they are cut off from the rest of the text. The movies told are all in the present tense which is, after all, the tense we naturally use in describing a film. The traditional tense of prose fiction is past though readers adapt to it in such a way as to imagine the story unfolding before them. The illusion of the present grows in this text not only because of the verb tense used but because cinema itself is so immediate. Susanne Langer compared it to the dream, in which different senses are enthralled and co-mingled: "The 'dreamed reality' on the screen can move forward or backward because it is really an eternal and ubiquitous virtual present. The action of drama goes inexorably forward because it creates a future . . . the dream mode is an endless Now." In *El beso de la mujer araña* that "endless now" is the convergence and reliving of film narratives rescued from the past.

The past becomes present in memory. Although memory is central in the novel, we find the past tense only in the dry, bureaucratic prose of the day-by-day police report, here truly depersonalized and reified in describing the end of a life. Molina always tries to remember, urged on by Valentín when he falters: "Hacé memoria"; "es que la memoria me falla." At another moment, "Y a todo esto se me olvidó decirte que a la mañana ella con todo cariño siempre le pone alpiste al canario, y le cambia el agua, y el canario canta," followed by a quick shift to the ongoing text: "Y llega por fin el marido." Repeatedly we are reminded that Molina pieces together his stories from memory: "Bueno ahora lo que sigue no me acuerdo si es esa misma noche, creo que sí, la otra se vuelve a la casa."

Memory and narrative are the hallmarks of our consciousness. Indeed, our consciousness is nothing else but the tying of memory to projected actions, the creation of a vicarial self that exists not just now, but before and after. Julian Jaynes calls such projections "narratization." We create a self in time "spatialized into a journey of my days and years." That self does not really exist in the here and now except in so far as I make it part of the story I tell myself about it. Consciousness means telling stories, narrating. "It is not just our now 'analog I' that we are narratizing; it is everything else in consciousness. A stray fact is narratized to fit with some other stray fact. A child cries in the street and we narratize the event into a mental picture of a lost child and a parent searching for it." This narratization transforms the jumbled here and now into a coherent story. Metz goes so far as to say that narrative, by its very existence, suppresses the now (accounts of current life) or the here (live television coverage). "Reality does not tell stories, but memory, because it is an account, is entirely imaginative." For that reason, he tells us, "a process of unrealization ("irrealization") is at the heart of every narrative act."

This is the secret of narrative's fascination for us. Because we narratize our selves, we are ever in need of models of action. We are intrigued by all the different ways of narratizing. We want to see how others do it. We listen to gossip (a much maligned form of narration), we read novels, we go to the movies. Nowadays many of us prefer the movies to novels. Puig's book gives us both, a kind of double feature. Or rather a carefully spun web that twines the reader's memories into the fabricated lives of Molina and Valentín, a web that seems to stretch out in time and space, linking a prison cell in Buenos Aires and Velázquez and Ovid and Rita Hayworth.

But memory retrieves other things as well. Because we find in Puig's novel a common store of remembered films, we cannot help but consider the basis of that coincidence of recollection. We remember that the movie industry of this world, the First World, has produced and sold, both here and in the Third World, the movies—and the ideologies which go with them—that have conditioned or influenced all of us. The cinema is one of the most forceful modes of communication and social indoctrination, as well as a primary stimulus to the spread of a consumer mentality that is a necessary support of capitalism in our day. "Trade follows the film" was a favorite dictum of the economic expansionists of the 1920s. All Puig's novels show an obsession with the products of an advanced and often useless technology; for example, in *La traición de Rita Hayworth* and *Boquitas pintadas*, cosmetics, home appliances, the shifts of fashion in clothing, furniture, and hair styles are central topics in the dialogues and thoughts of the characters. North Americans and South Americans share the images of Donald Duck (see Dorfman and Mattlehart's excellent study of Disney comics), Rita Hayworth, the iconography of horror films, science fiction, and the western. Economic and cultural imperialism unifies the world, providing a shared cultural heritage.

Obviously we share it in different ways. The communality of the movie culture stands in sharp contrast to the economic dichotomy on which it is based, the polarization between the metropolis and the periphery of the world capitalist system. There are no political or economic analyses in the novel except in the mouth of Valentín, where often enough they sound urgent and shallow. Yet the reader is conscious throughout of the contradictions within which the work is situated and to which it points. In a dependent Argentina two men are jailed by a regime that must defend an economic system and its accompanying cultural myths with a ferocity and brutality unnecessary in the metropolis, in the "advanced industrial world." Homosexuality and militant leftist politics violate both Hollywood's moving picture code of the 1930s and 1940s and the social code of today's Argentina. Different applications of those codes are dictated by distinct historical moments: the moralistic sentimentality of the movies is an indirect repression of "aberrant" sexual and political behavior; the imprisonment and threat of torture and death is a direct repression of deviation or opposition to established order.

Against repression, the two prisoners have only their thoughts and fantasies. Yet Molina's narratives call up the creative collaboration of readers and viewers. Arachne spins an Ariadne thread that makes a path outwards, even though it is only imaginary. Molina and Valentín put the ideologies and images of Hollywood to their own use and we are invited to do likewise. We may not have seen "The Kiss of the Panther Woman" but we have seen enough movies like it to visualize sets, lighting, and camera angles. We picture a jail cell in Buenos Aires; beyond that we picture not the elements of the everyday visible reality of the First World—a middle class apartment, furniture, a woman's face—but rather those elements contained in films we remember. Although the book would have us find our materials in the movies we all know, our visual imagining is freed from the inalterable features of a given actor or set; we are allowed to cast and direct our own film. Wolfgang Iser, speaking of the disappointment readers feel on seeing a novelistic hero on screen (a person previously pictured but not seen), says that the reader's perception is simultaneously richer and more private than that of the film-viewer confined to physical perception. This novel, stimulating our movie memories, leads us back and forth between two media so that our perception becomes certainly richer and more private, but more communal as well, because we sense the continuity of movie viewers from Chicago to General Villegas. This continuity, this sharing of a culture no matter how "degraded" in the eyes of some, permits a collaborative artistic activity that retrieves and refashions works made for indoctrination and manipulation.

For Valentín, Molina is the spider woman who draws people into her web. In an alternate image he sees her in the deepest jungle trapped in the web, but then, no, the web grows out of her body. The narrative too pulls us inward and reaches out, releasing us to picture and narratize in the extendable space and time of imagination. At one point Valentín is sad because the picture has ended and he says that it is as if the characters had died. But we all know (as Unamuno keeps telling us) that they come alive again in a reader's world, say in Barcelona or Ann Arbor.

El beso de la mujer araña, like any good novel, shows the artist at work. The activity of art is set against the repressions of our society. By appropriating its power to enthrall, the artist turns the commercial product against itself. Our dreams may be prostituted by Hollywood, but ultimately our own dreaming comes to the rescue. The text shows us that an ordinary person, Molina, the reader, Puig the storyteller, can make art out of anything. Art does not exist in some special, sacred place, the creation of a mind different and better than ours. It is the inventive force in all of us.

The Transformation of Privilege
in the Work of Elena Poniatowska

Bell Gale Chevigny

"We write in Latin America to reclaim a space to discover ourselves in the presence of others, of human community—so that they may see us, so that they may love us—to form the vision of the world, to acquire some dimension—so they can't erase us so easily. We write so as not to disappear."

These remarks of Elena Poniatowska at a conference at Wellesley College in the spring of 1980 drew their coloration from her anguish over the "disappearance" of Latin Americans by political forces, but they aptly characterize her most important work as well. The evanescent or invisible, the silent or the silenced, those who elude official history or vanish from it, make the subject of the two of Poniatowska's works from which her fame and influence chiefly derive. Her testimonial novel, *Hasta no verte Jesús mío* (1969, *Until I See You, My Jesus*) presents in first-person narration the story of an adventuring peasant woman, fighter in the Mexican revolution and survivor of its inhospitable aftermath. Hitherto such characters had been presented only externally, and Poniatowska's distillation of her subject's dense and highly-colored idiom became a new literary resource. *La noche de Tlatelolco* (1970, translated as *Massacre in Mexico*) is a dramatic collage of interviews with participants in the 1968 student movement and with witnesses to the massacre of hundreds during a peaceful meeting in Mexico City, an event obfuscated by government agencies and the press alike.

A close reader of Poniatowska's work may also interpret her words at Wellesley to mean that as her writing brings Latin America into being, so has Latin America made Poniatowska emerge as a writer; the two formations are intimately related. This interpretation gains force when we consider that Poniatowska's identification with Latin America and its language

From *Latin American Literary Review* no. 26 (July–December 1985). © 1985 by *Latin American Literary Review*.

357

were both deliberate choices, the land and the tongue of her childhood being other. While her mother was Mexican and her father was Polish, both were in many important ways French. Poniatowska was born and raised in Paris. Even after the family returned to Mexico when Poniatowska was nine, only French and English were spoken at home. Most of her family still identify themselves as European. Poniatowska's choosing to cast her lot with Latin America and to write in Spanish with a highly Mexican inflection, point to a deliberateness of self-formation that is reinforced by other choices. For Poniatowska's social roots are aristocratic and her political antecedents are conservative. Generations of exile from reform and revolution in Mexico and Poland produced in France Poniatowska's parents and Poniatowska herself. Against such a background, Poniatowska's two most celebrated works stand in high relief; they delineate the dual trajectory of her career. In *Hasta no verte, Jesús mío*, she journeys to the opposite end of woman's world of social possibility and, in *La noche de Tlatelolco*, she journeys to the alternate pole of political possibility. Each journey may be seen as metaphor and impetus of the other. Like her choice of Latin America, her choosing to write of a woman with no resources but her self and of political insurgents has everything to do with her authorial self-creation.

In this connection, her rejection in 1970 of Mexico's most prestigious literary award, the Xavier Villaurrutia Prize for *La noche de Tlatelolco* takes on added significance. In an open letter to the new president, Luís Echevarría, Poniatowska asked who was going to give prizes to the dead. In 1968 Echevarría had been Minister of the Interior, responsible for all internal security forces. In Poniatowska's rejection of the prize lie two refusals: a refusal to help Echevarría symbolically dissociate himself from the massacre and treat as settled the problem raised by the students, and a refusal to identify herself with established power. She rejects the implications of closure which the awarding and accepting of such a prize chiefly signify.

It is arguable that Poniatowska's rejection of the Villaurrutia Prize was an aesthetic as well as a political gesture; in refusing closure with the massacred subjects of her book, she acknowledges the sources of her art. I will try to show that the particular force of Poniatowska's work derives from the emptiness she found in her position as a woman of privilege and from her using that position to cultivate a readiness of imagination and spirit; when this readiness met with vivid exposure to the dispossessed, she converted equivocal privilege into real strength. Such an evolution would make her links to the dispossessed a continuing necessity.

I will trace this evolution by looking first at works of hers which treat women, seeking to discern in them her progressive identification of her career as a writer. I will then look at the writings which treat more general political and social issues in an endeavor to show how her evolution as a woman informed her vision of these issues.

I

When socially privileged, Poniatowska's female characters are cursed with feverish instability. In *De noche vienes* (1979; *You Come at Night*) a volume of stories written over several years, the protagonist or narrator is almost always a woman. Sensuousness, an antic humor, and a lyrical eagerness stamp the stories which are also often edged with intimations of death or of isolation without remedy. Three of them offer patently autobiographical moments. In "Canción de cuña" (Lullaby), dedicated to "una señorita bien educada" (a well-bred young lady), Poniatowska offers a paradigmatic image of that condition. An undefined narrator speaks fancifully to a woman disqualified from experience by her very position of privilege. She is counselled to march through her day with the steps of a sergeant, to end it with prayers and fall asleep to a lullaby:

> Lovely little sparrow
> with a coral beak
> I bring you a cage
> of pure crystal.

But with lids closed she feels beneath her body the earth and its grottos, its rivers with their crossing roads, its fire and its gold, its diamonds submerged in coal and still lower the deaf beat of the lava. She feels the elements which erupt in volcanos, and without opening her eyes she hears a voice whispering the most tender declarations of passion. It is important that the explosion of repressed love and longing comes from the earth, that one subterranean realm ignites the other, that despite her crystal cage, the señorita is not out of touch with earth. Although such women are cut off from life by sex, class, and rearing, their predicament does not jail their imaginations, their sense of the possible.

In "El limbo" (Limbo), Monica, a kindred protagonist, tries to take action, carrying the unwanted infant of Rose, a housemaid, to the hospital, there trying absurdly first to get preferential treatment and then to organize a group of mothers to protest bad hospital conditions. At home, her aristocratic grandmother is repelled by the girl's raw indignation ("if you went about it à la Tolstoy, I would overlook it, but you are the most dreadful fabricator of commonplaces I have ever heard in my life"). Finally her mother half distracts her with thoughts of a dance, but Monica weeps over her supper:

> She cried because she would never make a bomb in the basement
> of her house . . . —the powder was damp beforehand—but she
> cried above all because she was Monica and no one else, because
> the death of Rose's baby was not her death and she couldn't ex-
> perience it, because she knew very well she would dance Saturday
> in her red dress, O Bahía, ay, ay, tapping with her heels on the

heart of the child, she would dance over the women whose babies fell between their legs like rotten fruit, she would dance . . . because after all, one's own life is stronger than that of the rest.

The desperation underlying this self-assertion finds only ironic relief in the experience privilege affords mature women. In them the potential of the señorita of Canción de Cuña is warped. The narrator of "El inventario" (The Inventory), the young mistress of an ancestral house being dismantled, is one of those observers on whom nothing is lost. She is closest to the servant, a woman as cold as all the years not lived in that house, as implacable as the furniture which is the essence, in this bitter sketch, of family. This servant, whose kneeling makes the narrator feel kneeled-*on* is named Ausencia (absence). *Ausencia* might as well be the name of the narrator, of the ancestral estate, of the life it affords well-bred ladies. In an amazing scene, an Aunt Veronica, who lives to command the furniture and its care, loses herself in the miasma of sweet wood smells and turpentine oils in the shop of a furniture restorer.

> Aunt Veronica stopped giving orders. I think she even forgot why she had come. She sniffed excitedly and hid behind the sound of the saw. Slowly, ever so slowly, she ran her slender fingers over the corners of a table, slipping them into this or that crack and leaving one of them inside with indescribable pleasure. Finger and cleft fit delicately together, immersed in each other, and, I don't know precisely how or why, my aunt's excitement was contagious. For the first time I was seeing something unknown and mysterious. Aunt Veronica was breathing hard, as if her body were brushing up against something alive and demanding, something inexhaustible which rose with her as her breathing filled with desire. Then she gave instructions with a vague softness, her eyes sated, and something came out of her, something not like her usual words, her swollen lips betraying her. And then I understood that furniture is made to receive our bodies or for us to touch it lovingly. Not in vain did it have laps, backs, and quilted arms to play horsey on; not in vain were the shoulders so broad, the seats so cozy. Furniture was neither virgin nor innocent; on the contrary, it was heavy with awareness. Every piece was covered with glances, with the licked corners of mouths, with chinks, with sculpted flanks. There were corners filled with a secret light and an animal force rose unmistakably from the wood.

Again, as with the Señorita and Monica, imagination and the need to give and receive love have nowhere to go. They can offer only this delicious and perverse insight into chairs. It may forever alter our casual sense of them—but is that enough? The flight of fancy here is symptom and protest against the crystal cage of class and gender. And clearly here, the crystal cage is the stronger for being made in Europe. The narrator's family, troubled by her outbursts, determine to keep her more indoors—or to send her to Europe (two versions of the same idea, as it turns out, because for the narrator Europe is an old pullman car with dusty curtains, seats of wine-colored plush, toothless fringes; it is threadbare, it smells bad).

It is tempting to read *Querido Diego, te abraza Quiela* (1978; *Dear Diego, with Hugs from Quiela*) as that sort of covert autobiography which magically fends off possible destinies; in it Poniatowska, a Pole raised in Paris and in love with Mexico, seems to measure the cage she has had to flee. For Quiela is Angelina Beloff, a Russian painter who lived in Paris ten years with Diego Rivera before he left her for Mexico promising to write for her to follow. Drawn to this woman left on history's margin, Poniatowska has taken scraps of her letters and imagined them whole, imagined what Quiela felt, recalling the cold winter when their infant son died, living through another winter trying to keep her love alive and give new birth to her painting. All fails, motherhood, painting, and love—even the letters are (and were) never answered. Poniatowska has found a *form* that follows the contours of unrequited love and pathetically enduring hope, an epistolary novel of dead letters, a duet for one instrument. What is her object? Poniatowska explores the depths of female dependency, casting her light in that abyss to banish its terrors, for herself and the rest of us. In all these works Poniatowska demystifies privileged gentility so that it can no longer seduce any woman or be honored or used as weapon of control over them. Angelina's story may exorcise a ghost of Poniatowska's, but it is not her story. For she would have been already there in Mexico, like Rivera, but making her own mural of the revolution.

A mural of revolution: that partly describes *Hasta no verte, Jesús mío.* Jesusa Palancares, the speaker of this extraordinary *novela-testimonio*, is the antithesis of Angelina Beloff, sharing with her only a will to survive and a need to break silence, to assert herself (Angelina before an indifferent man, Jesusa before an indifferent society). They have in common also Elena Poniatowska, who sees in Angelina how one kind of female sensibility feeds dependence and in Jesusa how another kind feeds an independence that is almost—though not absolutely—complete.

The *novela-testimonio* lends itself peculiarly to a sort of symbiosis in which the author explores through the presentation of the subject her or his own potential strengths and weaknesses. In Cuba, for example, Miguel Barnet sees in the black centenarian who fled slavery and fought for Cuban independence what is the stuff of independence (*Biografía de un cimarrón,* 1968, translated as *Autobiography of a Runaway Slave*); in the spunky vedette Rachel, who fought for marginal bourgeois existence in republican Cuba, he sees how inevitably her thoughts and feelings were compromised (*Canción de Rachel,* 1970; *Rachel's Song*). Barnet, who was transforming himself from a privileged bourgeois into a revolutionary clearly used these books as aspiration and catharsis, and his method, it seems to me, might also be

Poniatowska's. He writes: "*Canción de Rachel* speaks of her, of her life, just as she told it to me and just as I then told it to her." As the writers become ventriloquists for their subjects, so is the reverse true.

What we know of Poniatowska's life bears out such an interpretation. When she was brought to Mexico at the age of nine, she was placed for three years in an English school. As only French and English were spoken at home, she learned Spanish from the servants; her regard for these speakers and their world is bound up with her love for the language as they speak it. She has said that she feels that she is Mexican because this idiom comes now more definitively from within herself than any other. When she first saw Jesusa, she was working as a journalist, interviewing important figures daily for the Mexican newspaper *Novedades*, but she was more attracted to Jesusa than to anyone else, she says, "because she spoke so coarsely, so vehemently—I loved her language—because she was always fighting and because she is very short like me." Jesusa did not want to be interviewed, however, and Poniatowska for some time visited Jesusa once a week in what appears a tacit understanding of an equalizing ritual. Jesusa would set her to the task of taking her thirteen hens, a little leash tied to a leg of each, out into the sun. Gradually Jesusa began to talk of her life, and after Poniatowska's period of initiation, reverted to the coarse and figurative speech that had so drawn the writer. Poniatowska says that sometimes Jesusa did not want to talk—Jesusa needed to fix a drain, get fish for the cat, take a nap—but that she learned things from these encounters as well ("when we took a nap I found wonderful sayings embroidered on her pillows.") The ensuing creative process was symbiotic. Although Poniatowska has said she made up details, her deference to Jesusa is patent in everything she says about her. For example, in speaking of Jesusa's wish to die alone, Poniatowska said, "She needs no one, but I need her, and perhaps others need her."

The passage to which she refers ends the book and expresses as powerfully as any Jesusa's poignant self-sufficiency, in which the crucial relationships of her life form a part, and the mysteries of society, nature, and death are acknowledged and integrated:

> It's really hard not dying when you're supposed to. When I don't feel well I keep my door shut—I spend days on end barricaded in. At most I'll boil some tea or gruel or something like that. But I don't go out stirring up trouble and nobody comes to my door. One day I'll be all twisted up in here and my door will be bolted shut. That's why I ask God to let me die up in the hills. If he answered my prayers, all I'd need would be the strength to climb to the top. But since He doesn't give scorpions wings, who knows? That's what I pray for, but if He says no . . . then let His will be done. I'd like to go back and die where I used to gallivant about when I was young and sit under a tree over there, let the buzzards

surround me, and that's it. Then if anyone came looking for me I'd be up there happy as can be flying in the buzzards' guts. Otherwise your neighbors come and peer in while you're dying, to see how horrible you look, all twisted and tangled and bloated, with your legs splayed and your mouth gaping and your eyes popped out. Some life, to die like that! That's why I bolt myself in. Casimira, the landlady, will have to break the door down to get me when I'm stiff as a board and starting to stink. They'll have to drag me out. But no one's going to come in and see if this or that . . . no one. It'll be just God and me. That's why I don't want to die in Mexico City. No. I want to be on a hillside or in a ditch like my father, who died under a tree in an open field. God give me the strength to get there! It's a good thing to know the hour of your death. I ask Him to let me know so I can get ready, and be on my way. I'll become fodder for the animals out there. For the coyotes, like Pedro, my husband. It's not that I don't want to be buried, but who's going to bury me? They'll say: "Praise the Lord, that old mule's finally bit the dust." I don't think people are good. Only Jesus Christ, but I never met him. And my father, who I never knew if he loved me or not. But here on earth, how can you expect people to be good? Now fuck off. Go away. Let me sleep.

Here and throughout this book, Poniatowska's language becomes much more definitively Mexican than it has been in earlier work. She exploits the resources of Mexican campesino speech, making a thick brew of its errors and earthiness, its domesticating diminutives and strong images. For a European, she has said, writing is a way of belonging to an adopted country, and in Jesusa's speech there is no trace of the old Pullman.

Much of the power of *Hasta no verte* lies in the surprise it plays on official history, which has left Jesusa out of its accounting. Poniatowska not only adds her in, but gives us a Jesusa who recasts it wholly. That's one surprise. Another is that Jesusa gains prodigious authority from a range of activities on which society confers no authority. She is by turns a motherless child, a punching-bag for her father, a servant to her stepmothers, neglected by all but the revolutionary soldier husband Pedro who likes to beat her; the pension she is promised after riding and fighting in the revolution, even leading Pedro's troops after his death, is later denied her; she lives as a vagrant, picking up work when she can in laundries, restaurants, factories, bars, fine houses; a haunter of vestibules and corners of the houses of others, she becomes also a handy street-brawler and a protector, willing or not, of superfluous children and dogs. Orphaned, victimized, deluded, fired, cheated, beaten, and often jailed, Jesusa tells with unflagging zest of language how she fought back on each occasion; she delivers judgments as fresh as they are convincing on Mexican heroes, politics in general, marriage, the relation of men to women, of humans to the earth, to evil, and to death. How is this alchemy worked? I believe that Jesusa offered the anecdotal skeleton, that the styles of discourse are essentially hers, but that it was Poniatowska who heard what she said, who broke through the noise of disordered reminiscence (another kind of silence), and *saw* the strength hidden in weakness. Human gain buried in human loss, the diamond in the coal, these are the strengths granted woman in general that women artists are especially gifted in releasing. For a woman, writing is converting her loss into gain. And as Barnet's writing moves him from the bourgeoisie to the revolution, Poniatowska's moves her from the implosions of the haut-bourgeois—self-serenades, orgasms with furniture, dead letters—to the explosions of Jesusa. At the same time, the imaginative attention to things which distinguished the idle high-born ladies is now present in Jesusa's scrupulously detailed accounts of her work.

Poniatowska does not romanticize Jesusa's strength. When her difficulties seem overwhelming, Jesusa seeks consolation, from time to time, in confusion, in the mystifying light of the Obras Espirituales. This spiritualist sect, with its creed of reincarnation, plays on her naiveté, and her desire for a more fulfilling past and future and for a justification for her current suffering. Jesusa's engagement with the revolution responded in part to her quest for family, for community and for meaning; when it was foiled she sought them in individual terms, in the specious family and opportunistic meanings of the sect. In a sense, in her later work, Poniatowska makes Jesusa's quest her own.

Hasta no verte Jesús mío appears to have led Poniatowska past the impasse of adolescent Monica who felt, even while despising her own life, that it was stronger than that of the rest. Finding Jesusa's strength, she could begin to cultivate her own.

II

Listening to Jesusa in order to break the silence about her side of Mexican history prepared Poniatowska to understand the silence at the heart of contemporary Mexican political life. Profoundly shaken by the events of 1968, she brought to them and subsequent political events imaginative resources developed in her evolving treatment of women. These include an uncanny ear and eye, and a vigilance for opportunities to identify the self in action and to locate the values of intimacy and family in a community which dominates no one.

In the summer of 1968 an escalating series of student demonstrations culminated in the call for a huge and public dialogue with the government. This last demand reveals the students' acumen with regard to the PRI, the Institutionalized Revolutionary Party—the bitter paradox of that name had become insufferable. The students saw that with its monolithic dominance of politics, of the economy, of the labor unions and of the press, the PRI offered less than a monologue—in effect, silence. The chants of the student movement were thus important but the dialogues they initiated were more so. The students of UNAM, the National Autonomous University of Mexico, bridged the chasms of class in making common cause with the students of the National Polytechnical Institute; women began to share positions of leadership with men; and their lightning meetings and imaginative street theatre began to tell in working-class districts.

The form of Poniatowska's chronicle *Massacre in Mexico* captures this excitement over dialogue itself. Extracts of the testimony of students and faculty leaders, other participants, workers, passersby, journalists, critics and informers are interwoven with leaflets, slogans, and official statements. Poniatowska edits and orchestrates, but adding no words to those of her sources, makes history seem to flow from the voices of the participants and gives us an uncanny experience of the simultaneous spontaneity and inevitability of events. And the feeling of immediacy is balanced by the historical sense of those who saw this movement against the backdrop of the railroad strike of 1958, the killing of Zapatista peasant organizer Ruben Jaramillo in 1962, and the repression of the doctors' movement in 1964. The euphoria of the movement at high tide is epitomized in the students' occupation of UNAM. They converted the university into a model or alternate society, an exemplary state, a self-proclaimed "territorio libre de Mexico." Poniatowska later wrote, with her characteristic susceptibility to dislocated domesticity, the university now "really functioned like an *alma mater*, an amorous mother who sheltered and covered with her protecting wings." Students fell asleep, she reports, to the cradle song of the mimeograph machine.

The army's occupation of the free territory of UNAM on September 18 and later of the Polytechnical Institute brought an end to this dialogue. Although the students had promised not to interfere with the Olympic games scheduled to open October 12, the government grew frantic at the prospect of menace to this star in its crown, conclusive proof of Mexico's alleged superiority in the Hispanic world. The horror of Tlatelolco represents the loss of the trophy of world opinion in the effort to secure it. On October 2, while 10,000 people gathered to hear speeches from the National Strike Committee at the Tlatelolco housing unit, 5,000 soldiers and police surrounded the square. Flares in the sky gave the signal to open fire, and those who tried to flee were met by columns approaching in a pincer play. Over 2,000 were jailed, many of them for years. The dead proved harder to count; after careful investigation the British newspaper *The Guardian* offered what may be the estimate: 325. On October 3, the Mexican press estimated variously 20 to 26 dead.

The press's irresponsibility was backed by deepened government silence as it refused to investigate the massacre. Poniatowska, who defines literature as "un largo grito" (a long shout), constructed her narrative to amplify her protest against silence: the book's first part recounts the events before and after October 2; the second is the prolonged cry of anguish and rage which is the telling of the night of Tlatelolco.

Significantly, Poniatowska differs in her interpretation of that night from her good friend Octavio Paz, the poet and critic who in 1968 resigned his ambassadorial post in India in protest and also wrote the introduction to the United States edition of *Massacre in Mexico*. In his analysis, *The Other Mexico: A Critique of the Pyramid* (1972), he argues that the "invisible history" of the country, the survival in modern Mexico of Aztec hierarchic domination and ritual sacrifice, explains the bloodletting. As Poniatowska challenges the publicists who claim for Mexico an enlightenment that excepts it from the rest of Latin America, so she disputes the fatalism which for Paz distinguishes his land.

Without making nationalist claims, Poniatowska discerns exceptional persons and moments which animate belief in change. Of the several massive marches on the Zocalo in 1968, she gives her sharpest attention in *Massacre in Mexico* to the silent march of September 13, which happened also to be the largest. On that date some four hundred thousand participants marched in silence, some with their mouths taped shut—a silence than ran counter to the fiesta-like abandon said to be the quintessence of Mexican public events. This show of the capacity for change, more than any other march, brought onlookers off the benches and into the ranks. What engages Poniatowska, I believe, is the power of silence transformed into silence *heard*: as such it is the emblem of her later work, and gives her most recent book its title.

Hearkening to the nuances of silence, speaking for those who answer "no one" to the peremptory question, "who goes there?"—these are the disciplines that govern Poniatowska's five chronicles in *Fuerte es el silencio* (*Silence Is Strong*, 1980). Briefly, the first of these sketches the children who fly in and out of the capital selling chiclets or Kleenex and make their cardboard homes in the hundreds of "lost cities" surrounding it. She calls them "ángeles de la ciudad" (angels of the city) in a metaphoric strategy which makes visible those whom Mexico's miraculous "progress" brought into being and requires its proper citizens to ignore. We may recall the imaginative ingenuity by which Aunt Veronica transformed the furniture, but imagination is now and forever out of the house, discerning the vitality not of possessions but of the human dispossessed. The second chronicle traces the effects of 1968 in the next ten years, showing especially how Echevarría's attempt to co-opt the student movement without addressing its aims ended by reproducing 1968 in other forms; the picture of the PRI as a tightly-knit, self-indulgent family living in a blind fortress is fixed.

Poniatowska may have lived in crystal cages, but she never belonged to the PRI fortress. Through Jesusa's revolution and the students' brigades, she had glimpsed the promise of better "families." Her remaining three chronicles are linked by her exploration of alternative organizations, the fragmentary "families" that emerged after 1968. Echevarría's equivocal liberalization worked both to politicize oppressed groups and to generate a stronger, more autonomous military. As student protests gave way to urban guerilla activities and peasant land seizures, Mexico learned practices—especially disappearance and torture—it had censured in dictatorships. In a third chronicle, Poniatowska tries through interviews to grasp the motives of jailed guerillas. In a fourth, the diary of a 1978 hunger strike, she describes the four-day bivouac in the Cathedral of the capital by 83 mothers of disappeared persons. While this makeshift family arouses more of Poniatowska's sympathy than the guerillas do, she remains ambivalent. She appears to be groping toward a new form, as she permits her own troubled musings and fantasies to break the surface of documentary reportage. We feel again Monica's malaise over the tug between one's own life and that of others.

Far more successful as formal synthesis and as provocation to the reader is the last chronicle, the best in the book. While Poniatowska the interviewer disappears, she is perhaps more present than in any other work. The passionate force of this narrative derives partly from its temporary fulfillment of strivings expressed in other works. Here families of dispossessed "angels" find their home by making their own city in Morelos, the Colonia Rubén Jaramillo, (named for the assassinated peasant leader), as hundreds of Mexican groups were doing in the mid-seventies. The desire of the well-bred señorita to slip her cage and make her home in the earth here combines with Jesusa's search for a true revolutionary family. Indeed the populist idiom and spirit of this chronicle is more than any other work like that of *Hasta no verte Jesús mío*.

The extraordinary figure, Florencio Medrano, who leads the group, bears some resemblance to the better known Ruben Jaramillo, and other peasant leaders Genaro Vásquez Rojas and Lucio Cabañas killed in the seventies. Called "El Guëro" (the blond), he combines the intimate knowledge of recipes and remedies of a Jesusa with the charisma of a Zapata and a rare compassion. Using a strategy he developed during a visit to China, he led families in 1973 to form a commune on *ejido* land outside Cuernavaca as the first in a contemplated series of land seizures which would culminate in armed revolution.

In a series of vignettes, Poniatowska offers moments which suggest the range and complexity of her vision. El Guëro spurs thirty apprehensive families to leave Cuernavaca's slums for unused collective land; giving each a lot on condition they build their shanty in seventy-two hours and joining them in the work, he makes their very fear productive. In the name of Rubén Jaramillo, he then persuades them to divide their lots for latecomers. The guerilla patriarch inspires students to participate on his "Red Sundays" in construction of hospital, roads, and plumbing in the "first free territory in America" since UNAM. In perhaps the most powerful episode, when the terrified governor comes to promise the settlers light, water, all services, El Guëro shouts down their cheering, seeing in it evidence of their interiorized humiliation: "Don't thank them!" he insists. "The earth is yours, by legitimate right, you're not orphans, you're Mexicans, here you were sown and here you must grow. . . . The light is yours, the water is yours, yours because they expelled you, don't go on being grateful, you have nothing to thank anyone for—nothing, nothing, *nothing!*—except yourselves and your own work." And mysteriously his exhausted aspect gives those close to him an intuition of his death; it is as if the very absolutism of his claims for human justice promises to consume him.

Other episodes present growing contradictions. Overconfident, El Guëro tolerates suspected spies. Scheming about collecting arms, he neglects the Colonia, imperiling it. In long evenings of talk with women, he persuades them to speak their bitterness, and to assume responsibility but he becomes possessively jealous of Elena, his secretary and confidante. Finally he flees, with Elena, from the encroachment of the police, hiding in the mountains to pursue his revolutionary dream, now reduced to kidnappings. Although his followers cannot believe the news of his death, they lose their revolutionary verve. The chronicle ends with Poniatowska in 1980 watching a conventional beauty queen pageant, in which the children, without understanding it intone a song about the ultimate victory of Florencio Medrano. Only one in the crowd recalls Medrano and invites Elena Poniatowska to hear his story.

No other work of hers has more concentrated force and complexity than this. An explanation lies partly in her giving the intrinsically dramatic facts and particularity and emotional coloring of her own. As she could learn of only fragments of Medrano, she made him, she says, the way she wanted him to be. Wholly fictional is the sheltered and faded Elena who comes as a secretary to help and writes at nights about "El Guëro" and revolution, who learns the limitations of his scheme from the Colonia's thoughtful schoolteacher, and yet flees with him as his lover. As her name and her literary vocation broadly hint, she is a figure of autobiographical fantasy. But as Poniatowska both includes and goes beyond "Elena," this chronicle as a whole both embodies Mexican romanticism and points to its limits. All Poniatowska's work discloses reservations about the romanticism it depicts and expresses; here her irony also analyzes it. The chronicle epitomizes Poniatowska's literary project: in naming and cultivating the lives and rights of others, the writer is naming, integrating herself in ever more complex ways. One's own life is stronger but imaginative familiarity with others gives meaning to its strength.

This compelling fable makes us perceive the shape of a terrible historical impasse. Damned by their own state, the people of the Colonia would never have fought without the fearless leadership of a Medrano, but that very revolutionary zeal dictated that he sacrifice the Colonia and abandon it to its fate. Poniatowska both recognizes the heroic efforts of the marginated to move toward the center of their own lives, to displace the heartless state and—when those efforts fail—she salvages the drama to seek out the issues which Medrano's successors must begin by addressing. Medrano sweeps through the lives of the people like a wind, moving them forward and going beyond them. What are the alternatives? The practical wisdom of the teacher (whom Poniatowska *did* meet) could not command the loyalty of the people as El Guëro's daring could. With all that militates against them, can the people learn to define, and gain the strength to pursue, their own largest interest?

Poniatowska's work elicits such questions because her mixture of modes of knowing—investigative and empathetic—and of ways of telling—novelistic, testimonial, journalistic and confessional—engage the feelings and curiosity of the reader: the reader is implicated in pursuit of the story beyond its formal ending. To express it another way, Poniatowska herself practices a kind of alchemy related to that by which Jesusa derived great authority from her strong response to abuse. In Poniatowska's case an empty privilege is transformed into a full one—the fullest privilege is responsibility—but in the process, privilege and responsibility are stripped of their established social meanings. If Poniatowska's self-presentation is modest, her effect is not: for the reader, the conventional privilege is diminished as responsibility is enlarged.

Rhetorics of the Plot

Ronald Christ

At almost the exact midpoint of Mario Vargas Llosa's novel *Pantaleón y las visitadoras* (1973) a police official explains to the book's hero the behavior of some religious fanatics, saying: "One for all and all for one, like in *The Three Musketeers*, that movie with Cantinflas. Did you see that?" Casual as the remark may seem to be, it nevertheless encapsulates the novel by evoking the mock, comic hero and the intertwined destinies of the book's characters as well as their spiritual, sexual, militaristic and domestic endeavors that become mirror images of one another. "One for all and all for one" even applies to the novel's narrative technique, which insistently makes one event, one action, one character stand for all the others. Perhaps most significantly, the quotation reminds us to think of the novel in comparison with a film, and it is, after all, the cinematic technique of *Pantaleón* that singularly distinguishes it. So epitomizing is the policeman's statement that I want to use it as the epigraph for what I have to say about the book, and I hope you will forgive my somehow having gotten started without having put my epigraph where it belongs: at the beginning, before everything else. To begin with a beginning, then:

> *"One for all and all for one, like in* The Three Musketeers, *that movie with Cantinflas. Did you see that?"*
> —VARGAS LLOSA, *Pantaleón y las visitadoras*

Predating the invention of movies, literature always has been implicated in the development of this technological art form. Sergei Eisenstein

From *World Literature Today* 52, no. 1 (Winter 1978). © 1978 by the University of Oklahoma Press.

was among the first theoreticians of film to analyze the relation of the two mediums, and in his book *Film Form* he knowingly traced the development of much that seems technically peculiar to movies back to literary master-works—the device he called "cross montage," for example, to Flaubert's *Madame Bovary*. After Eisenstein, critics have customarily analyzed how various literary forms and contents find their way into movies, so we have many books with titles like *Novels into Film* and many university courses based on the comparison of preexisting novels with their subsequent movie counterparts. Only rarely have critics chosen to show the reverse pattern: how movies have infiltrated our contemporary literature.

The consequence has been debilitating, to say the least, with *The Waste Land*, for instance, still largely unperceived as cinematic montage owing as much to the newborn art of movies as to the equally contemporary rhythms of jazz. Narrowing my focus to Latin American literature of our day, I see the lack of such recognition as just as great. Almost all the so-called Boom writers have written about movies; some have written for movies, and many have consciously reflected movies in their work.

Among the latter, Guillermo Cabrera Infante, an important film critic, sometimes narrates with verbs like "to come in for a close-up" and "to pan," while Manuel Puig's characters, like those of Cabrera Infante, know Hollywood films better than most North Americans do. Yet when we stop to reflect on these two authors, we should be reluctant to say that their novels are *cinematographic*, a word reserved for books like Carlos Fuentes's recent *Terra Nostra*, where, in Margaret Sayers Peden's translation, we read these words of the novel's famous character, Julian:

> Why would you tell us only what we already know, without re-vealing what we still do not know? Why would you describe to us only this time and this space without all the invisible times and spaces our time contains? why, in short, would you content your-self with the painful dribble of the sequential when your pen offers you the fullness of the simultaneous? I choose my word well, Chronicler, and I say: content yourself. Discontented, you will aspire to simultaneity of times, spaces, and events, because men resign themselves to that patient dribble that drains their lives, they have scarcely forgotten their birth when it is time to confront their death; you, on the other hand, have decided to suffer, to fly in pursuit of the impossible on the wings of your unique freedom, that of your pen, though still bound to the earth by the chains of accursed reality that imprisons, reduces, weakens, and levels all things.

Another version of "All for one and one for all," *Terra Nostra* confronts the reader with quickly shifting points of view, rapid shuttles in time and space within the narrative itself rather than in the characters' minds, giving to prose something of the camera's sweep and something of the movie editor's abrupt splicing and chopping. (An abruptness, you will remember, that charmed Borges when he saw the early films of von Sternberg; an abruptness he incorporated into his own narrative style.) Whereas the works of Puig and Cabrera Infante pertain to movies by way of content and evocation, Fuentes's method—and that of Vargas Llosa as well—belongs to movie art by way of technique, by way of manipulating the movement of movement.

Let me explain. What characterizes movies is precisely movement, from which they get their first and most down-to-earth name. But this primary movement is of one kind, while the art of movie making depends on others. Consequently, there are at least three orders of movement in movies: (1) the primary movement of people and things projected on the screen; (2) the movement of the camera in filming those people and things for projecting on the screen; and (3) the movement imposed upon the previous two in the process of editing the film, a movement that is commonly called *montage.* Your average moviegoer only recognizes the first and so in recounting a movie does not express how the work would have been any different had it been presented, say, in a novel. In such perfect confluence with the technical medium, this moviegoer confuses the latter movements recorded on film and converted into meaning by sutures in that record with the movements of his own eye witnessing that film, so that for him, the work of the director, the cameraman and the editor is entirely invisible. Substituting his own physiological process for their craft, he eliminates their function in recounting what he thinks he has seen.

Something similar happens with readers of cinematic fiction who will recount the so-called plot of a book without ever acknowledging the cinematic process conveying that plot. Therefore, when we speak of cinematographic fiction, it is important to emphasize that we are talking almost exclusively about the third order of movement: the analytic *editing* of dialogue and action. (And notice how we say *cinematic* or *cinematographic* fiction—never *movie* fiction—to distinguish between the primary movement of gesture, dialogue and physical action, which we are not talking about, and the esthetic deployment of that primary movement by the author, who replaces director, cameraman and editor in focusing our attention in an intermittent, flashing mode. A corollary of this distinction is that while the cineastes have had to borrow the word *auteur* to confer proper status on the controlling intelligence of film, literati may have to borrow the cinematic sense of *editor* to acknowledge properly the analytic function of the cinematic novelist, whose work appears to postdate the composition of his narrative, just as the film editor's work postdates the writing of the script and the actual filming.) When we are talking about fiction's cinematic quality, then, we are talking about one thing and one thing only: the way the narrator *edits* action and dialogue in accordance with principles of movie montage, which, as Eisenstein argues (in Jay Leyda's translation), are characterized "By collision. By the conflict of two pieces in opposition to each

other. By conflict. By Collision." Everything else that pertains to movies—
if that term designates film works, early and late, based simply on the
ability to project movement (or its ironic absence, as in Warhol's *Sleep* and
Eat—has very little to do with cinema or cinematographic fiction, if this
phrase designates works whose principal esthetic basis is the manipulation
of primary movement in some evocative or significative way. Unless there
is planned movement of the primary movement in a discontinuous, multiple way, unless the narrative material is edited in some way akin to film
montage, we will not recognize fiction as potentially cinematographic, no
matter when it was written.

Pantaleón y las visitadoras is a cinematographic novel relying on two
principal types of montage to order the primary movement it presents. That
primary movement is itself dual, concerning, on the one hand, a dutiful
soldier, Pantaleón Pantoja, who has been put in charge of developing a
secret corps of prostitutes to service the Peruvian armed forces in the jungle
and, on the other hand, an evangelist who raises bands of followers called
"brothers" and "sisters" in a religious sect whose principal rite is a reen-
actment of the crucifixion. These two heroes, who are simultaneous in the
fictive world created by the text but who never come into direct contact
within the time or space referred to by that text, become equally burden-
some to their society, represented publicly and politically by the armed
forces, privately and domestically by the Pantoja family. As the novel pro-
gresses, the followers of these two organizers assume greater and greater
resemblances in devoutly adoring their respective leaders. At the novel's
climax the religious leader, Brother Francisco, has himself crucified, and
the Army forcibly represses his sect while Pantaleón comparably martyrs
himself by publicly admitting the Army's secret backing for his prostitutes,
with the consequence that he is removed from office, reprimanded and
sent to cool his heels in the hinterlands. Thus the parallel careers of these
too-dutiful leaders, respectively concerned with body and with soul, spiral
downward until all they have accomplished is ruined and what remains is
a hypocritically purged military and the cozy domesticity of the Pantoja
family. As almost always in comedy, the conclusion restores society to the
status quo of its existence before the eruption of the idea promoting the
comic disruption in the first place.

Even this sketchy, unjust summary of *Pantaleón*, which has the making
of a contemporary morality movie, reveals how the work descends from
nineteenth-century novels of multiple plots whose resolution always demands that apparently parallel lines eventually intersect or converge, a
convergence that Vargas Llosa preserves and extends in many ways. For
instance, he gives Pantaleón's mother and the prostitutes' leader the same
name (Leonor), and he inflicts physical suffering on Pantaleón that is explicitly termed a "martyrdom," comparable to Brother Francisco's crucifixion—even though in Panta's case it is an ignoble martyrdom of
hemorrhoids. But such are the respective idioms of body and soul in a

novel dramatizing a dual sense of *passion*, a novel whose comic contrasts only reinforce the bisecting construction of its constituent stories.

The primary movement of this bisection is presented on the page in a special, edited way so as to create parallelism in the reader's perception of the movement. Whereas Dickens might have kept his two narratives functioning in alternating chapters or sections, as he did in *Bleak House*, Vargas Llosa analyzes his dual narrative into smaller, discontinuous fragments that collide and alternate more rapidly. Laying this analyzed narrative matter side by side in a manner reflecting the parallel linearity of the printed page, Vargas Llosa creates a simultaneity of place and time where in fact none exists. We read the fragments sequentially but we simultaneously perceive their organization—one after or on top of the other on the page—as similar to the organization of an orchestral score, where we read in a dual direction that is both vertical and horizontal. Analogously, the arrangement also reminds the reader of what André Bazin in his book *What Is Cinema?* terms "parallel montage," as when "Griffith succeeded in conveying a sense of the simultaneity of two actions taking place at a geographical distance by means of alternating shots from each." Following a comparable procedure, Vargas Llosa's prose intentionally does not "flow": it collides and divides into fractions contriving a simultaneity on the page, reflecting neither the actual geography nor chronology of the incidents but instead an imposed, stylized order created through analytic editing and expressed by no words in the text. In ordering action this way, Vargas Llosa furthers Joyce's technique in the "Wandering Rocks" episode of *Ulysses*, which may have developed from nineteenth-century multiple plots. The qualitative difference between Vargas Llosa and Dickens (or Balzac for that matter) on this point is fundamentally quantitative, depending on the rhythm of the analytic conflict, which is usually much faster, more staccato in Vargas Llosa.

This paralleling of nonparallel action is present in *Pantaleón* starting from the first page, which begins with a domestic conversation between Panta and his wife, who are discussing where he will be sent next. The dialogue is offered with stage directions, almost like a script, and the sequence is discontinuous, as though made up of several short "takes" as their topic varies from Panta's assignment to Pocha's reading about Brother Francisco's symbolic crucifixion. The novel's first sequence of these "takes"—a matter of no more than a page and a half—is terminated with Panta's mother saying:

> "I wish they'd send us to Chiclayo again," Mother Leonor brushes the crumbs onto a plate and removes the tablecloth. "After all, we were so well off there, isn't that so? To me, the main thing is that they don't make us move too far from the coast. Get going, child. Good luck. You have my blessing."

This speech immediately and without typographical interruption collides with the non sequitur of an excerpt from one of Brother Francisco's services:

"In the name of the Father and the Holy Ghost and the Son WHO DIED ON THE CROSS," Brother Francisco raises his eyes to the night, lowers his eyes to the torches. "My hands are tied, the wood is an offering, make the sign of the cross for me."

In turn, this excerpt collides with a passage that conflicts with it as a non sequitur but depends from the action implied by the initial conversation: " 'Colonel López López is waiting for me, Miss,' Captain Pantaleón Pantoja says."

From even this brief chunk of the novel, you can see how the paratactic, conflictual montage of dialogue coordinates in parallel status the life of Pantaleón and Brother Francisco at the same time that it establishes a corollary parallelism of the domestic, spiritual and military situation in the novel. So, whether we are speaking as rhetoricians, cineastes or readers of the nineteenth-century novel, the word *parallel* describes the fundamental way that Vargas Llosa moves the action in his novel, complexly justifying the motto "All for one and one for all."

These parallel relations and many, many others like them constitute the basic plot of *Pantaleón;* and they are arranged—*plotted* in Aristotle's sense of the word—so that we can theoretically distinguish between Vargas Llosa's function as *author*—the function of composing parallel fictions in what is really a cruciform pattern—and his function as *editor*, the function of analyzing that pattern into the atomistic units or "takes." As such, the parallelism of the basic plot can be grasped only as an abstraction, a conception, an ideal armature for what is happening in the book. The discovery of this parallelism out of the apparent confusion with which the book begins is conducted through dialogue and actions of the characters themselves; the parallel plotting is implied by the words of the text itself. At this primary stage, plot is nowhere else visible in *Pantaleón*, yet its requirements are so exacting that some characters, whom Henry James would call *ficelles*, are sacrificed to its operation. The editing of this primary material, however, *is* visible—almost palpable to the reader—in the jolts and collisions of the text's articulation. Pointing to this cinematic editing on the page, we point, most often, to an empty spot between paragraphs. As in movies, manipulative montage, to the extent that it is visible at all, is visible *between* shots. Looking for the counterpart of that montage in fiction demands studying the breaks, the blank spaces—between the chapters of a Dickens or Balzac novel, for instance. In fact, to find montage in fiction, we must literally learn to read between the lines.

Beginning to do that, I showed how the first element of Vargas Llosa's cinematic construction in *Pantaleón* is *parallelism* or, to use the rhetorician's term for it, *balance.* Created by nothing in the text so much as by subdividing the scenes and then juxtaposing the fragments without connective transitions, this balance suspends narrative elements in an ongoing, comparative relation. Examining the apparent non sequiturs constituting the analyzed units of this relation, we see that they are in fact closely connected. That is, discontinuous and nonsequential according to standard principles of prose rhetoric and narrative procedure, they are progressive and cumulative according to the rhetoric of montage, which classifies their configuration as *dialectic* or *montage by attraction*.

Turning our attention, then, from the discontinuous fragments themselves and focusing on the editing of their relation, we see that Vargas Llosa is linking one episode to another by means of an image that not only connects but actually reinforces, extends and even creates a significance where none existed in the discrete, sequential fragments themselves. Such dialectical montage or editing by attraction—as in the attraction of opposed electrical charges—associates images from different episodes and, as Eisenstein argued, out of the energy of such collision, as in an internal combustion engine, achieves the dynamic force to drive the work forward. We can see the process when Mother Leonor says "You have my blessing" at the end of the first sequence, which immediately *attracts* the image of Brother Francisco giving his blessing to his spiritual children, saying "In the name of the Father," et cetera. The attraction here is obvious: even though in different times, places and circumstances, both Mother Leonor and Brother Francisco are giving blessings; but from the collision of Brother Francisco's benediction with Pantaleón's bland statement, "Colonel López López is waiting for me, Miss," we come to recognize Panta as someone with his hands metaphorically tied, as someone being offered up as a sacrifice, someone requiring the blessing of others as he begins his new undertaking. In other words, while Mother Leonor's and Brother Francisco's blessings attract each other because they are congruent—a consequence that will be conducted to its logical conclusion in the primary movement of the book—Brother Francisco's benediction and plea attracts Panta's simple declaration in such a way as to affect the latter, changing its resonance and implication. Test what I am saying. Try imagining Panta's simple statement "Colonel López López is waiting for me, Miss" without reading Brother Francisco's "My hands are tied, the wood is an offering, make the sign of the cross for me" directly before it. No, Panta's line is radically altered by the juxtaposition, which is to say that an *idea* of benediction *arises*, as Eisenstein would say, out of the collision of these seemingly unrelated episodes, and this idea, created by the author's analysis of textual content but not actually expressed in that text itself, is what gives the narrative its impetus.

No need to stress any theoretical novelty in the practice of Vargas Llosa's fiction at this point. I have suggested that it draws upon Eisenstein, Dickens, without, of course, meaning to suggest any such thing as influence. More appropriately, we should try to see how the analytic technique he practices accords with fundamental and therefore ever-new modes of human perception: with that of the impressionist painters who rediscovered that one color laid next to another in abrupt alternation affects the individual color radically; with that of Artistotle, of course, when he observed the phenomenon in watching dyers build up color in a fabric; with that of André Bresson in his *Notes on Cinematography* when he writes, "An image must be transformed by contrast with other images, as is a color by contrast with other colors. A blue is not the same blue beside a green, a yellow, a red. No art without transformation." Bresson's word *transformation* is crucial here because it clears our way to seeing that it is not with the change of subject matter—whether it be that of still life or naturalistic fiction—that the impressionist, the cinematographic artist concerns himself, but with the transformation of that matter by his deployment of it. Or, as Erwin Panofsky wrote about movies: "To restylize reality prior to tackling it amounts to dodging the problem. The problem is to manipulate and shoot unstylized reality in such a way that the result has style."

Precisely: Vargas Llosa's result has style, although it is a style often lost on those who do not see the transformation achieved through montage. No new subject matter in Vargas Llosa, then; rather, a new way of *editing* narrative through analytic decomposition that forces a new way of reading as it simultaneously recomposes our perceptions in what may be called, following Eisenstein again, the artist's *idea*. One truth about the expression of this idea is that, in spite of what some readers say, there is no difficulty in Vargas Llosa's text or in the text's meaning. None at all. What is difficult is reeducating our way of reading—and of summarizing too. The plot of *Pantaleón* can no more be reduced to hypotactic statements in linear sequence than the plot of *Potemkin*.

The variety of effects that Vargas Llosa extracts from montage range from the outright comic to the didactic. Comic collisions occur, for example, when in one line a character refers to the prostitutes, saying "Here come the girls," and in the very next line Mother Leonor appears, describing her entrance at one of Brother Francisco's meetings: "I should have known as soon as I got out of the taxi." Montage by attraction is also used to elucidate the complicated parallelism that might otherwise require the reader's intense analysis. For example, in the middle of the novel Mother Leonor is describing her horrifying vision of a small boy crucified at one of Brother Francisco's meetings, and this description is immediately followed by an Army chaplain's denouncing Panta's pint-sized assistant who distributes pornographic literature to the men waiting in line to use the prostitutes. Mother Leonor says: "Oh, God, Pochita, when I'm on my deathbed, I'll still see that poor little angel," which is immediately followed by "In other words, it wasn't just that one time or the initiative of that fiendish dwarf." Linking the crucified child and the runtish pimp cuts both ways in creating the meaning of their respective functions. Emphasizing their disparity, montage creates their identicality.

In order to examine more precisely the hooks and eyes of this montage, I am going to revert to a vocabulary older than that of the movies, to the vocabulary of classical rhetoric. Doing so may not be as outdated as it seems, since structuralism, with all its monstrous inventions, has also summoned the older terminology.

Looking at the first two episodes I alluded to—the respective blessings of Mother Leonor and Brother Francisco—we can see that the point of convergence is an abstract one in the space between paragraphs: a typographical synapse. Considering the two episodes rhetorically, however, we can see that the very last element in Mother Leonor's speech—"You have my blessing"—corresponds to the very first element in Brother Francisco's: "In the name of the Father," et cetera. Neither cinematically nor rhetorically are the elements identical; but their image, what they allude to, is, and that is what unites them. Now, in rhetoric there is a term that refers to the linking of the end of one syntactical structure to the beginning of the next by repeating an element, and this term, *anadiplosis,* may be just ugly enough and just arcane enough to appeal even to structuralist ardor. The roots of the word in Greek reveal the action it names: "doubled back." Looked at from the point of view of Eisenstein's theory of montage, Vargas Llosa's plot is impelled forward by a series of collisions; looked at from the point of view of rhetoric, the plot is ironically halted by a series of doublings back. Simultaneous driving forward and doubling back are, in fact, the principal actions imposed on the characters by Vargas Llosa's rhetoric of plot. No matter how busy these people—and the people in *Conversation in the Cathedral* too—may be in scurrying about for their independent and collective motives, the invisible action of the plot is constantly neutralizing those activites into a version of the status quo, the satiric meaning that is abundantly evident in the rhetoric itself.

The rhetorical figure of *anastrophe,* which refers to an inversion or unusual arrangement of words, retards the forward drive of the novel from its very first lines, where we discover an inverted subject and verb, which is quite typical of this novel where proper-noun subjects come at the end of narrative descriptions, far removed from the verbs they command. The retrograde action of this suspended sentence structure is again fully apparent in the etymology of the word *anastrophe,* which derives from Greek roots meaning "turned back." Every time Vargas Llosa uses this anastrophic construction (and he uses it in almost every description of a character's action in the book), he literally "turns back" the movement of the prose. Vargas Llosa has said that he instituted his shift in syntax for the sake of rhythm as well as to energize the usually inert portions of narration. With this in mind, we can see once more how energy and novelty in the text are carefully counterpoised by the rearguard action of rhetoric. However down-to-earth the characters in *Pantaleón* may talk, the figure of anastrophe in the descriptions framing that talk always calls attention to the artfully rhetorical nature of the work, alerting us to the critical countermovement within the book, reminding us to distinguish Vargas Llosa's recuperation of impersonal, public modes of discourse from ones in the fiction of Puig that predates *Pantaleón* in exploring ways to express intensely private sentiment and consciousness through vulgarly public and impersonal modes.

Turning back the drive of Vargas Llosa's prose, anastrophe places heavy emphasis on the ends of syntactical units, but Vargas Llosa also uses comparable rhetorical figures to emphasize the beginnings of such units for similar purposes. In many of the military dispatches, for example, Vargas Llosa uses a form of parallel grammatical construction to string together like grammatical elements—subordinate clauses in this instance. For the sake of brevity, I will quote only the beginnings of successive constructions from a typical report, one at the head of chapter 4, which begins:

> Rear Admiral Pedro G. Carrillo, Chief of the River Forces for the Amazon,
>
> CONSIDERING:
> I. That he has received a request from Captain PA (Quartermaster) Pantaleón Pantoja. . . .
> II. That the aforementioned request has the authorization of the Department of Administration. . . .
> III. That the administration of the Navy has considered the request for assistance favorably. . . .
> IV. That, having been consulted in the matter. . . .

Notice how each parallel clause of the dispatch begins with the same word: *that*. In contrast to the device of anadiplosis, which links syntactical units head to tail, Vargas Llosa is here using the figure of *anaphora*, the repetition of the same word or phrase at the beginning of successive syntactical structures. Now the Greek roots of the word *anaphora* again reveal exactly what the device accomplishes: the etymological meaning of *anaphora* is "a carrying back," and that is what this device does here. No matter how neatly the numbered paragraphs of these dispatches march down the page in a sequential parade, the repeated word *that* constantly reins them in, carrying the reader back to the starting verb. In contrast to the genuine analytics of Vargas Llosa's montage, these analytics of bureaucracy parody an institution's paralysis masked by intentioned activity. Even Pantaleón, benign embodiment of the analytic cast he shares in such deep but contrasting ways with his author, is in fact the analysand in a situation where he believes himself to be the analyst. The anaphora underscoring this motionless motion is something like the physical gesture of certain characters who, at moments of great excitement, jump up and down on the spot. Anaphora, like jumping up and down in one spot, is a fancy way of getting nowhere fast.

If anaphora characterizes the military mode of discourse in *Pantaleón*, it also marks the religious, for Brother Francisco, widely recognized rhetorician that he is, makes good use of the venerable device, as this typical quotation from one of his sermons shows:

With wood you make the fire that cooks your food, with wood you build the house where you live . . . With wood you make the harpoon that catches the fish.

Even the unnamed narrator resorts to anaphora for comic effect, as when we are given the description of Pantaleón's nightmare on the night of 16–17 August 1966:

But, meticulous, uncorruptible, punctual Lieutenant Pantoja is crossing the open area . . . But, rigid, Lieutenant Pantoja is now overseeing the distribution of breakfast to the soldiers . . . But now Lieutenant Pantoja, standing still as a statue, watches how some soldiers are unloading sacks of provisions from the truck . . . But now Lieutenant Pantoja is carefully tasting the contents of the kitchen kettles.

Permeating the verbal texture of the book so completely, anaphora also provides the fundamental armature for the ten chapters of the book's parallel narrative of body and soul. The first chapter begins with Pochita waking Panta by saying: "Wake up, Panta! It's eight o'clock already." Followed by her reading about Brother Francisco in the newspaper, this awakening gives way to the breakfast episode I have already quoted, intercut with Brother Francisco's benediction, itself interrupted by the entrance of Panta at the military headquarters where his superiors await him. Turning to chapter 5, the book's keystone, we read: "Wake up, Panta! It's six o'clock already," and the line is followed by a similar sequence involving Brother Francisco and the Army command. Chapter 10, which occurs after Brother Francisco's death, varies the pattern slightly by opening with Mother Leonor saying "Ah, you're already up, son," but goes on to follow through with a meeting between Panta and his superior officers. This anaphoric pattern of beginning the first, fifth and tenth chapters with the same image is brought to a fitting close when in the novel's last paragraph Pocha says once more and for the last time: "Panta, wake up, it's five o'clock already." The anaphora linking the chapters in this selected example is thus topped off by the figure of *epanalepsis*, which signifies the repetition at a structure's end of the same word or phrase with which it began. Once more the Greek roots of the term are illuminating: the etymological meaning of epanalepsis is "repetition" or "resumption."

And it is precisely with that—a repetition that is a resumption—that *Pantaleón* closes. The crying needs of the body and the soul have been silenced; the old order has been restored; neither the sexual nor the spiritual revolution has taken place. Although driven head on by the piston of filmic montage, Panta and the other characters have been constantly turned back by rhetorical devices of the plot. This contradiction of movement in place is evident in gesture throughout the book, as when a character's described actions get ahead of his dialogue only to be bridled back by the dialogue's coming in out of chronological sequence and creating the effect of an out-of-sync voice-over in a film. Here, for example, the radio announcer Sinchi, one of the loudest rhetoricians in the novel, is virtually tripping over his own lines as we read the staccato, almost Morse-code description of his being thrown out of Panta's office and into the river, only to read, *after* that, his lines as he is dragged from the office followed by the trailing off of his voice as he is dunked:

> "Listen here, don't cut your throat, don't be irresponsible, I'm a superman in Iquitos," Sinchi waves his arms, shoves, defends himself, slips, backs off, disappears, is soaked. "Let go of me! What does this mean! Listen, you're going to regret this, Pantoja, I came to help you. I'm your frien-n-n-d."

A narrative equivalent to playback in the movies or television, this innovation in prose backtracks the plot just as much as the anaphora at the chapter heads. In combination, all these devices show that Panta has not even been running in place throughout the novel. No, he's been running backwards, not even keeping up with the Red Queen, as Pocha first gets him up at 8:00 in chapter 1, next at 6:00 in chapter 5 and finally—gloomily and frigidly—at 5:00 in chapter 10.

Unlike old schoolroom clocks that registered time by moving one minute backward and then two minutes forward, the plot of *Pantaleón*, through the finely conflicting rhetorics of cinematography and prose, moves one step ahead and then one step back in order to register no movement whatsoever. Balance, apparent from the very beginning of this parallel plot—"All for one and one for all"—is what the book achieves in the process of reestablishing stasis, which is what comedy usually achieves. The beauty here is that the meaning of this balance, this stasis, is *critical* in every sense of the word, from the esthetic to the political. Yet, in the tradition of the very best literature, this total criticism is never explicitly stated. Instead, it is incarnate in the very form—the plot, the rhetoric—of the novel itself. Having developed his rhetorics of plot, Vargas Llosa has solved a problem of writing revolutionary literature without sounding like nothing more (or less) than a revolutionary. Vargas Llosa has turned mere "rhetoric" into the action of his plot, which is, has been and ever will be the substance of narrative fiction.

Beyond Magic Realism

Roger Kaplan

The Peruvian novelist Mario Vargas Llosa is known both for his interest in politics and for his realistic narratives, as contrasted with the experimental forms favored by a number of his Latin American contemporaries. In his most recent novel, *The War of the End of the World*, Vargas Llosa has expressed his views on the dynamics of his continent's politics more forthrightly than in any of his previous books. He has done so, moreover, by recreating with scrupulous precision a real historical event, and has even dedicated his work to the author of the primary source on this event, which carried within itself many if not most of the central elements, the important issues, of twentieth-century Latin American politics.

That Vargas Llosa should have been willing to go back nearly a hundred years to this event and ask himself how it resembles the contemporary scene is in itself an act of intellectual courage in a continent that has all too often dealt with its problems by denying them. It is altogether fitting that his courage should have been rewarded with so fine a novel.

The event in question was a rebellion in 1896–97 against the young Brazilian republic which had been established five years earlier upon the abdication of Pedro II. It was a fanatically, hopelessly anti-republican action led by a messianic figure by the name of Antônio Vicente Mendes Maciel, an itinerant preacher among the poorest of the poor, who referred to himself as *o Conselheiro*, the Counselor.

Four expeditions were required to subdue the Conselheiro insurrection, which was based in a locale called Canudos in the impoverished drought-stricken backlands of the province of Bahia. Accompanying the last such expedition as a journalist was a retired military engineer named Euclides da Cunha. The report he wrote, *Os Sertões* ("The Backlands,"

From *Commentary* 78, no. 6 (December 1984). © 1984 by the American Jewish Committee.

published in 1903; the 1944 English translation by Samuel Putnam, *Rebellion in the Backlands*, is still in print), was recognized immediately as a literary achievement of the first rank, one that would put Brazil, and indeed Latin America, on the world literary map. But comparatively little attention was paid to the work's prodigious importance as a political and historical document. The events it described in epic detail seem to have been outside the comprehension of a generation, in Brazil and beyond, that had not yet been shocked by world war and revolution into a somber appreciation of the nature of modern politics.

Not that the Brazilians had any difficulty understanding that the Conselheiro insurrection was a deadly serious affair. The first two reinforced police expeditions, in October and January 1896–97, were routed by the *jagunços* (backlanders), who evidently had passed from rural banditry into militant anti-republican utopianism under the leadership of the mad preacher, a figure who until then had been dismissed by Church and civil authorities alike as just another starving charismatic heretic. The political and military leaders in São Paulo now became deeply alarmed. Some of the most notorious bandits in the backlands had placed themselves in the service of the Counselor; whole families were going to Canudos; and the *jagunços* were expropriating arms and provisions from Bahia's great plantations, on which the slaves had been freed less than ten years earlier.

It became apparent that the *jagunços*, who proclaimed that the republic was the work of Satan and the Antichrist, posed a new type of military challenge to the state. Fighting irregularly, sustaining enormous losses relative to the numbers of soldiers they killed, they were driven less by territorial than by religio-political motives. Against them, Colonel Moreira Cesar, the aging hero of Brazilian republicanism, took command of a third expedition led by the crack troops of his own Seventh Regiment and supported by artillery. Moreira Cesar was every inch a political solider. His friends organized riots in São Paulo aimed at "monarchists" who, they claimed, were responsible for the rebellion and were plotting to prevent Brazil from achieving its great destiny; the idea was that Moreira would return in triumph, seize state power, and establish a "Jacobin" republic.

But Moreira Cesar was killed before Canudos on March 3. Having driven his regiment back, the *jagunços* were now convinced the millennium was at hand. The government called a national mobilization; under the command of General Arthur Oscar, six brigades in two columns, supported by the heaviest artillery available, laid siege to Canudos. Antônio Conselheiro died of starvation in September, but, fantastically, the city held out until October. Out of a population of 20,000 or more, 300 women, old men, and children surrendered and were executed. Among the *jagunço* combatants, there were no survivors. Wrote da Cunha:

> Canudos did not surrender. The only case of its kind in history,
> it held out to the last man. Conquered inch by inch, in the literal

meaning of the words, it fell on October 5. . . . There were only four of them left: an old man, two other full-grown men, and a child, facing a furiously raging army of five thousand soldiers.

Had Euclides da Cunha lived (born in 1866, he was assassinated in 1909), he might have revised his text to read: "The first case of its kind." In his genius, he understood that what he had witnessed was not just a weird New World throwback to the medieval uprisings of feverish millenarians. To be sure, the Counselor and his followers were gripped by the kinds of eschatological doctrines profoundly etched in the Christian mind and which the Church, whether Catholic or Protestant, had repressed only with the greatest difficulty well into the Reformation. They believed that King Sebastian, a sixteenth-century Portuguese monarch who had disappeared in Africa and into apocalyptic legend, would return after they had won their victory over the satanic republic, in anticipation of the second coming of Christ. Yet whereas it could be said that medieval millenarians were only demanding immediately what Church doctrine asserted would happen sooner or later anyway, modern millenarianism represented an attack on the modern world itself, which had rejected millenarianism. Couched either in the language of religion or the language of revolution (or both), it could not coexist with secular, pluralistic, democratic political cultures

Euclides da Cunha understood this as well as did Moreira Cesar, but he also saw in Canudos a profound tragedy for the modern spirit. Unlike Moreira, a would-be military dictator who regarded the *jagunços* as vermin and Antônio Conselheiro as a brazen insurgent in the pay of the monarchists (and the British empire), da Cunha saw in the whole affair evidence of the republic's shortcomings, of its arrogance, its lack of humanity. He believed that the republic, with whose fundamental objectives of political order and economic development he was of course in agreement, was spoiling its own enterprise by neglecting the backlands and treating its inhabitants like savages. Da Cunha was a man of science; he had no romantic illusions about Canudos; but he demanded a similar realism about the virtues of the republic. "What we had to face here," he wrote, "was the unlooked-for resurrection, under arms, of an old society, a dead society, galvanized into life by a madman." And then he added:

Caught up in the sweep of modern ideas, we abruptly mounted the ladder, leaving behind us in their centuries-old semi-darkness a third of our people in the heart of our country. Deluded by a civilization which came to us second-hand . . . and shunning, in our revolutionary zeal, the slightest compromise with the exigencies of our own national interests, we merely succeeded in deepening the contrast between our mode of life and that of our rude native sons, who were more alien to us in this land of ours than were the immigrants who came from Europe.

The significance of Canudos, and of da Cunha's *Os Sertões*, to Brazil and to Latin America as a whole, is apparent from even so cursory a summary. The clash between the coast, with its great capitals and human ferment, and the appallingly poor interior; and the conflict between the modernizing middle classes, who have often relied on the military both for personal advancement and social progress, and the inheritors of the land, aristocrats as well as bondsmen, represent some of the key givens of Latin American history. They also represent issues that have never been resolved satisfactorily. In Vargas Llosa's Peru, for example, the virtual exclusion of the vast majority of the people, who are Indians, from the political and economic life of the country, has been an urgent national problem at least since the 1920s.

Latin Americans have been cursed by political and cultural traditions that have been founded on, and maintained by, lies. They are not unique in this respect, but their case is an extreme one, as their own greatest writers (not to speak of Simón Bolívar, the Liberator) have admitted. The flat denial of the racial problem in countries like Mexico and Brazil is one instance. The habit of blaming their own political instability on the scheming of the United States—or, in an earlier era, on that of the British empire—is another. The contrasting honesty of da Cunha, who sought in the geographic, the political, even the racial realities of Brazil the answers to the problems raised by the crisis he had witnessed, is unusual in Latin American letters— and so is the fact that now, Mario Vargas Llosa has dedicated his novel to Euclides da Cunha, and made wholesale use of the Brazilian's material.

This aspect of *The War of the End of the World* has received scant, if any, attention from reviewers, but it is of the utmost significance, and for more than one reason. In his work, Vargas Llosa generally has avoided the paraphernalia of tricks going under the name of "magic realism"—the deliberate obscurities, linguistic games, and irrational narrative devices, not to speak of the arbitrary use of time and space and the introduction of fantasy, which have done so much damage to Latin American writing (while delighting European literary critics and their North American fellow-travelers). It is worth speculating, indeed, that the cultivation of literary difficulty by Latin American novelists may be less a consequence of modernist literary aspiration than a result of knowing that one's writing is based on false premises. A novelist who feels compelled to say that Yankee imperialism is responsible for his country's problems, and yet who knows perfectly well that this is untrue, is, understandably, going to seek refuge in stylistic games and literary cover-ups. Thus the renewal of a link with da Cunha is important not only because of the burning urgency of the great Brazilian's theme—the false and violently destructive alternatives of revolution and militarism—but also because it suggests a desire on the part of Vargas Llosa to return to a clear, lucid, and honest tradition in Latin American writing.

Vargas Llosa's work has long expressed a profound concern with the relationship between public and private corruption. He has always been interested in politics and, rather exceptionally for a Latin American writer, has championed liberal democracy while denouncing the bigotry of those who think Latin countries must choose between Marxist utopianism and rightist dictatorship. He refuses the patronizing advice of foreigners like Guenter Grass who seek a revolutionary heaven anywhere but in their own countries, and has written (in connection with Grass, who has suggested that Latin Americans follow the example of the Sandinistas) that "an intellectual who believes that freedom is necessary and possible for his own country cannot decide that it is a superfluous luxury for others."

When Mario Vargas Llosa was growing up (he was born in 1936), freedom and democracy were anything but superfluous luxuries in Peru. The country was ruled by a military dictator named Manuel Amoretti Odría. Most Peruvian intellectuals regarded Odría's soldiers as footstools of the rich, who relied on them to stave off APRA—the Popular American Revolutionary Association—which was considered well enough organized and sufficiently popular to be the sure winner in a genuinely democratic election. But other, Left-leaning intellectuals believed that APRA represented a fascist (later, Peronist) trend, and the party was thoroughly hated by the Communists.

All this is the background of Vargas Llosa's *Conversation in the Cathedral* (1970), a novel about a rich man and his estranged son during the Odría period that fairly drips with bitterness. Powerful as it is, however, in its examination of greed and cowardice and lust, it is also marked by the influence of Lima's San Marcos University, where the intellectual atmosphere was (and remains) heavily tainted by Marxists and Communists (in the party sense). This leads to certain distortions, notably a failure to consider that the Odría period could be understood differently from the way it is described here. Actually, General Odría was benign and even benevolent by the standards of his time, which was the time of Juan Peron in Argentina and Perez Jiménez in Venezuela (among others). These are not the standards self-respecting Latin Americans would want to be held to, and they should not be, but the dictatorial regime that emerges from an uninformed reading of *Conversation in the Cathedral* does not really correspond to Peru under General Odría, who relinquished power on the exact day he said he would, having fulfilled his mission, as he saw it, of restoring order and legality.

Before *Conversation in the Cathedral*, Vargas Llosa wrote a partly autobiographical novel about boys in a military academy, *The Time of the Hero* (1962), which was bleak and brutal enough to be burned by the officers of the academy the author had attended, and *The Green House* (1965), which is about the jungle just outside the city, or the animal within. Both these novels won important literary prizes and were widely acclaimed, and both have much to say about the way people are exploited by others more powerful than they. The trouble with them, especially the second, is that the author's control over his material often seems tenuous and sometimes seems to disappear entirely. In the burlesque and farcical *Captain Pantoja and the Special Service* (1973), which concerns the attempt by army officers to relieve the frustrations of enlisted men in a remote garrison, the very idea of authorial control seems to be caricatured.

After the loosening-up (if that is the term) of *Pantoja*, and the touching good humor of *Aunt Julia and the Scriptwriter* (1977; English translation, 1982), the latter more evidently autobiographical than any of his books since *The Time of the Hero* (and much funnier), Vargas Llosa was, it seems, ready for the most deeply political novel of his career, *The War of the End of the World*. When coming to the latest book by a very good writer, one frequently gets the impression that all his previous work has been a preparation. This is certainly the case here, but it is equally difficult not to see in the events of Vargas Llosa's lifetime a series of inducements to write about Canudos.

In his youth, he had lived through oligarchism and military dictatorship. Thereafter, APRA was kept out of power in Peru by a rather unholy alliance among the liberal Fernando Belaúnde Terry, the Communists, and the army. But in 1968 the soldiers took over again under the leadership of General Juan Velasco Alvarado, and this time they covered their public-relations flank with leftist, Third Worldist rhetoric, which for a time they took so seriously that even Fidel Castro began revising his views on the revolutionary potential of military officials. For Vargas Llosa, who like most of the young men of his time and place had supported the Castro revolution, the experience was instructive.

Velasco bought Soviet arms, and with these there arrived military advisers and political operatives; Communists were also placed in charge of government programs. The situation in Peru thus became, and remains, somewhat reminiscent of Italy (although APRA is still the strongest force on the Left). The Velasco period, which lasted until 1980 when Belaúnde Terry's Acción Popular, now situated on the Center-Right rather than the Center-Left, came back to power, corresponds in some ways to the Italian "opening to the Left" of the early 1960s, the net result of which was a huge increase of Communist influence at all levels. In Peru, the intelligentsia is overwhelmingly Marxist. The mayor of Lima (as of Rome) is a Communist. And, almost in imitation of the Italian Red Brigades, Peruvian extremists calling themselves *Sendero Luminoso* ("Shining Path") or Túpac Amaru (after an eighteenth-century Inca who led a rebellion against the colonial government in Peru) have picked up the gun, hoping to provoke a military repression while at the same time castigating the official (or "democratic") Left for going legal.

In the midst of this rising national crisis—perhaps one should say, this recurring national crisis—Vargas Llosa has come to settle on centrist, democratic pluralism as the best hope for his country and his continent. Despite certain old habits of mind with regard to the United States—he condemned the rescue invasion of Grenada last year, even while he recognized that it was welcomed by the Grenadians—what he wants for his country is, in all but name, the North American model. He even helped to found a pro-democracy, pro-free-market organization called the Institute for Liberty and Democracy—and was, in fact, offered the premiership of Peru by Belaúnde Terry (which he declined on the ground that his influence and that of the Institute would be more effective if exercised privately).

The War of the End of the World can be read as a rejection of the false choice between revolution, which at some level is always based on mille-narianism, and military dictatorship. Like the great classic from which it is explicitly drawn, it is a profound indictment of the lies that have brought Latin American countries repeatedly to the awful dilemma of such false choices.

Vargas Llosa despises the violent apocalypticism of the "theology of liberation"—the most influential theoretical treatise on which was written by the Peruvian priest, Gustavo Gutierrez—just as he hates the brutal and arbitrary simplicities of political soldiers. Violent religious leaders, brutal soldiers, men willing and able to make other men die for lies, are the villains of *The War of the End of the World*. Vargas Llosa's Moreira Cesar, like da Cunha's, is a ruthless and unscrupulously ambitious soldier who comes by his nickname—the Throatcutter—honestly. He is driven by his notion of what a properly regimented Brazil will be; as much a "Jacobin" for his times as Velasco was to be in Peru of the 1970s, he cannot believe his enormous country is big enough to hold both him and the (fictional) Baron of Canabrava, a great Bahia landowner and the leader of the conservative Autonomist party, which stands for traditional order and authority. As Moreira tells the Baron:

> There are people up in arms here who are refusing to accept the republic. Objectively, these people are the instruments of those who, like yourself, have accepted the republic the better to betray it. . . . There is now a civilian president, a party rule that divides and paralyzes the country. . . . [The army will] bring about na-tional unity . . . create a strong, modern country. We are going to remove the obstacles in the way, I promise you: Canudos, you, the English merchants, whoever blocks our path.

As for the rebellious Counselor and his acolytes, they do not express themselves quite so brutally; theirs is a rhetorical tradition based on such concepts as love and generosity and self-sacrifice. What is clear, however, is that their rhetoric is undercut by their deeds—in the quest for spiritual salvation, they are leading thousands to their doom.

Revolutionary utopians, irresponsible militarists—Vargas Llosa also has a score to settle with Third World groupies who (*à la* Guenter Grass) think they know what is best for other people's countries. The type does not appear in da Cunha's book, of course, but in Vargas Llosa's novel there is a European anarchist who goes by the assumed name Galileo Gall and who finds, in the rebels of the backlands, allies, however deluded by priestly superstitions, in the war against bourgeois order. About a third of the narrative is in fact carried by Gall's obsessive and pathetic (and fatal) attempt to be wherever the revolutionary action is.

The focus then shifts—against a canvas thick with the blood, dust, anguish, and hope of the Canudos war—to the story of Jurema, an illiterate backlander whom Gall has raped and widowed (characteristically, while trying to make himself useful to the international working class). Jurema, a witness to the sound and fury of Canudos, is a good novelistic idea, though she is not as vividly drawn as the major actors in the great drama.

As for the conservative Baron of Canabrava, he expresses a kind of mature wisdom about the world that contrasts favorably with the twin fanaticisms that engulf his province—but he too comes in for his share of the author's skepticism. Near the end of the story, he rapes his wife's maid, a rather mean touch intended perhaps to underline the point that no one gains anything from revolution, repression, and war. Or perhaps there is something of a sentimental streak in Mario Vargas Llosa. In the last line of the book the fiercest of the *jagunço* leaders is touched by an angel and goes up to heaven. We are, then, also meant to think that whereas men of power will always use their power—in little despicable ways if they cannot use it in great despicable ways—poor men will die fighting, in hope and glory, for what they believe.

These notes, variously jarring and pleasing, are sounded several times in the course of the novel; whether they serve it well or mar it depends on how intelligently and lucidly one feels Vargas Llosa has presented his complex theme. He has, in any event, like Euclides da Cunha before him, given us a powerful epic of the notions men have of themselves and their destiny, and of the terrible, destructive lengths they will go to realize them. He has also pointed the way toward a renewal in Latin American politics of the democratic faith, and in Latin American literature of a related and all but forgotten tradition of honest lucidity.

Mass Media Images of the Puertorriqueña in *La guaracha del Macho Camacho*

Stacey Schlau

In the five years since its first publication in 1976, Luis Rafael Sánchez's novel, *La guaracha del Macho Camacho*, has had at least seven editions. The English translation has just been published. Many newspaper articles, reviews, and interviews with the author have been written. The *Revista de Estudios Hispánicos* put out a special issue on Sánchez. Despite its apparently difficult structure and linguistic experimentation, the book has achieved enormous success from the beginning. One clue to understanding its popularity lies in the author's parodic use of mass media language. This includes disc jockeys' speeches, announcers' sales pitches, and billboard messages, familiar to most readers. Of course, the fictitious song that gives the novel its title, and at the same time serves as a unifying structural and thematic motif, dominates the other sounds as the ultimate parody of mass media-produced false reality. Certainly, the mass media as an instrument of acculturation—and ultimately indoctrination—permeates the text on almost every level, including characterization. Indeed, Sánchez's condemnation of his island's sociopolitical situation emerges in the fragmentary portrayal of a few characters' lives. In the case of female characters, his criticism springs from the ironic use of sex-role stereotyping, to a large extent.

The insistent and continuous drone of announcers' voices, the *guaracha* always playing in the background, and the Senator Vicente Reinosa's political speeches all symbolize the alienation and lack of meaning flowing from publicity language in contemporary human relationships. The four principal characters—La China Hereje, Graciela, Vicente, and Benny—appear throughout the novel waiting and alone. The only communication between two characters takes place between La Madre and doña Chon in the park. The rest is empty discourse: the song in a continuous recurring pattern, clichés, and publicity stunts. Colonized reality in this novel finally means alienation in its deepest and most modern sense. Mass media's presence forms and ultimately distorts all the characters' realities, particularly Graciela's and La China Hereje's.

La China Hereje is the first character we meet in the novel. After "Advertencia," in which Sánchez uses announcer's patter to ironically point out the contrast between the guaracha's illusory "La vida es una cosa fenomenal" and the characters' lives, the opening sequence reveals La China Hereje (although without mentioning her name), waiting for Vicente Reinosa's arrival. The narrator speaks to the readers, telling them to turn around and look at her. He describes her body in such a way as to suggest a movie camera's caress. The language is laden with pornographic implications; the reader becomes a *voyeur*:

> Si se vuelven ahora, recatadas la vuelta y la mirada, la verán esperar sentada, una calma o la sombra de una calma atravesándola. Cara de ausente tiene, cara de víveme y tócame, las piernas cruzadas en cruz. . . . Cuerpo de desconcierto tiene cuerpo de ay deja eso, ¿ven?, cuerpo que ella sienta, tiende y amontona en un sofá . . .

The camara's eye is then used to charge the visual representation with political significance: "el sol cumple aquí una vendetta impía, mancha el pellejo, emputece la sangre, borrasca el sentido: aquí en Puerto Rico, colonia sucesiva de dos imperios e isla del Archipélago de las Antillas." Thus, from the first page of the novel, a stereotypically sensual *mulata* becomes the symbol of a colonized, even prostituted, Puerto Rico. This kind of imagery is used throughtout.

The opening sequence ends with a reference to La China Hereje's shower half an hour earlier, during which the *guaracha* was playing, and in which we saw "guaracha y mujer matrimoniados por una agitación soberana." Thus the *guaracha* is seen as dominating her life; she is united with it as if in matrimony. Also, her movements prefigure her identification with Iris Chacón, developed later. La China Hereje sometimes works as a prostitute. She uses her affair with Vicente to get money for her son and her consumer needs. "El Nene" needs medical care and food; she needs new linoleum in her kitchen.

Her most important need, however, is a direct result of media promotion; she wants to be Iris Chacón. Of course, Iris Chacón has become the national sex symbol of Puerto Rico. (Cover stories have appeared about her in all the popular magazines, and she has a television variety show.) She is, claims the narrator, "la oferta suprema de una erótica nacional: envidia de culiguardadas, fantasía masturbante de treceañeros, sueño cachondo de varones, razón de la bellaquería realenga." The implications of this kind of sex-stereotyping for La China Hereje and the novel's development of an inauthentic reality are clear. From the mass media, she has learned exactly what she must do and be to achieve success and recognition. La China Hereje digests this information, and transforms it into the central fantasy of her life.

Most of Iris Chacón's description in this sequence occurs in La China Hereje's voice. The long paragraph undergoes a change in point of view in the middle, to first person singular. La China Hereje begins by complaining that Vicente has caused her to miss Iris Chacón's show twice, because he detained her too long. She continues:

> Y las dos veces que me he perdido el show de Iris Chacón en la televisión me han comentado que a Iris Chacón le pusieron la cámara en la barriga y esa mujer parece que se iba romper de tanto que se meneaba, como si fuera una batidora eléctrica. . . . Es que . . . tiene un salero entre cuero y carne: . . . Vuelta y vuelta: ay deja eso . . .

Thus, the television camera's lens, narrated by La China Hereje, again causes the reader to focus on an overt, stereotypical sexuality, based on close observation and exploitation of a fragmented female body. La China Hereje aspires to this kind of reifying sexuality. Her thoughts pass from Iris Chacón to herself: "El Viejo me pasa los pesos pero los pesos me los pasa quien yo quiera que me los pase . . . Señal de que yo no estoy buena porque estoy buenísima."

In a later interior monologue, La China Hereje explains why she admires Iris Chacón so much: "Porque Iris Chacón no está sujeta más que al impulso bailotero de su cuerpo." Thus, her vision of freedom resides in the narcissistic, but ultimately self-exploitative use of her own body to achieve fame and recognition. It is therefore false. This fantasy is so well-developed that La China Hereje has a name for herself in her new life: "irme de artista con el nombre de La Langosta, y hacerme famossssa y dar opiniones y firmar autógrafossss." Her ultimate dream is to be the object of the same kind of male attention as her role model.

Although La China Hereje has continued her five o'clock meetings with Vicente, whom she calls "El Viejo," for six months, he has little to do with her authentic sexual life. Their relationship retains an artifical, script-like quality in her narration, much like a grade B movie. They met in a supermarket, where she went to meet rich men. He has rented a studio; they meet there regularly at five o'clock. Each claims other evening commitments. She travels there by bus, and he in his Mercedes Benz, demonstrating their class difference. For him she is one in a long line of *mulata* mistresses. Their interaction is determined by his tastes, his likes and dislikes, his fantasies. For example, she waits for him nude, because he likes to find her that way. For Vicente, La China Hereje is the "oferta suprema de una erótica" he constantly seeks: "Las hembras de color me acaloran."

On the other hand, their encounters leave her cold. She makes an ironic comparison to Snow White and the dwarves when thinking about herself and "El Viejo." Thus, the relationship symbolizes another aspect of the mass media-fed dissociation between La China Hereje's reality and her fantasies. Even her mannerisms in the studio appear to be learned from the media: "¿Aprendió el dulce encanto del fingimiento de los manerismos repercutidos del grandioso teleculebrón *El hijo de Angela María* que convirtió en melaza el corazón isleño?"

In contrast, although still adhering to the "sensual *mulata* stereotype," she expresses a more authentic sexuality in a variety of erotic scenes with her cousins, beginning in early childhood. The flashbacks to these scenes occur in La China Hereje's memory while she waits for Vicente, who is caught in a traffic jam. Her cousins' names are Hugo, Paco, and Luis, from the *Donald Duck* cartoon series. The description of their sexual activity together is deliberately cinematic; it is interspersed with director's instructions on when to cut and how to film the sequence. This erotic scene's authenticity is nevertheless in doubt, since it ends with a commercial:

> Corte. Toma panorámica de cuerpos en convulsión culminante: interés especial en el frotado de los vientres: ombligo a ombligo: así se chicha. Corte . . . Toma panorámica de cuerpo de la autora de cerebro, cuerpo resbaloso, cuerpo vaselinado, cuerpo aceitado con bronceador Coppertone, cuerpo aceitado con fijador Johnson. Corte.

The consumerist interference continues when she meets one cousin years later, and begins another affair with him. The background for their sensual encounter is a store sale. She reclines on a shelf of plastic Halloween pumpkins and plastic Thanksgiving turkeys: "aquí no, sweetie pie, un pavo plástico como cinturón de castidad." Thus La China Hereje's potentially authentic sexuality is falsified in the artificial reality of an Americanized, consumerized Puerto Rico.

In her role caring for son "El Nene," La China Hereje is referred to only as "La Madre." The effects of mass media indoctrination are also apparent here. This is made particularly clear in La Madre's conversations with her friend doña Chon, who represents the old ways. Doña Chon's ignorance of the mass media in general allows her to see far more clearly than the other characters. La Madre's concept of maternity is derived principally from the Mexican film industry:

> La madre sabe muchas canciones de las madres, la madre sabe muchos pasodobles de las madres, la madre sabe muchos tangos de las madres. La madre ha visto mucho cine mexicano.

La Madre's motherhood has a grotesque quality quite apart from mass media's influence. "El Nene" is hydrocephalic. The language used to describe him de-emphasizes his humanity. Here is one example:

El nubarrón de moscas, euménides zumbonas que improvisaban un halo furioso sobre la gran cabeza. La Madre y doña Chon miraron la cara babosa y el baberío y la dormidera boba con lagartijo muerto en la mano: El Nene mordía la cabeza del lagartijo hasta que el rabo descansaba la guardia, el mismo rabo que trampado en la garganta convidaba al vómito.

The lizard image is later transferred into a simile describing El Nene himself: "como un réptil desperezándose, . . . vómito y baba escurriendo, . . . como un Bobón Niño de las Moscas." Ironically, the other son in the novel, Benny, is also a kind of monster, although of a very different sort. He is linked to El Nene in the final unifying device of the text, when he apparently kills him in a car accident with his Ferrari.

Another unifying device, which makes the reader realize that La China Hereje and La Madre are the same person, is the set of cross-references in their dialogues. One prevailing theme is Iris Chacón. She figures as much in La Madre's imagination as in La China Hereje's. In fact, the culmination of Iris Chacón's portrayal as a media-created fantasy figure occurs early in the novel, when La Madre states, "el día que Iris Chacón baile y cante la guaracha del macho Camacho será el día del despelote." Doña Chon, to whom this is addressed, responds, "Dios nos ampare ese día."

The contrast between doña Chon's and La Madre's attitudes reinforces the grotesque quality of the latter's motherhood, and ultimately, her inauthentic life. This is true despite La China Hereje's statement that "doña Chon es una derrotá igual que yo." Doña Chon's son is serving a seven-year jail sentence; she cooks to make money for his lawyers' fees. In spite of her misfortunes, she lives a more authentic reality than La Madre. In large measure, this is because she retains old ways and is generally ignorant of mass media reality. She is an excellent cook of *comida criolla*: "Doña Chon, clériga suma del arroz y la habichulela, invicta hacedora de rellenos de papa, . . . mater et magistra del asopao de pollo." The parody of theological language is immediately apparent here, and in many other places in the text. When doña Chon is first introduced, she is presented as: "vecina nuestra que estás en el Caño de Martin Peña." These linguistic parodies notwithstanding, doña Chon's attitude is characterized by what one critic has called "inconformidad pasiva." Although not consciously political, her attitudes reflect a political consciousness. She repeats that "La vida es un lío de ropa sucia," and in general cries out against the injustices she sees. When describing the legal system, she says, "a los ricos si te vi ya no me acuerdo . . . A los pobres siete años en la sombra."

Possibly the most poignant aspect of doña Chon's characterization is her vision of women as childbearers. Only women know real pain: "Ningún hombre podrá parir nunca." Being a woman means suffering: "Ahí mismo supe yo lo que era el dolor de nacer mujer." She describes her son's birth in great detail. It lasted three days, and was extremely painful. Nevertheless, doña Chon feels women are superior to men because they can have children:

> A los machos con todo y ser machos y ser los dueños del mandar, les falta el importante tornillo de la pujadera que es un tornillito importante que la mujer trae desde que nace en su parte de mujer.

Thus, although doña Chon is portrayed as displaying a more authentic existence than La China Hereje, her *raison d'être* is also founded on a stereotypical definition of woman—in this case, as mother.

There is one more mother in the novel. She is Graciela Alcántara y López de Montefrío, Vicente's wife and Benny's mother. Graciela, although belonging to a very different class reality than doña Chon and La China Hereje, also emerges as a product of the mass media's values and *modus operandi*. She is depicted as conforming to familial and social expectations of an upper-class woman. We initially encounter her waiting in her psychiatrist's office. The same technique of fragmentary visual representation of her physical appearance is used as when La China Hereje was first presented. In Graciela's case, however, the camera goes no farther than her painted fingernails, designer clothing, and expensive handbag. Graciela likes to think her hallmarks are Jane Fonda's in *Klute:* "Coolness y análisis." While waiting, she reads *Time* magazine. When she sees photographs of napalm bombing, her reaction is: "yo no nací para eso." On the other hand, photographs of Liz and Dick fascinate her so much that she turns back to them. Her fantasy role model, who also appears photographed in *Time*, is Jacqueline Onassis. Despite the differences between her fantasy aspirations and La China Hereje's both rely on the mass media to determine and foster them. Each one's vision falls into the precise categories assigned to her class, race, and sex by social expectations.

Flashbacks to Graciela's earlier life, all occurring in her memory, enable the reader to place her in her class and culture. She is the daughter of an old aristocratic family. Her upbringing has taught her to despise Puerto Rico, so that she lives in a continuously alienated state, alone. As a teenager, she was sent to finishing school in Switzerland. The sequence describing this contains an ironic contrast between "Suiza nevada y pura"—reinforced with her name, Montefrío—and "la estrepitosa vulgaridad insular." On her return to Puerto Rico, she married Vicente, whom she thought a refined gentleman, in her bourgeois terms. Their wedding night quickly disabuses her of any illusions in that regard. She and Vicente live in the same house, but rarely see each other. Nor does she have much contact with her son Benny, except to tell him to keep his friends' motorcycles out of her garden. Here she is counterpointed with La Madre, for whom El Nene is emotional contact with another human being.

Graciela's life is a model of bourgeois emptiness. Although she is often the object of the author's linguistic parody, she is also a victim of the false set of social expectations to which she conforms. She does nothing; her life is filled with discussions about her continual attempts to appear more beautiful and younger, which perfume she should buy, the country club, and the Casals festival as a "pasatiempo Trivia cultivado." Although she thinks about reading literature occasionally, she only reads magazines and *novelas*. By going to Dr. Severo Severino, the psychiatrist, she also conforms to her role expectations. The receptionist there says of the doctor's patients: "Mucha señora deprimida." Nevertheless, the doctor is also an example of a media-produced fantasy: "modal de Rossano Brazzi, modal de Raf Vallone, modal de Omar Sharif."

Graciela's frame of reference is largely a product of mass media. And, in order to unmask her class' language, movies, magazines, television, and commercials are used as the basis for linguistic parody against her. Her desire to be like Jacqueline Onassis, for example, is transformed into a long word play:

> Había una vez y dos son tres, una princesita llamada Jacqueline que se casó con el Rey de la Isla del Escorpión. . . . Graciela edita . . . : la Princesita Jacqueline en traje de montar en jabalí, la Princesita Jacqueline en traje de comer papas fritas, la Princesita Jacqueline en traje de dar limosnas a los pobres, la Princesita Jacqueline en traje de quitarse el Tampax, la Princesita Jacqueline en traje de llamar por teléfono a la Baroness Marie Hèlene Rothschild.

Her terrible fear of growing old, a preoccupation reinforced by advertisements for cold creams and cosmetics, is also couched in terms of movies and television, parodied by the narrator:

> La palabra otoñal la atosiga de recuerdos conmovidos, recuerdos lastimosos de una novela de televisión protagonizada por la profunda trágica Madeline Willemsen, la gran Madeline Willemsen destruida, capítulo tras capítulo por la perversidad absoluta de un ingeniero canalla que empeña el precioso collar de perlas que le regala un conde austríaco, conde austríaco que no era tal conde austríaco pero sí un apache de los bajos fondos de París, . . . y, Falso, falso, falso, amnesíaca, olvidadiza, la estrella de la novela.

This reality's absolute falsity is demonstrated through its constant fluctuation. Facts cannot be verified, and her feelings are triggered only in relation to a fictitious and false reality, product of the mass media.

Along with her fear of losing youth and beauty, Graciela's obsession with refinement and the external trappings of class lead her to constant critical self-examination. She is always looking in the mirror. Like La China Hereje, she sets herself up as a spectacle. Unlike her counterpart, however, her concern is with proper clothing and accessories, and other accoutrements of bourgeois appearance. It is for this reason that the symbolic contrast between the pristine mountains of Switzerland, where nobody spits, and Puerto Rico's vulgarity is so important:

No escupe porque en Suiza nevada y pura aprendió a no escupir.
Porque en Suiza nevada y pura no se escupe, en este bendito
Puerto Rico sí: . . . en este país se escupe donde quiera, . . . :
escupir: costumbre desclasada de país desclasado: Isabel y Fernando nunca debieron.

Nowhere, however, does the novel's linguisitic parody become sharper
than in the description of Graciela's repressed sexuality. Her counterpoint-
ing with La China Hereje—"Belle de Jour insular"—is also found principally
in this aspect of her characterization. Vicente contrasts her creamed face
and sexual distance with La China Hereje's skill, worthy of *Last Tango in
Paris*. Her fear of sex, and insistence on its vulgarity, are as stereotypically
class and race defined as La China's mercenary attitude toward her own
body and her enthusiastic sensuality. As such, both are representative
victims of women's role expectations, although on opposite ends of the
class scale.

The contrast between Graciela's wedding and her honeymoon typifies
her rigid adherence to bourgeois forms, and total rejection of any consciousness that negates them. She remembers herself at the wedding as:
"solemne y trémula, . . . pálida como la amada inmóvil, bellamente quieta
ante la turbulencia de las aclamaciones y los bravos." This is, of course, a
fantasy memory. Its glorious image is shattered in the realization of marriage's sexual reality. The parody is clear in these lines: "¿qué es eso Mama?,
. . . eso es la carnal penetración de su vergüenza en la tuya." Not until
one month after marriage, and long after their honeymoon, is the marriage
consummated. Graciela's repressed sexuality turns into disgust, and is generalized into her dissatisfaction with a "Puerto Rico desclasado," finally
symbolized in the *guaracha*. Unlike La China Hereje, whose body moves
to the *guaracha's* rhythm, Graciela rejects its validity. In this, she is alone.
Even Dr. Severo Severino likes it. Graciela's attitude is:

Ciérrate vaniti de señora señorísima fastidiada por los dejes insi-
diosos de esa música guarachosa que a ella le parece un voto de
confianza a la chabacanería desclasada que atraviesa como un rayo
que no cesa la isla de Puerto Rico.

Nevertheless, her inability to substitute any but another false reality—the
colonized bourgeois ideal—leaves Graciela trapped as well.

Among the multiple parodies of contemporary Puerto Rican society
interwoven in this novel, the *puertorriqueña's* stereotyping stands out. La
China Hereje typifies both the archetypical sensual seductress, and as La
Madre, the current maternal mythology. She also incarnates the themes of
youth culture and beauty as defined by the mass media, and is reified into
a reflection of these values. Ultimately, her situation symbolizes Puerto
Rico's colonization. Her friend doña Chon, on the other hand, retains the
old ways, and remains the stereotypical self-sacrificing mother. Graciela

Alcántara y López de Montefrío, although participating in a very different class reality, also emerges as a product of the mass media's acculturation process. She is the rich man's wife, occupied with keeping herself chic, consuming the appropriate goods, and maintaining her distance from whatever she considers unrefined and vulgar. She wishes to be Jacqueline Onassis; La China Hereje emulates Iris Chacón. Nevertheless, these female characters' differences also bring to light their commonality. Together, they form a constellation of stereotypical female characterizations, described and encouraged principally by the mass media.

The mass media in turn functions as a symbol of Puerto Rico's cultural colonization. As such, it serves as an instrument to foment sex, class, and race stereotypes. Sánchez's linguistic parody functions as a strong critique of contemporary Puerto Rican society. His attitude in the novel is clearly exemplified by his portrayal of female characters.

Plain Song: Sarduy's *Cobra*

Roberto González Echevarría

> *In some of his books Paul Valéry uses as epigraph a line from Góngora, and even though he misquotes it, his mistake is a perfect illustration of my argument. "En rocas de cristal," cites Valéry, "serpiente breve" (in crystal rocks a brief serpent). His own biases lead him to believe that those serpents must have wriggled across a static, contrasting surface, creating and destroying their letters in the process. He is searching for a background of immobility, "the crystal rocks" on which those dark games of the snakes can be performed. These lines are the beginning "La toma de Larache," which reads "en roscas de cristal serpiente breve" (in crystal curls a brief serpent). The difference between original and citation marks the desire, the prior vision that destroys the line's reality.*
> —JOSÉ LEZAMA LIMA, "Luis de Gongora's Serpent"

The snow that covers Havana at the end of the last story in *De donde son los cantantes* anticipates the Tibetan snow that closes *Cobra* and opens *Maitreya*. Whiteness is death, absence, the empty page on which will be inscribed, as excess, Sarduy's most recent work which both distances him from and returns him to the Cuban literary tradition. Like the final story in *De donde son los cantantes*, these works are geographical and historical phantasies, allegorical pilgrimages during which Sarduy moves from the Europe of drug-dealing motorcycle gangs to China, Tibet, Ceylon, Havana, and the Miami of Cuban exiles. There appear in the accounts of these voyages decisive historical events such as the Chinese Revolution, the Cuban Revolution, and even the more recent upheavals in Iran. Despite or perhaps because of the obvious remoteness of such places and accounts, Sarduy's works are a return to and a recovering of the work of Lezama, but through a process very different from that practiced by Lezama's more direct *Orígenes* disciples. The Lezama Sarduy recovers here is not the one we find in Vitier's *Lo cubano en la poesia*, but the more historical and more radically experimental Lezama of *La expresíon americana* and *Las eras imaginarias*, as well as, of course, the Lezama of *Paradiso*. Or better even, what will ultimately be recovered is the text of *Paradiso* more than Lezama himself. This process of recovering takes as its point of departure the most remote of the components that make up Cuban culture: the oriental elements whose significance I shall sketch in the following pages, and which immediately reveals its Lezamian slant—the farthest is the closest, that at which one arrives through an oblique experience.

If *De donde son los cantantes* reverses the journey of *Lo cubano en la poesía*, *Cobra*, *Maitreya*, and books of essays such as *Barroco* and *La simulación* reread another book that was initially a series of lectures given in Havana in 1957: Lezama's *La expresión americana*. *La expresión americana* is the first systematic exposition of the method through which Lezama interpreted history, if one can call Lezama's reading of history an interpretation. *La expresión americana* is also the work in which Lezama expounds his theories of the Baroque. Relying on the methodology introduced in *La expresión americana*, Lezama amplifies his historical meditation in *Las eras imaginarias*. The vast geographical and historical spirals of *Cobra* and *Maitreya*, much like the theories of *Barroco* in which different cultures and distinct historical periods confront each other, are supported by the method of the interplay of events and places that Lezama proposes in his texts, although with notable differences. It is necessary to add to this context another text which also poses an interplay of cultures and historical epochs: Octavio Paz's *Conjunctions and Disjunctions* (1969).

Lezama's dazzling originality cannot make us lose sight of the intellectual context in which his essays were written, which is of course the same as Vitier's. Lezama, whose only language was Spanish, was philosophically formed by the work of promotion and dissemenination carried out by Ortega y Gasset and his disciples. To be sure, Lezama added to their approach a strong dosage of variegated and heterodox readings—occultism, kabbalah, oriental religions—not to mention his immeasurable capacity for transmutation, as well as his very original reading of the poetic tradition of the West. But in the thirties, when Lezama was young, what circulated in Havana were the writings of Ortega and his disciples, the *Revista de Occidente,* and soon, after the Spanish Civil War, Ortega's disciples in the flesh. Among those, Maria Zambrano was the one with the most direct impact on the members of the *Orígenes* group, a very hispanophile circle, one might add. Some of its members, like the distinguished composer Julián Orbón, had spent critical years in Spain. Furthermore, the *Orígenes* poets—some, like Fina García Marruz, still in their teens—were initiated into poetry by Juan Ramon Jimenez's visit to Havana in 1936. Juan Ramon's visit was crucial to the development of Cuban literature, above all Cuban poetry. The founding of literary journals and the activities of the *Orígenes* group were, to a large extent, a continuation, in Cuba, of artistic-philosophical movements initiated in Spain. The group's Catholicism, for instance—let us not forget the presence of the poet/priest Angel Gaztelu in its midst—reflects that continuity. More so than Ortega himself, his disciples, for example Manuel García Morente, attempted to wed the Catholicism inherent in the Spanish tradition with the new philosophical and aesthetic trends. This refurbished, and thus at times somewhat tortured but nevertheless creative, Catholicism, was the heritage not of the Cuban but the Spanish avant-garde. To all this should be added that the most distinguished painter of the group, Wifredo Lam (whose influence on Sarduy is vast), had participated, with quite a few other fellow Cubans, in the Civil War and then married and settled in Spain. Lezama's interest in the classics of the Spanish Baroque stemmed in part from his affinity with the poets of the Generation '27 in Spain, a group that rediscovered the work of Góngora, as is notorious.

In *La expresión americana*, and later in the essays collected in *Las eras imaginarias*, Lezama elaborates a poetic theory of history that can be summarized as follows: there are elements in each culture that resemble those in other cultures removed in time and space. Those supra-temporal analogies make possible the conception of "imaginary eras" in which those common features are combined. It is the "metaphoric subject" who interweaves those analogous characteristics in order to shape the eras: "A determinate mass of natural or cultural objects suddenly acquires immense resonances. In a space counterpointed by the imago and the metaphoric subject, objects such as expressions, fables or the ruins of Pergamon acquire new life, like the plant or the dominated space. The metamorphosis of a natural object into an imaginary cultural object depends on this contrapuntal space" (*La expresion*). The proximity of his method to that of Spengler in *The Decline of the West* made it necessary for Lezama to establish a clear distinction which is worth citing here before we look more closely at some of the other concepts and questions that his formulations raise:

> Let us preempt any conclusion that may be inferred, with false delight and equal carelessness, from the similarity in appearance of my theory with those of some irreducible sectors on whom Oswald Spengler seems to have exerted a dazzling influence with what contemporary historiography has called homologous events. If we compare the shape of a bull's horns to that of the Byzantine emperors' tiara, which according to Spenglerian precepts, are homologous, we pose a parallelism of cultural symbols, which acquire precisely that symbolic value by being situated in the value-system of a morphology. But my belief in cultural analogy presupposes the participation, across a contrapuntal space, of the metaphoric subject. We could perhaps say that that metaphoric subject acts as a temporal factor that prevents the natural and cultural objects from remaining *gelee* [sic] in their sterile plain.
>
> (*La expresión*)

The "metaphoric subject" (that is, the poet), caught within his own temporality, perceives relations that suddenly make of nature a super-nature, which is the image, that is, the imaginary era, made up of fragments of other eras. But Lezama is even more ambitious. That image is not the reflection of a reality, but, once configured on the basis of elements that themselves already are cultural creations, acts upon reality. This process, whose agent is the "metaphoric subject," is an act of charity, of love, that blurs the boundary between subject and object ("subject and object consume each other and disappear," *La expresión*). As Lezama put it in "La imagen histórica":

> The image extracts from the enigma a glimmer, with whose ray of light we can penetrate, or at least live while in wait for resurrection. The image, in this sense we give it, attempts to reduce the supernatural to man's transfigured senses. The natural thus empowered and laden with potentialities moves closer to the unreal, to be able to give back the word's charisma with a surfeit of love, by revealing a similarity that involves a boundless act of charity. Poetry appears in this guise as the probable form of *the charity that accepts everything, caritas omnia credit.*
>
> (*La expresión*)

"Charity" (*caridad*) here means love; the "metaphoric subject" creates, through love, those images of gyrating cultures in which all is possible, where nothing is fantastic or unreal. In this new creation there is at work a sort of intertextuality *avant la lettre*, "the original invents its citations, charging them with more meaning within the new body on which they are grafted than what they had on the body from which they were extracted" (*Las eras*). This weave of quotations, this text, which is image, supernature, imaginary era, poetry, arises from the interchangeability of subject and object, a movement that is like a network of metaphoric correspondences in which time and space have been abolished, except for the time of the "metaphoric subject." But who is that being? Clearly, the answer must come from mythological thinkers—Plato, Vico, Jung, Eliot—who attribute to the individual the ability to capture or express elemental forms, forms of the origin that are common to all of humankind. Lezama says this in a lapidary phrase in *La expresión americana*: "Memory is the plasma of the soul, it is always creative, spermatic, thus we remember from the very depths of the species." If we remember by drawing from a collective well, like the individual in the Platonic cave, we extract from within ourselves something everyone shares—the inner light is the spark of the light of universal truths. But Lezama wants to go further back toward a mythological reason where, instead of ideas, what exists are fables: "Vico intuits that there is in man a sense, let us call it the birth of another reason that is mythological, which is neither Greek nor Cartesian rationality, in order to explain the transformation of the fabulous into the mythological. Confronted with the world of *physis*, Descartes finds shelter in his clear and distinct ideas. Confronted with the "dark and muddled" details of the origins, Vico places before Plato's universal ideas his concept of fantastic or imaginary universals" (*Las eras*). For Lezama, the image is the product of a metaphoric activity which, by joining dispersed elements, reshapes forms that are present in the memory. It is a kind of monism whose magnetic force is love, the desire that joins together and breaks, approximating elements of reality and facilitating the interpenetration of subject and object.

It may be naive to think of Lezama's theory as original. His formulations correspond to the Romantics' ideas about creation, as they had arrived at conclusions similar to those of Vico, for the most part without having read him. At its most abstract level, Lezama's theory is not an original aesthetic. But in its application as a poetics of history, geography, and culture, it is no doubt a powerful and attractive poetic system. It should be added that Lezama believed that the kingdom of the image anticipated the kingdom of resurrection, which is by definition the realm of that which is farthest removed, of the hypertelos, that which surpasses the end, or the goal. Poetry is thus the dwelling-place of fulfilled prophecies which have been realized in the strong sense of the term. In Heidegger being is for death; in Bataille death generates an excess which is creation, culture. In Lezama the hypertelos announces, prefigures resurrection. It is not difficult to see why the Baroque, the art of the excessive, should have become so important in such a system. Sarduy's theory of the Baroque relies on certain aspects of Lezama's system, although it differs considerably from that of the master in its Freudian basis and its quasi-scientific tone, which is derived from Sarduy's association with *Tel Quel*.

There is a group of Latin American essayists, both prior to and contemporary with Lezama, which recovers the Latin American Baroque—the "barroco de Indias"; I am thinking mainly of Alfonso Reyes, Pedro Henríquez Ureña, and Mariano Picón Salas. But Lezama is the first to declare the Latin American Baroque, the "señor barroco," the origin of American consciousness and of American art. Lezama breaks away from those attempting to locate the origin of Americanness in the indigenous cultures or in a certain simplicity and purity of form associated with Renaissance Spain. In contrast to the purity of a primitive origin, Lezama proposes a complex, excessive origin, which is not simply an admixture of the different cultural traditions that can be found in the New World, but the creative flash sparked by that fusion. The founding figures, for Lezama, are Sor Juana Inés de la Cruz, Carlos de Sigüenza y Góngora, Aleijahndino, and Indio Kondori. Lezama attributes to the American Baroque a capacity for creation, for innovation generally associated with Romanticism, above all because of its igneous quality: "First, there is a tension in the Baroque; second, there is a Plutonism, an originary fire that tears apart the fragments as well as unifies them" (*La expresión*); "In the beautiful works of the Indio Kondori, in whose originary fire the banal pride of the contemporary architects could find a lot to learn" (*La expresión*). Because, against those who would situate the origin of an American identity in Romanticism, Lezama wields the Baroque as an already original anxiety of creation and innovation—Lezama's Baroque is a romantic Baroque, a Baroque endowed with the fundamental features of German Romanticism.

Sarduy's theory of the Baroque shares with Lezama's the conjoining of different periods and the confrontation, through analogy, of diverse cultures, but his bases and his language aspire to be more scientific, and the "metaphoric subject," if it does not altogether disappear, is at least transfigured. Like the theories of Sigüenza y Góngora, Sarduy's theory is cosmological, mainly because he relates astronomy and psychology. Sarduy suggests an analogy between the cosmological theories of the Baroque period and those of today. The former theories discovered the elliptical orbit of the stars in the solar system, the latter formulate the theory of the *Big Bang* about the creation of the universe—the universe is the product of an initial explosion, which sets in motion and expands the particles that constitute it. Modernity: explosion/expansion. In the Baroque period the figure—geometrical and rhetorical—that was very much in fashion in art and literature was precisely that of the ellipse, the deformed circle with two centers, one of which is displaced. In our time psychoanalysis was invented, a theory of the subject based on repression, that is, the suppression of an origin, which is experienced as a lack or defect, around which meaning is constructed as a form of defense: writing, figures. The *Big Bang*, in short, is a cosmological theory that finds its equivalent in psychoanalysis. Both take the ellipse as their primary figure, in the same way that in the Baroque age the ellipse served as the basis for the conception of planetary movement and determined the organization of the plastic arts and literature. The resemblance to the theory of Lezama is obvious, but the differences are also very pronounced, above all in how each theory conceives of the subject.

What moves the "metaphoric subject" in Lezama, as we have seen, is love which abundantly replenishes "the word's charisma" (its graces, offerings, or gifts) through acts of combination, and whose outcome is, therefore, an overflow: the cornucopia of the Baroque banquet. Sarduy defines more specifically the mechanism through which the subject engenders baroque language:

> The baroque metaphor would identify itself with a mode radically different from *suppression,* a mode that consists of a change of structure; *repression* (Verdrängung/refoulement). It is at the level of the system of the Unconscious that the process unfolds through which the representations of representations that are tied to certain impulses [*pulsiones*] are pushed away or maintained at a distance. In the same manner in which one perceives the organization of "original" deficiency—, repression sets off a sort of metonymic reaction which implies the indefinite flight of the object of the drive; but, in the same way that one can foresee, through the symptom, a return to that which has been repressed—in the economy of neurosis the symptom is its signified—it blends *exactly* into metaphor.

> (*Barroco*)

Sarduy, quite obviously, avails himself of a Lacanian terminology, which becomes even less accessible due to his substitution of the Spanish word "pulsion" for instinct or drive (such as the death drive). In any case, we can translate Sarduy's pronouncements in the following way: The Baroque metaphor compensates for the deficiency on which being is founded. The desire, the impulse to cover the lack, and the way in which it is covered is a function of this absence itself, which is repressed in the process of being covered. The act of covering functions metonymically as a chain of signifiers. Given that these figures—which are much like the symptoms that the analyst interprets—include the absence, although it is erased, their function is ultimately metaphoric, not metonymic. The memory of the repressed object props up what it represents in the present. In cosmological terms, the movement of the stars (metonymy) makes up a planetary system that covers (metaphor) the black hole created by the original explosion. The metaphoric system of the Baroque covers a repressed signified that can be retrieved through a reading of signifiers which, although they ostensibly allude to other things, call attention to it. It is important to note here the mutual reflections between lack and excess, between blank and explosion, and between the infinite rays that mark the trajectory of the stars and the graphs of writing. Lack and excess are the interchangeable inversion and reversal of Sarduy's metaphoric system. Sarduy's "metaphoric subject" does not remember from "the very depths of the species," but constitutes itself in the mechanisms of memory. Those mechanisms erase it: "In the Baroque the poetic is a Rhetoric: language, the autonomous and tautological code, does not admit into its *charged*, dense web the possibility of a creative *I*, an individual referent, a center, which expresses itself—the Baroque functions in a vacuum—which channels or arrests the flow of signs" (*Barroco*). We do not, quite obviously, believe, that the subject is annulled, in part because language, no matter how tautological it may be, can speak of itself only indirectly, and one of the tangential themes it needs to bring forth a discourse about itself is the subject and its history. This, I believe, is rendered evident in Sarduy's fiction. But *Barroco* makes a formal effort to integrate the annihilation of the subject in the process that constitutes the essay itself: the opening of the book, which follows a numerical scheme, is a zero, "the echo chamber." That "echo chamber" is the authorial *I* at the beginning of writing: its essence is absence, whiteness encircled by the blackness of the graphic figure—whiteness of the beginning, of snow, of cocaine that expands consciousness—the invisible wall from which voice bounces back as voices: the whiteness of death. White means death in Afro-Cuban cosmology.

It is not difficult to perceive the relationship between Sarduy's theory of the Baroque and Lezama's. American identity is an absence, a deficiency from which emerges a culture that always seems to be wrought in the zero of the beginning. Culture consists in simulating that there is neither lack nor contradiction; it creates itself. According to this concept of culture, being is a hypostasis of rhetoric, a necessary entelechy of language, not its source. But the differences between Lezama's Baroque and that of Sarduy are equally notable. In Lezama the "metaphoric subject" is manifest in its product—the imaginary eras, the texts—whereas in Sarduy it seeks to manifest itself in its function, its transport and passion, grasped and constituted in the web of language. This is particularly obvious in *Cobra*, the fictional hinge of Sarduy's work, the last text to appeal to the jargon of *Tel Quel*, and which, through a severe askesis, dismantles language and breaks it down into its most elemental particles in order from there to begin again to recover Cuba, this time through the text of *Paradiso*.

II

In the heat of the party [José Arcadio] exhibited his unusual masculinity on the bar, completely covered with tattoos of words in several languages intertwined in blue and red.

ONE HUNDRED YEARS OF SOLITUDE

If *De donde son los cantantes* marked Sarduy as one of the most audacious writers in Latin America, the publication of *Cobra* in 1972 turned him into a polemical figure. *Cobra* is Sarduy's most difficult work, the one that least surrenders to a reader mostly used to the Latin American novel of the Boom. Although the impact of *Cobra* on writers such as Juan Goytisolo and Carlos Fuentes was enormous, it has never reached as wide an audience as the novels of the Spaniard and the Mexican, mainly because its oriental theme and its insistence on portraying the world of transvestites made it too foreign to most. If the Boom represents the popularity of the Latin American narrative, *Cobra*, like *De donde son los cantantes*, is a work of the anti-Boom. The novels of Carlos Fuentes, Gabriel García Márquez, Mario Vargas Llosa, and Juan Goytisolo experiment with the conventions of the modern novel and are part of an ideology whose fundamental issue is that of cultural identity. In *De donde son los cantantes* Sarduy challenges the question of cultural identity and its relation to language. *De donde son los cantantes* denounces the reduction of character implicit in the question of identity, which subordinates the various modes of discourse that constitute a culture to a single ideology. The aesthetic of the Boom novel still contains fundamental elements of the traditional novel: characters that follow mimetic conceptions; time that is recoverable despite fragmentation; an implicit faith in the authenticity of local color as a source of truth about culture and the propriety of language. Oliveira and La Maga, Jaguar, Artemio Cruz, Aureliano Buendía are all novelistic characters whose gender is prescribed by the cultural tradition to which they belong, who have biographies that explain their actions in the novel, and who speak and think in the Spanish corresponding to their nationality and social class. This is not the case with Auxilio and Socorro in *De donde son los cantantes*, whose existence is a function of rhetoric, whose speech is made up of bits and pieces from different kinds of discourse, and who, in the final analysis, represent the irreducible binary opposition at the origin of language. To be sure, the work of Cortázar, above all *Rayuela*, offers new experiments with language and with the form of the novel, such as the inclusion of dispensable chapters as the novel's pre-text. But the conception of the characters, including the narrator, is quite conventional. The same, and more, can be said about the works of Donoso, Goytisolo, and Vargas Llosa.

These elements of the traditional novel which survive, more or less intact, in the writers of the Boom are precisely the ones that are most charged with ideological implications and the ones that Sarduy dismantles most gleefully, above all, in *Cobra*. How can the gender and sexual roles of the characters and their linguistic manifestations not be fundamental? Or the way in which language relates the biography of a character? And if changes in point of view assume a correspondence between grammatical and real person, are they not based on an assumption burdened with ideological suggestions? In Sarduy language is always an enigma, against which each culture or discourse makes violent, but inescapable, decisions. The traditional novel has male or female characters, whereas Sarduy's text displays the mechanism governing this decision to repress other possibilities. The novel of the Boom functions, as long as it narrates, through tacit repressions. *Cobra* insists on making those repressions explicit. Sarduy's novel attempts to embody nothing less than the subconscious of the Latin American narrative. This is, above all, why *Cobra* has been repressed by many writers and critics, for some of whom Sarduy is anathema. Only after the systematic deconstruction of Cuban and by extension Latin American identity in *De donde son los cantantes* could Sarduy embark on such a dazzling and radical analysis of the discourse of Latin American literature.

Cobra consists (but this is, of course, a misrepresentation since it is impossible to "describe" a text like this without betraying it, but this, as we shall see, is also the point) of two stories which interweave and repeat each other at different levels, at times literally. It is difficult to separate those levels because their components do not always form meaningful sequences. When reading *Cobra*, we often feel as if the text lacks a focus of meaning that would bring coherence to the elements it assembles. In addition to the stories, which are presented mostly in dialogue, language constantly releases sparks of meaning which cannot be retraced to a center that emits or receives them, sparks that do not constitute unities of meaning belonging to an all-encompassing system. This characteristic trait of *Cobra*, however, does have meaning in global terms. As we can see in *De donde son los cantantes*, one of Sarduy's basic postulates is that the possibility of submitting language to a coherent meaning is an illusion that only sacred texts can sustain. But, in spite of that dissolution, we can still discern the contours of two stories in the novel.

The main story of the first part takes place in the Lyrical Puppet Theater, a burlesque that recalls the Shanghai of *De donde son los cantantes*, but which also immediately evokes the Derridean vision of Plato's Pharmacy, that is, the realm of writing and of pharmacopeia used for physical transformations. In his well-known essay, Derrida shows how the West has suppressed writing in favor of voice, how the former is associated with the East and embodied in an ambiguous god who poisons and cures at the same time and who keeps a record of the dead. The protagonist of the novel's first part is Cobra, the prima donna, who, together with the Señora—the owner of the joint—is obsessed with shrinking her feet which, because of their disproportionate size, are her only physical fault. After trying out various brews and concoctions made of different kinds of herbs, they finally discover an effective drug. But this drug proves so effective that it turns both Cobra and the Señora into dwarfs, whose names are now Cobrita (later Pup) and the Señorita. Now, however, there is a doubling. The "life size" Cobra sets out for India with Eustaquio the Delightful One, a "skin" painter in charge of the Theater's body-makeup, in search of colors for a planned *Féerie Orientale*. Eustaquio's zigzagging life—which alternates between the East and the West—is also being narrated, along with his virtuosity with brush and penis. While Cobra is gone, the Señora suggests that Pup regain her normal size to replace her double in the Theater. She is subjected to various attempts at enlargement, until snow is discovered to be the last recourse. It is possible that "snow" alludes here to cocaine because of its powers to "expand" the mind, but we cannot be altogether certain about this. The efforts to increase Pup's size are described in detail. However, all fails, despite the fact that these efforts almost kill her. Cobra returns from India to take her place.

These adventures are framed by several sentences about the "art of writing," which establish a clear correspondence between the Señora's pharmacopeia and the act of writing. Writing also functions through contraction and expansion in the form of rhetorical figures; the herbal alchemy of the Señora, her Celestinesque profession, corresponds perfectly to the figure of the Derridean god of writing; the fact that the metamorphoses (changes in size, Eustaquio's painting) are always physical and the origins of the techniques always oriental also fits the model of Plato's Pharmacy. This Derridean element in *Cobra* is clarified in the next sequence.

Here we find that Cobra has gone to Tanger in search of Dr. Ktazob, famous for his sex-change operations on transvestites who wish to perfect their physical appearance. The Señora and her disciples, in search of Cobra, set out for Spain where they meet Auxilio and Socorro, the characters from *De donde son los cantantes*. In Tanger four drug pushers from Amsterdam in search of raw materials send them to Dr. Ktazob, "who was enriched by the configuration of new Evas and the disfiguration of old Nazis." These are the characters of the novel's next section. Also in Tanger Cobra meets her rival, Cadillac, to whom Ktazob has surgically added a penis ("the inversion of inversion"). During surgery Cobra has a series of hallucinations in which the landscapes that appear at the end of the novel (the Indian Diary) are prefigured and in whose description language is reduced to such an extent that it turns into anagrams of the protagonist's name. During his chirurgical procedure Ktazob succeeds in diverting Cobra's pain to the dwarfed double Pup.

Like the Lyrical Theater, Tanger represents the realm of transformations; more specifically, it represents the hinge of the separation and difference between East and West. Writing, once more associated with ritualistic physical mutilation, is that which is repressed, which is why the West associates its birth, its origin, with the East. Orientalism begins to acquire here a precise meaning, one that has already been sketched in *De donde son los cantantes.* The oriental is the supplement, that which is beyond the end, because it is mostly a necessary invention of the West: *the Oriental is writing.* Therefore, the oriental is founded on death, writing arises from the opposition to voice, which is the uncontaminated origin. Cobra's castration has, therefore, a complex allegorical meaning: her appearance, that is, her apparent gender, her makeup, her being, arises from an incision, a lack created, inscribed by Dr. Ktazob. Writing inscribes itself on a tainted origin, on a carved negation—in this economy of gains and losses Cobra collects being. *Cobrar,* to collect, to acquire, to take on a characteristic; *cobrar,* to gather, to collect, to bring together, to join: *cobrar,* desire.

In the following section we find ourselves in an ultramodern city, where Cobra, dressed in black and wearing excessive makeup, reappears on a subway train. Here she is recognized by an old woman, presumably the Señora, who refers to Cobra in masculine terms: "—It's him." This scene leads us to the world of the drug dealers whom we have already met in Tanger. They turn out to be a motorcycle gang adept at Tantrism, which has joined forces with a group of Tibetan monks who were exiled after the Chinese invasion. Their names are Totem, Tiger, Scorpio, and Tundra, and they subject Cobra to an initiation ritual that leads to his/her death. They then perform with the body a complex Tantric funeral rite that ends, in a new section entitled "Blanco," with a series of prayers by each member of the group for someone whose identity they do not know. The motorcyclists have learned the ritual and other liturgical practices from the Tibetan monks, one of whom has assumed the posture of a *maharishi* who sells advice, relics, and drugs. All of them live from the production and distribution of drugs. It is obvious that both the initiation ritual and the funeral ceremony, above all in the details describing the mutilation of the body, repeat the alchemical activities of the Señora in the Lyrical Puppet Theater as well as the sexual surgery Ktazob performs in Tanger.

We have already seen the relationship of those rituals to writing—excision, cutting, the creation of a wound or deficiency that sustains the mark, the fixed graph that signifies absence and that, in its hieratic quality, suggests death. It is worth emphasizing the repetitive nature of ritual, the repetitions that punctuate the text of the novel itself. As we have already observed, Sarduy's metaphoric subject arises from and hides behind those repetitions, behind those metonymies that traverse the text at all levels, that pierce it, like a bird impaled on the wires of its cage. The passion and transport of Cobra in both stories are those of the metaphoric subject whose absence, as a center of meaning, we feel, in the strict and contradictory sense of the phrase: *we feel its absence*. The vanishing point, s/he who flees—Cobra in the subway—is the metaphoric subject, the marked (up) being, the carved one who covers the fault and embodies the symptoms of its absence, its re-production. Writing is the recurring sacrifice (the death foretold) of that center, of that subject who flees, like Velásquez in *Las Meninas* (flight becomes an obsession in *Colibrí*; it is implicit in the origin of Cuban literature, in the antislavery novel, which is literature of flight, of *marronage*). Cobra covers, Cobra culls; but what does Cobra collect? The fault is the debt collected, default avoided.

Like *De donde son los cantantes*, *Cobra* winds up in whiteness, which, in this case, turns out to be the prayers mentioned before. Whiteness is the end and the beginning, the white page, the goal, which of course alludes to the famous poem by Octavio Paz ("Blanco")—to hit on the bull's eye, "dar en el blanco," "blanco," that at which one aims, that which orients us. But, like the earlier novel, *Cobra* has not one, but at least two endings; if *De donde son los cantantes* ends with the author's "Note," *Cobra* closes with the "Indian Diary" in which appear the characters of the second part on their pilgrimage to Tibet. The action in *De donde son los cantantes* ends in the plain—in Havana—while *Cobra* ends in the mountains, the abode of the gods.

We do not know if the flight from the raid that puts an end to their drug dealings is the reason for the appearance, in the "Indian Diary," of the motorcyclists and the Tibetan monks, who are engaged in a return to the native land—the "Indian Diary" is a metaphoric *Cahier d'un retour au pays natal* in which the homeland has changed considerably. The exile of the motorcycle gang (from Europe) corresponds to the return of the monks (to Tibet), and this double movement cancels the sense of progression implicit in the pilgrimage. Departure and return occur simultaneously. The "Diary" marks the beginning of a journey of recovery, a return to the *monte*, the sacred mountain of Afro-Cuban lore: a flight that heals, that makes one recover. Cobra, *cubrir*, to cover. Tibet is the devastated space of the sacred, the ruined origin of the cult. Language becomes more and more impersonal, less and less accessible, as if it were only the text itself that embarked on this voyage to the Orient—reminiscent of Cobra's trip with Eustaquio, a return to the origin/supplement. Inserted in the text is a fragment of Columbus's *Diary*, which is entitled "The Indies," and the characters visit a nightclub called "Las Indias Gallantes," an allusion to the opera by Rameau, with its lavishly dressed Indians. The "Indian Diary" has the name of Columbus's *Diary*; it is a chronicle of the first voyage, the voyage of the beginning, of the origin, which is turned into metaphor and transfigured into the nightclub. A double movement, Columbus's text is a beginning, but it appears at the end, and it gives a name to the hovel where real Indians live together with those Indians Columbus invented by mistake. On their way to Tibet—in India—the motorcyclists question the exiled Great Lama, ask for his help, and consult him on the best way of reaching god. The Great Lama who, in his present situation, also lives by selling relics and advice responds in an oracular and impenetrable fashion. The text ends in the snows of the Chinese border, in total desolation, where the only possible language is the impersonal sounds the wind makes when it twirls the prayer wheels: "Further on, between the peaks, maybe the wind will make the prayer wheels spin, aligned upon the walls of the abandoned monasteries, upon the altars buried by the snow."

We return to Tibet, but to a Tibet from which the gods have fled as a result of the Chinese invasion which does not simply represent China's millennial imperialism but now a new, Western ideology—Communism. The "Indian Diary," then, traces a return to a sacred space, but that space, *el monte,* is found empty or corrupted. The realm of the sacred has been occupied by the profane, the plain on the mountain—the mountainous plain. History—the Chinese Revolution—has invaded the temple: it is a veritable explosion in the cathedral. The prayer wheels disseminate a sacred language that is without sender or recipient, set in motion by an invisible cosmic force. Scribbled, repeated white, the "Indian Diary" is an end that inaugurates a beginning, that *is* a beginning. Distanced from the two histories that repeat themselves, it is the product of a hypertelos, of that which exceeds closures. The realm of writing—the polyglot penis of José Arcadio—is removable, like Cobra's phallus.

But the "Indian Diary" does not content itself with such abstractions. It reflects its historical context in quite a direct fashion. The Chinese Revolution, the invasion of Tibet—whose different levels of meaning can be seen here and, later on, in *Maitreya*—are events that punctuate the plot, that fix its place in historical time. The "Indian Diary" was written at the end of the sixties, and it is that period that this text reflects.

The whole story about the motorcyclists and the monks has various meanings, and it is one of the ways in which *Cobra* performs a critical reading of Octavio Paz's *Conjunctions and Disjunctions.* To be able to understand how *Cobra* functions as a mechanism that reveals Latin America's literary subconscious, it is necessary first to consider its relationship with Paz's work. *Conjunctions and Disjunctions* is a book in which Paz enters the game of juggling cultures and histories, which Spengler initiated and which Lezama follows up in *La expresión americana.* Mexican Ambassador in New Delhi and profoundly interested in oriental culture, Paz asks himself in *Conjunctions and Disjunctions* about the nature of the cultural exchange between East and West. His meditation is also motivated by the student movement of the seventies, the popularity of drugs among the younger generation, as well as by certain Western poetic trends that looked toward the East for a kind of nirvana. At the center of Paz's meditation lies the way in which different cultures have conceived the mind-body distinction. By way of a structuralist approach, Paz charts a series of binary oppositions that embrace entire cultures. Paz's method is quite different from Lezama's, who assembled elements from various cultures in order to form what essentially were imaginary cultures. For Paz, the student movements of the sixties were a sign that the cultures that had not been founded on the negation of the body—the Eastern cultures—were in the process of replacing those of the West, at least in terms of their beliefs. Paz writes on the penultimate page of his passionate book:

> modern time—linear time, the homologue of the ideas of progress and history, ever propelled into the future, the time of the sign *non-body*, of the fierce will to dominate nature and tame instincts, the time of sublimation, aggression, and self-mutilation—is coming to an end. I believe that we are entering another time, a time that has not as yet revealed its form and about which we can saying nothing except that it will be neither linear time nor cyclical time. Neither history nor myth. . . . The return of the present: the time that is coming is defined by a *here* and a *now*. It is a negation of the sign *non-body* in all its Western versions: religious or atheist, philosophical or political, materialist or idealist. The present does not project us into any place beyond, any motley, other-worldly eternities or abstract paradises at the end of history. It projects us into the medulla, the invisible center of time: here and now. A carnal time, a mortal time: *the present is not unreachable, the present is not forbidden territory.* How can we touch it, how can we penetrate inside its transparent heart? I do not know, and I do not believe anybody knows . . . Perhaps the alliance of poetry and rebellion will give us a vision of it.

The center of Paz's poetic system is that present whose main feature is always transparency, but which is at the same time the kingdom of flesh and of objects bearing number, weight, and measure. This present in which the body is not denied and in which the symbolic capacity of language remains intact, is the whiteness that pervades his poetry and that is always found in the Orient, particularly in the landscapes. I cite the passage from *Conjunctions and Disjunctions* that appears as epigraph to the "Indian Diary" in *Cobra*: "The sky dips into the pool. There is no top or bottom: the world has been concentrated in this serene rectangle, a space which contains everything and is made up of nothing but air and a few images."

It is revealing that Paz insists on a romantic vision of the East, which perhaps corroborates his own theory in *Los hijos del limo*, according to which Latin Americans are products of a belated romanticism because they did not have a legitimate one at the proper time. It is also fascinating to observe how the elements that constitute the poetics of a great poet like Paz, once submitted to the discursiveness of prose, turn from seductive tropes into obvious contradictions: If the present is transparent, invisible, then how can it be a time of the flesh? In any case, we can now clearly see the relation of the second part of *Cobra* and the "Indian Diary" with *Conjunctions and Disjunctions*. The gang of drug-pushing motorcyclists represents the student movements to which Paz refers, with its return to the liturgy of oriental religions and the mind-altering powers of drugs. Above all, we can see that Sarduy's novel insists on rituals related to the body, living or dead, on the exaltation of the body's materiality. The alliance between the young-sters and the Tibetan monks would seem to corroborate Paz's contentions and make Sarduy's novel a sort of allegory of the latter's ideas. But it is quite the opposite.

There is in *Cobra* an interpenetration of East and West, a confluence of beginning and present, in which the beginning is a function of the present, and not the other way around. The motorcyclists have influenced the monks in the same way that the monks have influenced them. If we look closely, *Cobra* insists on the modernity of the Tibetans. The *maharishi* in the second part is quite emphatic about this: "I travel by jet, *not* by elephant." The landscape in the "Indian Diary" frequently abandons the purity of whiteness to become a junkyard, a kind of waste land, ruins of the modern that have left their indelible mark on the house of the gods: "The ringing of bicycles and car horns mingles with radios' high, syrupy soprano voices, xylophones, and harps. Rusty autobodies, broken engines, tires are all piled up to the porticos; rancid motor oil gushes from zinc; a pungent stench rises out of the scrap iron labyrinth." Some of the monks wear glasses, others drink Ovomaltine. And the Great Lama, hardened by the rigors of exile, reduced to much less than a god, commercializes the cult: "Yes, white shaggy monks, I am fulfilling my karma in this suburban hovel, selling the ancient tankas of the Order and trafficking in copper scepters, now rusted green, in order to support the last lamas of the Yellow Hat." The present in *Cobra* is not transparent; it is a fallen time, a time of exile, in which symbols are remade, recovered (*recobrados*), after the dev-astating blow of history. It is a *bricolage*, like the one we see in *De donde son los cantantes*, whose model in this case could be Lezama's imaginary era, constructed from fragments of different epochs and cultures, that is, from scraps of texts that within the actual mixture acquire a greater sig-nificance than they had in the original context from which they were torn.

A topic of Western letters that has been adopted by Latin American literature remains intact in Paz's ideas: the East as a utopia, America as its historical manifestation. Beautiful essays by Alfonso Reyes and pages from Carpentier's fiction have given linguistic reality to this topic, which is re-peated in writers as different as Onetti and García Márquez, and which has been studied in minute detail by Juan Duran in his beautiful book. Sarduy makes manifest in *Cobra*—and here we begin to glimpse his role as the subconscious of Latin American literature—how that topic is constituted, how it is part of a process of textual production. Paz prophetically announces the possible alliance between poetry and rebellion in order to embody the utopia of a present that would be like the West's conception of the oriental world. In Paz, not only history is suppressed, but also the mechanism through which poetic illusion is created; Sarduy shows its linguistic and scriptural constituency. Sarduy, being historical, proposes that the East of today is not the one of the origin that Paz invents, but instead the future of Latin America: a future of chaotic cities filled with misery and violence, where primitive cultures subsist and are reborn. This historical inversion—the East as America's future, not as its origin—is probably modeled on Lévi-Strauss's *Tristes tropiques*, where the anthropologist, before embarking on his journey to Brazil in search of a present origin of humanity among the Indians left in the jungle, offers us a chapter that describes his voyage to New Delhi, a hair-raising image of what will become the Latin American cities. Had he looked out of the window, Paz would have noticed that in the most transparent region of air, as Alfonso Reyes called Mexico, the air is very opaque, hardly breathable. In Sarduy, modernity is not only indelible in its effects—we are condemned to a time of recovery, to always having to collect the debt, not to possess the principal—but part of a dialectical process of creation. The destructiveness, the self-mutilation that Paz wishes to abolish, is part of that creativity.

Charred snow, tainted whiteness, the meaning of writing in *Cobra* is key to Sarduy's difference from Paz and perhaps from the entire generation to which the Mexican poet belongs. Writing, in Sarduy, does not simply represent a mode of communication, but is that through which the workings of language are made manifest. Language arises from difference, or in difference, in the incision between two elements which, in order to signify, to be, have to remain distinct from each other. Writing reflects this cut, the originary negativity of language, which is never the "white pearl on a white forehead," as Dante would have it, but black on white, or vice-versa. What *Cobra* dramatizes time and again is the ritualization of that cut, which, by being at the very heart of language, is at the beginning of being and of culture. One recovers (*se recobra*) upon leaving the incision that announces and denounces the fault. For Paz, the East is a possible nirvana, for Sarduy, it is Columbus's initial mistake. The origin is always multiple, contradictory, and deceptive; its truth, the truth of Columbus's India, of Cipango, is being founded on that mistake, which here is the fault (default) of the beginning, that which covers the present, that which erases itself but does not disappear completely. Therefore, while, for Paz, "nothing is written in advance," for Sarduy, everything is written, each sign already contains all writing.

The deepest stratum where we can see this economy of being and language in *Cobra* is in the title itself of the book, which is the object of many different word games in the text and which is related to one of Paz's own poems cited by Sarduy, appropriately, after the above passage from *Conjunctions and Disjunctions*:

>   *La boca habla*
>   La cobra
>   fabla de la obra
>   en la boca del abra
>   recobra
>   el habla:
>   El Vocablo.

Paz's poem describes and dramatizes how language is generated, a process
that thematically appears as the circular movement of the snake that swallows its own tail; sign against sign, ring against ring, which in its own
association creates the word and disappears at the same time. There is a
dialectic between the closure of the circle that evokes the Cobra and the
initial *o* and the aperture of the *a*, specifically in *abra*, which means opening
as well as gap, separation, entrance. Ebb and flow, opening and closure;
air that flows through the hollow circles of the vowels, arrested by the
barrier of the consonants. With the exception of the *c* however, the consonants are fricatives: intervocalic *b*'s (which may be inscribed as *b* or *v*), *r*
and *l*, liquid fricatives when combined with the intervocalic *b*. *Cobra, abra,
vocablo*: breath, life force, spirit that resides in air or wind, according to the
most venerable theories. The breath of air that flows through the written
letters of *cobra* creates language. It is a beginning, like the cobra itself, the
snake is found at the origin of all theogonies; the phallus which, in psychoanalysis, represents the separable, imaginary object at the origin of
representation. Envy and anxiety; motion. But we cannot forget that *cobra*
begins with a cut, with the incomplete *o* that is the *c*, an occlusive consonant
which, of course, closes, cuts the column of air, inaugurates the word with
a cut, breaks the ground for the house of language, removes the joint for
the erection of the word. Cobra is the embellished, disfigured, carved origin. From the smoothness of the *o* that opens onto the *c* we travel across
the mountain of the *br*, almost a cut, the *r* a detour around the *b*, which
guides us to the opening of the *a*.

From the irreducible dialectic at the origin of language proliferate meanings that cover the crevice, the opening: [c]obra, bar[r]oco, braço (arm,
hence *abrazo*, to embrace, to encircle, to wrap around as the snake wraps
around its victim, deadly embrace), [a]barco (to encompass, to contain),
[re]cobra, cubre, cobre (copper). The word that lies hidden under this elaborate series of mistakes is CUBA which has the same initial cut of the
incomplete *o* made occlusive and the same intervocalic fricative. Cuba, the
lost signified, object of a search within language, the word omitted from
the circumlocution in the title of *De donde son los cantantes*. Cobra is Cuba
deformed through pronunciation, through the mistake. The language of
the novel, like that of the characters, is the language of exile, language of
the plain, of the plain song, the *canto llano*, which recovers and at the same
time disfigures the source—baroque plainness of the mixed source. The
effaced metaphoric subject's obsession with being can be glimpsed at the

edges, a residue, a perimeter of errors around the absent center, the fleeing center, which is always deformed by the multiple reflections and echoes that collide with each other. We see, then, that Sarduy's version of Lezama's "metaphoric subject" also seems to be motivated by desire, but this desire is not the love to which the author of *Paradiso* refers, a love that supplements and augments, but rather a contradictory impulse that adds and subtracts at the same time. The "passion" of this "metaphoric subject" is reflected in the two rituals that are performed in the two main parts of *Cobra*. Within the text of the novel, what is simultaneously erased and added is the "Indian Diary" which is writing.

In Sarduy, Lezama's imaginary era becomes a vast machinery that attempts, in several ways, to make manifest the mechanisms through which language is created. To be sure, because of the nature of language itself, this demonstration has to be made through allusion to something else: That is to say, language is metaphorical even when it refers to itself. Hence the surgery and the funeral rites. The entire description of the process through which Ktazob "remakes" Cobra, in which he transfers the pain to Pup, shows how language covers one signified with another, or how the subconscious creates a false symptom that the analyst has to interpret. The castration itself, as has been mentioned, is an allegory of the workings of language, its play of negations and supplements. Lezama combines *attributes* of different cultures and epochs, whereas Sarduy shows how those attributes and elements are combined. Sarduy reduces language to monogrammatical particles: To his mind, COpenhagen, BRussels, Amsterdam yield COBRA. And Cobra, as I have suggested, may be a distortion of Cuba. For this reason we can say that everything is written in Sarduy.

To all this we can add another dimension of the novel: cosmology as reflected in the theory of the Big Bang. Pup is the name of a star, "white dwarf" (*enana blanca*) is a type of star. There exists, consequently, a correlation at the cosmic level between the stellar system, such as it is conceived today, and language. It is a saturation of language that pervades everything. In the works of the great Mexican Baroque writers Carlos de Sigüenza y Góngora (*Occidental planeta, Libra astronómica*) and Sor Juana (*Primero sueño*), we can also find this vision of the universe as a great combinatory of signs in motion, a stellar system of which we are part—a language that articulates us. Sarduy's cosmology poses the existence of a black hole at the origin of that constellation, which represents the initial explosion and which is comparable, within Sarduy's entire system, to the fault, the mistake, the germinating cut.

We have seen how *Cobra* unveils the way in which things oriental are turned into a topic in Latin American literature, and how this process is part of what I have called the subconscious of Latin American literature. But that process includes, above all, formal elements of the novel: characters, plot, language. The characters in *Cobra*—like the characters in *De donde son los cantantes*, but in an even more radical way—are not invested with elements of continuity or duration. In this sense, they are totally flat, without inner depth, much like the characters in an epic; everything is external to them, everything is visible. Sarduy touches bottom and reduces the novel to its functions. His characters, like the ones in an epic, are concentrations of ideas, ideologies: they are representations, in the most literal sense. Sarduy's characters are forged in the melting pot of the pure, undiluted values of Latin American and Western culture. Cobra and Cadillac exhibit an exaggerated version of *machismo*. Gender is based on a lack; it is a kind of literary transvestism. The Lyrical Puppet Theater thus represents a place of literary and cultural transformations, where language/culture shapes the features of each individual according to the laws of a system whose workings we have observed at various levels. Before being Traveler or Horacio, cultural decisions have been made about those fictional entities, decisions more significant than their features as characters in *Rayuela*. Latin American *machismo* grows out of a system of values that has been built on language; *Cobra* does not denounce *machismo* but exposes its artificiality, its being founded on a transvestism inherent in language itself.

The same is true with respect to the characters' language, which is shockingly artifical in *Cobra*. Sarduy's characters are made up of different kinds of discourse which turn them inside out in order constantly to betray them. The traditional novel, including that of the Boom, does the same but represses it. Exaggerated artificiality is a way of separating language from that which represses its artificial origin, from that which covers it up. As is already manifest in *Gestos*, Sarduy's first novel, falsity challenges the laws of mimesis, brings them to the surface. And the multiplicity of discursive modes through which the same character plays the same role is a form of alienation, a strategy through which language reveals its distance from the source. In this sense, Sarduy's language is deliberately one of exile, of recollection (re-cobro).

Little remains standing after *Cobra* (except for the oversized feet of the protagonist). Sarduy has toppled the ideology of Cuban identity to replace it with something more dialectical and polemically pluralistic. In *Cobra* he has rendered visible the mechanisms of that dialectic. As I have already suggested, that askesis, that reduction of the received legacy, and the annihilation of the metaphoric subject, are the counterparts of Cobra's passion, of his/her mutilation. After this rigorous deconstruction, we move with Sarduy toward recovering Cuba, not by way of the *Orígenes* ideology, but appropriately through the text of *Paradiso. Maitreya*, Sarduy's next work, emerges from a passage of Lezama's novel. Cuba is a text.

Notes on the Fiction of Nélida Piñón

Giovanni Pontiero

Among contemporary Brazilian authors Nélida Piñón has emerged as a writer of note and interest. Her novels and short stories . . . show the same deep concern with universal themes and individuality of style that characterizes the recent fiction from Spanish America. In general terms, her writing can be related to an existentialist tradition immersed in philosophical complexities. Appropriately enough, her prose strives for accuracy and conciseness on the one hand, and on the other, a poetic lyricism that depends for its effects upon nuances of expression and a carefully contrived tension in the verbal rhythm. And here Nélida Piñón adds a lightness of touch that one rarely finds in comparable writers.

The dominant symbol in all of the narratives in *Sala de armas* is that of a *journey*, sometimes physical, but often purely imaginative. Projecting the idea of the journey as something basic and essential in our earthly existence, the title story represents the cycle of life with its numerous possibilities and alternatives. To quote the narrator of this central story: "I have labored day and night in order to bring my eternity indoors. For the error of death has always inhabited me." The fascination of the unknown also provides the theme for "Fronteira natural" (Natural Frontier) where the sudden confrontation and way of life completely different from our own is described in dramatic terms underlining the irresistible attractions of a challenge and its inherent dangers. Man, beast, tree and flower express in their very manner of being a constant desire for change and that infinite quest for perpetual flux and transformation as defined by the philosophical teachings of Heraclitus. The nagging urge to be someone else in some other place, to discover and embrace new customs and even some new form of existence

From *Review* no. 19 (Winter 1976). © 1974 by the Center for Inter-American Relations, Inc.

is voiced in "Os Mistérios de Eleusis" (The Mysteries of Eleusis): "I persuaded myself that Eleusis was not the only mortal to abandon her body in the promise of some other form, for was I myself not imitating her?" Thus the journey invoked in these stories is no mere escape or opting out but, rather, a meaningful pursuit of self-discovery and illumination in some new and remote environment as hectic as that of New York or as exotic as that of the Far East.

There are no guarantees of success for those who embark upon these journeys. In "Illustração da graca" (The Illustration of Grace), Claudio warns the wayward woman in his life: "Look, should you decide to go, be sure to take a coat, for one never knows whether one will find summer or winter in certain forms of existence." The uncertainty that hovers over the outward journey also marks the traveller's return. The male protagonist in "Colheita" (Harvest) comes home still haunted by doubts and darkness only to find that the woman he left behind has not only grown in sheer intensity of feeling but also in powers of expression: "She did not cease to take possession of words and for the first time in years she was able to explain her life. She experienced the pleasure of gathering into her womb, like a tumour grating against its inner cavities, the sound of her own voice . . . she took delight in this new passion and embraced this new world hitherto shrouded in darkness, which now revealed itself with the man's return."

II

As human beings we appear to transform our lives in a number of ways, partly through our contact with certain surroundings and partly through our contact with other people, animals and objects. The image of the fencing room in Nélida Piñón's title begins to make sense when you start to consider the constant parrying with obscure forces in the relationships described in these stories. Stories where human motivations are scrupulously examined while weaknesses and deformities, both physical and mental, are cruelly exposed; stories where the abstract nature of power, faith, love, loyalty and dependence is closely questioned.

In these relationships the fundamental *rapport* between male and female, whether purely sexual or spiritual, reveals important differences in their physical and emotional make-up. Male supremacy is voiced by the gauche João Manco to his friend and benefactor Adamastor: "If a man doesn't tame his woman, Adamastor, what other animal can he hope to tame?" and in "Ave de paraíso" (Bird of Paradise), we find the woman "concealing herself in the shadow" of her husband. At the same time, we are left in no doubt as to who is the stronger partner. "A sagrada família" (The Holy Family), ironically enough, concerns a marriage contracted in hatred: "Life together ended in bitterness and in the hardening of misplaced estimations" but the feminine traits of patience and self-sacrifice ultimately bear fruit because in this fiction a woman's bid for freedom is something much deeper than mere social acceptance just as her outer delicacy and tact betray her inner security and her outer vulnerability, her inner strength. Moreover, as "Sangue esclarecido" makes clear, the miraculous act of procreation is hers alone: "He wanted to tell her that the product of his flesh in sweat and secretion, represented for him the palpable and afflicted signs of a world to which he had no admittance even though he, too, had sown in her body the generous seeds with which empires are born."

The margins between hatred and love are often obscure but the hero in "Colheita" comes round to recognizing that the woman in his life is capable of a much greater intensity in her emotions and that her range of sensitivity is beyond his powers. In women, the mystery of love remains intact and just as with the radiant Eleusis, everything they touch is tinged with magic.

Love, "however ugly and incalculable, is necessary" we are assured in "Sangue esclarecido" and for the chosen few, such as the punished lovers in "Cortejo do divino" (Divine Ceremonial), there are the delights of "an overwhelming voluptuousness and divinity through the powers of the flesh."

A primitive freedom and hedonistic sensuality prevail in these stories. The legend of Orpheus and Eurydice is re-enacted by many of the characters who are condemned to tragic destinies by their very excess of love. And what better setting for these pagan rites than an elemental world of river, tree, fruit and mineral untouched by social conventions or restrictions. In "Oriente próximo" (Near East) the Turkish visitors compare their happiness with "the freshness of figs" and elsewhere, the simple operation of peeling fruit becomes a solemn ritual of love and physical union. A surfeit of sensibility is everywhere in this enchanted forest and the love Nélida Piñón's women experience is instinctively . . . "exaggerated . . . intense . . . and excessive."

This same pursuit of spontaneous feeling and unbridled love and copulation leads on to a preference (common among existential writers) for the sentient world of animals uncomplicated by conscience or moral scruple. Her heroines Eleusis, Luz and Domina prosper in the solitude of a natural setting and the ugly, unwanted child of "O novo reino" (The New Kingdom) not only finds peace but establishes a new species there that makes any return to the civilization she once knew seem intolerable: "Her revulsion now, was that of someone who was visiting hell after having inhabited the paradise of animal love." The primitive world is not merely the domain of the "free beasts of the jungle" but that divine haven where living creatures can "co-exist with ardor" and freely surrender to the *concentrated richness of summer.*" Little wonder then that the little calf adopted as a family pet in "Vida de estimação" (Privileged Life) should spurn the world of men or that the murderer in "Sangue esclarecido" should find the law of the jungle the only law to which he is temperamentally fitted: "That savage love was the only kind that he had ever felt. And the only kind of love that he could not refuse."

III

Many of the dramatic situations created in these narratives stem not so much from encounters between man and woman, or man and beast, as between the hypersensitive individual and the uncomprehending masses. Hatred is shown to be much easier than love and the unwillingness or inability to understand other customs and modes of behavior is one of the saddest failings in the experience and history of mankind. In "Colheita" we encounter the familiar situation of the townsfolk "who rejected the conduct of those who inhabited strange lands." The sole woman character in "Oriente próximo" has a delicate and difficult task on her hands in trying to win the friendship and trust of the four Turkish gentlemen who disappear as mysteriously as they came by the end of the story, and in "Fronteira natural" most forcefully of all, we can observe that any sallies into foreign territory whether on earth, in heaven, hell or limbo, are necessarily fraught with danger and ultimately doomed to failure. The adventurer is free to pursue his dream but he must beware of "uneasy alliances" and resign himself to a lonely path. The eccentric who is determined to run against the current of accepted social patterns must be prepared for suffering and the fate of the outcast. If they persevere and survive the cruelties of their fellow-men, they will touch the stones of essential truth but the price can be high. This is the final lesson of "Fronteira natural" and "Cortejo do divino" where the characters endure public censure and hatred despite the worthiness of their ideals.

IV

The most ordinary domestic situation in Nélida Piñón's fiction is soon transformed into something quite extraordinary, impregnated with unsuspected mysteries and signs. For example, with the simple task of baking a chocolate cake in "Bird of Paradise" the characters take off into the realms of extravagance and fantasy on the slightest pretext. Nevertheless, these men and women are recognizable as people and they are not mere states of mind as in so much existential writing.

This brings us to the vital question of Nélida Piñón's creative approach to language. Her phrasing and vocabulary like those of another distinguished contemporary, Clarice Lispector, respond to her own special needs. Like Lispector, she poses herself some vital questions. How best to describe a world in which material accidents cloak intangible truths and a mysterious essence beyond human understanding? How best to analyze and describe *feeling?* Nélida Piñón stresses the extraordinary power of language and its ability to exhilarate the reader, transforming resentment into submission and distaste into admiration. Language carefully exploited can move, exalt and disturb the reader and when inspiration is upon the writer, *words* and *enchantment* become synonymous: "My words were her delight," the hero exclaims in "Luz" (Light). Her descriptive prose alternates between tense, dramatic phrasing and long-spun sensuous images. Recalling their ardent love affair, the hero of "Luz" declares: "I was the flowering of Luz. She would stroke my body extending her graceful arm, and her flesh became mine as she began to match my ardor."

The quest for understanding between men and nations is an arduous and even fruitless task as the well-intentioned woman in "Próximo oriente" soon learns in trying to cope with her exotic guests: "I acquired a passion for hospitality in dealing with those four little Turks as well as an instinct about crossing frontiers in which I began to confide. Our brothers from oppressed lands treasure their possessions more than we do—hence their great wealth and pride." Similar discoveries require a probing of linguistic differences as well as those of custom and tradition, because the Tower of Babel is still with us. The tutors in "Torre de Roccarosa" (The Tower of Roccarosa) are a case in point. "They wanted to say: 'I am happy,' but by some inexplicable process, they expressed themselves in a language un-known by all. Or when they finally succeeded in saying 'I am happy,' they incurred some error, since what they had really wanted to say beforehand was that they had probably been too late in liberating themselves."

The characters she creates and admires must be equal to the challenge of this garden of freedom and hedonistic pleasures where the breasts of the Sultan's seven virgins become "landscapes of golden crescents and repose" and where language is "cultivated like wheat."

The philosophical speculations that have found a new impetus in Latin American writing with figures such as Borges, Cortázar and Guimarães Rosa find a new emphasis in Nélida Piñón's work. Time-honoured com-plexities about the nature and purpose of all human activity are reexamined in her own imaginative vein. In the key story "Sala de armas," which bears a striking similarity to the theme and conclusions of Guimarães Rosa's brilliant narrative "The Other Bank of the River," the narrator sums up the basic difference between himself and the woman whom he loves: "She believed in the immortality of life. I, more sinister, invented the immortality of death and prepared myself for the banquet."

But if it is difficult to live, at times it appears to be even more difficult to die and characters remain hovering on the frontiers between hope and despair.

V

The initial paragraph of stories such as "Fronteira natural," "A sagrada família," "Sangue esclarecido" and most notably of all, "O novo reino" plunge us into dramatic situations and an atmosphere of tension reflected in landscape, men, animals and objects alike. In "O novo reino," the cruel world of men stands in stark contrast to the stillness and impassiveness of nature all around them: "The landscape of green vegetation, the light silhouetting beasts and things. The father walked in front, like a monarch. It was his task to slaughter the pigs, and he always sat at the head of the table. The procession behind him consisted of two women. Despite the intimacies of their flesh, the couple only had one daughter. Ugly and unloved, she followed them everywhere. When they visited the town, it was their custom to return through the forest by an open path that led to their home where they lived surrounded by trees and shrubs. And the immense countryside stretched all around them."

There is a pleasing sonority in this writer's prose and her exalted use of language is achieved on the whole without resorting to a blatant abuse of metaphor and imagery—a common failing among Latin American writers. Her choice of adjectives calls for attentive reading, e.g. *"concentrated* richness," *"distracted* appreciation"; her fondness for apparent contradictions, frequent antitheses and unusual juxtapositions also demands some probing for the fictional world she presents is one of constant transformations "under the effect of a seismic shock." It is a world full of ambiguities and contradictions that defy adequate expression; things constantly appear to be 'aggressive' yet 'innocent,' 'near' yet 'remote,' 'friendly' yet 'alien.'

Critics familiar with modern Brazilian literature might argue that Nélida Piñón lacks the linguistic virtuosity of the late Guimarães Rosa or the thematic coherence and consistency of Clarice Lispector whom she most closely resembles in her writing. But Nélida Piñón's creative talent is beyond question and the threads of imaginative speculation she weaves carry a refreshing note of irony and subdued optimism.

Voices in the Silence

Patricia Tobin

> Most people think voices don't matter; they regard voice as a ghost or a garment or a cosmetic; it is a very detachable attribute of the visible or tangible body. To most, sound is mere décor. To this boy, Llew, my voice was a standard machine of communication, a jalopy for getting around in, and the hell with the make. To me his voice, which for some minutes I ate with nauseated hunger, was the hateful blessed key to a return to the total variousness of life against which he and I were blaspheming.
>
> —ANTHONY BURGESS

The unilingual American, who reads his Latin American and French contemporary literature in translation, is immediately aware of the amplitude of the one and the confinement of the other. The Latin American novel—as it is being written by García Márquez, Lezama Lima, Donoso, Vargas Llosa, Carpentier—offers an ebullient, epic accommodation of everything that has been lost in the linear pursuits of the traditional European novel. Against this phenomenon of abundance—variously affirmed as *tropicalismo*, *el barroco férvoro*, *realismo mágico*—stands the *esprit géométrique* of the French *nouveau roman*, refining its technical experiments in pattern and surface. In *Clara*, Luisa Valenzuela has smudged these demarcations. To the isolated individual she has returned the experience of *lo real maravilloso*, playing it along his quivering pulses; and she has returned to the fictional character precisely what the French have subtracted, a psychology that is revealed by a voice.

The people in Valenzuela's short stories do not walk their native land; they hover over it. Appearing fully formed yet diaphanous, they hang suspended between the mundane and the unearthly, having firm roots in neither, reaching for both. Typically, they have a project for relieving a bare, unsatisfactory reality which escalates into the uncanny. A paradigm may be discovered in the hero of "The Alphabet" who, having resolved to act methodically all his life, respects only one letter of the alphabet for each of three months, and in the fourth month "without prior notice" dies of dysentery. He is not unlike the adolescent boy who takes a quantitative approach in seeking total absolution for his sins. To hedge against future sinning, he hoards the church wafers, fasts, and has himself beaten; and, having left off a heterosexual affair to begin a homosexual one, he ends

From *Review* no. 18 (Fall 1976). © 1976 by the Center for Inter-American Relations, Inc.

his confession with this question: "But I am worried, Father, and that's why I want you to tell me: how much time in Paradise can I add in my book for having given up Adela so much against my wishes?" Thus, when the Virgin Mary does not deliver a miracle ("Very pretty and all that, but what has She done for us? Not even a minor miracle. We're fed up, I can tell you"), the fisherpeople of the village stone her statue; thus, when the mute woman finally finds a man who "has a voice that could raise the dead," and her dead materialize with flesh hanging from their bones, she must kill him to stop his voice. The unnverving logic of psychopathology rides on the crisp tones of human determination.

Perhaps "Irka of the Horses" illustrates best the white space of silence within which Valenzuela wraps the voice in a short story—the voice as it floats on consciousness or as it is forced up from the unconscious, shaping alternate realities. Three women from the city have come to an isolated beach home on holiday. Bored with knitting and sunbathing, they light green candles to the invisible sorceress Irka, so that she might drive away the fascinating wild horses nearby. "In reality, however, they were not waiting for Irka but for Leda, their friend." Leda's car has broken down ("That's life—the right person is never there at the right time. Damn men who know nothing about nuts and bolts!"), and she takes a ride with a motorcyclist who has a skull printed on the back of his windbreaker. Her friends find her the next morning under the carob tree with Death the motorcyclist, whom she has strangled with her scarf. This Leda then speaks: "Go away, you loathsome sniffing dogs. This body is mine; my eyes are also bulging. I also want to disembowel him and see what's inside. That's better than possessing their souls while they're alive. That's better than trying to break their will. While they're alive, one can only wound them with words, crack the mask. Now I possess him, dead at my feet, defeated. I can open him with a knife, at last I can have a man, the insides of a man. I want to feel his viscous viscera, warm, slippery." For the three women "Irka no longer existed; only Leda, who must be punished, who must pay for her crime." But then " a strange gleam appeared in Antonia's eyes":

> "She said she strangled him. . . ."
> "And," Josefina added, "at the foot of the strangled, they say,
> a root grows, in the shape of a man. It screeches when it's torn,
> and it contains magic secrets. . . ."
> "It's the mandrake," cried Maria Carmela. "It's the charm Irka
> is sending us."
> "He's under the carob tree. . . ."
> "Lets go look!"

What grips us in these eerie stories is a force rather than a form, a voice that begins again and again without lapse or closure, speaking in each line the unpredictable. Perhaps this is why the novel *Clara* seems less satisfactory than the thirteen short stories in the volume. The novel's ongoing plot dictates that its form must swallow up the voice, allowing no moments of original suspension when time stumbles and there is nothing but voice. Because in this novel the events accommodate themselves to character, everything serves for the clarification of Clara—the contrast between her body as whore and her head as the carnival's Aztec Flower, the sadomasochistic patterns of her love affairs, the sea and the "red destiny" as her symbols. What emerges as the meaning of the book, borne on the back of the repetition that always signifies, is the self's autonomy. It is only in the short story's exquisitely unique and local it-only-happens-once that the unautonomous self speaks in the obsessive rhythms of division and dependence.

We should be grateful that to Luisa Valenzuela, the voice does matter. That in her short stories, if not in her novel, the voice is indeed "the hateful blessed key to a return to the total variousness of life."

The Dazzling World
of Friar Servando

Julio Ortega

Celestino antes del alba (''Celestino before Sunrise,'' 1967) by Reinaldo Arenas, one of the most important writers to have appeared in Cuba since the Revolution, is a poetic re-creation of childhood; but, far more important, it is an outstanding verbal exercise. Arenas uses the poetic technique of semi-independent phrases, which, as they accumulate, take the shape of a fragmentary text modified and remade in successive variations. The technique resembles the contrapuntal phrasing of surrealism, though it reminds one even more of the versicles of traditional poetry. Understandably, then, we find Arenas frequently quoting this poetry.

Hallucinations, his second novel, unfolds within a framework of the fantastic and the baroque but according to a very concrete and objective system of correlations. The fictional aspect of the work focuses on everyday facts and experiences—hunger, physical punishment, helplessness—all endowed with a dreamlike aura and a genuine, spontaneous intensity, which, nevertheless does not contaminate the physical dimension communicating through all the senses a multifarious accumulation of reality. Thus the capriciousness of an erratic existence and the reverberations of a hostile and magic world inform Arenas's narrational space and characterize his personal world from the very first page.

The book, of course, is an unrestrained verbal re-creation of the life of Friar Servando Teresa de Mier, an extraordinary character whom Lezama Lima, writing in *La expresión americana*, sees as an archetypal image supporting an extremely convincing reality populated with other, less extraordinary characters from nineteenth-century Latin America. And in depicting that existence which exceeds reality and acquires form in a mod-

From *Review* no. 10 (Winter 1973), translated by Tom J. Lewis. © 1973 by the Center for Inter-American Relations, Inc.

ifying imagination (by means of a combination Lezama himself formulated), *Hallucinations* develops that combination not as symbol, but as adventure:

> This is the life of Friar Servando Teresa de Mier. Such as it was, and could have been; such as I should have liked it to have been.
> It is meant to be simply a novel, rather than a biographical or historical novel.

So declares the author. "An Adventure Novel," reads the subtitle introducing Arenas's unrestricted fictional perspective which expands the historical-biographical material he uses chiefly as referential correlative— oriented, as much as possible, toward fiction. For example, Arenas's letter addressed to his main character serves as the book's prologue in which the author tells of looking for information on Friar Servando: the data he finally gathers is considerable, but he had difficulty finding it, and that data reduces his character from a public figure to a marginal personage within the story. From the very beginning, then, this historical figure *is* a fictional character, but one who maintains a secret fascination which doubly animates and justifies Arenas's novel.

A MULTI-PLANAR TEXT

On the one hand, Arenas is inspired by an almost revisionist sentiment— poetry is still capable of discovering a hidden meaning in history—as well as a desire to revive the marginal heroism of a rebel, and Arenas perceives in Servando's heroism an important option: a life radicalized by rebellion. (Recall the epilogue to *Explosion in a Cathedral*, where Alejo Carpentier takes inventory of Victor Hugo's sources supporting a notion of fact insofar as the origin of his text is concerned. In *Hallucinations* the historical sources uphold, instead, the notion of *fantasy*.) And on the other hand, Arenas sees his subject as a personal reflection:

> The amount of facts about your life that I assembled was actually quite large; but getting to know and love you was not really made easier by those wearisome, all too precise encyclopedias, or by those awful essays which were never precise enough. It was far more use to discover that you and I are the same person.

Arenas, then, does not feel obliged to limit himself to historical information; it is enough that he refer to the *Autobiography of Fray Servando*, which he quotes along with a few other sources, throughout the novel. Whereas Carpentier confronts an almost completely unknown character, Arenas engages one so accessible that he has left behind a detailed autobiography. In order to be faithful to reality Carpentier has to "re-create" profusely; Arenas has to "remake, de-realize," and the identification of the author with his character is, at base, a poetic mechanism establishing a norm for this fictional license, opening up spaces of imagination where fantasy revokes veristic naturalism and enables the author to replace conventions of biography and history with conventions of the novel itself. History, biography, novel—these are the elements Arenas employs to create a multi-planar text.

THREE PERSONS IN ONE TEXT

An adventure novel obviously requires spatial structure, so the chapters carry the names of different places where the "biography" unfolds. But in the fantastic adventure novel, this manner of division becomes a convention facilitating no more than a variety of parody and hyperbolic criticism. (The same thing occurs with the historical chronology of more than forty years.) The conventions function as a frame of reference for the text since the structural space is formed by the simultaneous presence of several speakers. The first person (Friar Servando), the second person (who amplifies and corrects the facts) and the third person (who provides the tones of a chronicle and parody simultaneously) establish three levels in the text, but always as a narrative convention, since the individual levels do not require separate, disjointed versions of the text, but function as a process of continuous unfolding, making and remaking the text. Essentially, this triple focus forms the fictional aspect of the biographical novel. The first person is the conventional form of the "autobiography," the second is the convention of the "historical chronicle" and the third is the convention of "fictional narrative." With considerable technical ability, Arenas creates a mirroring of perspectives, which is the writing itself unfolding in its avid questioning, persuasive criticism and humor.

This triple approach, which remakes facts in order to multiply them, confers on the text another distinct characteristic: its parodical aspect. Through continual modification and duplication, the facts are drawn out and extended in the commentary, in fantasy and in the irony of the absurd. All the realism of the novel is thus denied: the drama of the "biography" does not require emphasis because the humor accomplished that without a loss of effect while subordinating the dramatic facts (in that anxious and wrathful life) to a pious irony of excess and exaggeration. Humor does not render Arenas's character any less heroic (consider the example of *Don Quixote*); rather, it makes him a modern hero. But the parody does not stop here, showing up in the book's loquacity as well as in the conventional devices of an adventure story. The generous commentaries of the historical chronicles convert historical prolixity into comic hyperbole. And in that comedy of continual accidents and misfortunes, the fire of a destiny forms the hero of the true *revolution*.

A NOVEL REVOLUTIONARY

"At that time I suffered from loneliness and took refuge in literature," says Friar Servando on page forty. And, in fact, his persecutions—his prisons—began with his famous discourse on the Virgin of Guadalupe, who according to Friar Servando, appeared before the advent of the Spaniards. Thus, the origin of his adventures is his intellectual condition: he is persecuted for his ideas, and in the novel this fact becomes the central motivation. Having started his anti-official and critical speculations, Friar Servando becomes a marginal figure who is quickly pursued and captured, all of which points to the nature of his rebellion and, subsequently, to his American conscience: desire for Mexican and American independence. Servando's rebellion is anti-colonialist and his protest a permanent state of dissent: the Friar as total revolutionary shaped by a novel.

This perspective is set within yet another: the deranged fantasy which gives rise to a dazzling world. In childhood the main character has been defined ("All that he possessed now was imagination") and opened to all possibilities of adventure: "I could do for you what you have done or even imagined doing." This intervention by the author himself, creating the text and directing toward the character functions within the continual disclosure of facts and their resonances, within a series of hyperbolic variations. In the same respect, the intellectual dimension too is a magical activity: thus rebellion is reality—a vast exercise in pure anarchy, in radical protest.

KILL EVEN GOD IF NECESSARY

Let us follow the origin and development of that exercise for a few moments. On page seventy-eight Friar Servando, in prison, speaks with a friar who has grown disenchanted with the French revolution, a disenchantment he does not share:

> "No, no! It's better that it happened. Things should never *not* happen! This is the whole point!"
> "You say this because you have never really experienced anything momentous enough to shake your faith."

replies the other. And Friar Servando answers, "My faith is beyond my experience." "I believe," he says, "in myself, which means in almost everyone else. That's why I can never be betrayed." This all-encompassing and integrating perspective derives without a doubt from that tantalizing disclosure that had previously defined it. Upon this foundation his political attitude is formed as anarchical rebellion, but carried out as passion for justice and vision of a natural order. In Spain he rejects the role of the intellectuals who are subservient to power. Soon he wants to kill Godoy, the king, the pope and even God, if necessary. Fleeing his pursuers and seeking amends for the unjust punishment he received on account of his sermon about the Virgin of Guadalupe, Servando travels from Paris to Rome, where "he wants to leave his clerical robes and become a worldly priest." Upon leaving France he has a new insight: "I then realized that everything is a fraud in the world of politics." Once again in Spain, but still on the run, he regains the feeling of an experience based on his own sufferings, in the name of his ideas and the power he has gained will eventually dictate, the necessity of his rebellion after thirty years of clandestine living:

> . . . I entered this prison when I was still young, and now I'm being shipped off to another one as an old man near to death. Riddled with disease. My crime is being American . . .

His aim is now a program:

> . . . to see America free of all the evils caused by Europeans, and
> . . . this can be achieved only through complete independence.

But when political independence is won for his country, he still has to fight Iturbide. Again his nonconformist criticism leads him to prison. "The fact that I am again being imprisoned merely shows Mexico is still not free," he says. "Once in my cell, by the light of a spluttering candle I began writing against him [Iturbide] and prepared for the true revolution." Finally the intellectual bureaucracy gathers round and praises the new president, Guadalupe Victoria, amid galleries of martyrs and patriotic heroes: the republic is sinking into grandiloquent ridicule. The works of Friar Servando do not cease, even though his dream of total revolution now appears to be impossible, owing to human nature itself which will not allow of a perfect order, an order which is thought to be out of reach even in the heavenly realm. "He had a presentiment that during his whole life he had been deceived." His radical credo seeks ultimate answers but it is too late for him now. In the public celebration which pays an homage to him as a hero of the new republic, an homage which he ignores, he thinks of the inner deficiency that places limits on men and postpones the day of the real revolution.

This brief résumé shows the interweaving of history and fiction on an argumentative base modified by formal discontinuity—by diverse approaches which together form the "true documentary proof" of Friar Servando's greatness. Toward the second half of the book we note that the author intervenes, perhaps to unify a "fictional documentary" that accurately recovers the most living dimension of a historical character. Thus, fiction is read into history, bestowing on it a living character's complete presence: in fiction, history is better accomplished with the aid of an exemplarily depicted destiny.

UTOPIA'S CLAIM ON HISTORY

The critical power of Arenas's novel is also noteworthy. If Carpentier's *Explosion in a Cathedral* detailed the painful destruction of the French revolution in its echoes in the Antilles, *Hallucinations* details the failure of American emancipation, its prompt deterioration; but now it is not necessary to recount that process for it can easily be deduced from the radical rebellion Arenas's character experiences. That radicalism is utopia's claim on history, and its claim against politics. It is a claim that is not worked out in this novel—it was in Carpentier's—which does not therefore imply an ideological dispute, but simply a poetic choice. For in *Hallucinations* utopia is not a dream of the rational faculty but a movement of all-embracing desire, a claim of human nature against itself, or in spite of itself. History is again brought under question. And to remake it as fiction, to invent it in a splurge of language is to experience it with a freedom and abundance normally unavailable to us, which is also the case with the political disenchantment of *One Hundred Years of Solitude*. Once again fiction makes history in a literary movement that is typically ours, dramatically Latin American at least since the chronicles of Garcilaso el Inca. Fiction creates history not in order to judge it or reproduce it, but rather to modify it with the confusion of desire which gives barren reality the possibility of enchantment. It is writing that is thus doubly critical. For the function of utopia is the critical bipolarization of discourse, the preferred notion of truth that questions every accepted truth little by little, since it very rarely accords with a radical need and faith. Such a faith—(revolution, poetry)—inflames this book with brilliant spontaneity, a passionate sense of freedom.

Woman's Space, Woman's Text:
A New Departure in Inés Malinow's
Entrada libre

Doris Meyer

Entrada libre (*Free Entry*), published in 1978, is the second novel by the Argentine author Inés Malinow, known also as a writer of short stories, poetry, children's books and journalistic essays. It is a novel which, as its title indicates, offers free entry to its readers through the untrammeled directness of its prose, sparkling with poetic images, and through the intriguing story of a mother and daughter who are vacationing in Cuzco, Peru. Once entered, however, this novel resists a facile exit. Not unlike Juan Rulfo's *Pedro Páramo* in its incorporation of the otherwordly into an episodic narrative journey, *Free Entry* is a deceptively labyrinthine work which can be interpreted on various levels.

Most intriguing, in my opinion, is the unmistakably woman-centered quality of its structure and language. Using Hélène Cixous's terminology, *Free Entry* may be called a "woman-text" because it represents "a step forward, an adventure, an exploration of woman's power," and because, also in Cixous's words,

> [a woman-text is] really giving, making a *gift* of departure, allowing departure, allowing breaks, "parts," partings, separations. . . . When a woman writes in nonrepression she passes on her others, her abundance of non-ego/s in a way that destroys the form of the family structure, so that it is defamilialized, can no longer be thought in terms of the attribution of roles within a social cell: what takes place is an endless circulation of desire from one body to another, above and across sexual difference, outside those relations of power and regeneration constituted by the family.

From *Latin American Literary Review* no. 23 (Fall–Winter 1983). © 1983 by *Latin American Literary Review*.

In order to understand this definition of a woman-text more fully in terms of its application to *Free Entry*, we must begin with a discussion of the novel's inception and development.

The writing of *Entrada libre* grew out of a trip Malinow took to Peru in 1975 with her eldest daughter, Gabriela. Malinow had lived in Peru for several years as a child, so this was a journey of rediscovery. But it turned out to have an even deeper effect by touching her creative unconscious and inspiring a novel which was not autobiographical but rather an intuitive vision of a world she had once inhabited and lost from memory. In Malinow's own words:

> Los episodios de mi infancia fueron como un elemento generador, porque yo me transformé en un ser que lo veía todo de nuevo, con ojos asombrados de niñez. La tramazón de la novela es como un mapa de los signos que yo alcancé a percibir, itinerarios todavía curiosamente presentes, en los que estaban vívidos los momentos en que las gentes se conocieron, se enamoraron, vivieron, en fin.

> (The episodes of my childhood were like a generative element, because I transformed myself into a being who saw everything afresh, with the astonished eyes of a child. The plot structure of the novel is like a map of the signs that I managed to make out, itineraries still curiously present, in which I saw vividly the moments when people met each other, fell in love, and simply lived.)

The dreamlike quality of the narrative—in which reality and fantasy meet in total nonchalance—is thus a function of its visionary gestation, as is also the poetic quality of the prose. Malinow once said that she has come to see *Free Entry* as a kind of haiku, a poetic metaphor whose shape she was not aware of as she wrote. It is indeed a symbolic novel, but it is also more than that.

The mirror reflection of her journey to Cuzco in the imaginary journey of her text indicates a fictional representation of the voyage of rebirth and transformation or, in other words, the archetypal quest for selfhood. Essential to the success of this quest is the venture beyond ego-oriented social boundaries to the realm of the unconscious. Logos gives way to Eros and the hidden values of the psyche emerge from the repressed unconscious. The archetypal pattern most closely discernible in *Free Entry* is that of the matriarchal myth of Demeter and Kore and the rituals of the Eleusinian mysteries. In novels structured according to this myth, the mother-daughter relationship leads through a quest to the ultimate rebirth and transformation of one or both parties. At issue in both ancient and modern interpretations of the story of Demeter and Kore is woman's erotic autonomy following rape or abuse by a male figure. Such is the case in Malinow's novel.

Free Entry begins with the arrival of a mother (referred to only as "la

Madre") and daughter (named "Ana") in the legendary city of Cuzco, birthplace of the Incan empire. They go directly to a rented house in the neighborhood of Nueva Alta where mysterious unidentified presences in the form of "murmullos de risas" ["murmurs of laughter"] and "pasos y corridas" ["footsteps and running"] greet them but do not upset them, as they settle into their separate rooms immersed in their own private thoughts. Ana, who appears to be in her late teens, is obsessed with letters she writes but never sends to an ungiving and unnamed "Amada" ["Beloved Woman"]. Meanwhile, the mother meditates on the real motive for their trip but is unable to decide if it was for Ana's sake or her own. Recently separated from her husband, Roberto, who had left home without explanation, the mother seems ridden by guilt and in need of a vacation from her career as a dentist. She must sort out the reasons for her personal upheaval; after all, she reflects, "pensar es asomarse a una ventana y tomar el aire antes de la tormenta" ["to think is to lean out a window and breathe the air before a storm"]. Of Ana, there is almost no physical description. Of the mother, only a passing reference to "cabellera rojiza, el rostro dulce al sonreír" "reddish hair, a sweet face when smiling" (reminiscent of Malinow herself) and the noteworthy remark that she seems no older than Ana: "ambas altas, delgadas, flojas en las ropas de buen corte" ["both of them tall, slim, with loose-fitting, stylish clothes"].

Strange luggage in the corridors of the house is followed some time later by the appearance of nameless actors who, ghostlike, have inhabited the house for months and only ask permission to sleep there at night, promising not to disturb the new lodgers. As one of them explains, "Nos hemos acostumbrado a no mirar, a no exisitir casi . . . e incluso a dormir dos o tres horas, si podemos." ["We have accustomed ourselves to not looking, to practically not existing . . . and even to sleeping two or three hours, if we can."] After the mother reluctantly acquiesces, he adds, "un actor entiende lo que ocurre. También podemos acompañar." ["an actor understands what is happening. We can also accompany."]

The house in Nueva Alta becomes the point of departure for excursions that the mother and Ana make to Machu Picchu, Sacsahuamán, Pisac and different areas of Cuzco itself. They are tourists, yet Malinow does not exploit the pictorial aspect of their experience other than to suggest that the magical quality of the ancient Incan culture infuses all life there, past and present. When Ana asks a new companion—identified only by his Cuzqueño hat and his profession as a doctor—"¿Es muy viejo esto?" ["Is this very old?"], the doctor answers, "Viejo. Y májico. Cuando Machu Picchu lo decide, la cambia." ["Old. And magic. When Machu Picchu decrees it, people change."] The doctor, who had somehow anticipated their arrival in Cuzco, takes upon himself the difficult process of weaning Ana from dependency upon her obsessive letter-writing. Like the actor, he is less an individual than a facilitator. Through his attentions, Ana gradually learns to openly express her sexuality, though she continues to write sad, furtive notes to her Amada. Ana's homosexual dependency was apparently provoked by an incestuous relationship with Roberto. Roberto's aggression, suspected by the mother and confirmed by Ana's recollections of the hateful sensation of her father's hands on her body, haunts both women. Thus mother and daughter constitute two sides of an emotional triangle in which they are both allies and rivals. The absent Roberto, the abusive male whose lingering influence they must both overcome, is their mutual source of anguish.

While Ana gradually explores her own sexual identity, the mother likewise comes to grips with her need for sexual independence from her role as guilt-ridden wife and mother. The letters she wishes Roberto would write never arrive, and she slowly accepts their rupture as final. In the penetrating cold of a Cuzco night, the mother realizes that her life is beginning again: ". . . ya no importa la existencia de Roberto porque ella misma siente una fuerza que la envía hacia otras partes" [". . . Robert's existence no longer matters because she herself feels a strength that sends her toward other regions"]. Rational acceptance of this reality, however, does not preclude the mother's search for explanations. Roberto continues to haunt her consciousness, while at night her unconscious self reacts freely to the warmth of phantom presences at her side. First the actor and later the doctor come to her bed as if in a dream. The mother's perception of these presences is positive in that they offer her a comforting warmth. Along with the other inhabitants of Nueva Alta she discovers there the uninhibited pleasure of sexual companionship without possessiveness.

In a subplot woven into the episodic texture of the novel, we hear the story of another estranged couple whose marriage has been reduced to letters written by the husband, José, to his wife, Aurora, as he travels throughout Peru promoting his political campaign. These letters, left in the house in Nueva Alta by Aurora who once lived there, are read by the mother who sees in them a mirror of her own problems. Meanwhile, Aurora is still living secretly in Cuzco with her son, Carlos, fearful that José— ironically a political liberal—wants to control his son's life for his own ends. One of José's henchmen lurks around the house in Nueva Alta looking for Aurora and Carlos and writes reports back to José about the house and its strange inhabitants. His letters, like so many others in the novel, are an expression of myopic misunderstanding and not the connective communication they are meant to be.

Throughout the novel an omniscient narrator describes the house in Nueva Alta as a bulwark, a defense, essentially a refuge for wandering souls in search of themselves. Indeed, the house is characterized by its freedom of entry. Those who go there—the mother, Ana, the actors, even young Carlos looking for a toy he left behind—are openly received and comforted, as if the house were a metaphoric womb. Within its walls there is no patriarchal hierarchy, no censure of free expression, no rigidly imposed boundaries between the acceptable and the unacceptable. It is as if those who took refuge there were able to shed the inhibitions of the outside world and rediscover their own libidinal energies. Only the robotlike henchman, too conditioned by José's authority, is unable to enter easily into the community he observes from a distance.

Two incidents which take place in the house have ritualistic significance, comparable to the function of the mythological Eleusinian mysteries. On one occasion the mother dresses in elaborate costume and plays the part of Our Lady of Mercy, granting the wishes of all who ask her favor. Both benefactor and supplicant, the mother asks that Ana be granted the favor of forgetting the letters she continually writes; for herself, she requests the ability to forget Roberto and all the questions that plague her about the fateful triangle. On another occasion, toward the end of the novel, all the inhabitants of the house in Nueva Alta take part in an evening of revelry that ends in everyone undressing and joining in a rhythmic blend of nameless bodies. Like a ritual cleansing, identities are shed with the clothing: "La madre parece Ana, Ana la actriz de los pantalones ajustados, ésta la otra muchacha, el médico el actor, el actor uno de sus compañeros, curiosamente sin ropas han perdido su nombre. No están avergonzados de sus cuerpos, en realidad no les prestan atención porque se mueven por su cuenta." ["The mother seems to be Ana, Ana the actress in tight pants, the latter seems to be the other girl, the doctor the actor, the actor one of his companions—curiously, without clothes, they have lost their names. They are not ashamed of their bodies, in fact they pay no attention to them because they move of their own accord."] The two occasions—the first, of dressing as another, the second, undressing and becoming the other— symbolize the process of transformation and transcendence necessary to achieve psychic wholeness.

Essentially, the house in Nueva Alta has served as the symbolic or ritualistic space required for the liberation of the unconscious and the integration of the psyche. It resembles the maternal womb in that it makes possible a rebirth for those who seek it. A confirmation of this significance can be found in the mother's meditation on the two lives she has discovered: one with Roberto, one without him. She then immediately thinks of how it feels to await the birth of a child: "Es como el viento que sopla a la noche, no hay forma de ignorarlo." ["It's like the wind that blows in the night, there's no way to ignore it."] She describes the birthing experience in terms of this metaphor, recalling the birth of Ana, their life with Roberto and finally their trip to Cuzco

con sus nacimientos sorpresivos y penetrantes, las manos sin demasiados dueños, las esperas tácitas y necesarias. Toda Nueve Alta es una enorme primavera, los pomos de las puertas expectativas, cada noche una inmensa liberación y cada amanecer un hallazgo para partir con alegría y volver luego repleto a dar, ya en la lectura de la cartas de Aurora, ya en el sueño donde siempre

se encontraban reparaciones. Eso, Nueva Alta la había reparado
para poder otra vez iniciar los años, porque estaba entera.

(with its surprising and penetrating births, the hands without too
many owners, the tacit and necessary waiting. All Nueva Alta is
an enormous springtime, the handles of expectant doors, each
night an immense liberation and each dawn a discovery in order
to depart with joy and return again the fullness to give, be it in
the reading of Aurora's letters or in sleeping where she always
found renewal. That was it, Nueva Alta had renewed her so that
she could begin the years again, because she was whole.)

In a recent article assessing the current state of feminist criticism, Elaine
Showalter makes a strong case for what has been called the "double-voiced
discourse" of woman's writing. The image of the double voice recognizes
that however much the muted female segment of society may seek a mode
of expression all its own, echoes of the dominant male segment will persist
in the social, literary and cultural heritage from which it evolves. This is
not to say that women cannot or should not explore the uncharted terrain
of what has been called "woman's space" in search of a non-confining,
non-patriarchal truth. In fact there is much to be learned from French
feminist critics like Cixous, Irigaray or Kristeva who wish to deconstruct
traditional phallocentric language and reinvent a language that will inscribe
the female experience. But as Showalter points out, for the time being,
most women writers are the product of two worlds, and novels such as
Free Entry tend to reflect this ambivalence. It is a work rich in sociocultural
resonances such as the animistic nature of the Incan heritage, the oppressed
condition of the indigenous population, and the general lack of communication in human relationships. Nonetheless, the prevailing theme of *Free
Entry* is, in my opinion, the exploration of a woman's psychic and physical
space, thereby approaching what Cixous calls a woman-text. A brief textual
commentary will illustrate this further.

Both in the novel's title and in the loosely connected episodes of life
in the house in Nueva Alta there is an emphasis on the fluid movement
of bodies and emotions, the freedom of open rather than closed spaces,
the notion of space, in fact, not as separating but bringing together. Referring to women's texts, Claudine Herrmann has said: "Time and space
no longer participate in the artificial continuity imposed by social life, but
in a reality that is simply that of intimate life." In portraying the mother's
and Ana's gradual awakening to erotic autonomy, Malinow focuses on the
burden of neurosis and guilt which they carry with them as a product of
restrictive, patriarchal mores. Nueva Alta allows them to shed this burden.
There mother and daughter coexist as equals, at times protective of one
another, at times retreating into their own thoughts. With frequent references to the mirror motif, Malinow suggests that the mother and daughter
exchange roles and that the nature of identity is (in a Borgesian manner)

shared, circular, mythic rather than exclusive. When, for example, the mother reads José's letters to Aurora, she feels they also belong to her because "en realidad todas las vidas le pertenecen ahora que se está buscando otra diferente" ["in reality all lives belong to her now that she is looking for another one of her own"].

In "This Sex Which Is Not One" Luce Irigaray writes of the multiplicity of female sexuality, "a sort of universe in expansion for which no limits could be fixed" and in which "property and propriety are undoubtedly rather foreign." However, she adds, "Nearness . . . is not foreign to woman, a nearness so close that any identification of one or the other, and therefore any form of property, is impossible. Woman enjoys a closeness with the other that is *so near she cannot possess it, any more than she can possess herself*." *Free Entry* seems to reflect a similar view of female eroticism. The following passage represents the culminating moment of the mother's libidinal liberation. She is in bed alone, yet senses someone next to her. In what is apparently an autoerotic fantasy, she realizes that it is not Roberto giving her this pleasure

> . . . acaso se tratara del médico, pero ¿cómo el médico sabe la manera de? Únicamente Roberto, había pensado ella, es capaz de conmoverla pero es otra la palabra, alguien más la conoce—¿o ella era hábil para entender otras gargantas? ¿Era ella la que buscaba o era ella la hallada?—y piensa que no importa quién es. Se trata fundamentalmente de sus nupcias consigo misma, unas nupcias solemnes, las verdaderas para entender la voz de muchas gargantas. La mecen, la arrullan, juegan con ella; la madre siente achicarse la noche, disminuir el tamaño del cielo y del infierno puesto no está solo y puesto que Roberto no necesariamente es el esperado. Quiso agradecer, busca, devuelve, multiplica. Los canteros de la Plaza de Armas empezaron a lustrarse con el brillo de la madrugada.

> (. . . perhaps it was the doctor, but how does the doctor know how to? Only Roberto, she had thought, is capable of moving her, but the words are different, someone else knows them—or was she able to understand other throats? Was she the one searching or was she the one being found?—and she thinks it doesn't matter who it is. It was fundamentally a question of nuptials with her own self, solemn nuptials, the true ones for being able to understand the voice of many throats. They rock her, coo to her, play with her; the mother feels the night grow small, heaven and hell diminish in size now that she is not alone and now that Roberto is not necessarily the awaited one. She tried to thank, seek, give back, multiply. The edges of the Plaza de Armas began to shine in the glow of dawn.)

Coincidentally, Malinow's novel has more than a little in common with Irigaray's prose poem, "And the One Doesn't Stir without the Other," published a year after *Entrada libre*. Both works deal with the complexities of the mother-daughter relationship and indicate that "as women become subjects, mothers and daughters may become women, subjects and protagonists of their own reality rather than objects and antagonists in the Father's drama."

Once free of the confinement of phallocentric society and no longer silenced or, in Cixous's words, "decapitated" by its laws, woman begins to speak her own sexuality and to write "things that will constitute a feminine Imaginary." According to Cixous,

> all the feminine texts I've read are very close to the voice, very close to the flesh of language, much more so than masculine texts . . . perhaps because there's something in them that's freely given, perhaps because they don't rush into meaning, but are straightway at the threshold of feeling. There's *tactility* in the feminine text, there's touch, and this touch passes through the ear. Writing in the feminine is passing on what is cut out by the Symbolic, the voice of the mother, passing on what is most archaic. The most archaic force that touches a body is one that enters by the ear and reaches the most intimate point. This innermost touch always echoes in a woman text. So the movement, the movement of the text, doesn't trace a straight line. I see it as an outpouring.

In *Free Entry* Malinow conveys a sense of tactility in many ways. In one episode reminiscent of a dream dance sequence, the mother goes to sleep covering herself with a newly purchased Indian blanket, only to have the blanket removed from her and borrowed in turn by the actor, Ana, the doctor, an actress and then another man in the house, upon which the mother awakens and takes the blanket back to her bed. All the residents of Nueva Alta share the same real and symbolic need for warmth in order to reach the realm of the unconscious and "la manta está caliente, llena de privacía, porque habla de muchas cosas" ["the blanket is warm, full of privacy, because it speaks of many things"]. In another poetic passage, the mother dreams that she feels other people's urge to cry, as if she were crying the tears of the world:

> . . . supo que todo ese llanto es un sueño pero un sueño tan triste que ansía despertarse, mas las lágrimas continuaron, se le metieron por los pliegues del camisón, sintió su útero penetrado de lágrimas, son lágrimas tan tristes, si esa gente no podía llorar tanta tristeza, las paredes rezuman lágrimas como si Nueva Alta fuera una catarata, una marejada, un alud de lagrimones, todas las lágrimas del mundo habían estado en esa casa esperándola y ahora se desbarrancan sobre ella, lágrimas altas, densas, de gente que no supo

catalogarlas, lágrimas incatalogables de todo tipo de sufrimientos, lágrimas de dedos lastimados, de domingos y abortos, las lágrimas más austeras del mundo habían sollozado sobre el rostro de la madre que se despierta en la oscuridad, hace un gran movimiento y enciende la luz.

(. . . she knew that all that weeping was a dream but such a sad dream that she longed to wake up, but the tears continued, fell between the folds of her nightgown, she felt her uterus invaded by tears, they are such sad tears, hard to believe those people could weep so much sadness, the walls leaked tears as if Nueva Alta were a waterfall, a sea swell, an avalanche of big tears, all the tears of the world had been in that house waiting for her and now they were falling onto her, tall, dense tears of people who didn't know how to classify them, unclassifiable tears of all types of suffering, tears of hurt fingers, of Sundays, and abortions, the harshest tears of the world had sobbed over the fact of the mother who awakens in the darkness, makes a great effort and turns on the light.)

Through its fluctuating verb tenses and unrestrained structure, this powerful passage conveys the life force embodied in the mother as woman in addition to the image of the female unconscious as linked to the mythic Great Mother.

Inés Malinow's *Entrada libre* was critically acclaimed in Argentina, but it has not yet received the attention it deserves in North America. Even in Argentina its unique qualities as a woman's text were overlooked with the exception of one review in *La Prensa* written by another accomplished woman writer, Luisa Valenzuela. Her review concludes with this observation:

Si hasta hace poco se hablaba de la novela femenina con tono peyorativo, a partir de obras como *Entrada libre* sabemos que la escritura femenina nada tiene que ver con lo dulzón, chirle y barroco. Estamos frente a un libro que nos da la contrapartida de la escritura viril pero sin perder ni una gota de fuerza, de coraje, de poesía, de precisión. Más bien todo lo contrario.

(If up to recently one spoke of the feminine novel in a pejorative tone, after works like *Entrada libre* we know that feminine writing has nothing to do with the sweet, the prattling and the baroque. We have here a book that gives us the counterpart of manly writing, but without losing a single drop of strength, courage, poetry or precision. Rather, just the opposite.)

Chronology

1925   *Popol Vuh*, Miguel Angel Asturias.

1930   *Leyendas de Guatemala*, Miguel Angel Asturias.

1935   *Historia universal de la infamia*, Jorge Luis Borges.
          La última niebla, María Luisa Bombal.

1938   *La amortajada*, María Luisa Bombal.

1939   *El pozo*, Juan Carlos Onetti.

1943   *Perto do Coração Selvagem*, Clarice Lispector.

1944   *Ficciones*, Jorge Luis Borges.

1946   *Sagarana*, João Guimarães Rosa.
          El señor presidente, Miguel Angel Asturias.

1949   *El aleph*, Jorge Luis Borges.
          El reino de este mundo, Alejo Carpentier.
          Hombres de maíz, Miguel Angel Asturias.

1950   *La vida breve*, Juan Carlos Onetti.
          Viento fuerte, Miguel Angel Asturias.

1953   *Los pasos perdidos*, Alejo Carpentier.
          El llano en llamas, Juan Rulfo.

1954   *Lilus Kikus*, Elena Poniatowska.
          Papa verde, Miguel Angel Asturias.

1955   *Pedro Páramo*, Juan Rulfo.
          Veraneo, José Donoso.

1956   *Grande Sertão: Veredas*, João Guimarães Rosa.
          Los pasos perdidos, Alejo Carpentier.

447

1957   *Coronación*, José Donoso.
        El acoso, Alejo Carpentier.

1958   *La región más transparente*, Carlos Fuentes.

1959   *Los jefes*, Mario Vargas Llosa.

1960   *Los premios*, Julio Cortázar.
        Los ojos de los enterrados, Miguel Angel Asturias.
        Laços de família, Clarice Lispector.
        Así en la paz como en la guerra, Guillermo Cabrera Infante.

1961   *El coronel no tiene quien le escriba*, Gabriel García Márquez.
        El astillero, Juan Carlos Onetti.
        A maça no escuro, Clarice Lispector.

1962   *La muerte de Artemio Cruz*, Carlos Fuentes.
        Primeiras estórias, João Guimarães Rosa.
        Lunes mi enemigo, Inés Malinow.

1963   *Rayuela*, Julio Cortázar.
        Gestos, Severo Sarduy.
        Los recuerdos del porvenir, Elena Garro.
        La ciudad y los perros, Mario Vargas Llosa.

1964   *A paixão segundo G. H.*, Clarice Lispector.

1965   *Tres tristes tigres*, Guillermo Cabrera Infante.

1966   *Paradiso*, José Lezama Lima.
        Este domingo, José Donoso.
        El lugar sin limites, José Donoso.
        Hay que sonreir, Luisa Valenzuela.
        Tempo das frutas, Nélida Piñón.

1967   *Cien años de soledad*, Gabriel García Márquez.
        De donde son los cantantes, Severo Sarduy.
        Cambio de piel, Carlos Fuentes.
        Celestino antes del alba, Reinaldo Arenas.
        Las armas secretas, Julio Cortázar.
        Miguel Angel Asturias receives the Nobel Prize in literature.

1968   *62. Modelo para armar*, Julio Cortázar.
        La traición de Rita Hayworth, Manuel Puig.

1969   *Boquitas pintadas*, Manuel Puig.
        El mundo alucinante, Reinaldo Arenas.
        Conversación en la catedral, Mario Vargas Llosa.
        Hasta no verte, Jesús mío, Elena Poniatowska.

1970   *El obsceno pájaro de la noche*, José Donoso.
        El informe de Brodie, Jorge Luis Borges.

1971   *La noche de Tlatelolco: Testimonios de historia oral*, Elena Poniatowska.

1972   *Cobra*, Severo Sarduy.
        El gato eficaz, Luisa Valenzuela.

1973   *Sala de armas*, Nélida Piñón.
        Panteleón y las visitadoras, Mario Vargas Llosa.
        The Buenos Aires Affair, Manuel Puig.
        Libro de Manuel, Julio Cortázar.

1974   *Vista del amanecer en el trópico*, Guillermo Cabrera Infante.
        Concierto barroco, Alejo Carpentier.
        El recurso del método, Alejo Carpentier.

1975   *Terra Nostra*, Carlos Fuentes.
        El otoño del patriarca, Gabriel García Márquez.

1976   *El beso de la mujer araña*, Manuel Puig.
        Aquí pasan cosas raras, Luisa Valenzuela.
        La guaracha del Macho Camacho, Luis Rafael Sánchez.

1978   *Querido Diego, te abraza Quiela*, Elena Poniatowska.
        Entrada libre, Inés Malinow.

1980   *Andamos huyendo Lola*, Elena Garro.
        O calor das coisas, Nélida Piñón.

1981   *Crónica de una muerte anunciada*, Gabriel García Márquez.
        Termina el desfile, Reinaldo Arenas.

1982   *Otra vez el mar*, Reinaldo Arenas.
        Gabriel García Márquez receives the Nobel Prize in literature.

1983   *La tercera mitad*, Inés Malinow.

Biographical Notes

Jorge Luis Borges was born on August 24, 1899, in Buenos Aires, Argentina. He was educated in Buenos Aires and Geneva and traveled throughout Europe after World War I. During the 1920s, Borges was a leading member of the Ultraist literary movement, based loosely on surrealism and imagism, but he later disavowed its precepts. A perpetual student of occidental and oriental literature and culture, Borges's life consisted largely of reading and writing. His most famous works of short fiction, the genre for which he is most celebrated, may be found in *Historia universal de la infamia* (1935), *Ficciones* (1944), and *El aleph* (1949). His essays and criticism are collected in *Inquisiciones* (1925), *Discusión* (1932), and *Otras inquisiciones* (1952). *Elogio de la sombra* (1969) and *El otro, el mismo* (1969) are two of his many outstanding collections of poetry. Borges also collaborated with Adolpho Bioy Casares on a number of works, often under the pseudonyms of H. Bustos Domeq and B. Suarez Lynch. In 1961 he was awarded the International Publisher's Prize with Samuel Beckett. He held honorary degrees from Oxford, Harvard, and Columbia universities and lectured throughout Europe and the United States until his death in 1986.

Miguel Angel Asturias was born on October 19, 1899, in Guatemala City, Guatemala. He studied law at the National University of Guatemala and ancient American culture at the Sorbonne. While in Paris he published his translations and transcriptions of Mayan legends: *Popol Vuh* (1925) and *Leyendas de Guatemala* (1930), among them. His first novel, *El señor presidente* (1946) brought him much critical acclaim and he was awarded the Prix du Meilleur Roman Etranger for it in 1952. Subsequent novels include *Hombres de maíz* (1949), and the trilogy *Viento fuerte* (1950), *Papa verde* (1954), and *Los ojos de los enterrados* (1960). Asturias spent his life in and out of the Guatemalan diplomatic corps, depending upon the politics of the current regime. He was awarded the Nobel Prize in literature in 1967. He died on June 9, 1974.

Alejo Carpentier was born on December 26, 1904, in Havana, Cuba to parents of Russian and French origin. As a journalist, musicologist, editor, and writer, Carpentier participated in the Afro-Cuban cultural revival in the twenties, thirties, and forties. He edited the influential journal *Carteles* and was imprisoned in 1927 for support of a group that was against the current dictator Machado. He escaped from Cuba and spent some years in Paris where he was greatly influenced by the surrealist movement and the avant-garde of the time. Carpentier returned to Cuba in 1939 but a short time later he went into voluntary

film critic for *Carteles* and in 1959 he founded *Lunes,* of which he was editor until its banning in 1961. After a brief period as a cultural attache in the Cuban embassies in Belgium and Luxembourg, Cabrera Infante left Cuba permanently and took up residence in England, where he is now a naturalized citizen. He is the author of *Así en la paz como en la guerra* (1960), *Tres tristes tigres* (1965), and *Vista del amanecer en el trópico* (1974). This last novel is his most famous work and was awarded Seix-Barral's Biblioteca Breve prize in 1964 and the Prix du Meilleur Livre Etranger in 1971.

Manuel Puig was born on December 28, 1932, in General Villegas, Argentina. As a child he became enthralled with the world of Hollywood movies, which he attended religiously with his mother. His first novel, *La traición de Rita Hayworth* (1968) and *El beso de la mujer araña* (1976) make particular use of this experience, shifting between "literary" narrative and "filmic" narrative. Puig studied the "languages of film" (French, English, and Italian) in secondary school and, after attempting to earn degrees in philosophy and architecture at the University of Buenos Aires, he studied at Italy's Centro Sperimentale di Cinematografia. He also withdrew from this course of study and traveled throughout Europe and North America. His other works include *Boquitas pintadas* (1969) and *The Buenos Aires Affair* (1973).

Elena Poniatowska was born on May 19, 1933, in Paris. Her father was Polish, and her mother Mexican and she was raised in Europe and Mexico and educated in the United States. Her first novel, *Hasta no verte, Jesús mío* (1969) was awarded the Mazatlan award for fiction. *La noche de Tlatleloco: Testimonios de historia oral* (1971) is a documentary collage that makes use of Poniatowska's experience as a journalist. She currently lives in Mexico City.

Mario Vargas Llosa was born on March 28, 1936, in Arequipa, Peru. He attended the University of San Marcos in Lima and received his doctoral degree from the University of Madrid in 1959. He has taught at London University and at various universities in the U.S.A. *La huída,* a play, appeared in 1952 followed by a collection of stories, *Los jefes* (1958). He came to prominence with the novel *La ciudad y los perros* (1962), and *La casa verde* (1966) and *Conversación en la catedral* (1969) brought him international fame. *Panteleón y las visitadoras* (1973) and *La Guerra del fin del mundo* (1981) are among his more recent works. He has also written a critical study of *Madame Bovary, La orgía perpetua* (1975). He lives primarily in Paris.

Luis Rafael Sánchez was born in Puerto Rico in 1936. A dramatist, actor, poet, and short story writer, he is one of Puerto Rico's most important contemporary artists. *La guaracha del Macho Camacho* (1976) is the work for which he is best known.

Severo Sarduy was born on February 25, 1937, in Camaguey, Cuba. He studied art criticism at the Ecole du Louvre in 1964. Closely associated with the critics of the *Tel Quel* group, Sarduy has been greatly influenced by French post-structural criticism. *Gestos* appeared in 1963 and was followed by *De donde son los cantantes* (1967). *Escrito sobre un cuerpo* (1969) is a collection of essays and *Cobra* (1972), a novel about a Parisian transvestite, won the Prix Medicis. *Big Bang* (1974), *Flamenco* (1969), and *Mood Indigo* (1970) are collections of poetry.

Nélida Piñón was born in Rio de Janeiro, Brazil, in 1937. Throughout the 1960s, she worked as a journalist for *Cuadernos Brasileiros* and taught writing workshops, and traveled extensively in Europe and the United States. *Tempo das frutas,* a collection of stories, appeared in 1966, followed by *Sala de armas* (1973) and *O calor das coisas* (1980).

Luisa Valenzuela was born on November 26, 1938, in Buenos Aires, Argentina. She attended the University of Buenos Aires and later worked as an editor and freelance writer in Argentina. In 1978 she went to New York as writer-in-residence at Columbia University. *Hay que sonreir* (1966) and *Los heréticos* (1967) are two collections of short stories, and many of the stories from them have been translated into English. Among her other works are *El gato eficaz* (1972) and *Aquí pasan cosas raras* (1976). She currently spends her time in Mexico, organizing workshops and lecturing.

Reinaldo Arenas was born in Holguin, Cuba, in 1943. *Celestino antes del alba* (1967) and *El mundo alucinante* (1969) both received awards from the Havana Writers' Union but Arenas became increasingly dissatisfied and disillusioned in revolutionary Cuba. His collection of short stories, *Termina el desfile* (1981), recalls his experience in the revolution, his growing difficulty with the government, and his part in the 1980 exodus from Mariel. His most recent book is *Otra vez el mar* (1982).

Inés Malinow was born in Buenos Aires and has lived in Chile and Peru. She published a book of poems in 1949, but is known more for her novels *Lunes mi enemigo* (1962), *Entrada libre* (1978), and her collection of short stories *La tercera mitad* (1983). She was awarded the Premio del Fondo Nacional de las Artes in 1962.

Contributors

Harold Bloom, Sterling Professor of the Humanities at Yale University, is the author of *The Anxiety of Influence, Poetry and Repression*, and many other volumes of literary criticism. A MacArthur Prize Fellow, he is general editor of five series of literary criticism published by Chelsea House. During 1987–88, he served as Charles Eliot Norton Professor of Poetry at Harvard.

Carter Wheelock is a professor of Spanish-American literature at the University of Texas at Austin. He is the author of *The Mythmaker: A Study of Motif and Symbol in the Short Stories of Jorge Luis Borges*.

Sophia S. Morgan has taught comparative literature and semiotics at the University of Colorado. She is the author of *The Legend of Alexander of Macedon*.

Bella Brodzki teaches comparative literature at Smith College. She wrote her dissertation on the modern parables of S. Y. Agnon, Franz Kafka, and Jorge Luis Borges.

Ariel Dorfman was a professor of journalism and literature in Chile until 1973. He now lives near Washington D.C. A critic and essayist, he is the author of *Imaginación y violencia en America* and *Para leer al Pato Donald*, among other works.

Roberto González Echevarría is the chairman of the Department of Spanish and Portuguese at Yale University. He is the author of *Alejo Carpentier: The Pilgrim at Home*, and *Relecturas: Ensayos de literatura cubana*, as well as many articles and reviews on Spanish Golden Age literature and contemporary Latin American literature.

José Piedra is a graduate student in the Spanish department at Yale University.

457

Julie Jones teaches at Tulane University.

Allan Englekirk teaches in the Department of Foreign Languages at the University of South Carolina.

George Levine is a professor of English at Livingston College, Rutgers University. A specialist in the nineteenth-century novel, he has written *The Boundaries of Fiction: Carlyle, Macaulay, Newman* and *The Realistic Imagination: English Fiction from Frankenstein to Lady Chatterly.*

Phyllis Rodríguez-Peralta teaches at Temple University. She is the author of *José Santos Chocano*, a volume in the Twayne World Authors series.

Julio Cortázar was one of Latin America's major novelists. He is best known for his experimimental novel *Rayuela (Hopscotch).*

Severo Sarduy is a Cuban novelist and literary critic who lives in Paris. He has written a book of essays entitled *Escrito sobre un cuerpo,* among other works.

Saúl Sosnowski is an Argentine writer and critic. He is the author of numerous essays on Spanish-American literature, as well as many books, including *Borges y la cabala* and *Julio Cortázar, una búsqueda mítica.*

Barbara L. Hussey teaches at Purdue University.

Lois Parkinson Zamora teaches in the English department at the University of Texas at Austin. She is the editor of *The Apocalyptic Vision in America.*

Paul B. Dixon teaches Portuguese and Spanish at Purdue University. He is the author of *Reversible Readings: Ambiguity in Four Modern Latin American Novels.*

Steven Boldy is the author of numerous articles on Latin American literature.

Harry Enrique Rosser is a professor in the Department of Romance Languages at Boston University.

Alfred J. MacAdam is a professor of Spanish-American literature at Columbia University, and the author of *El individuo el otro: A Study of Julio Cortázar.*

Hélène Cixous teaches at the University of Paris at Vincennes and is part of a research group on the theory of femininity. She is the author of many essays and a few novels and plays, including *Portrait de Dora* and "Le rire de la medusa."

Marta Peixoto is a professor of Portuguese at Yale University. She has published articles on many Brazilian writers, and a book, *Poesia com coisas: Uma leitura de João Cabral de melo neto.*

Susanne Kappeler is a senior lecturer in English at the University of Rabat. She teaches a seminar on the literary interpretations of women, and has taught a similar course at the Faculty of English at Cambridge while she was a research fellow at Jesus College.

Patricia Tobin teaches literary criticism at Rutgers University. She often writes about Latin American fiction, and is the author of *Time and the Novel: The Genealogical Imperative.*

Claudette Kemper Columbus is a professor of English and comparative literature at Hobart and William Smith Colleges. Her several publications include *Mythological Consciousness and the Future: José María Arguedas.*

Jaime Alazraki is a professor of Romance Languages and Literature at Harvard University. He is the author of *Jorge Luis Borges, Poética y Poesía de Pablo Neruda, La prosa narrativa de Jorge Luis Borges,* and *Versiones, inversiones, reversiones.*

Wendy B. Faris is an associate professor of English and comparative literature at the University of Texas at Arlington. She has published a book on Carlos Fuentes and articles on modern Latin American, British, French, and North American fiction.

Stephanie Merrim teaches Latin American literature at Brown University. She is the author of *Logos and the Word: The Novel of Language and Linguistic Motivation in* Grande Sertão: Veredas *and* Tres tristes tigres.

Frances Wyers (Weber) is the author of *The Literary Perspective of Ramon Perez de Ayala* and a book on Miguel de Unamuno. She teaches at Indiana University, Bloomington.

Bell Gale Chevigny is a professor of English literature at the State University of New York at Purchase. A contributor to the *Village Voice,* she is the editor of *Twentieth-Century Interpretations of Beckett's* Endgame and author of *The Woman and the Myth: Margaret Fuller's Life and Writings.*

Ronald Christ is a professor of English at Livingston College, Rutgers University, and a psychotherapist in private practice. He is the author of *The Narrow Act: Borges' Art of Allusion,* and was the editor of *Review* (Center for Inter-American Relations) from 1970 to 1980.

Roger Kaplan is a novelist and critic whose work has appeared in *Commentary,* the *American Spectator,* the *Wall Street Journal,* and other periodicals.

Stacey Schlau has published essays on Spanish-American literature and teaches in the Department of Romance Languages at Lafayette College.

Giovanni Pontiero is a professor of Spanish and Portuguese at the University of Manchester in England. He has translated stories and poems of Clarice Lispector, Carlos Martinez Moreno, and Nélida Piñón (among others) and is the author of the *Poetry of Manuel Bandeira.*

Julio Ortega is a Peruvian author and literary critic who has taught at various universities in the United States. He now resides in Lima, Peru. He is the author of *La contemplación y la fiesta* and *The Poetics of Change,* among numerous other dramatic, poetic, and critical works.

Doris Meyer is a professor of Spanish at Brooklyn College of the City University of New York. She is the author of *Victoria Ocampo: Against the Wind and Tide* and a study of Francisco de Quevedo.

Bibliography

GENERAL

Brushwood, John S. *The Spanish American Novel.* Austin: University of Texas Press, 1975.

Carpentier, Alejo. *Tientos y Diferencias.* Havana: Union Nacional de Escritores y Artistas de Cuba, 1966.

Chevigny, Bell Gale and Gari Laguardia, eds. *Reinventing the Americas.* New York: Cambridge University Press, 1986.

Dixon, Paul B. *Reversible Readings: Ambiguity in Four Latin American Novels.* University: University of Alabama Press, 1985.

Harss, Luis and Barbara Dohman. *Into the Mainstream.* New York: Harper & Row, 1967.

Langford, Walter M. *The Mexican Novel Comes of Age.* Notre Dame: University of Notre Dame Press, 1971.

Lipski, John M. "Reading the Writers: Hidden Meta-Structures in the Modern Latin American Novel." *Perspectives of Contemporary Literature* 6 (1980): 117–24.

MacAdam, Alfred J. *Modern Latin American Narratives.* Chicago: University of Chicago Press, 1977.

Minc, Rose S., ed. *Latin American Fiction Today.* Tacoma Park, Md.: Hispamerica, 1979.

———, ed. *Literature and Popular Culture in the Hispanic World.* Gaithersburg, Md.: Ediciones Hispamerica, 1981.

Muller-Bergh, Klaus. "The Persistence of the Marvellous." *Review* no. 28 (Spring 1981): 25–26.

Ortega, Julio. *Poetics of Change: The New Spanish American Narrative.* Translated by Galen D. Greaser. Austin: University of Texas Press, 1984.

Reyes, Alfonso. "Fragmento sobre la interpretación social de las lettras." In *Ensayos sobre la historia del nuevo mundo.* Mexico: Instituto Panamericano de Geografia e Historia, 1951.

Sommers, Joseph. *After the Storm.* Albuquerque: University of New Mexico Press, 1968.

Souza, Raymond D. *Major Cuban Novelists.* Columbia: University of Missouri Press, 1976.

JORGE LUIS BORGES

Bell-Villada, Gene H. *Borges and His Fiction: A Guide to His Mind and Art.* Chapel Hill: University of North Carolina Press, 1981.

Christ, Ronald. *The Narrow Act.* New York: New York University Press, 1969.

Coleman, Alexander. "The Playful Atoms of Jorge Luis Borges." In *Auctor Ludens: Essays on Play in Literature,* edited by Gerald Guinness and Andrew Hurley. Philadelphia: Benjamins, 1986.

Cossio, M. E. "A Parody of Literariness: *Seis problemas para don Isidro Parodi.*" *Dispositio* 5–6 (1980/1981): 143–53.

Gutierrez-Movat, Ricardo. "Borges and the Center of the Labyrinth." *Romance Notes* 21 (1981): 287–92.

Irby, James E, Napoleón Murat, Carlos Penatta. *Encuentro con Borges.* Buenos Aires: Editorial Galerna, 1968.

McGurk, G. J. "Seminar on Jorge Luis Borges' 'Death and the Compass.' " *Renaissance and Modern Studies* 27 (1983): 47–60.

McMurray, George R. "Borges's 'The Secret Miracle': A Self-Conscious, Self-Begetting Fiction." In *In Honor of Boyd G. Carter: A Collection of Essays,* edited by Catherine Vera. Laramie: Department of Modern and Classical Languages, University of Wyoming, 1981.

Rodríquez-Monegal, Emir. *Jorge Luis Borges: A Literary Biography.* New York: E. P. Dutton, 1978.

Schehr, Lawrence R. "Unreading Borges's Labyrinths." *Studies in Twentieth Century Literature* 10 (1986): 177–89.

Sturrock, John. *Paper Tigers.* Oxford: Clarendon Press, 1977.

TriQuarterly 25 (1972). Special Borges issue.

MIGUEL ANGEL ASTURIAS

Martin, Gerald. "*El señor presidente* and How to Read It." *Bulletin of Hispanic Studies* 47 (1970): 223–43.

Review no. 15 (Fall 1975). Special Asturias issue.

Wilson, Diana Armas. "The Dynamics of Myth and Legend: Miguel Angel Asturias' *Men of Maize.*" *Denver Quarterly* 11 (1977): 177–84.

ALEJO CARPENTIER

Cheuse, Alan. "Hamlet in Haiti: Style in Carpentier's *The Kingdom of This World.*" *Caribbean Quarterly* 21, no. 4 (1975): 13–29.

Gonzalez, Eduardo. "Framing Carpentier." *MLN* 101 (1986): 424–29.

González Echevarría, Roberto. *The Pilgrim at Home.* Ithaca: Cornell University Press, 1977.

———. "Socrates among the Weeds: Blacks and History in Carpentier's *Explosion in a Cathedral.*" *Massachusetts Review* 24 (1983): 545–61.

Kirk, John M. "Concientizacion: Keystone to the Novels of Alejo Carpentier." *International Fiction Review* 8 (1981): 106–13.

Review no. 18 (Fall 1976). Special Carpentier issue.

JOÃO GUIMARÃES ROSA

Brasil, Francisco de Assis Almeida. *Guimarães Rosa.* Rio de Janeiro: Organização Simoes, 1969.

Harss, Luis and Barbara Dohmann. *Los Nuestros*. Buenos Aires: Editorial Suda-
    merica, 1971.
Lorenz, Gunter. *Dialogue con America Latina*. Santiago: Ediciones Universitarias de
    Valparaiso, 1972.
Merrim, Stephanie. *Logos and the Word*. Utah Studies in Literature and Linguistics
    23. Berne, N.Y.: Peter Lang, 1983.
————. "*Sagarana*: A Story System." *Hispania* 66 (1983): 502–10.
Vincent, Jon. *João Guimarães Rosa*. Boston: Twayne, 1978.

JUAN CARLOS ONETTI

Deredita, John F. "The Shorter Works of Juan Carlos Onetti." *Studies in Short
    Fiction* 8 (1971): 112–22.
Review no. 16 (Winter 1975). Special Onetti issue.

MARÍA LUISA BOMBAL

Brown, Catherine Meredith. "Haunted Hacienda." *Saturday Review of Literature* 30
    (May 30, 1947): 22.
Campbell, Margaret V. "The Vaporous World of María Luisa Bombal." *Hispania*
    44 (1961): 415–19.
Debicki, Andrew P. "Structure, Imagery and Experience in María Luisa Bombal's
    'The Tree.' " *Studies in Short Fiction* 8 (1971): 123–29.
Levine, Linda Gould. "María Luisa Bombal from a Feminist Perspective." *Revista
    Interamericana* 4 (1974): 148–61.

JOSÉ LEZAMA LIMA

Ortega, Julio. "Reading *Paradiso*." In *Poetics of Change: The New Spanish American
    Narrative*, translated by Galen D. Greaser with Susan Jean Pels, 60–84. Austin:
    University of Texas Press, 1984.
Review no. 12 (Fall 1974). Special Lezama Lima issue.

JULIO CORTÁZAR

Alazraki, Jaime and Ivar Ivask, eds. *The Final Island*. Norman: University of Okla-
    homa Press, 1976, 1978.
Bennett, Maurice J. "A Dialogue of Gazes: Metamorphosis and Epiphany in Julio
    Cortazar's 'Axolotl.' " *Studies in Short Fiction* 23 (1986): 57–62.
Boldy, Steven. *The Novels of Julio Cortázar*. Cambridge: Cambridge University Press,
    1980.
Casa de las Americas 25 (1984). Special Cortázar issue.
Filer, Malva E. "La Busqueda de la autenticidad." In *Homenaje a Julio Cortázar*,
    edited by Helmy F. Giacomen. New York: Las Americas, 1972.
Foster, David. *Currents in the Contemporary Argentine Novel*. Columbia: University
    of Missouri Press, 1975.
Hernandez del Castillo, Ana. *Keats, Poe, and the Shaping of Cortázer's Mythopoesis*.
    Amsterdam: Benjamins, 1981.
Holsten, Ken. "Notas sobre el 'Tablero de Dirección' en *Rayuela* de Julio Cortázar."
    Revista Iberoamericana 39 (1973): 683–88.

Ortega, Julio. "Hopscotch" and "Morelli on the Threshold." In *Poetics of Change: The New Spanish American Narrative*, translated by Galen D. Greaser, 42–53, 54–59. Austin: University of Texas Press, 1984.

Review no. 7 (Winter 1972). Special Cortázar issue.

Review of Contemporary Fiction 3 (1983). Special Cortázar issue.

Valentine, Robert V. "The Creative Personality in Cortázar's 'El persiguedor.' " *Journal of Spanish Studies: Twentieth Century* 2 (1974): 169–91.

———. "The Rhetoric of Haracio's Narration in *Rayuela*." *Bulletin of Hispanic Studies* 58 (1981): 339–44.

Vernon, Kathleen. "Cortázar's 3 R's: Reading, Rhetoric and Revolution in *Libro de Manuel*." *Modern Language Studies* 16 (1986): 264–70.

JUAN RULFO

Adams, M. Ian. "Landscape and Loss in Juan Rulfo's *Pedro Páramo*." *Chasqui* 9 (1979): 24–29.

Gyurko, Lanin A. "Rulfo's Aesthetic Nihilism: Narrative Antecedents of *Pedro Páramo*." *Hispanic Review* 40 (1972): 451–66.

Hayes, Aden W. "Rulfo's Counter-Epic: *Pedro Páramo* and the Stasis of History." *Journal of Spanish Studies: Twentieth Century* 7 (1979): 279–96.

Leal, Luis. "La estructura de *Pedro Páramo*." *Anvario de letras* 4 (1964): 287–94.

Lioret, Keith. "A Matter of Life and Death in *Pedro Páramo*." *Romance Notes* 17 (1976): 99–102.

Lippman, Carlee. "The Statue at Tuxcacuexco: Memory and Freedom in Juan Rulfo." *Southwest Review* 61 (1976): 193–99.

Ortega, Julio. "Pedro Páramo." In *Poetics of Change: The New Spanish American Narrative*, 33–41. Austin: University of Texas Press, 1984.

Ramirez, Arthur. "Spatial Form and Cinema Techniques in Rulfo's *Pedro Páramo*." *Revista de Estudio Hispánicos* 15 (1981): 233–49.

Rodriquez-Alcalá, Hugo. *El Arte de Juan Rulfo*. Mexico City: Instituto Nacional de Bellas Artes, 1965.

ELENA GARRO

Brushwood, John S. *Mexico in Its Novel*. Austin: University of Texas Press, 1966.

Langford, Walter M. *The Mexican Novel Comes of Age*. Notre Dame: Notre Dame University Press, 1971.

Mora, Gabriela. "A Thematic Exploration of the Works of Elena Garro." In *Latin American Women Writers: Yesterday and Today*, 91–97. Edited by Yvette E. Miller and Charles M. Tatum. Pittsburgh: Latin American Literary Review, 1977.

Rutherford, John. *Mexican Society during the Revolution*. Oxford: Oxford University Press, 1971.

JOSÉ DONOSO

Coleman, Alexander. "Some Thoughts on José Donoso's Traditionalism." *Studies in Short Fiction* 8 (1971): 155–58.

MacMurray, George R. "José Donoso's Tribute to Consciousness: *El obsceno pájaro de la noche*." *Chasqui* 3, no. 3 (1974): 40–48.

Martinez, Z. Nelly. "José Donoso: A Short Study of His Works." *Books Abroad* 49 (1975): 251–55.

Review no. 9 (Fall 1973). Special Donoso issue.
Tatum, Charles M. "*El obsceno pájaro de la noche:* Demise of a Feudal Society." *Latin American Literary Review* no. 2 (1973): 99–106.

CLARICE LISPECTOR

Cixous, Hélène. *Vivre l'orange/To live the orange.* Translated by Ann Liddle and Sarah Cornell. Paris: Des Femmes, 1979.
Fitz, Earle E. "Freedom and Self-Realization: Feminist Characterization in the Fiction of Clarice Lispector." *Modern Language Studies* 10 (1980): 51–61.
Lindstrom, Naomi. "Clarice Lispector: Articulating Women's Experience." *Chasqui* 8, no. 1 (1978): 43–52.
———. "A Feminist Discourse Analysis of Clarice Lispector's 'Daydreams of a Drunken Housewife.' " *Latin American Literary Review* no. 19 (1981): 7–16.
Rosowski, Susan J. "The Novel of Awakening." In *The Voyage In: Fictions of Female Development,* edited by Elizabeth Abel. Hanover, N.H.: University Press of New England, 1983.

GABRIEL GARCÍA MÁRQUEZ

Alvarez-Boland, Isabel. "From Mystery to Parody: (Re)Readings of García Márquez's *Crónica de una muerte anunciada.*" *Symposium* 38 (1984–85): 278–86.
Barros-Lemez, Alvaro. "Beyond the Prismatic Mirror: *One Hundred Years of Solitude* and Serial Fiction." *Studies in Latin American Popular Culture* 3 (1984): 105–14.
Bell-Villada, Gene H. "Names and Narrative Pattern in *One Hundred Years of Solitude.*" *Latin American Literary Review* no. 18 (1981): 37–46.
Books Abroad 47 (1981). Special García Márquez issue.
Buchanan, Rhonda L. "The Cycle of Rage and Order in García Márquez's *El otoño del patriarca.*" *Perspectives on Contemporary Literature* 10 (1984): 75–85.
González Echevarría, Roberto. "With Borges in Macondo." *Diacritics* 2, no. 1 (1972): 57–60.
Gullón, Ricardo. "Gabriel García Márquez and the Lost Art of Storytelling." Translated by José G. Sanchez. *Diacritics* 1, no. 1 (1971): 27–32.
Janes, Regina. *Gabriel García Márquez: Revolution in Wonderland.* Columbia: University of Missouri Press, 1981.
Latin American Literary Review no. 25 (1985). Special García Márquez issue.
Peel, Roger M. "The Short Stories of Gabriel García Márquez." *Studies in Short Fiction* 8 (1971): 159–68.
Tobin, Patricia. "García Márquez and the Genealogical Imperative." *Diacritics* 4, no. 2 (1974): 52–55.

CARLOS FUENTES

Brody, Robert and Charles Rossman, eds. *Carlos Fuentes: A Critical View.* Austin: University of Texas Press, 1982.
Costa, Luis F. "Patterns of Discovery and Conquest in Carlos Fuentes' *Terra Nostra.*" *Exploration* 9 (1981): 23–41.
Faris, Wendy. *Carlos Fuentes.* New York: Frederick Unger, 1983,
———. "Desyoizacion: Joyce /Cixous/ Fuentes and the Multi-Vocal Text." *Latin American Literary Review* no. 19 (1981): 31–39.
Grossman, Edith. "Myth and Madness in Carlos Fuentes' *A Change of Skin.*" *Latin American Literary Review* no. 5 (1974): 98–110.

Gyurko, Lanin A. "Structure and Theme in Fuentes' *La muerte de Artemio Cruz.*" *Symposium* 34 (1980): 29–41.

Janes, Regina. "*Terra Nostra:* Charting the Terrain." *Literary Review* 23 (1980): 261–71.

Kerr, Lucille. "The Paradox of Power and Mystery: Carlos Fuentes' *Terra Nostra.*" *PMLA* 95 (1980): 91–102.

Koldewyn, Philip. "Mediation and Regeneration in the Sacred Zones of Fiction: Carlos Fuentes and the Nature of Myth." *Journal of Latin American Lore* 7 (1981): 147–69.

Kooreman, Thomas E. "Reader Interest in *Aura:* A Search for Confirmation." Edited by Catherine Vera and George R. McMurray. In *In Honor of Boyd G. Carter: A Collection of Essays.* Laramie: Department of Modern and Classical Languages, University of Wyoming, 1981.

Leal, Luis. "Realism, Myth, and Prophecy in Fuentes' *Where the Air Is Clear.*" *Confluencia* 1 (1985): 75–81.

Swietlicki, Catherine. "*Terra Nostra:* Carlos Fuentes' Kabbalistic World." *Symposium* 35 (1981): 155–67.

Titiev, Janic Geasler. "Witchcraft in Carlos Fuentes' *Aura.*" *Revista de Estudios Hispanicos* 15 (1981): 377–93.

World Literature Today 57 (1983). Special Fuentes issue.

GUILLERMO CABRERA INFANTE

Lipski, John M. "Paradigmatic Overlapping in *Tres tristes tigres.*" *Dispositio* 1 (1976): 33–45.

Malcuzynski, M-Pierrette. "*Tres tristes tigres,* or the Treacherous Play on Carnival." *Ideologies and Literature* no. 15 (1981): 33–56.

Merrim, Stephanie. *Logos and the Word.* Utah Studies in Literature and Linguistics Volume 23. Berne; New York. Peter Lang, 1983.

Nelson, Ardis L. *Cabrera Infante in the Menippean Tradition.* Juan de la Cuesta Hispanic Monographs, 28. Newark, N.J.: Juan de la Cuesta, 1983.

Review nos. 4–5 (Winter 1971–Spring 1972). Special Cabrera Infante issue.

Rodríguez-Monegal, Emir. " Structure and Meaning in *Three Trapped Tigers.*" *Latin American Literary Review* no. 2 (1973): 19–35.

Rosa, Nicolás. "Cabrera Infante: Una Patología del Lenguaje." In *Critica y Significación.* Buenos Aires: Gelerna, 1970.

MANUEL PUIG

Borinsky, Alicia. "Castration: Artifices." *The Georgia Review* 29, no. 1 (1975): 95–114.

Kerr, Lucille. "The Fiction of Popular Design and Desire: Manuel Puig's *Boquitas pintadas.*" *MLN* 97 nos. 4–5 (1982): 411–21.

MacAdam, Alfred J. "Manuel Puig's Chronicles of Provincial Life." *Revista Hispánica Moderna* nos. 1–2 (1973): 50–65.

McCracken, Ellen. "Manuel Puig's *Heartbreak Tango:* Women and Mass Culture." *Latin American Literary Review* no. 18 (1981): 27–35.

Review nos. 4–5 (Winter 1971–Spring 1972). Special Puig issue.

ELENA PONIATOWSKA

Christ, Ronald. "The Author as Editor." *Review* no. 15 (Fall 1975): 78–79.

Hancock, Joel. "Elena Poniatowska's *Hasta no verte, Jesús mío:* Remaking the Image of Woman." *Hispania* 66 (1983): 353–59.

Tatum, Charles M. "Elena Poniatowska'a *Hasta no verte, Jesús mío.*" In *Latin American Women Writers: Yesterday and Today*, 49–58. Edited by Yvette E. Miller and Charles M. Tatum. Pittsburgh: Latin American Literary Review, 1977.

MARIO VARGAS LLOSA

Fenwick, M. J. *Dependency Theory and Literary Analysis: Reflections on Vargas Llosa's* The Green House. Minneapolis: Institute for the Study of Ideologies and Literature, 1981.

Flasher, John. "*Conversación en la catedral:* A Bleak Social, Political and Moral Vision of Lima." *The City in the Latin American Novel*, edited by Bobby J. Chamberlain, 45–56. East Lansing: Latin American Studies Center, Michigan State University, 1980.

Fletcher, M. D. "*Captain Pantoja and the Special Service* and the Peruvian Revolution." *Mosaic* 18 (1985): 44–60.

Kulin, Katalin. "The Discourse of *Conversation in the Cathedral.*" *Acta Literaria* 27 (1985): 365–94.

Prieto, Rene. "The Two Narrative Voices in Mario Vargas Llosa's *Aunt Julia and the Scriptwriter.*" *Latin American Literary Review* no. 22 (1983): 15–25.

Review no. 14 (Spring 1975). Special Vargas Llosa issue.

Texas Studies in Literature and Language 19 (1977). Special Vargas Llosa issue.

World Literature Today 52 (1978). Special Vargas Llosa issue.

SEVERO SARDUY

Ortega, Julio. "*From Cuba with a Song.*" In *Poetics of Change: The New Spanish American Narrative*, translated by Galen D. Greaser. Austin: University of Texas Press, 1984: 173–79.

Review no. 6 (Fall 1972). Special Sarduy issue.

Review no. 13 (Winter 1974). Special Sarduy issue.

REINALDO ARENAS

Review no. 8 (Spring 1973). Special Arenas issue.

Rodríguez-Monegal, Emir. "The Labyrinthine World of Reinaldo Arenas." *Latin American Literary Review* no. 16 (1980): 126–31.

INÉS MALINOW

Valenzuela, Luisa. "El juego de la ambiguedad y la puréza." *La Prensa* 14 (January 1979).

Acknowledgments

"Borges's New Prose" by Carter Wheelock from *TriQuarterly* no. 25 (Fall 1972), © 1972 by Northwestern University Press. Reprinted by permission of *TriQuarterly*, a publication of Northwestern University, and the author.

"Borges's 'Immortal': The Ritual Experience of Literature" (originally titled "Borges's 'Immortal': Metaliterature, Metaperformance") by Sophia S. Morgan from *Rite, Drama, Festival, Spectacle: Rehearsals toward a Theory of Cultural Performance*, edited by John J. MacAloon, © 1984 by the Institute for the Study of Human Issues. Reprinted by permission.

" 'She Was Unable Not to Think': Borges's 'Emma Zunz' and the Female Subject" by Bella Brodzki from *MLN* 100, no. 2 (March 1985), © 1985 by The Johns Hopkins University Press. Reprinted by permission.

"Myth as Time and Word" (originally titled "Men of Corn: Myth as Time and Word") by Ariel Dorfman, translated by Paula Speck, from *Review* no. 15 (Fall 1975), © 1975 by the Center for Inter-American Relations, Inc. Reprinted by permission.

"On *Reasons of State*" by Roberto Gonzalez Echevarría from *Review* no. 18 (Fall 1976), © 1976 by the Center for Inter-American Relations, Inc. Reprinted by permission.

"A Return to Africa with a Carpentier Tale" by José Piedra from *MLN* 97, no. 2 (March 1982), © 1982 by The Johns Hopkins University Press. Reprinted by permission.

"The Picaroon in Power: Alejo Carpentier's *El recurso del método*" by Julie Jones from *Revista Canadiense de Estudios Hispánicos* 7, no. 2 (Winter

1983), © 1983 by *Revista Canadiense de Estudios Hispánicos*. Reprinted by permission.

"The Destruction of Realism in the Short Prose Fiction of João Guimarães Rosa" by Allan Englekirk from *South Atlantic Review* 47, no. 1 (January 1982), © 1982 by South Atlantic Modern Language Association. Reprinted by permission.

"Anguish of the Ordinary" by George Levine from *Review* no. 16 (Winter 1975), © 1975 by the Center for Inter-American Relations, Inc. Reprinted by permission.

"María Luisa Bombal's Poetic Novels of Female Estrangement" by Phyllis Rodríguez-Peralta from *Revista de Estudios Hispánicos* 14, no. 1 (January 1980), © 1980 by the University of Alabama Press. Reprinted by permission.

"An Approach to Lezama Lima" by Julio Cortázar, translated by Paula Speck, from *Review* no. 12 (Fall 1974), © 1974 by the Center for Inter-American Relations, Inc. Reprinted by permission.

"A Cuban Proust" by Severo Sarduy, translated by Enrico-Mario Santí, from *Review* no. 12 (Fall 1974), © 1974 by the Center for Inter-American Relations, Inc. Reprinted by permission.

"Pursuers" by Saúl Sosnowski from *The Final Island: The Fiction of Julio Cortázar*, edited by Jaime Alazraki and Ivan Ivask, © 1976, 1978 by the University of Oklahoma Press. Reprinted by permission.

"*Rayuela*: Chapter 55 as Take-(away)" by Barbara L. Hussey from *International Fiction Review* 8, no. 1 (Winter 1981), © 1981 by the York Press. Reprinted by permission.

"Movement and Stasis, Film and Photo: Temporal Structures in the Recent Fiction of Julio Cortázar" by Lois Parkinson Zamora from *The Review of Contemporary Fiction* 3, no. 3 (1983), © 1983 by *The Review of Contemporary Fiction*. Reprinted by permission.

"Three Versions of *Pedro Páramo*" by Paul B. Dixon from *Reversible Readings: Ambiguity in Four Modern Latin American Novels* by Paul B. Dixon, © 1985 by the University of Alabama Press. Reprinted by permission.

"Authority and Identity in Rulfo's *El llano en llamas*" by Steven Boldy from *MLN* 101, no. 2 (1986), © 1986 by The Johns Hopkins University Press. Reprinted by permission.

Form and Content in Elena Garro's *Los recuerdos del porvenir*" by Harry Enrique Rosser from *Revista Canadiense de Estudios Hispánicos* 11, no. 3 (Spring 1978), © 1978 by Asociación Canadiense de Hispanitas, Carleton University. Reprinted by permission.

"Writing/Transvestism" by Severo Sarduy, translated by Alfred MacAdam, from *Review* no. 9 (Fall 1973), © 1973 by the Center for Inter-American Relations, Inc. Reprinted by permission.

"José Donoso: Endgame" by Alfred J. MacAdam from *Latin American Narratives: The Dreams of Reason* by Alfred J. MacAdam, © 1977 by The University of Chicago. Reprinted by permission of The University of Chicago Press and the author.

"Reading Clarice Lispector's 'Sunday before Going to Sleep' " by Hélène Cixous, translated by Betsy Wing, from *Boundary 2* 12, no. 2 (Winter 1984), © 1984 by *Boundary 2*. Reprinted by permission.

"*Family Ties:* Female Development" (originally titled "*Family Ties:* The Female Development in Clarice Lispector") by Marta Peixoto from *The Voyage In: Fictions of Female Development*, edited by Elizabeth Abel, Marianne Hirsch, and Elizabeth Langland, © 1983 by the Trustees of Dartmouth College. Reprinted by permission of the University Press of New England.

"Voices of Patriarchy: Gabriel García Márquez's *One Hundred Years of Solitude*" by Susanne Kappeler from *Teaching the Text*, edited by Susanne Kappeler and Norman Bryson, © 1983 by Susanne Kappeler. Reprinted by permission of Associated Book Publishers, Ltd.

"The Autumn of the Signifier: The Deconstructionist Moment of García Márquez" by Patricia Tobin from *Latin American Literary Review* no. 25 (January–June 1985), © 1985 by *Latin American Literary Review*. Reprinted by permission.

"The Heir Must Die: *One Hundred Years of Solitude* as a Gothic Novel" by Claudette Kemper Columbus from *Modern Fiction Studies* 32, no. 3 (Autumn 1986), © 1986 by the Purdue Research Foundation. Reprinted by permission.

"*Terra Nostra:* Coming to Grips with History" by Jaime Alazraki, translated by David Draper Clark, from *World Literature Today* 57, no. 4 (Autumn 1983), © 1983 by the University of Oklahoma Press. Reprinted by permission.

" 'Without Sin and with Pleasure': The Erotic Dimensions of Fuentes's Fiction" by Wendy B. Faris from *Novel: A Forum on Fiction* 20, no. 1 (Fall 1986), © 1986 by Novel Corp. Reprinted by permission.

"A Secret Idiom: The Grammar and Role of Language in *Tres tristes tigres*" by Stephanie Merrim from *Latin American Literary Review* no. 16 (Spring–Summer 1980), © 1980 by *Latin American Literary Review*. Reprinted by permission.

"Manuel Puig at the Movies" by Frances Wyers (Weber) from *Hispanic Review* 49, no. 2 (Spring 1981), © 1981 by the Trustees of the University of Pennsylvania. Reprinted by permission of *Hispanic Review*.

"The Transformation of Privilege in the Work of Elena Poniatowska" by Bell Gale Chevigny from *Latin American Literary Review* no. 26 (July–December 1985), © 1985 by *Latin American Literary Review*. Reprinted by permission.

"Rhetorics of the Plot" by Ronald Christ from *World Literature Today* 52, no. 1 (Winter 1978), © 1978 by the University of Oklahoma Press. Reprinted by permission.

"Beyond Magic Realism" by Roger Kaplan from *Commentary* 78, no. 6 (December 1984), © 1984 by the American Jewish Committee. Reprinted by permission of *Commentary* and the author.

"Mass Media Images of the Puertorriqueña in *La guaracha del Macho Camacho*" by Stacey Schlau from *Literature and Popular Culture in the Hispanic World*, edited by Rose S. Minc, © 1981 by Montclair State College. Reprinted by permission.

"Plain Song: Sarduy's *Cobra*" by Roberto González Echevarría, © 1990 by Roberto González-Echevarría. Published for the first time in this volume.

"Notes on the Fiction of Nélida Piñón" by Giovanni Pontiero from *Review* no. 19 (Winter 1976), © 1976 by the Center for Inter-American Relations, Inc. Reprinted by permission.

"Voices in the Silence" by Patricia Tobin from *Review* no. 18 (Fall 1976), © 1976 by the Center for Inter-American Relations, Inc. Reprinted by permission.

"The Dazzling World of Friar Servando" by Julio Ortega, translated by Tom J. Lewis from *Review* no. 10 (Winter 1973), © 1973 by the Center for Inter-American Relations, Inc. Reprinted by permission.

"Woman's Space, Woman's Text: A New Departure in Inés Malinaw's *Entrada libre*" by Doris Meyer from *Latin American Literary Review* no. 23 (Fall–Winter 1983), © 1983 by *Latin American Literary Review*. Reprinted by permission.

Index